350 THAI & CHINESE

LOW-FAT RECIPES FOR HEALTHY LIVING

350 THAI & CHINESE

LOW-FAT RECIPES FOR HEALTHY LIVING

Delicious spicy and aromatic dishes from South-East Asia in no-fat or low-fat versions, shown in over 1600 step-by-step photographs

CONTRIBUTING EDITORS:
JANE BAMFORTH, MAGGIE PANNELL AND JENNI FLEETWOOD

LORENZ BOOKS

This edition is published by Lorenz Books, an imprint of Anness Publishing Ltd
Hermes House, 88–89 Blackfriars Road, London SE1 8HA
tel. 020 7401 2077; fax 020 7633 9499

www.lorenzbooks.com; www.annesspublishing.com

If you like the images in this book and would like to investigate using them for
publishing, promotions or advertising, please visit our website www.practicalpictures.com
for more information.

UK agent: The Manning Partnership Ltd; tel. 01225 478444;
fax 01225 478440; sales@manning-partnership.co.uk
UK distributor: Grantham Book Services Ltd; tel. 01476 541080;
fax 01476 541061; orders@gbs.tbs-ltd.co.uk
North American agent/distributor: National Book Network;
tel. 301 459 3366; fax 301 429 5746; www.nbnbooks.com
Australian agent/distributor: Pan Macmillan Australia; tel. 1300 135 113;
fax 1300 135 103; customer.service@macmillan.com.au
New Zealand agent/distributor: David Bateman Ltd; tel. (09) 415 7664; fax (09) 415 8892

Publisher: Joanna Lorenz
Senior Managing Editor: Conor Kilgallon
Editors: Lucy Doncaster, Doreen Gillan, Joy Wotton and Elizabeth Woodland
Consultant Editors: Maggie Pannell and Jenni Fleetwood
Designers: Bill Mason, Nigel Partridge
Recipes: Catherine Atkinson, Alex Barker, Ghillie Basan, Judy Bastyra, Mridula Baljekar,
Jane Bamforth, Carla Capalbo, Kit Chan, Roz Denny, Joanna Farrow, Rafi Fernandez,
Jenni Fleetwood, Christine France, Silvano Franco, Linda Fraser, Yasuko Fukuoka,
Elaine Gardner, Sarah Gates, Shirley Gill, Brian Glover, Nicola Graimes, Deh-Ta Hsiung,
Shehzad Husain, Christine Ingram, Becky Johnson, Emi Kazuko, Soheila Kimberley,
Lucy Knox, Masaki Ko, Elizabeth Lambert Ortiz, Ruby Le Bois, Patricia Lousada,
Norma MacMillan, Lesley Mackley, Sue Maggs, Kathy Man, Sarah Maxwell, Maggie Mayhew,
Jane Milton, Sallie Morris, Janice Murfitt, Annie Nichols, Angela Nilsen, Maggie Pannell,
Keith Richmond, Anne Sheasby, Marlena Spieler, Liz Trigg, Hilaire Walden, Laura Washburn,
Steven Wheeler, Jenny White, Kate Whiteman, Elizabeth Wolf-Cohen
Home Economists: Julie Beresford, Carla Capalbo, Kit Chan, Joanne Craig, Joanna Farrow,
Annabel Ford, Nicola Fowler, Christine France, Carole Handslip, Jane Hartshorn, Tonia Hedley,
Shehzad Husain, Kate Jay, Becky Johnson, Wendy Lee, Sara Lewis, Lucy McKelvie,
Annie Nichols, Bridget Sargeson, Jennie Shapter, Jane Stevenson, Helen Trent, Sunil Vijayakar,
Steven Wheeler, Elizabeth Wolf-Cohen.
Photographers: Edward Allwright, Peter Anderson, David Armstrong, Steve Baxter,
Martin Brigdale, Nicki Dowey, James Duncan, Gus Filgate, Michelle Garrett,
Amanda Heywood, Janine Hosegood, Tim Hill, Becky Johnson, David Jordan, Dave King,
Don Last, William Lingwood, Patrick McLeavey, Michael Michaels, Thomas Odulate,
Peter Reilly, Craig Robertson, Simon Smith
Production Controller: Claire Rae

Ethical Trading Policy
Because of our ongoing ecological investment programme, you, as our customer, can have
the pleasure and reassurance of knowing that a tree is being cultivated on your behalf to
naturally replace the materials used to make the book you are holding. For further
information about this scheme, go to www.annesspublishing.com/trees

Main front cover image shows Curried Rice Vermicelli, see page 379

Notes
Bracketed terms are intended for American readers.
For all recipes, quantities are given in both metric and imperial measures and,
where appropriate, in standard cups and spoons. Follow one set, but not a mixture,
because they are not interchangeable.
Standard spoon and cup measures are level. 1 tsp = 5ml,
1 tbsp = 15ml, 1 cup = 250ml/8fl oz.
Australian standard tablespoons are 20ml. Australian readers should use 3 tsp in place of
1 tbsp for measuring small quantities of gelatine, salt etc.
The nutritional analysis given for each recipe is calculated per portion (i.e. serving or item),
unless otherwise stated. If the recipe gives a range, such as Serves 4–6, then the
nutritional analysis will be for the smaller portion size, i.e. 6 servings. Measurements for
sodium do not include salt added to taste. Medium (US large) eggs are used unless
otherwise stated.

Each recipe title in this book is followed by a symbol that indicates the following:
★ = 5g of fat or less per serving
★★ = 10g of fat or less per serving
★★★ = 15g of fat or less per serving

CONTENTS

INTRODUCTION 6

THE LOW-FAT THAI AND CHINESE
KITCHEN 8
HEALTHY EATING GUIDELINES 10
PLANNING A LOW-FAT DIET 12
VEGETABLES 14
FRUIT, NUTS AND SEEDS 18
HERBS, SPICES AND FLAVOURINGS 20
RICE 24
NOODLES 26
PANCAKES AND WRAPPERS 28
TOFU PRODUCTS 30
POULTRY AND MEAT 31
FISH AND SHELLFISH 32
FAT AND CALORIE CONTENTS 34

THE RECIPES 36
SOUPS 38
APPETIZERS 84
LIGHT BITES 112
VEGETARIAN MAIN DISHES 138
FISH 168
SHELLFISH 198
CHICKEN AND DUCK 230
LAMB, PORK AND BEEF 274
RICE 324
NOODLES 356
VEGETABLES AND SIDE DISHES 396
PICKLES AND SALADS 424
COLD DESSERTS 448
HOT DESSERTS 482

GLOSSARY 504
INDEX 506

INTRODUCTION

The food and cooking styles of Thailand and China are among the most popular in the world, and they can also be included among the healthiest. They feature simple and fresh ingredients, fragrant herbs and spices, and quick cooking techniques which preserve flavour and nutritional value.

The majority of people living in South-east Asia have a very healthy diet, which is low in fat, high in fibre, with plenty of vegetables and relatively small amounts of meat. Much of their protein comes from fish and tofu, both of which are low-fat foods. Noodles and rice form the bulk of most meals, and processed foods are seldom eaten. In part, this diet evolved through necessity. Subsistence workers could not afford to eat large quantities of meat on a daily basis, even though pork, duck and chickens were – and still remain – an important part of the diet. Unfortunately, increased prosperity has caused higher fat consumption in countries like China. In major cities like Beijing, where individuals have adopted a more Western diet, the incidence of coronary heart disease is on the rise.

Some of the dishes exported to the West are none too healthy either. Pork that has been dipped in batter, deep-fried in fat and then coated in a syrupy sauce is never going to make it to the list of best choices for optimum nutrition. Nor is the practice of enriching a dish by stirring in pure lard to be recommended.

Countries in South-east Asia can however provide a great source of healthy, low-fat recipes. Asian cooks are fussy about what they eat, and ingredients are chosen with considerable care. Visit any open-air market and you will see cooks sifting through piles of gourds to choose one that is at just the right state of ripeness for the meal they have planned. Meat and fish must be very fresh, a fact that

Right: The use of the wok has grown from its origins in Asia into a pan used all over the world for cooking all sorts of foods.

can be a bit daunting to the visitor invited to choose their meal while it is still swimming in a tank, but which proves beyond any doubt that the item in question will be fresh.

A HEALTHY WAY OF COOKING

Steaming and stir-frying are two of the most popular cooking methods in South-east Asia. Both these methods are ideal for the low-fat cook, since they require little or no oil to be used.

The wok is the principal utensil. This extraordinarily versatile pan, with its rounded bottom, was originally designed to fit snugly on a traditional Asian brazier or stove. Modern versions have flatter bases, to prevent wobble on electric stoves, but are still very efficient in the even way they conduct and retain

heat. The sloping sides mean that the food always returns to the centre, where the heat is most intense.

Many of the woks on sale today are non-stick. Although traditional carbonized steel woks are the ones purists choose, because they are so efficient, non-stick woks are better for low-fat cooking, since they make it possible to stir-fry with the smallest amount of oil.

When stir-frying, the best technique is to place the wok over the heat without any oil. When the pan is hot, dribble drops of oil in a circle on to the inner surface just below the rim. As the drops slither down the pan, they coat the sides, then puddle on the base. You can get away with using just about a teaspoon of oil if you follow this method.

Above: Chinese greens like pak choi (bok choy) and Chinese leaves (Chinese cabbage) are delicious raw in salads or stir-fried with just a drop of oil.

Add the food to be cooked when the oil is very hot, and keep it moving. This is done with a pair of chopsticks, but the easiest way is to use two spatulas or spoons, as when tossing a salad.

Add a metal trivet to a wok and it becomes a steamer. Better still, use a bamboo steamer. These attractive-looking utensils look rather like hat boxes, and come with tightly fitting domed lids. You can stack several tiers on top of each other over a wok partly filled with water. No fat will be needed and the food will taste delicious.

A HEALTHY LIFESTYLE

Most of us eat fats in some form or another every day and we all need a small amount of fat in our diet to maintain a healthy, balanced eating plan. However, many of us eat far too much fat, and we should all be looking to reduce our overall fat intake, especially of saturated fats, and choose the healthier unsaturated fats.

Regular exercise is also an important factor in a healthy lifestyle, and we should all be aiming to exercise three times a week for a minimum of half an hour each session. Swimming, brisk walking, jogging, dancing, skipping and cycling are all good forms of aerobic exercise promoting a healthy heart.

ABOUT THIS BOOK

This cookbook brings together a wide selection of delicious and nutritious dishes, all of which are low in fat, and are ideal to include as part of a healthy and low-fat eating plan.

The book includes plenty of useful and informative advice. A succinct introduction gives a blueprint for healthy eating and has helpful tips on low-fat and fat-free ingredients and cooking techniques. There are tips for reducing fat, especially saturated fat, in your diet, and the section on ingredients provides an insight into fruits, vegetables, meats and other essentials.

All the tempting recipes are designed to be enjoyed by the whole family. They range from soups, appetizers and light bites to hot and cold desserts and there are lots of delicious main course dishes for meat eaters and vegetarians. The emphasis throughout the book is on good food with maximum taste, and if you don't let on that the dishes are also low in fat, nobody is likely to guess.

THE LOW-FAT RECIPES

Each recipe includes a nutritional breakdown, proving an at-a-glance guide to calorie and fat content (including saturates and polyunsaturates content) per serving, as well as other key components such as protein, carbohydrate, calcium, cholesterol, fibre and sodium. All the recipes in this collection are low in fat. Many contain

Above: Keep the food moving when cooking in a wok. Large chopsticks like these are widely available in good Asian food stores.

five grams of total fat or less per serving, and a few are even lower in fat, with under one gram per serving. One or two classic recipes, such as Marinated Duck Curry (see page 268), and Beef in Oyster Sauce (see page 314), contain slightly more fat, but even these contain less than in the traditional versions.

For ease of reference, all recipes with a single * after the recipe title contain a maximum of five grams of total fat, those with ** contain a maximum of 10 grams of total fat and those with *** contain up to 15 grams of total fat per portion. Each recipe also has a complete breakdown of the energy, protein, carbohydrate, cholesterol, calcium, fibre and sodium values of the food.

Although the recipes are low in fat, they lose nothing in terms of flavour. This practical cookbook will enable you to enjoy healthy Asian food with a clear conscience. All the recipes are easy to cook and many are so quick that you'll have supper on the table in less time than it would have taken to collect a take-away.

Left: When food is cooked in a steamer, there is no need for any fat to be used. A bamboo steamer like this one is ideal. Several can be stacked on top of each other if you're cooking many dishes.

THE LOW-FAT
THAI AND CHINESE
KITCHEN

Cooks in Thailand and China have much to teach us about

low-fat cooking. Their traditional diet is largely composed of

vegetables, with a healthy proportion of carbohydrate in the

form of noodles or rice, protein in the form of tofu and only

small amounts of poultry, meat and seafood. You will find a

selection of many popular dishes from across South-east Asia

in this book, as well as some less well-known recipes, but they

are all delicious and perfect for a low-fat diet.

HEALTHY EATING GUIDELINES

A healthy diet provides us with all the nutrients we need. By eating the right types, balance and proportions of foods, we are more likely to have more energy and a higher resistance to infections and illnesses such as heart disease, cancers, bowel disorders and obesity.

By choosing a variety of foods every day, you are supplying your body with all the essential nutrients it needs. To get the balance right, it is important to know just how much of each type of food you should be eating.

Of the five main food groups, it is recommended that we eat at least five portions of fruit and vegetables a day, not including potatoes; carbohydrate foods such as noodles, cereals, rice and potatoes; moderate amounts of fish, poultry and dairy products; and small amounts of foods containing fat or sugar. A dish like Five-Flavour Noodles (see page 387) fits perfectly, with its balance of noodles, lean pork, cabbage, beansprouts and (bell) peppers.

THE ROLE OF FAT IN THE DIET

Fats shouldn't be cut out of our diets completely, as they are a valuable source of energy and make foods more palatable. However, lowering the fats, especially saturated fats, in your diet, may help you to lose weight, as well as reducing your risk of developing diseases.

Aim to limit your daily intake of fats to no more than 30–35 per cent of the total number of calories you consume. Each gram of fat provides nine calories, so a person eating 2,000 calories a day should not eat more than 70g/2¾oz of fat in total. Saturated fat should not comprise more than 10 per cent of the total calorie intake.

TYPES OF FAT

All fats in our foods are made up of building blocks of fatty acids and glycerol, and their properties vary according to each combination.

The two main types of fat are saturated and unsaturated. The unsaturated group is divided into two further categories – polyunsaturated and monounsaturated fats. There is usually a combination of these types of unsaturated fat in foods that contain fat, but the amount of each type varies from one kind of food to another.

SATURATED FATS

These fats are usually hard at room temperature. They are not essential in the diet, and should be limited, as they are implicated in raising the level of cholesterol in the blood, which can increase the likelihood of heart disease.

The main sources of saturated fats are animal products, such as fatty cuts of meat and meat products; spreading fats that are solid at room temperature, such as butter, lard and margarine; and dairy products such as cream and cheese. Aside from meat, these ingredients are seldom found in South-east Asian recipes, but it is also important to avoid coconut and palm oil, which are saturated fats of vegetable origin.

Above: Rice noodles come in various forms, from very thin strands called rice vermicelli. Easily reconstituted, they are virtually fat free.

Above: Tofu, which is also known as bean curd, is a highly nutritious vegetable protein. It is cholesterol-free and low in fat.

Above: South-east Asian cooks can use a wonderful assortment of shellfish, such as mussels, from the sea, lakes, rivers and canals.

More insidious are those fats which, when processed, change the nature of the fat from unsaturated fatty acids to saturated ones. These are called "hydrogenated" fats, and should be strictly limited, so look out for that term on food labels.

Saturated fats are also found in many processed foods, such as chips (French fries) and savoury snacks, as well as cookies, pastries and cakes.

POLYUNSATURATED FATS

Small amounts of polyunsaturated fats are essential for good health, as they provide energy, can help to reduce cholesterol levels and enable the absorption of the fat-soluble vitamins A and D. The body can't manufacture polyunsaturated fatty acids, so they must be obtained from food. There are two types: those of vegetable or plant origin, known as Omega-6, which are found in sunflower oil, soft margarine, nuts and seeds; and Omega-3 fatty acids, which come from oily fish such

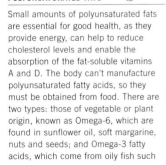

Left: Asian cooking makes use of a wide variety of herbs, spices and flavourings, including cinnamon, root ginger, garlic, lemon grass and kaffir limes.

as tuna, salmon, herring, mackerel and sardines as well as walnuts, soya beans, wheatgerm and rapeseed (canola) oil.

MONOUNSATURATED FATS

The best known monounsaturated fat is olive oil. This is not used in Asian cooking, but another monounsaturated oil, groundnut (peanut) oil, is a popular choice. It is ideal for stir-frying and gives food a delicious flavour. Monounsaturated fatty acids are also found in nuts such as almonds, and oily fish. They are thought to have the beneficial effect of reducing blood cholesterol levels.

THE CHOLESTEROL QUESTION

Cholesterol is a fat-like substance that occurs naturally in the body, and which we also acquire from food. It has a vital role, since it is the material from which many essential hormones and vitamin D are made. Cholesterol is carried around the body, attached to proteins called high density lipoproteins (HDLs), low density lipoproteins (LDLs) and very low density lipoproteins (VLDLs or triglycerides).

Eating too much saturated fat encourages the body to make more cholesterol than it can use or can rid itself of. After food has been consumed, the LDLs carry the fat in the blood to

the cells where it is required. Any surplus should be excreted from the body, but if there are too many LDLs in the blood, some of the fat will be deposited on the walls of the arteries. This furring up gradually narrows the arteries and is one of the most common causes of heart attacks and strokes.

By way of contrast, HDLs appear to protect against heart disease. Whether high triglyceride levels are risk factors remains unknown.

CUTTING DOWN ON FATS AND SATURATED FATS IN THE DIET

It is relatively easy to cut down on obvious sources of fat in the diet, like butter, oils, margarine, cream, whole milk and full-fat cheese, but it is also important to know about and check consumption of "hidden" fats.

By educating yourself and being aware of which foods are high in fats, and by making simple changes, you can reduce the total fat content of your diet quite considerably. Choose low-fat alternatives when selecting items like milk, cheese and salad dressings. If you are hungry, fill up on very low-fat foods, such as fruits and vegetables, and foods that are high in carbohydrates, such as bread, potatoes, rice or noodles.

PLANNING A LOW-FAT DIET

Cutting down on fat on an everyday basis means we need to keep a close eye on the fat content of everything we eat. These general guidelines on reducing fat are applicable to all cuisines.

CUTTING DOWN ON FAT IN THE DIET

Most of us eat far more fat than we require – consuming about 115g/4oz of fat every day. Yet just 10g/¼oz, the amount in a single packet of crisps (potato chips) or a thin slice of Cheddar cheese, is all that we actually need.

Current nutritional thinking is more lenient than this and suggests an upper daily limit of about 70g/2¾oz total fat.

Using low-fat recipes helps to reduce the overall daily intake of fat, but there are also lots of other ways of reducing the fat in your diet. Just follow the "eat less, try instead" suggestions below to discover how easy it can be.

• Eat less butter, margarine, other spreading fats, cooking oils and hard cooking fats, such as lard. Try reduced-fat spreads, low-fat spreads or fat-free spreads or polyunsaturated or monounsaturated oils, such as sunflower or corn oil, and don't use too much. Butter or hard margarine

Above: For fat-free snacks that are always available, keep an exotic supply of fresh fruit to hand including star fruit (carambola) and watermelons.

should be softened at room temperature so that they can be spread thinly. Try low-fat cream cheese or low-fat soft cheese for sandwiches and toast.
• Eat less full-fat dairy products such as whole milk, cream, butter, hard margarine, crème fraîche, whole-milk yogurts and hard cheese. Try instead semi-skimmed (low-fat) or skimmed milk, low-fat or reduced-fat milk products, such as low-fat yogurts and soft cheeses, reduced-fat hard cheeses such as Cheddar, and reduced-fat crème fraîche.
• Silken tofu can be used instead of cream in soups and sauces. It is a good source of calcium and an excellent protein food.
• Eat fewer fatty cuts of meat and high-fat meat products, such as pâtés, burgers, pies and sausages. Try instead naturally low-fat meats such as skinless chicken and turkey, ostrich and venison. When cooking lamb, beef or pork, use only the leanest cuts. Always cut away any visible fat and skin from meat before cooking. Try substituting low-fat protein ingredients like dried beans, lentils or tofu for some or all of the meat in a recipe.
• Eat more fish. It is easy to cook, tastes great, and if you use a steamer, you won't need to add any extra fat at all.
• Eat fewer rich salad dressings and less full-fat mayonnaise. Try reduced-fat or fat-free dressings, or just a squeeze of lemon juice. Use a reduced-fat mayonnaise and thin it with puréed silken tofu for an even greater fat saving.
• Eat less fried food. Try fat-free cooking methods like steaming, grilling (broiling), baking or microwaving. Use non-stick pans with spray oil. When roasting or grilling meat, place it on a rack and drain off excess fat frequently.
• Eat fewer deep-fried or sautéed potatoes. Boil or bake them instead, or use other carbohydrates. Avoid chow-mein noodles, which are high in fat.

Above: Tuna and salmon are good sources of Omega-3 fatty acids, phytochemicals and antioxidants, which work together for a healthy heart.

• Cut down on oil when cooking. Drain fried food on kitchen paper to remove as much oil as possible. Choose heavy, good-quality non-stick pans and use spray oil for the lightest coverage. Moisten food with fat-free or low-fat liquids such as fruit juice, defatted stock, wine or even beer.
• Eat fewer high-fat snacks, such as chocolate, cookies, chips (French fries) and crisps. Try instead a piece of fruit, some vegetable crudités or some home-baked low-fat fruit cake.

Below: Choose lean cuts of meat and naturally low-fat meats such as skinless chicken and turkey.

FAT-FREE COOKING METHODS

Asian cooking uses a variety of low-fat and fat-free cooking methods, and by incorporating recipes from this region into your daily diet it is easy to bring down your total fat consumption. Where possible, steam, microwave or grill (broil) foods, without adding extra fat. Alternatively, braise in a defatted stock, wine or fruit juice, or stir-fry with just a spray of vegetable oil.

• By choosing a good quality, non-stick wok, such as the one above, you can keep the amount of fat needed for cooking foods to the absolute minimum. When cooking meat in a regular pan, dry-fry the meat to brown it, then tip it into a sieve (strainer) and drain off the excess fat before returning it to the pan and adding the other ingredients. If you do need a little fat for cooking, choose an oil high in unsaturates, such as sunflower or corn oil and use a spray where possible.

• Eat less meat and more vegetables and noodles or other forms of pasta. A good method for making a small amount of meat such as beef steak go a long way is to place it in the freezer for 30 minutes and then slice it very thinly with a sharp knife. Meat prepared this way will cook very quickly with very little fat.

• When baking chicken or fish, wrap it in a loose package of foil or baking parchment, with a little wine or fruit juice. Add some fresh herbs or spices before sealing the parcel, if you like.

• It is often unnecessary to add fat when grilling (broiling) food. If the food shows signs of drying, lightly brush or spray it with a little unsaturated oil, such as sunflower, corn or olive oil. Microwaved foods seldom need the addition of fat, so add herbs or spices for extra flavour and colour.

• Steaming is the ideal way of cooking fish. If you like, arrange the fish on a bed of aromatic flavourings such as lemon or lime slices and sprigs of herbs. Alternatively, place finely shredded vegetables or seaweed in the base of the steamer to give the fish extra flavour.

• If you do not own a steamer, cook vegetables in a covered pan over low heat with just a little water, so that they cook in their own juices.
• Vegetables can be braised in the oven in low-fat or fat-free stock, wine or a little water with some chopped fresh or dried herbs.
• Try poaching foods such as chicken, fish or fruit in low-fat or fat-free stock or fruit juice.
• Plain rice or noodles make a very good low-fat accompaniment to most Thai and South-east Asian dishes.

• The classic Asian technique of adding moisture and flavour to chicken by marinating it in a mixture of soy sauce and rice wine, with a little sesame oil, can be used with other meats too. You can also use a mixture of alcohol, herbs and spices, or vinegar or fruit juice. The marinade will also help to tenderize the meat and any remaining marinade can be used to baste the food while it is cooking.
• When serving vegetables, resist the temptation to add butter. Instead, sprinkle with chopped fresh herbs.

Low-fat spreads in cooking
A huge variety of low-fat and reduced-fat spreads is available in supermarkets, along with some spreads that are very low in fat. Generally speaking, any very low-fat spreads with a fat content of around 20 per cent or less have a high water content. These are unsuitable for cooking and can only be used for spreading.

VEGETABLES

Naturally low in fat and bursting with vitamins and minerals, vegetables are one food group that should ideally make up the bulk of our daily diet. In China and Thailand, cooks use vegetables freely in stir-fries and braised dishes, and have evolved a wide range of delicious vegetarian main courses to make the most of the abundant choice of vegetables on sale in markets.

Many of these vegetables are now commonplace in other parts of the world. Chinese leaves (Chinese cabbage), pak choi (bok choy) and beansprouts are usually available in supermarkets, and other greens, such as mizuna, Chinese mustard greens and Chinese broccoli, are often grown by small producers and can be found at farmers' markets.

CHINESE LEAVES/CHINESE CABBAGE

Also known as Chinese cabbage or Napa cabbage, this vegetable has pale green, crinkly leaves with long, wide, white ribs. It is pleasantly crunchy, has a sweet, nutty flavour and tastes wonderful raw or cooked. When buying Chinese leaves, look out for firm, slightly heavy heads with pale green leaves without blemishes or bruises. To prepare, peel off the outer leaves, cut off the root and slice the cabbage thinly or thickly. When stir-fried, Chinese leaves lose their subtle cabbage taste and take on the flavour of other ingredients in the dish.

Above: Chinese leaves have a mild, delicate flavour.

Left: Pak choi tastes similar to spinach.

PAK CHOI (BOK CHOY)

Another member of the brassica family, pak choi (bok choy) has lots of noms-de-plume, including horse's ear, Chinese cabbage and Chinese white cabbage. There are several varieties, and one or other is usually on sale at the supermarket. Unlike Chinese leaves, pak choi doesn't keep well, so plan to use it within a day or two of purchase. The vegetable is generally cooked, although very young and tender pak choi can be eaten raw. The stems – regarded by many as the best part – need slightly longer cooking than the leaves.

CHOI SUM

Often sold in bunches, choi sum is a brassica with bright green leaves and thin, pale, slightly grooved stems. It has a pleasant aroma and mild taste, and remains crisp and tender if properly cooked. The leaves can be sliced, but are more often steamed whole. Choi sum will keep for a few days in the salad drawer, but is best used as soon as possible after purchase.

CHINESE BROCCOLI

With its somewhat straggly appearance, this brassica looks more like purple sprouting broccoli than prim Calabrese. Every part of Chinese broccoli is edible, and each has its own inimitable taste. To prepare, remove the tough outer leaves, then cut off the leaves. If the stems are tough, peel them. It is usual to blanch the vegetable briefly in salted boiling water or stock before stir-frying.

AUBERGINES (EGGPLANTS)

Popular throughout Thailand and Southeast Asia, aubergines come in a variety of shapes, sizes and colours. They have a smoky, slightly bitter taste and spongy flesh that readily absorbs other flavours and oils. To avoid the absorption of too much fat, cut the aubergine into slices, and dry-fry these in a wok over medium heat for 4–5 minutes. They can also be braised, stuffed or baked.

Above: Aubergines (eggplants) come in different sizes and varieties of purple.

MOOLI (DAIKON)

Also known as daikon, this Asian vegetable looks rather like a parsnip, but is actually related to the radish. The flavour is milder than that of most radishes, however, although the texture is similar: crisp and crunchy. Treat it like a carrot, scraping or peeling the outer skin and then slicing it in rounds or batons. It can be eaten raw or cooked.

Above: Mooli has a crisp, crunchy texture and is delicious raw.

Below: Potatoes and sweet potatoes.

POTATOES AND SWEET POTATOES

Although potatoes and sweet potatoes are unrelated, this was not appreciated when they first reached Asia, and they were both given the same Chinese name. In northern China white potatoes are a staple food, although not as important as noodles; in southern China they are far less significant. Sweet potatoes are popular in the Philippines. Both regular potatoes and sweet potatoes are prepared in the same way: after peeling, they are sliced or diced, then stir-fried or braised with seasonings or spices. Thai cooks make a very sweet dessert based on deep-fried sweet potatoes.

YAMS

Yams are believed to have originated in China, but are now grown in all tropical regions. The Chinese yam has fine whiskers and the flesh is creamy white.

TARO

This root vegetable requires warm, damp growing conditions and is usually harvested in the winter. Generally, it comes in two varieties. One is small and egg-shaped; the other is about 25cm/10in long and shaped like a barrel. Both are covered in short hairs with white purple-flecked flesh.

Along with sweet potatoes and yams, taro is used like a potato – mashed and baked, or added to soups, stews and curries. The larger variety is firm with a nutty flavour; the smaller one is creamier and sweeter, lending itself to sweet cakes and puddings. Taro roots are available in Asian stores as well as in some supermarkets.

LUFFA SQUASH

Dark green with ridges running lengthways, luffa squash has sweet and spongy flesh and is usually harvested when it is about 30cm/1ft long. Generally, it is sliced and used in stir-fries and soups, much the same way as you would cook a courgette (zucchini). Luffa squash is available in Asian markets.

If the luffa is young, all you need to do is wash and slice it. Luffas seldom need peeling, but sometimes the ridges toughen as the vegetable ripens, in which case remove the ridges but leave the skin between, so that the luffa is striped green and white. If the skin is very tough, it is best to peel it completely. Unlike cucumber or young, tender courgettes, luffa is never eaten raw. Keep fresh luffa in the refrigerator, but do not store it for too long as within 2–3 days of purchase it will start to go limp.

KABOCHA SQUASH

This is a stout, pumpkin-shaped vegetable with a beautiful dark-green skin patterned with yellow spots and green lines. The flesh is pale orange, fragrant, sweet and creamy, lending itself to a variety of dishes, including curries and desserts. An average kabocha weighs about 1–1.5kg/2–3lb and has edible skin. They are available in Asian markets and supermarkets.

WINTER MELON

Large, mild-flavoured gourds, winter melons can weigh 5.4kg/12lb or more and grow up to 25cm/10in in diameter. Egg- or pear-shaped and dark green, they are harvested in the summer (but traditionally stored for winter) and sold whole or cut into wedges. The white flesh tastes like marrow or courgette (zucchini) and is believed to cool fevers. Prepared and cooked in the same way as a pumpkin, winter melon is added to soups, stews and stir-fries, as the flesh absorbs the flavours of the dish. The rind must be cut off and the seeds and coarse fibres at the centre scooped out before the flesh is cut into strips or wedges. Winter melons and fuzzy melons can be used interchangeably, as they are similar in flavour. Both come in various shapes and sizes and are available in Asian markets and supermarkets.

BAMBOO SHOOTS

Fresh bamboo shoots are quite hard to buy outside Asia, but you may find them in big-city Asian markets. They must be parboiled before being cooked, as the raw vegetable contains a highly toxic oil. Remove the base and the hard outer leaves, then cut the core into chunks. Boil these in salted water for 30 minutes, then drain, rinse under cold water and drain again. Cut into slices, shreds or cubes for further cooking. Dried bamboo slices must be soaked in water for 2–3 hours before use. Canned bamboo shoots only need rinsing before being used.

WATER CHESTNUTS

Fresh, crisp water chestnuts are the corms of a plant that grows on the margins of rivers and lakes. Their snow-white flesh stays crunchy even after long cooking. Fresh water chestnuts are often available from Asian markets. They keep well in a paper bag in the refrigerator. Once released from their dark brown jackets, they must be kept submerged in water in a covered container and used within one week. Canned water chestnuts should be rinsed before being used.

Below: Canned and fresh water chestnuts.

Above: Beansprouts are a widely used ingredient in stir-fries.

BEANSPROUTS

Mung beans and soy beans are the varieties of beansprout most often used, and they are an important ingredient in the Asian kitchen. It is important to use them as fresh as possible. Better still, sprout the beans yourself. Before use, rinse them to remove the husks and tiny roots. Use them in salads or stir-fries, but take care not to overcook them, or they will become limp and tasteless.

MUSHROOMS

Several types of mushrooms are used in Asian cooking, and many of these are now available in Western supermarkets.

Shiitake mushrooms are prized in Asia, both for their flavour and their medicinal qualities. They have a slightly acidic taste and a meaty, slippery texture. They contain twice as much protein

as button mushrooms and their robust flavour makes them the ideal partner for noodles and rice. To prepare fresh shiitake mushrooms, remove the stems. The caps can be left whole, or sliced. If they are to be used in a salad, cook them briefly in low-fat stock first.

Dried shiitake mushrooms must be reconstituted before being used. Soak them in cold water overnight, or in a bowl of warm water for at least 30 minutes before using, then strain the liquid. Remove the stems before use. Oyster mushrooms have a mild flavour and are pastel-coloured in shades of pink, yellow or pearl grey. They need gentle handling. Tear, rather than cut, large specimens and don't overcook them, or they will become rubbery.

Enokitake mushrooms are tiny, with bud-like caps at the end of long, slender stems. To appreciate their crisp texture and sweet flavour, use them raw in salads.

Wood ear mushrooms, also known as cloud ears, tree mushrooms or simply dried black fungus, are widely used in China, Thailand and Vietnam. The dried fungi are thin and brittle, and look like pieces of charred paper.

Dried black mushrooms are widely used throughout Asia, and are exported around the world. Although they are frequently labelled as "Chinese", to distinguish them from other dried mushrooms, and have come to be widely known as such, the majority of dried black mushrooms sold in Asian stores actually come from Japan, which produces and exports far more dried black mushrooms than does China.

Shimeji is another popular Japanese mushroom. There are many varieties, but the most common has a light grey cap and grows to 2.5–10cm/1–4in in diameter. One of the varieties, called shaka shimeji, sports small caps with short stems that grow stuck together at the lower end giving it a unique appearance and greater popularity. It is this variety that is most commonly available in the West from Asian supermarkets.

Left: Fresh and dried shiitake mushrooms.

ONIONS

The common onion so widely used in the West is known as "foreign onion" in Asia, where shallots and spring onions are generally preferred. They come in a wide variety of sizes and colours from huge golden-skinned globes to smaller, milder red and white onions. The onion is a very versatile vegetable. It can be eaten fried, boiled, steamed or raw, and it is an essential component of a great number of sauces and dishes, such as curries and stews. There is no mistaking the strong aroma and flavour of the onion. It is used as a flavouring

Above: Small and large onions.

ingredient throughout Asia, but is seldon served on its own as a side vegetable. Fried onions are a popular garnish, especially in South-east Asia.

SPRING ONIONS (SCALLIONS)

Slender and crisp, spring onions (scallions) are appreciated by Asian cooks not only for their aroma and flavour, but also for their perceived cooling qualities. Use spring onions raw in salads or lightly cooked in stir-fries. They need very little preparation. Just trim off the roots, strip off the wilted outer leaves and separate the white and green parts. Spring onion green is sometimes used in Asian dishes as ribbon, to tie tiny parcels of food, in which case it is first blanched so that it becomes more flexible.

SHALLOTS

Although they belong to the same family as garlic, leeks, chives and onions – and look suspiciously like baby onions – shallots are very much their own vegetable. Sometimes called bunching onions, they have bulbs that multiply to produce clusters joined at the root end.

Shallots tend to be sweeter and much milder than large onions. Some Thai varieties are sweet enough to be used in desserts.

Indispensable in Asian kitchens, shallots are far more popular than both regular onions and spring onions (scallions) for everyday use. Ground with garlic, ginger and other aromatics, shallots form the standard marinade and are also an essential ingredient in curry pastes and satay sauce.

Preparation and cooking techniques: Trim the shallots, peel off the skin, then prise the bulbs apart.

Left: Thai pink shallots.

Leave these whole for braising, or chop as required. Thinly-sliced shallot rings are sometimes dry-fried until crisp, then used as a garnish.

CHINESE CHIVES

Although they belong to the same family, Chinese chives are quite different from the Western variety, both in their appearance and taste. Two species are available: one has long, flat green leaves like a small, thin leek, the other has long, tubular stalks with a single bud at the tip. Chinese chives have a much stronger aroma than the ones grown in the West. They don't really taste of onions, but have a flavour that resembles a cross between garlic and leek. They are seldom used as a garnish, but are either served as a vegetable in their own right, or used as an ingredient in cooked dishes, especially with seafood or meat. A very popular Chinese vegetarian dish features chopped chives cooked with scrambled eggs and tofu. This is not only colourful, but tastes delicious. Chinese chives are always sold as leaves only, without the bulb. Uniformly dark green leaves are good, and any that are turning yellow should be discarded. Wash well, drain, then chop or slice into short sections. Cantonese cooks often blanch chives in boiling water or stock for a minute or two before stir-frying.

Above: Chinese chives.

How to make spring onion curls
Spring onion curls make an attractive and edible garnish.

1 Trim off most of the green leaves from the spring onion bulbs to leave a 7.5cm/3in length.

2 Finely shred the spring onions to within about 1cm/½in of the root end.

3 Place the shredded spring onions in a bowl of iced water and chill for 15–20 minutes or until the shredded ends have curled.

FRUIT, NUTS AND SEEDS

When embarking on a low-fat eating plan, it is all too easy to concentrate solely on the fat content of foods while ignoring the amount of sugar they contain. Avoid following a sensible main course with a sugary dessert. Instead, end a meal with a piece of fresh fruit or a few nuts. The latter can be high in fat, but, with the exception of brazil nuts and coconuts, the fat in nuts is monounsaturated or polyunsaturated, and cholesterol-free.

LYCHEES

These moist fruits need no preparation once you have cracked the shells and peeled off the scaly red skin. The pearly white flesh inside can be sliced and used in a fruit salad or savoury dish. South-east Asian cooks like to pair lychees with pork.

MANGOSTEEN

Mangosteens are small, apple-shaped fruits with leathery brown skin that turns purple as they ripen. The flesh looks similar to that of a lychee, but tastes completely different. They are native to South-east Asia and are cultivated in Thailand.The tough skin surrounds delicious white flesh, which is divided into segments, each with a large seed. The pearly white flesh is fresh and fragrant. Some say it tastes like grapefruit. Mangosteens are always eaten raw, but the related kokum, which has a pleasant sour taste, is used as a souring agent in Indian cooking.

Below: Mangosteen can be eaten on its own or added to a fruit salad.

PINEAPPLES

The raw fruit and juice are very popular in Asia, but pineapple is also used in cooked sweet and savoury dishes. Fresh pineapple will keep in a cool place for up to a week. To prepare pineapple, cut off the leaves, then quarter lengthways or cut in slices. Remove the skin and "eyes".

DURIAN

Durian has a very unpleasant smell, often likened to the stench of raw sewage. The ripe flesh, however, is as delicious as the odour is awful: sweet and creamy, with a hint of strawberries.

MANGOES

Most mangoes are oval in shape with blushed gold or pink skin. The easiest way to obtain mango chunks is to cut a thick lengthways slice off each side of the unpeeled fruit. Score the flesh on each slice with criss-cross lines. Fold these slices inside out and slice off the flesh.

PAPAYAS

Papayas or paw-paws can be small and round, but are usually pear-shaped. When ripe, the flesh is eaten as it is or used in fruit salads and other desserts. Papayas that are not too ripe can be added to soups, curries or seafood dishes.

KUMQUATS

Although these look like tiny oranges, they are not in fact citrus fruits, but belong to a species of fruit classified as fortunella. The name comes from the Cantonese *kam kwat*, which translates as "golden orange". About the size of a large olive, the fruits have thin orange-coloured edible rind. This is sweet and provides an interesting contrast to the tangy, often quite bitter pulp it encloses. Kumquats can be eaten whole, halved or sliced into rings.

DRAGON FRUIT

These brightly coloured fruits are widely grown in Vietnam. They come in pink and yellow varieties. The pink ones are about 10cm/4in long, and are covered with pointed, green-tipped scales. The yellow ones are smaller and look more like prickly pears. The flesh is sweet and refreshing, and is best eaten chilled, sprinkled with a little lemon juice.

Above: Dragon fruit.

STAR FRUIT (CARAMBOLA)

The correct name for this fruit is carambola. Cylindrical in shape, the bright yellow waxy-looking fruit has five distinctive "wings" or protuberances which form the points of the star shapes revealed when the fruit is sliced. The flavour varies: fruits picked straight from the tree in Asia are inevitably sweet and scented, but those that have travelled long distances in cold storage can be disappointing.

Above: Asian pears.

ASIAN PEARS

Unlike European pears, Asian pears – from Japan, China and Korea – do not soften when ripe, and are valued for their crunch. There are several varieties, most of which are round, rather than the conventional pear-shape, with golden or russet skin.

LIME

These small, green and very sour citrus fruits are used extensively throughout the region. Fresh lime juice is served as a drink, with salt and sugar, and is also used in salad dressings.

COCONUT MILK AND CREAM

Coconut milk is high in fat but there is a version that is 88 per cent fat free. Coconut milk and cream are both made from the grated flesh of the coconut, and in the East, one can buy bags of freshly grated coconut for just this purpose. Warm water is added and the coconut is squeezed until the mixture is cloudy. When strained, this is coconut milk. If the milk is left to stand, coconut cream will float to the surface.

PEANUTS

One of the most important flavourings in Thai cooking, peanuts are not especially low in fat but a small amount can make all the difference to the character of a dish, so use sparingly. Raw peanuts have little smell, but once cooked they have a powerful aroma, a crunchy texture and a distinctive flavour. Peanuts play an important role in South-east Asian cuisine. The smaller ones are used for making oil, while the larger, less oily nuts are widely eaten, both as a snack food and as ingredients in salads and main courses.

WALNUTS

These have been cultivated in Asia for centuries. They have a delicious sweet-sour flavour, but go rancid quite quickly, so are best used as soon as possible after purchase.

CASHEW NUTS

Have a sweet flavour and crumbly texture. They are never sold in the shell, since removing the seed from its outer casing requires an extensive heating process.

Right: Lotus root and seeds.

Left: Coconut milk thick cream and dessicated coconut.

ALMONDS

These are valued for their aroma and crunchy texture.

GINKGO NUTS

Ginkgo nuts resemble lotus seeds in appearance and taste, but have a smoother and firmer texture and are somewhat less sweet.

CANDLENUTS

These look rather like macadamia nuts and are used as a thickener in Asian cooking. They are slightly toxic when raw, so must always be cooked.

CHINESE CHESTNUTS

These are sweeter and have a finer texture than the Japanese variety. They have a meaty texture and robust flavour, and taste particularly good with Chinese leaves (Chinese cabbage).

SESAME SEEDS

These tiny seeds are flat and pear-shaped. Raw sesame seeds have very little aroma and they are almost tasteless until they are roasted or dry-fried, which brings out their distinctive nutty flavour and aroma.

LOTUS SEEDS

Fresh lotus seeds are used as a snack food. The dried seeds must be soaked in water before use. The seeds are prized for their texture and ability to absorb other flavours. They are often added to soups.

HERBS, SPICES AND FLAVOURINGS

The principal flavourings favoured in South-east Asia have made a tremendous contribution to global cuisine. Ingredients like fresh ginger, lemon grass and kaffir lime now feature on menus the world over, not just in recipes that reflect their origin, but also in fusion food. Fish sauce is an essential seasoning for Thai and Vietnamese cooking, in much the same way that soy sauce is important to the Chinese and Japanese.

GARLIC

Often used with spring onions (scallions) and ginger, garlic is a vital ingredient in Asian dishes. The most common variety has a purple skin, a fairly distinctive aroma and a hint of sweetness. Garlic is strongest when crushed and mildest when left whole and roasted.

Above: Garlic bulb and cloves.

GALANGAL

Galangal is slightly harder than ginger, but used in much the same way. When young, the skin is creamy white with pink sprouts and the flavour is lemony. As galangal matures, the flavour intensifies and becomes more peppery.

Above: Galangal root.

GINGER

Valued not just as an aromatic, but also for its medicinal qualities, ginger is used throughout Asia. When young, ginger is juicy and tender, with a sharp flavour suggestive of citrus. At this stage it can easily be sliced, chopped or pounded to a paste. Older roots are tougher and may need to be peeled and grated. Pickled ginger is delicious.

PALM SUGAR

Widely used in South-east Asia, palm sugar is extracted from the sap of various palm trees. The sap is collected from incisions made in the trunks of the trees. Palm sugar is golden to toffee-brown in colour with a distinctive flavour. It is usually sold in blocks, often referred to as jaggery in Asian stores. The sugar palm tree is the symbol of Cambodia, where the sap is used in the production of medicine, wine and vinegar, among other products.

SICHUAN/SZECHUAN PEPPER

To call this "pepper" is misleading. This spice actually comes from the prickly ash tree, which is native to the Sichuan province in China, but also grows elsewhere in Asia. Unusually, it is the seed pods themselves, not the seeds they contain, that are used for the spice. The tiny reddish brown pods or husks are harvested when ripe, the bitter black seeds are removed and discarded, and the pods – Sichuan peppercorns – are either added whole to stewed dishes or dried and ground as a seasoning spice.

CHILLIES

Although they did not originate in South-east Asia, chillies have been embraced so fervently by Thailand that they are now irrevocably associated with the area. They are an essential ingredient in a variety of Asian cuisines. But it is for their flavour rather than their fire that they are most valued. Be careful when you handle chillies. They contain a substance called capsaicin, which is a powerful irritant. If this comes into contact with delicate skin or the eyes, it can cause pain.

LEMON GRASS

A perennial tufted plant with a bulbous base, lemon grass looks like a plump spring onion (scallion). When the stalk is cut or bruised, the lively citrus aroma becomes evident. There are two main ways of using lemon grass. The stalk can be kept whole, bruised, then cooked slowly in liquid until it releases its flavour and is removed, or the tender lower portion of the stalk can be sliced or finely chopped and then stir-fried.

Above: Sliced lemon grass stalks.

KAFFIR LIME LEAVES

These fruit are not true limes, but belong to a subspecies of the citrus family. Native to South-east Asia, they have green knobbly skins. The fruit is not edible, but the rind is sometimes used in cooking, and it is the leaves that are most highly prized. Kaffir lime leaves are synonymous with Thai cooking. The leaves are torn or finely shredded and used in soups and curries. Finely grated rind is added to fish or chicken dishes.

Right: Kaffir lime and leaves.

BASIL

Three types of basil are grown in Thailand, each with a slightly different appearance, flavour and use. Thai basil has a sweet, anise flavour and is used in red curries. Holy basil is pungent and tastes like cloves. Lemon basil is used in soups and is sprinkled on salads.

CORIANDER/CILANTRO

The entire coriander plant is used in Thai cooking – roots, stems, leaves and seeds. The fresh, delicate leaves are used in sauces, curries and for garnishes. The roots and stems are crushed and used for marinades. The seeds are ground to add flavour to various curry pastes.

MITSUBA

This herb has three light green, coriander-like leaves (hence the name, meaning three leaves) on top of thin whitish stalks about 15–20cm/6–8in long. A member of the parsley family, it is cultivated outside Japan and is available from Asian stores. Mitsuba is used for its unique aroma, so only a few leaves are put into clear soup, thick egg soup or used in hors d'oeuvres. It is also used for casserole dishes and the stalks can be fried.

CHINESE FIVE-SPICE POWDER

Close your eyes as you enter a Chinese supermarket or store and the distinctive aroma of Chinese five-spice powder seems to dominate. This reddish brown spice mixture is classically composed of equal quantities of Sichuan peppercorns, cassia or cinnamon, cloves, fennel seeds and star anise. Blends vary, however, and ginger, galangal, black cardamom and liquorice can

Right: Chinese five-spice and Japanese seven-spice powder.

be included. Ginger gives the spice blend a sweeter flavour, and this version is used in desserts. Five-spice powder is very popular in China, and goes particularly well with duck, pork, red cooked meats (cooked in soy sauce) and barbecued meats such as spare ribs. Make your own powder by grinding equal amounts of the five spices with a mortar and pestle, or buy the ready ground powder in small quantities and store in an airtight jar away from strong light. A five spice paste is now widely available in small jars from many of the larger supermarkets.

SEVEN-SPICE POWDER

Seven-spice powder, which is also known as seven-flavour seasoning or seven-taste powder, is a delicious condiment that the Japanese like to shake on to food at the table much as we would use salt and pepper. It is especially popular as a seasoning for soups and noodles and other dishes such as sukiyaki and tempura. It would be usual to buy this mixture ready prepared. Blends of this spice mixture vary, from mild to very sharp.

CURRY POWDERS

The word curry evolved from the Tamil word *kari,* meaning any food cooked in a sauce. There is little doubt that curry powder, a ready-made blend of spices, was an early convenience food, prepared for merchants, sailors and military men who had served in the East and wished to bring these exotic flavours home. In India, the spices would have been prepared in the kitchen on a daily basis.

Over the decades and centuries these spice and curry mixtures have changed and developed, as have our tastes, so that today our supermarket shelves carry a wealth of different spice mixtures from all parts of the globe.

For enthusiastic cooks it is fun and a creative challenge to make up your own curry powder. Keep experimenting until you find the balance of spicing which suits you and your family.

Above: Yellow curry paste.

CURRY PASTES

Most Thai curries are based on "wet" spice mixtures, made by grinding spices and aromatics in a heavy mortar with a rough surface. Red curry paste is used in beef dishes and robust chicken dishes. Green curry paste, made from herbs and fresh green chillies, is used for chicken curries. Yellow curry paste and, the mildest of all, Mussaman curry paste are used for chicken and beef curries.

TAMARIND PASTE

Tamarind is used in many curries, chutneys and dhals, and is an essential ingredient of Thai hot and sour soups. It is also one of the ingredients in Worcestershire sauce. Tamarind is available in a variety of forms. Blocks of compressed tamarind and slices of dried tamarind have been around for a while, but it is now also possible to buy jars of fresh tamarind and cartons of tamarind concentrate and paste. There is no substitute for tamarind. Some recipes may suggest using vinegar or lemon juice instead, but the results will not compare with using the real thing.

CHILLI BEAN PASTE

This is a Sichuan speciality. What makes it unique is the fact that the beans used are not soya beans, but a type of broad bean, hence the name *douban* or *toban* in Chinese. Outside China the sauce is sold under various names, including chilli bean sauce, hot bean sauce or just plain Sichuan sauce. There are several chilli bean pastes on the market, ranging from mild to hot, but all have a lovely "beany" aroma with a rich flavour.

SHRIMP PASTE

Whether you call it *blachan, terasi, kapi* or *ngapi*, shrimp paste is an essential ingredient in scores of savoury dishes throughout South-east Asia. It is made from tiny shrimps which have been salted, dried, pounded and then left to ferment in the hot humid conditions until the aroma is very pungent. The colour of the paste can be anything from oyster pink to purplish brown, depending upon the type of shrimp and the precise process used. It is compressed and sold in block form or packed in tiny tubs or jars.

WASABI

Sometimes described as horseradish mustard, this has much in common with both, although it is related to neither. Wasabi is Japanese seasoning, derived from a slow-growing plant that is found near mountain streams. The peeled root reveals vivid green flesh. This is finely grated, then dried or powdered. Wasabi powder is mixed with a little water to create a paste. Ready-made pastes are widely available.

Above: Wasabi powder and paste.

ANCHOVY SAUCE

Chinese in origin, this pungent, salty sauce is often used in combination with a sweet, fruity ingredient, such as ripe pineapple. Bottles of this thick, light-grey sauce can be found in Asian stores and markets.

SOY SAUCE

Made from fermented soya beans, this popular condiment is used all over Asia. Chinese soy sauce can be light, dark or a blend of the two. Japan has similar products. Shoyu is a full-flavoured sauce made from fermented soya beans, wheat and salt. *Koikuchi* is dark shoyu, and *usukuchi* is light shoyu. *Usukuchi* is an all-purpose shoyu and is slightly less salty than its Chinese equivalent. Miso is one of the oldest traditional Japanese ingredients, and it has a strong fermented bean flavour. There are three types: *shiro-miso*, which is the lightest in saltiness and flavour; *aka-miso*, which has a medium flavour; and *kuro-miso*, which has the strongest flavour.

OYSTER SAUCE

This thick, brown sauce is made from dried oyster extract, sugar, water and salt. Strongly flavoured and salty, it is used in moderation as a seasoning agent in Chinese-style dishes. It is available in Asian stores.

FISH SAUCE

Thai *nam pla* or fish sauce has a slightly stronger flavour and aroma than the Vietnamese or Chinese versions. It is used in Asia as a seasoning in all kinds of savoury dishes. It is also blended with extra flavourings such as finely chopped garlic and chillies, and sugar and lime juice to make a dipping sauce.

TUK TREY

Similar to *nuoc mam*, this is Cambodia's fish sauce. It is made in the same way as *nuoc mam*, by layering small fish and salt in wooden barrels and leaving them to ferment for months until the juices can be extracted and bottled. Bottles of *tuk trey* can be found in some Asian markets. Alternatively, use the Vietnamese fish sauce, *nuoc mam*, or the Thai version, *nam pla*, which are both useful substitutes.

NUOC MAM

The principal ingredient that is quintessentially Vietnamese is *nuoc mam*, which is a fermented fish sauce with a pungent smell. It is a condiment that most Vietnamese can't do without as it is splashed into practically every soup, stir-fry and marinade, as well as serving as a standard dipping sauce. Bottles are available in most Asian stores. Look for a rich, dark colour with the words *ngon* or *thuong hang* on the label as these indicate a good quality.

NUOC CHAM

This spicy Vietnamese sambal makes a delicious, if fiery, dipping sauce and is good served with crisp, fried spring rolls. To make about 105 ml/7 tbsp, you'll need 2 fresh seeded red chillies, 2 crushed garlic cloves, 15ml/1 tbsp sugar, 45ml/3 tbsp fish sauce, and the juice of 1 lime or ½ lemon. Place the chillies in a large mortar and pound to a paste using a pestle. Then transfer the chillies to a bowl and add the garlic, sugar and fish sauce. Stir in lime or lemon juice to taste.

PLUM SAUCE

Made from plum juice with sugar, salt, vinegar and a thickening agent, plum sauce is a sort of sweet-and-sour sauce. It is generally associated with Chinese food. Thai cooks are partial to plum sauce, but they tend to make their own, using preserved plums and sugar.

Right: Chinese plum sauce.

Above from left: Hoisin sauce, soy sauce and mirin.

HOISIN SAUCE

Another Cantonese speciality, hoisin is also known as barbecue sauce. Its Chinese name literally means "sea-flavour", which is a reflection on just how delicious it is, rather than an indication of its ingredients. Hoisin sauce does not contain so much as a trace of seafood, unlike oyster sauce and fish sauce. The main components of this very popular sauce are fermented beans, sugar, vinegar, salt, chilli, garlic and sesame oil, but there is no standard formula, so the aroma and flavour of different brands can vary considerably. A good quality product should have a fragrant aroma with a rich, warm, sweet yet salty flavour.

CHILLI SAUCE

The best known Asian chilli sauce comes from China, although the Vietnamese have a very hot version and there is also a thick, spicy chilli sauce made in Thailand. This Chinese bottled chilli sauce is quite hot and spicy, with a touch of fruitiness, as it is made from fresh red chillies, salt, vinegar and apples or plums. The Thai version includes both hot and sweet chillies, and adds ginger, spices and vinegar.

BLACK BEAN SAUCE

A mixture of puréed salted black beans with soy sauce, sugar and spice, this popular sauce is especially manufactured for the convenience of Western cooks, since people in China and South-east Asia generally use only whole fermented beans, and make their own sauce by crushing the beans in the wok while cooking. Black bean sauce should not be used cold straight from the jar or bottle, but should always be heated first. It is usually blended with other strongly flavoured seasonings such as spring onions, garlic, ginger and chillies before being added to stews, stir-fries, and braised or steamed dishes. Ready-made black bean sauces seasoned either with garlic or chillies. These should be heated before being used, to bring out the flavour.

YELLOW BEAN SAUCE

Also known as brown bean sauce or ground bean sauce, this Chinese favourite consists of crushed fermented soya beans which have been mixed with salt, wheat flour and sugar to make a paste which is not only useful on its own, but is also the basis of numerous more elaborate sauces. Regular yellow bean sauce has a wonderfully "beany" aroma with a delectable flavour. It is not as salty as black bean sauce, and cooks in every region of China add their own spices and seasonings to make individual blends.

CHILLI OIL

Chilli oil is made by infusing chopped dried red chillies, red chopped onions, garlic and salt in hot vegetable oil for several hours. There is also an "XO chilli oil", which is flavoured with dried scallops, and is much more expensive. Chilli oil is easy to make at home; simply put about 20 seeded and chopped dried chillies in a heatproof container. Heat 250ml/8fl oz/1 cup groundnut or corn oil until it just reaches smoking point, then leave to cool for 5 minutes. Carefully pour the oil into the heatproof container and leave to stand for at least an hour or two. Strain the oil, then use as required.

SESAME OIL

Extracted from sesame seeds, this oil is commonly used in stir-fried dishes. Two types are available: the plain, pale golden oil, which is mildly nutty and is good for frying; and the darker, richer tasting oil made from roasted sesame seeds, which is usually added in small quantities for flavour just before serving

RICE VINEGAR

Vinegar fermented from rice, or distilled from rice grains, is used extensively in Asian cooking. The former is dark amber in colour and is referred to in China as red or black vinegar; the latter is clear, so it is called white vinegar. Unless labelled *yonezu* (pure rice vinegar), most Japanese vinegars, called *su* or *kokumotso-su* (grain vinegar), contain other grains besides rice.

DASHI STOCK

Dashi is a fish stock made from water, konbu and dried skipjack tuna. It can be made at home, or you can buy freeze-dried granules called *dashi-no-moto* for an instant stock, if you prefer.

MIRIN

This amber-coloured, heavily sweetened sauce is made from distilled sake. It is only used in cooking, and adds a mild sweetness, a slight alcoholic flavour and a shiny glaze to food. It is used for simmered dishes and in glazing sauces.

SAKE

There are reputedly about 6,000 brands of sake produced by about 2,000 makers in Japan, ranging from mass-produced nationwide brands to smaller regional, exclusive names.

Right: Japanese sake.

RICE

This low-fat high carbohydrate food is immensley important in Asian cooking. Many Asians eat rice three times a day and it is no coincidence that the Chinese character for cooked rice, *fan*, also stands for nourishment and good health. Rice is the essential element of the meal and anything served with it is merely relish.

Rice is a non-allergenic food, rich in complex carbohydrates and low in salts and fats. It contains small amounts of easily digestible protein, together with phosphorous, magnesium, potassium and zinc. Brown rice, which retains the bran, yields vitamin E and some B-group vitamins, and is also a source of fibre. Although it is healthier than white rice, it is the latter that is preferred in South-east Asia.

There are thousands of varieties of rice, many of which are known only in the areas where they are cultivated. The simplest method of classification is by the length of the grain, which can be long, medium or short.

LONG GRAIN RICE

White long grain rice is the most commonly available and can come from any number of countries. It is three or four times as it is wide. When cooked, the individual grains separate. Long grain rice can be used in a variety of recipes. Brown long grain rice, sometimes called wholegrain rice, is the whole grain complete with bran. Most brown rice is consumed in the West, where is is considered a healthier alternative to white rice.

JASMINE RICE

Also known as fragrant or scented rice, this long grain variety is the staple food of the central and southern parts of Thailand. As the name suggests, jasmine rice has a delicate aroma. The flavour is slightly nutty, and it resembles Basmati rice from India. The uncooked grains are translucent and, when cooked, the rice is fluffy and white. Most of the crop comes from a

Above: Jasmine or fragrant rice has tender, aromatic grains and is popular throughout much of South-east Asia. It is widely available in supermarkets and Asian stores in the West.

region between central and north-eastern Thailand where the soil is a combination of clay and sand. Newly harvested rice from this region is prized for the delicate texture of the grains.

Plain boiled rice
Use long grain or jasmine rice. Allow 50g/2oz/generous ¼ cup raw rice per person.

1 Put the correct amount of dry rice you require in a colander and rinse it under cold running water.

2 Tip into a large pan, then pour in enough cold water to come 2cm/¾in above the surface of rice. (In Asia the traditional way of measuring this is with the help of the index finger. When the tip of the finger is touching the surface of the rice, the water level should just reach the first joint.)

3 Add a pinch of salt, and, if you like, about 5ml/1 tsp vegetable oil, stir once and bring to the boil.

4 Stir once more, reduce the heat to the lowest possible setting and cover the pan with a tight-fitting lid.

5 Cook for 12–15 minutes, then turn off the heat and leave the rice to stand, tightly covered, for about 10 minutes. Fluff up the rice with a fork before serving.

GLUTINOUS RICE

Commonly referred to as sweet or sticky rice, glutinous rice is the mainstay of the diet in the northern and north-eastern regions of Thailand. It is delicious and very filling. The name is derived entirely from its sticky texture, as rice does not contain any gluten. Easily cultivated on the hillsides and high plateaus of these regions, glutinous rice requires less water during the growing period than the wet rice of the central lowlands.

Glutinous rice comes in both short or round grain and long grain varieties. Thai people prefer the long grain variety; the short grain rice is more commonly used in Japanese and Chinese cooking. Some of the long grain varieties have a delicate, aromatic flavour, and these high-grade hybrids are sometimes labelled "jasmine sweet" or "jasmine glutinous rice", the adjective "jasmine" echoing the description used for their fragrant cousins in the non-glutinous rice family.

What makes this type of rice unusual is the way in which the grains clump together when cooked, enabling it to be eaten with the hands. Bitesize chunks of cooked rice are pulled off, one at a time, and rolled to a ball between the fingers and palm of the right hand. The ball is then dunked in a sauce or stew before being eaten. The process is not as messy as it sounds; if it is done correctly, then the grains stick to each other but not to the fingers or the palm. At the end of a meal, rolling the last piece of rice can actually have a cleansing effect, as the rice mops up any remaining juices or grease on the hand.

The starchiness of glutinous rice gives the uncooked grain a distinct opaque white colour, which is different from the more translucent appearance of regular rice grains. When soaked and steamed, however, the reverse is true. Glutinous rice becomes translucent, while regular rice turns opaque.

Although it is in the north and the north-eastern regions of Thailand that glutinous rice is most popular, it is also eaten elsewhere in the country, most frequently in sweet snacks or desserts. The rice is sweetened and flavoured with coconut milk, and is especially popular in the mango and durian season, when huge amounts of the coconut-flavoured rice are sold to eat with these precious fruits. Use low-fat coconut milk to keep the fat content as low as possible.

BLACK GLUTINOUS RICE

This wholegrain rice – that is, with only the husk removed – has a rich, nutty flavour that is distinctly different from the more subtle taste of white glutinous rice. It is generally sweetened with coconut milk and sugar and eaten as a snack or dessert, rather than being used as the staple of a savoury meal. Reduced-fat coconut milk makes an excellent substitute. It does tend to be quite heavy, filling and indigestible if eaten in quantity, so it is usually nibbled as a sweetmeat snack in the mid-afternoon or later in the evening, after the evening meal has been digested. A popular version of roasted glutinous rice, flattened into a cake, is *khao mow rang*, which is sold at all markets throughout Thailand.

In spite of its name, black rice isn't actually black in colour. If the grains are soaked in water for a few hours, the water will turn a deep burgundy red, showing the rice's true colour.

RICE PRODUCTS

Throughout Thailand and South-east Asia, rice, the staple carbohydrate, is used in many different ways.

Rice Flour

This flour may be made from either glutinous or non-glutinous raw rice that has been very finely ground. It is used to make the dough for fresh rice noodles and is also used to make desserts such as pancakes. Rice flour is readily available in Asian food stores. When the source is non-glutinous rice it is called *paeng khao jao* and when it is made from glutinous rice it is known as *paeng khao niao*. Store it as you would wheat flour.

Fermented Rice

Made by fermenting cooked glutinous rice, this is a popular sweetmeat, sold on market stalls and by street vendors.

Rice-pot Crust

In several cultures, the crust that forms on the base of the pan when rice is cooked in a particular way is highly prized. In Thailand, the crust is lifted off the base of the pan in sheets and is then dried out in the sun before being sold. *Khao tang* is lightly toasted or fried before being eaten.

Above: Black and white glutinous rice.

NOODLES

Second only to rice in importance in the Asian diet, noodles and wrappers are cooked in a vast number of ways. Noodles are eaten at any time of day, including breakfast, and if hunger strikes unexpectedly, one of the many roadside noodle carts will furnish a tasty snack. For the local population, soup noodles are easily the most popular dish, but tourists tend to plump for fried noodles. Wrappers are wrapped around all kinds of fillings.

There are a variety of noodles used in Chinese and Thai cooking. Most can be bought fresh in Asian stores, but it is more likely that you will find them dried. Noodles come in several sizes, from tiny transparent threads to large sheets. Many of them are made from rice, which serves to further emphasize the importance of the grain in the Thai diet. Other types of noodles are based on wheat flour or flour made from ground mung beans.

Unfortunately, the names of noodles are not standardized and the same type of noodle may go under several different names, depending on the manufacturer or which part of the country they come from. Noodles made without eggs are often labelled "imitation noodles" or "alimentary paste".

Below: Dried vermicelli rice noodles should be soaked, not boiled.

RICE NOODLES

Both fresh and dried rice noodles are available in Asian supermarkets as well as in most large food stores. Fresh noodles are highly perishable, and they must be cooked as soon as possible after purchase. Rice noodles are available in a wide range of shapes and widths from fine vermicelli to medium rice noodle nests.

Vermicelli Rice Noodles

These noodles are usually sold dried and must be soaked in boiling water before use. When dried, rice vermicelli are known as rice stick noodles and rice river noodles; these noodles are sold both dried and fresh, although the latter form is more popular. Fresh rice stick noodles tend to be rather sticky and need to be separated before being cooked.

Medium Rice Noodles

Resembling spaghetti, these noodles are usually sold dried. The city of Chanthaburi in Thailand is famous for *sen lek* noodles, which are sometimes called *Jantoboon* noodles after the nickname for the town.

Rice Noodle Nests

Although the Thai name of these fresh thick round rice noodles means Chinese noodles, these are actually a Thai speciality, made of rice flour. In the Lacquer Pavilion of Suan Pakkad Palace there is a panel showing the making of *khanom chine* as part of the preparations for the Buddha's last meal. *Khanom chine* are white and the strands are a little thicker than spaghetti. At most markets in Thailand, nests of these noodles are a familiar sight. They are sold freshly cooked. You buy them by the hundred nests and should allow four or five nests per person. Buy the cheaper ones, because they taste better although they are not so white as the more expensive noodle nests.

To prepare deep-fried rice noodles

1 Place the noodles in a large bowl and soak in cold water for 15 minutes. Drain them and lay them on kitchen paper to dry.

2 Heat about 1.2 litres/2 pints/5 cups vegetable oil in a large, high-sided frying pan or wok to 180°C/350°F/Gas 4. To test if the oil is ready, carefully drop in a couple of noodle strands. If they puff and curl up immediately, the oil is hot enough.

3 Very carefully, add a handful of dry noodles to the hot oil. As soon as they puff up, after about 2 seconds, flip them over with a long-handled strainer and cook for 2 seconds more.

4 Transfer to a large baking sheet lined with kitchen paper and leave to cool. When the fried noodles are cold they can be transferred to a sealed plastic bag and will stay crisp for about 2 days.

Fresh noodles are highly perishable, so, even though they are cooked, it makes sense to buy them early in the day, and steam them again when you get them home.

Preparing rice noodles is a simple matter. They need only to be soaked in hot water for a few minutes to soften them before serving.

Rice stick noodles puff up and become wonderfully crisp when they are deep-fried.

EGG NOODLES

These noodles owe their yellow colour to the egg used in their manufacture. Sold fresh in nests, they must be shaken loose before being cooked. They come in both flat and round shapes. Very thin noodles are known as egg thread noodles. The flat type of noodles are generally used for soups and the rounded type are preferred for

Above: Dried egg noodles.

Above: Dried cellophane noodles.

Above: Fresh udon noodles.

stir-frying. Egg noodles freeze well, provided that they are correctly wrapped. Thaw them thoroughly before using them in soup or noodles dishes.

Egg noodles should be cooked in boiling water for 4–5 minutes, or according to the packet instructions.

CELLOPHANE NOODLES

These thin, wiry noodles, also called glass, jelly or bean thread noodles, are made from mung beans. They are the same size as ordinary egg noodles but

---

Noodle know-how

Both dried and fresh noodles have to be cooked in boiling water before use – or soaked in boiling water until pliable. How long for depends on the type of noodle, their thickness and whether or not the noodles are going to be cooked again in a soup or sauce. As a rule, once they have been soaked, dried noodles require about 3 minutes' cooking, while fresh ones will often be ready in less than a minute and may need to be rinsed under cold water to prevent them from overcooking.

---

they are transparent, resembling strips of cellophane or glass. They are only available dried. Cellophane noodles are never served on their own, but always as an ingredient in a dish. Soak them in hot water for 10–15 minutes to soften, then drain and cut into shorter strands.

SOBA NOODLES

This uniquely Japanese noodle is made of buckwheat flour mixed with ordinary wheat flour. To make buckwheat flour, the black-skinned seeds are first coarsely ground, then the outer skins are removed, and the flour is finely ground. As soba made from just buckwheat flour lacks elasticity and stickiness, wheat flour is usually added to act as a smoothing, binding agent. The colour ranges from dark brownish grey to light beige, depending on how the buckwheat seeds were ground.

UDON

This is a thick wheat noodle, which is eaten all over the world and probably has the longest history. To make udon, wheat flour is mixed with salted water to

Right: Dried ramen noodles.

make a dough, then rolled out and thinly sliced. Fresh, raw udon is available in Japan but in the West it is usually either dried or cooked and frozen to be sold in packets.

RAMEN

Literally meaning stretched noodle, ramen originated in China, and is made of wheat flour with added eggs and alkali water. The chemical reaction between them makes the wheat dough smooth and stretchable to create very fine noodles.

PANCAKES AND WRAPPERS

The pancakes of Asia are quite different from their counterparts in the West. For a start, they are almost always made from plain dough, rather than a batter, and they are more often than not served with savoury fillings rather than sweet.

There are two types of pancakes in China, either thin or thick. Thin pancakes are also known as mandarin or duck pancakes, because they are used as wrappers for serving the famous Peking duck. They are also served with other savoury dishes, most notably, the very popular *mu-shu* or *moo-soo* pork, which consists of scrambled egg with pork and wood ears (dried black fungus). Making pancakes demands considerable dexterity, so many cooks prefer to buy them frozen from Asian supermarkets.

Thick pancakes are made with lard and flavoured with savoury ingredients such as spring onions (scallions) and rock salt. In northern China, they are eaten as a snack, or as part of a main meal, rather like the Indian paratha. Both thin and thick pancakes are sometimes served as a dessert, with a filling of sweetened bean paste.

Below: Thin pancakes are used as wrappers, notably for Peking duck, or served with savoury dishes.

Below: Thick pancakes are eaten as a savoury snack, or filled with sweet bean paste and served as a dessert.

NONYA SPRING ROLL PANCAKES

These are the exception to the rule that most pancakes in the East are made from dough. Typical of the Singaporean style of cooking known as Nonya, they are made from an egg, flour and cornflour batter and are traditionally served with a wide selection of fillings.

SPRING ROLL WRAPPERS

Spring rolls are called egg rolls in the USA, and pancake rolls in many other parts of the world. They must be one of the most popular Chinese snacks everywhere, including China itself. While the fillings may vary from region to region, or even between different restaurants and fast food stalls, the wrappers are always more or less the same. They are made from a simple flour and water dough, except in Vietnam, where wrappers are made from rice flour, water and salt.

There are three different sizes of ready-made spring roll wrappers available from the freezers of Asian stores: small, medium and large. They are all wafer-thin. The smallest wrappers, which are about 12cm/4½ in square, are used for making dainty, cocktail-style rolls. The standard-size wrappers measure 21–23cm/8½–9in square, and usually come in packets of 20 sheets. The largest, 30cm/12in square, are too big for general use, so they are usually cut in half or into strips for making samosas and similar snacks.

WONTON SKINS

These skins or wrappers are made from a flour and egg dough, which is rolled out to a smooth, flat thin sheet, as when making egg noodles. The sheet is usually cut into small squares, although round wonton skins are also available. Ready-made wonton skins are stacked in piles of 25 or 50, wrapped and sold fresh or frozen in Asian or Chinese stores.

Unlike spring roll wrappers, which have to be carefully peeled off sheet by sheet before use, fresh wonton skins are dusted with flour before being packed, This keeps each one separate from the others and so they are very

Above: Square wonton wrappers.

Preparing wontons

1 Place the filling in the centre of the wonton skin and dampen the edges.

2 Press the edges of the wonton skin together to create a little purse shape, sealing the filling completely.

easy to use. Frozen wrappers must, however, be thawed thoroughly before use, or they will tend to stick together. Any unused skins can be re-frozen, but should be carefully wrapped in foil so that they do not dry out in the freezer.

Above: Large spring roll wrappers can be cut into strips for making samosas.

There are several ways of using wonton skins. They can be deep-fried and served with a dip, filled and boiled, steamed or deep-fried, or simply poached in a clear broth. On most Chinese restaurant menus in the West, this last option is listed under soups, which is misleading, as in China and South-east Asia wonton soup is always served solo as a snack, never as a separate soup course as part of a meal.

RICE PAPERS

The rice paper used in Thai cooking is quite different from the rice paper that is used for writing and painting in China and Japan, nor does it bear any resemblance to the sheets of rice paper British cooks use as pan liners when baking macaroons. Made from rice flour, water and salt, it is a round, tissue-thin "crepe", dried on bamboo mats in the sun, which results in the familiar crosshatch pattern being embedded on each sheet.

Rice paper is used for wrapping spring rolls and small pieces of meat and fish to be eaten in the hand. The sheets are rather dry and brittle, so must be softened by soaking in warm water for a few seconds before use. Alternatively, they can be placed on damp dish towels and brushed with water until they are sufficiently pliable to be used.

Spring rolls are usually deep-fried, but this is not always the case. Chinese and Thai cooks also make a fresh version. Cooked pork, prawns (shrimp), beansprouts and vermicelli are wrapped in rice paper, which has been dipped in cold water until it is pliable and transparent. The filling can clearly be seen through the wrappers, and the rolls look very pretty.

Packaged and sold in 15cm/6in, 25cm/10in and 30cm/12in rounds, rice papers will keep for months in a cool, dry place, provided the packets are tightly sealed. When buying, look for sheets that are of an even thickness, with a clear, whitish colour. Broken pieces are a sign of bad handling, and are quite useless for wrapping, so avoid any packets that look as if they have been knocked about.

Reheating Chinese pancakes

1 Stack the pancakes, interleaving them with squares of baking parchment.

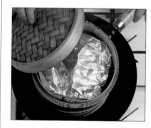

2 Carefully wrap the stacked pancakes in foil, folding over the sides of the foil so that the pancakes are completely sealed.

3 Put the foil parcel in a steamer and cover. Place the steamer on a trivet in a wok of simmering water. Steam for 3–5 minutes until the pancakes are hot.

Left: Rice papers are dried on bamboo mats, which give them their familiar cross-hatch pattern.

TOFU PRODUCTS

An inexpensive protein food invented by the Chinese, bean curd or tofu is now widely enjoyed throughout the world as an alternative to meat or fish.

TOFU

Soya beans are mainly used to make tofu, also known as bean curd. It is often referred to as "poor man's meat" throughout Asia. High in protein, incredibly low in calories and devoid of cholesterol, tofu provides essential amino acids, vitamins and minerals for good health. It is made by combining soya bean milk with a coagulant such as gypsum powder to form curds which are then pressed together into blocks.

Highly versatile, it lends itself to stir-frying, grilling (broiling), steaming, smoking or simmering. It is added to many vegetarian dishes for protein and texture, including stir-fries, soups and stuffings. On its own it is bland, but this is the beauty of it, as it has the ability to absorb flavours and is delicious when marinated in flavourings, then stir-fried and served with fresh basil leaves. Fresh tofu, sold in firm blocks packed in water, is available in most health stores. In Asian stores, you may find soft and medium types. Generally, the soft silken tofu is better for soups and steamed dishes, whereas the medium and firm varieties are best in stir-fries and fillings. Tofu is

best used straight away, but, if it is kept submerged in water which is changed daily, it can be stored for 3–4 days in the refrigerator.

Dried tofu

Also known as "bean curd sticks", this product is made by simmering soya milk until a thin skin forms on top. Traditionally, a long bamboo stick is used to lift the skin off the milk to hang on a line to dry. As they dry, the skins shrink a little and stiffen, until they resemble tongs or "sticks". Creamy coloured and delicate tasting, this dried tofu is sold in packages in Asian markets to be used in soups and stews. Before using, it must first be soaked in water for 20–30 minutes. Dried tofu is also available in sheets which can be used as wrappers for salads and other fillings.

Preserved tofu

Cubes of fermented tofu are preserved in salty brine for several months. Before use, the preserved cubes need to be rinsed thoroughly. Strong in flavour, they are used sparingly when added to stir-fries and soups. Preserved tofu can be found in Asian stores.

Above, clockwise from top: Deep-fried tofu, silken tofu, and cubes of fresh tofu, all varying in degrees of firmness and suited to stir-fries or soups.

Below: Pressed tofu has a firm texture.

Pressed tofu

This is fresh tofu that has been compressed until almost all the liquid has been squeezed out, leaving a solid block with a smooth texture. It is usually marinated in soy sauce and seasoned with five-spice powder, so is pale on the surface, but white inside.

Deep-fried tofu

This is fresh, firm beancurd that has been cut into cubes, squares or triangles, then deep-fried until light brown. Deep-fried beancurd has an interesting texture. It puffs up during cooking, and underneath the crispy brown skin the flesh is white and soft.

Fermented tofu

This is made by fermenting fresh tofu on beds of rice straw, then drying the curd in the sun before marinating with salt, alcohol and spices. Finally, it is stored in brine in sealed earthenware urns and left to mature for at least six months before being packaged and sold. It is definitely an acquired taste and is traditionally served either on its own with rice congee at breakfast, or used in marinating and cooking. Fermented tofu is available from South-east Asian markets and, once opened, must be stored in the refrigerator.

Silken tofu

Soft, silken tofu, drizzled with syrup, is sold by vendors as a warm street snack. It is also often used in soups.

POULTRY AND MEAT

It is traditional in Thailand and China for the meat element in a dish to be a relatively small percentage of the whole, with vegetables and noodles or rice forming the majority of the dish. This is good news for anypne on a low-fat diet. When meat is included, it is usually used in stir-fries, soups and braised or grilled (broiled) dishes, none of which require much additional fat. Chicken is immensely popular and is the leanest meat. Pork, which comes a close second, is not quite such a healthy choice, although the breeding of new and leaner animals has reduced the fat content of pork in recent years. Lamb is not widely eaten, but there is a burgeoning interest in beef, partly because of the proliferation of fast-food restaurants in major cities.

CHICKEN

A whole chicken is a popular purchase almost everywhere in South-east Asia. The breast portion will be sliced or diced for a stir-fry; the rest of the meat will be carefully cut off the carcass and used in a red-cooked dish or a curry, and the bones will be simmered in water to make a stock or soup. The giblets are also valued, as are the feet.

DUCK

Much higher in saturated fat than chicken, especially if you eat the skin, duck is best kept for very occasional treats, or used in small quantities to flavour a substantial broth. When buying duck, look for a bird with a long body and a plump breast. The skin should be unmarked and should look

Left: Duck is often served whole in dishes reserved for festive occasions.

creamy and slightly waxy. The healthiest way of cooking duck breast fillets is to steam them for about an hour, having first removed the skin. The meat can then be sliced and moistened with a little of the water from the steamer. Duck cooked this way is delicious in a salad.

PORK

The leanest cut of pork is fillet (tenderloin). There's very little waste with this cut, and it is perfect for stir-frying. Choose fillets that are pale pink all over. The flesh should be fairly firm, and should be slightly moist to the touch. Avoid any meat with discoloured areas. To prepare pork fillet, pull away the membrane that surrounds the meat, removing any fat at the same time. The sinew, which looks like a tougher strip of membrane, must be sliced away.

BEEF

In much of Asia, the cow was for many centuries regarded solely as a beast of burden, thus too precious to be slaughtered for food. Today, however, thanks to the fast-food industry, beef consumption is on the increase all over China, and even in Japan, which was for centuries a Buddhist (and therefore vegetarian) culture. When buying beef, look for deep red meat. For slow-cooked dishes, a generous marbling of fat is required, but if the meat is to be stir-fried, a leaner cut such as fillet (tenderloin) or rump (round) steak should be used.

LAMB

Although not as popular as pork or beef, lamb is nevertheless an important ingredient in some classic Asian dishes, particularly those that originated in Mongolia or Tibet. Remove any visible fat before cooking, and use sparingly, padding out the meal with vegetables or carbohydrates.

Above: Lean leg steaks, fillet and spare ribs are the preferred cuts of pork.

PRESERVED MEATS

Some traditional Thai and Chinese ingredients are quite high in fat and should be used sparingly.

Chinese Sausages/Wind-dried Sausages

Although these are always described as Chinese sausages, wind-dried sausages are made throughout South-east Asia, and are widely available in the West. There are basically two types: a pink and white sausage, which is made from pork and pork fat, and a darker sausage, in which the pork is mixed with duck liver. The sausages are about 15cm/6in long and about 2cm/¾in wide, and are sold in pairs, tied together with string. Chinese sausages are very versatile. They must be cooked before eating. The best way of cooking them is to cut them diagonally into thin slices, then steam them on top of rice for 10 minutes or so. Alternatively, the whole sausage can be steamed for 10 minutes, then skinned and sliced before adding to dishes such as fried rice.

Pork Crackling

Also known as chicaron, pork crackling is made from pork rind that has been deep-fried, forming crisp puffy crackers. It is served as a crunchy contrast alongside curries, or sliced in salads. The deep-fried rind has a meaty aroma with a subtle flavour. It has a firm yet spongy texture that absorbs other strongly flavoured ingredients. It is used in soups, stews and casseroles.

FISH AND SHELLFISH

Fish is an extremely important source of protein throughout Thailand, China and South-east Asia, whose many coastal waters, rivers and lakes provide an abundant harvest. From a healthy eating perspective, sea bass, cod, grouper, monkfish, red snapper, grey mullet, sea bream, sole and plaice are excellent low-fat protein foods, but the darker-fleshed oily fish like tuna, salmon, carp, trout, mackerel, sardines and herring excite even more interest to those in search of a healthy diet. The Omega-3 fatty acids these fish contain benefit the heart. Scientific research has proved that they can help lower cholesterol and triglyceride levels and reduce the risk of high blood pressure. Scallops and squid are also a good source of Omega-3 fatty acids, and these, along with prawns (shrimp), crab and clams are used to great effect by Chinese and Thai cooks.

Before you purchase your fish, try to take an interest in where your food comes from. Many varieties of fish are in danger of over-fishing, including sea bass, Atlantic cod and wild salmon, so try to be aware of where and how the fish is caught and whether they come from sustainable stocks. If in doubt, choose organically farmed fish.

COD

This large family of fish includes haddock, hake, ling, whiting and many other related species of white-fleshed fish. Cod holds its texture well and can be cooked in many different ways, but it is vitally important not to overcook it.

GREY MULLET

Varieties of grey mullet are found all over the world. The beautiful silvery fish resemble sea bass, but have larger scales and small mouths. A good grey mullet has lean, slightly soft, creamy white flesh with quite a pleasant flavour.

PLAICE

These distinctive-looking fish have smooth, dark greyish-brown skin with orange spots and the underside is pearly white. They have soft, rather bland white flesh, which can sometimes lack flavour.

Above: Lemon and Dover sole.

SOLE

Arguably the finest fish of all. Dover have a firm, delicate flesh with a superb flavour. Sole are best three days after they are caught, so if you are sure that you are buying fish straight from the sea, keep them a couple of days before cooking. The skin should be sticky and the underside very white.

EELS

There are more than twenty members of the eel family. All are snake-like fish with smooth slippery skin and spineless fins. Eels have been a popular food throughtout Asia. They should be bought alive, as they go off very quickly once dead. Ask the fishmonger to kill and skin them and to chop them up into 5cm/2in lengths.

SALMON

The finest wild salmon has a superb flavour and is an excellent healthy choice being full of Omega-3 acids. It is a costly fish, however, and so it may not be affordable on a regular basis. Responsibly farmed salmon is more economical to buy, and although the flavour is not quite as good as that of wild salmon, it is still delicious. The rosy flesh is beautifully moist and responds very well to being poached or baked, either on its own or with herbs and spices or aromatics. Salmon can take quite robust flavours. Try it with sweet soy sauce and noodles for a quick supper. When buying fresh salmon, have a good fishmonger cut you a chunk from a large salmon for really excellent results; do not use ready-cut steaks.

SEA TROUT

They closely resemble salmon, but have smaller less pointed heads and squarer tails. The have fine, dark pink flesh, which is beautifully succulent and has a delicate, mellow flavour.

SEA BASS

Characterized by the delicate flavour of its flesh, sea bass is enjoyed throughout Asia. It holds its shape when cooked, and can be grilled (broiled), steamed, baked or barbecued whole. Sea bass fillets taste delicious when they have been marinated, then cooked on a ridged griddle pan. Chunks or strips make a sensational stir-fry.

GROUPER

These are members of the extensive sea bass family. They look extremely gloomy, with upturned protruding lips. Groupers are available all year round, and can be cooked in the same ways as sea bass.

SNAPPER

There are more than 250 species of snapper throughout the world. The best-known is the red snapper, which is bright red all over. Snapper is a versatile fish that can be baked, poached, pan-fried, grilled (broiled) and steamed.

Above: Red and Emperor Snappers.

MONKFISH

The monkfish tail is one of the finest of all fish, with a superb firm texture and a delicious sweetness, rather like lobster meat. Monkfish is available all year, but is best in spring and summer before spawning. It is sold as whole tails, fillets or medallions. Generally speaking, the larger the tail, the better the quality; avoid thin, scraggy tails.

CARP

This freshwater fish is widely farmed in Asia. It has meaty, moist flesh that can taste a little muddy to those unfamiliar with the distinctive taste. When buying carp, ask the fishmonger to remove the scales and strong dorsal fins. A favourite way of cooking carp is to stuff it with ginger and spring onions (scallions) and serve it with a sweet pickle sauce.

TUNA

This very large fish is usually sold as steaks, which can be pink or red, depending on the variety. Avoid steaks with heavy discoloration around the bone, or which are brownish and dull-looking. The flesh should be solid and compact. Tuna loses its colour and can become dry when overcooked, so cook it only briefly over high heat, or stew it gently with moist ingredients like tomatoes and peppers.

SQUID

The cardinal rule with squid is to either cook it very quickly, or simmer it for a long time. Anything in between will result in seafood that is tough and rubbery. Squid is an ideal candidate for stir-frying with flavours like ginger, garlic, spring onion (scallion) and chilli, and it will also make an interesting salad. For a slow-cooked dish, try squid cooked in a clay pot with chillies and noodles.

LOBSTER

This luxury shellfish is usually served as a restaurant dish. To cook a live lobster, put it in a pan of ice cold water, cover the pan tightly and bring the water to the boil. The shell will turn bright red and the flesh will be tender and succulent when the lobster is cooked.If you buy a ready-cooked lobster the tail should spring back into a curl when pulled out straight.

CRAB

Several varieties of crab are found in Asian waters. Off the coast of Vietnam and Cambodia, the saltwater variety can grow huge, at least 60cm/2ft in diameter. Crab meat has a distinctive taste that goes well with Thai, Chinese and South-east Asian flavours. A popular variety is the soft-shell crabs are blue crabs that shed their hard carapaces, leaving them deliciously tender, with sweet creamy fish. They are extremely delicate so they are generally sold frozen.

SCALLOPS

The tender, sweet flesh of this seafood needs very little cooking. Whenever possible, buy scallops fresh. If they are to be used for sashimi, the coral (roe), black stomach and frill must be removed first. In cooked dishes, the coral can be retained and is regarded as a delicacy.

MUSSELS

This shellfish is widely used in Thai and Asian cooking. Farmed mussels are now readily available and they are usually relatively free of barnacles. They are generally sold in quantities of 1kg/2¼lb, sufficient for a main course for two or three people. Look for good-sized specimens with glossy shells. Discard any that are not closed, or which fail to shut when

Left: If you buy a fresh lobster, make sure the pincers are secured.

tapped. Use the back of a short stout knife to scrape away any barnacles, pull away the hairy "beards", then wash the shellfish thoroughly. The best way to cook mussels is to steam them in a small amount of flavoured liquor in a large lidded pan for 3–4 minutes until the shells open. Use finely chopped fresh root ginger, lemon grass, torn lime leaves and some fish sauce to add flavouring to the mussels.

SHRIMPS AND PRAWNS

If you ask for shrimp in Britain, then you will be given tiny crustaceans, while in the United States, the term is used to describe the larger shellfish which the British refer to as prawns. However, Asian cooks use both words fairly indiscriminately, so check what a recipe requires. Buy raw shellfish whenever possible, and then cook it yourself. This applies to fresh and frozen mixed seafood. If the shellfish are frozen, thaw them slowly and pat them dry before cooking. Since they are low in fat, they are one of the healthiest forms of protein. Dried shrimps are especially popular in China and Thailand. THey are pale pink in colour, having been boiled before being spread out in the sun to dry. Dry shrimps have a very strong smell, and the flavour is sharp and salty. Because of their strong taste, they are usually used as seasoning rather than an independent ingredient, and are often used in rice dishes and to garnish salads.

Butterfly prawns/shrimp

Prawns (shrimp) prepared this way cook quickly and curl attractively.

1 Remove the heads and body shells, but leave the tails. Pull out the intestinal cords using tweezers.

2 Make a cut through the belly of each prawn.

3 Gently open out the two halves of the prawn so that they will look like butterfly wings.

FAT AND CALORIE CONTENTS

The figures show the weight of fat (g) and the energy content per 100g (3½oz) of each of the following typical foods used in Chinese and Thai cooking. Use the table to help work out the fat content of favourite dishes.

	fat (g)	Energy kcals/kJ		fat (g)	Energy kcals/kJ
MEATS			**VEGETABLES**		
Beef minced (ground), raw	16.2	225kcal/934kJ	Asparagus	0.0	12.5kcal/52.5kJ
Beef, rump (round) steak, lean only	4.1	125kcal/526kJ	Aubergine (eggplant)	0.4	15kcal/63kJ
Beef, fillet (tenderloin) steak	8.5	191kcal/799kJ	Bamboo shoots	0.0	29kcal/120kJ
Chicken, minced (ground), raw	8.5	106kcal/449kJ	Beansprouts	1.6	10kcal/42kJ
Chicken fillet, raw	1.1	106kcal/449kJ	(Bell) peppers	0.4	32kcals/128kJ
Chicken thighs, without skin, raw	6.0	126kcal/530kJ	Beans, fine green	0.0	7kcal/29kJ
Duck, without skin, cooked	9.5	182kcal/765kJ	Beetroot (beets)	0.1	36kcal/151kJ
Lamb leg, lean, cooked	6.3	198kcal/831kJ	Broccoli	0.9	33kcal/138kJ
Liver, lamb's, raw	6.2	137kcal/575kJ	Carrot	0.3	35kcal/156kJ
Pork, average, lean, raw	4.0	123kcal/519kJ	Celery	0.2	7kcal/142kJ
Pork, lean roast	4.0	163kcal/685kJ	Chilli, fresh	0.0	30kcal/120kJ
Pork, minced (ground), raw	4.0	123kcal/519kJ	Chinese leaves (Chinese cabbage)	0.0	8kcal/35kJ
Pork, ribs, raw	10.0	114kcal/480kJ	Courgettes (zucchini)	0.4	18kcal74kJ
Turkey, meat only, raw	1.6	105kcal/443kJ	Cucumber	0.1	10kcal/40kJ
Turkey, minced (ground), raw	6.5	170kcal/715kJ	Leek	0.3	20kcal/87kJ
			Lotus root, raw	0.0	74kcal/310kJ
FISH AND SHELLFISH			Mangetouts (snow peas)	0.4	81kcal/339kJ
Cod, raw	0.7	80kcal/337kJ	Mung beans, cooked	0.1	70kcal/295kJ
Crab meat, raw	0.5	54kcal/230kJ	Mushrooms, button (white)	0.5	24kcal/100kJ
Mackerel, raw	16.0	221kcal/930kJ	Mushrooms, shiitake	0.2	55kcal/230kJ
Monkfish, raw	1.5	76kcal/320kJ	Mushrooms, dried	0.0	56kcal/240kJ
Mussels, raw, weight without shells	1.8	74kcal/312kJ	Onion	0.2	36kcal/151kJ
Mussels, raw, weight with shells	0.6	24kcal/98kJ	Pak choi (bok choy)	0.0	13kcal/53kJ
Oysters, raw	4.2	120kcal/508kJ	Spinach (fresh, cooked)	0.0	20kcal/87kJ
Prawns (shrimp)	1.0	76kcal/320kJ	Spring onion (scallion)	0.0	17kcal/83kJ
Salmon, steamed	13.0	200kcal/837kJ	Sweet potato (peeled, boiled)	0.0	84kcal/358kJ
Scallops, raw	1.6	105kcal/440kJ	Water chestnuts	0.0	98kcal/410kJ
Sardine fillets, grilled	10.4	195kcal/815kJ			
Sardines, grilled, weight with bones	6.3	19kcal/497kJ	**NUTS AND SEEDS**		
Sea bass, raw	2.0	97kcal/406kJ	Cashew nuts	48.0	573kcal/2406kJ
Squid, boiled	1.0	79kcal/330kJ	Chestnuts	2.7	169kcal/714kJ
Swordfish, grilled	5.1	155kcal/649kJ	Peanuts	26.9	586kcal/2464kJ
Tuna, grilled	6.3	184kcal/770kJ	Sesame seeds	47.0	507kcal/2113kJ

Below: Red meat such as beef, lamb and pork have a higher quantity of fat per 100g than white meat.

Below: Seafood is a good source of vitamins, minerals and protein. Oily fish contains high levels of Omega-3 fatty acids.

FRUIT	fat (g)	Energy kcals/kJ
Apples, eating	0.1	47kcal/199kJ
Bananas	0.3	95kcal/403kJ
Grapefruit	0.1	30kcal/126kJ
Grapes (green)	0.0	56kcal/235kJ
Lychees	0.1	58kcal/248kJ
Mangoes	0.0	60Kcal/251kJ
Nectarine	0.0	40kcal/169kJ
Oranges	0.1	37kcal/158kJ
Papayas	0.0	36kcal/153kJ
Peaches	0.0	31kcal/132kJ
Pineapple, fresh	0.0	50Kcal/209kJ
Pineapple, canned chunks	0.2	63Kcal/264kJ
Raspberries	0.0	28Kcal/117kJ
Star fruit (carambola)	0.0	25Kcal/105kJ
Strawberries	0.0	27kcal/113kJ
Watermelon	0.0	23kcal/95kJ

BEANS, NOODLES, RICE AND TOFU		
Aduki beans, cooked	0.2	123kcal/525kJ
Noodles, cellophane	trace	351kcal/1468kJ
Noodles, egg	0.5	62kcal/264kJ
Noodles, plain wheat	2.5	354kcal/1190kJ
Noodles, rice	0.1	360kcal/1506kJ
Noodles, soba	0.1	99kcal/414kJ
Rice, brown, uncooked	2.8	357kcal/1518kJ
Rice, white, uncooked	3.6	383kcal/1630kJ
Tofu, firm	4.2	73kcal/304kJ
Tofu, silken	2.5	55kcal/230kJ

BAKING AND PANTRY		
Cornflour (cornstarch)	0.7	354kcal/1508kJ
Flour, plain (all-purpose) white	1.3	341kcal/1450kJ
Flour, self-raising (self-rising)	1.2	330kcal/1407kJ
Flour, wholemeal (whole-wheat)	2.2	310kcal/1318kJ
Tapioca	0.0	28kcal/119kJ
Honey	0.0	288kcal/1229kJ
Soy sauce, per 5ml/1 tsp	0.0	9kcal/40kJ
Sugar, white	0.3	94kcal/1680kJ

FATS, OILS AND EGGS	fat (g)	Energy kcals/kJ
Butter	81.7	737kcal/3031kJ
Low-fat spread	40.5	390kcal/1605kJ
Very low-fat spread	25.0	273kcal/1128kJ
Oil, corn, per 1 tbsp/15ml	13.8	124kcal/511kJ
Oil, groundnut (peanut), per 1 tbsp/15ml	14.9	134kcal/552kJ
Oil, sesame seed, per 1 tbsp/15ml	14.9	134kcal/552kJ
Oil, sunflower, per 1 tbsp/15ml	13.8	124kcal/511kJ
Eggs	10.8	147kcal/612kJ
Coconut milk	17.0	225kcal/944kJ
Coconut milk, reduced-fat	8.6	137kcal/575kJ
Coconut cream	68.8	669kcal/2760kJ

DAIRY PRODUCTS		
Cheese, hard	34.4	412kcal/1708kJ
Cheese, hard, reduced fat	15.0	261kcal/1091kJ
Cheese, cottage	3.9	98kcal/413kJ
Cheese, cream	47.4	439kcal/1807kJ
Cream, double (heavy)	48.0	449kcal/1849kJ
Cream, reduced-fat double (heavy)	24.0	243kcal/1002kJ
Cream, single (light)	19.1	198kcal/817kJ
Cream, whipping	39.3	373kcal/1539kJ
Crème fraîche	40.0	379kcal/156kJ
Crème fraîche, reduced fat	15.0	165kcal/683kJ
Fromage frais, plain	7.1	113kcal/469kJ
Fromage frais, very low-fat	0.2	58kcal/247kJ
Milk, full cream (whole)	3.9	66kcal/275kJ
Milk, semi-skimmed (low-fat)	1.5	35kcal/146kJ
Milk, skimmed	0.1	33kcal/130kJ
Yogurt, low-fat natural (plain)	0.8	56kcal/236kJ
Yogurt, Greek (US strained plain)	9.1	115kcal/477kJ

Below: Vegetables are very low in fat. Eat them raw for a filling snack, or steam them to retain maximum nutritional value.

Below: Soya products, such as tofu, soya milk and soya beans, contain isoflavones that are thought to lower cholesterol levels.

THE
RECIPES

Some of the world's most exciting

and well-known dishes come from

Thailand and China. Although both

countries have their own distinct

cuisine, there is a common emphasis

on serving food that is as fresh as

possible. In the following chapters,

you will find an extensive

collection of exotic dishes that are

not only delicious, but also

low in fat and perfect for

every occasion.

SOUPS

In China, Thailand and South-east Asian countries such as Indonesia and Malaysia, soups are often served alongside the meal. They offer a healthy, low-fat flavoursome choice that provides the palate with tastes and textures that complement or contrast with main dishes. Any of these soups are also ideal as a light lunch or supper, and there's something to please everyone; try comforting Congee with Chinese Sausage, fragrant Thai Fish Broth or classic Beef Noodle Soup.

SPICY GREEN BEAN SOUP ★

*THIS POPULAR SOUP IS MADE WITH BEANS, BUT ANY SEASONAL VEGETABLES CAN BE ADDED OR
SUBSTITUTED. THE RECIPE ALSO INCLUDES SHRIMP PASTE, WHICH GIVES IT A RICH FLAVOUR.*

2 Finely grind the chopped garlic, macadamia nuts or almonds, shrimp paste and the coriander seeds to a paste using a pestle and mortar or in a food processor.

3 Heat the oil in a wok, and fry the onion until transparent. Remove with a slotted spoon. Add the nut paste to the wok and fry it for 2 minutes without allowing it to brown.

4 Add the reserved vegetable water to the wok and stir well. Add the reduced-fat coconut milk to the wok, bring to the boil and add the bay leaves. Cook the soup, uncovered, for 15–20 minutes.

SERVES 8

INGREDIENTS

225g/8oz green beans
1.2 litres/2 pints/5 cups lightly
  salted water
1 garlic clove, roughly chopped
2 macadamia nuts or 4 almonds,
  finely chopped
1cm/1/2 in cube shrimp paste
10–15ml/2–3 tsp coriander seeds,
  dry fried
15ml/1 tbsp sunflower oil
1 onion, finely sliced
400ml/14fl oz can reduced-fat
  coconut milk
2 bay leaves
225g/8oz/4 cups
  beansprouts
8 thin lemon wedges
30ml/2 tbsp lemon juice
salt and ground black pepper

1 Trim the beans, then cut them into small pieces. Bring the lightly salted water to the boil, add the beans to the pan and cook for 3–4 minutes. Drain, reserving the cooking water. Set the beans aside.

COOK'S TIP
Dry fry the coriander seeds for about 2 minutes until the aroma is released.

5 Just before serving, reserve a few green beans, fried onions and beansprouts for garnish and stir the rest into the soup and heat through. Add the lemon wedges, lemon juice and seasoning; stir well. Pour into individual soup bowls and serve, garnished with reserved green beans, onion and beansprouts.

Energy 51kcal/212kJ; Protein 2.2g; Carbohydrate 5.2g, of which sugars 4.2g; Fat 2.5g, of which saturates 0.4g; Cholesterol 3mg; Calcium 43mg; Fibre 1.2g; Sodium 84mg.

UDON NOODLE SOUP ★

THIS DELICATE, FRAGRANT SOUP IS FLAVOURED WITH JUST A HINT OF CHILLI. IT IS BEST SERVED AS A LIGHT LUNCH OR AS A FIRST COURSE. IT LOOKS VERY PRETTY WITH THE NOODLES AND VEGETABLES.

SERVES 4

INGREDIENTS

45ml/3 tbsp *aka-miso*
200g/7oz/scant 2 cups udon noodles, soba noodles or egg noodles
30ml/2 tbsp sake or dry sherry
15ml/1 tbsp rice or wine vinegar
45ml/3 tbsp shoyu or soy sauce
115g/4oz asparagus tips or mangetouts (snow peas), thinly sliced diagonally
50g/2oz/scant 1 cup shiitake mushrooms, stalks removed and caps thinly sliced
1 carrot, sliced into julienne strips
3 spring onions (scallions), thinly sliced diagonally
salt and ground black pepper
5ml/1 tsp dried chilli flakes, to serve

4 Thoroughly combine the sake or sherry, vinegar and soy sauce in a small bowl, then add to the pan of boiling water.

5 Boil the mixture gently for 3 minutes, then reduce the heat and stir in the miso mixture.

6 Add the asparagus or mangetouts, mushrooms, carrot and spring onions, and simmer for 2 minutes until the vegetables are just tender. Season.

7 Divide the noodles among four warm bowls and pour the soup over the top. Serve sprinkled with the chilli flakes.

1 Bring 1 litre/1¾ pints/4 cups water to the boil in a pan. Pour 150ml/¼ pint/⅔ cup of the boiling water over the miso and stir until it has dissolved.

2 Meanwhile, bring another large pan of lightly salted water to the boil, add the noodles and cook according to the packet instructions until they are just tender.

3 Drain the noodles in a colander. Rinse under cold water, then drain again.

COOK'S TIP

Miso is a thick fermented paste based on cooked soya beans with rice or a similar cereal. It adds a savoury flavour to dishes. There are various types, *aka-miso* being medium strength.

Energy 223kcal/942kJ; Protein 7.5g; Carbohydrate 40.9g, of which sugars 3.8g; Fat 3.4g, of which saturates 0.1g; Cholesterol 0mg; Calcium 29mg; Fibre 2.5g; Sodium 807mg.

OMELETTE SOUP ★

*A VERY SATISFYING BUT HEALTHY SOUP THAT IS QUICK AND EASY TO PREPARE. IT IS VERSATILE, TOO,
IN THAT YOU CAN VARY THE VEGETABLES ACCORDING TO WHAT IS AVAILABLE.*

<u>SERVES 4</u>

INGREDIENTS

1 egg
5ml/1 tsp sunflower oil
900ml/1½ pints/3¾ cups
  vegetable stock
2 large carrots, finely diced
4 leaves pak choi (bok choy),
  shredded
30ml/2 tbsp soy sauce
2.5ml/½ tsp granulated sugar
2.5ml/½ tsp ground black pepper
fresh coriander (cilantro) leaves,
  to garnish

VARIATION
Use Savoy cabbage instead of pak choi.
In Thailand there are about forty
different types of pak choi, including
miniature versions.

1 Put the egg in a bowl and beat lightly
with a fork. Heat the oil in a small frying
pan until it is hot, but not smoking.
Pour in the egg and swirl the pan so
that it coats the base evenly. Cook over
a medium heat until the omelette has
set and the underside is golden. Slide
it out of the pan and roll it up like a
pancake. Slice into 5mm/¼in rounds
and set aside for the garnish.

2 Put the stock into a large pan. Add
the carrots and pak choi and bring
to the boil. Reduce the heat and simmer
for 5 minutes, then add the soy sauce,
granulated sugar and pepper.

3 Stir well, then pour into warmed
bowls. Lay a few omelette rounds on the
surface of each portion and complete
the garnish with the coriander leaves.

Energy 52kcal/217kJ; Protein 3.4g; Carbohydrate 4.1g, of which sugars 3.8g; Fat 2.6g, of which saturates 0.6g; Cholesterol 48mg; Calcium 100mg; Fibre 1.7g; Sodium 628mg.

MIXED VEGETABLE SOUP ★

IN THAILAND, THIS TYPE OF SOUP IS USUALLY MADE IN LARGE QUANTITIES AND THEN REHEATED FOR CONSUMPTION OVER SEVERAL DAYS. CHILL LEFTOVER SOUP RAPIDLY AND REHEAT BEFORE SERVING.

SERVES 4

INGREDIENTS
    15ml/1 tbsp sunflower oil
    15ml/1 tbsp magic paste (see
      Cook's Tip)
    90g/3½oz Savoy cabbage or
      Chinese leaves (Chinese cabbage),
      finely shredded
    90g/3½oz mooli (daikon),
      finely diced
    1 medium cauliflower,
      coarsely chopped
    4 celery sticks, coarsely chopped
    1.2 litres/2 pints/5 cups
      vegetable stock
    130g/4½oz fried tofu, cut into
      2.5cm/1in cubes
    5ml/1 tsp palm sugar or light
      muscovado (brown) sugar
    45ml/3 tbsp light soy sauce

1 Heat the sunflower oil in a large, heavy pan or wok. Add the magic paste and cook over a low heat, stirring frequently, until it gives off its aroma. Add the shredded Savoy cabbage or Chinese leaves, mooli, cauliflower and celery. Pour in the vegetable stock, increase the heat to medium and bring to the boil, stirring occasionally. Gently stir in the tofu cubes.

2 Add the sugar and soy sauce. Reduce the heat and simmer for 15 minutes, until the vegetables are cooked and tender. Taste and add a little more soy sauce if needed. Serve hot.

COOK'S TIP
Magic paste is a mixture of crushed garlic, white pepper and coriander. Look for it at Thai markets.

Energy 75kcal/311kJ; Protein 3.6g; Carbohydrate 4g, of which sugars 3.8g; Fat 5g, of which saturates 0.6g; Cholesterol 0mg; Calcium 196mg; Fibre 1g; Sodium 825mg.

CHEAT'S SHARK'S FIN SOUP ★

*SHARK'S FIN SOUP IS A RENOWNED DELICACY. IN THIS VEGETARIAN VERSION TRANSPARENT
CELLOPHANE NOODLES MASQUERADE AS SHARK'S FIN NEEDLES, WITH REMARKABLE EFFECTS.*

SERVES 4–6

INGREDIENTS

4 dried Chinese mushrooms
25ml/1½ tbsp dried cloud ear
  (wood ear) mushrooms
115g/4oz cellophane noodles
30ml/2 tbsp vegetable oil
2 carrots, cut into fine strips
115g/4oz canned bamboo shoots,
  rinsed, drained and cut into strips
1 litre/1¾ pints/4 cups
  vegetable stock
15ml/1 tbsp light soy sauce
15ml/1 tbsp arrowroot or
  potato flour
1 egg white, beaten (optional)
5ml/1 tsp sesame oil
salt and ground black pepper
2 spring onions (scallions), finely
  chopped, to garnish
Chinese red vinegar, to
  serve (optional)

1 Soak the mushrooms and cloud ears
in separate bowls of warm water for
20 minutes. Drain.

2 Remove the mushroom stems from
the water and slice the caps thinly. Cut
the cloud ears into fine strips,
discarding any hard bits.

3 Soak the noodles in hot water until
soft. Drain and cut into short lengths.

4 Heat the oil in a large pan. Add the
mushrooms and stir-fry for 2 minutes.

5 Add the cloud ears, stir-fry for
2 minutes, then stir in the carrots,
bamboo shoots and noodles.

COOK'S TIP
Also known as mung bean or transparent
noodles, cellophane noodles retain their
firm texture when cooked.

6 Add the stock to the pan. Bring to the
boil, then simmer for 15–20 minutes.

7 Season with salt, pepper and soy
sauce. Blend the arrowroot or potato
flour with about 30ml/2 tbsp water.
Pour into the soup, stirring all the time
to prevent lumps from forming as the
soup continues to simmer.

8 Remove the pan from the heat. Stir
in the egg white, if using, so that it sets
to form small threads in the hot soup.
Stir in the sesame oil, then pour the
soup into individual heated bowls.

9 Sprinkle with chopped spring onions
and offer the Chinese red vinegar
separately, if you are using it.

Energy 124kcal/518kJ; Protein 2.4g; Carbohydrate 18.9g, of which sugars 1.2g; Fat 4.4g, of which saturates 0.5g; Cholesterol 0mg; Calcium 11mg; Fibre 0.5g; Sodium 184mg.

CELLOPHANE NOODLE SOUP ★

EXOTIC DRIED LILY FLOWERS ARE FROM CHINA. THESE EDIBLE FLOWERS ARE ALSO KNOWN AS TIGER LILY BUDS OR GOLDEN NEEDLES, AND ARE USED IN A VARIETY OF SOUPS AND OTHER DISHES.

SERVES 4

INGREDIENTS
4 large dried shiitake mushrooms
15g/½oz dried golden needles
(lily buds)
½ cucumber, coarsely chopped
2 garlic cloves, halved
90g/3½oz white cabbage, chopped
1.2 litres/2 pints/5 cups boiling water
115g/4oz cellophane noodles
30ml/2 tbsp soy sauce
15ml/1 tbsp palm sugar or light
muscovado (brown) sugar
90g/3½oz block silken tofu, diced
fresh coriander (cilantro) leaves,
to garnish

1 Soak the shiitake mushrooms in warm water for 30 minutes. In a separate bowl, soak the dried golden needles in warm water, also for 30 minutes.

2 Meanwhile, put the cucumber, garlic and cabbage in a food processor and process to a smooth paste. Scrape the mixture into a large pan and add the measured boiling water.

3 Bring to the boil, then reduce the heat and cook for 2 minutes, stirring occasionally. Strain this stock into another pan, return to a low heat and bring to simmering point.

4 Drain the golden needles, rinse under cold running water, then drain again. Cut off any hard ends. Add to the stock with the noodles, soy sauce and sugar and cook for 5 minutes more.

5 Strain the mushroom soaking liquid into the soup. Discard the mushroom stems, then slice the caps. Divide them and the tofu among four bowls. Pour the soup over, garnish and serve.

Energy 148kcal/618kJ; Protein 4.1g; Carbohydrate 29.7g, of which sugars 5.7g; Fat 1.1g, of which saturates 0.1g; Cholesterol 0mg; Calcium 139mg; Fibre 0.7g; Sodium 546mg.

HOT AND SOUR SOUP ★

THIS SPICY, WARMING SOUP REALLY WHETS THE APPETITE AND IS THE PERFECT INTRODUCTION TO A SIMPLE CHINESE MEAL. USE HOME-MADE VEGETABLE STOCK FOR THE BEST POSSIBLE FLAVOUR.

SERVES 4

INGREDIENTS
    10g/¼oz dried cloud ear
      (wood ear) mushrooms
    8 fresh shiitake mushrooms
    75g/3oz firm tofu
    50g/2oz/½ cup sliced, drained,
      canned bamboo shoots
    900ml/1½ pints/3¾ cups
      vegetable stock
    15ml/1 tbsp caster (superfine) sugar
    45ml/3 tbsp rice vinegar
    15ml/1 tbsp light soy sauce
    1.5ml/¼ tsp chilli oil
    2.5ml/½ tsp salt
    large pinch of ground white pepper
    15ml/1 tbsp cornflour (cornstarch)
    15ml/1 tbsp cold water
    1 egg white
    5ml/1 tsp sesame oil
    2 spring onions (scallions),
      cut into fine rings

1 Soak the dried cloud ears in hot water for 20 minutes or until soft. Drain, trim off and discard the hard base from each cloud ear and then chop the fungus roughly.

2 Remove and discard the stems from the shiitake mushrooms. Cut the caps into thin strips.

3 Cut the tofu into 1cm/½in cubes and shred the bamboo shoots finely.

4 Place the stock, mushrooms, tofu, bamboo shoots and cloud ear mushrooms in a large pan. Bring the stock to the boil, lower the heat and simmer for about 5 minutes.

5 Stir in the sugar, vinegar, soy sauce, chilli oil, salt and pepper. Mix the cornflour to a paste with the water. Add the mixture to the soup, stirring constantly with a spoon or whisk until it thickens slightly.

6 Lightly beat the egg white, then pour it slowly into the soup in a steady stream, stirring constantly. Cook, stirring, until the egg white changes colour and becomes thready.

7 Add the sesame oil just before serving. Ladle into heated bowls and top each portion with spring onion rings.

COOK'S TIP
To transform this tasty soup into a nutritious light meal, simply add extra mushrooms, tofu, bamboo shoots and noodles.

Energy 60kcal/254kJ; Protein 3.2g; Carbohydrate 8.4g, of which sugars 4.6g; Fat 1.8g, of which saturates 0.3g; Cholesterol 0mg; Calcium 103mg; Fibre 0.5g; Sodium 287mg.

TOFU SOUP WITH MUSHROOMS AND TOMATO ★

THIS BROTH IS PERFECT TO BALANCE A MEAL THAT MAY INCLUDE SOME HEAVIER DISHES. AS THE SOUP IS RELIANT ON AN AROMATIC BROTH, THE BASIC STOCK NEEDS TO BE RICH IN TASTE.

SERVES 4

INGREDIENTS

115g/4oz/scant 2 cups dried shiitake
   mushrooms, soaked in water for
   20 minutes
5ml/1 tsp sunflower oil
2 shallots, halved and sliced
2 Thai chillies, seeded and sliced
4cm/1½ in fresh root ginger, peeled
   and grated or finely chopped
15ml/1 tbsp *nuoc mam* or other
   fish sauce
350g/12oz tofu, rinsed, drained
   and cut into bitesize cubes
4 tomatoes, skinned, seeded and
   cut into thin strips
salt and ground black pepper
1 bunch coriander (cilantro),
   stalks removed, finely chopped,
   to garnish

For the stock

1 meaty chicken carcass
25g/1oz dried squid or shrimp,
   soaked in water for 15 minutes
2 onions, peeled and quartered
2 garlic cloves, crushed
7.5cm/3in fresh root ginger, chopped
15ml/1 tbsp *nuoc mam* or other
   fish sauce
6 black peppercorns
2 star anise
4 cloves
1 cinnamon stick
sea salt

1 To make the stock, put the chicken carcass in a deep pan. Drain and rinse the dried squid or shrimp. Add to the pan with the remaining stock ingredients, except the salt, and pour in 2 litres/3½ pints/8 cups water. Bring to the boil, and boil for a few minutes, skim off any foam, then reduce the heat and simmer with the lid on for 1½–2 hours.

2 Remove the lid and continue simmering the stock for a further 30 minutes to reduce. Skim off any fat, season, then strain and measure out 1.5 litres/2½ pints/6¼ cups.

3 Squeeze dry the soaked shiitake mushrooms, remove the stems and slice the caps into thin strips. Heat the oil in a large pan or wok and stir in the shallots, chillies and ginger. As the fragrance begins to rise, stir in the *nuoc mam*, followed by the stock.

4 Add the tofu, mushrooms and tomatoes and bring to the boil. Reduce the heat and simmer for 5–10 minutes. Season to taste and sprinkle the finely chopped fresh coriander over the top. Serve piping hot.

Energy 100kcal/418kJ; Protein 8.8g; Carbohydrate 5.2g, of which sugars 4.5g; Fat 5g, of which saturates 0.7g; Cholesterol 0mg; Calcium 480mg; Fibre 1.8g; Sodium 32mg.

Miso Broth with Tofu ★

This is a simple but highly nutritious soup. It is makes a warming breakfast, and can also be eaten with rice or noodles for a more filling snack later in the day.

3 Heat the mixture gently until it is boiling, then lower the heat and simmer for 10 minutes. Strain, return to the pan and reheat until simmering.

4 Add the green portion of the sliced spring onions or leeks to the soup with the pak choi or greens and tofu. Cook for 2 minutes.

5 Mix 45ml/3 tbsp of the miso with a little of the hot soup in a bowl, then stir it into the soup. Taste the soup and add more miso with soy sauce to taste.

6 Chop the reserved coriander leaves roughly and stir most of them into the soup with the white part of the spring onions or leeks.

7 Cook for 1 minute, then ladle the soup into warmed serving bowls. Sprinkle with the remaining coriander and the fresh red chilli, if using, and serve at once.

SERVES 4

INGREDIENTS

   1 bunch of spring onions (scallions)
     or 5 baby leeks
   15g/½ oz fresh coriander (cilantro),
     including the stalks
   3 thin slices fresh root ginger
   2 star anise
   1 small dried red chilli
   1.2 litres/2 pints/5 cups dashi stock
     or vegetable stock
   225g/8oz pak choi (bok choy) or
     other Asian greens, thickly sliced
   200g/7oz firm tofu, cut into
     2.5cm/1in cubes
   60ml/4 tbsp red miso
   30–45ml/2–3 tbsp shoyu or other
     soy sauce
   1 fresh red chilli, seeded and
     shredded (optional)

1 Cut the coarse green tops off the spring onions or baby leeks and slice the rest finely on the diagonal. Place the tops in a large pan.

2 Remove the coriander leaves from the stalks, and set the leaves aside. Add the coriander stalks, fresh root ginger, star anise and dried chilli to the pan. Pour in the dashi or vegetable stock.

COOK'S TIP
- Dashi powder is available in most Asian and Chinese stores. Alternatively, make your own by gently simmering 10–15cm/4–6in konbu seaweed in 1.2 litres/2 pints/5 cups water for 10 minutes. Do not boil the stock vigorously as this makes the dashi bitter. Remove the konbu, then add 15g/½oz dried bonito flakes and bring to the boil. Strain immediately through a fine sieve.
- If you prefer not to use dashi stock, you can substitute instant or home-made vegetable stock in its place.

Energy 71kcal/297kJ; Protein 7.2g; Carbohydrate 4.2g, of which sugars 3.5g; Fat 2.9g, of which saturates 0.4g; Cholesterol 0mg; Calcium 372mg; Fibre 2.6g; Sodium 884mg

HOT AND SWEET VEGETABLE AND TOFU SOUP ★

AN INTERESTING COMBINATION OF HOT, SWEET AND SOUR FLAVOURS. IT IS QUICK TO MAKE AS THE SPINACH AND TOFU ARE SIMPLY PLACED IN BOWLS AND COVERED WITH THE FLAVOURED HOT STOCK.

SERVES 4

INGREDIENTS
1.2 litres/2 pints/5 cups
 vegetable stock
5–10ml/1–2 tsp Thai red
 curry paste
2 kaffir lime leaves, torn
40g/1½oz/3 tbsp palm sugar or light
 muscovado (brown) sugar
30ml/2 tbsp soy sauce
juice of 1 lime
1 carrot, cut into thin batons
50g/2oz baby spinach leaves, any
 coarse stalks removed
225g/8oz block silken tofu, diced

1 Heat the stock in a large pan, then add the red curry paste. Stir constantly over a medium heat until the paste has dissolved. Add the lime leaves, sugar and soy sauce and bring to the boil.

2 Add the lime juice and carrot to the pan. Reduce the heat and simmer for 5–10 minutes. Place the spinach and tofu in four individual serving bowls and pour the hot stock on top to serve.

Energy 98kcal/412kJ; Protein 5.3g; Carbohydrate 12.7g, of which sugars 12.3g; Fat 3.3g, of which saturates 0.4g; Cholesterol 0mg; Calcium 318mg; Fibre 0.6g; Sodium 558mg.

TOFU AND BEANSPROUT SOUP ★

THIS LIGHT AND REFRESHING SOUP IS AN EXCELLENT PICK-ME-UP. THE AROMATIC, SPICY BROTH IS SIMMERED FIRST, AND THEN THE TOFU, BEANSPROUTS AND NOODLES ARE ADDED.

SERVES 4

INGREDIENTS

150g/5oz dried thick rice noodles
1 litre/1¾ pints/4 cups
  vegetable stock
1 red chilli, seeded and
  finely sliced
15ml/1 tbsp light soy sauce
juice of ½ lemon
10ml/2 tsp sugar
5ml/1 tsp finely sliced garlic
5ml/1 tsp finely chopped fresh
  root ginger
200g/7oz firm tofu, cubed
90g/3½oz beansprouts
50g/2oz peanuts
15ml/1 tbsp chopped fresh
  coriander (cilantro)
spring onion (scallion) slivers and
  red chilli slivers, to garnish

1 Spread out the noodles in a shallow dish and and cook according to the packet instructions until they are just tender. Drain, rinse and set aside.

2 Meanwhile, place the stock, red chilli, soy sauce, lemon juice, sugar, garlic and ginger in a wok over high heat. Bring to the boil, cover, reduce to low heat and simmer gently for 10–12 minutes.

3 Cut the tofu into cubes. Add it to the wok with the drained noodles and beansprouts. Cook the mixture gently for 2–3 minutes.

4 Roast the peanuts in a dry non-stick wok, then chop them. Stir the coriander into the soup. Serve in warm bowls with peanuts, spring onions and chilli on top.

Energy 190kcal/795kJ; Protein 6.7g; Carbohydrate 34.7g, of which sugars 3.5g; Fat 2.3g, of which saturates 0.3g; Cholesterol 0mg; Calcium 266mg; Fibre 0.4g; Sodium 275mg.

NORTHERN PRAWN AND SQUASH SOUP ★

THIS TRADITIONAL NORTHERN THAILAND SOUP IS QUITE A HEARTY DISH. THE BANANA FLOWER ISN'T AN ESSENTIAL INGREDIENT, BUT IT DOES ADD A UNIQUE AND AUTHENTIC FLAVOUR.

SERVES 4

INGREDIENTS

1 butternut squash, about 300g/11oz
1 litre/1¾ pints/4 cups
   vegetable stock
90g/3½oz/scant 1 cup green beans,
   cut into 2.5cm/1in pieces
45g/1¾oz dried banana
   flower (optional)
15ml/1 tbsp Thai fish sauce
225g/8oz raw prawns (shrimp)
small bunch fresh basil
cooked rice, to serve
For the chilli paste
115g/4oz shallots, sliced
10 drained bottled green peppercorns
1 small fresh green chilli, seeded and
   finely chopped
2.5ml/½ tsp shrimp paste

1 Peel the squash and cut it in half. Scoop out the seeds and discard, then cut the flesh into neat cubes. Set aside.

2 Make the chilli paste by pounding the sliced shallots, peppercorns, chilli and shrimp paste together using a mortar and pestle or puréeing them in a spice blender.

3 Heat the vegetable stock gently in a large pan, then stir in the chilli paste. Add the squash, beans and banana flower, if using. Bring to the boil and cook for 15 minutes.

4 Add the fish sauce, prawns and basil. Simmer for 3 minutes. Serve in warmed bowls, accompanied by rice.

Energy 73kcal/307kJ; Protein 11.8g; Carbohydrate 5.2g, of which sugars 3.9g; Fat 0.7g, of which saturates 0.2g; Cholesterol 113mg; Calcium 90mg; Fibre 1.7g; Sodium 669mg.

PIQUANT PRAWN LAKSA ★

THIS SPICY SOUP TASTES JUST AS GOOD WHEN MADE WITH FRESH CRAB MEAT OR ANY FLAKED
COOKED FISH. IF YOU ARE SHORT OF TIME OR CAN'T FIND ALL THE SPICY PASTE INGREDIENTS,
BUY READY-MADE LAKSA PASTE, WHICH IS AVAILABLE FROM MANY ASIAN STORES.

2 To make the spicy paste, place the freshly prepared chopped lemon grass, seeded and chopped red chillies, sliced fresh root ginger, shrimp paste, chopped garlic cloves, ground turmeric and tamarind paste in a mortar and pound with a pestle to form a paste. Alternatively, put the ingredients in a food processor and whizz until a smooth paste is formed.

3 Heat the vegetable oil in a large pan, add the spicy paste and fry, stirring constantly, for a few moments to release all the flavours, but be careful not to let it burn.

SERVES 3

INGREDIENTS
   115g/4oz rice vermicelli or noodles
   10ml/2 tsp vegetable oil
   750ml/1¼ pints/3 cups fish stock
   200ml/7fl oz/scant 1 cup coconut milk
   30ml/2 tbsp fish sauce
   ½ lime
   18 cooked peeled prawns (shrimp)
   salt and cayenne pepper
   60ml/4 tbsp fresh coriander (cilantro)
     sprigs, chopped, to garnish
For the spicy paste
   2 lemon grass stalks, finely chopped
   2 fresh red chillies, seeded
     and chopped
   2.5cm/1in piece fresh root ginger,
     peeled and sliced
   2.5ml/½ tsp dried shrimp paste
   2 garlic cloves, chopped
   2.5ml/½ tsp ground turmeric
   30ml/2 tbsp tamarind paste

1 Cook the rice vermicelli or noodles in a large pan of boiling salted water according to the instructions on the packet. Tip the vermicelli or noodles into a large strainer, then rinse them under cold water until the liquid runs clear and drain. Keep warm.

VARIATION
Replace the rice vermicelli or noodles with fresh egg noodles for a more substantial soup.

4 Add the fish stock and coconut milk and bring to the boil. Stir in the fish sauce, then simmer for 5 minutes. Season with salt and cayenne to taste, adding a squeeze of lime. Add the prawns and heat through for a few seconds.

5 Divide the noodles among three soup plates. Pour over the soup, making sure that each portion includes an equal number of prawns. Garnish with coriander and serve piping hot.

Energy 224kcal/939kJ; Protein 15.7g; Carbohydrate 33.7g, of which sugars 3.6g; Fat 2.9g, of which saturates 0.5g; Cholesterol 130mg; Calcium 108mg; Fibre 0.5g; Sodium 206mg.

BROTH <u>WITH</u> STUFFED CABBAGE LEAVES ★

A SUBTLY SPICY FILLING OF PRAWNS, PORK AND VEGETABLES IS FLAVOURED WITH TRADITIONAL THAI INGREDIENTS. THE HEALTHY LOW-FAT FILLING IS WRAPPED IN CABBAGE LEAVES AND SIMMERED IN A WONDERFULLY AROMATIC CHICKEN STOCK FOR FULL FLAVOUR WITHOUT FAT.

SERVES 4

INGREDIENTS

10 Chinese leaves (Chinese cabbage) or Savoy cabbage leaves, halved, main ribs removed
4 spring onions (scallions), green tops left whole, white part finely chopped
5–6 dried cloud ear (wood ear) mushrooms, soaked in hot water for 15 minutes
115g/4oz minced (ground) lean pork
115g/4oz prawns (shrimp), shelled, deveined and finely chopped
1 Thai chilli, seeded and chopped
30ml/2 tbsp *nuoc mam* or other fish sauce
15ml/1 tbsp soy sauce
4cm/1½in fresh root ginger, peeled and very finely sliced
chopped fresh coriander (cilantro), to garnish

For the stock
1 meaty chicken carcass
2 onions, peeled and quartered
4 garlic cloves, crushed
4cm/1½in fresh root ginger, chopped
30ml/2 tbsp *nuoc mam* or other fish sauce
30ml/2 tbsp soy sauce
6 black peppercorns
a few sprigs of fresh thyme
sea salt

1 To make the chicken stock, put the chicken carcass into a deep pan. Add all the other stock ingredients except the sea salt and pour over 2 litres/3½ pints/8 cups of water. Bring to the boil, and boil for a few minutes, skim off any foam, then reduce the heat and simmer gently with the lid on for 1½–2 hours.

2 Remove the lid and simmer for a further 30 minutes to reduce the stock. Skim off any fat, season with sea salt, then strain the stock and measure out 1.5 litres/2½ pints/6¼ cups. It is important to skim off any froth or fat, so that the broth is light and fragrant.

3 Blanch the cabbage leaves in boiling water for about 2 minutes, or until tender. Remove with a slotted spoon and refresh under cold water. Add the green tops of the spring onions to the boiling water and blanch for a minute, or until tender, then drain and refresh under cold water. Carefully tear each piece into five thin strips and set aside.

4 Squeeze dry the cloud ear mushrooms, then trim and finely chop and mix with the pork, prawns, spring onion whites, chilli, *nuoc mam* and soy sauce. Lay a cabbage leaf flat on a surface and place a teaspoon of the filling about 1cm/½in from the bottom edge – the edge nearest to you.

5 Fold this bottom edge over the filling, and then fold in the sides of the leaf to seal it. Roll all the way to the top of the leaf to form a tight bundle. Wrap a piece of blanched spring onion green around the bundle and tie it so that it holds together. Repeat with the remaining leaves and filling.

6 Bring the stock to the boil in a wok or deep pan. Stir in the finely sliced ginger, then reduce the heat and drop in the cabbage bundles. Bubble very gently over a low heat for about 20 minutes to ensure that the filling is thoroughly cooked. Serve immediately, ladled into bowls with a sprinkling of fresh coriander leaves.

Energy 80kcal/334kJ; Protein 12.7g; Carbohydrate 3.9g, of which sugars 3.7g; Fat 1.5g, of which saturates 0.5g; Cholesterol 74mg; Calcium 68mg; Fibre 1.4g; Sodium 891mg.

PUMPKIN, PRAWN AND COCONUT SOUP ★

IN THIS LOVELY LOOKING SOUP, THE NATURAL SWEETNESS OF THE PUMPKIN IS HEIGHTENED BY THE ADDITION OF A LITTLE SUGAR, BUT THIS IS BALANCED BY THE CHILLIES, SHRIMP PASTE AND DRIED SHRIMP. REDUCED-FAT COCONUT MILK BLURS THE BOUNDARIES BEAUTIFULLY.

SERVES 6

INGREDIENTS
- 450g/1lb pumpkin
- 2 garlic cloves, crushed
- 4 shallots, finely chopped
- 2.5ml/½ tsp shrimp paste
- 1 lemon grass stalk, chopped
- 2 fresh green chillies, seeded
- 15ml/1 tbsp dried shrimp soaked for 10 minutes in warm water to cover
- 600ml/1 pint/2½ cups chicken stock
- 600ml/1 pint/2½ cups reduced-fat coconut milk
- 30ml/2 tbsp Thai fish sauce
- 5ml/1 tsp granulated sugar
- 115g/4oz small cooked shelled prawns (shrimp)
- salt and ground black pepper
To garnish
- 2 fresh red chillies, seeded and thinly sliced
- 10–12 fresh basil leaves

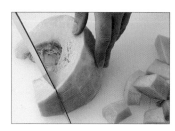

1 Peel the pumpkin and cut it into quarters with a sharp knife. Scoop out the seeds with a teaspoon and discard. Cut the flesh into chunks about 2cm/¾in thick and set aside.

2 Put the garlic, shallots, shrimp paste, lemon grass, green chillies and salt to taste in a mortar. Drain the dried shrimp, discarding the soaking liquid, and add them, then use a pestle to grind the mixture into a paste. Alternatively, place all the ingredients in a food processor and process to a paste.

3 Bring the chicken stock to the boil in a large pan. Add the ground paste and stir well to dissolve.

4 Add the pumpkin chunks and bring to a simmer. Simmer for 10–15 minutes, or until the pumpkin is tender.

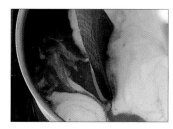

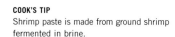

5 Stir in the coconut milk, then bring the soup back to simmering point. Do not let it boil. Add the fish sauce, sugar and ground black pepper to taste.

6 Add the prawns and cook for a further 2–3 minutes, until they are heated through. Serve in warm soup bowls, garnished with chillies and basil leaves.

COOK'S TIP
Shrimp paste is made from ground shrimp fermented in brine.

Energy 63kcal/269kJ; Protein 6g; Carbohydrate 9g, of which sugars 8.2g; Fat 0.7g, of which saturates 0.3g; Cholesterol 50mg; Calcium 101mg; Fibre 1g; Sodium 611mg.

P R A W N AND P O R K   S O U P WITH R I C E   S T I C K S ★

THIS LOW-FAT AND HEALTHY SOUP IS A SPECIALITY OF HO CHI MINH CITY (FORMERLY SAIGON), WHERE THE PORK STOCK IS ENHANCED WITH THE INTENSE SWEET AND SMOKY FLAVOUR OF DRIED SQUID. IT IS ALSO A POPULAR EVERYDAY SOUP IN CAMBODIA.

SERVES 4

INGREDIENTS

    225g/8oz lean pork tenderloin
    225g/8oz dried rice sticks
      (vermicelli), soaked in lukewarm
      water for 20 minutes
    20 prawns (shrimp), shelled
      and deveined
    115g/4oz/½ cup beansprouts
    2 spring onions (scallions),
      finely sliced
    2 green or red Thai chillies, seeded
      and finely sliced
    1 garlic clove, finely sliced
    1 bunch each coriander (cilantro)
      and basil, stalks removed, leaves
      roughly chopped
    1 lime, cut into quarters, and *nuoc
      cham* or other fish sauce, to serve
For the stock
    25g/1oz dried squid
    450g/1lb pork ribs
    1 onion, peeled and quartered
    225g/8oz carrots, peeled and cut
      into chunks
    15ml/1 tbsp fish sauce
    15ml/1 tbsp soy sauce
    6 black peppercorns
    salt

1 To make the stock, soak the dried squid in water for 30 minutes, rinse and drain. Put the ribs in a large pan and cover with approximately 2.5 litres/4½ pints/10 cups water. Bring to the boil, skim off any fat, and add the dried squid with the remaining stock ingredients. Cover the pan and simmer for 1 hour, then skim off any foam or fat and continue to simmer, uncovered, for a further 1½ hours.

2 Strain the stock and check the seasoning. You should have roughly 2 litres/3½ pints/8 cups.

COOK'S TIP
To serve the soup on its own, add bitesize pieces of soaked dried shiitake mushrooms or cubes of firm tofu.

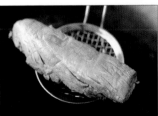

3 Pour the stock into a wok or deep pan and bring to the boil. Reduce the heat, add the pork tenderloin and simmer for 25 minutes. Lift the tenderloin out of the stock, place it on a board and cut it into thin slices. Meanwhile, keep the stock simmering gently over a low heat.

4 Bring a pan of water to the boil. Drain the rice sticks and add to the water. Cook for about 5 minutes, or until tender, separating them with chopsticks if they stick together. Drain the rice sticks and divide them among four warm bowls.

5 Drop the prawns into the simmering stock for 1 minute. Lift them out with a slotted spoon and layer them with the slices of pork on top of the rice sticks. Ladle the hot stock over them and sprinkle with beansprouts, spring onions, chillies, garlic and herbs. Serve each bowl of soup with a wedge of lime to squeeze over it and *nuoc cham* to splash on top.

Energy 234kcal/981kJ; Protein 26.2g; Carbohydrate 24.8g, of which sugars 1.6g; Fat 3.3g, of which saturates 1g; Cholesterol 137mg; Calcium 84mg; Fibre 1.1g; Sodium 681mg.

CLEAR SOUP WITH SEAFOOD STICKS ★

*THIS DELICATE JAPANESE-STYLE SOUP, WHICH IS OFTEN EATEN WITH FISH, IS VERY QUICK TO MAKE IF
YOU PREPARE THE FIRST DASHI BEFOREHAND OR IF YOU USE FREEZE-DRIED DASHI-NO-MOTO.*

SERVES 4

INGREDIENTS

    4 mitsuba sprigs or 4 chives and
      a few sprigs of mustard and cress
    4 seafood sticks
    400ml/14fl oz/1⅔ cups first dashi
      stock, or the same amount of
      water and 5ml/1 tsp dashi-
      no-moto
    15ml/1 tbsp shoyu or soy sauce
    7.5ml/1½ tsp salt

1 Mitsuba leaves are normally sold with
the stems and roots on to retain
freshness. Cut off the root, then cut
5cm/2in from the top, retaining both the
long straw-like stem and the leaf.

COOK'S TIP
Dashi-no-moto is freeze-dried stock
granules for making a quick dashi stock.

2 Blanch the stems in hot water from
the kettle. If you use chives, choose
them at least 10cm/4in in length and
blanch them, too.

3 Take a seafood stick and carefully tie
around the middle with a mitsuba stem
or chive, holding it in place with a knot.
Do not pull too tightly, as the bow will
easily break. Repeat the process to
make four tied seafood sticks.

4 Hold one seafood stick in your hand.
With your finger, carefully loosen both
ends to make it look like a tassel.

5 Place one seafood stick in each soup
bowl, then put the four mitsuba leaves
or mustard and cress on top.

6 Heat the stock in a pan and bring to
the boil. Add shoyu and salt to taste.
Pour the stock gently over the mitsuba
and seafood stick.

VARIATION
You can use small prawns (shrimp)
instead of seafood sticks. Blanch 12 raw
prawns in boiling water until they curl
up and form a full circle. Drain. Tie
mitsuba stems to make four bows.
Arrange three prawns side by side in
each bowl and put the mitsuba bows
and leaves on top.

Energy 30kcal/125kJ; Protein 5.4g; Carbohydrate 1g, of which sugars 0.9g; Fat 0.5g, of which saturates 0.1g; Cholesterol 23mg; Calcium 36mg; Fibre 0.2g; Sodium 877mg.

COCONUT AND SEAFOOD SOUP ★

THE LIST OF INGREDIENTS COULD MISLEAD YOU INTO THINKING THAT THIS SOUP IS TIME-CONSUMING TO MAKE. IN FACT, IT IS EXTREMELY EASY TO PUT TOGETHER AND THE FLAVOURS WORK BEAUTIFULLY.

SERVES 4

INGREDIENTS
750ml/1¼ pints/3 cups fish stock
5 thin slices fresh root ginger
2 lemon grass stalks, chopped
3 kaffir lime leaves, shredded
bunch garlic chives, about 25g/1oz
small bunch fresh coriander
  (cilantro), about 15g/½oz
5ml/1 tsp sunflower oil
4 shallots, chopped
250ml/8fl oz/1 cup reduced-fat
  coconut milk
30–45ml/2–3 tbsp Thai
  fish sauce
45ml/3 tbsp Thai green
  curry paste
350g/12oz raw large prawns
  (shrimp), peeled and deveined
350g/12oz prepared squid
a little fresh lime juice (optional)
salt and ground black pepper
30ml/2 tbsp crisp fried shallot
  slices, to serve

1 Pour the fish stock into a large pan and add the slices of ginger, the chopped lemon grass and half the shredded kaffir lime leaves.

VARIATIONS
• Instead of squid, you could add 400g/14oz firm white fish, such as monkfish, cut into small pieces.
• You could also replace the squid with mussels. Steam 675g/1½lb live mussels in a tightly covered pan for 3–4 minutes, or until they have opened. Discard any that remain shut, then remove them from their shells and add to the soup.

2 Reserve a few garlic chives for the garnish, then chop the remainder. Add half the chopped garlic chives to the pan. Strip the coriander leaves from the stalks and set the leaves aside. Add the stalks to the pan. Bring to the boil, reduce the heat to low and cover the pan, then simmer gently for 20 minutes. Strain the stock into a bowl.

3 Rinse and dry the pan. Add the oil and shallots. Cook over a medium heat for 5–10 minutes, until the shallots are just beginning to brown.

4 Stir in the strained stock, coconut milk, the remaining kaffir lime leaves and 30ml/2 tbsp of the fish sauce. Heat gently until simmering and cook over a low heat for 5–10 minutes.

5 Stir in the curry paste and prawns, then cook for 3 minutes. Add the squid and cook for a further 2 minutes. Add the lime juice, if using, and season, adding more fish sauce to taste. Stir in the remaining chives and the reserved coriander leaves. Serve in bowls and sprinkle each portion with fried shallots and whole garlic chives.

Energy 164kcal/692kJ; Protein 29.7g; Carbohydrate 4.5g, of which sugars 3.4g; Fat 3.1g, of which saturates 0.7g; Cholesterol 368mg; Calcium 137mg; Fibre 0.5g; Sodium 363mg.

SEAFOOD WONTON SOUP ★

THIS IS A VARIATION ON THE POPULAR WONTON SOUP THAT IS TRADITIONALLY PREPARED USING PORK.
IN THIS VERSION THE FAT CONTENT IS REDUCED BY SUBSTITUTING PRAWNS, SCALLOPS AND COD.

SERVES 4

INGREDIENTS
   50g/2oz raw tiger prawns
     (jumbo shrimp)
   50g/2oz queen scallops
   75g/3oz skinless cod fillet,
     roughly chopped
   15ml/1 tbsp finely chopped chives
   5ml/1 tsp dry sherry
   1 small egg white, lightly beaten
   2.5ml/½ tsp sesame oil
   1.5ml/¼ tsp salt
   large pinch of ground white pepper
   20 wonton wrappers
   900ml/1½ pints/3¾ cups fish stock
   2 cos lettuce leaves, shredded
   fresh coriander (cilantro) leaves and
     garlic chives, to garnish

1 Peel the prawns, then devein them using the point of a sharp knife. Rinse them well, pat them dry on kitchen paper and cut them into small pieces.

2 Rinse the scallops in a sieve (strainer) under cold water. Pat them dry, using kitchen paper. Chop them into small pieces so that they are the same size as the prawns.

3 Place the cod in a food processor and process until a smooth paste is formed. Scrape the paste into a bowl and stir in the prawns, scallops, chives, sherry, egg white, sesame oil, salt and pepper.

4 Mix all of the ingredients thoroughly, cover with clear film (plastic wrap) and leave in a cool place to marinate for at least 20 minutes.

5 Make the wontons. Place a teaspoonful of the seafood filling in the centre of a wonton wrapper, then bring the corners together to meet at the top.

6 Twist the edges of the wonton together to completely enclose the filling. Fill the remaining wonton wrappers in the same way.

7 Pour the fish stock into a pan and heat it gently over low heat. Do not let it boil, but ensure that it is piping hot.

COOK'S TIP
The filled wonton wrappers can be made ahead, then frozen for several weeks and cooked in boiling water for 8 minutes straight from the freezer.

8 Bring a large pan of water to the boil. Add the wontons to the pan using a spoon. When the water returns to the boil, lower the heat and simmer the wontons gently for 5 minutes or until they float to the surface. Drain the wontons and divide them among four heated soup bowls.

9 Add a portion of shredded lettuce to each bowl. Ladle the hot fish stock into each bowl, garnish each portion with coriander leaves and garlic chives and serve immediately.

Energy 113kcal/478kJ; Protein 11.3g; Carbohydrate 15.7g, of which sugars 0.9g; Fat 0.8g, of which saturates 0.2g; Cholesterol 39mg; Calcium 53mg; Fibre 0.9g; Sodium 75mg.

CRAB AND ASPARAGUS SOUP ★

ASPARAGUS IS OFTEN COMBINED WITH CRAB IN VIETNAM, AND MAKES A DELICIOUS LOW-FAT SOUP.
SERVE THIS SOUP AS A LIGHT LUNCH OR SUPPER WITH PLAIN NOODLES ON THE SIDE.

SERVES 6

INGREDIENTS

350g/12oz asparagus spears,
  trimmed and halved
900ml/1½ pints/3¾ cups chicken
  stock, preferably home-made
15ml/1 tbsp sunflower oil
6 shallots, chopped
115g/4oz crab meat, fresh or
  canned, chopped
15ml/1 tbsp cornflour (cornstarch),
  mixed to a paste with water
30ml/2 tbsp Thai fish sauce
1 egg, lightly beaten
chopped chives, plus extra chives
  to garnish
salt and ground black pepper to taste

1 Cook the asparagus spears in the chicken stock for 5–6 minutes until tender. Drain, reserving the stock.

2 Heat the oil and stir-fry the shallots for 2 minutes. Add the asparagus spears, crab meat and chicken stock.

3 Bring the mixture to the boil and cook for 3 minutes, then remove the wok or pan from the heat and spoon some of the liquid into the cornflour mixture. Return this to the wok or pan and stir until the soup begins to thicken slightly.

4 Stir in the fish sauce, with salt and pepper to taste, then pour the beaten egg into the soup, stirring briskly so that the egg forms threads. Finally, stir the chopped chives into the soup and serve immediately, garnished with chives.

COOK'S TIP
If fresh asparagus isn't available, use 350g/12oz can asparagus. Drain and halve the spears.

Energy 75kcal/313kJ; Protein 6.6g; Carbohydrate 5.2g, of which sugars 2.4g; Fat 3.3g, of which saturates 0.6g; Cholesterol 46mg; Calcium 49mg; Fibre 1.2g; Sodium 476mg.

SEAFOOD SOUP WITH NOODLES ★★

AUDIBLE SOUNDS OF ENJOYMENT ARE A COMPLIMENT TO THE CHINESE COOK, SO SLURPING THIS SUPERB SEAFOOD SOUP IS NOT ONLY PERMISSIBLE, BUT POSITIVELY DESIRABLE.

SERVES 6

INGREDIENTS
  175g/6oz tiger prawns (jumbo
    shrimp), peeled and deveined
  225g/8oz monkfish fillet, cut
    into chunks
  225g/8oz salmon fillet, cut
    into chunks
  5ml/1 tsp vegetable oil
  15ml/1 tbsp dry white wine
  225g/8oz/2 cups dried
    egg vermicelli
  1.2 litres/2 pints/5 cups
    fish stock
  1 carrot, thinly sliced
  225g/8oz asparagus, cut into
    5cm/2in lengths
  30ml/2 tbsp dark soy sauce
  5ml/1 tsp sesame oil
  salt and ground black pepper
  2 spring onions (scallions), cut
    into thin rings, to garnish

1 Mix the prawns and fish together in a bowl. Add the vegetable oil and wine with 1.5ml/¼ tsp salt and a little ground pepper. Mix lightly, cover with clear film (plastic wrap) and marinate in a cool place for 15 minutes.

2 Bring a large pan of lightly salted water to the boil and cook the noodles for 4 minutes until just tender, or according to the instructions on the noodle packet.

3 Drain the noodles thoroughly and divide them among four deep serving bowls. Set to one side and keep the bowls of noodles hot.

4 Bring the fish stock to the boil over high heat in a separate pan. Add the prawns and monkfish, cook for 1 minute, then add the salmon and cook for 2 minutes more.

5 Using a slotted spoon, lift the fish and prawns out of the stock, add to the noodles in the bowls and keep hot.

6 Strain the stock through a sieve (strainer) lined with muslin or cheesecloth into a clean pan. Bring to the boil and cook the carrot and asparagus for 2 minutes, then add the soy sauce and sesame oil, with salt to taste. Stir well.

7 Pour the stock and the vegetables over the hot noodles and seafood, garnish with the spring onions and serve immediately.

Energy 274kcal/1147kJ; Protein 23.2g; Carbohydrate 31.5g, of which sugars 2g; Fat 5.9g, of which saturates 1g; Cholesterol 81mg; Calcium 57mg; Fibre 0.9g; Sodium 442mg.

CHINESE FISH BALL SOUP ★

THIS LIGHT CHINESE SOUP CAN BE FOUND IN COFFEE SHOPS AND AT THE TZE CHAR STALLS. OFTEN EATEN AS A SNACK OR LIGHT LUNCH, THE SOUP IS GARNISHED WITH SPRING ONIONS AND CHILLIES.

SERVES 4–6

INGREDIENTS

For the fish balls
  450g/1lb fresh fish fillets (such as
    haddock, cod, whiting or bream),
    boned and flaked
  15–30ml/1–2 tbsp rice flour
  salt and ground black pepper

For the soup
  1.5 litres/2½ pints/6¼ cups fish
    or chicken stock
  15–30ml/1–2 tbsp light soy sauce
  4–6 mustard green leaves,
    chopped
  90g/3½oz mung bean thread
    noodles, soaked in hot water
    until soft

For the garnish
  2 spring onions (scallions), trimmed
    and finely sliced
  1 red or green chilli, seeded and
    finely sliced
  fresh coriander (cilantro) leaves,
    finely chopped

1 To make the fish balls, grind the flaked flesh to a paste, using a mortar and pestle or food processor. Season with salt and pepper and stir in 60ml/4 tbsp water. Add enough rice flour to form a paste.

COOK'S TIP
Add cubed tofu pieces to the soup along with the fish balls for a more filling dish.

2 Take small portions of fish paste into your hands and squeeze them to mould into walnut-size balls.

3 Meanwhile, bring the stock to the boil in a deep pan and season to taste with soy sauce. Drop in the fish balls and simmer for 5 minutes. Add the shredded mustard greens and cook for 1 minute.

4 Divide the noodles among four to six bowls. Using a slotted spoon, add the fish balls and greens to the noodles, then ladle over the hot stock. Garnish with the spring onions and chilli and sprinkle the chopped coriander on top.

Energy 127kcal/533kJ; Protein 14.9g; Carbohydrate 14.8g, of which sugars 0.5g; Fat 0.6g, of which saturates 0.1g; Cholesterol 35mg; Calcium 17mg; Fibre 0.2g; Sodium 408mg.

HOT-AND-SOUR FISH SOUP ⋆

THIS TANGY SOUP IS FOUND THROUGHOUT ASIA. CHILLIES PROVIDE THE HEAT, TAMARIND PRODUCES THE TARTNESS AND THE DELICIOUS SWEETNESS COMES FROM PINEAPPLE.

SERVES 4

INGREDIENTS

1 catfish, sea bass or red snapper, about 1kg/2¼lb, filleted
60–75ml/4–5 tbsp *nuoc mam* or other fish sauce
2 garlic cloves, finely chopped
25g/1oz dried squid, soaked in water for 30 minutes
10ml/2 tsp vegetable oil
2 spring onions (scallions), sliced
2 shallots, sliced
4cm/1½in fresh root ginger, peeled and chopped
2–3 lemon grass stalks, cut into strips and crushed
30ml/2 tbsp tamarind paste
2–3 Thai chillies, seeded and sliced
15ml/1 tbsp sugar
225g/8oz fresh pineapple, peeled and diced
3 tomatoes, skinned, seeded and roughly chopped
50g/2oz canned sliced bamboo shoots, drained
1 small bunch fresh coriander (cilantro), stalks removed, leaves finely chopped
salt and ground black pepper
115g/4oz/½cup beansprouts and 1 bunch dill, fronds roughly chopped, to garnish
1 lime, cut into quarters, to serve

1 Cut the fish into bitesize pieces, mix with 30ml/2 tbsp of the fish sauce and garlic and leave to marinate. Save the head, tail and bones for the stock. Drain and rinse the soaked dried squid.

2 Heat the oil in a deep pan and stir in the spring onions, shallots, ginger, lemon grass and dried squid. Add the reserved fish head, tail and bones, and sauté them gently for a minute or two. Pour in 1.2 litres/2 pints/5 cups water and bring to the boil. Reduce the heat and simmer for 30 minutes.

3 Strain the stock into another deep pan and bring to the boil. Stir in the tamarind paste, chillies, sugar and the remaining fish sauce and simmer for 2–3 minutes. Add the pineapple, tomatoes and bamboo shoots and simmer for a further 2–3 minutes. Stir in the fish pieces and the chopped fresh coriander, and cook until the fish turns opaque.

4 Season to taste and ladle the soup into hot bowls. Garnish with beansprouts and dill, and serve with the lime quarters to squeeze over.

VARIATIONS
• Depending on your mood, or your palate, you can adjust the balance of hot and sour by adding more chilli or tamarind to taste. Enjoyed as a meal in itself, the soup is usually served with plain steamed rice but in Ho Chi Minh City in Vietnam it is served with chunks of fresh baguette, which are perfect for soaking up the spicy, fruity, tangy broth.
• Other fresh herbs, such as chopped mint and basil leaves, also complement this soup.

Energy 166kcal/704kJ; Protein 23.1g; Carbohydrate 10.9g, of which sugars 10g; Fat 3.7g, of which saturates 0.6g; Cholesterol 51mg; Calcium 113mg; Fibre 3g; Sodium 116mg.

RICE IN GREEN TEA WITH SALMON ★

HERE IS THE PERFECT RECIPE FOR TEA LOVERS. IT IS VERY SIMPLE TO MAKE TOO.

3 Using scissors, cut the nori into short, narrow strips about 20 x 5mm/³⁄₄ x ¹⁄₄in long, or leave as long narrow strips, if you prefer.

4 If the cooked rice is warm, put equal amounts into individual rice bowls or soup bowls. If the rice is cold, put it in a sieve (strainer) and pour hot water from a kettle over it to warm it up. Drain, then spoon it into the bowls. Place the salmon pieces on top of the rice.

5 Put the *sencha* leaves in a teapot. Bring 600ml/1 pint/2¹⁄₂ cups water to the boil, remove from the heat and allow to cool slightly.

SERVES 4

INGREDIENTS
150g/5oz salmon fillet
¹⁄₄ sheet nori seaweed
250g/9oz/1¹⁄₄ cups Japanese short
  grain rice cooked using 350ml/
  12fl oz/1¹⁄₂ cups water
15ml/1 tbsp *sencha* leaves
5ml/1 tsp wasabi paste (optional)
20ml/4 tsp shoyu or soy sauce
salt

1 Thoroughly salt the salmon fillet and leave for 30 minutes. If the salmon fillet is thicker than 2.5cm/1in, slice it in half and salt both halves.

2 Wipe the salt off the salmon with kitchen paper and grill (broil) the fish under a preheated grill (broiler) for about 5 minutes until cooked through. Remove the skin and any bones, then roughly flake the salmon with a fork.

6 Pour into the teapot and wait for 45 seconds. Strain the tea gently and evenly over the top of the rice and salmon. Add some nori and wasabi, if using, to the top of the rice, then trickle shoyu over and serve.

COOK'S TIP
Sencha leaves are what the popular Japanese green tea is made from. They are often packaged as loose tea leaves.

Energy 294kcal/1229kJ; Protein 12.4g; Carbohydrate 50.3g, of which sugars 0.4g; Fat 4.5g, of which saturates 0.7g; Cholesterol 19mg; Calcium 21mg; Fibre 0g; Sodium 373mg

RED SNAPPER SOUP ★★★

TAMARIND GIVES THIS LIGHT, FRAGRANT NOODLE SOUP A SLIGHTLY SOUR TASTE.

SERVES 4

INGREDIENTS

2 litres/3½ pints/8 cups water
1kg/2¼lb red snapper (or other
   red fish such as mullet)
1 onion, sliced
50g/2oz tamarind pods
15ml/1 tbsp fish sauce
15ml/1 tbsp sugar
30ml/2 tbsp vegetable oil
2 garlic cloves, finely chopped
2 lemon grass stalks, very
   finely chopped
4 ripe tomatoes, peeled and
   coarsely chopped
30ml/2 tbsp yellow bean paste
225g/8oz rice vermicelli, soaked in
   warm water until soft
115g/4oz/½ cup beansprouts
8–10 fresh basil or mint sprigs
25g/1oz/¼ cup roasted
   peanuts, ground
salt and ground black pepper

1 Bring the water to the boil in a pan. Lower the heat and add the fish and onion, with 2.5ml/½ tsp salt. Simmer gently until the fish is cooked through.

2 Remove the fish from the stock; set aside. Add the tamarind, fish sauce and sugar to the stock. Cook for 5 minutes, then strain the stock into a large bowl. Carefully remove all of the bones from the fish, keeping the flesh in big pieces.

3 Heat the oil in a large frying pan. Add the garlic and lemon grass and cook for a few seconds. Stir in the tomatoes and bean paste. Cook gently for 5–7 minutes, until the tomatoes are soft. Add the stock, bring back to a simmer and adjust the seasoning. Stir to mix.

COOK'S TIP
Use about 1 tbsp prepared tamarind paste instead of the pods.

4 Drain the vermicelli and divide among individual serving bowls. Add the beansprouts, fish and basil or mint, and sprinkle the ground peanuts on top. Top up each bowl with the hot soup.

Energy 495kcal/2079kJ; Protein 43.1g; Carbohydrate 55.5g, of which sugars 9.1g; Fat 11.4g, of which saturates 1.9g; Cholesterol 65mg; Calcium 108mg; Fibre 2.4g; Sodium 165mg

THAI FISH BROTH ★

LEMON GRASS, CHILLIES AND GALANGAL ARE AMONG THE FLAVOURINGS USED IN THIS FRAGRANT SOUP.

SERVES 3

INGREDIENTS

1 litre/1¾ pints/4 cups fish or
  light chicken stock
4 lemon grass stalks
3 limes
2 small fresh hot red chillies,
  seeded and thinly sliced
2cm/¾in piece fresh galangal,
  peeled and thinly sliced
6 fresh coriander (cilantro) stalks
2 kaffir lime leaves,
  finely chopped
350g/12oz monkfish fillet, skinned
  and cut into 2.5cm/1in pieces
15ml/1 tbsp rice vinegar
45ml/3 tbsp Thai fish sauce
30ml/2 tbsp chopped coriander
  (cilantro) leaves, to garnish

1 Pour the stock into a pan and bring it to the boil. Meanwhile, slice the bulb end of each lemon grass stalk diagonally into pieces about 3mm/⅛in thick. Peel off four wide strips of lime rind with a potato peeler, taking care to avoid the white pith underneath which would make the soup bitter. Squeeze the limes and reserve the juice.

2 Add the sliced lemon grass, lime rind, chillies, galangal and coriander stalks to the stock, with the kaffir lime leaves. Simmer for 1–2 minutes.

VARIATIONS

Prawns (shrimp), scallops, squid or sole can be substituted for the monkfish. If you use kaffir lime leaves, you will need the juice of only 2 limes.

3 Add the monkfish, rice vinegar and Thai fish sauce, with half the reserved lime juice. Simmer for about 3 minutes, until the fish is just cooked. Lift out and discard the coriander stalks, taste the broth and add more lime juice if necessary; the soup should taste quite sour. Sprinkle with the coriander leaves and serve very hot.

Energy 88kcal/373kJ; Protein 19.2g; Carbohydrate 1.5g, of which sugars 1.3g; Fat 0.6g, of which saturates 0.1g; Cholesterol 16mg; Calcium 40mg; Fibre 0.4g; Sodium 1112mg.

BAMBOO SHOOT, FISH AND RICE SOUP ★

THIS IS A REFRESHING SOUP MADE WITH FRESHWATER FISH SUCH AS CARP OR CATFISH.

SERVES 4

INGREDIENTS
   75g/3oz/scant ½ cup long grain rice,
     well rinsed
   250ml/8fl oz/1 cup reduced-fat
     coconut milk
   30ml/2 tbsp fish sauce
   2 lemon grass stalks, trimmed
     and crushed
   25g/1oz galangal, thinly sliced
   2–3 Thai chillies
   4 garlic cloves, crushed
   15ml/1 tbsp palm sugar
   1 fresh or canned bamboo shoot,
     peeled, boiled in water for 10
     minutes, and sliced
   450g/1lb freshwater fish fillets,
     such as carp or catfish, skinned
     and cut into bitesize pieces
   1 small bunch fresh
     basil leaves
   1 small bunch fresh coriander
     (cilantro), chopped, and 1 chilli,
     finely sliced, to garnish
   rice or noodles, to serve
For the stock
   450g/1lb pork ribs
   1 onion, quartered
   225g/8oz carrots, cut
     into chunks
   25g/1oz dried squid or dried shrimp,
     soaked in water for 30 minutes,
     rinsed and drained
   15ml/1 tbsp fish sauce
   15ml/1 tbsp soy sauce
   6 black peppercorns
   salt

1 To prepare the stock, put the ribs in a large pan and cover with 2.5 litres/4¼ pints/10 cups water. Bring to the boil, skim off any fat, and add the remaining stock ingredients. Cover the pan and simmer for 1 hour, then skim off any foam or fat.

2 Simmer the stock, uncovered, for a further 1–1½ hours, until it has reduced. Check the seasoning and strain the stock into another pan. There should be approximately 2 litres/3½ pints/7¾ cups of stock.

3 Bring the pan of stock to the boil. Stir in the rice and reduce the heat. Add the coconut milk, fish sauce, lemon grass, galangal, chillies, garlic and sugar. Simmer for about 10 minutes to let the flavours mingle. The rice should be just cooked, with bite to it.

4 Add the sliced bamboo shoot and the pieces of fish. Simmer for 5 minutes, until the fish is cooked. Check the seasoning and stir in the basil leaves. Ladle the soup into bowls, garnish with the chopped coriander and chilli, and serve with the rice or noodles.

Energy 269kcal/1130kJ; Protein 35.5g; Carbohydrate 23.2g, of which sugars 7.9g; Fat 3.8g, of which saturates 1.1g; Cholesterol 87mg; Calcium 109mg; Fibre 2.6g; Sodium 214mg.

GINGER, CHICKEN AND COCONUT SOUP ★

THIS AROMATIC AND COMFORTING SOUP IS RICH WITH COCONUT MILK AND INTENSELY FLAVOURED
WITH GALANGAL, LEMON GRASS AND KAFFIR LIME LEAVES. IT IS VERY EASY TO MAKE.

SERVES 6

INGREDIENTS

4 lemon grass stalks, roots trimmed
2 × 400ml/14fl oz cans reduced-fat
  coconut milk
475ml/16fl oz/2 cups chicken stock
2.5cm/1in piece galangal, peeled and
  thinly sliced
10 black peppercorns, crushed
10 kaffir lime leaves, torn
300g/11oz chicken breast fillets,
  cut into thin strips
115g/4oz/1 cup button (white)
  mushrooms
50g/2oz/¹⁄₂ cup baby corn cobs,
  quartered lengthways
60ml/4 tbsp lime juice
45ml/3 tbsp Thai fish sauce
fresh red chillies, spring onions and
  fresh coriander (cilantro), to garnish

1 Cut off the lower 5cm/2in from each lemon grass stalk and chop it finely. Bruise the remaining pieces of stalk. Bring the coconut milk and chicken stock to the boil in a large pan. Add all the lemon grass, the galangal, peppercorns and half the lime leaves, lower the heat and simmer gently for 10 minutes. Strain into a clean pan.

2 Return the soup to the heat, then add the chicken, mushrooms and corn. Simmer for 5–7 minutes or until the chicken is cooked.

3 Stir in the lime juice and Thai fish sauce, then add the remaining lime leaves. Serve hot, garnished with chopped chillies, spring onions and coriander.

HOT-AND-SOUR PRAWN SOUP ★

THIS IS A CLASSIC THAI SEAFOOD SOUP – KNOWN AS TOM YAM KUNG – AND IT IS PROBABLY
ONE OF THE MOST POPULAR AND WELL-KNOWN SOUP FROM THAT COUNTRY.

SERVES 6

INGREDIENTS

450g/1lb raw king prawns (jumbo
  shrimp), thawed if frozen
1 litre/1³⁄₄ pints/4 cups chicken
  stock or water
3 lemon grass stalks, root trimmed
10 kaffir lime leaves, torn in half
225g/8oz can straw mushrooms
45ml/3 tbsp Thai fish sauce
60ml/4 tbsp lime juice
30ml/2 tbsp chopped spring onion
  (scallion)
15ml/1 tbsp fresh coriander
  (cilantro) leaves
4 fresh red chillies, seeded
  and thinly sliced
salt and ground black pepper

1 Shell the prawns, putting the shells in a colander. Devein and set aside.

2 Rinse the shells under cold water to remove all grit and sand, then put in a large pan with the chicken stock or water. Bring to the boil.

3 Bruise the lemon grass stalks with a pestle or mallet and add them to the stock with half the lime leaves. Simmer gently for 5–6 minutes, until the stock is fragrant.

4 Strain the stock, return it to the clean pan and reheat. Add the drained mushrooms and the prawns, then cook until the prawns turn pink.

5 Stir in the Thai fish sauce, lime juice, spring onion, coriander, chillies and the remaining lime leaves. Taste and adjust the seasoning. The soup should be sour, salty, spicy and hot.

Top: Energy 90kcal/383kJ; Protein 13.2g; Carbohydrate 7.4g, of which sugars 7.2g; Fat 1.1g, of which saturates 0.4g; Cholesterol 35mg; Calcium 44mg; Fibre 0.3g; Sodium 807mg.
Bottom: Energy 69kcal/292kJ; Protein 14.5g; Carbohydrate 1.1g, of which sugars 1g; Fat 0.8g, of which saturates 0.1g; Cholesterol 146mg; Calcium 81mg; Fibre 0.9g; Sodium 682mg.

CHICKEN RICE SOUP WITH LEMON GRASS ★

THIS IS CAMBODIA'S ANSWER TO THE CHICKEN NOODLE SOUP THAT IS POPULAR IN THE WEST.
LIGHT AND FAT-FREE, THIS TANGY AND DELICIOUS SOUP IS THE PERFECT CHOICE FOR A HOT DAY,
AS WELL AS A GREAT PICK-ME-UP WHEN YOU ARE FEELING LOW OR TIRED.

SERVES 4

INGREDIENTS
    2 lemon grass stalks, trimmed,
        cut into 3 pieces, and lightly
        bruised
    15ml/1 tbsp Thai fish sauce
    90g/3½oz/½ cup short grain
        rice, rinsed
    1 small bunch coriander (cilantro)
        leaves, finely chopped, and 1
        green or red chilli, seeded
        and cut into thin strips,
        to garnish
    1 lime, cut in wedges, to serve
    sea salt
    ground black pepper
For the stock
    1 small chicken or 2 meaty
        chicken legs
    1 onion, quartered
    2 cloves garlic, crushed
    25g/1oz fresh root ginger,
        sliced
    2 lemon grass stalks, cut in half
        lengthways and bruised
    2 dried red chillies
    30ml/2 tbsp *nuoc mam* or fish sauce

1 Put the chicken into a deep pan. Add all the other stock ingredients and pour in 2 litres/3½ pints/7¾ cups water. Bring to the boil for a few minutes, then reduce the heat and simmer gently with the lid on for 2 hours.

2 Skim off any fat from the stock, strain and reserve. Remove the skin from the chicken and shred the meat. Set aside.

3 Pour the stock back into the deep pan and bring to the boil. Reduce the heat and stir in the lemon grass stalks and fish sauce. Stir in the rice and simmer, uncovered, for about 40 minutes. Add the shredded chicken and season to taste.

4 Ladle the piping hot soup into warmed individual bowls, garnish with chopped coriander and the thin strips of chilli and serve with lime wedges to squeeze over.

COOK'S TIPS
• The fresh, citrus aroma of lemon grass and lime, combined with the warmth of the chillies, is invigorating and awakens the senses. However, many Vietnamese and Cambodians often spike the soup with additional chillies as a garnish, or served on the side.
• Variations of this soup crop up all over Cambodia and Vietnam, where it is often served as a meal in itself.

Energy 194kcal/817kJ; Protein 26.2g; Carbohydrate 18.4g, of which sugars 0.3g; Fat 1.6g, of which saturates 0.3g; Cholesterol 70mg; Calcium 36mg; Fibre 0.6g; Sodium 268mg.

AROMATIC BROTH WITH ROAST DUCK, PAK CHOI AND EGG NOODLES ★

SERVED ON ITS OWN, THIS CHINESE-INSPIRED DUCK AND NOODLE SOUP MAKES A DELICIOUS AUTUMN OR WINTER MEAL. THIS RECIPE CAN BE MADE WITH LEFTOVER DUCK MEAT FROM A ROASTED DUCK OR BY ROASTING A DUCK, SAVING MEAT FOR THE SOUP, AND THEN USING THE CARCASS TO MAKE A STOCK.

SERVES 6

INGREDIENTS
    5ml/1 tsp sunflower oil
    2 shallots, thinly sliced
    4cm/1½in fresh root ginger,
        peeled and sliced
    15ml/1 tbsp soy sauce
    5ml/1 tsp five-spice powder
    10ml/2 tsp sugar
    175g/6oz pak choi (bok choy)
    450g/1lb fresh egg noodles
    225g/8oz roast duck, thinly sliced
    sea salt
For the stock
    1 chicken carcass
    2 carrots, peeled and quartered
    2 onions, peeled and quartered
    4cm/1½in fresh root ginger, peeled
        and cut into chunks
    2 lemon grass stalks, chopped
    30ml/2 tbsp *nuoc mam* or fish sauce
    15ml/1 tbsp soy sauce
    6 black peppercorns
For the garnish
    4 spring onions (scallions), sliced
    1–2 red Serrano chillies, seeded and
        finely sliced
    1 bunch each coriander (cilantro) and
        basil, stalks removed, leaves
        chopped

1 To make the stock, put the chicken carcass into a deep pan. Add all the other stock ingredients and pour in 2.5 litres/4½ pints/10¼ cups water. Bring to the boil, and boil for a few minutes, skim off any foam, then reduce the heat and simmer gently with the lid on for 2–3 hours. Remove the lid and continue to simmer for a further 30 minutes to reduce the stock. Skim off any fat, season with salt, then strain the stock. Measure out 2 litres/3½ pints/8 cups.

2 Heat the oil in a wok or deep pan and stir in the shallots and ginger. Add the soy sauce, five-spice powder, sugar and stock and bring to the boil. Season with a little salt, reduce the heat and simmer for 10–15 minutes.

3 Meanwhile, cut the pak choi diagonally into wide strips and blanch in boiling water to soften them. Drain and refresh under cold running water to prevent them cooking any further. Bring a large pan of water to the boil, then add the fresh noodles. Cook for 5 minutes, then drain well.

4 Divide the noodles among six soup bowls, lay some of the pak choi and sliced duck over them, and then ladle over generous amounts of the simmering broth. Garnish with the spring onions, chillies and herbs, and serve immediately.

COOK'S TIP
If you can't find fresh egg noodles, substitute dried egg noodles instead. Soak the dried noodles in lukewarm water for 20 minutes, then cook, one portion at a time, in a sieve (strainer) lowered into the boiling water. Use a chopstick to untangle them as they soften. Ready-cooked egg noodles are also available in supermarkets.

Energy 337kcal/1411kJ; Protein 12.1g; Carbohydrate 62.5g, of which sugars 1.1g; Fat 3.3g, of which saturates 0.8g; Cholesterol 41mg; Calcium 66mg; Fibre 0.7g; Sodium 269mg.

CORN AND CHICKEN SOUP ★

A VERY POPULAR SOUP, SERVED BEFORE THE MAIN FEAST. USING A COMBINATION OF CHICKEN,
CREAMED CORN AND WHOLE KERNELS GIVES THIS CLASSIC CHINESE SOUP A LOVELY TEXTURE.

SERVES 4–6

INGREDIENTS

1 skinless chicken breast fillet,
   about 115g/4oz, cubed
10ml/2 tsp light soy sauce
15ml/1 tbsp Chinese rice wine
5ml/1 tsp cornflour (cornstarch)
60ml/4 tbsp cold water
5ml/1 tsp sesame oil
15ml/1 tbsp vegetable oil
5ml/1 tsp grated fresh root ginger
1 litre/1¾ pints/4 cups
   chicken stock
425g/15oz can creamed corn
225g/8oz can whole kernel corn
2 eggs, beaten
2–3 spring onions (scallions), green
   parts only, cut into tiny rounds
salt and ground black pepper

VARIATION

For a seafood twist, add 175g/6oz/1 cup
drained canned crab meat in place of
the chicken.

1 Mince (grind) the chicken in a
food processor, taking care not to
over-process. Transfer the chicken
to a bowl and stir in the soy sauce, rice
wine, cornflour, water, sesame oil and
seasoning. Cover with clear film (plastic
wrap) and leave for about 15 minutes
to absorb the flavours.

2 Heat a wok over medium heat. Add
the vegetable oil and swirl it around.
Add the ginger and stir-fry for a few
seconds. Pour in the stock with the
creamed corn and corn kernels.
Bring to just below boiling point.

3 Spoon about 90ml/6 tbsp of the hot
liquid into the chicken mixture until it
forms a smooth paste and stir. Return to
the wok. Slowly bring to the boil, stirring
constantly, then simmer for 2–3 minutes
or until the chicken is cooked.

4 Pour the beaten eggs into the soup
in a slow steady stream, using a fork or
chopsticks to stir the top of the soup
in a figure-of-eight pattern. The egg
should set in lacy shreds. Serve
immediately with the spring onions
sprinkled over.

Energy 196kcal/831kJ; Protein 10g; Carbohydrate 29.9g, of which sugars 10.7g; Fat 4.7g, of which saturates 1g; Cholesterol 77mg; Calcium 17mg; Fibre 1.6g; Sodium 447mg.

MISO SOUP WITH PORK AND VEGETABLES ★★

THIS IS QUITE A RICH-TASTING AND FILLING SOUP. IT IS A WARM AND REFRESHING DISH. ALTHOUGH IT MAKES A TASTY MEAL IN ITSELF, IT IS OFTEN CONSUMED ALONGSIDE THE MAIN MEAL.

SERVES 4

INGREDIENTS

200g/7oz lean boneless pork
15cm/6in piece *gobo* or 1 parsnip
50g/2oz daikon (mooli)
4 fresh shiitake mushrooms
½ *konnyaku* or 115g/4oz firm tofu
15ml/1 tbsp sesame oil, for stir-frying
600ml/1 pint/2½ cups instant
  dashi stock
70ml/4½ tbsp miso
2 spring onions (scallions), chopped
5ml/1 tsp sesame seeds

1 Slice the meat horizontally into very thin long strips, then cut the strips crossways into stamp-size pieces. Set the pork aside.

2 Peel the *gobo*, then cut it diagonally into 1cm/½in thick slices. Quickly plunge the slices into a bowl of cold water. If you are using parsnip, peel, cut it in half lengthways, then cut it into 1cm/½in thick half-moon-shaped slices.

3 Peel and slice the daikon into 1.5cm/⅔in thick discs. Shave the edge of the discs, then cut into 1.5cm/⅔in cubes.

4 Remove the shiitake stalks and cut the caps into quarters.

5 Cook the *konnyaku* in a pan of boiling water for 1 minute. Drain and cool. Cut in quarters lengthways, then crossways into 3mm/⅛in thick pieces.

6 Heat the sesame oil in a heavy pan. Stir-fry the pork, then add tofu, if using, *konnyaku* and all the vegetables except the spring onions. As soon as the colour of the meat changes, add the stock.

7 Bring to the boil over a medium heat. Keep skimming off the foam until the soup looks clear. Reduce the heat, cover, and simmer for 15 minutes.

8 Mix the miso with 60ml/4 tbsp hot stock to make a smooth paste. Stir one-third into the soup. Taste and add more if required. Add the spring onions and remove the pan from the heat. Serve hot in soup bowls and sprinkle with sesame seeds.

Energy 134kcal/558kJ; Protein 14.4g; Carbohydrate 3.4g, of which sugars 1.9g; Fat 7.1g, of which saturates 1.4g; Cholesterol 32mg; Calcium 173mg; Fibre 1.4g; Sodium 308mg.

CRISPY WONTON SOUP ★

THE FRESHLY COOKED CRISP WONTONS ARE SUPPOSED TO SIZZLE AND "SING" IN THE HOT SOUP AS THEY ARE TAKEN TO THE TABLE. ALTHOUGH IT CONTAINS WONTONS THIS RECIPE IS VERY LOW IN FAT.

2 Place the wonton wrappers under a slightly dampened dish towel so that they do not dry out. Next, dampen the edges of a wonton wrapper. Place about 5ml/1 tsp of the filling in the centre of the wrapper. Gather it up like a purse and pinch together well. Fill the remaining wontons in the same way.

3 Make the soup. Drain the cloud ears, trim away any rough stems, then slice thinly. Bring the stock to the boil, add the ginger and the spring onions and simmer for 3 minutes. Add the sliced cloud ears, shredded spring greens, bamboo shoots and soy sauce. Simmer for 10 minutes, then stir in the sesame oil. Season to taste with salt and pepper, cover and keep hot.

SERVES 6

INGREDIENTS
2 cloud ear (wood ear) mushrooms, soaked for 30 minutes in warm water to cover
1.2 litres/2 pints/5 cups home-made chicken stock
2.5cm/1in piece fresh root ginger, peeled and grated
4 spring onions (scallions), chopped
2 rich-green inner spring greens (collards) leaves, finely shredded
50g/2oz drained canned bamboo shoots, sliced
25ml/1½ tbsp dark soy sauce
2.5ml/½ tsp sesame oil
salt and ground black pepper
For the filled wontons
2.5ml/½ tsp sesame oil
½ small onion, finely chopped
10 drained canned water chestnuts, finely chopped
115g/4oz minced (ground) lean pork
24 wonton wrappers
1 egg white
5ml/1 tsp sunflower oil

1 Make the filled wontons. Heat the sesame oil in a small pan. When hot, add the finely chopped onion and water chestnuts and the lean pork and cook, stirring often, until the meat is no longer pink but not overbrown. Tip the mixture into a bowl, season to taste and leave to cool.

VARIATION
For a delicious soup that is even lower in fat, replace the pork with an equivalent quantity of minced (ground) lean chicken or turkey breast fillets. Season well with freshly ground black pepper.

4 Meanwhile, preheat the oven to 240°C/475°F/Gas 9. Lightly whisk the egg white with the sunflower oil and water. Brush the wontons generously with egg white and place them on a non-stick baking sheet. Bake for about 5 minutes, until browned and crisp. Ladle the soup into six warmed soup bowls and share the wontons among them. Serve immediately.

COOK'S TIP
The wontons can be sprinkled with 5ml/1 tsp toasted sesame seeds for extra flavour and crunch. To toast sesame seeds, put them in a dry frying pan and place over a medium heat until the seeds change colour. Shake the pan constantly so that the seeds brown evenly and do not burn.

Energy 132kcal/554kJ; Protein 8.4g; Carbohydrate 17g, of which sugars 3.4g; Fat 3.9g, of which saturates 0.7g; Cholesterol 12mg; Calcium 140mg; Fibre 2.7g; Sodium 332mg.

CONGEE WITH CHINESE SAUSAGE ★★★

ALSO KNOWN AS RICE SOUP, CONGEE IS GENTLE ON THE STOMACH. IT IS A POPULAR AND SUBSTANTIAL BREAKFAST AND LUNCH DISH, AND IS TRADITIONALLY SERVED TO CONVALESCENTS.

SERVES 2–3

INGREDIENTS

115g/4oz/generous ½ cup long-grain rice
25g/1oz/3 tbsp glutinous rice
1.2 litres/2 pints/5 cups water
about 2.5ml/½ tsp salt
5ml/1 tsp sesame oil
thin slice of fresh root ginger, peeled and bruised
2 Chinese sausages
1 egg, lightly beaten (optional)
2.5ml/½ tsp light soy sauce
roasted peanuts, chopped, and thin shreds of spring onion (scallion)

3 About 15 minutes before serving, add salt to taste and the sesame oil, together with the piece of ginger.

VARIATION
If you prefer, use roast duck instead of Chinese sausages. Congee is also popular with tea eggs. It is also delicious with fish fillets.

4 Steam the Chinese sausages for about 10 minutes, then slice and stir into the congee. Cook for 5 minutes.

5 Just before serving, remove the ginger and stir in the lightly beaten egg, if using. Add the peanuts and spring onions and drizzle of soy sauce. Serve hot.

1 Wash both rices thoroughly. Drain and place in a large pan. Add the water, bring to the boil and immediately reduce to the lowest heat, using a heat diffuser if you have one.

2 Cook gently for 1¼–1½ hours, stirring from time to time. If the congee thickens too much, stir in a little boiling water. It should have the consistency of creamy pouring porridge.

Energy 301kcal/1254kJ; Protein 7.2g; Carbohydrate 40.4g, of which sugars 0.8g; Fat 12g, of which saturates 4.2g; Cholesterol 16mg; Calcium 23mg; Fibre 0.2g; Sodium 610mg.

TOMATO AND BEEF SOUP ★

MAKE THIS BEEF BROTH IN LATE SUMMER, WHEN FARMERS' MARKETS AND ROADSIDE STALLS SELL FRESHLY PICKED RIPE TOMATOES. IT TAKES VERY LITTLE TIME TO COOK AND TASTES SUPERB.

SERVES 4

INGREDIENTS

75g/3oz rump (round) steak,
  trimmed of fat
900ml/1½ pints/3¾ cups
  beef stock
30ml/2 tbsp tomato purée (paste)
6 tomatoes, halved, seeded
  and chopped
10ml/2 tsp caster (superfine)
  sugar
15ml/1 tbsp cornflour (cornstarch)
15ml/1 tbsp cold water
1 egg white
2.5ml/½ tsp sesame oil
2 spring onions (scallions),
  finely shredded
salt and ground black pepper

1 Cut the beef into thin strips and place it in a pan. Pour over boiling water to cover. Cook for 2 minutes, then drain thoroughly and set aside.

VARIATION
Instead of using spring onions, top with finely chopped red (bell) peppers.

2 Bring the stock to the boil in a clean pan. Stir in the tomato purée, then the tomatoes and sugar. Add the beef strips, allow the stock to boil again, then lower the heat and simmer for 2 minutes.

3 Mix the cornflour to a paste with the water. Add the mixture to the soup, stirring constantly until it thickens slightly. Lightly beat the egg white in a cup.

4 Pour the egg white into the soup in a steady stream, stirring all the time. As soon as the egg white changes colour and becomes thready, add salt and pepper, stir the soup and pour it into heated bowls.

5 Drizzle each portion of soup with a few drops of sesame oil, sprinkle the shredded spring onions over the top and serve immediately.

Energy 68kcal/287kJ; Protein 6.2g; Carbohydrate 7.7g, of which sugars 7.7g; Fat 1.6g, of which saturates 0.5g; Cholesterol 11mg; Calcium 16mg; Fibre 1.5g; Sodium 56mg.

Beef and Vegetables in Table-top Broth ★★★

THE PERFECT INTRODUCTION TO ASIAN COOKING, THIS DISH IS GREAT FUN FOR A SPECIAL DINNER PARTY AS GUESTS CHOOSE THEIR OWN INGREDIENTS AND COOK THEM AT THE TABLE.

SERVES 4–6

INGREDIENTS
    450g/1lb lean sirloin beef,
        fat trimmed off
    1.75 litres/3 pints/7 1/2 cups water
        with 1/2 sachet instant dashi
        powder, or 1/2 vegetable (bouillon)
        stock cube
    150g/5oz carrots
    6 spring onions (scallions),
        trimmed and sliced
    150g/5oz Chinese leaves (Chinese
        cabbage), roughly shredded
    225g/8oz daikon (mooli),
        peeled and shredded
    275g/10oz udon or fine wheat
        noodles, cooked
    115g/4oz canned bamboo
        shoots, sliced
    175g/6oz firm tofu, cubed
    10 shiitake mushrooms, sliced
For the sesame dipping sauce
    30ml/2 tbsp tahini paste
    120ml/4fl oz/1/2 cup instant
        dashi stock or vegetable stock
    60ml/4 tbsp dark soy sauce
    10ml/2 tsp sugar
    30ml/2 tbsp sake (optional)
    10ml/2 tsp wasabi powder (optional)
For the ponzu dipping sauce
    75ml/5 tbsp lemon juice
    15ml/1 tbsp rice wine or
        white wine vinegar
    75ml/5 tbsp dark soy sauce
    15ml/1 tbsp tamari sauce
    15ml/1 tbsp mirin or 1 tsp sugar
    1.5ml/1/4 tsp instant dashi powder
        or 1/4 vegetable stock (bouillon) cube

1 Slice the meat thinly with a large knife or cleaver. Arrange neatly on a plate, cover and set aside.

2 In a covered, flameproof casserole that is unglazed on the outside, bring the dashi powder or stock cube and water to the boil. Cover and simmer for 8–10 minutes over a low heat.

3 Place the casserole on a hot tray or a similar heat source, on the table.

4 Shred the daikon finely. Peel the carrots and cut grooves along their length with a canelle knife, then slice thinly into rounds. Bring a pan of lightly salted water to the boil. Blanch the sliced carrots, spring onions, Chinese leaves and daikon separately in the boiling water.

5 Drain the vegetables and arrange on a platter with the noodles, bamboo shoots, tofu and mushrooms.

6 Make the sesame dipping sauce by mixing all of the ingredients well and pouring them into a shallow dish.

7 To make the ponzu dipping sauce, put the ingredients into a screw-top jar and shake well. Provide your guests with chopsticks and bowls, so they can cook their choice of meat and vegetables in the stock and flavour with either the sesame or ponzu dipping sauces.

8 Near the end of the meal, each guest takes a portion of noodles and ladles the stock over them.

Energy 376kcal/1583kJ; Protein 27.2g; Carbohydrate 41.8g, of which sugars 7.5g; Fat 12.3g, of which saturates 2.2g; Cholesterol 44mg; Calcium 244mg; Fibre 3.4g; Sodium 1250mg.

BEEF NOODLE SOUP ★

SOME WOULD SAY THAT THIS CLASSIC NOODLE SOUP IS VIETNAM IN A BOWL. MADE WITH BEEF OR CHICKEN, IT IS FAST FOOD, STREET FOOD, WORKING MEN'S FOOD AND FAMILY FOOD. IT IS NUTRITIOUS, PARTICULARLY LOW IN FAT, AND MAKES AN INTENSELY SATISFYING MEAL.

SERVES 6

INGREDIENTS
 250g/9oz beef sirloin, trimmed
 500g/1¼lb dried noodles, soaked in
  lukewarm water for 20 minutes
 1 onion, halved and finely sliced
 6–8 spring onions (scallions),
  cut into long pieces
 2–3 red Thai chillies, seeded and
  finely sliced
 115g/4oz/½ cup beansprouts
 1 large bunch each fresh coriander
  (cilantro) and mint, stalks removed,
  leaves chopped
 2 limes, cut in wedges, and hoisin
  sauce, *nuoc mam*, *nuoc cham* or
  other fish sauce to serve
For the stock
 1.5kg/3lb 5oz oxtail, trimmed of fat
  and cut into thick pieces
 1kg/2¼lb beef shank or brisket
 2 large onions, peeled and quartered
 2 carrots, peeled and cut into chunks
 7.5cm/3in fresh root ginger,
  cut into chunks
 6 cloves
 2 cinnamon sticks
 6 star anise
 5ml/1 tsp black peppercorns
 30ml/2 tbsp soy sauce
 45–60ml/3–4 tbsp *nuoc mam*
 salt

1 To make the stock, put the oxtail into a large, deep pan and cover it with water. Bring it to the boil and blanch the meat for about 10 minutes. Drain the meat, rinsing off any scum, and clean out the pan. Put the blanched oxtail back into the pan with the other stock ingredients, apart from the *nuoc mam* and salt, and cover with about 3 litres/5¼ pints/12 cups water. Bring it to the boil, reduce the heat and simmer, covered, for 2–3 hours.

2 Remove the lid and simmer for another hour, until the stock has reduced to about 2 litres/3½ pints/ 8 cups. Skim off any fat and then strain the stock into another pan.

3 Cut the beef sirloin across the grain into thin pieces, the size of the heel of your hand. Bring the stock to the boil once more, stir in the *nuoc mam*, season to taste, then reduce the heat and leave the stock simmering until ready to use.

4 Meanwhile, bring a pan filled with water to the boil, drain the noodles and add to the water. Cook for about 5 minutes or until tender – you may need to separate them with a pair of chopsticks if they look as though they are sticking together.

5 Drain the noodles and divide them equally among six wide soup bowls. Top each serving with the slices of beef, onion, spring onions, chillies and beansprouts.

6 Ladle the hot stock over the top of these ingredients, top with the fresh herbs and serve with the lime wedges to squeeze over. Pass around the hoisin sauce, *nuoc mam* or *nuoc cham* for those who like a little sweetening, fish flavouring or extra fire.

COOK'S TIPS
• The key to this soup is a tasty, light stock flavoured with ginger, cinnamon, cloves and star anise, so it is worth cooking it slowly and leaving it to stand overnight to allow the flavours to develop.
• To enjoy this dish, use your chopsticks to lift the noodles through the layers of flavouring and slurp them up. This is the essence of Vietnam.

Energy 391kcal/1633kJ; Protein 14.9g; Carbohydrate 70.5g, of which sugars 1.9g; Fat 4.3g, of which saturates 1.6g; Cholesterol 24mg; Calcium 41mg; Fibre 1.1g; Sodium 398mg.

BEEF, VEGETABLE AND NOODLE SOUP ★★★

THIS RICH, SATISFYING SOUP IS PACKED WITH ALL SORTS OF FLAVOURS AND TEXTURES, BROUGHT TOGETHER WITH DELICIOUS EGG NOODLES. THE GINGER GIVES IT A DELIGHTFUL TANG.

SERVES 4

INGREDIENTS

10g/¼oz dried porcini mushrooms
6 spring onions (scallions)
115g/4oz carrots
350g/12oz lean rump (round) steak
about 30ml/2 tbsp oil
1 garlic clove, crushed
2.5cm/1in fresh root ginger,
  finely chopped
1.2 litres/2 pints/5 cups beef stock
45ml/3 tbsp light soy sauce
60ml/4 tbsp sake or dry sherry
75g/3oz dried thin egg noodles
75g/3oz spinach, shredded
salt and ground black pepper

1 Break the dried porcini into small pieces, place them in a small heatproof bowl and pour over 150ml/¼ pint/⅔ cup boiling water. Cover the bowl and leave the mushrooms to soak for 15 minutes.

2 Cut the spring onions and carrots into fine 5cm/2in-long strips. Trim any fat off the meat and slice into thin strips.

3 Heat the oil in a large pan and cook the beef in batches until browned, adding a little more oil if necessary. Remove the beef with a slotted spoon and drain on kitchen paper.

4 Add the garlic, ginger, spring onions and carrots to the pan and stir-fry for 3 minutes.

5 Add the beef stock, the mushrooms and their soaking liquid, the soy sauce, sherry and plenty of seasoning. Bring to the boil, reduce the heat and simmer, covered, for 10 minutes.

6 Break up the noodles slightly and add to the pan, with the spinach. Simmer gently for 5 minutes, or until the beef is tender. Adjust the seasoning before serving in warmed bowls.

COOK'S TIP
Chilling the beef briefly in the freezer will make it much easier to slice into thin strips.

Energy 273kcal/1143kJ; Protein 22.9g; Carbohydrate 17.6g, of which sugars 4.2g; Fat 10.9g, of which saturates 2.6g; Cholesterol 57mg; Calcium 57mg; Fibre 1.9g; Sodium 923mg.

NOODLE AND MEATBALL SOUP ★★★

EGG NOODLES AND SPICY MEATBALLS MAKE THIS A REALLY SUSTAINING MAIN MEAL SOUP. IN THE EAST IT IS OFTEN SERVED FROM STREET STALLS, TO MAKE A CONVENIENT LUNCH FOR OFFICE WORKERS.

SERVES 6

INGREDIENTS

    450g/1lb dried medium egg noodles
    30ml/2 tbsp vegetable oil
    1 large onion, finely sliced
    2 garlic cloves, crushed
    2.5cm/1in fresh root ginger,
        cut into thin matchsticks
    1.2 litres/2 pints/5 cups beef stock
    30ml/2 tbsp dark soy sauce
    2 celery sticks, sliced, leaves reserved
    6 Chinese leaves (Chinese cabbage),
        cut into small pieces
    1 handful mangetouts (snow peas),
        cut into strips
    salt and ground black pepper
For the meatballs
    1 large onion, roughly chopped
    1–2 fresh red chillies, seeded
        and chopped
    2 garlic cloves, crushed
    1cm/½in cube shrimp paste
    450g/1lb/2 cups lean minced
        (ground) beef
    15ml/1 tbsp ground coriander
    5ml/1 tsp ground cumin
    10ml/2 tsp dark soy sauce
    5ml/1 tsp dark brown sugar
    juice of ½ lemon
    a little beaten egg

1 To make the meatballs, put the onion, chillies, garlic and shrimp paste in a food processor. Process in short bursts, taking care not to over-chop the onion.

2 Put the meat in a large bowl. Stir in the onion mixture. Add the ground coriander and cumin, soy sauce, sugar, lemon juice and seasoning.

3 Bind the mixture with a little beaten egg and shape into small balls.

4 Cook the noodles in a large pan of boiling, salted water for 3–4 minutes, or until just tender.

5 Drain in a colander and rinse with plenty of cold water. Set aside.

6 Heat the oil in a wide pan and fry the onion, garlic and ginger until soft but not browned. Add the stock and soy sauce and bring to the boil.

COOK'S TIP
Shrimp paste, or terasi, has a strong, salty, distinctive flavour and smell. Use sparingly if unsure of its flavour.

7 Add the meatballs, half-cover and simmer until they are cooked, about 5–8 minutes. Just before serving, add the sliced celery. Cook for 2 minutes more, then add the Chinese leaves and mangetouts. Adjust the seasoning. Divide among soup bowls. Garnish with the reserved celery leaves.

Energy 464kcal/1955kJ; Protein 27.2g; Carbohydrate 58.6g, of which sugars 5.6g; Fat 15.0g, of which saturates 4.8g; Cholesterol 66mg; Calcium 44mg; Fibre 2.9g; Sodium 905mg.

APPETIZERS

Follow the low-fat recipes in this section and treat your
dinner guests to a tasty yet healthy first course. Garlic,
ginger, coriander, chillies and vegetables combine to make
appetizers that are both irresistible and delicious, including
Mussels in Black Bean Sauce, Scented Chicken Wraps, and
Cabbage and Noodle Parcels. Even fried appetizers such as
Oriental Scallops with Ginger Relish can be amazingly low in
cholesterol and prove a healthy-eating choice.

WAKAME <u>WITH</u> PRAWNS <u>AND</u> CUCUMBER ★

THIS LOW-FAT SALAD-STYLE DISH USES WAKAME SEAWEED, WHICH IS NOT ONLY RICH IN MINERALS,
B COMPLEX VITAMINS AND VITAMIN C, BUT ALSO MAKES YOUR HAIR SHINY.

2 Peel the prawns, including the tails. Insert a cocktail stick (toothpick) into the back of each prawn and gently scoop up the thin black vein running down its length. Pull it out, then throw it away.

3 Add the prawns to a pan of lightly salted boiling water and cook until they curl up completely to make full circles. Drain and cool.

4 Halve the cucumber lengthways. Peel away half of the green skin with a zester or vegetable peeler to create green and white stripes. Scoop out the centre with a tablespoon. Slice the cucumber very thinly with a sharp knife or a mandolin. Sprinkle with 5ml/1 tsp salt, and leave for 15 minutes in a sieve (strainer), to draw out excess liquid.

SERVES 4

INGREDIENTS
  10g/¼oz dried wakame seaweed
  12 medium raw tiger prawns
    (jumbo shrimp), heads removed
    but tails intact
  ½ cucumber
  salt
For the dressing
  60ml/4 tbsp rice vinegar
  15ml/1 tbsp shoyu
  7.5ml/1½ tsp caster
    (superfine) sugar
  2.5cm/1in fresh root ginger, peeled
    and cut into thin strips,
    to garnish

1 Soak the wakame in a pan or bowl of cold water for 15 minutes until fully open. The wakame expands to three to five times its original size. Drain.

VARIATION
For a vegetarian version, replace the shellfish with some toasted pine nuts.

5 Bring a large pan of water to the boil and blanch the wakame briefly. Drain and cool under cold running water. Add to the cucumber in the sieve.

6 Press the cucumber and wakame to remove the excess liquid. Repeat the rinsing, draining and pressing process two to three times.

7 Mix the dressing ingredients in a mixing bowl. Stir well until the sugar has dissolved. Add the wakame and cucumber to the dressing and mix.

8 Pile up the wakame mixture in four small bowls or on four plates. Prop the prawns against the heap. Garnish with ginger and serve immediately.

Energy 37kcal/154kJ; Protein 6.9g; Carbohydrate 1.7g, of which sugars 1.7g; Fat 0.3g, of which saturates 0g; Cholesterol 73mg; Calcium 35mg; Fibre 0.2g; Sodium 339mg.

SALT AND PEPPER PRAWNS ★

THESE SUCCULENT SHELLFISH ARE SO TANTALIZING THAT THEY BEG TO BE EATEN SIZZLINGLY HOT WITH THE FINGERS, SO PROVIDE FINGER BOWLS OR HOT CLOTHS FOR YOUR GUESTS.

SERVES 4

INGREDIENTS
15–18 large raw prawns (shrimp),
    in the shell, about 450g/1lb
15ml/1 tbsp sunflower oil
3 shallots or 1 small onion,
    very finely chopped
2 garlic cloves, crushed
1cm/¹/₂in piece fresh root
    ginger, peeled and very
    finely grated
1–2 fresh red chillies, seeded and
    finely sliced
2.5ml/¹/₂ tsp sugar or
    to taste
3–4 spring onions (scallions),
    shredded, to garnish
For the fried salt
    10ml/2 tsp salt
    5ml/1 tsp Sichuan peppercorns

1 Make the fried salt by dry frying
the salt and peppercorns in a
heavy frying pan over medium heat
until the peppercorns begin to release
their aroma. Leave the mixture until
cool, then tip it into a mortar and crush
it with a pestle.

COOK'S TIP
"Fried salt" is also known as "Cantonese
salt" or simply "salt and pepper mix".
It is widely used as a table condiment or
as a dip for deep fried or roasted food,
but can also be an ingredient in a recipe,
as here. Black or white peppercorns
can be substituted for the Sichuan
peppercorns. For the best flavour, make
the fried salt when needed.

2 Carefully remove the heads and legs
from the raw prawns and discard. Leave
the body shells and the tails in place.
Pat dry with sheets of kitchen paper.

3 Heat the oil in a shallow pan until very
hot. Fry the prawns for 2–3 minutes
each side until cooked through, then
lift them out and drain thoroughly on
kitchen paper.

4 Reheat the oil in the frying pan.
Add the fried salt, together with the
shallots or onion, garlic, ginger, chillies
and sugar. Toss together for 1 minute,
then add the prawns and toss them
over the heat for 1 minute more until
they are coated and the shells are
impregnated with the seasonings.
Serve immediately, garnished with the
spring onions.

Energy 122kcal/514kJ; Protein 20.1g; Carbohydrate 2.7g, of which sugars 2.4g; Fat 3.5g, of which saturates 0.5g; Cholesterol 219mg; Calcium 97mg; Fibre 0.3g; Sodium 1197mg.

GRILLED PRAWNS <u>WITH</u> LEMON GRASS ★

NEXT TO EVERY FISH STALL IN AN ASIAN MARKET YOU MAY FIND SOMEONE COOKING UP FRAGRANT, CITRUS-SCENTED SNACKS FOR YOU TO EAT AS YOU WANDER AROUND.

2 Put the *nuoc mam* in a small bowl with the sugar, and beat together until the sugar has dissolved completely. Add the oil and lemon grass and mix well.

3 Pour the marinade over the prawns, using your fingers to rub it all over the prawns and inside the shells too. Cover the dish with clear film (plastic wrap) and chill for at least 4 hours.

4 Cook the prawns on a barbecue or under a conventional grill (broiler) for 2–3 minutes each side. Serve with little bowls of water for rinsing sticky fingers.

SERVES 4

INGREDIENTS
   16 king prawns (jumbo shrimp),
     cleaned, with shells intact
   120ml/4fl oz/½ cup *nuoc mam* or
     other fish sauce
   30ml/2 tbsp sugar
   15ml/1 tbsp sunflower oil
   3 lemon grass stalks, trimmed and
     finely chopped

COOK'S TIP
Big, juicy king prawns are best for this recipe, but you can use smaller ones if the large king prawns are not available.

1 Using a small sharp knife, carefully slice open each king prawn shell along the back and pull out the black vein, using the point of the knife. Try to keep the rest of the shell intact. Place the deveined prawns in a shallow dish and set aside.

Energy 97kcal/409kJ; Protein 9.2g; Carbohydrate 8.8g, of which sugars 8.7g; Fat 3.1g, of which saturates 0.4g; Cholesterol 98mg; Calcium 46mg; Fibre 0g; Sodium 897mg.

STUFFED CHILLIES ★

WITH LESS THAN 3 GRAMS OF TOTAL FAT, THIS IS A GOOD CHOICE FOR A FIRST COURSE OR FOR SERVING WITH DRINKS. IT ISN'T TOO HOT — UNLESS YOU'VE CHOSEN ESPECIALLY FIERY CHILLIES.

SERVES 4

INGREDIENTS

    10 fat fresh green chillies
    115g/4oz lean pork, chopped
    75g/3oz raw tiger prawns (jumbo
    shrimp), peeled and deveined
    15g/½oz/½ cup fresh coriander
    (cilantro) leaves
    5ml/1 tsp cornflour (cornstarch)
    10ml/2 tsp sake or dry sherry
    10ml/2 tsp soy sauce
    5ml/1 tsp sesame oil
    2.5ml/½ tsp salt
    15ml/1 tbsp cold water
    1 fresh red and 1 fresh green chilli,
    seeded and sliced into rings, and
    cooked peas, to garnish

3 Fill each half chilli with some of the meat mixture. Have ready a steamer or a heatproof plate and a pan with about 5cm/2in boiling water in the bottom.

COOK'S TIP

If you prefer a slightly hotter taste, leave seeds in some of the chillies.

4 Place the stuffed chillies in the steamer or on a plate, meat side up, and cover them with a lid or foil.

5 Steam steadily for 15 minutes or until the meat filling is cooked. Serve immediately, garnished with the chilli rings and peas.

1 Cut all the chillies in half lengthways, keeping the stalk. Scrape out and discard the seeds and set the chillies aside.

2 Mix the chopped pork, prawns and coriander leaves in a food processor. Process until smooth. Scrape into a bowl and mix in the cornflour, sherry, soy sauce, sesame oil, salt and water. Cover the bowl and leave to marinate for 10 minutes.

Energy 74kcal/309kJ; Protein 9.9g; Carbohydrate 3.1g, of which sugars 1.8g; Fat 2.2g, of which saturates 0.6g; Cholesterol 55mg; Calcium 27mg; Fibre 0.6g; Sodium 237mg.

SEAWEED-WRAPPED PRAWNS ★

NORI SEAWEED IS USED TO ENCLOSE THE FRAGRANT FILLING OF PRAWNS, WATER CHESTNUTS
AND FRESH HERBS AND SPICES IN THESE STEAMED ROLLS WHICH ARE VIRTUALLY FAT-FREE.

SERVES 4

INGREDIENTS

675g/1½lb raw tiger prawns (jumbo
  shrimp), peeled and deveined
1 fresh red chilli, seeded
  and chopped
5ml/1 tsp finely grated garlic
5ml/1 tsp finely grated fresh
  root ginger
5ml/1 tsp finely grated lime rind
60ml/4 tbsp very finely chopped
  fresh coriander (cilantro)
1 egg white, lightly beaten
30ml/2 tbsp chopped water
  chestnuts
4 sheets nori seaweed
salt and ground black pepper
shoyu, to serve

1 Place the prawns in a food processor with the red chilli, garlic, ginger, lime rind and coriander. Process until smooth, add the egg white and water chestnuts, season and process until combined. Scrape the mixture into a bowl, cover and chill in the refrigerator for 3–4 hours.

2 Lay the nori sheets rough-side up on a clean, dry surface and spread the prawn mixture over each sheet, leaving a 2cm/¾in border at one end. Roll up to form tight rolls, wrap in clear film (plastic wrap) and chill for 2–3 hours.

3 Unwrap the rolls and place on a board. Using a sharp knife, cut each roll into 2cm/¾in lengths.

4 Cut several pieces of baking parchment to fit the tiers of a bamboo steamer. Cut a few holes in each piece of parchment to allow the steam to circulate.

5 Place the rolls in the steamer, cover and place over a wok of simmering water (making sure the water does not touch the steamer). Steam for 6–8 minutes. Serve warm or at room temperature with the shoyu.

Energy 138kcal/581kJ; Protein 31g; Carbohydrate 0.9g, of which sugars 0.3g; Fat 1.1g, of which saturates 0.2g; Cholesterol 329mg; Calcium 137mg; Fibre 0.3g; Sodium 337mg.

MUSSELS <u>IN</u> BLACK BEAN SAUCE ★

LARGE GREEN-SHELLED MUSSELS ARE PERFECT FOR THIS DELICIOUS DISH. BUY THE COOKED MUSSELS ON THE HALF SHELL, AND TAKE CARE NOT TO OVERCOOK THEM, OR THEY WILL BE TOUGH.

SERVES 4

INGREDIENTS

15ml/1 tbsp vegetable oil
2.5cm/1in piece fresh root ginger, finely chopped
2 garlic cloves, finely chopped
1 fresh red chilli, seeded and chopped
15ml/1 tbsp black bean sauce
15ml/1 tbsp sake or dry sherry
5ml/1 tsp caster (superfine) sugar
5ml/1 tsp sesame oil
10ml/2 tsp dark soy sauce
20 cooked (New Zealand) green-shelled mussels
2 spring onions (scallions), 1 shredded and 1 cut into fine rings

1 Heat the vegetable oil in a small frying pan until very hot. Fry the ginger, garlic and chilli with the black bean sauce for a few seconds, then add the sake or sherry and caster sugar and cook for 30 seconds more.

2 Remove the sauce from the heat and stir in the sesame oil and soy sauce. Mix thoroughly, using a pair of chopsticks or a wooden spoon.

3 Place a trivet in the base of a heavy pan, then pour in boiling water to a depth of 5cm/2in. Place the mussels on a heatproof plate that will fit over the trivet. Spoon over the sauce.

4 Sprinkle the spring onions over the mussels, cover the plate tightly with foil and place it on the trivet in the pan.

5 Steam the mussels over a high heat for about 10 minutes or until the mussels have heated through.

6 Lift the plate carefully out of the pan and serve immediately.

COOK'S TIP
Large scallops in their shells taste delicious when they are cooked in the same way. Do not overcook the shellfish or it will become rubbery.

Energy 83kcal/348kJ; Protein 6.6g; Carbohydrate 3.5g, of which sugars 1.5g; Fat 4.4g, of which saturates 0.7g; Cholesterol 21mg; Calcium 22mg; Fibre 0.2g; Sodium 413mg.

PAN-STEAMED MUSSELS <u>WITH</u> LEMON GRASS, CHILLI <u>AND</u> THAI HERBS ★

LIKE SO MANY SOUTH-EAST ASIAN DISHES, THIS IS VERY EASY TO PREPARE AND VERY LOW IN FAT. THE LEMON GRASS AND KAFFIR LIME LEAVES ADD A REFRESHING TANG TO THE MUSSELS.

SERVES 6

INGREDIENTS
    500g/1¼lb fresh mussels
    1 lemon grass stalk, finely chopped
    2 shallots, chopped
    2 kaffir lime leaves, coarsely torn
    1 fresh red chilli, sliced
    15ml/1 tbsp Thai fish sauce
    30ml/2 tbsp fresh lime juice
    thinly sliced spring onions (scallions)
        and coriander (cilantro) leaves,
        to garnish

1 Clean the mussels by pulling off the beards, scrubbing the shells well and removing any barnacles. Discard any mussels that are broken or which do not close when tapped sharply.

2 Place the mussels in a large, heavy pan and add the lemon grass, shallots, kaffir lime leaves, chilli, fish sauce and lime juice. Mix well. Cover the pan tightly and steam the mussels over a high heat, shaking the pan occasionally, for 5–7 minutes, until the shells have opened.

3 Using a slotted spoon, transfer the cooked mussels to a warmed serving dish or individual bowls. Discard any mussels that have failed to open.

4 Garnish the mussels with the thinly sliced spring onions and coriander leaves. Serve immediately.

Energy 26kcal/112kJ; Protein 4.5g; Carbohydrate 1g, of which sugars 0.8g; Fat 0.5g, of which saturates 0.1g; Cholesterol 10mg; Calcium 52mg; Fibre 0.1g; Sodium 231mg.

GREEN CURRIED MUSSELS AND CLAMS WITH COCONUT MILK ★

LEMON GRASS HAS A DISTINCTIVE AND AROMATIC FLAVOUR AND IS WIDELY USED WITH ALL KINDS OF SEAFOOD IN THAILAND AS THE FLAVOURS MARRY SO PERFECTLY.

SERVES 6

INGREDIENTS

900g/2lb fresh mussels
225g/8oz baby clams
120ml/4fl oz/½ cup dry white wine
1 bunch spring onions (scallions),
  chopped
1 lemon grass stalk, chopped
3 kaffir lime leaves, chopped
10ml/2 tsp Thai green curry paste
120ml/4fl oz/½ cup reduced-fat
  coconut milk
30ml/2 tbsp chopped fresh
  coriander (cilantro)
salt and ground black pepper
garlic chives, to garnish

1 Clean the mussels by pulling off the beards, scrubbing the shells well and scraping off any barnacles with the blade of a knife. Scrub the clams. Discard any mussels or clams that are damaged or broken or which do not close immediately when tapped sharply.

2 Put the wine in a large pan with the spring onions, lemon grass and lime leaves. Stir in the curry paste. Simmer until the wine has almost evaporated.

COOK'S TIPS
• It is unwise to gather fresh shellfish yourself. Those available from stores have either been farmed or have undergone a purging process to clean them.
• Depending on where you live, you may have difficulty obtaining clams. If so, use a few extra mussels instead.

3 Add the mussels and clams to the pan and increase the heat to high. Cover tightly and steam the shellfish for 5–6 minutes, until they open.

4 Using a slotted spoon, transfer the mussels and clams to a heated serving bowl, cover and keep hot. Discard any shellfish that remain closed. Strain the cooking liquid into a clean pan through a sieve lined with muslin (cheesecloth) and simmer briefly to reduce to about 250ml/8fl oz/1 cup.

5 Stir the coconut milk and chopped coriander into the sauce and season with salt and pepper to taste. Heat through. Pour the sauce over the mussels and clams, garnish with the garlic chives and serve immediately.

Energy 73kcal/309kJ; Protein 10.5g; Carbohydrate 2.1g, of which sugars 1.8g; Fat 1.2g, of which saturates 0.2g; Cholesterol 26mg; Calcium 129mg; Fibre 0.7g; Sodium 271mg.

CRAB CAKES WITH GINGER AND WASABI ★★★

THERE'S MORE THAN A HINT OF HEAT IN THESE CRAB CAKES, THANKS TO WASABI, A POWERFUL CONDIMENT, AND ROOT GINGER. THE DIPPING SAUCE DOUBLES THE DRAMATIC IMPACT.

SERVES 6

INGREDIENTS

4 spring onions (scallions)
450g/1lb fresh dressed crab meat (brown and white meat)
2.5cm/1in piece fresh root ginger, grated
30ml/2 tbsp chopped fresh coriander (cilantro)
30ml/2 tbsp low-fat mayonnaise
2.5–5ml/½–1 tsp wasabi paste
15ml/1 tbsp sesame oil
50–115g/2–4oz/1–2 cups fresh white breadcrumbs
30ml/2 tbsp vegetable oil, for frying
salt and ground black pepper
For the dipping sauce
5ml/1 tsp wasabi paste
90ml/6 tbsp soy sauce

1 Make the dipping sauce. Mix the wasabi and soy sauce in a small bowl. Set aside.

2 Chop the spring onions. Mix the crab meat, spring onions, ginger, coriander, mayonnaise, wasabi paste and sesame oil in a bowl. Season and stir in enough breadcrumbs to make a mixture that is firm enough to form patties. Chill the mixture for 30 minutes.

COOK'S TIPS

• Fresh crab meat will have the best flavour, but if it is not available, use frozen or canned crab meat.
• Wasabi is often described as horseradish mustard, although this Japanese paste is unrelated to either condiment. It is very hot.

3 Form the crab mixture into 12 cakes. Heat the oil in a non-stick frying pan and fry the crab cakes for about 3–4 minutes on each side, until browned.

4 Serve with the dipping sauce. Chilli and spring onion slices can be used as a garnish, and the crab cakes served with lettuce and lime slices.

Energy 190kcal/795kJ; Protein 16.2g; Carbohydrate 7.1g, of which sugars 0.6g; Fat 11g, of which saturates 1.4g; Cholesterol 55mg; Calcium 35mg; Fibre 0.3g; Sodium 388mg.

SOFT-SHELL CRABS WITH CHILLI AND SALT ★★

IF FRESH SOFT-SHELL CRABS ARE UNAVAILABLE, YOU CAN BUY FROZEN ONES IN ASIAN SUPERMARKETS. ALLOW TWO SMALL CRABS PER SERVING, OR ONE IF THEY ARE VERY LARGE.

SERVES 4

INGREDIENTS
    8 small soft-shell crabs, thawed
      if frozen
    50g/2oz/½ cup plain
      (all-purpose) flour
    15ml/1 tbsp sunflower oil
    2 large fresh red chillies, or
      1 green and 1 red, seeded and
      thinly sliced
    4 spring onions (scallions) or a
      small bunch of garlic chives,
      chopped
    coarse sea salt and ground
      black pepper
To serve
    shredded lettuce, mooli (daikon)
      and carrot
    light soy sauce

1 Pat the crabs dry with kitchen paper. Season the flour with pepper and coat the crabs lightly with the mixture.

2 Heat the oil in a shallow pan until very hot, then put in the crabs (you may need to do this in two batches). Fry for 2–3 minutes on each side, until the crabs are golden brown but still juicy in the middle. Drain the cooked crabs on kitchen paper and keep hot.

3 Add the sliced chillies and spring onions or garlic chives to the oil remaining in the pan and cook gently for about 2 minutes. Sprinkle over a generous pinch of salt, then spread the mixture on to the crabs.

4 Mix the shredded lettuce, mooli and carrot together. Arrange on plates, top each portion with two crabs and serve, with light soy sauce for dipping.

Energy 133kcal/558kJ; Protein 11.1g; Carbohydrate 10g, of which sugars 0.4g; Fat 5.7g, of which saturates 0.7g; Cholesterol 36mg; Calcium 21mg; Fibre 0.5g; Sodium 211mg.

LEMON GRASS SNAILS ★

THE LIVE SNAILS SOLD IN MARKETS ARE USUALLY DESTINED FOR THIS POPULAR DELICACY. SERVED STRAIGHT FROM THE BAMBOO STEAMER, THESE LEMON GRASS-INFUSED MORSELS ARE SERVED AS AN APPETIZER, OR AS A SPECIAL SNACK, DIPPED IN NUOC CHAM OR A SWEET CHILLI SAUCE.

SERVES 4

INGREDIENTS
    12 fresh snails in their shells
    115g/4oz lean minced (ground) pork,
      passed through the mincer twice
    2 lemon grass stalks, trimmed
      and finely chopped or ground
      (reserve the outer leaves)
    1 spring onion (scallions),
      finely chopped
    15g/¹/₂oz fresh root ginger, peeled
      and finely grated
    1 red Thai chilli, seeded and
      finely chopped
    5ml/1 tsp sesame oil
    sea salt and ground black pepper
    nuoc cham or other fish sauce,
      for dipping

1 Pull the snails out of their shells and place them in a colander. Rinse the snails thoroughly in plenty of cold water and pat dry with kitchen paper. Rinse the shells and leave to drain.

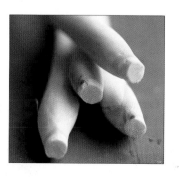

2 Chop the snails finely and put them in a bowl. Add the minced pork, lemon grass, spring onions, ginger, chilli and oil. Season with salt and pepper and mix all the ingredients together.

3 Select the best of the lemon grass leaves and tear each one into thin ribbons, roughly 7.5cm/3in long. Bend each ribbon in half and put it inside a snail shell, so that the ends are poking out. The idea is that each diner pulls the ends of the lemon grass ribbon to gently prise the steamed morsel out of its shell.

COOK'S TIP
Freshwater snails in their shells are available in South-east Asian markets, and some supermarkets and delicatessens. The idea of eating snails may have come from the French, who colonized Vietnam and Cambodia in the 19th and 20th centuries, but the method of cooking them in Vietnam is very different. Snails are plucked live from the water, straight into the bamboo steamer. If you ask for snails in a Vietnamese restaurant, they are likely to be cooked this way.

4 Using your fingers, stuff each shell with the snail and pork mixture, gently pushing it between the lemon grass ends to the back of the shell so that it fills the shell completely.

5 Fill a wok or large pan a third of the way up with water and bring it to the boil. Arrange the snail shells, open side up, in a steamer that fits the wok or pan.

6 Place the lid on the steamer and steam for about 10 minutes, until the mixture is cooked. Serve hot with *nuoc cham* or another strong-flavoured dipping sauce of your choice, such as soy sauce spiked with chopped chillies.

Energy 85kcal/357kJ; Protein 12g; Carbohydrate 0.4g, of which sugars 0.4g; Fat 4g, of which saturates 1.2g; Cholesterol 36mg; Calcium 29mg; Fibre 0.7g; Sodium 38mg.

ORIENTAL SCALLOPS ~~WITH~~ GINGER RELISH ★★

BUY SCALLOPS IN THEIR SHELLS TO BE SURE OF THEIR FRESHNESS; YOUR FISHMONGER WILL OPEN THEM FOR YOU IF YOU FIND THIS DIFFICULT. KEEP THE SHELLS AS THEY MAKE EXCELLENT SERVING DISHES.

SERVES 4

INGREDIENTS
   8 king or queen scallops
   4 whole star anise
   30ml/2 tbsp vegetable oil
   salt and ground white pepper
   fresh coriander (cilantro) sprigs and
     whole star anise, to garnish
For the relish
   ½ cucumber, peeled
   salt, for sprinkling
   5cm/2in piece fresh root
    ginger, peeled
   10ml/2 tsp caster (superfine) sugar
   45ml/3 tbsp rice wine vinegar
   10ml/2 tsp syrup from a jar of
    preserved stem ginger
   5ml/1 tsp sesame seeds,
    for sprinkling

1 To make the relish, halve the cucumber lengthways, scoop out all of the seeds with a teaspoon and discard.

2 Cut the cucumber into 2.5cm/1in pieces, place in a colander and sprinkle liberally with salt. Set the cucumber aside, placing it in the sink to drain for 30 minutes.

3 To prepare the scallops, cut each into 2–3 slices leaving the corals attached. Coarsely grind the star anise using a mortar and pestle.

4 Place the scallop in a bowl and add the star anise and seasoning. Cover the bowl and marinate the scallops in the refrigerator for about 1 hour.

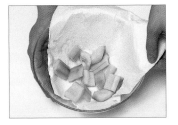

5 Rinse the cucumber under cold water, then drain and pat dry with kitchen paper. Place the cucumber in a bowl.

6 Cut the ginger into thin julienne strips and add to the cucumber with the sugar, rice wine and syrup. Mix well, then cover with clear film (plastic wrap) and chill until the relish is needed.

7 Heat the wok and add the oil. When the oil is very hot, add the scallop slices and stir-fry them for 2–3 minutes. Place the cooked scallops on kitchen paper to drain off any excess oil.

8 Garnish with sprigs of coriander and whole star anise, and serve with the cucumber relish, sprinkled with sesame seeds.

Energy 130kcal/542kJ; Protein 12.1g; Carbohydrate 4.9g, of which sugars 3.2g; Fat 7g, of which saturates 1g; Cholesterol 24mg; Calcium 31mg; Fibre 0.3g; Sodium 92mg.

LEMON SOLE AND FRESH OYSTER SALAD ★★★

FRESH OYSTERS, WITH A RICE VINEGAR DRESSING, TASTE WONDERFUL WITH THE MARINATED LEMON SOLE. THIS COOL AND REFRESHING SALAD IS A TYPICAL USE OF THE CATCH OF THE DAY.

SERVES 4

INGREDIENTS
1 very fresh lemon sole, skinned and
   filleted into 4 pieces
105ml/7 tbsp rice vinegar
dashi-konbu (dried kelp for stock), in 4
   pieces, big enough to cover the fillets
50g/2oz Japanese cucumber, ends
   trimmed, or ordinary salad
   cucumber with seeds removed
50g/2oz celery sticks, strings removed
450g/1lb large broad (fava)
   beans, podded
1 lime, ½ thinly sliced
60ml/4 tbsp walnut oil
seeds from ½ pomegranate
salt
For the oysters
   15ml/1 tbsp rice vinegar
   30ml/2 tbsp shoyu or other
     soy sauce
   15ml/1 tbsp sake or dry sherry
   12 large fresh oysters, opened
   25g/1oz daikon (mooli), peeled
     and very finely grated
   8 chives

1 Sprinkle salt on the sole fillets. Cover and cool in the refrigerator for 1 hour.

2 Mix the rice vinegar and a similar amount of water in a bowl. Wash the fish fillets in the mixture, then drain well. Cut each fillet in half lengthways.

3 Lay one piece of *dashi-konbu* on a work surface. Place a pair of sole fillets, skinned sides together, on to it, then lay another piece of *konbu* on top. Cover all the fillets like this and chill for 3 hours.

4 Halve the cucumber crossways and slice thinly lengthways. Then slice again diagonally into 2cm/¾in wide pieces. Do the same for the celery. Sprinkle the cucumber with salt and leave to soften for 30–60 minutes. Gently squeeze to remove the moisture. Rinse if it tastes too salty, but drain well.

5 Boil the broad beans in lightly salted water for 15 minutes, or until soft. Drain and cool under running water, then peel off the skins to reveal the bright green beans inside. Sprinkle with salt.

6 Mix the rice vinegar, shoyu and sake for the oysters in a small bowl.

7 Slice the sole very thinly with a sharp knife. Remove the slightly chewy *dashi-konbu* first, if you prefer.

8 Place pieces of cucumber and celery in a small mound in the centre of four serving plates, then lay lime slices on top. Garnish with some chopped chives.

9 Place the oysters to one side of the cucumber, topped with a few broad beans, then season with 5ml/1 tsp of the vinegar mix and 10ml/2 tsp grated daikon. Arrange the sole sashimi on the other side and drizzle walnut oil and a squeeze of lime juice on top. Add pomegranate seeds and serve.

Energy 248kcal/1036kJ; Protein 20g; Carbohydrate 14.1g, of which sugars 1.9g; Fat 12.7g, of which saturates 1.3g; Cholesterol 41mg; Calcium 108mg; Fibre 7.6g; Sodium 167mg.

CUBED <u>AND</u> MARINATED RAW TUNA ★

TUNA IS A ROBUST, MEATY FISH. IT MAKES GREAT SASHIMI, ESPECIALLY IF YOU MARINATE IT BRIEFLY IN A MIXTURE OF SHOYU — A JAPANESE SOY SAUCE — WASABI PASTE AND FINELY CHOPPED SPRING ONIONS. MAKE SURE YOU USE ONLY THE FRESHEST TUNA STEAKS YOU CAN FIND.

<u>SERVES 4</u>

INGREDIENTS
    400g/14oz very fresh tuna, skinned
    1 carton mustard and cress or
        land cress (optional)
    20ml/4 tsp wasabi paste
    60ml/4 tbsp shoyu or other
        soy sauce
    8 spring onions (scallions), green
        part only, finely chopped
    4 shiso leaves, cut into thin
        slivers lengthways

COOK'S TIP
As the tuna is not cooked, make sure
that you use very fresh fish from a
reputable supplier.

1 Chill the tuna briefly so that it
becomes firmer and easier to slice.

2 Cut the tuna into 2cm/³⁄₄in cubes. If
using mustard and cress or land cress,
tie into pretty bunches or arrange as a
bed in four small serving bowls or plates.

3 Just 5–10 minutes before serving,
blend the wasabi paste with the shoyu
in a bowl, then add the tuna and spring
onions. Mix well and leave to marinate
for 5 minutes. Divide among the bowls
and add a few slivers of shiso leaves on
top. Serve immediately.

Energy 149kcal/627kJ; Protein 24.5g; Carbohydrate 1.9g, of which sugars 1.7g; Fat 4.9g, of which saturates 1.3g; Cholesterol 28mg; Calcium 27mg; Fibre 0.4g; Sodium 78.3mg.

PORK PÂTÉ IN A BANANA LEAF ★★

THIS PÂTÉ HAS A VIETNAMESE TWIST: IT IS STEAMED IN BANANA LEAVES AND HAS A SLIGHTLY SPRINGY
TEXTURE AND DELICATE FLAVOUR. BAGUETTES ARE A COMMON SIGHT ALONGSIDE THE NOODLES AND
VEGETABLES IN SOUTHERN MARKETS AND FREQUENTLY EATEN SMEARED WITH PÂTÉ.

SERVES 6

INGREDIENTS
   45ml/3 tbsp *nuoc mam* or other
     fish sauce
   15ml/1 tbsp vegetable or sesame oil
   15ml/1 tbsp sugar
   10ml/2 tsp five-spice powder
   2 shallots, peeled and finely chopped
   2 garlic cloves, crushed
   675g/1½lb/3 cups minced
     (ground) pork
   25g/1oz/¼ cup potato starch
   7.5ml/1½ tsp baking powder
   1 banana leaf, trimmed into a strip
     25cm/10in wide
   vegetable oil, for brushing
   salt and ground black pepper
   nuoc cham or other fish sauce and a
     baguette or salad, to serve

1 In a bowl, beat the *nuoc mam* and oil
with the sugar and five-spice powder.
Once the sugar has dissolved, stir in
the shallots and garlic. Add the minced
pork and seasoning, and knead well
until thoroughly combined. Cover and
chill for 2–3 hours.

2 Knead the mixture again, thumping it
down into the bowl to remove any air.
Add the potato starch and baking
powder and knead until smooth and
pasty. Mould the pork mixture into a fat
sausage, about 18cm/7in long, and
place it on an oiled dish.

COOK'S TIP
You can find banana leaves in African,
Caribbean and Asian markets. To prepare
them, trim the leaves to fit the steamer,
using a pair of scissors, making sure that
there is enough to fold over the pâté. If
you cannot find banana leaves, you can
use large spring green (collard) leaves,
or several Savoy cabbage leaves instead.

VARIATION
This pâté can also be added to noodles,
soups and stir-fried dishes, in which it is
complemented by fresh herbs and spices.

3 Lay the banana leaf on a flat surface,
brush it with a little vegetable oil, and
place the pork sausage across it. Lift
up the edge of the banana leaf nearest
to you and fold it over the sausage
mixture, tuck in the sides, and roll it
up into a firm, tight bundle. Secure
the bundle with a piece of string, so
that it doesn't unravel during the
cooking process.

4 Fill a wok one-third full with water.
Balance a bamboo steamer, with its lid
on, above the level of the water. Bring
to the boil, lift the lid and place the
banana leaf bundle on the rack, being
careful not to burn yourself. Re-cover and
steam for 45 minutes. Leave the pâté to
cool in the leaf, open it up and cut it
into slices. Drizzle with *nuoc cham*, and
serve with a baguette or salad.

Energy 187kcal/783kJ; Protein 24.5g; Carbohydrate 6.7g, of which sugars 3.2g; Fat 6.9g, of which saturates 1.9g; Cholesterol 71mg; Calcium 13mg; Fibre 0.2g; Sodium 79mg.

POPIAH ★

Here is the Malaysian version of the spring roll. Do not be put off by the number of ingredients; it takes a little time to get everything together but once it is all on the table the cook can retire as guests assemble their own.

MAKES ABOUT 24 PANCAKES

INGREDIENTS
40g/1½oz/⅓ cup cornflour
 (cornstarch)
215g/7½oz/generous 1¾ cups
 plain (all-purpose) flour
salt
450ml/¾ pint/scant 2 cups water
6 eggs, beaten
spray sunflower oil, for frying
For the cooked filling
15ml/1 tbsp sunflower oil
1 onion, finely chopped
2 garlic cloves, crushed
115g/4oz cooked lean pork, chopped
115g/4oz crab meat or peeled
 cooked prawns (shrimp), thawed
 if frozen
115g/4oz drained canned bamboo
 shoot, thinly sliced
1 small yam bean, peeled and grated
 or 12 drained canned water
 chestnuts, finely chopped
15–30ml/1–2 tbsp yellow
 salted beans
15ml/1 tbsp light soy sauce
ground black pepper
For the fresh fillings
2 hard-boiled eggs, chopped
2 Chinese sausages, steamed
 and sliced
115g/4oz packet fried tofu, each
 piece halved
225g/8oz/4 cups beansprouts
115g/4oz crab meat or peeled
 cooked prawns (shrimp)
½ cucumber, cut into matchsticks
small bunch of spring onions
 (scallions), finely chopped
20 lettuce leaves, rinsed and dried
fresh coriander (cilantro) sprigs,
 to garnish
selection of sauces, including
 bottled chopped chillies, bottled
 chopped garlic and hoisin sauce,
 to serve

COOK'S TIP
Yam beans are large tubers with a mild
sweet texture similar to water chestnuts.

1 Sift the flours and salt into a bowl. Add the measured water and eggs and mix to a smooth batter.

2 Spray a heavy non-stick frying pan with sunflower oil, then pour in just enough batter to cover the base.

3 As soon as it sets, flip and cook the other side. The pancakes should be quite thin. Repeat with the remaining batter to make 20–24 pancakes in all. Pile the cooked pancakes on top of each other, with a layer of baking parchment between each to prevent them sticking. Wrap in foil and keep warm in a low oven.

4 Make the cooked filling for the popiah. Heat the oil in a wok and stir-fry the onion and garlic together for 5 minutes until softened but not browned. Add the pork, crab meat or prawns, bamboo shoot and grated yam bean or water chestnuts. Stir-fry the mixture over a medium heat for 2–3 minutes.

5 Add the salted yellow beans and soy sauce to the wok, with pepper to taste. Cover and cook the beans gently for 15–20 minutes, adding a little boiling water if the mixture starts to dry out. Spoon into a serving bowl and allow to cool.

6 Meanwhile, arrange the chopped hard-boiled eggs, sliced Chinese sausages, sliced tofu, beansprouts, crab meat or prawns, cucumber matchsticks, finely chopped spring onions and lettuce leaves in piles on a large platter or in separate bowls. Spoon the bottled chopped chillies, bottled chopped garlic and hoisin into small bowls.

7 To serve, arrange the popiah on a large warm platter. Each person makes up his or her own popiah by spreading a very small amount of chopped chilli, garlic or hoisin sauce on a pancake, adding a lettuce leaf, a little of the cooked filling and a small selection of the fresh ingredients. The pancake wrapper should not be over-filled.

8 The ends can be tucked in and the pancake rolled up in typical spring roll fashion, then eaten in the hand. They also look attractive simply rolled with the filling showing. The popiah can be filled and rolled before guests arrive, in which case, garnish with sprigs of coriander. It is more fun though for everyone to fill and roll their own.

Energy 94kcal/396kJ; Protein 6.7g; Carbohydrate 10g, of which sugars 0.7g; Fat 3.4g, of which saturates 0.8g; Cholesterol 88mg; Calcium 60mg; Fibre 0.6g; Sodium 109mg.

MINI PHOENIX ROLLS ★★

THESE FILLED OMELETTE PARCELS ARE SO TASTY THAT THEIR FAME IS ALMOST AS LEGENDARY AS THAT OF THE MYTHICAL BIRD AFTER WHICH THEY ARE NAMED. THE SLICES LOOK GOOD AND TASTE BETTER.

4 Scrape the pork paste into a bowl. Stir in the egg white, sherry, remaining water, salt and pepper. Mix thoroughly, cover the bowl and leave in cool place for about 15 minutes.

5 Half-fill a steamer with boiling water and fit the insert, making sure it is clear of the water.

SERVES 4

INGREDIENTS
  2 large eggs, plus 1 egg white
  7ml/5 tbsp cold water
  5ml/1 tsp vegetable oil
  175g/6oz lean pork, diced
  75g/3oz/½ cup drained, canned
    water chestnuts
  5cm/2in piece fresh root
    ginger, grated
  4 dried Chinese mushrooms, soaked
    in hot water until soft
  15ml/1 tbsp dry sherry
  1.5ml/¼ tsp salt
  large pinch of ground white pepper
  30ml/2 tbsp rice vinegar
  2.5ml/½ tsp caster (superfine) sugar
  fresh coriander (cilantro) or flat leaf
    parsley, to garnish

1 Lightly beat the 2 whole eggs with 45ml/3 tbsp of the water. Heat a 20cm/8in non-stick omelette pan and brush with a little of the oil.

2 Pour in a quarter of the egg mixture, swirling the pan to coat the base lightly. Cook the omelette until the top is set. Slide it on to a plate. Make three more omelettes in the same way.

3 Mix the pork and water chestnuts in a food processor. Add 5ml/1 tsp of the root ginger. Drain the mushrooms, chop the caps roughly and add these to the mixture. Process until smooth.

COOK'S TIP
These rolls can be prepared a day in advance and steamed just before serving.

6 Divide the pork mixture among the omelettes and spread into a large square shape in the centre of each of the omelettes.

7 Bring the sides of each omelette over the filling and roll up from the bottom to the top. Arrange the rolls in the steamer. Cover tightly and steam over a high heat for 15 minutes.

8 Make a dipping sauce by mixing the remaining ginger with the rice vinegar and sugar in a small dish.

9 Lift the rolls out of the steamer, then cut them diagonally in 1cm/½in slices, arrange them on a plate, garnish with the coriander or flat leaf parsley leaves and serve with the sauce.

Energy 110kcal/460kJ; Protein 13.8g; Carbohydrate 0.8g, of which sugars 0.5g; Fat 5.4g, of which saturates 1.5g; Cholesterol 123mg; Calcium 22mg; Fibre 0.3g; Sodium 82mg.

SAVOURY CHIFFON CUSTARDS ★★

IT IS THE CONTRAST IN TEXTURES THAT MAKES THESE LITTLE POTS SO APPEALING. THE PORK AND
MUSHROOM MIXTURE IS TOPPED WITH EGG, WHICH BECOMES A VELVETY CUSTARD WHEN STEAMED.

SERVES 4

INGREDIENTS
15g/½oz dried shrimps
4 dried Chinese mushrooms
175g/6oz lean pork, roughly chopped
3 large eggs
475ml/16fl oz/2 cups chicken stock
salt and ground white pepper
30ml/2 tbsp chopped chives
plaited whole chives, to garnish

1 Soak the dried shrimps in water to cover for about 1 hour or until softened.

2 Soak the mushrooms in a bowl of hot water for 30 minutes until soft. Drain, remove the hard stems, then cut the mushroom caps into small pieces.

3 Place the pork and mushrooms in a food processor. Drain the shrimps, then add them with 1.5ml/¼ tsp salt and a pinch of pepper. Process until finely ground. Scrape into a bowl and set aside.

4 Break the eggs into a bowl, then whisk in the stock. Add 2.5ml/½ tsp salt and a large pinch of pepper. Beat well, then strain into a jug (pitcher).

5 Stir a little of the egg mixture into the pork mixture to loosen it. Divide among four 300ml/½ pint/1¼ cup soufflé dishes and divide the remaining egg mixture equally among the soufflé dishes.

6 Sprinkle over the chives. Cover tightly with clear film (plastic wrap) and then foil and place in a steamer.

7 Bring a pan containing about 5cm/2in water to the boil.

8 Cover the steamer and position above the pan of boiling water.

9 Steam the custards for about 10 minutes, then lower the heat and continue steaming for a further 20 minutes until the custards are just set.

10 Serve the custards immediately, garnished with plaited whole chives.

VARIATION
For a delicious alternative, replace the pork mixture with fresh or frozen white crabmeat; this gives a more subtle taste. The crabmeat custards would make a great appetizer.

Energy 118kcal/493kJ; Protein 16.2g; Carbohydrate 0g, of which sugars 0g; Fat 6g, of which saturates 1.8g; Cholesterol 189mg; Calcium 70mg; Fibre 0g; Sodium 246mg.

LION'S HEAD MEAT BALLS ★★★

THESE LARGER-THAN-USUAL PORK BALLS ARE FIRST FRIED, THEN SIMMERED IN STOCK. THEY ARE OFTEN SERVED WITH A FRINGE OF GREENS SUCH AS PAK CHOI TO REPRESENT THE LION'S MANE.

SERVES 2–3

INGREDIENTS

450g/1lb lean pork, minced (ground)
   finely with a little fat
4–6 drained canned water
   chestnuts, finely chopped
5ml/1 tsp finely chopped fresh
   root ginger
1 small onion, finely chopped
30ml/2 tbsp dark soy sauce
beaten egg, to bind
30ml/2 tbsp cornflour (cornstarch),
   seasoned with salt and ground
   black pepper
30ml/2 tbsp groundnut (peanut) oil
300ml/½ pint/1¼ cups
   chicken stock
2.5ml/½ tsp sugar
115g/4oz pak choi (bok choy),
   stalks trimmed and the leaves
   rinsed
salt and ground black pepper

1 Mix the pork, water chestnuts, ginger and onion with 15ml/1 tbsp of the soy sauce in a bowl. Add salt and pepper to taste, stir in enough beaten egg to bind, then form into 8 or 9 balls. Toss a little of the cornflour into the bowl and make a paste with the remaining cornflour and water.

2 Heat the oil in a large frying pan and brown the meat balls all over. Using a slotted spoon, transfer the meat balls to a wok or deep frying pan.

3 Add the stock, sugar and the remaining soy sauce to the oil that is left in the pan. Heat gently, stirring to incorporate the sediment on the bottom of the pan. Pour over the meat balls, cover and simmer for 20–25 minutes.

4 Increase the heat and add the pak choi. Continue to cook for 2–3 minutes or until the leaves are just wilted.

5 Lift out the greens and arrange on a serving platter. Top with the meat balls and keep hot. Stir the cornflour paste into the sauce. Bring to the boil, stirring, until it thickens. Pour over the meat balls and serve immediately.

Energy 326kcal/1363kJ; Protein 35.2g; Carbohydrate 13.1g, of which sugars 3.3g; Fat 15g, of which saturates 3.4g; Cholesterol 139mg; Calcium 91mg; Fibre 1.1g; Sodium 893mg.

SCENTED CHICKEN WRAPS ★

FOR A SOPHISTICATED FIRST COURSE, THESE LEAF-WRAPPED CHICKEN BITES TAKE A LOT OF BEATING.
THEY ARE SURPRISINGLY EASY TO MAKE AND CAN BE DEEP-FRIED IN MINUTES IN THE WOK.

SERVES 4

INGREDIENTS
400g/14oz skinless chicken
  thighs, boned
45ml/3 tbsp soy sauce
30ml/2 tbsp finely grated garlic
15ml/1 tbsp cumin
15ml/1 tbsp ground coriander
15ml/1 tbsp golden caster
  (superfine) sugar
5ml/1 tsp finely grated fresh
  root ginger
1 fresh bird's eye chilli
30ml/2 tbsp oyster sauce
15ml/1 tbsp fish sauce
1 bunch of pandanus leaves,
  to wrap
vegetable oil, for deep-frying
sweet chilli sauce or chilli sambal,
  to serve

1 Using a cleaver or sharp knife, cut the chicken into bitesize pieces and place in a large mixing bowl.

2 Place the soy sauce, garlic, cumin, coriander, sugar, ginger, chilli, oyster sauce and fish sauce in a blender and process until smooth. Pour over the chicken, cover and leave to marinate in the refrigerator for 6-8 hours.

3 When ready to cook, drain the chicken from the marinade and wrap each piece in a pandanus leaf (you will need to cut the leaves to size) and secure with a cocktail stick (toothpick).

4 Fill a wok one-third full of oil and heat to 180°C/350°F or until a cube of bread, dropped into the oil, browns in 45 seconds. Carefully add the chicken parcels, 3–4 at a time, and deep-fry for 3–4 minutes, or until cooked through. Drain on kitchen paper and serve with the chilli sauce or sambal. (Do not eat the leaves!)

COOK'S TIP
Pandanus leaves are usually available from Asian supermarkets.

Energy 159kcal/669kJ; Protein 24.5g; Carbohydrate 6.8g, of which sugars 6.6g; Fat 3.9g, of which saturates 0.6g; Cholesterol 70mg; Calcium 10mg; Fibre 0.1g; Sodium 1055mg.

DRUNKEN CHICKEN ★

AS THE CHICKEN IS MARINATED FOR SEVERAL DAYS, IT IS IMPORTANT TO USE A VERY FRESH BIRD FROM
A REPUTABLE SUPPLIER. "DRUNKEN" FOODS ARE USUALLY SERVED COLD AS PART OF AN APPETIZER.

3 Pour 300ml/½ pint/1¼ cups stock into a jug (pitcher). Freeze the remainder.

4 Remove the skin from the chicken, joint it neatly. Divide each leg into a drumstick and thigh. Make two portions from the wings and some of the breast, then cut away the remainder of the breast pieces (still on the bone) and divide each into two even-size portions.

5 Arrange the chicken portions in a single layer in a shallow dish. Rub salt into the chicken and cover closely with clear film (plastic wrap). Leave in a cool place for several hours or overnight in the refrigerator.

SERVES 4–6

INGREDIENTS
  1 chicken, about 1.3kg/3lb
  1cm/½in piece fresh root ginger, peeled and thinly sliced
  2 spring onions (scallions), trimmed
  1.75 litres/3 pints/7½ cups water or to cover
  15ml/1 tbsp salt
  300ml/½ pint/1¼ cups sake or dry sherry
  spring onions (scallions), shredded, and fresh herbs, to garnish

1 Rinse and dry the chicken inside and out. Place the ginger and spring onions in the body cavity. Put the chicken in a large pan or flameproof casserole and just cover with water. Bring to the boil, skim and cook for 15 minutes.

6 When the stock has cooled completely, lift off any fat that has congealed on the surface. Mix the sherry and reserved stock in a jug (pitcher) and pour over the chicken. Cover again and leave in the refrigerator to marinate for a further 2 or 3 days.

VARIATION
To serve as a cocktail snack, take the meat off the bones, cut it into bitesize pieces, then spear each piece on a cocktail stick (toothpick).

2 Turn off the heat, cover the pan or casserole tightly and leave the chicken in the cooking liquid for 3–4 hours, by which time it will be cooked. Drain well.

7 When ready to serve, cut the chicken through the bone into chunky pieces and arrange on a serving platter garnished with spring onion shreds and herbs.

Energy 200kcal/843kJ; Protein 32.2g; Carbohydrate 0.8g, of which sugars 0.8g; Fat 1.5g, of which saturates 0.4g; Cholesterol 93mg; Calcium 12mg; Fibre 0.1g; Sodium 1068mg.

LETTUCE PARCELS ★★

KNOWN AS SANG CHOY IN HONG KONG, THIS IS A POPULAR "ASSEMBLE-IT-YOURSELF" TREAT.
THE FILLING IS SERVED WITH CRISP LETTUCE LEAVES, WHICH ARE USED AS WRAPPERS.

SERVES 6

INGREDIENTS

2 chicken breast fillets, total weight
 about 350g/12oz
4 dried Chinese mushrooms, soaked
 for 20 minutes in warm water
 to cover
30ml/2 tbsp vegetable oil
2 garlic cloves, crushed
6 drained canned water chestnuts,
 thinly sliced
30ml/2 tbsp light soy sauce
5ml/1 tsp Sichuan peppercorns,
 dry fried and crushed
4 spring onions (scallions),
 finely chopped
5ml/1 tsp sesame oil
vegetable oil, for deep frying
50g/2oz cellophane noodles
salt and ground black
 pepper (optional)
1 crisp lettuce and 60ml/4 tbsp
 hoisin sauce, to serve

4 Add the sliced mushrooms, water
chestnuts, soy sauce and peppercorns.
Toss for 2–3 minutes, then season, if
needed. Stir in half the spring onions,
then the sesame oil. Remove from the
heat and set aside.

5 Cook the noodles in a large pan
of lightly salted boiling water for
3–4 minutes or according to the
packet instructions. Drain thoroughly.

6 Add the cooked noodles to the wok
and toss over a high heat to warm
through. Transfer to a serving dish and
add the remaining spring onions. Wash
the lettuce leaves, pat dry and arrange
on a large platter.

7 Toss the chicken and noodles together
using chopsticks or wooden spoons.

8 Invite guests to take one or two
lettuce leaves, spread the inside with
hoisin sauce and add a spoonful of
filling, before rolling them into a parcel.

1 Remove the skin from the chicken
breast fillets, if they have any, then pat
the fillets dry with kitchen towel. Chop
the chicken into thin strips.

2 Drain the soaked mushrooms.
Cut off and discard the mushroom
stems. Slice the caps finely and set
them aside.

3 Heat the vegetable oil in a wok or large
frying pan over high heat. When
the oil is very hot, add the garlic, then
add the chicken strips and stir-fry for
2–3 minutes until the pieces of chicken
are cooked through and no longer pink.

Energy 168kcal/705kJ; Protein 15.6g; Carbohydrate 7.5g, of which sugars 1.2g; Fat 8.6g, of which saturates 1.1g; Cholesterol 41mg; Calcium 14mg; Fibre 0.6g; Sodium 393mg.

CRISPY TURKEY BALLS *

TURKEY IS LOW IN SATURATED FAT, SO ALTHOUGH IT IS NOT TRADITIONALLY USED IN CHINESE COOKING, IT IS AN EXCELLENT CHOICE FOR HEALTHY EATING AND WORKS WELL IN THIS RECIPE.

SERVES 4–6

INGREDIENTS

4 thin slices white bread,
  crusts removed
5ml/1 tsp vegetable oil
225g/8oz skinless, boneless
  turkey meat, roughly chopped
50g/2oz/⅓ cup drained, canned
  water chestnuts
2 fresh red chillies, seeded and
  roughly chopped
1 egg white
10g/¼oz/¼ cup fresh coriander
  (cilantro) leaves
5ml/1 tsp cornflour (cornstarch)
2.5ml/½ tsp salt
1.5ml/¼ tsp ground white
  pepper
30ml/2 tbsp light soy sauce
5ml/1 tsp sugar
30ml/2 tbsp rice vinegar
2.5ml/½ tsp chilli oil
shredded fresh red chillies and
  fresh coriander (cilantro) sprigs,
  to garnish

1 Preheat the oven to 120°C/250°F/ Gas ½. Brush the bread slices lightly with vegetable oil and cut them into 5mm/¼in cubes. Spread on a baking sheet and bake for 15 minutes they are until dry and crisp.

2 Meanwhile, mix the turkey meat, water chestnuts and chillies in a food processor. Process to a coarse paste. Add the egg white, coriander leaves, cornflour, salt and pepper. Pour in half the soy sauce and process for about 30 seconds. Scrape into a bowl, cover and leave in a cool place for 20 minutes.

3 Remove the toasted bread cubes from the oven and set them aside. Raise the oven temperature to 200°C/400°F/ Gas 6. With dampened hands, divide the turkey mixture into 12 portions and form into balls.

4 Roughly crush the toasted bread cubes, then transfer to a plate. Roll each ball in turn over the toasted crumbs until coated. Place on a baking sheet and bake for about 20 minutes or until the coating is brown and the turkey filling has cooked through.

5 In a small bowl, mix the remaining soy sauce with the sugar, rice vinegar and chilli oil. Serve the sauce with the turkey balls, garnished with shredded chillies and coriander sprigs.

VARIATION
Chicken can be used instead of turkey, with equally delicious results.

Energy 93kcal/393kJ; Protein 11.4g; Carbohydrate 9.7g, of which sugars 1g; Fat 1.2g, of which saturates 0.2g; Cholesterol 21mg; Calcium 23mg; Fibre 0.4g; Sodium 472mg.

CABBAGE AND NOODLE PARCELS ★★

*THE NOODLES AND CHINESE MUSHROOMS GIVE A DELIGHTFUL ORIENTAL FLAVOUR TO THE FILLING FOR
THESE TRADITIONAL CABBAGE ROLLS, WHICH ARE SIMMERED IN A TASTY TOMATO SAUCE.*

SERVES 6

INGREDIENTS

    4 dried Chinese mushrooms, soaked
      in hot water until soft
    50g/2oz cellophane noodles, soaked
      in hot water until soft
    450g/1lb/2 cups minced (ground) pork
    2 garlic cloves, finely chopped
    8 spring onions (scallions)
    30ml/2 tbsp Thai fish sauce
    12 large outer green cabbage leaves
For the sauce
    15ml/1 tbsp vegetable oil
    1 small onion, finely chopped
    2 garlic cloves, crushed
    400g/14oz can chopped
      plum tomatoes
    pinch of sugar
    salt and ground black pepper

1 Drain the mushrooms, discard the
stems and chop the caps. Put them in
a bowl. Next, drain the noodles and cut
them into short lengths. Add to the bowl
with the pork and garlic.

2 Chop two of the spring onions and
add to the bowl. Season with the fish
sauce and pepper.

3 Blanch the cabbage leaves a few at
a time in a pan of boiling, lightly salted
water for about 1 minute. Remove the
leaves from the pan with a spoon and
refresh under cold water.

4 Drain the leaves and dry them well on
kitchen paper. Blanch the remaining six
spring onions in the same fashion.
Drain well.

5 Fill one of the cabbage leaves with
a generous spoonful of the pork and
noodle filling.

6 Taking hold of the corner closest to
yourself, roll up the leaf sufficiently
to enclose the filling, then tuck in the
sides and continue rolling the leaf
to make a tight parcel. Make more
parcels in the same way.

7 Split each spring onion lengthways
by cutting through the bulb and then
tearing upwards.

8 Tie each of the cabbage parcels with
a length of spring onion.

9 To make the sauce, heat the oil in a
large frying pan and add the onion and
garlic. Fry for 2 minutes until soft. Tip
the tomatoes into a bowl. Mash with a
fork, then add to the onion mixture.

10 Season with salt, pepper and a pinch
of sugar, then bring to simmering point.
Add the cabbage parcels. Cover and
cook gently for 20–25 minutes. Check
the seasoning and serve immediately.

Energy 159kcal/670kJ; Protein 18g; Carbohydrate 9.8g, of which sugars 3.4g; Fat 5.6g, of which saturates 1.4g; Cholesterol 47mg; Calcium 20mg; Fibre 1.3g; Sodium 238mg.

LIGHT
BITES

These bites are light in every sense of the word. Not only are they served in relatively small, easy-to-digest portions, but they are also low in fat. In visual terms, they are immensely satisfying, thanks to the Asian cook's passion for perfect presentation. This is clearly evident in recipes such as Chicken and Vegetable Bundles, Crunchy Summer Rolls, Egg Foo Yung Cantonese Style, Prawn Toasts with Sesame Seeds, and Steamed Pork Buns, to name but a few.

GRILLED VEGETABLE STICKS ★★

FOR THIS TASTY DISH, MADE WITH TOFU, KONNYAKU AND AUBERGINE, YOU WILL NEED 40 BAMBOO SKEWERS, SOAKED IN WATER TO PREVENT THEM FROM BURNING WHILE BEING COOKED.

SERVES 4

INGREDIENTS
- 1 × 285g/10¼oz packet firm tofu
- 1 × 250g/9oz packet *konnyaku*
- 2 small aubergines (eggplants)
- 25ml/1½ tbsp toasted sesame oil

For the yellow and green sauces
- 45ml/3 tbsp *shiro miso*
- 15ml/1 tbsp caster (superfine) sugar
- 5 young spinach leaves
- 2.5ml/½ tsp *sansho* pepper
- salt

For the red sauce
- 15ml/1 tbsp *aka miso*
- 5ml/1 tsp caster (superfine) sugar
- 5ml/1 tsp mirin

To garnish
- pinch of white poppy seeds
- 15ml/1 tbsp toasted sesame seeds

1 Drain the liquid from the tofu packet and wrap the tofu in three layers of kitchen paper.

2 Set a plate on top to press out the remaining liquid. Leave for 30 minutes until the excess liquid has been absorbed by the kitchen paper. Cut into eight 7.5 × 2 × 1cm/3 × ¾ × ½in slices.

3 Drain the liquid from the *konnyaku*. Cut it in half and put in a small pan with enough water to cover. Bring to the boil and cook for about 5 minutes. Drain and cut it into eight 6 × 2 × 1cm/ 2½ × ¾ × ½in slices.

4 Halve the aubergines lengthways, then halve the thickness to make four flat slices. Soak in cold water for 15 minutes. Drain and pat dry.

5 To make the yellow sauce, mix the *shiro miso* and the sugar in a pan, then cook over a low heat, stirring to dissolve the sugar. Remove the pan from the heat. Place half the sauce in a small bowl.

6 Blanch the spinach leaves in rapidly boiling water with a pinch of salt for 30 seconds and drain, then cool under running water. Squeeze out as much of the water as possible and chop finely.

7 Transfer the chopped spinach to a mortar and pound to a paste using a pestle. Mix the paste and *sansho* pepper into the bowl of yellow sauce to make the green sauce.

8 Put all the red sauce ingredients in a small pan and cook over a low heat, stirring constantly, until the sugar has dissolved. Remove from the heat.

9 Pierce the slices of tofu, *konnyaku* and aubergine with two bamboo skewers each. Heat the grill (broiler) to high. Brush the aubergine slices with sesame oil and grill (broil) for 7–8 minutes each side. Turn several times.

10 Grill the konnyaku and tofu slices for 3–5 minutes each side, or until lightly browned. Remove them from the heat but keep the grill hot.

11 Spread the red miso sauce on the aubergine slices. Spread one side of the tofu slices with green sauce and one side of the *konnyaku* with the yellow miso sauce from the pan. Grill the slices for 1–2 minutes. Sprinkle the aubergines with poppy seeds. Sprinkle the *konnyaku* with sesame seeds and serve all together.

Energy 132kcal/549kJ; Protein 11.8g; Carbohydrate 6.5g, of which sugars 5.8g; Fat 6.7g, of which saturates 0.9g; Cholesterol 0mg; Calcium 711mg; Fibre 1.3g; Sodium 291mg.

POTATO, SHALLOT AND GARLIC SAMOSAS ★

TRADITIONALLY, SAMOSAS ARE DEEP-FRIED. THESE ARE BAKED, MAKING THEM A HEALTHIER OPTION.
THEY ARE PERFECT FOR PARTIES, SINCE THE PASTRIES NEED NO LAST-MINUTE ATTENTION.

3 Add the drained diced potato, coconut milk, red or green curry paste, peas and lime juice to the frying pan. Mash together coarsely with a wooden spoon. Season to taste with salt and pepper and cook over a low heat for 2–3 minutes, then remove the pan from the heat and set aside until the mixture has cooled a little.

MAKES 25

INGREDIENTS
1 large potato, about 250g/
  9oz, diced
15ml/1 tbsp sunflower oil
2 shallots, finely chopped
1 garlic clove, finely chopped
60ml/4 tbsp reduced-fat
  coconut milk
5ml/1 tsp Thai red or green
  curry paste
75g/3oz/¾ cup peas
juice of ½ lime
25 samosa wrappers or 10 x 5cm/
  4 x 2in strips of filo pastry
salt and ground black pepper
oil, for brushing

1 Preheat the oven to 220°C/425°F/ Gas 7. Bring a small pan of water to the boil, add the diced potato, cover and cook for 10–15 minutes, until tender. Drain and set aside.

2 Meanwhile, heat the sunflower oil in a large frying pan and cook the shallots and garlic over a medium heat, stirring occasionally, for 4–5 minutes, until softened and golden.

COOK'S TIP
Many Asian food stores sell what is described as a samosa pad. This is a packet, usually frozen, containing about 50 oblong pieces of samosa pastry. Filo pastry, cut to size, can be used instead.

4 Lay a samosa wrapper or filo strip flat on the work surface. Brush with a little oil, then place a generous teaspoonful of the potato mixture in the middle of one end. Turn one corner diagonally over the filling to meet the long edge.

5 Continue folding over the filling, keeping the triangular shape as you work down the strip. Brush with a little more oil if necessary and place on a baking sheet. Prepare all the other samosas in the same way.

6 Bake for 15 minutes, or until the pastry is golden and crisp. Leave to cool slightly before serving.

Energy 42kcal/178kJ; Protein 1.2g; Carbohydrate 8.5g, of which sugars 0.6g; Fat 0.6g, of which saturates 0.1g; Cholesterol 0mg; Calcium 14mg; Fibre 0.5g; Sodium 4mg.

SPICY CAULIFLOWER AND GINGER SAMOSAS ★

SAMOSAS ARE USUALLY SOLD BY STREET VENDORS THROUGHOUT SOUTH-EAST ASIA. BAKING THEM RETAINS ALL THE SPICY FLAVOURS, AND HELPS TO KEEP THE FAT CONTENT TO A MINIMUM.

MAKES ABOUT 20

INGREDIENTS
1 packet 25cm/10in square spring
   roll wrappers, thawed if frozen
30ml/2 tbsp plain (all-purpose) flour,
   mixed to a paste with water
about 15ml/1 tbsp sunflower oil
coriander (cilantro) leaves,
   to garnish
cucumber, carrot and celery,
   cut into matchsticks, to serve
   (optional)
For the filling
15ml/1 tbsp sunflower oil
1 small onion, finely chopped
1cm/1/2in piece fresh root ginger,
   peeled and chopped
1 garlic clove, crushed
2.5ml/1/2 tsp chilli powder
1 large potato, about 225g/8oz,
   cooked until just tender and
   finely diced
50g/2oz/1/2 cup cauliflower florets,
   lightly cooked, finely chopped
50g/2oz/1/2 cup frozen peas, thawed
5–10ml/1–2 tsp garam masala
15ml/1 tbsp chopped fresh coriander
   (cilantro) leaves and stems
squeeze of lemon juice
salt

2 Preheat the oven to 200°C/400°F/ Gas 6. Cut the spring roll wrappers into three strips (or two for larger samosas). Brush the edges with a little flour paste. Place a small spoonful of filling about 2cm/3/4in in from the edge of one strip.

3 Fold one corner over the filling to make a triangle and continue this folding until the entire strip has been used and a triangular pastry has been formed. Seal open edges with flour and water paste, adding more water if the paste is thick.

4 Place the samosas on a non-stick baking sheet and brush with oil. Bake for about 10 minutes, until crisp. Serve hot garnished with coriander leaves and accompanied by cucumber, carrot and celery matchsticks, if you like.

COOK'S TIP
Filo pastry can be used instead of spring roll wrappers. Cut the pastry into 8.5cm/ 3in wide strips.

1 Heat the oil in a large wok and fry the onion, ginger and garlic for 5 minutes until the onion has softened. Add the chilli powder, cook for 1 minute, then stir in the potato, cauliflower and peas. Sprinkle with garam masala and set aside to cool. Stir in the chopped coriander, lemon juice and salt.

Energy 44kcal/186kJ; Protein 1.2g; Carbohydrate 8.3g, of which sugars 0.6g; Fat 0.9g, of which saturates 0.1g; Cholesterol 0mg; Calcium 17mg; Fibre 0.6g; Sodium 2mg.

TUNG TONG ★

Known as "gold bags" in Thailand, these crisp pastry purses have a coriander-flavoured filling based on water chestnuts and corn. They are the perfect vegetarian snack.

MAKES 18

INGREDIENTS

18 spring roll wrappers, about
   8cm/3¼in square, thawed
   if frozen
1 egg white
5ml/1 tsp sunflower oil
plum sauce, to serve
For the filling
4 baby corn cobs
130g/4½oz can water chestnuts,
   drained and chopped
1 shallot, coarsely chopped
1 egg, separated
30ml/2 tbsp cornflour (cornstarch)
60ml/4 tbsp water
small bunch fresh coriander
   (cilantro), chopped
salt and ground black pepper

1 Make the filling. Place the baby corn, water chestnuts, shallot and egg yolk in a food processor or blender. Process to a coarse paste.

2 Place the egg white in a cup, add the sunflower oil and 5ml/1 tsp water, and whisk it lightly with a fork.

3 Preheat the oven to 180°C/350°F/ Gas 4. Put the cornflour in a small pan and stir in the water until smooth. Add the corn mixture and chopped coriander and season with salt and pepper to taste. Cook over a low heat, stirring constantly, until the mixture boils and thickens.

4 Leave the filling for the pastry purses to cool slightly. Prepare a non-stick baking sheet or line a baking sheet with baking parchment.

5 Place 5ml/1 tsp of filling in the centre of a spring roll wrapper. Brush the edges lightly with the beaten egg white, then gather up the points and press them firmly together to make a pouch or bag.

6 Repeat with remaining wrappers and filling. Brush each pouch generously with the egg white, and place on the baking sheet. Bake for 12–15 minutes, until golden brown. Serve hot, with the plum sauce.

VARIATION
Rice paper wrappers can be used in place of spring roll wrappers if you are following a wheatfree diet. Simply reconstitute the wrappers by brushing them on both sides with warm water to soften them immediately before you use them.

Energy 36kcal/151kJ; Protein 1.5g; Carbohydrate 6.4g, of which sugars 0.4g; Fat 0.7g, of which saturates 0.1g; Cholesterol 11mg; Calcium 17mg; Fibre 0.5g; Sodium 73mg.

GREEN CURRY PUFFS ★

SHRIMP PASTE AND GREEN CURRY SAUCE, USED JUDICIOUSLY, GIVE THESE PUFFS THEIR DISTINCTIVE, SPICY, SAVOURY FLAVOUR, AND THE ADDITION OF CHILLI STEPS UP THE HEAT.

MAKES 24

INGREDIENTS

    24 small wonton wrappers, about
       8cm/3¼in square, thawed if frozen
    15ml/1 tbsp cornflour (cornstarch),
       mixed to a paste with 30ml/
       2 tbsp water
    5ml/1 tsp sunflower oil
For the filling
    1 small potato, about 115g/4oz,
       boiled and mashed
    25g/1oz/3 tbsp cooked petits pois
       (baby peas)
    25g/1oz/3 tbsp cooked corn
    few sprigs fresh coriander
       (cilantro), chopped
    1 small fresh red chilli, seeded and
       finely chopped
    ½ lemon grass stalk, finely chopped
    15ml/1 tbsp soy sauce
    5ml/1 tsp shrimp paste or fish sauce
    5ml/1 tsp Thai green curry paste

1 Combine the filling ingredients. Lay out one wonton wrapper and place a teaspoon of the filling in the centre.

2 Brush a little of the cornflour paste along two sides of the square. Fold the other two sides over to meet them, then press together to make a triangular pastry and seal in the filling. Make more pastries in the same way, thinning the paste with a little water if it becomes too thick.

3 Preheat the oven to 240°C/475°F/ Gas 9 and prepare a non-stick baking tray or line a baking tray with baking parchment. Lightly whisk the egg white with the oil and 5ml/1 tsp water.

4 Brush the pastries generously with the egg white and place on the baking sheet. Bake for about 5–8 minutes, until browned and crisp. If you intend serving the puffs hot, place them in a low oven while cooking successive batches. The puffs also taste good cold.

COOK'S TIP
Wonton wrappers dry out quickly, so keep them covered, using clear film (plastic wrap), until you are ready to use them.

Energy 32kcal/134kJ; Protein 1g; Carbohydrate 6.7g, of which sugars 0.4g; Fat 0.3g, of which saturates 0g; Cholesterol 1mg; Calcium 16mg; Fibre 0.4g; Sodium 58mg.

ROLLED OMELETTE ★★★

THIS IS A FIRMLY SET, ROLLED OMELETTE, CUT INTO NEAT PIECES AND SERVED COLD. THE TEXTURE
SHOULD BE SMOOTH AND SOFT, NOT LEATHERY, AND THE FLAVOUR IS SWEET-SAVOURY.

SERVES 4

INGREDIENTS
    4 eggs
    30ml/2 tbsp sugar
    10ml/2 tsp shoyu, plus extra
      to serve
    45ml/3 tbsp sake or dry white wine
    30ml/2 tbsp vegetable oil, for cooking
    wasabi and pickled ginger, to garnish

COOK'S TIP
Use the wasabi sparingly as it is
extremely hot.

1 Crack the eggs into a large bowl
and lightly mix them, using a pair
of chopsticks and a cutting action.

2 Mix the sugar with the soy sauce and
sake or wine in a small bowl. Lightly stir
this mixture into the eggs.

3 Heat a little of the oil in a non-stick
frying pan, then wipe off the excess.
Pour a quarter of the egg mixture
into the pan, tilting the pan to coat
it thinly. When the edge has set, but
the middle is still moist, roll up the
omelette towards you.

4 Moisten a paper towel with a little
of the oil and grease the empty side of
the pan. Pour a third of the remaining
egg into the pan. Carefully lift up the
rolled egg with your chopsticks and let
the raw egg run underneath it. When
the edge has set, roll the omelette up
in the opposite direction, tilting the
pan away from you.

5 Slide the roll towards you, grease
the pan and pour in half the remaining
mixture, letting the egg run under.

6 When the egg is set, insert chopsticks
in the side of the rolled omelette, then
flip over towards the opposite side. Cook
the remainder in the same way. Slide the
roll so that its join is underneath. Cook
for 10 seconds.

7 Slide the roll out on to a bamboo
mat and roll up tightly, then press
neatly into a rectangular shape. Leave to
cool. Slice the cold omelette into
2.5cm/1in pieces, arrange on a platter
and garnish with a little wasabi and
some *gari* (pickled ginger). Serve
with soy sauce.

Energy 161kcal/671kJ; Protein 6.4g; Carbohydrate 8.1g, of which sugars 8.1g; Fat 11.1g, of which saturates 2.2g; Cholesterol 190mg; Calcium 34mg; Fibre 0g; Sodium 249mg.

EGG FOO YUNG – CANTONESE STYLE ★★★

HEARTY AND FULL OF FLAVOUR, THIS CAN BE COOKED EITHER AS ONE LARGE OMELETTE OR AS INDIVIDUAL OMELETTES. EITHER WAY, IT IS A CLEVER WAY OF USING UP LEFTOVER ROAST PORK.

SERVES 4

INGREDIENTS
6 dried Chinese mushrooms soaked
   for 20 minutes in warm water
50g/2oz/1 cup beansprouts
6 drained canned water chestnuts,
   finely chopped
50g/2oz baby spinach
   leaves, washed
45ml/3 tbsp vegetable oil
50g/2oz lean roast pork, cut
   into strips
3 eggs
2.5ml/½ tsp sugar
5ml/1 tsp rice wine or dry sherry
salt and ground black pepper
fresh coriander (cilantro) sprigs,
   to garnish

1 Drain the mushrooms. Cut off and discard the stems; slice the caps finely and mix with the beansprouts, water chestnuts and spinach leaves. Heat 15ml/1 tbsp oil in a large heavy frying pan. Add the pork and vegetables and toss over the heat for 1 minute.

2 Beat the eggs in a bowl. Add the meat and vegetables and mix well.

3 Wipe the frying pan and heat the remaining oil. Pour in the egg mixture and tilt the pan so that it covers the base. When the omelette has set on the underside, sprinkle the top with salt, pepper and sugar.

4 Invert a plate over the pan, turn both the pan and the plate over, and slide the omelette back into the pan to cook on the other side. Drizzle with rice wine or sherry and serve immediately, garnished with sprigs of coriander.

Energy 153kcal/634kJ; Protein 8.1g; Carbohydrate 0.7g, of which sugars 0.5g; Fat 13.1g, of which saturates 2.3g; Cholesterol 151mg; Calcium 46mg; Fibre 0.5g; Sodium 80mg.

CRUNCHY SUMMER ROLLS ★

THESE DELIGHTFUL RICE PAPER ROLLS ARE LIGHT AND REFRESHING, EITHER AS A SNACK OR AS AN APPETIZER TO A MEAL, AND ARE PARTICULARLY ENJOYED ALL OVER SOUTH-EAST ASIA.

2 Work with one paper at a time. Place a lettuce leaf towards the edge nearest to you, leaving about 2.5cm/1in to fold over. Place a mixture of the vegetables on top, followed by some mint and coriander leaves.

3 Fold the edge nearest to you over the filling, tuck in the sides, and roll tightly to the edge on the far side. Place the filled roll on a plate and cover with clear film (plastic wrap), so it doesn't dry out. Repeat with the remaining rice papers and vegetables.

4 Serve with a dipping sauce of your choice. If you are making these summer rolls ahead of time, keep them in the refrigerator under a damp dish towel, so that they remain moist.

COOK'S TIPS
• In Vietnam, these crunchy filled rolls are often served with a light peanut dipping sauce. In Cambodia, they are accompanied by a dipping sauce called *tuk trey* (also the name of the national fish sauce), which is similar to the Vietnamese dipping sauce, *nuoc cham*, except that it has chopped peanuts in it. They are, in fact, delicious with any dipping sauce.
• Rice papers can be bought in Chinese and South-east Asian markets.

VARIATION
This recipe only uses vegetables, which are cut into equal lengths, but you can also add pre-cooked shredded lean chicken, pork or prawns (shrimp) to summer rolls.

SERVES 4

INGREDIENTS
12 round rice papers
1 lettuce, leaves separated and ribs removed
2–3 carrots, cut into julienne strips
1 small cucumber, peeled, halved lengthways and seeded, and cut into julienne strips
3 spring onions (scallions), trimmed and cut into julienne strips
225g/8oz mung beansprouts
1 bunch fresh mint leaves
1 bunch coriander (cilantro) leaves
dipping sauce, to serve
(see Cook's Tips)

1 Pour some lukewarm water into a shallow dish. Soak the rice papers, 2–3 at a time, for about 5 minutes until they are pliable. Place the soaked papers on a clean dish towel and cover with a second dish towel to keep them moist.

Energy 107kcal/447kJ; Protein 3.9g; Carbohydrate 20.6g, of which sugars 4.4g; Fat 0.9g, of which saturates 0.1g; Cholesterol 0mg; Calcium 62mg; Fibre 2.9g; Sodium 16mg.

CORN FRITTERS ★

THESE LOW-FAT FRITTERS, PACKED WITH CRUNCHY CORN, FRESH CORIANDER AND CHILLI AND
ACCOMPANIED BY DELICIOUS SWEET CHILLI SAUCE, ARE VERY EASY TO PREPARE AND VERY POPULAR.

MAKES 12

INGREDIENTS

3 corn cobs, total weight
  about 250g/9oz
1 garlic clove, crushed
small bunch fresh coriander
  (cilantro), chopped
1 small fresh red or green chilli,
  seeded and finely chopped
1 spring onion (scallion),
  finely chopped
15ml/1 tbsp soy sauce
75g/3oz/¾ cup rice flour or plain
  (all-purpose) flour
2 eggs, lightly beaten
60ml/4 tbsp water
spray oil, for shallow frying
salt and ground black pepper
sweet chilli sauce,
  to serve

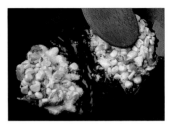

1 Using a sharp knife, slice the kernels from the corn cobs and place them in a large bowl. Add the crushed garlic, chopped coriander, chopped and seeded red or green chilli, chopped spring onion, soy sauce, flour, beaten eggs and water and mix well. Season with salt and pepper to taste and mix again. The mixture should be firm enough to hold its shape, but not stiff.

2 Spray a little oil into a large non-stick frying pan. Add spoonfuls of the corn mixture, gently spreading each one out to make a roundish fritter. Cook for 1–2 minutes on each side until golden-brown and cooked through.

3 Drain on kitchen paper and keep hot while frying more fritters in the same way. Serve hot with sweet chilli sauce.

Energy 49kcal/208kJ; Protein 2.3g; Carbohydrate 7.5g, of which sugars 0.6g; Fat 1.3g, of which saturates 0.3g; Cholesterol 32mg; Calcium 21mg; Fibre 0.6g; Sodium 102mg.

SEAFOOD TEMPURA ★★★

THIS POPULAR DISH CAN ALSO BE MADE WITH VEGETABLES SUCH AS ASPARAGUS AND AUBERGINE. THE
TEMPURA BATTER DOES NEEDS A LITTLE EFFORT, SO TAKE YOUR TIME AND ENJOY THE PROCESS.

SERVES 4

INGREDIENTS
8 large raw prawns (shrimp), heads
  and shells removed, tails intact
130g/4½oz squid body, cleaned
  and skinned
115g/4oz whiting fillets
4 fresh shiitake mushrooms,
  stalks removed
8 okra
⅛ nori sheet, 5 × 4cm/2 × 1½in
20g/¾oz dried cellophane noodles (a
  packet is a 150–250g/5–9oz mass)
vegetable oil and sesame oil,
  for deep-frying
plain (all-purpose) flour, for dusting
salt
For the dipping sauce
400ml/14fl oz/1⅔ cups second dashi
  stock, or the same amount of water
  mixed with 5ml/1 tsp dashi-no-moto
200ml/7fl oz/scant 1 cup shoyu
200ml/7fl oz/scant 1 cup mirin
For the condiment
450g/1lb daikon, peeled
4cm/1½in fresh root ginger, peeled
  and finely grated
For the tempura batter
ice-cold water
1 large (US extra large) egg, beaten
200g/7oz/2 cups plain flour, sifted
2–3 ice cubes

1 Remove the vein from the prawns,
then make 4 × 3mm/⅛in deep cuts
across the belly to stop the prawns
curling up. Snip the tips of the tails and
gently squeeze out any liquid. Pat dry.

2 Cut open the squid body. Lay flat,
inside down, on a chopping board, and
make shallow criss-cross slits on one
side. Cut into 2.5 × 6cm/1 × 2½in
rectangular strips. Cut the whiting fillets
into similar-size strips.

3 Make two notched slits on the shiitake
caps, in the form of a cross. Sprinkle
your hands with some salt and rub over
the okra, then wash the okra under
running water to clean the surface.

4 Cut the nori into four long strips
lengthways. Loosen the cellophane
noodles from the block and cut both
ends with scissors to get a few strips.
Make four bunches and tie them in the
middle by wrapping with a nori strip.
Wet the end to fix it.

5 Make the dipping sauce. In a pan,
mix all the dipping-sauce ingredients
and bring to the boil, then immediately
remove from the heat. Set aside and
keep warm.

6 Prepare the condiment. Grate the
daikon very finely. Drain in a sieve, then
squeeze out any excess water by hand.
Lay clear film (plastic wrap) over an egg
cup and press about 2.5ml/½ tsp grated
ginger into the bottom. Add 30ml/2 tbsp
grated daikon. Press and invert on to a
small plate. Make three more.

7 Half-fill a pan or wok with 3 parts
vegetable oil to 1 part sesame oil. Bring
to 175°C/347°F over a medium heat.

8 Meanwhile, make the tempura batter.
Add enough ice-cold water to the egg
to make 150ml/¼ pint/⅔ cup, then pour
into a large bowl. Add the flour and mix
roughly with chopsticks. Do not beat;
leave the batter lumpy. Add some ice
cubes later to keep the temperature cool.

9 Dip the okra into the batter and deep-
fry until golden. Drain on a rack. Batter
the underside of the shiitake. Deep-fry.

10 Increase the heat a little, then fry
the noodles by holding the nori tie with
chopsticks and dipping them into the oil
for a few seconds. The noodles instantly
turn crisp and white. Drain on kitchen
paper and sprinkle with salt.

11 Hold the tail of a prawn, dust with
flour, then dip into the batter. Do not
put batter on the tail. Slide the prawn
into the hot oil very slowly. Deep-fry one
to two prawns at a time until crisp.

12 Dust the whiting strips, dip into the
batter, then deep-fry until golden. Wipe
the squid strips well with kitchen paper,
dust with flour, then dip in batter. Deep-
fry until the batter is crisp.

13 Drain excess oil from the tempura
on a wire rack for a few minutes, then
arrange them on individual plates. Set
the condiment alongside the tempura.
Reheat the dipping sauce to warm
through, then pour into four small bowls.

14 Serve. Ask your guests to mix the
condiment into the dipping sauce and
dunk the tempura as they eat.

Energy 505kcal/2129kJ; Protein 28.3g; Carbohydrate 69.9g, of which sugars 26.2g; Fat 14.4g, of which saturates 2.1g; Cholesterol 231mg; Calcium 172mg; Fibre 2.8g; Sodium 3741mg

FIRECRACKERS ★

IT'S EASY TO SEE HOW THESE PASTRY-WRAPPED PRAWN SNACKS GOT THEIR NAME (KRATHAK *IN* THAI) *SINCE AS WELL AS RESEMBLING FIREWORKS, THEIR CONTENTS EXPLODE WITH FLAVOUR.*

2 Mix the curry paste with the fish sauce in a shallow dish. Add the prawns and turn them in the mixture until they are well coated. Cover and leave to marinate for 10 minutes.

3 Place a wonton wrapper on the work surface at an angle so that it forms a diamond shape, then fold the top corner over so that the point is in the centre. Place a prawn, slits down, on the wrapper, with the tail projecting from the folded end, then fold the bottom corner over the other end of the prawn.

4 Fold each side of the wrapper over in turn to make a tightly folded roll. Tie a noodle in a bow around the roll and set it aside. Repeat with the remaining prawns and wrappers.

5 Preheat the oven to 240°C/475°F/ Gas 9. Prepare a non-stick baking sheet or line a baking sheet with baking parchment. Lightly whisk the egg white with the oil and 5ml/1 tsp water. Brush the wrapped prawns generously with egg white, so they are well moistened, and place on the baking sheet. Bake for 5–6 minutes, until crisp and lightly browned.

MAKES 16

INGREDIENTS
16 large, raw king prawns (jumbo shrimp), heads and shells removed but tails left on
5ml/1 tsp red curry paste
15ml/1 tbsp Thai fish sauce
16 small wonton wrappers, about 8cm/3¼ in square, thawed if frozen
16 fine egg noodles, soaked (see Cook's Tip)
1 egg white
5ml/1 tsp sunflower oil

1 Place the prawns on their sides and cut two slits through the underbelly of each, one about 1cm/½in from the head end and the other about 1cm/½in from the first cut, cutting across the prawn. This will prevent the prawns from curling when they are cooked.

COOK'S TIP
Soak the fine egg noodles used as ties for the prawn rolls in a bowl of boiling water for 2–3 minutes, until softened, then drain, refresh under cold running water and drain well again.

Energy 37kcal/155kJ; Protein 2.1g; Carbohydrate 6g, of which sugars 0.2g; Fat 0.6g, of which saturates 0.1g; Cholesterol 13mg; Calcium 13mg; Fibre 0.2g; Sodium 88mg.

PRAWN TOASTS WITH SESAME SEEDS ★

THIS HEALTHY VERSION OF THE POPULAR APPETIZER HAS LOST NONE OF ITS CLASSIC CRUNCH AND TASTE. SERVE IT AS A SNACK, TOO. THESE ARE GREAT FOR GETTING A PARTY OFF TO A GOOD START.

SERVES 4–6

INGREDIENTS

6 slices medium-cut white bread,
  crusts removed
225g/8oz raw tiger prawns (jumbo
  shrimp), peeled and deveined
50g/2oz/⅓ cup drained,
  canned water chestnuts
1 egg white
5ml/1 tsp sesame oil
2.5ml/½ tsp salt
2 spring onions (scallions),
  finely chopped
10ml/2 tsp dry sherry
15ml/1 tbsp sesame seeds, toasted
  (see Cook's Tip)
shredded spring onion (scallion),
  to garnish

3 Scrape the mixture into a bowl, stir in the chopped spring onions and sherry and set aside for 10 minutes at room temperature to allow the flavours to mix.

COOK'S TIP
To toast sesame seeds, put them in a dry frying pan and place over a medium heat until the seeds change colour. Shake the pan constantly so the seeds brown evenly and do not burn.

4 Remove the toast from the oven and raise the temperature to 200°C/400°F/ Gas 6. Spread the prawn mixture on the toast, sprinkle with the sesame seeds and bake for 12 minutes. Garnish the prawn toasts with spring onion and serve hot or warm.

1 Preheat the oven to 120°C/250°F/ Gas ½. Cut each slice of bread into four triangles. Spread out on a baking sheet and bake for 25 minutes or until crisp.

2 Meanwhile, put the prawns in a food processor with the water chestnuts, egg white, sesame oil and salt. Process the mixture, using the pulse facility if you have it, until a coarse purée is formed.

Energy 120kcal/506kJ; Protein 10.1g; Carbohydrate 13.8g, of which sugars 1g; Fat 2.8g, of which saturates 0.3g; Cholesterol 73mg; Calcium 80mg; Fibre 0.8g; Sodium 223mg.

FISH CAKES WITH CUCUMBER RELISH ★

THESE WONDERFUL SMALL FISH CAKES ARE A VERY FAMILIAR AND POPULAR APPETIZER IN THAILAND AND INCREASINGLY THROUGHOUT SOUTH-EAST ASIA. THEY ARE USUALLY SERVED WITH THAI BEER.

MAKES ABOUT 12

INGREDIENTS
    5 kaffir lime leaves
    300g/11oz cod, cut into chunks
    30ml/2 tbsp red curry paste
    1 egg
    30ml/2 tbsp Thai fish sauce
    5ml/1 tsp sugar
    30ml/2 tbsp cornflour (cornstarch)
    15ml/1 tbsp chopped fresh
      coriander (cilantro)
    50g/2oz green beans, finely sliced
    spray vegetable oil, for frying
    Chinese mustard cress,
      to garnish
For the cucumber relish
    60ml/4 tbsp coconut or rice vinegar
    50g/2oz/¼ cup sugar
    1 head pickled garlic
    15ml/1 tbsp fresh root ginger
    1 cucumber, cut into matchsticks
    4 shallots, finely sliced

1 Make the cucumber relish. Bring the vinegar and sugar to the boil in a small pan with 60ml/4 tbsp water, stirring until the sugar has dissolved. Remove from the heat and cool.

2 Separate the pickled garlic into cloves. Chop these finely along with the ginger and place in a bowl. Add the cucumber and shallots, pour over the vinegar mixture and mix lightly.

3 Reserve two kaffir lime leaves for garnish and thinly slice the remainder. Put the chunks of fish, curry paste and egg in a food processor and process to a smooth paste. Transfer the mixture to a bowl and stir in the fish sauce, sugar, cornflour, sliced kaffir lime leaves, coriander and green beans. Mix well, then shape the mixture into about twelve 5mm/¼in thick cakes, measuring about 5cm/2in in diameter.

4 Spray the oil in a non-stick wok or deep-frying pan. Fry the fish cakes, a few at a time, for about 4–5 minutes until cooked and evenly brown.

5 Lift out the fish cakes and drain them on kitchen paper. Keep each batch hot while frying successive batches. Garnish with the reserved kaffir leaves and Chinese mustard cress. Serve with the cucumber relish.

Energy 54kcal/228kJ; Protein 5.4g; Carbohydrate 6.4g, of which sugars 5g; Fat 0.9g, of which saturates 0.2g; Cholesterol 27mg; Calcium 12mg; Fibre 0.2g; Sodium 22mg.

STEAMED CRAB DIM SUM <u>WITH</u> CHINESE CHIVES ★

THESE DELECTABLE CHINESE-STYLE DUMPLINGS HAVE A WONDERFULLY STICKY TEXTURE AND MAKE A PERFECT APPETIZER. YOU CAN MAKE THEM IN ADVANCE, AND STEAM THEM JUST BEFORE SERVING.

<u>SERVES 4</u>

INGREDIENTS
150g/5oz fresh white crab meat
115g/4oz/½ cup lean minced
   (ground) pork
30ml/2 tbsp chopped Chinese chives
15ml/1 tbsp finely chopped red
   (bell) pepper
30ml/2 tbsp sweet chilli sauce
30ml/2 tbsp hoisin sauce
24 fresh dumpling wrappers
   (available from Asian stores)
Chinese chives, to garnish
chilli oil and soy sauce, to serve

1 Place the crab meat, pork and chopped chives in a bowl. Add the red pepper, sweet chilli and hoisin sauces and mix well to combine.

2 Working with 2–3 wrappers at a time, put a small spoonful of the crab meat and pork mixture into the centre of each wrapper.

3 Brush the edges of each wrapper with water and fold over to form a half-moon shape. Press and pleat the edges to seal, and tap the base of each dumpling to flatten.

4 Cover with a clean, damp cloth and make the remaining dumplings in the same way.

VARIATION
To make a delicious variation on these crab dim sum, try using chopped raw tiger prawns (jumbo shrimp) in place of the crab meat.

5 Arrange the dumplings on one or more lightly oiled plates and fit inside one or more tiers of a bamboo steamer.

6 Cover the steamer and place over a wok of simmering water (making sure the water does not touch the steamer). Steam for 8–10 minutes, or until the dumplings are cooked through and become slightly translucent.

7 Make a dipping sauce by mixing equal amounts of chilli oil and soy sauce in a bowl.

8 Divide the dumplings among four plates. Garnish with Chinese chives and serve immediately with the sauce.

Energy 146kcal/617kJ; Protein 15.3g; Carbohydrate 14.8g, of which sugars 5.2g; Fat 3.3g, of which saturates 0.7g; Cholesterol 45mg; Calcium 35mg; Fibre 0.5g; Sodium 961mg

STEAMED FLOWER ROLLS ★

THESE ELEGANT STEAMED ROLLS ARE DELICIOUS AND ARE SO PRETTY THAT THEY LOOK ALMOST TOO GOOD TO EAT. THE TECHNIQUE FOR MAKING THEM IS A BIT TRICKY, BUT WELL WORTH THE EFFORT. SERVE WITH A SMALL BOWL OF CONDENSED MILK TO DIP THEM IN FOR A SWEETER SNACK.

MAKES 16

INGREDIENTS
  1 quantity basic dough (see Steamed
  Pork Buns, page 132) made using
  only 5ml/1 tsp sugar
  15ml/1 tbsp sesame seed oil
  chives, to garnish

1 Divide the risen and flattened dough into two equal portions. Roll each into a rectangle measuring 30 x 20cm/ 12 x 8in. Brush the surface of one with sesame oil and lay the other on top. Roll up like a Swiss roll (jelly roll). Cut into 16 pieces.

2 Take each piece of dough in turn and press down firmly on the rolled side with a chopstick making 6 or 7 indents in a row.

3 Pinch the opposite ends of each roll with the fingers of both hands, then pull the ends underneath and seal. The dough should separate into petals.

4 Place the buns on baking parchment in a steamer and leave to double in bulk. Steam over rapidly boiling water for 30–35 minutes. Serve hot, garnished with chives.

COOK'S TIP
When lining the steamer, fold the paper several times, then cut small holes like a doily. This lets the steam circulate, yet prevents the steamed flower rolls from sticking to the steamer.

Energy 84kcal/353kJ; Protein 1.8g; Carbohydrate 14.9g, of which sugars 0.6g; Fat 2.3g, of which saturates 0.3g; Cholesterol 0mg; Calcium 27mg; Fibre 0.6g; Sodium 1mg.

CRISPY SPRING ROLLS ★

IT IS SAID THAT THESE FAMOUS SNACKS WERE TRADITIONALLY SERVED WITH TEA WHEN VISITORS CAME TO CALL AFTER THE NEW YEAR. AS THIS WAS SPRINGTIME, THEY CAME TO BE KNOWN AS SPRING ROLLS. BUY FRESH OR FROZEN SPRING ROLL WRAPPERS FROM ASIAN STORES.

MAKES 12

INGREDIENTS
12 spring roll wrappers, thawed
   if frozen
30ml/2 tbsp plain (all-purpose) flour
   mixed to a paste with water
For the filling
6 Chinese dried mushrooms,
   soaked for 30 minutes in
   warm water
150g/5oz fresh firm tofu
15ml/1 tbsp sunflower oil
225g/8oz finely minced (ground)
   lean pork
225g/8oz peeled cooked prawns
   (shrimp), roughly chopped
2.5ml/$\frac{1}{2}$ tsp cornflour (cornstarch),
   mixed to a paste with 15ml/1 tbsp
   light soy sauce
75g/3oz each shredded bamboo shoot
   or grated carrot, sliced water
   chestnuts and beansprouts
6 spring onions (scallions) or 1 young
   leek, finely chopped
2.5ml/$\frac{1}{2}$ tsp sesame oil
For the dipping sauce
100ml/3$\frac{1}{2}$ fl oz/scant $\frac{1}{2}$ cup
   light soy sauce
15ml/1 tbsp chilli sauce or finely
   chopped fresh red chilli
a little sesame oil
rice vinegar, to taste

1 Make the filling. Drain the mushrooms. Cut off and discard the stems and slice the caps finely. Cut the tofu into slices of a similar size.

2 Heat the oil in a wok and stir-fry the pork for 2–3 minutes or until the colour changes. Add the prawns, cornflour paste and bamboo shoot or carrot. Stir in the water chestnuts.

COOK'S TIP
Thaw frozen spring roll wrappers at room temperature. Separate with a metal spatula. Cover with a damp cloth until needed.

3 Increase the heat, add the beansprouts and finely chopped spring onions or leek and toss the mixture for 1 minute. Stir in the dried Chinese mushrooms and tofu.

4 Off the heat, season the mixture to taste, and then stir in the sesame oil. Cool quickly on a large platter.

5 Separate the spring roll wrappers (see Cook's Tip). Place a wrapper on the work surface with one corner nearest you. Spoon some of the filling near the centre of the wrapper and fold the nearest corner over the filling. Smear a little of the flour paste on the free sides, turn the sides to the middle and roll up. Repeat this procedure with the remaining wrappers and filling.

6 Preheat the oven to 200°C/400°F/ Gas 6. Prepare a non-stick baking sheet or line a baking sheet with non-stick baking parchment. Lightly whisk the egg white with the oil and 5ml/1 tsp water. Generously brush the spring rolls with egg white, so they are moistened all over, and place on the baking sheet. Bake for about 20 minutes, until crisp and golden.

Energy 83kcal/349kJ; Protein 9.5g; Carbohydrate 7.9g, of which sugars 1.4g; Fat 1.7g, of which saturates 0.4g; Cholesterol 48mg; Calcium 97mg; Fibre 0.5g; Sodium 645mg.

STEAMED PORK BUNS ★★★

THESE DELICIOUSLY LIGHT STUFFED BUNS PUSH THE BOUNDARIES WHEN IT COMES TO THE FAT CONTENT,
SO SAVE THEM FOR SERVING AS OCCASIONAL TREATS. THE MEAT FILLING IS SWEET AND SPICY.

SERVES 4

INGREDIENTS
For the basic dough
   250ml/8fl oz/1 cup hand-hot water
   30ml/2 tbsp golden caster
   (superfine) sugar
   10ml/2 tsp dried yeast
   300g/11oz/2¾ cups plain
   (all-purpose) flour
   30ml/2 tbsp sunflower oil
   10ml/2 tsp baking powder
For the filling
   250g/9oz good quality lean
   pork sausages
   15ml/1 tbsp barbecue sauce
   30ml/2 tbsp oyster sauce
   15ml/1 tbsp sweet chilli sauce
   15ml/1 tbsp Chinese rice wine
   15ml/1 tbsp hoisin sauce
   5ml/1 tsp chilli oil

1 To make the dough, pour the water into a bowl. Add the sugar and stir to dissolve. Stir in the yeast, cover and leave in a warm place for 15 minutes.

2 Sift the flour into a large mixing bowl and make a well in the centre with the back of a spoon. Pour the sugar and yeast mixture into the well, together with the sunflower oil. Fold the mixture together, using your fingers, until it forms a ball. Turn out on to a lightly floured surface.

3 Knead the dough for 8–10 minutes until it becomes smooth and elastic. Place the dough in a lightly oiled bowl, cover with a perfectly clean dish towel and leave the dough to rise in a warm place for 3–4 hours.

4 When the dough has risen, place it on a lightly floured surface, knock back (punch down) and shape it into a large circle with your hands.

5 Sprinkle the baking powder in the centre of the dough circle, bring all the edges towards the centre and knead for 6–8 minutes.

6 Divide the dough into 12 balls of equal size, cover with a clean, damp dishtowel and set aside.

7 Squeeze the sausage meat from the casings into a large bowl and stir in the barbecue sauce, oyster sauce, sweet chilli sauce, rice wine, hoisin sauce and chilli oil. Mix thoroughly, using clean fingers, to combine.

8 Press each dough ball with the palm of your hand to form a round, 12cm/4½in in diameter.

9 Place a large spoonful of the pork mixture in the centre of each round of dough and bring the edges up to the centre, then press together firmly to seal and form a bun shape.

10 Arrange the pork buns on several tiers of a large bamboo steamer. Bring a large pan or wok of water to the boil.

11 Cover the steamer, position over the pan or wok of simmering water and steam the pork buns for 20–25 minutes, or until the buns have puffed up and the pork is cooked through. Serve the buns immediately.

Energy 498kcal/2100kJ; Protein 17.6g; Carbohydrate 77.7g, of which sugars 14.3g; Fat 15.0g, of which saturates 3.9g; Cholesterol 34mg; Calcium 194mg; Fibre 3.3g; Sodium 1542mg.

STEAMED PORK BALLS <u>WITH</u> DIPPING SAUCE ★★★

BITESIZE BALLS OF STEAMED PORK AND MUSHROOMS ROLLED IN JASMINE RICE MAKE A FABULOUS SNACK
TO SERVE WITH PRE-DINNER DRINKS, OR AS PART OF A SELECTION OF DIM SUM.

SERVES 4

INGREDIENTS

30ml/2 tbsp vegetable oil
200g/7oz/scant 3 cups finely
 chopped shiitake mushrooms
400g/14oz lean minced (ground) pork
4 spring onions (scallions), chopped
2 garlic cloves, crushed
15ml/1 tbsp fish sauce
15ml/1 tbsp soy sauce
15ml/1 tsp grated fresh root ginger
60ml/4 tbsp finely chopped
 coriander (cilantro)
1 egg, lightly beaten
salt and ground black pepper
200g/7oz/1 cup cooked jasmine rice
For the dipping sauce
 120ml/4fl oz/½ cup sweet
  chilli sauce
 105ml/7 tbsp soy sauce
 15ml/1 tbsp Chinese rice wine
 5–10ml/1–2 tsp chilli oil

1 Heat the oil in a large wok, then add
the mushrooms and stir-fry over a high
heat for 2–3 minutes. Transfer to a food
processor with the pork, spring onions,
garlic, fish sauce, soy sauce, ginger,
coriander and beaten egg. Process
for 30–40 seconds.

2 Scrape the pork mixture into a bowl
and make sure all the ingredients are
well combined. Cover and chill in the
refrigerator for 3–4 hours or overnight.

3 Place the jasmine rice in a bowl.
With wet hands, divide the mushroom
mixture into 20 portions and roll each
one into a firm ball. Roll each ball in
the rice then arrange the balls, spaced
apart, in two baking parchment-lined
tiers of a bamboo steamer.

4 Cover the steamer and place over
a wok of simmering water. Steam for
1 hour 15 minutes.

5 Meanwhile, combine all the dipping
sauce ingredients in a small bowl.

6 When the pork balls are fully cooked,
remove them from the steamer and
serve them warm with the spicy
dipping sauce.

COOK'S TIP
Check the water level in the wok
regularly and top up as required.

Energy 322kcal/1353kJ; Protein 25.8g; Carbohydrate 29.9g, of which sugars 14.3g; Fat 11.8g, of which saturates 2.7g; Cholesterol 111mg; Calcium 39mg; Fibre 0.8g; Sodium 893mg.

YAKITORI CHICKEN ★

THESE ARE JAPANESE-STYLE KEBABS. THEY ARE EASY TO EAT AND IDEAL FOR BARBECUES OR PARTIES.
THE YAKITORI SAUCE IS SO TASTY THAT YOU WILL WANT TO MAKE EXTRA TO SERVE WITH THE KEBABS.

SERVES 4

INGREDIENTS
6 skinless boneless chicken thighs
bunch of spring onions (scallions)
shichimi togarashi (seven-flavour
  spice), to serve (optional)
For the yakitori sauce
60ml/4 tbsp sake
75ml/5 tbsp shoyu or other
  soy sauce
15ml/1 tbsp mirin
15ml/1 tbsp caster (superfine)
  sugar
2.5ml/½ tsp cornflour (cornstarch)
  blended with 5ml/1 tsp water

1 Soak 12 bamboo skewers in water
for at least 30 minutes.

2 In a small pan, mix the ingredients for
the sauce, except the cornflour liquid.

3 Bring the sauce to the boil, then
reduce the heat and simmer for about
10 minutes, or until the sauce has
reduced slightly.

4 Add the cornflour liquid and stir the
mixture over the heat until the sauce is
thick. Transfer to a small bowl.

5 Cut each chicken thigh into bite-size
pieces and set aside.

6 Cut the spring onions into 3cm/
1¼in pieces. Preheat the grill or light
the barbecue.

7 Thread the chicken and spring onions
alternately on to the drained skewers.
Grill under medium heat or cook on
the barbecue, brushing several times
with the sauce. Allow 5–10 minutes,
until the chicken is cooked but moist.

8 Serve with a little extra yakitori sauce,
offering *shichimi* (seven-flavour spice)
with the kebabs if available.

COOK'S TIP
Paprika can be used instead of *shichimi
togarashi*, if that is difficult to obtain.

Energy 129kcal/545kJ; Protein 24.7g; Carbohydrate 5.1g, of which sugars 5g; Fat 1.2g, of which saturates 0.3g; Cholesterol 70mg; Calcium 16mg; Fibre 0.3g; Sodium 596mg.

GRILLED CHICKEN BALLS ON SKEWERS ★

*THESE LITTLE MORSELS MAKE A GREAT LOW-FAT SNACK. HAVING THE CHICKEN BALLS ON SKEWERS
MAKES THEM EASY TO EAT IN THE HAND, SO THEY ARE PERFECT FOR SERVING WITH DRINKS.*

SERVES 4

INGREDIENTS
300g/11oz skinless chicken,
  minced (ground)
2 eggs
2.5ml/½ tsp salt
10ml/2 tsp plain (all-purpose) flour
10ml/2 tsp cornflour (cornstarch)
90ml/6 tbsp dried breadcrumbs
2.5cm/1in piece fresh root
  ginger, grated
shichimi togarashi (seven-flavour
  spice), to serve (optional)
For the yakitori sauce
60ml/4 tbsp sake
75ml/5 tbsp shoyu or other
  soy sauce
15ml/1 tbsp mirin
15ml/1 tbsp caster (superfine) sugar
2.5ml/½ tsp cornflour
  (cornstarch) blended with
  5ml/1 tsp water

1 Soak eight bamboo skewers for
about 30 minutes in water. Put all the
ingredients for the chicken balls, except
the ginger, in a food processor and
process to blend well.

2 Wet your hands and scoop about a
tablespoonful of the mixture into your
palm. Shape it into a small ball about
half the size of a golf ball. Make a
further 30–32 balls in the same way,
wetting your hands as necessary.

3 Squeeze the juice from the grated
ginger into a small mixing bowl. Discard
the pulp. Preheat the grill (broiler) or
light the barbecue.

4 Add the ginger juice to a small pan
of boiling water. Add the chicken balls,
and boil for about 7 minutes, or until
the colour of the meat changes and the
balls float to the surface. Scoop the
balls out using a slotted spoon and
drain on kitchen paper.

5 In a small pan, mix all the ingredients
for the yakitori sauce, except the
cornflour liquid. Bring to the boil, then
reduce the heat and simmer for about
10 minutes, or until the sauce has
reduced slightly. Add the cornflour
liquid and stir over the heat until the
sauce is thick. Transfer to a small bowl.

6 Drain the skewers and thread 3–4 balls
on each. Cook under a medium grill
(broiler) or on a barbecue, keeping the
skewer handles away from the fire. Turn
them frequently for a few minutes, or
until the balls start to brown. Brush with
sauce and return to the heat. Repeat
the process twice. Serve, sprinkled
with *shichimi togarashi*, if you like.

Energy 217kcal/917kJ; Protein 24.2g; Carbohydrate 22.3g, of which sugars 1.2g; Fat 4.1g, of which saturates 1g; Cholesterol 148mg; Calcium 53mg; Fibre 0.6g; Sodium 787mg.

CHICKEN AND VEGETABLE BUNDLES ★

LEEKS FORM THE WRAPPERS FOR THESE ENCHANTING LITTLE VEGETABLE BUNDLES. THESE PARCELS TASTE GOOD ON THEIR OWN, BUT EVEN BETTER WITH THE SOY AND SESAME OIL DIP.

SERVES 4

INGREDIENTS
 4 skinless, boneless
  chicken thighs
 5ml/1 tsp cornflour (cornstarch)
 10ml/2 tsp sake or dry sherry
 30ml/2 tbsp light soy sauce
 2.5ml/½ tsp salt
 large pinch of ground
  white pepper
 4 fresh shiitake mushrooms
 50g/2oz/½ cup sliced, drained,
  canned bamboo shoots
 1 small carrot
 1 small courgette (zucchini)
 1 leek, trimmed
 1.5ml/¼ tsp sesame oil

3 Remove and discard the mushroom stems, then cut each mushroom cap in half (or in slices if very large). Cut the carrot and courgette into eight batons, each about 5cm/2in long, then mix the mushroom halves and bamboo shoots together in a bowl.

5 Divide the marinated chicken into eight portions. Do the same with the vegetables. Wrap each strip of leek around a portion of chicken and vegetables to make eight neat bundles. Half-fill a pan with boiling water and place the bundles in a bamboo steamer making sure that it is clear of the water.

1 Remove any fat from the chicken thighs before cutting each thigh lengthways into eight strips. Place the strips in a bowl.

4 Bring a small pan of water to the boil. Add the leek and blanch until soft. Drain thoroughly, then slit the leek down its length. Separate each layer to give eight long strips.

6 Cover and steam over a high heat for 12–15 minutes or until the filling is cooked.

7 Meanwhile, mix the remaining soy sauce with the sesame oil and use as a sauce for the bundles.

VARIATION
You could use skinless, boneless turkey thighs, if preferred.

COOK'S TIP
Chicken is a good low-fat source of protein and B vitamins, especially if you poach, grill or steam it. Those on a low-fat diet should remove the skin where possible before cooking, as it makes up about 50 per cent of the total fat content of chicken.

2 Add the cornflour, sherry and half the soy sauce to the chicken in the bowl. Stir in the salt and pepper and mix well. Cover with clear film (plastic wrap) and leave in a cool place to marinate for 10 minutes.

Energy 136kcal/576kJ; Protein 25.7g; Carbohydrate 4.5g, of which sugars 2.8g; Fat 1.5g, of which saturates 0.4g; Cholesterol 70mg; Calcium 25mg; Fibre 1.4g; Sodium 600mg.

VEGETARIAN
MAIN DISHES

*Vegetarians are well catered for in South-east Asia, but it is
important to ask precisely what a dish contains as some
stocks and sauces may not be suitable. As cooking for
vegetarian and vegan guests at home can prove challenging,
this chapter introduces some alternative ingredients that you
may not be familiar with. Recipes like Snake Beans with
Tofu, and Daikon, Beetroot and Carrot Stir-fry are
excellent low-fat choices.*

SPICED VEGETABLES WITH COCONUT ★

THIS SPICY AND SUBSTANTIAL DISH MAKES A DELICIOUS VEGETARIAN MAIN COURSE FOR TWO. SERVE IT WITH PLENTY OF PLAIN BOILED RICE FOR MOPPING UP THE DELICIOUS COCONUT AND GINGER STOCK.

SERVES 2

INGREDIENTS

1 fresh red chilli
6 celery stalks
2 large carrots
1 bulb fennel
15ml/1 tbsp vegetable oil
2.5cm/1in piece fresh root ginger,
  peeled and grated
1 garlic clove, crushed
3 spring onions (scallions), sliced
200ml/7fl oz/scant 1 cup
  reduced-fat coconut milk
200ml/7fl oz/scant 1 cup
  vegetable stock
15ml/1 tbsp fresh coriander
  (cilantro), chopped
salt and ground black pepper
coriander (cilantro) sprigs, to garnish

COOK'S TIP
If necessary, wear rubber gloves to protect your hands when handling the chillies.

1 Cut the chilli in half lengthways, remove the seeds and chop it finely.

2 Slice the celery stalks and the carrots on the diagonal using a sharp knife or cleaver, if you have one.

3 Trim the fennel and cut it into slices or chunks, using a sharp knife.

4 Heat the wok, then add the oil. When the oil is hot, add the ginger and garlic, chilli, carrots, celery, fennel and spring onions and stir-fry for 2 minutes. Add the coconut milk and vegetable stock. Stir with a spoon to mix well, then bring to the boil. Stir in the chopped coriander with salt and pepper to taste, and serve garnished with coriander sprigs.

Energy 59kcal/248kJ; Protein 2.2g; Carbohydrate 11.3g, of which sugars 10.9g; Fat 0.9g, of which saturates 0.3g; Cholesterol 0mg; Calcium 105mg; Fibre 4.8g; Sodium 175mg.

MUSHROOMS <u>WITH</u> GARLIC <u>AND</u> CHILLI SAUCE ★

*THE AMOUNT OF SATURATED FAT IN THIS DELICIOUS MUSHROOM DISH IS NEGLIGIBLE AND EVEN THE
TOTAL FAT LEVELS ARE VERY LOW INDEED, SO YOU CAN ENJOY IT WITH A CLEAR CONSCIENCE.*

SERVES 4

INGREDIENTS

    12 large field (portabello),
      chestnut or oyster mushrooms
      or a mixture
    4 garlic cloves,
      roughly chopped
    6 coriander (cilantro) roots,
      roughly chopped
    15ml/1 tbsp sugar
    30ml/2 tbsp light soy sauce
    ground black pepper
For the dipping sauce
    15ml/1 tbsp sugar
    90ml/6 tbsp rice vinegar
    5ml/1 tsp salt
    1 garlic clove, crushed
    1 small fresh red chilli, seeded
      and finely chopped

1 If using wooden skewers, soak eight
of them in cold water for at least
30 minutes to prevent them from
burning when exposed to direct heat.

2 Make the dipping sauce by heating
the sugar, rice vinegar and salt in a
small pan, stirring occasionally until
the sugar and salt have dissolved.

3 Add the garlic and chilli to the
mixture, pour into a serving dish and
keep warm.

4 In a mortar or spice grinder pound
or blend the garlic and coriander roots.

5 Scrape the mixture into a bowl and
mix with the sugar, soy sauce and a
little pepper.

6 Trim and wipe the mushrooms and
cut them in half.

7 Thread three mushroom halves on to
each skewer. Lay the filled skewers side
by side in a shallow dish.

8 Brush the soy sauce mixture over the
mushrooms and leave to marinate for
15 minutes.

9 Prepare the barbecue or preheat the
grill (broiler) and cook the mushrooms
for 2–3 minutes on each side. Serve
with the dipping sauce.

Energy 51kcal/215kJ; Protein 2.5g; Carbohydrate 9.7g, of which sugars 8.7g; Fat 0.5g, of which saturates 0.1g; Cholesterol 0mg; Calcium 12mg; Fibre 1.3g; Sodium 1031mg.

MIXED VEGETABLES MONK-STYLE ★

CHINESE MONKS EAT NEITHER MEAT NOR FISH, SO "MONK-STYLE" DISHES ARE FINE FOR VEGETARIANS.
THIS SUBSTANTIAL DISH IS CHOLESTEROL-FREE AND VERY LOW IN FAT.

SERVES 4

INGREDIENTS
   50g/2 oz dried tofu sticks
   115g/4oz fresh lotus root,
      or 50g/2oz dried
   10g/¼oz dried cloud ear
      (wood ear) mushrooms
   8 dried Chinese mushrooms
   6 golden needles (lily
      buds) (optional)
   15ml/1 tbsp vegetable oil
   75g/3oz/¾ cup drained, canned
      straw mushrooms
   115g/4oz/1 cup baby corn cobs,
      cut in half
   30ml/2 tbsp light soy sauce
   15ml/1 tbsp sake or dry sherry
   10ml/2 tsp caster (superfine) sugar
   150ml/¼ pint/⅔ cup
      vegetable stock
   75g/3oz mangetouts (snow peas)
   5ml/1 tsp cornflour (cornstarch)
   15ml/1 tbsp cold water
   salt

1 Put the tofu sticks in a bowl. Cover them with hot water and leave to soak for 1 hour.

2 If using fresh lotus root, peel it and slice it; if using dried lotus root, place it in a bowl of hot water and leave it to soak for 1 hour.

COOK'S TIP
The flavour of this tasty vegetable mix improves on keeping, so any leftovers would taste even better next day. Simply reheat in a wok or large pan until it is piping hot.

3 Prepare the wood ears and dried Chinese mushrooms by soaking them in separate bowls of hot water for 20 minutes.

4 Drain the wood ears, trim off and discard the hard base from each and cut the rest into bite-size pieces.

5 Drain the soaked Chinese mushrooms in a sieve (strainer), trim off and discard the stems and slice the caps roughly. If using golden needles, tie them into a bundle with kitchen string.

6 Drain the tofu sticks. Cut them into 5cm/2in long pieces, discarding any hard pieces. If using dried lotus root, drain well.

7 Heat the oil in a non-stick frying pan or wok. Stir-fry the wood ears, Chinese mushrooms and lotus root with the golden needles, if using, for about 30 seconds.

8 Add the pieces of tofu, straw mushrooms, baby corn cobs, soy sauce, sherry, caster sugar and stock. Bring to the boil, then cover, lower the heat and simmer for about 20 minutes.

9 Trim the mangetouts and cut them in half. Add to the vegetable mixture, with salt to taste, and cook, uncovered, for 2 minutes more. Mix the cornflour to a paste with the water and add to the pan or wok. Cook, stirring, until the sauce thickens. Serve immediately.

Energy 95kcal/399kJ; Protein 3.3g; Carbohydrate 12g, of which sugars 4.6g; Fat 3.6g, of which saturates 0.4g; Cholesterol 0mg; Calcium 91mg; Fibre 1.4g; Sodium 885mg.

DAIKON, BEETROOT AND CARROT STIR-FRY ★★

THIS IS A DAZZLINGLY COLOURFUL DISH WITH A CRUNCHY TEXTURE AND FRAGRANT TASTE. IT IS LOW IN SATURATED FAT AND CHOLESTEROL-FREE AND WOULD BE IDEAL FOR A SUMMER LUNCH.

2 Using a sharp knife, cut the daikon, beetroot and carrots into long, thin strips. Keep them separate on a chopping board.

3 Reheat the wok or frying pan, then add the oil. When the oil is hot, add the daikon, raw beetroot and carrots and stir-fry for 2–3 minutes.

4 Remove the vegetables from the wok and set aside.

5 Cut the orange in half. Squeeze the juice, using a citrus juicer or a reamer, and pour the juice into a bowl.

6 Arrange the vegetables attractively on a warmed platter, sprinkle over the coriander and season to taste with salt and ground black pepper.

7 Reheat the wok or frying pan, then pour in the orange juice and simmer for 2 minutes.

SERVES 4

INGREDIENTS
    25g/1oz/¼ cup pine nuts
    115g/4oz daikon (mooli),
        peeled
    115g/4oz raw beetroot (beet),
        peeled
    115g/4oz carrots, peeled
    15ml/1 tbsp vegetable oil
    1 orange
    30ml/2 tbsp chopped fresh
        coriander (cilantro)
    salt and ground black pepper

1 Heat a non-stick wok or frying pan. Add the pine nuts and toss over medium heat until golden brown. Remove and set aside.

8 Drizzle the reduced orange juice over the top of the stir-fried vegetables, sprinkle the top with the pine nuts, and serve immediately.

Energy 103kcal/427kJ; Protein 2.1g; Carbohydrate 7.8g, of which sugars 7.5g; Fat 7.2g, of which saturates 0.7g; Cholesterol 0mg; Calcium 33mg; Fibre 2.1g; Sodium 31mg.

CHOI SUM AND MUSHROOM STIR-FRY ★

USE THE MUSHROOMS RECOMMENDED FOR THIS DISH – WILD OYSTER AND SHIITAKE MUSHROOMS HAVE PARTICULARLY DISTINCTIVE, DELICATE FLAVOURS THAT WORK WELL WHEN STIR-FRIED.

SERVES 4

INGREDIENTS
    4 dried black Chinese mushrooms
    150ml/¼ pint/⅔ cup hot water
    450g/1lb choi sum
    50g/2oz/¾ cup oyster mushrooms,
      preferably wild
    50g/2oz/¾ cup shiitake mushrooms
    15ml/1 tbsp vegetable oil
    1 garlic clove, crushed
    30ml/2 tbsp vegetarian oyster sauce

1 Soak the dried Chinese mushrooms in the hot water for 15 minutes to soften.

2 Tear the choi sum into bitesize pieces with your fingers. Place in a bowl and set aside.

3 Halve any large oyster and shiitake mushrooms, using a sharp knife.

4 Strain the Chinese mushrooms and cut off the stems. Heat a wok, then add the oil. When the oil is hot, stir-fry the garlic until it has softened but not coloured.

5 Add the choi sum to the wok and stir-fry for 1 minute. Toss in the oyster and shiitake mushrooms with the Chinese mushroom caps, and stir-fry for 1 minute.

6 Add the oyster sauce, toss well and serve immediately.

COOK'S TIP
Choi sum is one of the most popular and widely used vegetables in Hong Kong. The flavour is like a cross between spinach and cabbage. Choi sum can be boiled, stir-fried, steamed, and is often added to soups.

Energy 57kcal/237kJ; Protein 3.7g; Carbohydrate 2.1g, of which sugars 1.8g; Fat 3.8g, of which saturates 0.5g; Cholesterol 0mg; Calcium 193mg; Fibre 2.7g; Sodium 159mg

VEGETARIAN STIR-FRY WITH PEANUT SAUCE ★★

STIR-FRIED VEGETABLES ARE POPULAR THROUGHOUT SOUTH-EAST ASIA. WHEREVER YOU GO, THERE WILL BE SOME VARIATION ON THE THEME. IN CAMBODIA, THE VEGETABLES ARE SOMETIMES DRIZZLED IN A PEANUT SAUCE LIKE THIS ONE, PARTICULARLY AMONG THE BUDDHIST COMMUNITIES.

SERVES 4–6

INGREDIENTS
- 6 Chinese black mushrooms (dried shiitake), soaked in lukewarm water for 20 minutes
- 20 tiger lily buds, soaked in lukewarm water for 20 minutes
- 225g/8oz tofu
- 60ml/4 tbsp sesame or groundnut (peanut) oil
- 1 large onion, halved and finely sliced
- 1 large carrot, finely sliced
- 300g/11oz pak choi (bok choy), the leaves separated from the stems
- 225g/8oz can bamboo shoots, drained and rinsed
- 50ml/2fl oz/¼ cup soy sauce
- 10ml/2 tsp sugar

For the peanut sauce
- 15ml/1 tbsp groundnut (peanut) or sesame oil
- 2 garlic cloves, finely chopped
- 2 red chillies, seeded and finely chopped
- 90g/3½oz/generous ½ cup unsalted roasted peanuts, finely chopped
- 150ml/5fl oz/⅔ cup coconut milk
- 30ml/2 tbsp hoisin sauce
- 15ml/1 tbsp soy sauce
- 15ml/1 tbsp sugar

1 To make the sauce, heat the oil in a small wok or heavy pan. Stir in the garlic and chillies, stir-fry until they begin to colour, then add all the peanuts except 15ml/1 tbsp. Stir-fry for a few minutes until the natural oil from the peanuts begins to weep.

VARIATION
The popular piquant peanut sauce is delicious served hot with stir-fried, deep-fried or steamed vegetables. Alternatively, leave it to cool, garnish with a little chopped mint and coriander (cilantro) and serve it as a dip for raw vegetables, such as strips of carrot, cucumber and celery.

2 Add the remaining ingredients and bring to the boil. Reduce the heat and cook gently until the sauce thickens a little and specks of oil appear on the surface. Put aside.

3 Drain the mushrooms and lily buds and squeeze out any excess water. Cut the mushroom caps into strips and discard the stalks. Trim off the hard ends of the lily buds and tie a knot in the centre of each one. Put the mushrooms and lily buds aside.

4 Cut the tofu into slices. Heat 30ml/2 tbsp of the oil in a wok or heavy pan and brown the tofu on both sides. Drain on kitchen paper and cut it into strips.

5 Heat a wok or heavy pan and add the remaining oil. Stir in the onion and carrot and stir-fry for a minute. Add the pak choi stems and stir-fry for 2 minutes. Add the mushrooms, lily buds, tofu and bamboo shoots and stir-fry for a minute more. Toss in the pak choi leaves, followed by the soy sauce and sugar. Stir-fry until heated through.

6 Heat up the peanut sauce and drizzle over the vegetables in the wok, or spoon the vegetables into individual bowls and top with a little sauce. Garnish with the remaining peanuts and serve.

Energy 157kcal/656kJ; Protein 5.5g; Carbohydrate 13g, of which sugars 11.4g; Fat 9.6g, of which saturates 2.1g; Cholesterol 0mg; Calcium 110mg; Fibre 5.5g; Sodium 65mg.

STUFFED SWEET PEPPERS ★

*THIS IS AN UNUSUAL RECIPE IN THAT THE STUFFED PEPPERS ARE STEAMED RATHER THAN BAKED. THE
FILLING INCORPORATES TYPICAL THAI INGREDIENTS SUCH AS RED CURRY PASTE AND KAFFIR LIME LEAVES.*

SERVES 4

INGREDIENTS
  3 garlic cloves, finely chopped
  2 coriander (cilantro) roots,
    finely chopped
  400g/14oz/3 cups
    mushrooms, quartered
  5ml/1 tsp Thai vegetarian red
    curry paste
  1 egg, lightly beaten
  15ml/1 tbsp light soy sauce
  2.5ml/½ tsp granulated sugar
  3 kaffir lime leaves, finely chopped
  4 yellow (bell) peppers, halved
    lengthways and seeded

VARIATIONS
For extra colour use red or orange (bell)
peppers if you prefer, or a combination
of the two.

1 In a mortar or spice grinder pound
or blend the garlic with the coriander
roots. Scrape into a bowl.

2 Put the mushrooms in a food
processor and pulse briefly until they
are finely chopped. Add to the garlic
and coriander mixture, then stir in the
curry paste, egg, soy sauce, sugar and
lime leaves.

3 Place the pepper halves in a single
layer in two steamer baskets. Spoon the
mushroom mixture loosely into the
pepper halves. Do not pack the mixture
down tightly or the filling will dry out too
much. Bring the water in the steamer
to the boil, then lower the heat to a
simmer. Steam the peppers for
15 minutes, or until the flesh is tender.
Serve hot.

Energy 95kcal/399kJ; Protein 5.6g; Carbohydrate 12.8g, of which sugars 12g; Fat 2.8g, of which saturates 0.7g; Cholesterol 48mg; Calcium 53mg; Fibre 4.5g; Sodium 301mg.

HERB AND CHILLI AUBERGINES ★★★

PLUMP AND JUICY AUBERGINES TASTE SENSATIONAL STEAMED UNTIL TENDER AND THEN TOSSED IN A
FRAGRANT MINT AND CORIANDER DRESSING WITH CRUNCHY WATER CHESTNUTS.

SERVES 4

INGREDIENTS
    500g/1¼lb firm baby
        aubergines (eggplants)
    30ml/2 tbsp vegetable oil
    6 garlic cloves, very
        finely chopped
    15ml/1 tbsp very finely
        chopped fresh root ginger
    8 spring onions (scallions), cut
        diagonally into 2.5cm/1in lengths
    2 red chillies, seeded
        and thinly sliced
    45ml/3 tbsp light soy sauce
    15ml/1 tbsp Chinese rice wine
    15ml/1 tbsp golden caster
        (superfine) sugar or palm sugar
    a large handful of mint leaves
    30–45ml/2–3 tbsp roughly chopped
        coriander (cilantro) leaves
    115g/4oz water chestnuts
    50g/2oz roasted peanuts,
        roughly chopped
    steamed egg noodles or rice,
        to serve

4 Place the oil in a wok and place over medium heat. When hot, add the garlic, ginger, spring onions and chillies and stir-fry for 2–3 minutes.

5 Remove from the heat and stir in the soy sauce, rice wine and sugar.

6 Add the mint leaves, chopped coriander, water chestnuts and peanuts to the cooled aubergine and toss.

7 Pour the garlic-ginger mixture evenly over the vegetables, toss gently and serve with steamed egg noodles or rice.

COOK'S TIP
When steaming the aubergines, check the water level frequently and top up with extra water if needed.

1 Cut the aubergines in half lengthways and place them on a heatproof plate.

2 Place a steamer rack in a wok and add 5cm/2in of water. Bring the water to the boil over high heat, then carefully lower the plate on to the rack and reduce the heat to low.

3 Cover the plate and steam the aubergines for 25–30 minutes, until they are cooked through. Remove the plate from on top of the steamer and set the aubergines aside to cool.

Energy 170kcal/709kJ; Protein 5.8g; Carbohydrate 10.6g, of which sugars 8.9g; Fat 12g, of which saturates 1.9g; Cholesterol 0mg; Calcium 37mg; Fibre 4g; Sodium 540mg.

AUBERGINE CURRY <u>WITH</u> COCONUT MILK ★

AUBERGINE CURRIES ARE POPULAR THROUGHOUT SOUTH-EAST ASIA, THE THAI VERSION BEING THE MOST FAMOUS. ALL ARE HOT AND AROMATIC, ENHANCED WITH REDUCED-FAT COCONUT MILK.

2 Stir in the coconut milk and stock, and add the aubergines and lime leaves.

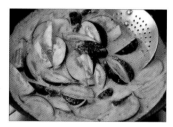

3 Partially cover the pan and simmer over a gentle heat for about 25 minutes until the aubergines are tender. Stir in the basil and check the seasoning. Serve with jasmine rice and lime wedges.

COOK'S TIP
Kroeung is a Cambodian herb paste made from a blend of lemon grass, galangal, garlic and turmeric.

SERVES 4

INGREDIENTS
   15ml/1 tbsp sunflower oil
   4 garlic cloves, crushed
   2 shallots, sliced
   2 dried chillies
   45ml/3 tbsp *kroeung*
   15ml/1 tbsp palm sugar
   300ml/½ pint/1¼ cups reduced-fat
     coconut milk
   550ml/18fl oz/2¼ cups vegetable stock
   4 aubergines (eggplants), trimmed
     and cut into bitesize pieces
   6 kaffir lime leaves
   1 bunch fresh basil, stalks removed
   jasmine rice and 2 limes, cut into
     quarters, to serve
   salt and ground black pepper

1 Heat the sunflower oil in a wok or heavy pan until sizzling. Stir in the crushed garlic cloves, sliced shallots and whole chillies and stir-fry for a few minutes until they begin to colour. Stir in the palm sugar and *kroeung*, and stir-fry until the mixture begins to darken.

Energy 80kcal/338kJ; Protein 1g; Carbohydrate 12.3g, of which sugars 11.9g; Fat 3.4g, of which saturates 0.6g; Cholesterol 0mg; Calcium 47mg; Fibre 1.2g; Sodium 139mg.

CORN AND CASHEW NUT CURRY ★★

A SUBSTANTIAL CURRY, THIS COMBINES ALL THE ESSENTIAL FLAVOURS OF SOUTHERN THAILAND. THIS DISH IS DELICIOUSLY AROMATIC, BUT THE FLAVOUR STILL REMAINS FAIRLY MILD.

SERVES 4

INGREDIENTS

5ml/1 tsp sunflower oil
4 shallots, chopped
50g/2oz/½ cup cashew nuts
5ml/1 tsp Thai vegetarian red
  curry paste
400g/14oz potatoes, peeled and cut
  into chunks
1 lemon grass stalk, finely chopped
200g/7oz can chopped tomatoes
600ml/1 pint/2½ cups boiling water
200g/7oz/generous 1 cup drained
  canned whole kernel corn
4 celery sticks, sliced
2 kaffir lime leaves, rolled into
  cylinders and thinly sliced
15ml/1 tbsp tomato ketchup
15ml/1 tbsp light soy sauce
5ml/1 tsp palm sugar or light
  muscovado (brown) sugar
4 spring onions (scallions), sliced
small bunch fresh basil, chopped

1 Heat the oil in a large, heavy pan or wok. Add the shallots and stir-fry over a medium heat for 2–3 minutes, until softened. Add the cashew nuts and stir-fry for a few minutes until golden.

2 Stir in the red curry paste. Stir-fry for 1 minute, then add the potatoes, lemon grass, tomatoes and boiling water.

3 Bring back to the boil, then reduce the heat to low, cover and simmer gently for 15–20 minutes, or until the potatoes are tender.

4 Stir the corn, celery, lime leaves, tomato ketchup, soy sauce and sugar into the pan or wok. Simmer for a further 5 minutes, until heated through, then spoon into warmed serving bowls. Sprinkle with the sliced spring onions and basil and serve.

COOK'S TIP
Rolling the lime leaves into cylinders before slicing produces very fine strips – a technique known as cutting *en chiffonnade*. Remove the central rib from the leaves before cutting them.

Energy 246kcal/1037kJ; Protein 6.9g; Carbohydrate 38.3g, of which sugars 12.7g; Fat 8.3g, of which saturates 1.6g; Cholesterol 0mg; Calcium 40mg; Fibre 3.5g; Sodium 535mg.

THAI VEGETABLE CURRY WITH LEMON GRASS RICE ★

A FRESH BOWL OF FRAGRANT JASMINE RICE, SUBTLY FLAVOURED WITH LEMON GRASS AND CARDAMOM, IS THE PERFECT ACCOMPANIMENT FOR THIS RICHLY SPICED VEGETABLE CURRY.

SERVES 4

INGREDIENTS

    10ml/2 tsp sunflower oil
    200ml/7fl oz/scant 1 cup reduced-fat
      coconut milk
    550ml/18fl oz/2½ cups
      vegetable stock
    225g/8oz new potatoes, halved or
      quartered, if large
    8 baby corn cobs
    5ml/1 tsp golden caster
      (superfine) sugar
    185g/6½oz/1¼ cups broccoli florets
    1 red (bell) pepper, seeded and
      sliced lengthways
    115g/4oz spinach, tough stalks
      removed, leaves shredded
    30ml/2 tbsp chopped fresh
      coriander (cilantro)
    salt and ground black pepper
For the spice paste
    1 fresh red chilli, seeded
      and chopped
    3 fresh green chillies, seeded
      and chopped
    1 lemon grass stalk, outer leaves
      removed and lower 5cm/2in
      finely chopped
    2 shallots, chopped
    finely grated rind of 1 lime
    2 garlic cloves, chopped
    5ml/1 tsp ground coriander
    2.5ml/½ tsp ground cumin
    1cm/½in piece fresh galangal,
      finely chopped, or 2.5ml/½ tsp
      dried galangal (optional)
    30ml/2 tbsp chopped fresh
      coriander (cilantro)
    15ml/1 tbsp chopped fresh
      coriander (cilantro) roots and
      stems (optional)
For the rice
    225g/8oz/1¼ cups jasmine
      rice, rinsed
    6 cardamom pods, bruised
    1 lemon grass stalk, outer leaves
      removed, cut into 3 pieces
    475ml/16fl oz/2 cups water

1 Make the spice paste. Place all the ingredients in a food processor and process to a coarse paste. Heat the oil in a large, heavy pan. Add the paste and stir-fry over a medium heat for 1–2 minutes, until fragrant.

2 Pour in the coconut milk and stock and bring to the boil. Reduce the heat, add the potatoes and simmer gently for about 15 minutes, until almost tender.

3 Meanwhile, put the rice into a large pan with the cardamoms and lemon grass. Pour in the water. Bring to the boil, reduce the heat, cover, and cook for 10–15 minutes, until the water has been absorbed and the rice is tender.

4 When the rice is cooked and slightly sticky, season to taste with salt, then replace the lid and leave to stand for about 10 minutes.

5 Add the baby corn to the potatoes, season with salt and pepper to taste, then cook for 2 minutes. Stir in the sugar, broccoli and red pepper, and cook for 2 minutes more, or until the vegetables are tender.

6 Stir the shredded spinach and half the fresh coriander into the vegetable mixture. Cook for 2 minutes, then spoon the curry into a warmed serving dish.

7 Remove and discard the cardamom pods and lemon grass from the rice and fluff up the grains with a fork. Garnish the curry with the remaining fresh coriander and serve with the rice.

COOK'S TIP
Cardamom pods may be dark brown, cream, or pale green. The brown pods are usually larger, coarser and do not have such a good flavour as the others. Always remove them before serving.

Energy 313kcal/1313kJ; Protein 9.8g; Carbohydrate 61.4g, of which sugars 7.7g; Fat 3.2g, of which saturates 0.5g; Cholesterol 0mg; Calcium 134mg; Fibre 4.1g; Sodium 439mg.

VEGETABLE FOREST CURRY ★

THIS IS A THIN, SOUPY CURRY WITH LOTS OF FRESH GREEN VEGETABLES AND ROBUST FLAVOURS.
IN THE FORESTED REGIONS OF THAILAND, WHERE IT ORIGINATED, IT WOULD BE MADE USING EDIBLE
WILD LEAVES AND ROOTS. SERVE IT WITH RICE OR NOODLES FOR A SIMPLE LUNCH OR SUPPER.

SERVES 2

INGREDIENTS
600ml/1 pint/2½ cups water
5ml/1 tsp Thai vegetarian red
  curry paste
5cm/2in piece fresh galangal or fresh
  root ginger
90g/3½oz/scant 1 cup green beans
2 kaffir lime leaves, torn
8 baby corn cobs, halved widthways
2 heads Chinese broccoli, chopped
90g/3½oz/generous
  3 cups beansprouts
15ml/1 tbsp drained bottled green
  peppercorns, crushed
10ml/2 tsp granulated sugar
5ml/1 tsp salt

1 Heat the water in a large pan. Add the red curry paste and stir until it has dissolved completely. Bring to the boil.

2 Meanwhile, using a sharp knife, peel and finely chop the fresh galangal or root ginger.

3 Add the galangal or ginger, green beans, lime leaves, baby corn cobs, broccoli and beansprouts to the pan. Stir in the crushed peppercorns, sugar and salt. Bring back to the boil, then reduce the heat to low and simmer for 2 minutes. Serve immediately.

Energy 154kcal/643kJ; Protein 14.9g; Carbohydrate 14.1g, of which sugars 11.8g; Fat 4.5g, of which saturates 0.8g; Cholesterol 0mg; Calcium 173mg; Fibre 9.1g; Sodium 678mg.

JUNGLE CURRY ★

VARIATIONS OF THIS FIERY, FLAVOURSOME VEGETARIAN CURRY CAN BE FOUND ALL OVER SOUTHERN VIETNAM. A FAVOURITE WITH THE BUDDHIST MONKS AND OFTEN SOLD FROM COUNTRYSIDE STALLS, IT IS BEST SERVED WITH PLAIN RICE OR NOODLES, OR EVEN CHUNKS OF CRUSTY BREAD.

SERVES 4

INGREDIENTS

    15ml/1 tbsp sunflower oil
    2 onions, roughly chopped
    2 lemon grass stalks, roughly
      chopped and bruised
    4 green Thai chillies, seeded and
      finely sliced
    4cm/1½in galangal or fresh root
      ginger, peeled and chopped
    3 carrots, peeled, halved lengthways
      and sliced
    115g/4oz long beans
    grated rind of 1 lime
    10ml/2 tsp soy sauce
    15ml/1 tbsp rice vinegar
    5ml/1 tsp black peppercorns,
      crushed
    15ml/1 tbsp sugar
    10ml/2 tsp ground turmeric
    115g/4oz canned bamboo shoots
    75g/3oz spinach, steamed and
      roughly chopped
    150ml/¼ pint/⅔ cup reduced-fat
      coconut milk
    salt
    chopped fresh coriander (cilantro)
      and mint leaves, to garnish

COOK'S TIPS
• Also known as yard-long beans or asparagus beans, snake beans are eaten all over South-east Asia. They may grow up to 40cm/16in long and can be found in Asian stores. There are two common varieties, pale green and darker green, the latter have the better flavour. When buying, choose young, narrow specimens with under-developed seeds, as these will be the most tender. They do not have strings, and preparation is simply trimming and chopping them into short lengths. As they mature, snake beans can become quite tough. They should be used before they turn yellow.
• Jungle curry should be fiery, almost dominated by the chilli. In Vietnam it is often eaten for breakfast or a great pick-me-up at any time of day.

1 Heat a wok or heavy pan and add the oil. Once hot, stir in the onions, lemon grass, chillies and galangal or ginger. Add the carrots and beans with the lime rind and stir-fry for 1–2 minutes.

2 Add the soy sauce and rice vinegar to the wok and stir well. Add the crushed peppercorns, sugar and turmeric, then stir in the bamboo shoots and the chopped spinach.

3 Stir in the coconut milk and simmer for about 10 minutes, until the vegetables are tender. Season with salt, and serve hot, garnished with fresh coriander and mint.

Energy 119kcal/496kJ; Protein 3.8g; Carbohydrate 18.6g, of which sugars 15.3g; Fat 3.8g, of which saturates 0.5g; Cholesterol 0mg; Calcium 125mg; Fibre 4.3g; Sodium 60mg.

AUBERGINE AND SWEET POTATO STEW WITH COCONUT MILK ★

THIS DISH IS SCENTED WITH FRAGRANT LEMON GRASS, GINGER AND LOTS OF GARLIC, CREATING A PARTICULARLY GOOD COMBINATION OF FLAVOURS. AUBERGINES AND SWEET POTATOES GO EXTREMELY WELL TOGETHER AND THE COCONUT MILK ADDS A CREAMY, MELLOW NOTE.

SERVES 6

INGREDIENTS

400g/14oz baby aubergines
 (eggplant) or 2 standard aubergines
15ml/1 tbsp sunflower oil
225g/8oz Thai red shallots or other
 small shallots or pickling onions
5ml/1 tsp fennel seeds,
 lightly crushed
4–5 garlic cloves, thinly sliced
25ml/1½ tbsp finely chopped fresh
 root ginger
475ml/16fl oz/2 cups vegetable stock
2 lemon grass stalks, outer layers
 discarded, finely chopped
 or minced
15g/½oz/⅔ cup fresh coriander
 (cilantro), stalks and leaves
 chopped separately
3 kaffir lime leaves, lightly bruised
2–3 small fresh red chillies
45ml/3 tbsp Thai green curry paste
675g/1½lb sweet potatoes, peeled
 and cut into thick chunks
400ml/14fl oz/1⅔ cups reduced-fat
 coconut milk
2.5–5ml/½–1 tsp palm sugar
250g/9oz/3½ cups mushrooms,
 thickly sliced
juice of 1 lime, to taste
salt and ground black pepper
boiled rice and 18 fresh Thai basil
 or ordinary basil leaves, to serve

1 Trim the aubergines. Slice baby aubergines in half lengthways. Cut standard aubergines into chunks.

2 Heat half the oil in a wide pan or deep, lidded frying pan. Add the aubergines and cook (uncovered) over a medium heat, stirring occasionally, until lightly browned on all sides. Remove from the pan and set aside.

3 Slice 4–5 of the shallots. Cook the whole shallots in the oil remaining in the pan, until lightly browned. Set aside with the aubergines. Add the remaining oil to the pan and cook the sliced shallots, fennel seeds, garlic and ginger over a low heat for 5 minutes.

4 Pour in the vegetable stock, then add the lemon grass, chopped coriander stalks and any roots, lime leaves and whole chillies. Cover and simmer over a low heat for 5 minutes.

5 Stir in 30ml/2 tbsp of the curry paste and the sweet potatoes. Simmer gently for about 10 minutes, then return the aubergines and browned shallots to the pan and cook for a further 5 minutes.

6 Stir in the coconut milk and the sugar. Season to taste with salt and pepper, then stir in the mushrooms and simmer gently for 5 minutes, or until all the vegetables are cooked and tender.

7 Stir in the remaining curry paste and lime juice to taste, followed by the chopped coriander leaves. Adjust the seasoning and ladle the vegetables into warmed bowls. Sprinkle basil leaves over the stew and serve with rice.

COOK'S TIP
Although this is called a stew, green curry paste is an important ingredient, as it is in most of these recipes. The quantity given is only a guide, however, so use less if you prefer.

Energy 147kcal/627kJ; Protein 3.2g; Carbohydrate 29.1g, of which sugars 11.3g; Fat 3g, of which saturates 0.6g; Cholesterol 0mg; Calcium 72mg; Fibre 4.9g; Sodium 125mg.

GLAZED PUMPKIN IN COCONUT MILK ★

PUMPKINS, BUTTERNUT SQUASH AND WINTER MELONS CAN ALL BE COOKED IN THIS WAY. VARIATIONS OF THIS DISH ARE SERVED AS A MAIN COURSE OR AS AN ACCOMPANIMENT TO RICE OR A SPICY CURRY.

SERVES 4

INGREDIENTS
    200ml/7fl oz/scant 1 cup
      reduced-fat coconut milk
    15ml/1 tbsp *kroeung*
    30ml/2 tbsp palm sugar
    15ml/1 tbsp sunflower oil
    4 garlic cloves, finely chopped
    25g/1oz fresh root ginger, peeled and
      finely shredded
    675g/1½lb pumpkin flesh, cubed
    ground black pepper
    a handful of curry or basil leaves,
      to garnish
    fried onion rings, to garnish
    plain rice, to serve

1 In a bowl, beat the coconut milk and the *kroeung* with the sugar, until it has dissolved. Set aside.

2 Heat the oil in a wok or heavy pan and stir in the garlic and ginger. Stir-fry until they begin to colour, then stir in the pumpkin cubes, mixing well.

3 Pour in the reduced-fat coconut milk and mix well. Reduce the heat, cover and simmer for about 20 minutes, until the pumpkin is tender and the sauce has reduced. Season with ground black pepper and garnish with curry or basil leaves and fried onion rings. Serve hot with plain rice.

Energy 92kcal/386kJ; Protein 1.8g; Carbohydrate 14.4g, of which sugars 13.5g; Fat 3.4g, of which saturates 0.6g; Cholesterol 0mg; Calcium 93mg; Fibre 2.3g; Sodium 60mg.

BRAISED TOFU WITH MUSHROOMS ★

THE SHIITAKE AND OYSTER MUSHROOMS FLAVOUR THE TOFU BEAUTIFULLY TO MAKE THIS A PERFECTLY DELICIOUS VEGETARIAN MAIN COURSE. IT CONTAINS VERY LITTLE SATURATED FAT.

SERVES 4

INGREDIENTS

350g/12oz tofu
2.5ml/½ tsp sesame oil
10ml/2 tsp light soy sauce
15ml/1 tbsp vegetable oil
2 garlic cloves, finely chopped
2.5ml/½ tsp grated fresh root ginger
115g/4oz/1 cup fresh shiitake
  mushrooms, stems removed
175g/6oz/2½ cups fresh
  oyster mushrooms
115g/4oz/1½ cups drained, canned
  straw mushrooms
115g/4oz/1½ cups button
  mushrooms, cut in half
15ml/1 tbsp dry sherry
15ml/1 tbsp dark soy sauce
90ml/6 tbsp vegetable stock
5ml/1 tsp cornflour (cornstarch)
15ml/1 tbsp cold water
salt and ground white pepper
2 spring onions (scallions), shredded

4 Mix the cornflour to a paste with the water. Stir into the pan or wok and cook, stirring, until thickened.

VARIATION
If fresh shiitake mushrooms are not available, use dried Chinese mushrooms soaked in hot water.

5 Carefully add the pieces of tofu, toss gently to coat thoroughly and simmer for 2 minutes.

6 Sprinkle the shredded spring onions over the top of the mixture, then transfer to a warm serving dish and serve immediately.

1 Put the tofu in a dish and sprinkle with the sesame oil, light soy sauce and a large pinch of pepper. Leave to marinate for 10 minutes, then drain. Use a sharp knife to cut the tofu into 2.5 x 1cm/1 x ½in pieces.

2 Heat the vegetable oil in a non-stick frying pan or wok. When it is very hot, fry the garlic and ginger for a few seconds. Add all the mushrooms and stir-fry for 2 minutes.

3 Stir in the sherry, soy sauce and stock, with salt, if needed, and pepper. Simmer for 4 minutes.

Energy 92kcal/386kJ; Protein 9.6g; Carbohydrate 2.9g, of which sugars 1g; Fat 4.3g, of which saturates 0.6g; Cholesterol 0mg; Calcium 456mg; Fibre 1.4g; Sodium 456mg.

SIMMERED TOFU WITH VEGETABLES ★

A TYPICAL DINNER AT HOME GENERALLY CONSISTS OF A SOUP, THREE DIFFERENT DISHES AND A BOWL OF RICE. ONE OF THE THREE DISHES IS ALWAYS A SIMMERED ONE LIKE THIS MUSHROOM MIXTURE.

SERVES 4

INGREDIENTS
4 dried shiitake mushrooms
450g/1lb daikon (mooli)
350g/12oz firm tofu
115g/4oz/¾ cup green beans,
5ml/1 tsp rice (any except for
    fragrant Thai or white basmati)
115g/4oz carrot, peeled and cut
    into 1cm/½in thick slices
300g/11oz baby potatoes, unpeeled
750ml/1¼ pints/3 cups
    vegetable stock
30ml/2 tbsp caster (superfine) sugar
75ml/5 tbsp shoyu or other
    soy sauce
45ml/3 tbsp sake
15ml/1 tbsp mirin

1 Put the dried shiitake in a bowl. Add 250ml/8fl oz/1 cup water and soak for 2 hours. Drain, discarding the liquid. Remove and discard the stems.

2 Peel the daikon and slice it into 1cm/½in discs. Shave the edge off the daikon discs to ensure they will cook evenly. Put the slices in cold water to prevent them from discolouring.

3 Drain and rinse the tofu, then pat dry with kitchen paper. Cut the tofu into pieces of about 2.5 × 5cm/1 × 2in.

4 Bring a pan of lightly salted water to the boil. Meanwhile, top and tail the beans, then cut them in half.

5 Blanch the beans in the boiling water for 2 minutes. Drain them in a sieve (strainer) and cool them under running water. Drain again.

6 Put the daikon slices in the clean pan. Pour in water to cover and add the rice. Bring to the boil, then reduce the heat and simmer for 15 minutes. Drain off the liquid and the rice.

7 Add the drained mushrooms, carrot and potatoes to the daikon in the pan.

8 Pour in the vegetable stock, bring the liquid to the boil, then reduce the heat to low and simmer.

9 Skim off any scum that comes to the surface of the liquid. Add the sugar, shoyu and sake and shake the pan gently to mix the ingredients thoroughly.

10 Cut a piece of baking parchment to a circle 1cm/½in smaller than the pan lid. Place the paper inside the pan, over the ingredients within.

11 Cover the pan with the lid and simmer for 30 minutes, or until the sauce has reduced by at least half.

12 Add the tofu and green beans and warm through for 2 minutes.

13 Remove the paper and add the mirin. Taste the sauce and adjust with shoyu if required. Serve immediately in warmed bowls.

COOK'S TIP
Once you have opened a packet of tofu, any that is unused should be rinsed and put in a bowl with fresh water to cover. Change the water every day and use the tofu within 5 days.

Energy 181kcal/762kJ; Protein 10.3g; Carbohydrate 26.8g, of which sugars 14.8g; Fat 4.4g, of which saturates 0.7g; Cholesterol 0mg; Calcium 496mg; Fibre 3.1g; Sodium 833mg.

TOFU AND GREEN BEAN RED CURRY ★

THIS IS ONE OF THOSE VERSATILE RECIPES THAT SHOULD BE IN EVERY COOK'S REPERTOIRE. THIS VERSION USES GREEN BEANS, BUT OTHER TYPES OF VEGETABLE WORK EQUALLY WELL. THE LOW-FAT TOFU TAKES ON THE FLAVOUR OF THE SPICE PASTE AND ALSO BOOSTS THE NUTRITIONAL VALUE.

SERVES 4

INGREDIENTS
200ml/7fl oz/scant 1 cup reduced-fat coconut milk
15ml/1 tbsp Thai vegetarian red curry paste
10ml/2 tsp palm sugar or light muscovado (brown) sugar
225g/8oz/3¼ cups button (white) mushrooms
400ml/14fl oz/1⅔ cups vegetable stock
115g/4oz/1 cup green beans, trimmed
175g/6oz firm tofu, rinsed, drained and cut in 2cm/¾ in cubes
4 kaffir lime leaves, torn
2 fresh red chillies, seeded and sliced
fresh coriander (cilantro) leaves, to garnish

1 Pour the reduced-fat coconut milk into a wok or pan. Cook until the coconut milk starts to separate and an oily sheen appears on the surface.

2 Add the red curry paste and sugar to the coconut milk. Mix thoroughly, then add the mushrooms. Stir and cook for 1 minute.

3 Stir in the stock. Bring back to the boil, then add the green beans and tofu cubes. Simmer gently for 4–5 minutes more.

4 Stir in the kaffir lime leaves and sliced red chillies. Spoon the curry into a serving dish, garnish with the coriander leaves and serve immediately.

Energy 67kcal/282kJ; Protein 5.3g; Carbohydrate 6.5g, of which sugars 6g; Fat 2.4g, of which saturates 0.4g; Cholesterol 0mg; Calcium 253mg; Fibre 1.3g; Sodium 60mg.

SNAKE BEANS WITH TOFU ★★

ANOTHER NAME FOR SNAKE BEANS IS YARD-LONG BEANS. THIS IS SOMETHING OF AN EXAGGERATION BUT THEY DO GROW TO LENGTHS OF 40CM/16IN AND MORE. LOOK FOR THEM IN ASIAN STORES AND MARKETS, BUT IF YOU CAN'T FIND ANY, SUBSTITUTE OTHER GREEN BEANS.

SERVES 4

INGREDIENTS

500g/1¼lb snake or yard-long
   beans, thinly sliced
200g/7oz silken tofu, cut
   into cubes
2 shallots, thinly sliced
200ml/7fl oz/scant 1 cup
   reduced-fat coconut milk
25g/1oz roasted peanuts, chopped
juice of 1 lime
10ml/2 tsp palm sugar or light
   muscovado (brown) sugar
60ml/4 tbsp soy sauce
5ml/1 tsp dried chilli flakes

VARIATION

For a brightly coloured variation, stir in sliced yellow or red (bell) pepper.

1 Bring a pan of lightly salted water to the boil. Add the beans and blanch them for 30 seconds.

2 Drain the beans immediately, then refresh under cold water and drain again, shaking well to remove as much water as possible. Place in a serving bowl and set aside.

3 Put the tofu and shallots in a pan with the coconut milk. Heat gently, stirring, until the tofu begins to crumble.

4 Add the peanuts, lime juice, sugar, soy sauce and chilli flakes. Heat, stirring, until the sugar has dissolved. Pour the sauce over the beans, toss to combine and serve immediately.

Energy 167kcal/697kJ; Protein 9.9g; Carbohydrate 12.9g, of which sugars 9.3g; Fat 10g, of which saturates 1g; Cholesterol 7mg; Calcium 327mg; Fibre 3.4g; Sodium 191mg.

TOFU AND VEGETABLE THAI CURRY ★★

*TRADITIONAL THAI INGREDIENTS — CHILLIES, GALANGAL, LEMON GRASS AND KAFFIR LIME LEAVES —
GIVE THIS CURRY A WONDERFULLY FRAGRANT AROMA. THE TOFU SHOULD BE LEFT TO MARINATE
FOR AT LEAST 2 HOURS, SO BEAR THIS IN MIND WHEN TIMING YOUR MEAL.*

SERVES 4

INGREDIENTS

    175g/6oz firm tofu
    45ml/3 tbsp dark soy sauce
    5ml/1 tsp sesame oil
    5ml/1 tsp chilli sauce
    2.5cm/1in piece fresh root ginger,
      peeled and finely grated
    1 head broccoli, about 225g/8oz
    ½ head cauliflower, about 225g/8oz
    15ml/1 tbsp sunflower oil
    1 onion, sliced
    200ml/7fl oz/scant 1 cup reduced-fat
      coconut milk
    350ml/12fl oz/1½ cups water
    1 red (bell) pepper, seeded
      and chopped
    175g/6oz/generous 1 cup green
      beans, halved
    115g/4oz/1½ cups shiitake or button
      (white) mushrooms, halved
    shredded spring onions (scallions),
      to garnish
    boiled jasmine rice or noodles,
      to serve
For the curry paste
    2 fresh red or green chillies, seeded
      and chopped
    1 lemon grass stalk, chopped
    2.5cm/1in piece fresh
      galangal, chopped
    2 kaffir lime leaves
    10ml/2 tsp ground coriander
    a few fresh coriander (cilantro)
      sprigs, including the stalks
    45ml/3 tbsp water

1 Rinse and drain the tofu. Using a sharp knife, cut it into 2.5cm/1in cubes. Place the cubes in the base of an ovenproof dish in a single layer.

2 Mix together the soy sauce, sesame oil, chilli sauce and grated ginger in a jug (pitcher) and pour over the tofu. Toss gently to coat all the cubes evenly, cover with clear film (plastic wrap) and leave to marinate for at least 2 hours or overnight if possible, turning and basting the tofu occasionally.

3 Make the curry paste. Place the chillies, lemon grass, galangal, lime leaves, ground coriander and fresh coriander in a food processor and process until well blended. Add the water and process to a thick paste.

4 Preheat the oven to 190°C/375°F/Gas 5. Cut the broccoli and cauliflower into small florets. Cut any stalks into thin slices.

5 Heat the sunflower oil in a frying pan and add the sliced onion. Cook over a low heat for about 8 minutes, until soft and lightly browned. Stir in the curry paste and the coconut milk. Add the water and bring to the boil.

6 Stir in the red pepper, green beans, broccoli and cauliflower. Transfer to a Chinese sand pot or earthenware casserole. Cover and place towards the bottom of the oven.

7 Stir the tofu and marinade, then place the dish on a shelf near the top of the oven. Cook for 30 minutes. Remove both the dish and the sand pot or casserole from the oven. Add the tofu, with any remaining marinade, to the curry, with the mushrooms, and stir well.

8 Return the sand pot or casserole to the oven, reduce the temperature to 180°C/350°F/Gas 4 and cook for about 15 minutes, or until the vegetables are tender. Garnish with the spring onions and serve with the rice or noodles.

COOK'S TIP
Tofu or beancurd is made from soya beans and is sold in blocks. It is a creamy white colour and naturally low in fat. Tofu has a bland flavour and its absorbent nature means that it takes on the flavours of marinades or other foods with which it is cooked.

Energy 155kcal/646kJ; Protein 10.9g; Carbohydrate 12.2g, of which sugars 10.5g; Fat 7.2g, of which saturates 1.1g; Cholesterol 0mg; Calcium 333mg; Fibre 5.3g; Sodium 875mg.

SWEET AND SOUR VEGETABLES WITH TOFU ★

BIG, BOLD AND BEAUTIFUL, THIS IS A HEARTY STIR-FRY THAT WILL SATISFY THE HUNGRIEST GUESTS. IT IS PACKED WITH COLOURFUL VEGETABLES INCLUDING CORN COBS, RED PEPPERS AND GREEN MANGETOUTS.

SERVES 4

INGREDIENTS
4 shallots
3 garlic cloves
15ml/1 tbsp sunflower oil
250g/9oz Chinese leaves (Chinese cabbage), shredded
8 baby corn cobs, sliced on the diagonal
2 red (bell) peppers, seeded and thinly sliced
200g/7oz/1¾ cups mangetouts (snow peas), trimmed and sliced
250g/9oz tofu, rinsed, drained and cut in 1cm/½in cubes
60ml/4 tbsp vegetable stock
30ml/2 tbsp light soy sauce
15ml/1 tbsp granulated sugar
30ml/2 tbsp rice vinegar
2.5ml/½ tsp dried chilli flakes
small bunch coriander (cilantro), chopped

1 Slice the shallots thinly using a sharp knife. Finely chop the garlic.

2 Heat the oil in a wok or large frying pan and cook the shallots and garlic for 2–3 minutes over a medium heat, until golden. Do not let the garlic burn or it will taste bitter.

3 Add the shredded cabbage, toss over the heat for 30 seconds, then add the corn cobs and repeat the process.

4 Add the red peppers, mangetouts and tofu in the same way, each time adding a single ingredient and tossing it over the heat for about 30 seconds before adding the next ingredient.

5 Pour in the stock and soy sauce. Mix together the sugar and vinegar in a small bowl, stirring until the sugar has dissolved, then add to the wok or pan. Sprinkle over the chilli flakes and coriander, toss to mix well and serve.

Energy 144kcal/604kJ; Protein 5.2g; Carbohydrate 23.7g, of which sugars 18.2g; Fat 3.7g, of which saturates 0.5g; Cholesterol 0mg; Calcium 73mg; Fibre 4.7g; Sodium 611mg.

SPICY TOFU WITH BASIL AND PEANUTS ★★

AROMATIC PEPPER LEAVES ARE OFTEN USED AS THE HERB ELEMENT IN THAILAND BUT, BECAUSE THESE ARE QUITE DIFFICULT TO FIND OUTSIDE SOUTH-EAST ASIA, YOU CAN USE BASIL LEAVES INSTEAD.

SERVES 4

INGREDIENTS

3 lemon grass stalks, finely chopped
45ml/3 tbsp soy sauce
2 red Serrano chillies, seeded and
    finely chopped
2 garlic cloves, crushed
5ml/1 tsp ground turmeric
10ml/2 tsp sugar
300g/11oz tofu, rinsed, drained,
    patted dry and cut into
    bitesize cubes
15ml/1 tbsp sunflower oil
15ml/1 tbsp roasted peanuts,
    chopped
1 bunch fresh basil, stalks removed
salt

1 In a bowl, mix together the lemon grass, soy sauce, chillies, garlic, turmeric and sugar until the sugar has dissolved. Add a little salt to taste and add the tofu, making sure it is well coated. Leave to marinate for 1 hour.

VARIATION
Replace the fresh basil with kaffir lime leaves, coriander (cilantro) leaves or curry leaves, all of which would work well in this simple stir-fry.

2 Heat a wok or heavy pan. Pour in the oil, add the marinated tofu, and cook, stirring frequently, until it is golden brown on all sides. Add the peanuts and most of the basil leaves.

3 Divide the marinated tofu and peanut mixture among individual serving dishes. Then sprinkle the remaining basil leaves over the top and serve hot or at room temperature.

Energy 115kcal/480kJ; Protein 7.4g; Carbohydrate 4.5g, of which sugars 3.9g; Fat 7.6g, of which saturates 1g; Cholesterol 0mg; Calcium 388mg; Fibre 0.2g; Sodium 804mg.

FISH

Fish is an excellent source of protein, vitamins and minerals. It has very little carbohydrate and contains oils that have a positive impact on health. Oily fish contains Omega-3 fatty acids, which help lower cholesterol and reduce blood pressure. Serving a fish whole, rather than cutting it into portions, has great appeal in Asia. Here, you'll find some of the finest fish recipes from South-east Asia, including delicious Sweet and Sour Fish, Eel Braised in a Caramel Sauce, and Steamed Red Snapper.

HOT AND FRAGRANT TROUT ★

THIS WICKEDLY HOT SPICE PASTE COULD ALSO BE USED AS A MARINADE FOR ANY FISH OR MEAT.

SERVES 4

INGREDIENTS

2 large fresh green chillies, seeded
  and coarsely chopped
5 shallots, peeled
5 garlic cloves, peeled
30ml/2 tbsp fresh lime juice
30ml/2 tbsp Thai fish sauce
15ml/1 tbsp palm sugar or light
  muscovado (brown) sugar
4 kaffir lime leaves, rolled
  into cylinders and thinly sliced
2 trout or similar firm-fleshed
  fish, about 350g/12oz
  each, cleaned
fresh garlic chives, to garnish
boiled rice, to serve

1 Wrap the chillies, shallots and garlic in a foil package. Place under a hot grill (broiler) for 10 minutes, until softened.

2 When the package is cool enough to handle, tip the contents into a mortar or food processor and pound with a pestle or process to a paste.

3 Add the lime juice, fish sauce, sugar and lime leaves and mix well. With a teaspoon, stuff this paste inside the fish. Smear a little on the skin too. Grill (broil) the fish for about 5 minutes on each side, until just cooked through. Lift the fish on to a platter, garnish with garlic chives and serve with rice.

Energy 117kcal/490kJ; Protein 14.8g; Carbohydrate 7.9g, of which sugars 6.7g; Fat 3.1g, of which saturates 0.7g; Cholesterol 59mg; Calcium 36mg; Fibre 0.7g; Sodium 57mg.

TROUT WITH TAMARIND AND CHILLI SAUCE ★★

SOMETIMES TROUT CAN TASTE RATHER BLAND, BUT THIS CHILLI SAUCE REALLY GIVES IT A ZING.

SERVES 4

INGREDIENTS

4 trout, cleaned
6 spring onions (scallions), sliced
60ml/4 tbsp soy sauce
spray sunflower oil, for frying
30ml/2 tbsp chopped fresh coriander
  (cilantro) and strips of fresh red
  chilli, to garnish

For the sauce

50g/2oz tamarind pulp
105ml/7 tbsp boiling water
2 shallots, coarsely chopped
1 fresh red chilli, seeded and
  chopped
1cm/½in piece fresh root ginger,
  peeled and chopped
5ml/1 tsp soft light brown sugar
45ml/3 tbsp Thai fish sauce

3 Make the sauce. Put the tamarind pulp in a small bowl and pour on the boiling water. Mash well with a fork until softened. Tip the tamarind mixture into a food processor or blender, and add the shallots, fresh chilli, ginger, sugar and fish sauce. Process to a coarse pulp. Scrape into a bowl.

4 Spray a large frying pan with oil. Heat and cook the trout, one at a time if necessary, for about 5 minutes on each side, until the skin is crisp and browned and the flesh cooked. Put on warmed plates and spoon over some of the sauce. Sprinkle with the coriander and chilli and serve with the remaining sauce.

1 Slash the trout diagonally four or five times on each side. Place them in a shallow dish that is large enough to hold them all in a single layer.

2 Fill the cavities with spring onions and douse each fish with soy sauce. Carefully turn the fish over to coat both sides with the sauce. Sprinkle any remaining spring onions over the top.

Energy 215kcal/904kJ; Protein 35.4g; Carbohydrate 3.2g, of which sugars 2.7g; Fat 6.8g, of which saturates 1.6g; Cholesterol 144mg; Calcium 60mg; Fibre 0.2g; Sodium 932mg.

THAI-STYLE TROUT ★★

THE COMBINATION OF CLASSIC THAI AROMATIC INGREDIENTS — GINGER, LEMON GRASS, COCONUT MILK AND LIME — GIVES THIS SIMPLE DISH A FABULOUS FLAVOUR. SERVE STRAIGHT FROM THE PAN WITH PLENTY OF STEAMED THAI FRAGRANT RICE TO SOAK UP THE DELICIOUS SAUCE.

SERVES 4

INGREDIENTS

   200g/7oz spinach leaves
   1 lemon grass stalk, finely chopped
   2.5cm/1in piece fresh root ginger,
     peeled and finely grated
   2 garlic cloves, crushed
   200ml/7fl oz/scant 1 cup reduced-fat
     coconut milk
   30ml/2 tbsp lime juice
   15ml/1 tbsp soft light brown sugar
   4 trout fillets, each about 200g/7oz
   salt and ground black pepper
   steamed Thai fragrant rice, to serve

COOK'S TIP

To steam Thai fragrant rice, cook it in a pan of salted boiling water for three-quarters of the time noted on the packet. Transfer it to a colander lined with muslin or cheesecloth and steam over simmering water for 5–10 minutes until just tender.

1 Preheat the oven to 200°C/400°F/ Gas 6. Place the spinach in a pan, with just the water that adheres to the leaves after washing. Cover with a lid and cook gently for 3–4 minutes until the leaves have just wilted. Drain the spinach in a colander and press it with the back of a spoon to remove any excess moisture.

2 Transfer the spinach to a mixing bowl and stir in the chopped lemon grass, grated ginger and garlic.

3 Combine the coconut milk, lime juice, sugar and seasoning in a jug (pitcher). Place the trout fillets side by side in a shallow baking dish and pour the coconut milk mixture over.

4 Bake the trout for 20–25 minutes until cooked. Place on individual serving plates, on top of the steamed Thai fragrant rice. Toss the spinach mixture in the juices remaining in the dish, spoon on top of the fish and serve.

Energy 266kcal/1119kJ; Protein 40.5g; Carbohydrate 7.9g, of which sugars 7.7g; Fat 8.3g, of which saturates 0.2g; Cholesterol 0mg; Calcium 140mg; Fibre 1.7g; Sodium 177mg.

GRILLED FISH ᵂᴵᵀᴴ MUNG BEANSPROUTS ★

*A WHOLE FISH GRILLED OVER CHARCOAL IS USUALLY SERVED WITH FRESH SALAD LEAVES, HERBS,
CHOPPED PEANUTS, AND A STRONG-FLAVOURED SAUCE ON THE SIDE. CHUNKS OF THE COOKED
FISH ARE WRAPPED IN THE SALAD LEAVES AND THEN DIPPED IN THE SAUCE.*

SERVES 4

INGREDIENTS

  1 good-sized fish, such as trout,
    snakehead, barb or carp, gutted and
    rinsed, head removed, if you like
  225g/8oz mung beansprouts
  1 bunch each fresh basil, coriander
    (cilantro) and mint, stalks removed,
    leaves chopped
  1 lettuce, broken into leaves
  15ml/1 tbsp roasted unsalted
    peanuts, finely chopped
  steamed rice, to serve
For the sauce
  3 garlic cloves, chopped
  2 red Thai chillies, seeded
    and chopped
  25g/1oz fresh root ginger, peeled
    and chopped
  15ml/1 tbsp palm sugar
  45ml/3 tbsp *tuk trey* or other
    fish sauce
  juice of 1 lime
  juice of 1 coconut

4 Lay out the beansprouts, herbs and
lettuce leaves on a large plate and place
the peanuts in a bowl. Put everything
on the table, including the cooked fish,
sauce and rice. Using chopsticks, if you
like, lift up the charred skin and tear off
pieces of fish. Place each piece on a
lettuce leaf, sprinkle with beansprouts,
herbs and peanuts, wrap it up and dip
it into the sauce.

1 First prepare the sauce. Using a
mortar and pestle, grind the garlic,
chillies and ginger with the sugar to
form a paste.

2 Add the *tuk trey*, lime juice and
coconut juice and blend well. Pour the
sauce into a serving bowl.

3 Prepare the barbecue. Place the
fish over the charcoal and grill it for
2–3 minutes each side, until cooked
right through. Alternatively, use a
conventional grill (broiler).

Energy 143kcal/604kJ; Protein 18.9g; Carbohydrate 9.1g, of which sugars 6.2g; Fat 3.7g, of which saturates 0.8g; Cholesterol 64mg; Calcium 84mg; Fibre 2.5g; Sodium 69mg.

THAI MARINATED SEA TROUT ★

SEA TROUT HAS A SUPERB TEXTURE AND A FLAVOUR LIKE THAT OF WILD SALMON. LIKE MANY OTHER FISH, IT IS BEST SERVED WITH STRONG BUT COMPLEMENTARY FLAVOURS, SUCH AS CHILLIES AND LIME.

3 Spray a hinged wire fish basket or grill rack with oil. Remove the cutlets from the marinade and place them in the fish basket or directly on the grill rack. Cook the fish for 4 minutes on each side, trying not to move them. They may stick to the grill rack if not seared first.

4 Strain the remaining marinade into a pan, reserving the contents of the sieve. Bring the marinade to the boil, then simmer gently for 5 minutes, stirring. Stir in the contents of the sieve and continue to simmer for 1 minute more. Add the Thai fish sauce and the remaining Thai basil.

SERVES 6

INGREDIENTS
  6 sea trout cutlets, each about
    115g/4oz
  2 garlic cloves, chopped
  1 fresh long red chilli, seeded
    and chopped
  45ml/3 tbsp chopped
    Thai basil
  15ml/1 tbsp granulated sugar
  3 limes
  400ml/14fl oz/1²⁄₃ cups
    reduced-fat coconut milk
  spray sunflower oil
  15ml/1 tbsp Thai fish sauce

1 Place the sea trout cutlets side by side in a shallow dish. Using a pestle, pound the chopped garlic and chilli in a large mortar to break both up roughly. Add 30ml/2 tbsp of the chopped Thai basil with the sugar and continue to pound the mixture until it forms a rough paste.

2 Grate the rind from 1 lime and squeeze it. Mix the rind and juice into the chilli paste, with the reduced-fat coconut milk. Pour the mixture over the cutlets. Cover and chill for about 1 hour. Cut the remaining limes into wedges.

5 Lift each fish cutlet on to a plate, pour over the sauce and serve with the lime wedges.

COOK'S TIP
Sea trout is best cooked when the barbecue is cool to medium hot, and the coals have a medium to thick coating of ash. Take care when cooking any fish in a marinade, as the residue can cause flare-ups if it drips on to the coals.

VARIATION
If you prefer you could substitute wild or farmed salmon for the sea trout. Be careful not to overcook it.

Energy 158kcal/666kJ; Protein 23.1g; Carbohydrate 6.1g, of which sugars 6.1g; Fat 4.7g, of which saturates 0.1g; Cholesterol 0mg; Calcium 48mg; Fibre 0.4g; Sodium 142mg.

ESCABECHE ★

THIS PICKLED FISH DISH IS EATEN WHEREVER THERE ARE — OR HAVE BEEN — SPANISH SETTLERS.
IT IS ESPECIALLY POPULAR IN THE PHILIPPINES WHERE IT IS SERVED WITH BOILED OR STEAMED RICE.

SERVES 6

INGREDIENTS

675–900g/1¹/₂–2lb white fish fillets,
  such as sole or plaice
45–60ml/3–4 tbsp seasoned flour
sunflower oil, for shallow frying
For the sauce
  2.5cm/1in piece fresh root ginger,
    peeled and thinly sliced
  2–3 garlic cloves, crushed
  1 onion, cut into thin rings
  15ml/1 tbsp sunflower oil
  ¹/₂ large green (bell) pepper,
    seeded and cut in small
    neat squares
  ¹/₂ large red (bell) pepper, seeded
    and cut in small neat squares
  1 carrot, cut into matchsticks
  25ml/1¹/₂ tbsp cornflour (cornstarch)
  450ml/³/₄ pint/scant 2 cups water
  45–60ml/3–4 tbsp herb or
    cider vinegar
  15ml/1 tbsp light soft brown sugar
  5–10ml/1–2 tsp Thai fish sauce
  salt and ground black pepper
  1 small chilli, seeded and sliced
    and spring onions (scallions), finely
    shredded, to garnish (optional)
  boiled rice, to serve

1 Wipe the fish fillets and leave them
whole, or cut into serving portions, if
you like. Pat dry on kitchen paper then
dust lightly with seasoned flour.

2 Heat oil for shallow frying in a frying
pan and fry the fish in batches until
golden and almost cooked. Transfer to
an ovenproof dish and keep warm.

3 Make the sauce in a wok or large
frying pan. Fry the ginger, garlic and
onion in the oil for 5 minutes or until
the onion is softened but not browned.

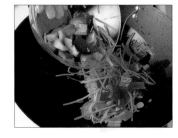

4 Add the pepper squares and carrot
strips and stir-fry for 1 minute.

5 Put the cornflour in a small bowl
and add a little of the water to make
a paste. Stir in the remaining water,
the vinegar and the sugar. Pour the
cornflour mixture over the vegetables in
the wok and stir until the sauce boils
and thickens a little. Season with fish
sauce and salt and pepper if needed.

6 Add the fish to the sauce and reheat
briefly without stirring. Transfer to a
warmed serving platter and garnish with
chilli and spring onions, if liked. Serve
with boiled rice.

COOK'S TIP
Red snapper or small sea bass could be
used for this recipe, in which case ask
your fishmonger to cut them into fillets.

Energy 130kcal/550kJ; Protein 21.3g; Carbohydrate 9.3g, of which sugars 5.2g; Fat 1.1g, of which saturates 0.2g; Cholesterol 52mg; Calcium 34mg; Fibre 1g; Sodium 74mg.

CHINESE-STYLE STEAMED FISH ★★

*THIS IS THE CLASSIC CHINESE WAY OF COOKING WHOLE FISH, WITH GARLIC, SPRING ONIONS, GINGER
AND BLACK BEANS. THE FISH MAKES A SPLENDID CENTREPIECE FOR A CHINESE MEAL.*

2 Mash half the black beans with the
sugar in a small bowl and then stir in
the remaining whole beans.

3 Place a little ginger and garlic inside
the cavity of each fish and then lay
them on a plate or dish that will fit
inside a large steamer.

4 Rub the bean mixture into the fish,
especially into the slashes, then
sprinkle the remaining ginger and garlic
over the top.

5 Cover the fish with clear film (plastic
wrap) and chill for 30 minutes.

SERVES 4–6

INGREDIENTS
  2 sea bass, grey mullet or trout,
    each weighing about 675–800g/
    1½–1¾lb, cleaned
  25ml/1½ tbsp salted black beans
  2.5ml/½ tsp sugar
  30ml/2 tbsp finely shredded
    fresh root ginger
  4 garlic cloves, thinly sliced
  30ml/2 tbsp Chinese rice wine
    or dry sherry
  30ml/2 tbsp light soy sauce
  4–6 spring onions (scallions), finely
    shredded or sliced diagonally
  10ml/2 tsp sesame oil

1 Wash the fish inside and out under
cold running water, then pat them dry
on kitchen paper. Using a sharp knife,
slash three or four deep cross shapes
on each side of each fish, taking care
not to cut right through.

6 Place the steamer over a pan of
simmering water. Sprinkle the rice wine
or sherry and half the soy sauce over
the fish, place them in the steamer and
steam them for 15–20 minutes, or until
just cooked.

7 Sprinkle the steamed fish with the
remaining soy sauce and the sesame
oil, then scatter with the spring onions.
Serve immediately.

Energy 260kcal/1095kJ; Protein 41.9g; Carbohydrate 1.5g, of which sugars 1g; Fat 9.1g, of which saturates 2g; Cholesterol 171mg; Calcium 69mg; Fibre 0.2g; Sodium 512mg.

STEAMED FISH WITH CHILLI SAUCE ★

STEAMING IS ONE OF THE HEALTHIEST METHODS OF COOKING FISH. BY LEAVING THE FISH WHOLE AND ON THE BONE, MAXIMUM FLAVOUR IS RETAINED AND THE FLESH REMAINS BEAUTIFULLY MOIST.

SERVES 4

INGREDIENTS

 1 large or 2 medium firm fish such
 as sea bass or grouper, scaled
 and cleaned
 30ml/2 tbsp rice wine
 3 fresh red chillies, seeded and
 thinly sliced
 2 garlic cloves, finely chopped
 2cm/¾in piece fresh root ginger,
 peeled and finely shredded
 2 lemon grass stalks, crushed and
 finely chopped
 2 spring onions (scallions), chopped
 30ml/2 tbsp Thai fish sauce
 juice of 1 lime
 1 fresh banana leaf
For the chilli sauce
 10 fresh red chillies, seeded
 and chopped
 4 garlic cloves, chopped
 60ml/4 tbsp Thai fish sauce or other
 fish sauce
 15ml/1 tbsp granulated sugar
 75ml/5 tbsp fresh lime juice

1 Thoroughly rinse the fish under cold running water. Pat it dry with kitchen paper. With a sharp knife, slash the skin of the fish a few times on both sides.

2 Mix together the rice wine, chillies, garlic, shredded ginger, lemon grass and spring onions in a non-metallic bowl. Add the fish sauce and lime juice and mix to a paste. Place the fish on the banana leaf and spread the spice paste evenly over it, rubbing it in well where the skin has been slashed.

3 Put a rack or a small upturned plate in the base of a wok. Pour in boiling water to a depth of 5cm/2in. Lift the banana leaf, together with the fish, and place it on the rack or plate. Cover with a lid and steam for 10–15 minutes, or until the fish is cooked.

4 Meanwhile, make the sauce. Place all the ingredients in a food processor and process until smooth. If the mixture seems to be too thick, add a little cold water. Scrape into a serving bowl.

5 Serve the fish hot, on the banana leaf if you like, with the sweet chilli sauce to spoon over the top.

Energy 147kcal/619kJ; Protein 28.4g; Carbohydrate 5.5g, of which sugars 5.3g; Fat 1.3g, of which saturates 0.2g; Cholesterol 69mg; Calcium 56mg; Fibre 1g; Sodium 898mg.

STEAMED FISH WITH FIVE WILLOW SAUCE ★★

A FISH KETTLE WILL COME IN USEFUL FOR THIS RECIPE. CARP IS TRADITIONALLY USED, BUT ANY CHUNKY FISH THAT CAN BE COOKED WHOLE MAY BE GIVEN THIS TREATMENT.

SERVES 4

INGREDIENTS

- 1–2 carp or similar whole fish, total weight about 1kg/2¼lb, cleaned and scaled
- 2.5cm/1in piece fresh root ginger, peeled and thinly sliced
- 4 spring onions (scallions), cut into thin strips
- 2.5ml/½ tsp salt

For the five willow sauce
- 375g/13oz jar *chow chow* (Chinese sweet mixed pickles)
- 300ml/½ pint/1¼ cups water
- 30ml/2 tbsp rice vinegar
- 25ml/1½ tbsp sugar
- 25ml/1½ tbsp cornflour (cornstarch)
- 15ml/1 tbsp light soy sauce
- 15ml/1 tbsp rice wine or medium-dry sherry
- 1 small green (bell) pepper, seeded and diced
- 1 carrot, peeled and cut into matchsticks
- 1 tomato, peeled, seeded and diced

1 Rinse the fish under running cold water inside and out. Pat dry with kitchen paper.

2 Thoroughly mix the ginger, spring onions and salt in a small bowl, then tuck the mixture into the body cavity of each fish.

3 Create a support for each fish by folding one or two broad strips of foil to make a long wide strip.

4 Place the fish on the foil and then lift the fish on to the trivet. Lower the trivet into the fish kettle and tuck the ends of the foil over the fish.

5 Pour boiling water into the fish kettle to a depth of 2.5cm/1in. Bring to a rolling boil, then lower the heat and cook until the flesh flakes, topping with boiling water as necessary. Allow about 20–25 minutes for a 1kg/2¼ lb fish; 15–20 minutes for a 675g/1½ lb fish.

6 Meanwhile, prepare the sauce. Tip the *chow chow* into a sieve (strainer) placed over a bowl. Reserve the liquid. Cut each of the pickles in half. Pour 250ml/8fl oz/ 1 cup of the water into a pan and bring to the boil. Add the vinegar and sugar and stir until dissolved.

COOK'S TIP
If using one large fish that is too long to fit in a fish kettle, cut it in half and cook it on a rack placed over a large roasting tin. Pour in a similar quantity of boiling water as for the fish kettle, cover with foil and cook on top of the stove. Reassemble the halved fish before coating it with the sauce.

7 In a small bowl, mix the cornflour to a paste with the remaining water. Stir in the soy sauce and rice wine or sherry and combine thoroughly.

8 Add the cornflour mixture to the sauce and bring to the boil, stirring until it thickens and becomes quite glossy. Add all the vegetables, the chopped pickles and the pickle liquid and cook over a gentle heat for 2 minutes.

9 Using the foil strips as a support, carefully transfer the cooked fish to a platter, then ease the foil away. Spoon the warm sauce over the fish and serve.

Energy 231kcal/973kJ; Protein 25.8g; Carbohydrate 20.3g, of which sugars 1.3g; Fat 5.8g, of which saturates 0.1g; Cholesterol 0mg; Calcium 126mg; Fibre 2.3g; Sodium 912mg.

FISH <u>IN</u> COCONUT CUSTARD ★★

HERE, THE FISH IS STEAMED IN A CUSTARD, MADE WITH COCONUT MILK AND FLAVOURED WITH KROEUNG — A HERB PASTE MADE FROM A BLEND OF LEMON GRASS, GALANGAL, GARLIC AND TURMERIC.

<u>SERVES 4</u>

INGREDIENTS

   2 x 400ml/14oz cans reduced-fat
     coconut milk
   3 eggs
   80ml/3fl oz *kroeung*
   15ml/1 tbsp *tuk trey* or other fish sauce
   10ml/2 tsp palm sugar or honey
   1 kg/2¼lb fresh, skinned white fish
     fillets, cut into 8 pieces
   1 small bunch chopped fresh coriander
     (cilantro), plus a few whole sprigs,
     to garnish
   jasmine rice or crusty bread and salad,
     to serve

VARIATION

This dish can also be cooked in the oven in a bain marie. Cook at 160°C/325°F/Gas 3 for about 50 minutes.

1 Half fill a wok or large pan with water. Set a bamboo or stainless-steel steamer over it and put the lid on. Bring the water to the boil.

2 In a bowl, beat the reduced-fat coconut milk with the eggs, *kroeung*, *tuk trey* and sugar or honey, until everything is well blended and the sugar has dissolved.

3 Place the fish fillets in a heatproof dish that will fit in the steamer. Pour the coconut mixture over the fish and place the dish in the steamer. Put the lid back on the steamer and reduce the heat so that the custard won't curdle. Steam over gently simmering water until the fish is cooked. Garnish with coriander and serve immediately with jasmine rice or crusty bread and salad.

Energy 314kcal/1324kJ; Protein 51.1g; Carbohydrate 13.6g, of which sugars 13.6g; Fat 6.5g, of which saturates 1.8g; Cholesterol 258mg; Calcium 102mg; Fibre 0g; Sodium 423mg.

FISH CAKES AND VEGETABLES ★★★

THIS IS A SIMPLE DISH BUT YOU WILL NEED TO MAKE THE FISH BALLS AND CAKES OR BUY THEM FROM AN ASIAN FOOD STORE. YOU WILL BE ABLE TO GET THE OTHER UNUSUAL INGREDIENTS THERE TOO.

SERVES 4

INGREDIENTS
30 × 7.5cm/12 × 3in *dashi-konbu*
675g/1½lb daikon (mooli), peeled and cut into 4cm/1½in lengths
12–20 ready-made fish balls and cakes (4 of each kind)
1 *konnyaku*
1 piece deep-fried tofu
8 small shiitake mushrooms, stems removed
4 medium potatoes, unpeeled, soaked in a bowl of water (to remove some of the starch)
4 hard-boiled eggs, unshelled
285g/10½oz packet tofu block, cut into 8 cubes
English (hot) mustard, to serve
For the soup stock
1.5 litres/2¼ pints/6½ cups water and 10ml/2 tsp instant dashi powder
75ml/5 tbsp sake
15ml/1 tbsp salt
40ml/8 tsp shoyu or other soy sauce

1 Wrap the *dashi-konbu* in a wet, clean dish towel and leave for 5 minutes, or until it is soft enough to bend easily by hand without breaking.

2 Snip the softened *dashi-konbu* in half crossways with a pair of scissors, then cut each piece lengthways into four ribbons. Tie a loose knot in the centre of each "ribbon".

COOK'S TIP
Konnyaku is a dense, gelatinous cake made from a yam-like plant.

3 Slightly shave the edges of each of the pieces of daikon. Place all the fish balls and cakes, *konnyaku* and *atsu-age* in a large pan. Add enough hot water to cover the ingredients, then drain.

4 Cut the *konnyaku* in quarters, then cut each quarter in half diagonally to make eight triangles. Cut large fish cakes in half. Put two shiitake mushrooms on to each of four bamboo skewers.

5 Mix all the ingredients for the soup stock, but only fill the pot or casserole by two-thirds. Add the daikon and potatoes and bring to the boil. Add the hard-boiled eggs.

6 Reduce the heat to low and simmer for an hour, uncovered, skimming off any scum occasionally.

7 Increase the heat to medium and add the other ingredients except for the mustard. Cover and cook for 30 minutes. Transfer to a casserole or pot that can be kept hot at the table on a hot tray or burner. Serve with the mustard.

VARIATIONS
Prawn Balls Combine 200g/7oz raw peeled small prawns (shrimp), 50g/2oz pork fat, 15ml/1 tbsp grated ginger juice, 1 egg white, 15ml/1 tbsp salt and 15ml/1 tbsp cornflour in a food processor, and shape into balls.
Squid and Ginger Balls Blend 200g/7oz chopped squid, 1 egg white, 15ml/1 tbsp cornflour, 10ml/2 tsp grated ginger juice and 15ml/1 tbsp salt in a food processor. Mix with 10ml/2 tsp chopped ginger, and shape into balls.

Energy 370kcal/1555kJ; Protein 37.2g; Carbohydrate 28.8g, of which sugars 5.8g; Fat 10.4g, of which saturates 2.4g; Cholesterol 237mg; Calcium 452mg; Fibre 3.1g; Sodium 1926mg.

NORTHERN FISH CURRY ★★

THIS IS A THIN, SOUPY CURRY WITH WONDERFULLY STRONG AROMATIC FLAVOURS. SERVE IT IN
BOWLS WITH LOTS OF STICKY RICE TO SOAK UP THE DELICIOUS JUICES.

3 Pour the stock into a large, heavy pan and bring it to the boil over a medium heat. Add the shallots, garlic, galangal, lemon grass, chilli flakes, fish sauce and sugar. Bring back to the boil, stir well, then reduce the heat and simmer gently for 15 minutes.

4 Add the fish, bring back to the boil, then turn off the heat. Leave the curry to stand for 10–15 minutes until the fish is cooked through, then serve.

SERVES 4

INGREDIENTS
 350g/12oz salmon fillet
 500ml/17fl oz/2¼ cups
  vegetable stock
 4 shallots, finely chopped
 2 garlic cloves, finely chopped
 2.5cm/1in piece fresh galangal,
  finely chopped
 1 lemon grass stalk, finely chopped
 2.5ml/½ tsp dried chilli flakes
 15ml/1 tbsp Thai fish sauce
 5ml/1 tsp palm sugar or light
  muscovado (brown) sugar

1 Place the salmon in the freezer for 30–40 minutes to firm up the flesh slightly.

2 Remove and discard the skin, then use a sharp knife to cut the fish into 2.5cm/1in cubes, removing any stray bones with your fingers or with tweezers as you do so.

VARIATION
Fillets of cod or haddock would work just as well in place of the salmon.

Energy 172kcal/717kJ; Protein 18.2g; Carbohydrate 3.2g, of which sugars 2.5g; Fat 9.7g, of which saturates 1.7g; Cholesterol 44mg; Calcium 24mg; Fibre 0.3g; Sodium 307mg.

GREY MULLET WITH PORK ★★

THIS ASIAN ANSWER TO SURF AND TURF COMBINATION MAKES A SPECTACULAR MAIN DISH AND TAKES VERY LITTLE EFFORT. THERE'S ONLY A SMALL AMOUNT OF PORK SO FAT LEVELS ARE NOT TOO HIGH.

SERVES 4

INGREDIENTS

1 grey mullet, red snapper
  or ponpano, about 900g/2lb,
  gutted and cleaned
50g/2oz lean pork
3 dried Chinese mushrooms, soaked
  in hot water until soft
2.5ml/½ tsp cornflour (cornstarch)
30ml/2 tbsp light soy sauce
15ml/1 tbsp vegetable oil
15ml/1 tbsp finely shredded fresh
  root ginger
15ml/1 tbsp shredded spring
  onion (scallions)
salt and ground black pepper
rice, to serve
sliced spring onion (scallion),
  to garnish

1 Make four diagonal cuts on either side of the fish and rub with a little salt; place the fish on a large shallow heatproof serving dish.

2 Cut the pork into thin strips. Place in a bowl. Drain the mushrooms, remove the stems and slice the caps thinly.

3 Add the mushrooms to the pork, with the cornflour and half the soy sauce. Stir in 5ml/1 tsp of the oil and plenty of black pepper. Arrange the pork mixture along the length of the fish. Sprinkle the ginger shreds over the top.

COOK'S TIP
If the fish is too big to fit into the steamer whole, cut the fish in half for cooking, then reassemble it later.

4 Set a trivet in a roasting pan that is large enough to hold the serving dish in which the pork stands.

5 Put the dish on the trivet and place the roasting pan on the stovetop. Pour boiling water into the roasting pan to a depth of about 5cm/2in. Cover and steam the fish.

6 Remove the foil and test the fish by pressing the flesh gently. If it comes away from the bone with a slight resistance, then the fish is cooked.

7 Lift the dish out of the pan and carefully pour away any excess liquid.

8 Heat the remaining oil in a small pan. Fry the shredded spring onion for a few seconds, then pour it over the fish, taking care as it will splatter. Drizzle over the remaining soy sauce, garnish with spring onion and serve with rice.

Energy 228kcal/960kJ; Protein 34.7g; Carbohydrate 0.7g, of which sugars 0.6g; Fat 9.8g, of which saturates 2.3g; Cholesterol 62mg; Calcium 46mg; Fibre 0g; Sodium 647mg.

JUNGLE FISH COOKED <u>IN</u> BANANA LEAVES ★

STEAMING FRESHWATER FISH IN BANANA LEAVES OVER HOT CHARCOAL IS A TRADITIONAL METHOD OF COOKING IN THE JUNGLE. BANANA LEAVES ARE LARGE AND TOUGH, AND SERVE AS COOKING VESSELS.

SERVES 4

INGREDIENTS

    350g/12oz freshwater fish fillets,
      such as trout, cut into
      bitesize chunks
    6 banana leaves (see Cook's Tip)
    spray sunflower vegetable oil
    sticky rice, noodles or salad, to serve
For the marinade
    2 shallots
    5cm/2in turmeric root, peeled
      and grated
    2 spring onions (scallions),
      finely sliced
    2 garlic cloves, crushed
    1–2 green Thai chillies, seeded
      and finely chopped
    15ml/1 tbsp *nuoc mam*
    2.5ml/½ tsp raw cane sugar
    salt and ground black pepper

1 To make the marinade, grate the shallots into a bowl, then combine with the other marinade ingredients, Season with salt and pepper. Toss the chunks of fish in the marinade, then cover and chill for 6 hours, or overnight.

VARIATION
This dish can be made with any of the catfish or carp family, or even tilapia.

2 Prepare a barbecue. Place one of the banana leaves on a flat surface and spray it with oil. Place the marinated fish on the banana leaf, spreading it out evenly, then fold over the sides to form an envelope. Place this envelope, fold side down, on top of another leaf and fold that one in the same manner. Repeat with the remaining leaves until they are all used up.

3 Secure the last layer of banana leaf with a piece of bendy wire. Place the banana leaf packet on the barbecue. Cook for about 20 minutes, turning it over from time to time to make sure it is cooked on both sides – the outer leaves will burn. Carefully untie the wire (it will be hot) and unravel the packet. Check that the fish is cooked and serve with sticky rice, noodles or salad.

COOK'S TIP
Banana leaves are available in some African and Asian stores and markets. If you can't find them, wrap the fish in vine leaves that have been soaked in cold water, or large flexible cabbage leaves. You can also use foil.

Energy 84kcal/352kJ; Protein 16.3g; Carbohydrate 1.5g, of which sugars 1.1g; Fat 1.4g, of which saturates 0.2g; Cholesterol 40mg; Calcium 12mg; Fibre 0.2g; Sodium 320mg.

SEA BASS WITH CHINESE CHIVES ★★

THIS SIMPLE TREATMENT IS JUST RIGHT FOR SEA BASS, ENHANCING THE FISH'S EXCELLENT FLAVOUR
WITHOUT OVERWHELMING IT. IT IS IMPORTANT TO KEEP THE CHUNKS OF FISH FAIRLY LARGE.

SERVES 4

INGREDIENTS
    450g/1lb sea bass
    5ml/1 tsp cornflour (cornstarch)
    30ml/2 tbsp vegetable oil
    175g/6oz Chinese chives
    15ml/1 tbsp Chinese rice wine or
       dry sherry
    5ml/1 tsp caster (superfine) sugar
    salt and ground pepper
    Chinese chives with flowerheads,
       to garnish

1 Remove the scales from the bass by scraping the fish with the back of a knife, working from the tail end to the head end.

2 Cut the fish into large chunks and dust them lightly with cornflour, salt and pepper.

COOK'S TIP
Chinese chives are widely available in Asian supermarkets but if you are unable to buy them, use half a large Spanish (Bermuda) onion, finely sliced, instead.

3 Heat the wok, then add the oil. When the oil is hot, toss in the chunks of fish briefly to seal, remove the fish with a slotted spoon and set aside.

4 Cut the Chinese chives into 5cm/2in lengths and discard the flowers. Add the Chinese chives to the wok and stir-fry for 30 seconds.

5 Return the fish to the wok and add the rice wine, then stir in the sugar. Lower the heat and cook the fish for a futher 2–3 minutes.

6 Spoon the fish into heated bowls, garnish with some flowering Chinese chives, and serve with a side dish of crisp mixed lettuce salad.

Energy 180kcal/754kJ; Protein 23g; Carbohydrate 2.7g, of which sugars 1.7g; Fat 8.7g, of which saturates 1.1g; Cholesterol 90mg; Calcium 221mg; Fibre 0.9g; Sodium 140mg.

SEA BASS STEAMED IN COCONUT MILK ★★★

THIS RECIPE ALSO WORKS WELL IN THE OVEN — SIMPLY PLACE THE FISH, TUCKED IN FOIL, ON A
BAKING TRAY AND BAKE. SERVE THIS DISH WITH PLAIN OR STICKY RICE OR A VEGETABLE SALAD.

3 Scatter half the basil leaves over the top of the fish and pull the foil packet almost closed. Lay the packet in a steamer. Cover the steamer, bring the water to the boil, reduce the heat and simmer for 20–25 minutes, or until just cooked. Alternatively, place the foil packet on a baking tray and cook in a preheated oven at 180°C/350°F/Gas 4.

4 Roast the cashew nuts in the frying pan, adding extra oil if necessary. Drain the nuts on kitchen paper, then grind them to crumbs. When the fish is cooked, lift it out of the foil and transfer it to a serving dish. Spoon the cooking juices over, sprinkle with the cashew nut crumbs and garnish with the remaining basil leaves. Serve with rice and a salad.

SERVES 4

INGREDIENTS
  200ml/7fl oz coconut milk
  10ml/2 tsp raw cane or muscovado
    (molasses) sugar
  about 15ml/1 tbsp vegetable oil
  2 garlic cloves, finely chopped
  1 red Thai chilli, seeded and
    finely chopped
  4cm/1½in fresh root ginger,
    peeled and grated
  750g/1lb 10oz sea bass, gutted
    and skinned on one side
  1 star anise, ground
  1 bunch fresh basil, stalks removed
  30ml/2 tbsp cashew nuts
  sea salt and ground black pepper
  rice and salad, to serve

1 Heat the coconut milk with the sugar in a small pan, stirring until the sugar dissolves, then remove from the heat. Heat the oil in a small frying pan and stir in the garlic, chilli and ginger. Cook until they begin to brown, then add the mixture to the coconut milk and mix well to combine.

2 Place the fish, skin side down, on a wide piece of foil and tuck up the sides to form a boat-shaped container. Using a sharp knife, cut several diagonal slashes into the flesh on the top and rub with the ground star anise. Season with salt and pepper and spoon the coconut milk over the top, making sure that the fish is well coated.

Energy 235kcal/983kJ; Protein 26g; Carbohydrate 8g, of which sugars 6g; Fat 11g, of which saturates 2g; Cholesterol 100mg; Calcium 217mg; Fibre 0.3g; Sodium 300mg.

TUNA <u>WITH</u> CUCUMBER, GARLIC <u>AND</u> GINGER ★★

THIS POPULAR DISH CAN BE MADE WITH MANY TYPES OF THICK-FLESHED FISH. TUNA IS PARTICULARLY SUITABLE BECAUSE IT IS DELICIOUS PAN-SEARED AND SERVED A LITTLE RARE.

SERVES 4

INGREDIENTS
  1 small cucumber
  10ml/2 tsp sesame oil
  2 garlic cloves, crushed
  4 tuna steaks
For the dressing
  4cm/1½in fresh root ginger, peeled
    and roughly chopped
  1 garlic clove, roughly chopped
  2 green Thai chillies, seeded and
    roughly chopped
  45ml/3 tbsp raw cane sugar
  45ml/3 tbsp fish sauce
  juice of 1 lime
  60ml/4 tbsp water

1 To make the dressing, grind the ginger, garlic and chillies to a pulp with the sugar, using a mortar and pestle. Stir in the fish sauce, lime juice and water, and mix well. Leave the dressing to stand for 15 minutes.

2 Cut the cucumber in half lengthways and remove the seeds. Cut the flesh into long, thin strips. Toss the cucumber in the dressing and leave to soak for at least 15 minutes.

3 Wipe a heavy pan with the oil and rub the garlic around it. Heat the pan and add the tuna steaks. Sear for a few minutes on both sides, so that the outside is slightly charred but the inside is still rare. Lift the steaks on to a warm serving dish. Using tongs or chopsticks, lift the cucumber strips out of the dressing and arrange them around the steaks. Drizzle the dressing over the tuna, and serve immediately.

Energy 228kcal/959kJ; Protein 36.2g; Carbohydrate 1.5g, of which sugars 1.4g; Fat 8.6g, of which saturates 2g; Cholesterol 42mg; Calcium 55mg; Fibre 1g; Sodium 76mg.

FRESH TUNA SHIITAKE TERIYAKI ★★

TUNA IS A ROBUST FISH, WELL ABLE TO COPE WITH THE STRONG FLAVOURS IN THE TERIYAKI SAUCE. SHIITAKE MUSHROOMS ARE AN INSPIRED ADDITION, TURNING A SIMPLE DISH INTO A RARE TREAT.

2 Mix together the fish and sliced mushrooms, pour the teriyaki sauce over them and set aside to marinate for a further 20–30 minutes, or longer if you have the time.

3 Drain the tuna steaks, reserving the marinade and mushrooms. Cook the tuna under a preheated moderate grill (broiler) or on a barbecue for 8 minutes, turning once.

4 Transfer the sliced mushrooms and the marinade to a stainless-steel pan and simmer the mixture over a medium heat for 3–4 minutes.

5 Slice the daikon and carrots thinly, then shred finely with a chopping knife. Arrange in heaps on four serving plates and add the fish.

6 Spoon over the mushrooms and the sauce. Serve with plain boiled rice.

SERVES 4

INGREDIENTS
  4 x 175g/6oz fresh tuna or yellowfin
    tail steaks
  175g/6oz shiitake mushrooms, sliced
  225g/8oz daikon (mooli), peeled
  2 large carrots, peeled
  salt
  boiled rice, to serve
For the teriyaki sauce
  45ml/3 tbsp shoyu or other
    soy sauce
  45ml/3 tbsp sake
  45ml/3 tbsp mirin
  15ml/1 tbsp plus 10ml/2 tsp
    caster (superfine) sugar

1 Season the tuna steaks with a sprinkling of salt, then set aside for 20 minutes. Meanwhile, make the teriyaki sauce by mixing the shoyu, sake, mirin and sugar in a small pan. Heat gently, stirring until the sugar has dissolved. Pour into a bowl and cool.

VARIATION
If you don't like – or have trouble locating – daikon, use celeriac instead, but make sure you toss it in lemon juice to prevent discoloration.

Energy 277kcal/1165kJ; Protein 43.4g; Carbohydrate 7.2g, of which sugars 6.7g; Fat 8.5g, of which saturates 2.2g; Cholesterol 49mg; Calcium 57mg; Fibre 2g; Sodium 1883mg.

SALMON TERIYAKI ★★★

FOR THIS POPULAR DISH A SWEET SAUCE IS USED FOR MARINATING AS WELL AS FOR GLAZING THE FISH AND VEGETABLES, GIVING THE WHOLE MEAL A MOUTHWATERING AND SHINY GLOSS.

SERVES 4

INGREDIENTS

  4 small salmon fillets with skin,
    each weighing about 115g/4oz
  50g/2oz/¼ cup beansprouts, washed
  50g/2oz mangetouts (snow peas),
    ends trimmed
  20g/¾oz carrot, cut into thin strips
  salt
For the teriyaki sauce
  45ml/3 tbsp shoyu or other
    soy sauce
  45ml/3 tbsp sake
  45ml/3 tbsp mirin
  15ml/1 tbsp plus 10ml/2 tsp
    caster (superfine) sugar

1 Mix all the ingredients for the teriyaki sauce except for the 10ml/2 tsp sugar, in a pan. Heat to dissolve the sugar. Remove and cool for 1 hour.

2 Place the salmon fillets in a shallow glass or china dish and pour over the teriyaki sauce. Leave to marinate for 30 minutes.

3 Meanwhile, blanch the vegetables in lightly salted water. First add the beansprouts, then after 1 minute, the mangetouts. Leave for 1 minute again, and then add the thin carrot strips. Remove the pan from the heat after 1 minute, then drain the vegetables and keep warm.

4 Preheat the grill (broiler) to medium. Take the salmon fillet out of the sauce and pat dry with kitchen paper. Reserve the sauce.

5 Lightly oil a grill (broiling) pan. Grill (broil) the salmon for 6 minutes, turning once, until golden on both sides.

6 Pour the sauce into the pan. Add the remaining sugar and heat until dissolved. Remove from the heat. Brush the salmon with the sauce, then grill until the surface of the fish bubbles. Turn over and repeat on the other side.

7 Heap the vegetables on to four heated serving plates. Place the salmon on top and spoon over the rest of the sauce. Serve immediately.

Energy 239kcal/995kJ; Protein 24.8g; Carbohydrate 2.1g, of which sugars 1.7g; Fat 13.3g, of which saturates 2.3g; Cholesterol 58mg; Calcium 93mg; Fibre 0.3g; Sodium 323mg.

VEGETABLES AND SALMON IN A PARCEL ★★★

IN THIS RECIPE, THE VEGETABLES AND SALMON ARE WRAPPED AND STEAMED WITH SAKE IN THEIR OWN MOISTURE. WHEN YOU OPEN THE PARCEL, YOU'LL FIND A COLOURFUL AUTUMN GARDEN INSIDE.

4 Slice the carrot very thinly, then with a Japanese vegetable cutter or sharp knife, cut out 8–12 maple-leaf or flower shapes. Carefully slice the spring onions in half lengthways with a sharp knife. Trim the mangetouts.

5 Cut four sheets of foil, each about 29 × 21cm/11½ × 8½in wide. Place the long side of one sheet facing towards you. Arrange the salmon and *shimeji* mushrooms in the centre, then place a spring onion diagonally across them. Put two shiitake on top, three to four mangetouts in a fan shape and then sprinkle with a few carrot leaves.

SERVES 4

INGREDIENTS
450g/1lb salmon fillet, skinned
30ml/2 tbsp sake or dry sherry
15ml/1 tbsp shoyu or other soy
  sauce, plus extra to serve
  (optional)
about 250g/9oz/3 cups fresh
  shimeji mushrooms
8 fresh shiitake mushrooms
2.5cm/1in carrot
2 spring onions (scallions)
115g/4oz mangetouts (snow peas)
salt

1 Cut the salmon into bitesize pieces. Marinate in the sake and shoyu for about 15 minutes, then drain and reserve the marinade. Preheat the oven to 190°C/375°F/Gas 5.

2 Clean the *shimeji* mushrooms and chop off the hard root. Remove and discard the stems from the shiitake.

3 Carve a shallow slit on the top of each shiitake with a sharp knife inserted at a slant. Repeat from the other side to cut out a notch about 4cm/1½in long, then rotate the shiitake 90° and carefully carve another notch to make a small white cross in the brown top.

6 Sprinkle the marinade and a good pinch of salt over the top. Fold the two longer sides of the foil together, then fold the shorter sides to seal. Repeat to make four parcels.

7 Place the parcels on a baking sheet and bake for 15–20 minutes in the middle of the preheated oven. When the foil has expanded into a balloon, the dish is ready to serve. Serve the parcels unopened with a little extra shoyu, if required.

Energy 231kcal/964kJ; Protein 25.2g; Carbohydrate 3.9g, of which sugars 3.3g; Fat 12.9g, of which saturates 2.2g; Cholesterol 56mg; Calcium 49mg; Fibre 2g; Sodium 328mg.

SWEET AND SOUR FISH ★★★

WHEN FISH SUCH AS RED MULLET OR SNAPPER IS COOKED IN THIS WAY THE SKIN BECOMES CRISP, WHILE THE FLESH REMAINS JUICY. THIS SWEET AND SOUR SAUCE COMPLEMENTS THE FISH BEAUTIFULLY.

SERVES 4–6

INGREDIENTS

1 large or 2 medium fish, such as
  snapper or mullet, heads removed
20ml/4 tsp cornflour (cornstarch)
120ml/4fl oz/½ cup vegetable oil
15ml/1 tbsp chopped garlic
15ml/1 tbsp chopped fresh
  root ginger
30ml/2 tbsp chopped shallots
225g/8oz cherry tomatoes
30ml/2 tbsp red wine vinegar
30ml/2 tbsp sugar
30ml/2 tbsp tomato ketchup
15ml/1 tbsp fish sauce
45ml/3 tbsp water
salt and ground black pepper
coriander (cilantro) leaves and
  shredded spring onions
  (scallions), to garnish

1 Rinse and dry the fish. Score the skin diagonally on both sides, then coat the fish lightly all over with 15ml/3 tsp of the cornflour. Shake off any excess.

2 Heat the oil in a wok or large frying pan. Add the fish and cook over a medium heat for 6–7 minutes. Turn the fish over and cook for 6–7 minutes more, until it is crisp and brown.

3 Remove the fish and place on a large platter. Pour off all but 30ml/ 2 tbsp of the oil from the wok or pan and reheat. Add the garlic, ginger and shallots and cook over a medium heat, stirring occasionally, for about 4 minutes, until golden.

4 Add the cherry tomatoes and cook until they burst open. Stir in the vinegar, sugar, tomato ketchup and fish sauce. Lower the heat and simmer gently for 1–2 minutes, then taste and adjust the seasoning.

5 In a cup, mix the remaining 5ml/1 tsp cornflour to a paste with the water. Stir into the sauce. Heat, stirring, until it thickens. Pour the sauce over the fish, garnish with coriander leaves and shredded spring onions and serve.

Energy 233kcal/969kJ; Protein 21.9g; Carbohydrate 6.3g, of which sugars 3g; Fat 13.5g, of which saturates 1.6g; Cholesterol 54mg; Calcium 16mg; Fibre 0.5g; Sodium 335mg.

RED SNAPPER IN BANANA LEAVES ★

WHOLE SNAPPERS INFUSED WITH COCONUT CREAM, HERBS AND CHILLI MAKE AN IMPRESSIVE MAIN COURSE. BANANA LEAVES ARE USED EXTENSIVELY IN THAILAND FOR STEAMING AND ROASTING FOOD.

SERVES 4

INGREDIENTS

  4 small red snapper, gutted and
    cleaned
  4 large squares of banana leaf
  50ml/2fl oz/¼ cup coconut cream
  90ml/6 tbsp chopped coriander
    (cilantro)
  90ml/6 tbsp chopped mint
  juice of 3 limes
  3 spring onions (scallions),
    finely sliced
  4 kaffir lime leaves, finely shredded
  2 fresh red chillies, seeded
    and finely sliced
  4 lemon grass stalks, split lengthways
  salt and ground black pepper
  steamed rice and steamed
    Asian greens, to serve

1 Using a small sharp knife, score the fish diagonally on each side. Half fill a wok with water and bring to the boil.

2 Dip each square of banana leaf into the boiling water in the wok for 15–20 seconds so they become pliable. Lift out carefully, rinse under cold water and dry with kitchen paper.

3 Place the coconut cream, chopped herbs, lime juice, spring onions, lime leaves and chillies in a bowl and stir. Season well.

COOK'S TIP
Banana leaves can also be used for mats, lining dishes, as platters and to make attractive containers that can be secured with bamboo sticks.

4 Lay the banana leaves flat and place a fish and a split lemon grass stalk in the centre of each of them. Spread the herb mixture over each fish and fold over each banana leaf to form a neat parcel. Secure each parcel tightly with a bamboo skewer.

5 Place the parcels in a single layer in one or two tiers of a large bamboo steamer and place over a wok of simmering water. Cover tightly and steam for 15–20 minutes, or until the fish is cooked through.

6 Remove the fish from the steamer and serve in their banana-leaf wrappings, with steamed rice and greens.

Energy 185kcal/781kJ; Protein 39.4g; Carbohydrate 0.9g, of which sugars 0.8g; Fat 2.7g, of which saturates 0.6g; Cholesterol 74mg; Calcium 87mg; Fibre 0.1g; Sodium 168mg

STEAMED RED SNAPPER ★

THIS ELEGANTLY PRESENTED DISH WOULD TRADITIONALLY FEATURE A WHOLE RED SNAPPER WRAPPED IN LAYERED PAPER SOAKED IN SAKE AND TIED WITH RIBBONS. THIS VERSION IS A LITTLE EASIER.

SERVES 4

INGREDIENTS

4 small red snapper fillets, no greater than 18 × 6cm/7 × 2½in, or whole snapper, 20cm/8in long, gutted but with head, tail and fins intact
1 lime
8 asparagus spears, hard ends snapped off
4 spring onions (scallions)
60ml/4 tbsp sake
5ml/1 tsp shoyu or other soy sauce (optional)
salt

1 Sprinkle the red snapper fillets with salt on both sides and leave in the refrigerator for 20 minutes.

2 Preheat the oven to 180°C/350°F/Gas 4. Cut the lime in half. Grate one half and thinly slice the other.

3 To make the parcels, lay baking parchment measuring 38 × 30cm/15 × 12in on a work surface. Use two pieces for extra strength. Fold up one-third of the paper and turn back 1cm/½in from one end to make a flap.

4 Fold 1cm/½in in from the other end to make another flap. Fold the top edge down to fold over the first flap. Interlock the two flaps to form a long rectangle.

VARIATION
You could use any firm fish you like, such as salmon, trout, tuna or swordfish, in place of the red snapper in this quick and easy recipe.

5 At each end, fold the top corners down diagonally, then fold the bottom corners up to meet the opposite folded edge to make a triangle. Press flat with your palm. Repeat the process to make four parcels.

6 Cut 2.5cm/1in from the tip of the asparagus, and slice in half lengthways. Slice the asparagus stems and spring onions diagonally into thin ovals. Par-boil the tips for 1 minute in a small pan of lightly salted water and drain. Set aside.

7 Open the paper parcels. Place the asparagus slices and the spring onions inside. Sprinkle with salt and place the fish on top. Add more salt and some sake, then sprinkle in the lime rind. Refold the parcels.

8 Pour hot water from a kettle into a deep roasting pan fitted with a wire rack to 1cm/½in below the rack. Place the parcels on the rack. Cook in the centre of the preheated oven for 20 minutes. Check that the fish is cooked by carefully unfolding a parcel from one triangular side. The fish should have changed from translucent to white.

9 Transfer the parcels on to individual plates. Unfold both triangular ends on the plate and lift open the middle a little. Insert a thin slice of lime and place two asparagus tips on top. Serve immediately, asking the guests to open their own parcels. Add a little shoyu, if you like.

Energy 112kcal/471kJ; Protein 20.6g; Carbohydrate 1g, of which sugars 0.9g; Fat 1.5g, of which saturates 0.3g; Cholesterol 37mg; Calcium 52mg; Fibre 0.6g; Sodium 79mg.

MARINATED ᴬⁿᵈ GRILLED SWORDFISH ★★

*THERE'S A TENDENCY FOR SWORDFISH TO TASTE RATHER DRY, SO FOR THIS RECIPE IT IS MARINATED IN
A MISO MIXTURE WHICH KEEPS IT SUCCULENT EVEN WHEN COOKED ON THE BARBECUE.*

2 Mix the miso and sake, then spread
half across the bottom of the cleaned
dish. Cover with a sheet of muslin or
cheesecloth the size of a dish towel,
folded in half, then open the fold.

3 Place the swordfish, side by side,
on top, and cover with the muslin.
Spread the rest of the miso mixture on
the muslin. Make sure the muslin is
touching the fish. Marinate for 2 days
in the coolest part of the refrigerator.

4 Preheat the grill (broiler) to medium.
Oil the wire rack and grill (broil) the fish
slowly for about 8 minutes on each side,
turning every 2 minutes. If the steaks
are thin, check them frequently to see
if they are ready.

SERVES 4

INGREDIENTS
    4 × 175g/6oz swordfish steaks
    2.5ml/½ tsp salt
    300g/11oz *shiro miso*
    45ml/3 tbsp sake
For the asparagus
    25ml/1½ tbsp soy sauce
    25ml/1½ tbsp sake or dry sherry
    8 asparagus spears, the hard ends
      snapped off, each spear cut
      into three

COOK'S TIP
Shiro miso is a lightly flavoured
yellow soyabean paste.

1 Place the swordfish in a shallow dish.
Sprinkle evenly with the salt on both
sides and leave for 2 hours. Drain and
wipe the fish with kitchen paper.

5 Mix the soy sauce and sake in a bowl.
Grill the asparagus for 2 minutes on
each side, then dip into the mixture.
Return to the grill for 2 minutes more
on each side. Dip in the sauce again
and set aside.

6 Serve the fish hot on four individual
serving plates. Garnish with the drained,
grilled asparagus.

Energy 203kcal/851kJ; Protein 32g; Carbohydrate 0.7g, of which sugars 0.6g; Fat 7.3g, of which saturates 1.6g; Cholesterol 72mg; Calcium 12mg; Fibre 0.2g; Sodium 495mg.

SWORDFISH WITH CITRUS DRESSING ★★★

FOR THIS BEAUTIFULLY PRESENTED SALAD, FRESH SWORDFISH IS SEARED AND SLICED THINLY, THEN SERVED WITH SALAD LEAVES AND VEGETABLES WITH A FLAVOURSOME DRESSING.

SERVES 4

INGREDIENTS

    75g/3oz daikon (mooli), peeled
    50g/2oz carrot, peeled
    1 cucumber
    10ml/2 tsp vegetable oil
    300g/11oz skinned fresh swordfish
      steak, cut against the grain
    2 cartons mustard and cress
      (fine curled cress)
    15ml/1 tbsp toasted sesame seeds
For the dressing
    105ml/7 tbsp shoyu or other soy sauce
    105ml/7 tbsp water and 5ml/1 tsp
      instant dashi powder
    30ml/2 tbsp toasted sesame oil
    juice of ½ lime
    rind of ½ lime, shredded into
      thin strips

6 Cut the swordfish steak in half lengthways before slicing it into 5mm/¼in thick pieces in the other direction, against the grain.

7 Arrange the fish slices into a ring on individual plates. Mix the vegetable strands, mustard and cress (fine curled cress) and sesame seeds.

8 Shape the vegetable strands into a sphere. Gently place it on the swordfish. Pour the dressing around the plate's edge and serve immediately.

COOK'S TIP
If you cannot locate mustard and cress or fine curled cress, serve on a pile of wild rocket (arugula) leaves. You could also add grapefruit segments.

1 Make the vegetable garnishes first. Use a very sharp knife, mandoline or vegetable slicer with a julienne blade to make very thin (about 4cm/1½in long) strands of daikon, carrot and cucumber.

2 Soak the daikon and carrot in ice-cold water for 5 minutes, then drain well and keep in the refrigerator.

3 Mix together all the ingredients for the dressing and stir well, then chill.

4 Heat the oil in a small frying pan until smoking hot. Sear the fish for 30 seconds on all sides.

5 Plunge the fish into cold water to stop the cooking. Dry on kitchen paper and wipe off as much oil as possible.

Energy 182kcal/758kJ; Protein 15.2g; Carbohydrate 2.4g, of which sugars 2.3g; Fat 12.5g, of which saturates 2g; Cholesterol 31mg; Calcium 63mg; Fibre 1.1g; Sodium 645mg.

CATFISH COOKED <u>IN A</u> CLAY POT ★

WONDERFULLY EASY AND TASTY, THIS DISH IS A CLASSIC. CLAY POTS ARE REGULARLY USED FOR COOKING AND THEY ENHANCE BOTH THE LOOK AND TASTE OF THIS TRADITIONAL DISH.

SERVES 4

INGREDIENTS
  30ml/2 tbsp sugar
  15ml/1 tbsp sunflower oil
  2 garlic cloves, crushed
  45ml/3 tbsp *nuoc mam* or other
    fish sauce
  350g/12oz catfish fillets, cut
    diagonally into 2 or 3 pieces
  4 spring onions (scallions), cut
    into bitesize pieces
  ground black pepper
  chopped fresh coriander (cilantro),
    to garnish
  fresh bread, to serve

1 Place the sugar in a clay pot or heavy pan, and add 15ml/1 tbsp water to wet it. Heat the sugar until it begins to turn golden brown, then add the oil and crushed garlic.

2 Stir the *nuoc mam* into the caramel mixture and add 120ml/4fl oz/¹/2 cup boiling water, then toss in the catfish pieces, making sure they are well coated with the sauce. Cover the pot, reduce the heat and simmer for about 5 minutes.

3 Remove the lid, season with ground black pepper and gently stir in the spring onions. Simmer for a further 3–4 minutes to thicken the sauce, garnish with fresh coriander, and serve immediately straight from the pot with chunks of fresh bread.

Energy 128kcal/537kJ; Protein 16.4g; Carbohydrate 8.3g, of which sugars 8.3g; Fat 3.4g, of which saturates 0.4g; Cholesterol 40mg; Calcium 18mg; Fibre 0.2g; Sodium 54mg.

EEL BRAISED IN A CARAMEL SAUCE ★★★

ALTHOUGH THIS DISH IS FOUND IN MANY PARTS OF SOUTH-EAST ASIA, IT IS TRADITIONALLY A VIETNAMESE DISH AND IT IS THERE, IN THE HIGHLANDS, THAT IT IS BEST SAMPLED.

SERVES 4

INGREDIENTS

    45ml/3 tbsp raw cane sugar
    30ml/2 tbsp soy sauce
    45ml/3 tbsp *nuoc mam* or other
        fish sauce
    2 garlic cloves, crushed
    2 dried chillies
    2–3 star anise
    4–5 black peppercorns
    350g/12oz eel on the bone,
        skinned, cut into 2.5cm/1in-thick
        chunks
    200g/7oz butternut squash, cut
        into bitesize chunks
    4 spring onions (scallions), cut
        into bitesize pieces
    30ml/2 tbsp sesame or vegetable oil
    5cm/2in fresh root ginger, peeled
        and cut into matchsticks
    salt
    cooked rice or noodles, to serve

1 Put the sugar in a wok or heavy pan with 30ml/2 tbsp water, and gently heat it until it turns golden. Remove the pan from the heat and stir in the soy sauce and *nuoc mam* with 120ml/4fl oz/½ cup water. Add the garlic, chillies, star anise and peppercorns and return to the heat.

COOK'S TIP
If you can't find eel, use mackerel for this dish. The fat rendered from these fish melts into the caramel sauce, making it deliciously velvety. It is often served with chopped fresh coriander (cilantro) on top.

2 Add the eel chunks, squash and spring onions, making sure the fish is well coated in the sauce, and season with salt. Reduce the heat, cover the pan and simmer gently for about 20 minutes, until the eel and vegetables are tender.

3 Meanwhile, heat a small wok, pour in the oil and stir-fry the ginger until crisp and golden. Remove and drain on kitchen paper.

4 Serve with rice or noodles, with the crispy ginger sprinkled on top.

Energy 204kcal/857kJ; Protein 11g; Carbohydrate 20g, of which sugars 14g; Fat 10g, of which saturates 1g; Cholesterol 0mg; Calcium 76mg; Fibre 1g; Sodium 110mg.

SHELLFISH

Shellfish are very popular ingredients in the Asian diet. They
can easily be steamed, stir-fried, baked, grilled, cooked with
fresh spices or herbs, and served in curries and sauces. Impress
your guests with luxurious dishes like Chilli-Seared Scallops on
Pak Choi, Five-spice Squid with Black Bean Sauce, and Curried
Seafood with Coconut Milk. There are also lightly cooked
delights to try, such as Stir-Fried Prawns with Mangetouts, and
Lobster and Crab Steamed in Beer.

STIR-FRIED BABY SQUID WITH GINGER, GARLIC AND LEMON ★★

THE THRIVING MARKETS OF THAILAND ARE SUSTAINED BY THE ABUNDANCE OF FISH AROUND THE GULF OF THAILAND. THE MARKETS SERVE THE RESTAURANT AND HOTEL TRADE AND DELICIOUS FRESHLY CAUGHT SEAFOOD IS USED IN DISHES SUCH AS THIS BY THE BUSY STREET TRADERS.

SERVES 2

INGREDIENTS

4 ready-prepared baby squid,
   total weight about 250g/9oz
15ml/1 tbsp sunflower oil
2 garlic cloves, finely chopped
30ml/2 tbsp soy sauce
2.5cm/1in piece fresh root ginger,
   peeled and finely chopped
juice of ½ lemon
5ml/1 tsp granulated sugar
2 spring onions (scallions), chopped

VARIATIONS
This dish is often prepared with fresh
galangal rather than ginger and works
well with most kinds of seafood,
including prawns (shrimp) and scallops.

1 Rinse the squid well and pat dry with
kitchen paper. Cut the bodies into rings
and halve the tentacles, if necessary.

2 Heat the oil in a wok or frying pan and
cook the garlic until golden brown, but
do not let it burn. Add the squid and
stir-fry for 30 seconds over a high heat.

3 Add the soy sauce, ginger, lemon
juice, sugar and spring onions. Stir-fry
for a further 30 seconds, then serve.

COOK'S TIP
Squid has an undeserved reputation for
being rubbery in texture. This is always
a result of overcooking it.

Energy 169kcal/709kJ; Protein 20g; Carbohydrate 5.3g, of which sugars 3.6g; Fat 7.7g, of which saturates 1.2g; Cholesterol 281mg; Calcium 26mg; Fibre 0.3g; Sodium 1207mg.

GRIDDLED SQUID AND TOMATOES IN A TAMARIND DRESSING ★

THIS IS A LOVELY FLAVOURSOME DISH — SWEET, CHARRED SQUID SERVED IN A TANGY DRESSING MADE WITH TAMARIND, LIME AND FISH SAUCE. IT IS BEST MADE WITH BABY SQUID BECAUSE THEY ARE TENDER AND SWEET. THE TOMATOES AND HERBS ADD WONDERFUL FRESH FLAVOURS.

SERVES 4

INGREDIENTS
    spray sunflower oil, for greasing
    2 large tomatoes, skinned, halved
        and seeded
    500g/1¼lb fresh baby squid
    1 bunch each fresh basil, coriander
        (cilantro) and mint, stalks removed,
        leaves chopped
For the dressing
    15ml/1 tbsp tamarind paste
    juice of half a lime
    30ml/2 tbsp fish sauce
    15ml/1 tbsp raw cane sugar
    1 garlic clove, crushed
    2 shallots, halved and finely sliced
    2 Serrano chillies, seeded and sliced

3 Clean the griddle, then heat it up again and spray with a little more oil. Griddle the squid for 2–3 minutes each side, pressing them down with a spatula, until nicely browned. Transfer to the bowl with the tomatoes, add the herbs and the dressing and toss well. Serve immediately.

COOK'S TIPS
• To prepare squid yourself, get a firm hold of the head and pull it from the body. Reach down inside the body sac and then pull out and discard the transparent backbone, as well as any stringy parts. Rinse the body sac inside and out and pat dry. Cut the tentacles off above the eyes and add to the pile of squid you're going to cook. Discard everything else.
• Griddled scallops and prawns (shrimp) are also delicious in this tangy dressing.

VARIATION
Traditionally, the squid are steamed for this dish: this creates a delicious low-fat meal. Steam the squid for 10–15 minutes.

1 Put the dressing ingredients in a bowl and stir until well mixed. Set aside.

2 Heat a ridged griddle, spray the pan with a little oil, and griddle the tomatoes until lightly charred on both sides. Transfer them to a board, chop into bitesize chunks, and place in a bowl.

Energy 153kcal/651kJ; Protein 20.4g; Carbohydrate 13.2g, of which sugars 11.3g; Fat 2.6g, of which saturates 0.6g; Cholesterol 281mg; Calcium 54mg; Fibre 1.6g; Sodium 149mg.

SPICY SQUID SALAD ★★

THE GENERAL RULE WITH SQUID IS THAT IT MUST EITHER BE COOKED VERY QUICKLY OR SIMMERED VERY SLOWLY. FOR THIS SUPERB SALAD THE FORMER METHOD IS USED WITH SPECTACULAR SUCCESS.

3 Cut the body open lengthways and wash thoroughly. Score criss-cross patterns on the inside, taking care not to cut through the squid, then cut into 7.5 x 5cm/3 x 2in pieces.

4 Bring the fish stock to the boil in a wok or pan. Add the squid, lower the heat and cook for about 2 minutes until they are tender and have curled. Drain.

5 In a separate pan of lightly salted boiling water, cook the beans for 3–4 minutes over medium heat until crisp-tender. Drain, refresh under cold water, then drain again. Mix the squid and beans in a serving bowl, and set aside.

SERVES 4

INGREDIENTS
    450g/1lb squid
    300ml/½ pint/1¼ cups fish stock
    175g/6oz green beans, trimmed
      and halved
    45ml/3 tbsp fresh coriander
      (cilantro) leaves
    10ml/2 tsp caster (superfine) sugar
    30ml/2 tbsp rice vinegar
    5ml/1 tsp sesame oil
    15ml/1 tbsp light soy sauce
    15ml/1 tbsp vegetable oil
    2 garlic cloves, finely chopped
    10ml/2 tsp finely chopped fresh
      root ginger
    1 fresh chilli, seeded and chopped
    salt

1 Prepare the squid. Holding the body in one hand, gently pull the head and tentacles away from the body with the other hand. Discard the head; trim and reserve the tentacles.

2 Remove the transparent "quill" from inside the body and peel off the purplish skin on the outside.

6 In a small bowl or jug (pitcher), mix the coriander leaves, sugar, rice vinegar, sesame oil and soy sauce. Pour the mixture over the squid and beans.

7 Heat the vegetable oil in a wok or small pan until very hot. Stir-fry the garlic, ginger and chilli for a few seconds, then pour the dressing over the squid mixture. Toss gently and leave for at least 5 minutes. Add salt to taste and serve warm or cold.

Energy 121kcal/507kJ; Protein 10.4g; Carbohydrate 7.5g, of which sugars 3.9g; Fat 5.6g, of which saturates 1.1g; Cholesterol 23mg; Calcium 84mg; Fibre 1.9g; Sodium 126mg.

SQUID <u>WITH</u> BROCCOLI ★★

THE SLIGHTLY CHEWY SQUID CONTRASTS BEAUTIFULLY WITH THE CRISP CRUNCH OF THE BROCCOLI TO GIVE THIS DISH THE PERFECT COMBINATION OF TEXTURES SO BELOVED BY THE CHINESE.

SERVES 4

INGREDIENTS
    300ml/½ pint/1¼ cups fish stock
    350g/12oz prepared squid, cut into
        large pieces
    225g/8oz broccoli
    15ml/1 tbsp vegetable oil
    2 garlic cloves, finely chopped
    15ml/1 tbsp Chinese rice wine
        or dry sherry
    10ml/2 tsp cornflour (cornstarch)
    2.5ml/½ tsp caster (superfine) sugar
    45ml/3 tbsp cold water
    15ml/1 tbsp oyster sauce
    2.5ml/½ tsp sesame oil
    noodles, to serve

3 Heat the vegetable oil in a wok or non-stick frying pan. When the oil is hot, add the garlic, stir-fry for a few seconds, then add the squid, broccoli and sherry. Stir-fry the mixture over medium heat for about 2 minutes.

4 Mix the cornflour and sugar to a paste with the water. Stir the mixture into the wok or pan, with the oyster sauce. Cook, stirring, until the sauce thickens slightly. Just before serving, stir in the sesame oil. Serve with noodles.

1 Bring the fish stock to the boil in a wok or pan. Add the squid pieces and cook for 2 minutes over medium heat until they are tender and have curled. Drain the squid pieces and set aside until required.

2 Trim the broccoli and cut it into small florets. Bring a pan of lightly salted water to the boil, add the broccoli and cook for 2 minutes until crisp-tender. Drain thoroughly.

Energy 143kcal/602kJ; Protein 18.2g; Carbohydrate 5.4g, of which sugars 3.6g; Fat 5.6g, of which saturates 0.9g; Cholesterol 253mg; Calcium 32mg; Fibre 1g; Sodium 124mg.

CLAY POT OF CHILLI SQUID ★★★

*THIS DISH IS DELICIOUS IN ITS OWN RIGHT, OR SERVED AS PART OF A LARGER CHINESE MEAL, WITH
OTHER MEAT OR FISH DISHES AND RICE. DON'T OVERCOOK THE SQUID OR IT WILL TOUGHEN.*

SERVES 2–4

INGREDIENTS

675g/1½lb fresh squid
30ml/2 tbsp vegetable oil
3 slices fresh root ginger,
  finely chopped
2 garlic cloves, finely chopped
1 red onion, thinly sliced
1 carrot, thinly sliced
1 celery stick, sliced diagonally
50g/2oz sugar snap peas
5ml/1 tsp sugar
15ml/1 tbsp chilli bean paste
2.5ml/½ tsp chilli powder
75g/3oz cellophane noodles, soaked
  in hot water until soft
120ml/4fl oz/½ cup chicken stock
  or water
15ml/1 tbsp light soy sauce
15ml/1 tbsp oyster sauce
5ml/1 tsp sesame oil
pinch of salt
fresh coriander (cilantro) leaves,
  to garnish

1 Prepare the squid. Holding the body
in one hand, pull away the head and
tentacles with the other hand. Discard
the head; trim and reserve the tentacles.

2 Remove the "quill" from inside the
body of the squid. Peel off the brown
skin on the outside. Rub salt into the
squid and wash under water.

COOK'S TIP
To vary the flavour of this dish, the
vegetables can be altered according
to what is available.

3 Cut the body into rings or split it open
lengthways, score criss-cross patterns
on the inside of the body and cut it into
5 x 4cm/2 x 1½in pieces.

4 Heat the oil in a large, flameproof
casserole or wok. Add the ginger, garlic
and onion and fry for 1–2 minutes.
Add the squid, carrot, celery and sugar
snap peas. Fry until the squid curls up.
Season with salt and sugar and then
stir in the chilli bean paste and powder.
Transfer to a bowl and set aside.

5 Drain the soaked noodles and add to
the casserole or wok. Stir in the chicken
stock or water, light soy sauce and
oyster sauce. Cover and cook over
medium heat for 10 minutes or until
the noodles are tender.

6 Return the squid and vegetable
mixture to the pot. Cover and cook
for a further 5–6 minutes, until all the
flavours are combined. Season to taste.

7 Spoon the mixture into a warmed clay
pot and drizzle with the sesame oil.
Sprinkle with the coriander leaves
and serve immediately.

Energy 292kcal/1229kJ; Protein 29.1g; Carbohydrate 21.2g, of which sugars 5.1g; Fat 10.8g, of which saturates 1.9g; Cholesterol 385mg; Calcium 45mg; Fibre 1.5g; Sodium 762mg.

SEAFOOD CHOW MEIN ★★★

CHOW MEIN IS A CHINESE DISH MEANING SIMPLY "STIR-FRIED NOODLES". IT IS USUALLY MEAT-BASED BUT TASTES JUST AS MARVELLOUS WHEN MADE WITH SQUID, PRAWNS AND SCALLOPS.

SERVES 4

INGREDIENTS
    75g/3oz fresh squid, cleaned
    75g/3oz raw prawns (shrimp)
    3–4 fresh scallops, prepared
    ½ egg white
    15ml/1 tbsp cornflour paste
     (see Cook's Tip)
    250g/9oz egg noodles
    30ml/2 tbsp vegetable oil
    50g/2oz mangetouts (snow peas)
    2.5ml/½ tsp salt
    2.5ml/½ tsp light brown sugar
    15ml/1 tbsp Chinese rice wine
    30ml/2 tbsp light soy sauce
    2 spring onions (scallions), shredded
    vegetable stock, (optional)
    few drops sesame oil

1 Open up the squid and score the inside in a criss-cross pattern. Cut the squid into pieces, each about the size of a postage stamp. Soak the squid in a bowl of boiling water until all the pieces curl up. Rinse in cold water and drain.

2 Peel and devein the prawns, then cut each of them in half lengthways.

3 Cut each scallop into 3–4 slices. Mix the scallops and prawns with the egg white and cornflour paste and set aside.

4 Cook the noodles in boiling water according to the packet instructions.

COOK'S TIP
To make cornflour paste, mix 4 parts dry cornflour with about 5 parts cold water until smooth.

5 Meanwhile, heat the oil in a preheated wok until hot. Stir-fry the mangetouts, squid, prawns and scallops for about 2 minutes, then add the salt, sugar, rice wine, half of the soy sauce and about half the spring onions. Blend well and add a little stock, if necessary. Transfer to a bowl and keep warm.

6 Drain the noodles and toss with the remaining soy sauce.

7 Place the noodles in a large serving dish, pour the seafood topping on top, garnish with the remaining spring onions and sprinkle with sesame oil. Serve hot or cold.

Energy 359kcal/1515kJ; Protein 19.5g; Carbohydrate 47.6g, of which sugars 2.9g; Fat 11.4g, of which saturates 2.3g; Cholesterol 106mg; Calcium 53mg; Fibre 2.3g; Sodium 1101mg.

FIVE-SPICE SQUID <u>WITH</u> BLACK BEAN SAUCE ★★

SQUID IS PERFECT FOR STIR-FRYING AS COOKING IT QUICKLY HELPS TO KEEP IT TENDER. THIS SPICY BLACK BEAN AND MUSHROOM SAUCE IS THE IDEAL ACCOMPANIMENT.

SERVES 6

INGREDIENTS

450g/1lb cleaned small squid
30ml/2 tbsp vegetable oil
2.5cm/1in piece fresh root
  ginger, grated
1 garlic clove, crushed
8 spring onions (scallions), cut
  diagonally into 2.5cm/1in lengths
1 red (bell) pepper, seeded and
  cut into strips
1 fresh green chilli, seeded and
  thinly sliced
6 fresh shiitake mushrooms, stems
  removed, caps sliced
5ml/1 tsp five-spice powder
30ml/2 tbsp black bean sauce
30ml/2 tbsp soy sauce
5ml/1 tsp granulated sugar
15ml/1 tbsp rice wine or dry sherry

1 Prepare the squid. Holding the body in one hand, gently pull away the head and tentacles with the other hand. Discard the head; trim and reserve the tentacles.

2 Peel off the brown skin on the outside of the squid. Remove the "quill" from inside the body. Rub salt into the squid and wash under water.

3 Slit the squid open and score the outside into diamonds with a sharp knife. Cut the squid into strips.

4 Heat the oil in a wok until hot. Stir-fry the squid quickly. Remove the squid from the wok with a slotted spoon; set aside. Add the ginger, garlic, spring onions, red pepper, chilli and mushrooms to the oil remaining in the wok and toss over the heat for 2 minutes.

5 Return the squid to the wok and stir in the five-spice powder using chopsticks. Stir in the black bean sauce, soy sauce, sugar and rice wine or sherry. Bring to the boil and cook, stirring, for 1 minute. Serve in heated bowls, with steamed rice or egg noodles.

Energy 112kcal/469kJ; Protein 12.6g; Carbohydrate 4g, of which sugars 2.9g; Fat 5.2g, of which saturates 0.8g; Cholesterol 169mg; Calcium 20mg; Fibre 0.8g; Sodium 797mg.

THREE SEA FLAVOURS STIR-FRY ★

THIS DELECTABLE SEAFOOD COMBINATION CONTAINS VERY LITTLE SATURATED FAT AND IS IDEAL FOR A SPECIAL OCCASION MEAL. FRESH ROOT GINGER AND SPRING ONIONS ENHANCE THE FLAVOUR.

SERVES 4

INGREDIENTS

  4 large scallops, with the corals
  225g/8oz firm white fish fillet, such
    as monkfish or cod
  115g/4oz raw tiger prawns
    (jumbo shrimp)
  300ml/½ pint/1¼ cups fish stock
  15ml/1 tbsp vegetable oil
  2 garlic cloves, roughly chopped
  5cm/2in piece of fresh root ginger,
    thinly sliced
  8 spring onions (scallions), cut into
    4cm/1½in pieces
  30ml/2 tbsp dry white wine
  5ml/1 tsp cornflour (cornstarch)
  15ml/1 tbsp cold water
  salt and ground white pepper
  noodles or rice, to serve

1 Separate the corals and slice each scallop in half horizontally. Cut the fish into chunks. Peel and devein the prawns.

2 Bring the fish stock to the boil in a pan. Add the seafood, lower the heat and poach gently for 1–2 minutes until the fish, scallops and corals are just firm and the prawns have turned pink.

3 Remove the seafood, using a slotted spoon, and set aside. Reserve about 60ml/4 tbsp of the stock.

4 Heat the oil in a non-stick frying pan or wok over a high heat until very hot. Stir-fry the garlic, ginger and spring onions for a few seconds.

5 Add the seafood and wine. Stir-fry for 1 minute, then add the reserved stock and simmer for 2 minutes.

VARIATION
For a more economical version of this dish, substitute 275g/10oz smoked haddock for the scallops and white fish.

6 Mix the cornflour to a paste with the water. Add the mixture to the pan or wok and cook, stirring gently just until the sauce thickens.

7 Season the stir-fry with salt and pepper to taste. Serve immediately, with noodles or rice.

Energy 159kcal/668kJ; Protein 26.2g; Carbohydrate 3.3g, of which sugars 0.6g; Fat 4.1g, of which saturates 0.6g; Cholesterol 103mg; Calcium 50mg; Fibre 0.3g; Sodium 172mg.

STIR-FRIED SCALLOPS AND PRAWNS ★

SERVE THIS LIGHT, DELICATE DISH FOR LUNCH OR SUPPER ACCOMPANIED BY AROMATIC STEAMED RICE OR FINE RICE NOODLES AND STIR-FRIED PAK CHOI. THIS COMBINATION OF FRESH SEAFOOD AND LIGHTLY COOKED VEGETABLES PRODUCES A DISH THAT IS HIGH IN FLAVOUR AND LOW IN FAT.

SERVES 4

INGREDIENTS
15ml/1 tbsp sunflower oil
500g/1¼lb raw tiger prawns
  (shrimp), peeled
1 star anise
225g/8oz scallops, halved if large
2.5cm/1in piece fresh root ginger,
  peeled and grated
2 garlic cloves, thinly sliced
1 red (bell) pepper, seeded and cut
  into thin strips
115g/4oz/1¾ cups shiitake
  or button (white) mushrooms,
  thinly sliced
juice of 1 lemon
5ml/1 tsp cornflour (cornstarch)
30ml/2 tbsp light soy sauce
chopped fresh chives,
  to garnish
salt and ground black pepper

1 Heat the oil in a wok until very hot. Put in the prawns and star anise and stir-fry over a high heat for 2 minutes. Add the scallops, ginger and garlic and stir-fry for 1 minute more, by which time the prawns should have turned pink and the scallops should be opaque. Season with a little salt and plenty of pepper and then remove from the wok using a slotted spoon. Discard the star anise.

2 Add the red pepper and mushrooms to the wok and stir-fry for 1–2 minutes.

3 Make a cornflour paste by combining the cornflour with 30ml/2 tbsp cold water. Stir until smooth.

4 Pour the lemon juice, cornflour paste and soy sauce into the wok, bring to the boil and bubble for 1–2 minutes, stirring all the time, until the sauce is smooth and slightly thickened.

VARIATIONS
Other types of shellfish can be used in this dish. Try it with thinly sliced rings of squid, or use mussels or clams. You could even substitute bitesize chunks of firm white fish, such as monkfish, cod or haddock, for the scallops. These can be added to the dish in step 1, as with the scallops.

Energy 212kcal/892kJ; Protein 36.2g; Carbohydrate 6.6g, of which sugars 3.3g; Fat 4.6g, of which saturates 0.8g; Cholesterol 270mg; Calcium 122mg; Fibre 1g; Sodium 877mg.

BANANA BLOSSOM SALAD <u>WITH</u> PRAWNS ★

BANANA BLOSSOM IS VERY POPULAR — THE PURPLISH-PINK SHEATHS ARE USED FOR PRESENTATION, THE PETALS AS A GARNISH, AND THE POINTED, CREAMY YELLOW HEART IS TOSSED IN SALADS, WHERE IT IS COMBINED WITH LEFTOVER GRILLED CHICKEN OR PORK, STEAMED OR GRILLED PRAWNS, OR TOFU.

SERVES 4

INGREDIENTS
2 banana blossom hearts
juice of 1 lemon
225g/8oz prawns (shrimp), cooked
  and shelled
30ml/2 tbsp roasted peanuts, finely
  chopped, fresh basil leaves and
  lime slices, to garnish
For the dressing
juice of 1 lime
30ml/2 tbsp white rice vinegar
60ml/4 tbsp fish sauce
45ml/3 tbsp palm sugar
3 red Thai chillies, seeded and
  finely sliced
2 garlic cloves, peeled and finely
  chopped

2 To make the dressing, beat the lime juice, vinegar, and fish sauce with the sugar in a small bowl, until it has dissolved. Stir in the chillies and garlic and set aside.

3 Drain the sliced banana blossom and put it in a bowl. Add the prawns and pour over the dressing. Toss well and garnish with the roasted peanuts, basil leaves and lime slices.

1 Cut the banana blossom hearts into quarters lengthways and then slice them very finely crosswise. To prevent them discolouring, tip the slices into a bowl of cold water mixed with the lemon juice and leave to soak for about 30 minutes.

COOK'S TIP
Banana blossom doesn't actually taste of banana. Instead, it is mildly tannic, similar to an unripe persimmon – a taste and texture that complements chillies, lime and fish sauce.

VARIATION
If you cannot find banana blossom hearts in Asian supermarkets, you can try this recipe with raw, or lightly steamed or roasted, fresh artichoke hearts.

Energy 103kcal/438kJ; Protein 11g; Carbohydrate 15g, of which sugars 13g; Fat 0.5g, of which saturates 0.1g; Cholesterol 110mg; Calcium 54mg; Fibre 0.7g; Sodium 109mg.

STIR-FRIED PRAWNS WITH TAMARIND ★

THE SOUR, TANGY FLAVOUR THAT IS CHARACTERISTIC OF MANY THAI DISHES COMES FROM TAMARIND.
FRESH PODS FROM THE TAMARIND TREE CAN SOMETIMES BE BOUGHT, BUT PREPARING THEM FOR
COOKING IS A LABORIOUS PROCESS. IT IS MUCH EASIER TO USE A BLOCK OF TAMARIND PASTE.

SERVES 4–6

INGREDIENTS

6 dried red chillies
15ml/1 tbsp sunflower oil
30ml/2 tbsp chopped onion
30ml/2 tbsp palm sugar or light
  muscovado (brown) sugar
30ml/2 tbsp water
15ml/1 tbsp Thai fish sauce
90ml/6 tbsp tamarind juice, made
  by mixing tamarind paste with
  warm water
450g/1lb raw prawns
  (shrimp), peeled
15ml/1 tbsp fried chopped garlic
30ml/2 tbsp fried sliced shallots
2 spring onions (scallions), chopped,
  to garnish

1 Heat a wok or large frying pan, but do not add any oil at this stage. Add the dried chillies and dry-fry them by pressing them against the surface of the wok or pan with a spatula, turning them occasionally. Do not let them burn. Set them aside to cool slightly.

2 Add the oil to the wok or pan and reheat. Add the chopped onion and cook over a medium heat, stirring occasionally, for 2–3 minutes, until softened and golden brown.

3 Add the sugar, water, fish sauce, dry-fried red chillies and the tamarind juice, stirring constantly until the sugar has dissolved. Bring to the boil, then lower the heat slightly.

4 Add the prawns, garlic and shallots. Toss over the heat for 3–4 minutes, until the prawns are cooked. Garnish with the spring onions and serve.

COOK'S TIP
Leave a few prawns in their shells for a garnish, if you like.

Energy 100kcal/422kJ; Protein 13.6g; Carbohydrate 6.6g, of which sugars 6g; Fat 2.3g, of which saturates 0.3g; Cholesterol 146mg; Calcium 65mg; Fibre 0.3g; Sodium 321mg.

STIR-FRIED LONG BEANS WITH PRAWNS ★★

POPULAR THROUGHOUT SOUTH-EAST ASIA, LONG BEANS — LIKE MANY OTHER VEGETABLES — ARE OFTEN STIR-FRIED WITH FRESH GARLIC AND GINGER. THIS TRADITIONAL SOUTH-EAST ASIAN RECIPE WITH PRAWNS, GALANGAL AND LIMES WORKS EXTREMELY WELL WHEN SERVED WITH RICE OR NOODLES.

SERVES 4

INGREDIENTS

30ml/2 tbsp sunflower oil
2 garlic cloves, finely chopped
25g/1oz galangal, finely
 shredded
450g/1lb fresh prawns (shrimp),
 shelled and deveined
1 onion, halved and finely sliced
450g/1lb long beans, trimmed
 and cut into 7.5cm/3in lengths
120ml/4fl oz/½ cup soy sauce
For the marinade
30ml/2 tbsp *tuk trey* or other
 fish sauce
juice of 2 limes
10ml/2 tsp sugar
2 garlic cloves, crushed
1 lemon grass stalk, trimmed
 and finely sliced

1 To make the marinade, beat the *tuk trey* and lime juice in a bowl with the sugar, until it has dissolved. Stir in the garlic and lemon grass. Toss in the prawns, cover, and chill for 1–2 hours.

2 Heat half the oil in a wok or heavy pan. Stir in the chopped garlic and galangal. Just as they begin to colour, toss in the marinated prawns. Stir-fry for a minute or until the prawns turn pink. Lift the prawns out on to a plate, reserving as much of the oil, garlic and galangal as you can.

3 Add the remaining oil to the wok. Add the onion and stir-fry until slightly caramelized. Stir in the beans, then pour in the soy sauce. Cook for a further 2–3 minutes, until the beans are tender. Add the prawns and stir-fry for a minute until heated through. Serve immediately.

Energy 187kcal/782kJ; Protein 22.6g; Carbohydrate 9.3g, of which sugars 7.9g; Fat 6.9g, of which saturates 0.9g; Cholesterol 219mg; Calcium 156mg; Fibre 3.2g; Sodium 485mg.

SINIGANG ★

THIS SOURED HEALTHY SOUP-LIKE STEW IS EXTREMELY LOW IN FAT. IT IS USUALLY SERVED WITH NOODLES OR RICE, AND FISH IS OFTEN ADDED FOR GOOD MEASURE.

SERVES 6

INGREDIENTS

15ml/1 tbsp tamarind pulp
150ml/¼ pint/⅔ cup warm water
2 tomatoes
115g/4oz spinach or Chinese leaves
   (Chinese cabbage)
115g/4oz peeled cooked large prawns
   (shrimp), thawed if frozen
1.2 litres/2 pints/5 cups prepared
   fish stock (see Cook's Tip)
½ mooli (daikon), peeled and diced
115g/4oz green beans, cut into
   1cm/½in lengths
225g/8oz piece of cod or haddock
   fillet, skinned and cut into strips
Thai fish sauce, to taste
squeeze of lemon juice, to taste
salt and ground black pepper
boiled rice or noodles, to serve

1 Put the tamarind pulp in a bowl and pour over the warm water. Set aside while you peel and chop the tomatoes, discarding the seeds. Strip the spinach or Chinese leaves from the stems and tear into small pieces.

2 Remove the heads and shells from the prawns, leaving the tails intact.

3 Pour the prepared fish stock into a large pan and add the diced mooli. Cook the mooli for 5 minutes, then add the beans and continue to cook for 3–5 minutes more.

4 Add the fish strips, tomato and spinach. Strain in the tamarind juice and cook for 2 minutes. Stir in the prawns and cook for 1–2 minutes to heat. Season with salt and pepper and add a little fish sauce and lemon juice to taste. Transfer to individual serving bowls and serve immediately, with rice or noodles.

COOK'S TIP

A good fish stock is essential for this dish. Ask your fishmonger for about 675g/1½lb fish bones. Wash them, then place in a large pan with 2 litres/ 3½ pints/8 cups water. Add half a peeled onion, a piece of bruised peeled ginger, and a little salt and pepper. Bring to the boil, skim, then simmer for 20 minutes. Cool slightly, then strain. Freeze unused fish stock.

Energy 52kcal/218kJ; Protein 10.6g; Carbohydrate 1.3g, of which sugars 1.3g; Fat 0.5g, of which saturates 0.1g; Cholesterol 55mg; Calcium 31mg; Fibre 0.6g; Sodium 62mg.

STIR-FRIED PRAWNS WITH MANGETOUTS ★

MANGETOUT MEANS "EAT ALL" AND YOU CAN SAFELY DO JUST THAT WHEN A RECIPE IS AS LOW IN FAT AS THIS ONE IS. THE PRAWNS REMAIN BEAUTIFULLY SUCCULENT AND THE SAUCE IS DELICIOUS.

SERVES 4

INGREDIENTS

300ml/½ pint/1¼ cups fish stock
350g/12oz raw tiger prawns (jumbo
  shrimp), peeled and deveined
15ml/1 tbsp vegetable oil
1 garlic clove, finely chopped
225g/8oz/2 cups mangetouts
  (snow peas)
1.5ml/¼ tsp salt
15ml/1 tbsp mirin or dry sherry
15ml/1 tbsp oyster sauce
5ml/1 tsp cornflour (cornstarch)
5ml/1 tsp caster (superfine) sugar
15ml/1 tbsp cold water
1.5ml/¼ tsp sesame oil

1 Bring the fish stock to the boil in a frying pan. Add the prawns. Cook gently for 2 minutes until the prawns have turned pink, then lift them out on a slotted spoon and set aside.

2 Heat the vegetable oil in a non-stick frying pan or wok. When the oil is very hot, add the chopped garlic and cook for a few seconds, then add the mangetouts. Sprinkle with the salt. Stir-fry for 1 minute.

3 Add the prawns and mirin or sherry to the pan or wok. Toss the ingredients together over the heat for a few seconds, then add the oyster sauce and toss again.

4 Mix the cornflour and sugar to a paste with the water. Add to the pan and cook, stirring constantly, until the sauce thickens slightly. Drizzle with sesame oil.

Energy 125kcal/524kJ; Protein 17.6g; Carbohydrate 5.2g, of which sugars 3.6g; Fat 3.4g, of which saturates 0.4g; Cholesterol 171mg; Calcium 96mg; Fibre 1.3g; Sodium 436mg.

GINGERED PRAWNS WITH NOODLES ★

DRIED PORCINI MUSHROOMS ARE OFTEN REGARDED BY MANY AS HAVING A RICHER FLAVOUR THAN CHINESE DRIED MUSHROOMS, SO THEY ARE THE PREFERRED CHOICE FOR THIS FUSION RECIPE.

2 Put the sliced spring onions, grated ginger and diced red pepper into a pan with the mushrooms and their liquid.

3 Bring to the boil, cover the pan and cook for about 5 minutes until the vegetables are tender.

4 Stir in the sliced water chestnuts, then add the soy sauce and sherry. Toss in the prawns and mix them with the sauce. Cover and cook gently for 2 minutes.

SERVES 4–6

INGREDIENTS

15g/½oz dried porcini mushrooms
300ml/½ pint/1¼ cups hot water
bunch of spring onions (scallions),
  cut into thick diagonal slices
2.5cm/1in piece fresh root ginger,
  peeled and grated
1 red (bell) pepper, seeded and diced
225g/8oz can water chestnuts, sliced
45ml/3 tbsp light soy sauce
30ml/2 tbsp sherry
350g/12oz large cooked prawns
  (shrimp), peeled
225g/8oz egg noodles

1 Put the dried porcini mushrooms into a bowl. Pour over the hot water and set aside to soak for 20 minutes.

5 Cook the egg noodles according to the instructions on the packet. Drain, heap on a warmed serving dish, spoon the hot prawns on top and serve immediately.

Energy 224kcal/947kJ; Protein 16.7g; Carbohydrate 31.3g, of which sugars 4.3g; Fat 3.8g, of which saturates 1g; Cholesterol 125mg; Calcium 73mg; Fibre 2.3g; Sodium 717mg.

SWEET AND SOUR PRAWNS ★

HEALTHIER THAN CONVENTIONAL SWEET AND SOUR PRAWNS, THESE ARE NOT DEEP-FRIED BUT RATHER JUST HEATED THROUGH IN THE TASTY SAUCE. COOKED THIS WAY, THEY STAY SUCCULENT.

SERVES 4–6

INGREDIENTS

1 small cos or romaine lettuce
350g/11oz cooked tiger prawns
   (jumbo shrimps) in their shells
For the sauce
15ml/1 tbsp vegetable oil
15ml/1 tbsp finely chopped
   spring onions (scallions)
10ml/2 tsp finely chopped fresh
   root ginger
30ml/2 tbsp light soy sauce
30ml/2 tbsp soft light
   brown sugar
45ml/3 tbsp rice vinegar
15ml/1 tbsp Chinese rice wine or
   dry sherry
about 120ml/4fl oz/½ cup chicken
   or vegetable stock
15ml/1 tbsp cornflour
   (cornstarch) paste
few drops sesame oil

1 Separate the lettuce leaves and rinse them under cold running water. Arrange them on a platter.

2 Pull the soft legs off the cooked prawns without removing the shells. Dry the peeled prawns well with kitchen paper and set aside.

3 To make the sauce, heat the oil in a preheated wok. Add the spring onions and ginger and toss to mix. Drizzle over the soy sauce, sugar, rice vinegar, Chinese rice wine or dry sherry. Add the stock, and bring to the boil.

4 Add the prawns to the sauce and toss over the heat to coat them thoroughly and heat them through. Thicken the sauce with the cornflour paste, stirring until smooth. Sprinkle with the sesame oil. Serve on a bed of lettuce.

VARIATION
It is not essential to use tiger prawns (jumbo shrimp). The smaller common prawns (shrimp) are not as luxurious, but still work well.

Energy 49kcal/208kJ; Protein 5.2g; Carbohydrate 2g, of which sugars 0.5g; Fat 2g, of which saturates 0.3g; Cholesterol 61mg; Calcium 27mg; Fibre 0g; Sodium 707mg.

GONG BOA PRAWNS ★

THERE'S SOMETHING DECADENT ABOUT TIGER PRAWNS, BUT WITH A TOTAL FAT CONTENT OF WELL UNDER 5 GRAMS AND A LOW SATURATED FAT CONTENT, THIS RECIPE CAN BE ENJOYED REGULARLY.

SERVES 4

INGREDIENTS
   350g/12oz raw tiger prawns
   (jumbo shrimp)
   ½ cucumber, about 75g/3oz
   300ml/½ pint/1¼ cups fish stock
   15ml/1 tbsp vegetable oil
   2.5ml/½ tsp crushed dried chillies
   ½ green (bell) pepper, seeded and
   cut into 2.5cm/1in strips
   1 small carrot, thinly sliced
   30ml/2 tbsp tomato ketchup
   45ml/3 tbsp rice vinegar
   15ml/1 tbsp caster sugar
   150ml/¼ pint/⅔ cup vegetable stock
   50g/2oz/½ cup drained canned
   pineapple chunks
   10ml/2 tsp cornflour (cornstarch)
   15ml/1 tbsp cold water
   salt

1 Peel and devein the prawns. Rub them gently with 2.5ml/½ tsp salt; leave them for a few minutes and then wash and dry thoroughly.

2 Using a narrow peeler or cannelle knife, pare strips of skin off the cucumber to give a stripy effect. Cut the cucumber in half lengthways and scoop out the seeds with a teaspoon. Cut the flesh into 5mm/¼in crescents.

3 Bring the fish stock to the boil in a pan. Add the prawns, lower the heat and poach the prawns for 2 minutes until they turn pink, then lift them out using a slotted spoon and set aside.

4 Heat the oil in a non-stick frying pan or wok over a high heat. Fry the chillies for a few seconds, then add the pepper strips and carrot slices and stir-fry for 1 minute more.

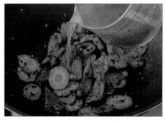

5 Spoon the tomato ketchup into a jug (pitcher) and stir in the vinegar, sugar and vegetable stock, with 1.5ml/¼ tsp salt. Pour into the pan and cook for 3 minutes more.

6 Add the prawns, cucumber and pineapple to the pan and cook for 2 minutes more. Mix the cornflour to a paste with the water.

7 Add the mixture to the pan and cook, stirring constantly, until the sauce thickens. Serve immediately.

COOK'S TIP
Omit the chillies if you like, or increase the quantity for a spicier dish.

Energy 147kcal/617kJ; Protein 16.3g; Carbohydrate 13.2g, of which sugars 10.7g; Fat 3.5g, of which saturates 0.5g; Cholesterol 171mg; Calcium 88mg; Fibre 1.1g; Sodium 296mg.

CHILLI-SEARED SCALLOPS <u>on</u> PAK CHOI ★★

TENDER, SUCCULENT SCALLOPS ARE SIMPLY DIVINE MARINATED IN FRESH CHILLI, FRAGRANT MINT AND AROMATIC BASIL, THEN QUICKLY SEARED IN A PIPING HOT WOK AND SERVED ON WILTED GREENS.

SERVES 4

INGREDIENTS

20–24 king scallops or 24 queen
  scallops, cleaned
30ml/2 tbsp vegetable oil
finely grated rind and juice of
  1 lemon
15ml/1 tbsp finely chopped
  fresh mint
15ml/1 tbsp finely chopped
  fresh basil
1 fresh red chilli, seeded and
  finely chopped
salt and ground black pepper
500g/1¼lb pak choi (bok choy)
extra chopped fresh mint and basil,
  to garnish (optional)

1 Place the scallops in a shallow, non-metallic bowl in a single layer. In a clean bowl, whisk together the oil, lemon rind and juice, chopped herbs and chilli and spoon over the scallops. Season well with salt and black pepper, cover the bowl and set aside for 10 minutes to allow the flavours to blend.

2 Using a sharp knife, cut each pak choi lengthways into four pieces.

3 Heat a frying pan or wok over a high heat. When the pan or wok is hot, drain the scallops (reserving the marinade) and add to the wok. Cook the scallops for 1 minute on each side, or until cooked to your liking.

4 Pour the marinade over the scallops and heat through briefly, then remove the wok from the heat and cover to keep warm.

5 Cook the pak choi for 2–3 minutes in a steamer over a pan of simmering water until the leaves are wilted.

6 Divide the greens among four warmed serving plates, then top with the reserved scallops and their juices.

7 Add more chopped herbs as a garnish if you like, and serve immediately.

Energy 199kcal/833kJ; Protein 26.7g; Carbohydrate 5.4g, of which sugars 1.9g; Fat 7.9g, of which saturates 1.2g; Cholesterol 47mg; Calcium 242mg; Fibre 2.6g; Sodium 355mg.

TIGER PRAWNS WITH HAM, CHICKEN AND EGG NOODLES ★★★

THIS RECIPE COMBINES PRAWNS WITH HAM AND CHICKEN, WHICH MAY SEEM UNCONVENTIONAL UNTIL YOU REMEMBER THAN THE SPANISH DO SOMETHING VERY SIMILAR IN THEIR PAELLA.

SERVES 4–6

INGREDIENTS
30ml/2 tbsp vegetable oil
2 garlic cloves, sliced
5ml/1 tsp fresh root ginger, peeled
   and chopped
2 fresh red chillies, seeded
   and chopped
75g/3oz lean ham, thinly
   sliced (optional)
1 skinless chicken breast fillet,
   thinly sliced
16 uncooked tiger prawns (jumbo
   shrimp), peeled, tails left intact
   and deveined
115g/4oz green beans, trimmed
225g/8oz beansprouts
50g/2oz Chinese chives
450g/1lb egg noodles, cooked in
   boiling water until tender
30ml/2 tbsp dark soy sauce
15ml/1 tbsp oyster sauce
salt and ground black pepper
5ml/1 tsp sesame oil
2 spring onions (scallions), cut into
   strips, and fresh coriander (cilantro)
   leaves, to garnish

1 Heat 15ml/1 tbsp of the oil in a wok or large frying pan. When the oil is hot, fry the garlic, ginger and chillies for 2 minutes.

2 Add the prepared ham, chicken, prawns and green beans to the wok or frying pan.

3 Stir-fry the meat for about 2 minutes over high heat or until the chicken and prawns are thoroughly cooked. Transfer the mixture to a bowl and set aside.

4 Heat the remaining oil in the wok or frying pan. When the oil is hot, add the beansprouts and Chinese chives. Stir-fry for 1–2 minutes.

5 Add the noodles and toss and stir to mix. Season with soy sauce, oyster sauce, salt and pepper.

6 Return the prawn mixture to the wok. Reheat and mix well with the noodles. Sprinkle with the sesame oil.

7 Serve garnished with the spring onions and coriander leaves.

VARIATIONS
You could use lean bacon, trimmed of fat, in place of the ham; and skinless turkey breast fillet in place of the chicken. You could also add extra green beans, mangetouts (snow peas) or sugar snap peas in place of the ham and chicken, if you prefer.

COOK'S TIP
Chinese chives, sometimes called garlic chives, have a delicate garlic/onion flavour. If they are not available, use regular chives, the green parts of spring onions (scallions), or just substitute 2 finely chopped shallots and a crushed garlic clove.

Energy 397kcal/1674kJ; Protein 21.3g; Carbohydrate 56.4g, of which sugars 3.2g; Fat 11.1g, of which saturates 2.4g; Cholesterol 89mg; Calcium 72mg; Fibre 3.3g; Sodium 567mg.

GREEN PRAWN CURRY ★

GREEN CURRY HAS BECOME A FIRM FAVOURITE IN THE WEST, AND THIS PRAWN DISH IS JUST ONE OF A RANGE OF DELICIOUS GREEN CURRY RECIPES. HOME-MADE GREEN CURRY PASTE HAS THE BEST FLAVOUR, BUT YOU CAN ALSO BUY IT FROM GOOD SUPERMARKETS IF YOU ARE SHORT OF TIME.

2 Add the prawns, kaffir lime leaves and chopped lemon grass. Fry for 2 minutes, until the prawns are pink.

3 Stir in the coconut milk and bring to a gentle boil. Simmer, stirring for about 5 minutes or until the prawns are tender.

SERVES 6

INGREDIENTS
    15ml/1 tbsp sunflower oil
    30ml/2 tbsp green curry paste
    450g/1lb raw king prawns (jumbo
      shrimp), peeled and deveined
    4 kaffir lime leaves, torn
    1 lemon grass stalk, bruised
      and chopped
    250ml/8fl oz/1 cup reduced-fat
      coconut milk
    30ml/2 tbsp Thai fish sauce
    ½ cucumber, seeded and cut into
      thin batons
    10–15 basil leaves
    4 green chillies, sliced, to garnish

1 Heat the sunflower oil in a wok or large pan until sizzling hot. Add the green curry paste and fry over a gentle heat for several minutes until bubbling and fragrant, stirring the mixture continually with chopsticks.

4 Stir in the fish sauce, cucumber batons and whole basil leaves, then top with the green chillies and serve from the pan.

VARIATION
Strips of skinless chicken breast fillet can be used in place of the prawns if you prefer. Add them to the pan in step 2 and fry until browned on all sides.

Energy 92kcal/385kJ; Protein 13.7g; Carbohydrate 2.6g, of which sugars 2.5g; Fat 3g, of which saturates 0.5g; Cholesterol 146mg; Calcium 92mg; Fibre 0.4g; Sodium 191mg.

PRAWNS WITH YELLOW CURRY PASTE ★

FISH AND SHELLFISH, SUCH AS PRAWNS, AND COCONUT MILK, WERE MADE FOR EACH OTHER. THIS IS A VERY QUICK RECIPE IF YOU MAKE THE YELLOW CURRY PASTE IN ADVANCE, OR BUY IT READY-MADE. IT KEEPS WELL IN A SCREW-TOP JAR IN THE REFRIGERATOR FOR UP TO FOUR WEEKS.

SERVES 6

INGREDIENTS

600ml/1 pint/2½ cups reduced-fat
  coconut milk
30ml/2 tbsp yellow curry paste
15ml/1 tbsp Thai fish sauce
2.5ml/½ tsp salt
5ml/1 tsp granulated sugar
450g/1lb raw king prawns (jumbo
  shrimp), peeled and deveined
225g/8oz cherry tomatoes
juice of ½ lime
red (bell) peppers, seeded and
  cut into thin strips, and fresh
  coriander (cilantro) leaves,
  to garnish

1 Put half the coconut milk in a wok or large pan and bring to the boil. Add the yellow curry paste and stir until it disperses. Lower the heat and simmer gently for about 10 minutes.

2 Add the fish sauce, salt, sugar and remaining coconut milk to the sauce. Simmer for 5 minutes more.

3 Add the prawns and cherry tomatoes. Simmer very gently for about 5 minutes until the prawns are pink and tender.

4 Spoon into a serving dish, sprinkle with lime juice and garnish with strips of pepper and coriander.

COOK'S TIPS
• Unused coconut milk can be stored in the refrigerator for 1–2 days, or poured into a freezer container and frozen for up to a month.
• If making your own coconut milk, instead of discarding the spent coconut, it can be reused to make a second batch of coconut milk. However, this will be of a poorer quality and it should only be used to extend a good quality first quantity of milk.
• To make coconut cream, leave newly made coconut milk to stand for 10 minutes. The coconut cream will float to the top – skim it off with a spoon and use in the usual way.

Energy 94kcal/397kJ; Protein 13.8g; Carbohydrate 7g, of which sugars 6.9g; Fat 1.4g, of which saturates 0.4g; Cholesterol 146mg; Calcium 92mg; Fibre 0.4g; Sodium 434mg.

SAMBAL GORENG <u>WITH</u> PRAWNS ★

*THIS IS AN IMMENSELY USEFUL AND ADAPTABLE LOW-FAT SAUCE. HERE IT IS COMBINED WITH
PRAWNS AND GREEN PEPPER, BUT YOU COULD ADD FINE STRIPS OF FRESHLY COOKED CALF'S LIVER,
CHICKEN LIVERS, TOMATOES, GREEN BEANS OR EVEN HARD-BOILED EGGS TO THE DISH.*

SERVES 6

INGREDIENTS
    350g/12oz peeled cooked
      prawns (shrimp)
    1 green (bell) pepper, seeded
      and sliced
    60ml/4 tbsp tamarind juice
    pinch of sugar
    45ml/3 tbsp reduced-fat
      coconut milk
    boiled rice, to serve
    lime rind and red onion, to garnish
For the sambal goreng
    2.5cm/1in cube shrimp paste
    2 onions, roughly chopped
    2 garlic cloves, roughly chopped
    2.5cm/1in piece fresh galangal,
      peeled and sliced
    10ml/2 tsp chilli sambal
    1.5ml/¼ tsp salt
    15ml/1 tbsp sunflower oil
    45ml/3 tbsp tomato purée (paste)
    600ml/1 pint/2½ cups water

1 Make the sambal goreng. Grind the
shrimp paste with the onions and garlic
using a mortar and pestle. Alternatively
put in a food processor and process
to a paste. Add the galangal, chilli
sambal and salt. Process or pound to
a fine paste.

COOK'S TIP
Store the remaining sauce in the
refrigerator for up to 3 days or freeze
it for up to 3 months.

2 Heat the oil in a wok or frying pan
and fry the paste for 1–2 minutes,
without browning, until the mixture
gives off a rich aroma. Stir in the tomato
purée and the stock or water and cook
for 10 minutes. Ladle half the sauce
into a bowl and leave to cool. This
leftover sauce can be used in another
recipe (see Cook's Tip).

3 Add the prawns and green pepper
to the remaining sauce. Cook over a
medium heat for 3–4 minutes, then
stir in the tamarind juice, sugar and
coconut milk. Spoon into warmed
serving bowls and garnish with strips of
lime rind and sliced red onion. Serve
immediately with boiled rice.

VARIATIONS
• To make tomato sambal goreng, add
450g/1lb peeled coarsely chopped
tomatoes to the sauce mixture, before
stirring in the stock or water.
• To make egg sambal goreng, add three
or four chopped hard-boiled eggs, and two
peeled chopped tomatoes to the sauce.

Energy 86kcal/359kJ; Protein 11.6g; Carbohydrate 4.6g, of which sugars 4.1g; Fat 2.4g, of which saturates 0.3g; Cholesterol 118mg; Calcium 67mg; Fibre 0.9g; Sodium 175mg

PRAWN AND CAULIFLOWER CURRY ★

THIS IS A BASIC FISHERMAN'S CURRY ORIGINALLY FROM THE SOUTHERN COAST OF VIETNAM. SIMPLE TO MAKE, IT WOULD USUALLY BE EATEN FROM A COMMUNAL BOWL, OR FROM THE WOK ITSELF, AND SERVED WITH NOODLES, RICE OR CHUNKS OF BAGUETTE TO MOP UP THE DELICIOUSLY FRAGRANT SAUCE.

SERVES 4

INGREDIENTS

   450g/1lb raw tiger prawns (jumbo
     shrimp), shelled and cleaned
   juice of 1 lime
   15ml/1 tbsp sunflower oil
   1 red onion, roughly chopped
   2 garlic cloves, roughly chopped
   2 Thai chillies, seeded and chopped
   1 cauliflower, broken into florets
   5ml/1 tsp sugar
   2 star anise, dry-fried and ground
   10ml/2 tsp fenugreek, dry-fried
    and ground
   450ml/¾ pint/2 cups reduced-fat
    coconut milk
   chopped fresh coriander (cilantro)
    leaves, to garnish
   salt and ground black pepper

1 In a bowl, toss the prawns in the lime juice and set aside. Heat a wok or heavy pan and add the oil. Stir in the onion, garlic and chillies. As they brown, add the cauliflower. Stir-fry for 2–3 minutes.

VARIATION
Other popular combinations include prawns with butternut squash or pumpkin.

2 Toss in the sugar and spices. Add the coconut milk, stirring to make sure it is thoroughly combined. Reduce the heat and simmer for 10–15 minutes, or until the liquid has reduced and thickened a little. Add the prawns and lime juice and cook for 1–2 minutes, or until the prawns turn opaque. Season to taste, and sprinkle with coriander. Serve hot.

Energy 157kcal/664kJ; Protein 24.7g; Carbohydrate 10.4g, of which sugars 9.4g; Fat 2.2g, of which saturates 0.6g; Cholesterol 219mg; Calcium 169mg; Fibre 2.7g; Sodium 352mg.

STEAMED MUSSELS <u>WITH</u> CHILLI <u>AND</u> GINGER ★

THIS SIMPLE DISH IS THE ASIAN VERSION OF THE FRENCH CLASSIC, MOULES MARINIÈRE. HERE, THE MUSSELS ARE STEAMED OPEN IN A HERB-INFUSED STOCK RATHER THAN IN WHITE WINE.

<u>SERVES 4</u>

INGREDIENTS
    600ml/1 pint/2½ cups chicken
        stock
    1 Thai chilli, seeded and chopped
    2 shallots, finely chopped
    3 lemon grass stalks,
        finely chopped
    1 bunch ginger or basil leaves
    1kg/2¼lb fresh mussels, cleaned
        and bearded
    salt and ground black pepper

COOK'S TIP
Aromatic ginger leaves are hard to find outside Asia. If you can't find them, basil or coriander (cilantro) will work well.

1 Pour the chicken stock into a deep pan. Add the chopped chilli, shallots, lemon grass and most of the ginger or basil leaves, retaining a few leaves for the garnish. Bring to the boil. Cover and simmer for 10–15 minutes, then season to taste.

2 Discard any mussels that remain open when tapped, then add the remaining mussels to the stock. Stir well, cover and cook for 2 minutes, or until the mussels have opened. Discard any that remain closed. Ladle the mussels and cooking liquid into individual bowls.

CLAMS AND SPRING ONIONS ★

SHELLFISH ARE A VERY POPULAR FOOD IN SOUTH-EAST ASIA, AND CLAMS ARE A FIRM FAVOURITE. IN SEASON, THEY BECOME SWEET AND JUICY, AND ARE EXCELLENT WITH THIS SWEET-AND-SOUR DRESSING.

SERVES 4

INGREDIENTS

   900g/2lb carpet shell clams or
   cockles, or 300g/11oz can baby
   clams in brine, or 130g/4½oz
   cooked and shelled cockles
   15ml/1 tbsp sake
   8 spring onions (scallions), green
   and white parts separated, then
   chopped in half
   10g/¼oz dried wakame
For the *nuta* dressing
   60ml/4 tbsp shiro miso
   20ml/4 tsp caster (superfine) sugar
   30ml/2 tbsp sake
   15ml/1 tbsp rice vinegar
   about 1.5ml/¼ tsp salt
   7.5ml/1½ tsp English (hot) mustard
   sprinkling of dashi-no-moto (if using
   canned shellfish)

1 If using fresh clams or cockles, wash the shells under running water. Discard any that remain open when tapped.

2 Pour 1cm/½in water into a small pan and add the clams or cockles. Sprinkle with the sake, cover, then bring to the boil. Cook over a vigorous heat for 5 minutes after the water reaches boiling point. Remove from the heat and leave to stand for 2 minutes. Discard any shells which remain closed.

3 Drain the shells and keep the liquid in a small bowl. Wait until the shells have cooled slightly, then remove the meat from most of the shells.

4 Cook the white part of the spring onions in a pan of rapidly boiling water, then add the remaining green parts after 2 minutes. Cook for 4 minutes altogether. Drain well.

5 Mix the shiro miso, sugar, sake, rice vinegar and salt for the *nuta* dressing, in a small pan. Stir in 45ml/3 tbsp of the reserved clam liquid, or the same amount of water and dashi-no-moto, if using canned shellfish.

6 Put the pan on a medium heat and stir constantly. When the sugar has dissolved, add the mustard. Check the seasoning and add a little more salt if desired. Remove from the heat and leave to cool.

7 Soak the wakame in a bowl of water for 10 minutes. Drain and squeeze out excess moisture by hand.

8 Mix together the clams or cockles, onions, wakame and dressing in a bowl. Heap up in a large bowl or divide among four small bowls and serve cold.

Energy 114kcal/482kJ; Protein 12.8g; Carbohydrate 13.2g, of which sugars 11.6g; Fat 0.6g, of which saturates 0.2g; Cholesterol 50mg; Calcium 71mg; Fibre 0.3g; Sodium 1762mg.

LOBSTER AND CRAB STEAMED IN BEER ★

IN SPITE OF ITS APPEARANCE ON MENUS IN RESTAURANTS THAT SPECIALIZE IN THE COMPLEX IMPERIAL DISHES OF VIETNAM, THIS RECIPE IS VERY EASY TO MAKE.

3 Add the remaining flavouring ingredients to the beer with the fish sauce and lemon juice. Pour into a dipping bowl and serve immediately with the hot lobsters and crabs, with extra splashes of fish sauce if you like.

VARIATIONS
Prawns (shrimp) and mussels are also delicious cooked this way. Replace the lemon with lime if you like.

COOK'S TIP
Whether you cook the lobsters and crabs at the same time depends on the number of people you are cooking for and the size of your steamer. However, they don't take long to cook so it is easy to steam them in batches. In the markets and restaurants of Vietnam, you can find crabs that are 60cm/24in in diameter, which may feed several people but require a huge steamer. Depending on the size and availability of the lobsters and crabs, you can make this recipe for as many people as you like, because the quantities are simple to adjust. For those who like their food fiery, splash a little chilli sauce into the beer broth.

SERVES 4–6

INGREDIENTS
- 4 uncooked lobsters, about 450g/1lb each
- 4 uncooked crabs, about 225g/8oz each
- 600ml/1 pint/2½ cups beer
- 4 spring onions (scallions), trimmed and chopped into long pieces
- 4cm/1½in fresh root ginger, peeled and finely sliced
- 2 green or red Thai chillies, seeded and finely sliced
- 3 lemon grass stalks, finely sliced
- 1 bunch fresh dill, fronds chopped
- 1 bunch each fresh basil and coriander (cilantro), stalks removed, leaves chopped
- about 30ml/2 tbsp fish sauce, plus extra for serving
- juice of 1 lemon
- salt and ground black pepper

1 Clean the lobsters and crabs thoroughly and rub them with salt and pepper. Place them in a large steamer and pour the beer into the base.

2 Sprinkle half the spring onions, ginger, chillies, lemon grass and herbs over the lobsters and crabs, and steam for about 10 minutes, or until the lobsters turn red. Lift them on to a warmed serving dish.

Energy 190kcal/801kJ; Protein 35.2g; Carbohydrate 1.5g, of which sugars 1.4g; Fat 4.9g, of which saturates 0.7g; Cholesterol 158mg; Calcium 86mg; Fibre 0.8g; Sodium 589mg.

ASPARAGUS WITH CRAB MEAT SAUCE ★★

THE SUBTLE FLAVOUR OF FRESH ASPARAGUS IS ENHANCED BY THE EQUALLY DELICATE TASTE OF THE CRAB MEAT IN THIS CLASSIC DISH. THIS IS PERFECT SERVED UP AS PART OF A LARGE DINNER.

SERVES 4

INGREDIENTS

  450g/1lb asparagus, trimmed
  15ml/1 tbsp vegetable oil
  4 thin slices of fresh root ginger
  2 garlic cloves, finely chopped
  115g/4oz/⅔ cup fresh or thawed
    frozen white crab meat
  5ml/1 tsp sake or dry sherry
  150ml/¼ pint/⅔ cup
    semi-skimmed (low-fat) milk
  15ml/1 tbsp cornflour (cornstarch)
  45ml/3 tbsp cold water
  salt and ground white pepper
  1 spring onion (scallion), thinly
    shredded, to garnish

3 Add the crab meat to the flavoured oil and toss to mix. Drizzle over the sherry, then pour in the milk. Cook, stirring often, for 2 minutes.

4 Meanwhile, put the cornflour in a small bowl with the water and mix to a smooth paste.

5 Add the cornflour paste to the pan, stirring constantly, then cook the mixture, continuing to stir, until it forms a thick and creamy sauce.

6 Season to taste with salt and pepper, spoon over the asparagus, garnish with shreds of spring onion and serve.

1 Bring a large pan of lightly salted water to the boil. Poach the asparagus for about 5 minutes until just crisp-tender. Drain well and keep hot in a shallow serving dish.

2 Bruise the slices of ginger with a rolling pin. Heat the oil in a non-stick frying pan or wok. Add the ginger and garlic for 1 minute and cook to release their flavour, then lift them out with a slotted spoon and discard them.

Energy 199kcal/833kJ; Protein 26.7g; Carbohydrate 5.4g, of which sugars 1.9g; Fat 7.9g, of which saturates 1.2g; Cholesterol 47mg; Calcium 242mg; Fibre 2.6g; Sodium 355mg.

CURRIED SEAFOOD WITH COCONUT MILK ★

THIS CURRY IS BASED ON A THAI CLASSIC. THE LOVELY GREEN COLOUR IS IMPARTED BY THE FINELY CHOPPED CHILLI AND FRESH HERBS ADDED DURING THE LAST FEW MOMENTS OF COOKING.

SERVES 4

INGREDIENTS
225g/8oz small ready-prepared squid
225g/8oz raw tiger prawns
   (jumbo shrimp)
400ml/14fl oz/1²⁄₃ cups reduced-fat
   coconut milk
2 kaffir lime leaves, finely shredded
30ml/2 tbsp Thai fish sauce
450g/1lb firm white fish fillets,
   skinned, boned and cut into chunks
2 fresh green chillies, seeded and
   finely chopped
30ml/2 tbsp torn fresh basil or
   coriander (cilantro) leaves
squeeze of fresh lime juice
cooked Thai jasmine rice, to serve
For the curry paste
   6 spring onions (scallions),
      coarsely chopped
   4 fresh coriander (cilantro) stems,
      coarsely chopped, plus 45ml/3 tbsp
      chopped fresh coriander (cilantro)
   4 kaffir lime leaves, shredded
   8 fresh green chillies, seeded and
      coarsely chopped
   1 lemon grass stalk,
      coarsely chopped
   2.5cm/1in piece fresh root ginger,
      peeled and coarsely chopped
   45ml/3 tbsp chopped fresh basil
   5ml/1 tsp sunflower oil

1 Make the curry paste. Put all the ingredients, except the oil, in a food processor and process to a paste. Alternatively, pound together in a mortar with a pestle. Stir in the oil.

2 Rinse the squid and pat dry with kitchen paper. Cut the bodies into rings and halve the tentacles, if necessary.

3 Heat a wok until hot, add the prawns and stir-fry, without any oil, for about 4 minutes, until they turn pink.

4 Remove the prawns from the wok and leave to cool slightly, then peel off the shells, saving a few shells on for the garnish. Make a slit along the back of each one and remove the black vein.

5 Pour the coconut milk into the wok, then bring to the boil over a medium heat, stirring constantly. Add 30ml/ 2 tbsp of curry paste, the shredded lime leaves and fish sauce and stir well to mix. Reduce the heat to low and simmer gently for about 10 minutes.

6 Add the squid, prawns and chunks of fish and cook for about 2 minutes, until the seafood is tender. Take care not to overcook the squid as it will become tough very quickly.

7 Just before serving, stir in the chillies and the torn basil or coriander leaves. Taste and adjust the flavour with a squeeze of lime juice. Garnish the curry with prawns in their shells, and serve with Thai jasmine rice.

VARIATIONS
• You can use any firm-fleshed white fish for this curry, such as monkfish, cod, haddock or John Dory.
• If you prefer, you could substitute shelled scallops for the squid. Slice them in half horizontally and add them with the prawns (shrimp). As with the squid, be careful not to overcook them.

Energy 211kcal/894kJ; Protein 39.8g; Carbohydrate 5.9g, of which sugars 5.2g; Fat 3.3g, of which saturates 0.7g; Cholesterol 288mg; Calcium 116mg; Fibre 0.6g; Sodium 351mg.

CHICKEN AND DUCK

In China, where thrift is highly prized, cooks tend to buy whole birds. The breast portions are sliced for a stir-fry, the rest of the meat used in a curry, and the bones simmered to make soup or stock. Chicken and duck are the most favoured birds to eat, but from a low-fat perspective, chicken is a more sensible choice than duck. Remove the skin and any obvious fat and use a low-fat cooking method like steaming, stir-frying or cooking in vegetable stock.

CHICKEN SATAY <u>WITH</u> PEANUT SAUCE ★★

THESE MOUTHWATERING MINIATURE KEBABS ARE POPULAR ALL OVER SOUTH-EAST ASIA. THE PEANUT DIPPING SAUCE IS THE PERFECT PARTNER FOR THE MARINATED CHICKEN.

SERVES 4

INGREDIENTS
  4 skinless, chicken breast fillets
For the marinade
  2 garlic cloves, crushed
  2.5cm/1in piece fresh root ginger,
    finely grated
  10ml/2 tsp Thai fish sauce
  30ml/2 tbsp light soy sauce
  15ml/1 tbsp clear honey
For the satay sauce
  45ml/3 tbsp crunchy peanut butter
  1/2 fresh red chilli, seeded and
    finely chopped
  juice of 1/2 lime
  30ml/2 tbsp reduced-fat
    coconut milk
  salt

1 First, make the satay sauce. Put all the ingredients in a food processor or blender. Process until smooth, then check the seasoning and add more salt or lime juice if necessary. Spoon the sauce into a bowl, cover with clear film (plastic wrap) and set aside.

2 Using a sharp knife, slice each chicken breast into four long strips. Put all the marinade ingredients in a large bowl and mix well, then add the chicken strips and toss together until thoroughly coated. Cover and leave for at least 30 minutes in the refrigerator to marinate. Meanwhile, soak 16 wooden satay sticks or kebab skewers in water, to prevent them from burning during cooking.

3 Preheat the grill (broiler) to high or prepare the barbecue. Drain the satay sticks or skewers. Drain the chicken strips. Thread one strip on to each satay stick or skewer. Grill (broil) for 3 minutes on each side, or until the chicken is golden brown and cooked through. Serve immediately with the satay sauce.

Energy 236kcal/992kJ; Protein 38.8g; Carbohydrate 3.4g, of which sugars 2.6g; Fat 7.5g, of which saturates 1.9g; Cholesterol 105mg; Calcium 15mg; Fibre 0.6g; Sodium 672mg.

BANG BANG CHICKEN ★★

DESPITE HAVING A RICH SAUCE BASED ON TOASTED SESAME PASTE, THIS CHICKEN DISH IS RELATIVELY LOW IN FAT, WITH SATURATED FAT LEVELS THAT ARE WELL WITHIN ACCEPTABLE LIMITS.

SERVES 4

INGREDIENTS
    3 skinless boneless chicken breast
        fillets, about 450g/1lb
    1 garlic clove, crushed
    2.5ml/½ tsp black peppercorns
    1 small onion, halved
    1 large cucumber
    salt and ground black pepper
For the sauce
    45ml/3 tbsp toasted sesame paste
    15ml/1 tbsp light soy sauce
    15ml/1 tbsp wine vinegar
    2 spring onions (scallions),
        finely chopped
    2 garlic cloves, crushed
    5cm/2½in fresh root ginger, peeled
        and cut into matchsticks
    15ml/1 tbsp Sichuan peppercorns,
        dry fried and crushed
    5ml/1 tsp light brown sugar
    15ml/1 tbsp chilli sauce, to serve

1 Place the chicken fillets in a pan. Just cover with water, add the garlic, peppercorns and onion and bring the water to the boil. Skim off any scum as it rises to the surface, stir in salt and pepper to taste, then cover the pan.

2 Cook for 25 minutes or until the chicken is just tender. Drain, reserving the stock in a bowl.

3 Make the sauce by mixing the toasted sesame paste with 45ml/3 tbsp of the chicken stock. Add the soy sauce, vinegar, spring onions, garlic, ginger and crushed peppercorns to the sesame mixture. Stir in sugar to taste.

4 Peel the cucumber, then cut in half lengthways and remove the seeds. Cut into batons. Spread on a platter. Cut the chicken fillets into pieces of about the same size as the cucumber and pile them on top. Pour over the sesame sauce, sprinkle over the chilli sauce and serve.

Energy 200kcal/838kJ; Protein 29.5g; Carbohydrate 2.8g, of which sugars 2.4g; Fat 7.9g, of which saturates 1.3g; Cholesterol 79mg; Calcium 89mg; Fibre 1.2g; Sodium 338mg.

FRAGRANT GRILLED CHICKEN ★

IF YOU HAVE TIME, PREPARE THE CHICKEN IN ADVANCE AND LEAVE IT TO MARINATE IN THE
REFRIGERATOR FOR SEVERAL HOURS — OR EVEN OVERNIGHT — UNTIL READY TO COOK.

3 Cover with clear film and set aside to marinate in a cool place for at least 20 minutes. Meanwhile, make the sauce.

4 Heat the vinegar in a small pan, add the sugar and stir until dissolved. Add the salt and stir until the mixture begins to thicken. Add the remaining sauce ingredients, stir well, then spoon the sauce into a serving bowl.

5 Preheat the grill (broiler) and cook the chicken for 5 minutes. Turn and baste with the marinade, then cook for 5 minutes more, or until cooked through and golden.

6 Serve with rice and the sauce, garnished with lime wedges.

SERVES 4

INGREDIENTS
    450g/1lb chicken breast fillets,
      with the skin on
    15ml/1 tbsp sesame oil
    2 garlic cloves, crushed
    2 coriander (cilantro) roots,
      finely chopped
    2 small fresh red chillies, seeded
      and finely chopped
    30ml/2 tbsp Thai fish sauce
    5ml/1 tsp sugar
    cooked rice, to serve
    lime wedges, to garnish
For the sauce
    90ml/6 tbsp rice vinegar
    60ml/4 tbsp sugar
    2.5ml/½ tsp salt
    2 garlic cloves, crushed
    1 small fresh red chilli, seeded
      and finely chopped
    115g/4oz/4 cups fresh coriander
      (cilantro), finely chopped

1 Lay the chicken breast fillets between two sheets of clear film (plastic wrap), baking parchment or foil and beat with the side of a rolling pin or the flat side of a meat tenderizer until the meat is about half its original thickness. Place in a large, shallow dish or bowl.

2 Mix together the sesame oil, garlic, coriander roots, red chillies, fish sauce and sugar in a jug (pitcher), stirring until the sugar has dissolved. Pour the mixture over the chicken and turn to coat.

Energy 221kcal/934kJ; Protein 28.3g; Carbohydrate 17.8g, of which sugars 17.7g; Fat 4.5g, of which saturates 0.8g; Cholesterol 79mg; Calcium 97mg; Fibre 2.1g; Sodium 82mg.

CHICKEN TERIYAKI ★

WHEN YOU ARE SHORT OF TIME, THIS IS THE PERFECT RECIPE. IT TAKES LESS THAN HALF AN HOUR, INCLUDING MARINATING THE CHICKEN, AND HAS LESS FAT THAN MANY ALTERNATIVE LIGHT MEALS.

SERVES 4

INGREDIENTS
450g/1lb skinless chicken
  breast fillets
orange segments and mustard
  and cress (fine curled cress),
  to garnish
For the marinade
5ml/1 tsp sugar
15ml/1 tbsp rice wine
15ml/1 tbsp dry sherry
30ml/2 tbsp dark soy sauce
rind of 1 orange, finely grated

1 Lay the chicken portions on a board. Using a sharp knife, slice each breast into long, thin strips.

2 Combine the sugar, rice wine, dry sherry and dark soy sauce in a bowl.

3 Place the chicken in a separate, large bowl, pour over the marinade and cover with clear film (plastic wrap). Leave to marinate in the refrigerator for at least 15 minutes. If you have time, leave it to marinate overnight.

4 Heat a wok, and stir-fry the chicken and marinade for 4–5 minutes.

5 Serve garnished with orange segments and mustard and cress

COOK'S TIP
Make sure that the marinade is brought to the boil in the wok, and that it cooks for at least 5 minutes, because it has been in contact with raw chicken.

VARIATIONS
• Turkey can be substituted for chicken in this recipe. Buy turkey steaks, place them between pieces of clear film (plastic wrap) and flatten them with a rolling pin before cutting them into thin strips for cooking. Any white fish can also be used in this dish.
• You could also serve the chicken with steamed rice and a side serving of vegetables, such as shredded cabbage.

Energy 149kcal/630kJ; Protein 27.4g; Carbohydrate 3.8g, of which sugars 3.8g; Fat 1.3g, of which saturates 0.4g; Cholesterol 79mg; Calcium 21mg; Fibre 0.5g; Sodium 70mg.

CHICKEN WITH MIXED VEGETABLES ★

ASIAN COOKS ARE EXPERTS IN MAKING DELICIOUS DISHES FROM A RELATIVELY SMALL AMOUNT OF MEAT AND A LOT OF VEGETABLES, WHICH IS GOOD NEWS FOR ANYONE TRYING TO EAT LESS FAT.

2 Bring the stock to the boil in a pan. Add the chicken fillets and cook for 12 minutes, or until tender. Drain and slice, reserving 75ml/5 tbsp of the chicken stock.

3 Heat the remaining oil in a non-stick frying pan or wok, add all the vegetables and stir-fry for 2 minutes. Stir in the sherry, oyster sauce, caster sugar and reserved stock. Add the chicken to the pan and cook for 2 minutes more.

SERVES 4

INGREDIENTS

350g/12oz skinless chicken
  breast fillets
20ml/4 tsp vegetable oil
300ml/½ pint/1¼ cups
  chicken stock
75g/3oz/¾ cup drained, canned
  straw mushrooms
50g/2oz/½ cup sliced, drained,
  canned bamboo shoots
50g/2oz/⅓ cup drained, canned
  water chestnuts, sliced
1 small carrot, sliced
50g/2oz/½ cup mangetouts (snow peas)
15ml/1 tbsp dry sherry
15ml/1 tbsp oyster sauce
5ml/1 tsp caster (superfine) sugar
5ml/1 tsp cornflour (cornstarch)
15ml/1 tbsp cold water
salt and ground white pepper

1 Put the chicken in a shallow bowl. Add 5ml/1 tsp of the oil, 1.5ml/¼ tsp salt and a pinch of pepper. Cover and set aside for 10 minutes in a cool place.

COOK'S TIP
Water chestnuts give a dish great texture as they remain crunchy, no matter how long you cook them for.

4 Mix the cornflour to a paste with the water. Add the mixture to the pan and cook, stirring, until the sauce thickens slightly. Season to taste with salt and pepper and serve immediately.

Energy 154kcal/646kJ; Protein 22.2g; Carbohydrate 4.9g, of which sugars 3.4g; Fat 4.3g, of which saturates 0.7g; Cholesterol 61mg; Calcium 17mg; Fibre 1g; Sodium 61mg.

CHICKEN <u>AND</u> SWEET POTATO CURRY ★★★

SOUTH-EAST ASIAN MARKETS ARE HOME TO MANY STALLS SPECIALIZING IN CURRIES LIKE THIS ONE.
THEY ALL USE INDIAN CURRY POWDER AND COCONUT MILK, AND ARE VERY SIMPLE TO MAKE.

SERVES 4

INGREDIENTS

45ml/3 tbsp Indian curry powder
15ml/1 tbsp ground turmeric
500g/1¼lb skinless boneless chicken
  thighs or chicken breast fillets
25ml/1½ tbsp raw cane sugar
30ml/2 tbsp sesame oil
2 shallots, chopped
2 garlic cloves, chopped
4cm/1½in galangal, peeled
  and chopped
2 lemon grass stalks, chopped
10ml/2 tsp chilli paste or dried
  chilli flakes
2 medium sweet potatoes,
  peeled and cubed
45ml/3 tbsp chilli sambal
600ml/1 pint/2½ cups coconut milk
1 small bunch each fresh basil
  and coriander (cilantro),
  stalks removed
salt and ground black pepper

4 Add the sweet potatoes, then the chilli sambal, syrup, coconut milk and 150ml/1/4 pint/2/3 cup water, mixing thoroughly to combine the flavours.

5 Bring to the boil, reduce the heat and cook for about 15 minutes until the chicken is cooked through. Season and stir in half the basil and coriander. Spoon into warmed bowls, garnish with the remaining herbs and serve immediately.

1 In a small bowl, mix together the curry powder and turmeric. Put the chicken in a bowl and coat with half of the spice. Set aside.

2 Heat the sugar in a small pan with 7.5ml/11/2 tsp water, until the sugar dissolves and the syrup turns golden. Remove from the heat and set aside.

3 Heat a wok or heavy pan and add the oil. Stir-fry the shallots, garlic, galangal and lemon grass. Stir in the rest of the turmeric and curry powder with the chilli paste or flakes, followed by the chicken, and stir-fry for 2–3 minutes.

Energy 384kcal/1621kJ; Protein 29.5g; Carbohydrate 39.7g, of which sugars 20.7g; Fat 13.1g, of which saturates 2.5g; Cholesterol 131mg; Calcium 181mg; Fibre 5.8g; Sodium 373mg.

TABLE-TOP HOTPOT ★★★

COOKING YOUR OWN FOOD FROM A COMMUNAL POT ON THE TABLE IS GREAT FUN. IT IS A HEALTHY OPTION, TOO, IF YOU USE STOCK INSTEAD OF OIL FOR COOKING, AND USE LEAN MEAT AND FISH.

SERVES 4

INGREDIENTS
225g/8oz piece of white fish fillet,
    such as sea bream, cod, plaice
    or haddock
4 x 5cm/2in thick salmon steaks
300g/11oz skinless chicken thighs,
    cut into large chunks, with bones
4 leaves from the head of Chinese
    leaves (Chinese cabbage),
    base trimmed
115g/4oz spinach
1 large carrot
2 thin leeks, washed and cut
    diagonally into 5cm/2in lengths
8 fresh shiitake mushrooms, stalks
    removed, or 150g/5oz oyster
    mushrooms, base trimmed
285g/10¼oz packet firm tofu,
    drained and cut into 16 cubes
salt
For the hot-pot liquid
    12 × 6cm/4½ × 2½in piece
    dashi-konbu
    1.2 litres/2 pints/5 cups water
    120ml/4fl oz/½ cup sake or
    dry sherry
For the condiments
    90g/3½oz daikon (mooli), peeled
    1 dried chilli, halved, seeded and
    cut into 2–3 strips
    1 lemon, cut into 16 wedges
    4 spring onions (scallions), chopped
    2 × 5g/⅛oz packets *kezuri-bushi*
    shoyu or other soy sauce

1 Trim the white fish fillet neatly, then cut it into four equal portions. Place the white fish, salmon steaks and the chunks of chicken in separate bowls.

2 Boil plenty of water in a large pan and cook the Chinese leaves for 3 minutes. Lift out and drain in a sieve (strainer) and leave to cool. Add a pinch of salt to the water and boil the spinach for 1 minute, then drain in a sieve under running water.

3 Squeeze the spinach and lay on a sushi rolling mat, then roll it up firmly. Leave to rest, then unwrap and take the cylinder out. Lay the Chinese leaves next to each other on the mat. Put the spinach cylinder in the middle and roll again firmly. Leave for 5 minutes, then unroll and cut into 5cm/2in long cylinders.

4 Using a sharp knife, cut the carrot into rounds, then into flowers.

5 Transfer the cabbage and spinach cylinders to the platter along with all the remaining vegetables and the tofu.

6 Lay the *dashi-konbu* on the bottom of a clay pot or flameproof casserole. Mix the water and sake or sherry in a bowl.

7 Cut the peeled daikon in half and insert a wooden skewer in two or three places. Insert the chilli pieces. Leave for 20 minutes, then grate finely. Drain in a fine-meshed sieve and squeeze the liquid out. Shape the grated daikon into a mound and put in a bowl. Put the other condiments into small bowls.

8 Fill the pot or casserole with two-thirds of the water and sake mixture. Bring to the boil, then reduce the heat.

9 Put the carrot, leeks and shiitake mushrooms into the pot and cook until the carrot is tender. Transfer the pot to a table-top burner. Add a batch of meat and fish to the pot, and, when they have changed colour, add some tofu.

10 Each guest pours a little soy sauce into a small bowl, squeezes in a little lemon juice, then mixes these with a condiment. The food is picked from the pot with chopsticks and dipped into the sauce. More ingredients can be cooked as needed and the water and sake can be topped up when necessary.

COOK'S TIP
Kezuri-bushi is ready-shaved, dried *katsuo* (skipjack tuna) flakes sold in packets for use in dashi fish stock.

Energy 283kcal/1186kJ; Protein 41.7g; Carbohydrate 5.1g, of which sugars 4.2g; Fat 10.7g, of which saturates 1.8g; Cholesterol 89mg; Calcium 454mg; Fibre 2.3g; Sodium 940mg.

CUBED CHICKEN AND VEGETABLES ★

THIS POPULAR COOKING STYLE SIMMERS VEGETABLES OF DIFFERENT TEXTURES WITH A SMALL AMOUNT OF MEAT TOGETHER IN A TASTY DASHI STOCK. THIS CHICKEN REMAINS MOIST AND TENDER.

SERVES 4

INGREDIENTS

2 skinless chicken thighs, about
    200g/7oz, boned
1 large carrot, trimmed
1 *konnyaku*
300g/11oz *satoimo* or small potatoes
500g/1¼lb canned bamboo shoots
30ml/2 tbsp vegetable oil
300ml/½ pint/1¼ cups water and
    7.5ml/1½ tsp instant dashi powder
salt
For the simmering seasonings
    75ml/5 tbsp shoyu or other soy sauce
    30ml/2 tbsp sake or dry sherry
    30ml/2 tbsp caster (superfine) sugar
    30ml/2 tbsp mirin

1 Cut the chicken into bitesize pieces. Chop the carrot into 2cm/¾in triangular chunks by cutting it diagonally and turning it 90 degrees each time you cut.

2 Boil the *konnyaku* in rapidly boiling water for 1 minute, then drain in a sieve (strainer) under running water. Cool, then slice it crossways into 5mm/¼in thick rectangular strips.

3 Cut a 4cm/1½in slit down the centre of a strip of cooled *konnyaku* without cutting the ends. Carefully push the top of the strip through the slit to make a decorative tie. Repeat with all of the *konnyaku* strips.

4 Peel and halve the *satoimo* or the new potatoes, if using. Put the pieces in a colander and sprinkle with a generous amount of salt. Rub well and wash under running water. Drain.

5 Drain and halve the canned bamboo shoots, then cut them into the same shape as the carrot.

6 In a medium pan, heat the vegetable oil and stir-fry the chicken pieces until the surface of the meat turns white.

7 Add the carrot, *konnyaku* ties, *satoimo* or potato and bamboo shoots. Stir well to thoroughly combine each time you add a new ingredient.

8 Add the dashi stock and bring to the boil. Cook on a high heat for 3 minutes then reduce to medium-low.

9 Add the shoyu, sake, sugar and mirin, cover the pan, then simmer for 15 minutes, until most of the liquid has evaporated, shaking the pan from time to time.

10 When the *satoimo* or potato is soft, remove the pan from the heat and spoon the chicken and vegetables into a large serving bowl. Serve immediately.

COOK'S TIP
When you cut *satoimo*, it produces a sticky juice. Rinsing with salt and water is the best way of washing it off the surface of the *satoimo*, your hands and any other surfaces it may have come into contact with.

Energy 101kcal/430kJ; Protein 8.4g; Carbohydrate 16.1g, of which sugars 4.8g; Fat 0.8g, of which saturates 0.2g; Cholesterol 18mg; Calcium 65mg; Fibre 2.7g; Sodium 906mg

KABOCHA SQUASH WITH CHICKEN SAUCE ★

IN THIS LOW-FAT DISH, THE MILD SWEETNESS OF KABOCHA SQUASH, WHICH TASTES RATHER LIKE SWEET POTATO, GOES VERY WELL WITH THE CHICKEN AND SAKE SAUCE.

SERVES 4

INGREDIENTS

1 kabocha squash, about 500g/1¼lb
½ lime
20g/¾oz mangetouts (snow peas)
salt
For the chicken sauce
  100ml/3½fl oz/scant ½ cup water
  30ml/2 tbsp sake or dry sherry
  300g/11oz lean chicken,
    minced (ground)
  60ml/4 tbsp caster (superfine) sugar
  60ml/4 tbsp shoyu or other soy sauce
  60ml/4 tbsp mirin

1 Halve the kabocha, then remove the seeds and fibre around the seeds. Halve again to make four wedges. Trim the stem end of each kabocha wedge.

2 Partially peel each wedge, cutting off two strips lengthways about 1–2.5cm/ ½–1in wide. The kabocha wedges will now have green (skin) and yellow (flesh) stripes. This will help preserve the kabocha's most tasty part just beneath the skin, and also allows it to be cooked until soft as well as being decorative.

3 Chop each wedge into large bitesize pieces. Place them side by side in a pan. Pour in enough water to cover, then sprinkle with some salt. Cover and cook for 5 minutes over a medium heat, then lower the heat and simmer for 15 minutes until tender.

4 Test the kabocha by pricking with a skewer. When soft enough, remove from the heat, cover and leave for 5 minutes.

5 Slice the lime into thin discs, then hollow out the inside of the skin to make rings of peel. Cover with a sheet of clear film (plastic wrap) until needed. Blanch the mangetouts in lightly salted water. Drain and set aside.

6 To make the chicken sauce, bring the water and sake to the boil in a pan. Add the chicken, and when the colour of the meat has changed, add the sugar, shoyu and mirin. Whisk together until the liquid has almost all evaporated.

7 Pile up the kabocha on a large plate, then pour the hot meat sauce on top. Add the mangetouts and serve, garnished with lime rings.

VARIATION

Use tofu for a vegetarian sauce. Wrap in kitchen paper and leave for 30 minutes. Mash with a fork, then add instead of the chicken in step 6.

Energy 165kcal/701kJ; Protein 19.2g; Carbohydrate 18.8g, of which sugars 18.1g; Fat 1.1g, of which saturates 0.4g; Cholesterol 53mg; Calcium 51mg; Fibre 1.4g; Sodium 47mg.

STIR-FRIED CHICKEN WITH BASIL AND CHILLI ★

THAI BASIL, WHICH IS SOMETIMES KNOWN AS HOLY BASIL, HAS A UNIQUE, PUNGENT FLAVOUR THAT IS BOTH SPICY AND SHARP. SKINLESS, BONELESS CHICKEN BREAST FILLETS ARE ESPECIALLY LOW IN FAT.

SERVES 6

INGREDIENTS

15ml/1 tbsp sunflower oil
4 garlic cloves, thinly sliced
2–4 fresh red chillies, seeded and
   finely chopped
450g/1lb skinless chicken
   breast fillets, cut into
   bitesize pieces
45ml/3 tbsp Thai fish sauce
10ml/2 tsp dark soy sauce
5ml/1 tsp granulated sugar
10–12 fresh Thai basil leaves
2 fresh red chillies, seeded and
   finely chopped, and 18 deep-fried
   Thai basil leaves, to garnish (optional)

1 Heat the oil in a wok or large, heavy frying pan. Add the garlic and chillies and stir-fry over a medium heat for 1–2 minutes until the garlic is golden. Take care not to let the garlic burn, otherwise it will taste bitter.

2 Add the pieces of chicken to the wok or pan, in batches if necessary, and stir-fry until the chicken changes colour.

3 Stir in the fish sauce, soy sauce and sugar. Continue to stir-fry the mixture for 3–4 minutes, or until the chicken is fully cooked and golden brown.

4 Stir in the fresh Thai basil leaves. Spoon the mixture on to a warm platter, or into individual dishes. Garnish with the chopped chillies and deep-fried Thai basil and serve immediately.

COOK'S TIP
To deep-fry Thai basil leaves, first make sure that the leaves are completely dry or they will splutter when they are added to the oil. Heat vegetable or sunflower oil in a wok or deep-fryer to 190°C/375°F or until a cube of bread, added to the oil, browns in about 45 seconds. Add the leaves and deep-fry them briefly until they are crisp and translucent – this will take only about 30–40 seconds. Lift out the leaves using a slotted spoon or wire basket. Drain them well on kitchen paper before using.

Energy 113kcal/474kJ; Protein 19.1g; Carbohydrate 2.9g, of which sugars 1.6g; Fat 2.8g, of which saturates 0.5g; Cholesterol 53mg; Calcium 22mg; Fibre 0.7g; Sodium 582mg.

CHICKEN WITH HIJIKI SEAWEED ★★

THE TASTE OF HIJIKI — A TYPE OF SEAWEED — IS SOMEWHERE BETWEEN RICE AND VEGETABLE. IT GOES WELL WITH MEAT OR TOFU PRODUCTS, ESPECIALLY WHEN STIR-FRIED IN THE WOK WITH A LITTLE OIL.

SERVES 2

INGREDIENTS

90g/3½oz dried hijiki seaweed
150g/5oz chicken breast fillet
½ small carrot, about 5cm/2in
15ml/1 tbsp vegetable oil
100ml/3fl oz/scant ½ cup instant
   dashi powder plus 1.5ml/¼ tsp
   dashi-no-moto
30ml/2 tbsp sake
30ml/2 tbsp caster (superfine) sugar
45ml/3 tbsp shoyu or other soy sauce
a pinch of cayenne pepper

1 Soak the hijiki in cold water for about 30 minutes. It will be ready to cook when it can be easily crushed between the fingers. Pour into a sieve (strainer) and wash under running water. Drain.

2 Peel the skin from the chicken and par-boil the skin in rapidly boiling water for 1 minute, then drain. With a sharp knife, shave off all the yellow fat from the skin. Discard the clear membrane between the fat and the skin as well. Cut the skin into thin strips about 5mm/¼in wide and 2.5cm/1in long. Cut the meat into small, bitesize chunks.

3 Peel and chop the carrot into long, narrow matchsticks.

4 Heat the oil in a wok or frying pan and stir-fry the strips of chicken skin for 5 minutes, or until golden and curled up. Add the chicken meat and keep stirring until the colour changes.

5 Add the hijiki and carrot, then stir-fry for a further minute. Add the remaining ingredients. Lower the heat and toss over the heat for 5 minutes more.

6 Remove the wok from the heat and stand for 10 minutes. Season and serve in small individual bowls.

Energy 154kcal/644kJ; Protein 10g; Carbohydrate 10.4g, of which sugars 10.2g; Fat 8.4g, of which saturates 2g; Cholesterol 39mg; Calcium 76mg; Fibre 1.1g; Sodium 884mg.

CHICKEN WITH MUSHROOMS ★★

THIS IS TRADITIONALLY A ONE-POT MEAL. THE COMBINATION OF RICE AND SHIITAKE MUSHROOMS
WITH THE CHICKEN AND TOFU MAKES THIS A VERY FILLING, HEALTHY AND LOW-FAT DISH.

SERVES 4

INGREDIENTS
225–275g/8–10oz/generous
    1–1½ cups Jasmine rice or
    glutinous rice
30ml/2 tbsp vegetable oil
2 garlic cloves, crushed
2.5cm/1in piece fresh root
    ginger, grated
5 spring onions (scallions),
    diagonally sliced
1 fresh green chilli, seeded and
    finely sliced
3 skinless chicken breast portions,
    cut into thin strips
150g/5oz tofu, cut into small cubes
115g/4oz/1¾ shiitake mushrooms,
    stems discarded and cups sliced
15ml/1 tbsp sake or dry sherry
30ml/2 tbsp light soy sauce
10ml/2 tsp granulated sugar
400ml/14fl oz/1⅔ cups chicken stock

1 Cook the rice in lightly salted boiling water following the instructions on the packet.

2 While the rice is cooking, heat the oil in a large frying pan. Stir-fry the garlic, ginger, spring onions and chilli for 1–2 minutes until slightly softened.

3 Add the strips of chicken and fry, in batches if necessary, until all the pieces are evenly browned.

4 Transfer the chicken mixture to a plate using a slotted spoon, and add the tofu to the pan.

5 Stir-fry the tofu for a few minutes, then add the mushrooms. Stir-fry for 2–3 minutes over medium heat until the mushrooms are tender.

6 Stir in the sake or sherry, soy sauce and sugar and cook the mixture briskly for 1–2 minutes, stirring all the time.

7 Return the chicken to the pan, toss over the heat for about 2 minutes, then pour in the stock. Stir well and cook over a gentle heat for 5–6 minutes until the sauce is bubbling.

8 Spoon the cooked rice into individual serving bowls and pile the chicken mixture on top, making sure that each portion gets a generous amount of chicken sauce.

COOK'S TIP
Once the rice is cooked, leave it covered until you are ready to serve. It will stay warm for about 30 minutes. Fork through lightly to fluff up just before serving.

Energy 408kcal/1709kJ; Protein 35.2g; Carbohydrate 46.3g, of which sugars 1.1g; Fat 8.8g, of which saturates 1.2g; Cholesterol 79mg; Calcium 216mg; Fibre 0.5g; Sodium 605mg.

CHICKEN WITH CASHEW NUTS ★

BASED ON THE CLASSIC DISH, BUT CONSIDERABLY LOWER IN FAT, THIS VERSION OF CASHEW NUT
CHICKEN ADDS CUBES OF BAMBOO SHOOTS, CARROTS AND CUCUMBER TO THE SAVOURY SAUCE.

SERVES 4

INGREDIENTS

   350g/12oz skinless chicken
      breast fillets
   1.5ml/¼ tsp salt
   pinch of ground white pepper
   15ml/1 tbsp dry sherry
   300ml/½ pint/1¼ cups
      chicken stock
   5ml/1 tsp cornflour (cornstarch)
   15ml/1 tbsp light soy sauce
   5ml/1 tsp caster (superfine) sugar
   15ml/1 tbsp vegetable oil
   1 garlic clove, finely chopped
   1 small carrot, cut into cubes
   ½ cucumber, about 75g/3oz, cut
      into 1cm/½in cubes
   50g/2oz/½ cup drained canned
      bamboo shoots, cut into
      1cm/½in cubes
   25g/1oz/¼ cup dry roasted
      cashew nuts
   2.5ml/½ tsp sesame oil
   noodles, to serve

1 Cut the chicken fillets into 2cm/¾in cubes using a sharp knife or a cleaver, if you have one. Place the cubes in a bowl, stir in the salt, pepper and sherry, cover with clear film (plastic wrap) and marinate for 15 minutes.

2 Bring the stock to the boil in a large pan. Add the chicken and cook, stirring, for 3 minutes. Drain, reserving 90ml/ 6 tbsp of the stock, and set aside.

3 Mix the cornflour with the soy sauce and sugar in a small bowl. Stir until it forms a smooth paste.

4 Heat the vegetable oil in a non-stick frying pan until very hot, add the garlic and stir-fry for a few seconds. Add the carrot, cucumber and bamboo shoots and continue to stir-fry over medium heat for 2 minutes.

5 Stir the chicken into the pan with the reserved stock and cornflour paste. Cook, stirring, until the sauce thickens slightly. Add the cashew nuts and sesame oil. Toss to mix thoroughly, then serve with noodles.

Energy 153kcal/645kJ; Protein 22.9g; Carbohydrate 5.1g, of which sugars 2.8g; Fat 4.3g, of which saturates 0.9g; Cholesterol 61mg; Calcium 14mg; Fibre 0.7g; Sodium 342mg.

CHICKEN WITH LEMON SAUCE ★

SUCCULENT CHICKEN WITH A REFRESHING LEMONY SAUCE AND JUST A HINT OF LIME IS A SURE
WINNER AS A FAMILY MEAL THAT IS ALSO QUICK AND VERY EASY TO PREPARE.

2 Mix together the egg white and cornflour. Add the mixture to the chicken and turn the chicken with tongs until thoroughly coated. Heat the sunflower oil in a non-stick frying pan or wok and fry the chicken fillets for about 15 minutes until they are golden brown on both sides.

3 Meanwhile, make the sauce. Combine all the ingredients in a small pan. Add 1.5ml/¼ tsp salt. Bring to the boil over a low heat, stirring constantly until the sauce is smooth and has thickened.

SERVES 4

INGREDIENTS
   4 small skinless chicken breast fillets
   5ml/1 tsp sesame oil
   15ml/1 tbsp dry sherry
   1 egg white, lightly beaten
   30ml/2 tbsp cornflour (cornstarch)
   15ml/1 tbsp sunflower oil
   salt and ground white pepper
   chopped coriander (cilantro) leaves
     and spring onions (scallions) and
     lemon wedges, to garnish
For the sauce
   45ml/3 tbsp fresh lemon juice
   30ml/2 tbsp sweetened lime juice
   45ml/3 tbsp caster (superfine) sugar
   10ml/2 tsp cornflour (cornstarch)
   90ml/6 tbsp cold water

1 Arrange the chicken in a single layer in a bowl. Mix the sesame oil with the sherry and add 2.5ml/½ tsp salt and 1.5ml/¼ tsp pepper. Pour over the chicken, cover and marinate for 15 minutes.

VARIATIONS
Turkey fillets can be substituted for chicken in this recipe. Any white fish can also be used in this dish.

4 Cut the chicken into pieces and place on a warm serving plate. Pour the sauce over, garnish with the coriander leaves, spring onions and lemon wedges.

Energy 235kcal/995kJ; Protein 30.9g; Carbohydrate 23.3g, of which sugars 14.1g; Fat 2.2g, of which saturates 0.5g; Cholesterol 88mg; Calcium 15mg; Fibre 0g; Sodium 97mg.

SOY SAUCE AND STAR ANISE CHICKEN ★★

*THE PUNGENT FLAVOUR OF STAR ANISE PENETRATES THE CHICKEN FILLETS AND ADDS A WONDERFUL
ANISEEDY KICK TO THE SMOKY FLAVOUR OF THE BARBECUE. SERVE WITH A REFRESHING SALAD.*

SERVES 4

INGREDIENTS
    4 skinless chicken breast fillets
    2 whole star anise
    30ml/2 tbsp soy sauce
    30ml/2 tbsp vegetable oil
    ground black pepper

1 Lay the skinless chicken breast fillets side by side in a shallow, non-metallic dish and add both pieces of star anise, keeping them whole.

2 Place the soy sauce in a small bowl. Add the oil and whisk together with a fork until the mixture emulsifies. Season to taste with black pepper to make a simple marinade.

3 Pour the marinade over the chicken and stir to coat each breast fillet all over. Cover the dish with clear film (plastic wrap) and chill for up to 8 hours.

4 Prepare a barbecue. Cook the chicken fillets for 8–10 minutes on each side, spooning over the marinade from time to time, until the chicken is cooked through. Serve immediately.

Energy 210kcal/884kJ; Protein 36.1g; Carbohydrate 0.3g, of which sugars 0.3g; Fat 7.2g, of which saturates 1.2g; Cholesterol 105mg; Calcium 8mg; Fibre 0g; Sodium 357mg.

STIR-FRIED GIBLETS WITH GINGER ★★

AS ALMOST EVERY PART OF THE BIRD IS USED IN CHINESE COOKING, THERE ARE SPECIFIC RECIPES FOR WHICH THEY ARE DESTINED. GIBLETS ARE OFTEN STIR-FRIED AND SERVED WITH RICE.

SERVES 2–4

INGREDIENTS
    30ml/2 tbsp groundnut (peanut) oil
    2 shallots, halved and finely sliced
    2 garlic cloves, finely chopped
    1 Thai chilli, seeded and finely sliced
    25g/1oz fresh root ginger, peeled
      and shredded
    225g/8oz chicken livers, trimmed
      and finely sliced
    115g/4oz mixed giblets, finely sliced
    15–30ml/1–2 tbsp fish sauce
    1 small bunch coriander (cilantro),
      finely chopped
    ground black pepper
    steamed rice, to serve

1 Heat the oil in a wok or heavy pan. Stir in the shallots, garlic, chilli and ginger, and stir-fry until golden. Add the chicken livers and mixed giblets and stir-fry for a few minutes more, until browned.

2 Stir in the fish sauce, adjusting the quantity according to taste, and half the chopped coriander. Season with ground black pepper and garnish with the rest of the coriander. Serve hot, with steamed fragrant rice.

Energy 134kcal/556kJ; Protein 15g; Carbohydrate 1.5g, of which sugars 1.1g; Fat 7.4g, of which saturates 1.3g; Cholesterol 290mg; Calcium 12mg; Fibre 0.2g; Sodium 360mg.

BARBECUE CHICKEN ★

CHICKEN COOKED ON A BARBECUE IS SERVED ALMOST EVERYWHERE IN THAILAND, FROM ROADSIDE STALLS TO SPORTS STADIA. THIS IS THE PERFECT DISH FOR A SUMMER PARTY.

SERVES 4–6

INGREDIENTS

1 chicken, about 1.5kg/3–3½lb,
    cut into 8–10 pieces
lime wedges and fresh red chillies,
    to garnish
For the marinade
2 lemon grass stalks, roots trimmed
2.5cm/1in piece fresh root ginger,
    peeled and thinly sliced
6 garlic cloves, coarsely chopped
4 shallots, coarsely chopped
½ bunch coriander (cilantro)
    roots, chopped
15ml/1 tbsp palm sugar or light
    muscovado (brown) sugar
120ml/4fl oz/½ cup reduced-fat
    coconut milk
30ml/2 tbsp Thai fish sauce
30ml/2 tbsp light soy sauce

1 Make the marinade. Cut off the lower 5cm/2in of the lemon grass stalks and chop them coarsely. Put into a food processor with the ginger, garlic, shallots, coriander, sugar, coconut milk and sauces and process until smooth.

2 Place the chicken pieces in a dish, pour over the marinade and stir to mix well. Cover the dish and leave in a cool place to marinate for at least 4 hours, or leave it in the refrigerator overnight.

3 Prepare the barbecue or preheat the oven to 200°C/400°F/Gas 6. Drain the chicken, reserving the marinade. If you are cooking in the oven, arrange the chicken pieces in a single layer on a rack set over a roasting pan.

4 Cook the chicken on the barbecue over moderately hot coals or on medium heat for a gas barbecue, or bake in the oven for 20–30 minutes. Turn the pieces and brush with the reserved marinade once or twice during cooking.

5 As soon as the chicken pieces are golden brown and cooked through, transfer them to a serving platter, garnish with the lime wedges and red chillies and serve immediately.

COOK'S TIPS
• Coriander roots are more intensely flavoured than the leaves, but the herb is not always available with the roots intact. One answer is to grow your own, but if this is impractical, use the bottom portion of the stem as a substitute.
• Coconut milk is available in cans or cartons from Asian food stores and most supermarkets. Reduced-fat versions contain less than half the fat.

Energy 145kcal/610kJ; Protein 28.5g; Carbohydrate 2.3g, of which sugars 2g; Fat 2.4g, of which saturates 0.7g; Cholesterol 108mg; Calcium 14mg; Fibre 0.1g; Sodium 458mg.

CHICKEN <u>WITH</u> YOUNG GINGER ★★

GINGER PLAYS A BIG ROLE IN CHINESE COOKING, PARTICULARLY IN THE STIR-FRIED DISHES.
WHENEVER POSSIBLE, THE JUICIER AND MORE PUNGENT YOUNG GINGER IS USED.

SERVES 4

INGREDIENTS

  30ml/2 tbsp groundnut (peanut) oil
  3 garlic cloves, finely sliced
    in strips
  50g/2oz fresh young root ginger,
    finely sliced in strips
  2 Thai chillies, seeded and finely
    sliced in strips
  4 chicken breasts or 4 boned
    chicken legs, skinned and cut
    into bitesize chunks
  30ml/2 tbsp fish sauce
  10ml/2 tsp sugar
  1 small bunch coriander (cilantro)
    stalks removed, roughly chopped
  ground black pepper
  jasmine rice and crunchy salad or
    baguette, to serve

1 Heat a wok or heavy pan and add the oil. Add the garlic, ginger and chillies, and stir-fry until fragrant and golden. Add the chicken and toss it around the wok for 1–2 minutes.

COOK'S TIP
Young ginger is available in Chinese and South-east Asian markets.

2 Stir in the fish sauce and sugar, and stir-fry for a further 4–5 minutes until cooked. Season with pepper and add some of the fresh coriander. Transfer the chicken to a serving dish and garnish with the remaining coriander. Serve hot with jasmine rice and a crunchy salad with fresh herbs, or with chunks of freshly baked baguette.

Energy 222kcal/935kJ; Protein 36.4g; Carbohydrate 3g, of which sugars 2.9g; Fat 7.3g, of which saturates 1.1g; Cholesterol 105mg; Calcium 32mg; Fibre 0.6g; Sodium 100mg.

STIR-FRIED CHICKEN WITH LEMON GRASS ★★

THERE ARE VARIATIONS OF THIS DISH, USING PORK OR SEAFOOD, THROUGHOUT SOUTH-EAST ASIA SO, FOR A SMOOTH INTRODUCTION TO THE COOKING OF THE REGION, THIS IS A GOOD PLACE TO START.

SERVES 4

INGREDIENTS

    15ml/1 tbsp sugar
    30ml/2 tbsp sesame or groundnut
       (peanut) oil
    2 garlic cloves, finely chopped
    2–3 green or red Thai chillies,
       seeded and finely chopped
    2 lemon grass stalks, finely sliced
    1 onion, finely sliced
    350g/12oz skinless chicken breast
       fillets, cut into bitesize strips
    30ml/2 tbsp soy sauce
    15ml/1 tbsp fish sauce
    1 bunch fresh coriander (cilantro),
       stalks removed, leaves chopped
    salt and ground black pepper
    nuoc cham, to serve

2 Heat a large wok or heavy pan and add the sesame or groundnut oil. Stir in the chopped garlic, chillies and lemon grass, and stir-fry until they become fragrant and golden. Add the onion and stir-fry for 1 minute, then add the chicken strips.

3 When the chicken is cooked through, add the soy sauce, fish sauce and caramel sauce. Stir to mix and heat through, then season with a little salt and pepper. Toss the coriander into the chicken and serve with *nuoc cham* to drizzle over it.

1 To make a caramel sauce, put the sugar into a pan with 5ml/1 tsp water. Heat gently until the sugar has dissolved and turned golden. Set aside.

Energy 202kcal/847kJ; Protein 22g; Carbohydrate 9g, of which sugars 7g; Fat 9g, of which saturates 1g; Cholesterol 61mg; Calcium 32mg; Fibre 0.6g; Sodium 800mg.

FRAGRANT RICE WITH CHICKEN ★

THIS REFRESHING DISH CAN BE SERVED SIMPLY, DRIZZLED WITH NUOC CHAM, OR AS PART OF A MEAL THAT MIGHT INCLUDE FISH OR CHICKEN, AND ACCOMPANIED BY PICKLES AND A TABLE SALAD.

2 Put the rice in a heavy pan and stir in the stock. When the rice settles, check that the stock sits roughly 2.5cm/1in above the rice; if not, top it up. Bring the liquid to the boil, cover the pan and cook for about 25 minutes, or until all the water has been absorbed.

3 Remove the pan from the heat and, using a fork, add the shredded chicken, shallots and most of the mint. Cover the pan again and leave the flavours to mingle for 10 minutes. Tip the rice into bowls, or on to a serving dish, garnish with the remaining mint and the spring onions, and serve with *nuoc cham*.

SERVES 4

INGREDIENTS
    350g/12oz/1¾ cups long grain rice,
    rinsed and drained
    2–3 shallots, halved and finely sliced
    1 bunch of fresh mint, stalks
    removed, leaves finely shredded
    2 spring onions (scallions), finely
    sliced, to garnish
    nuoc cham to serve
For the stock
    2 meaty chicken legs
    1 onion, peeled and quartered
    4cm/1½in fresh root ginger, peeled
    and coarsely chopped
    15ml/1 tbsp fish sauce
    3 black peppercorns
    1 bunch of fresh mint
    sea salt

1 To make the stock, put the chicken legs into a deep pan. Add all the other ingredients, except the salt, and pour in 1 litre/1¾ pints/4 cups water. Bring the water to the boil, skim off any foam, then reduce the heat and simmer gently with the lid on for 1 hour. Remove the lid, increase the heat and simmer for a further 30 minutes to reduce the stock. Skim off any fat, strain the stock and season with salt. Measure 750ml/1¼ pints/3 cups stock. Remove the chicken meat from the bone and shred.

VARIATIONS
Any meat or fish can be added to this basic recipe. Try strips of stir-fried pork, slices of Chinese sausage or a handful of prawns (shrimp). Simply toss into the rice along with the shredded chicken.

Energy 426kcal/1784kJ; Protein 25.6g; Carbohydrate 72.9g, of which sugars 1.8g; Fat 3.1g, of which saturates 0.7g; Cholesterol 92mg; Calcium 53mg; Fibre 0.5g; Sodium 82mg.

STIR-FRIED SWEET <u>AND</u> SOUR CHICKEN ★★★

AS WELL AS BEING QUICK AND VERY EASY TO MAKE, THIS POPULAR ASIAN DISH IS DECIDEDLY TASTY AND YOU WILL FIND YOURSELF BEING ASKED TO MAKE IT AGAIN AND AGAIN.

SERVES 3–4

INGREDIENTS

275g/10oz dried medium egg noodles
30ml/2 tbsp vegetable oil
3 spring onions (scallions), chopped
1 garlic clove, crushed
2.5cm/1in fresh root ginger, grated
5ml/1 tsp paprika
5ml/1 tsp ground coriander
3 skinless chicken breast
  fillets, sliced
225g/8oz sugar snap peas, trimmed
115g/4oz baby corn cobs, halved
225g/8oz/4 cups beansprouts
15ml/1 tbsp cornflour (cornstarch)
45ml/3 tbsp light soy sauce
45ml/3 tbsp lemon juice
15ml/1 tbsp sugar
45ml/3 tbsp chopped fresh coriander
  (cilantro), to garnish

1 Bring a large pan of lightly salted water to the boil. Add the egg noodles and cook until they are just soft and pliable, following the instructions on the packet. Tip into a colander and drain thoroughly, then cover and keep warm.

2 Heat the oil. Add the spring onions, garlic, ginger, paprika and coriander and stir-fry for 1 minute.

3 Stir in the chicken and stir-fry for 3–4 minutes. Add the sugar snap peas, corn cobs and beansprouts and cook briefly.

4 Add the noodles and toss lightly to mix with the other ingredients.

5 Combine the cornflour, soy sauce, lemon juice and sugar in a small bowl. Add to the wok and simmer briefly to thicken. Serve garnished with chopped fresh coriander.

Energy 501kcal/2116kJ; Protein 37.4g; Carbohydrate 63g, of which sugars 9.8g; Fat 12.8g, of which saturates 2.6g; Cholesterol 91mg; Calcium 70mg; Fibre 4.7g; Sodium 1319mg.

SICHUAN CHICKEN WITH KUNG PO SAUCE ★★★

ONE OF THE BEST WAYS OF ADDING FLAVOUR TO LOW-FAT DISHES IS BY SKILFUL USE OF SPICES, SOMETHING FOR WHICH SICHUAN COOKING IS FAMOUS. THIS IS A POPULAR CHICKEN RECIPE.

SERVES 4

INGREDIENTS

3 skinless chicken breast fillets, about 500g/1¼lb
1 egg white
10ml/2 tsp cornflour (cornstarch)
2.5ml/½ tsp salt
30ml/2 tbsp yellow salted beans
15ml/1 tbsp hoisin sauce
5ml/1 tsp light brown sugar
15ml/1 tbsp rice wine or medium-dry sherry
15ml/1 tbsp wine vinegar
4 garlic cloves, crushed
150ml/¼ pint/⅔ cup chicken stock
30ml/2 tbsp vegetable oil
2–3 dried chillies, broken into small pieces
50g/2oz/2½ cups roasted cashew nuts
fresh coriander (cilantro), to garnish

1 Cut the chicken into neat pieces. Lightly whisk the egg white in a dish, whisk in the cornflour and salt, then add the chicken and stir until coated.

COOK'S TIP
Peanuts are the classic ingredient in this dish, but cashew nuts have an even better flavour and have become popular both in home cooking and in restaurants.

2 In a separate bowl, mash the beans with the back of a spoon. Stir in the hoisin sauce, brown sugar, rice wine or sherry, vinegar, garlic and stock.

3 Heat a wok, add the oil and when the oil is very hot, add the chicken and fry, turning constantly, for about 1 minute.

4 Add the chillies and continue to stir-fry for a further minute or until the chicken is tender.

5 Pour in the bean sauce mixture. Bring to the boil and then stir in the cashew nuts.

6 Spoon into a heated serving dish and garnish with fresh coriander leaves.

Energy 270kcal/1131kJ; Protein 33.6g; Carbohydrate 4.3g, of which sugars 2.6g; Fat 13.2g, of which saturates 2.3g; Cholesterol 88mg; Calcium 14mg; Fibre 0.4g; Sodium 928mg.

THAI CHICKEN CURRY ★★

THIS FLAVOURFUL AND CREAMY THAI-STYLE CURRY IS VERY SIMPLE TO MAKE EVEN THOUGH IT INCLUDES A VARIETY OF INTERESTING INGREDIENTS. SERVE WITH FRAGRANT THAI RICE.

SERVES 6

INGREDIENTS
  400ml/14oz can unsweetened
    coconut milk
  6 skinless, chicken breast fillets,
    finely sliced
  225g/8oz can bamboo shoots,
    drained and sliced
  30ml/2 tbsp fish sauce
  15ml/1 tbsp soft light brown sugar
  cooked jasmine rice, to serve
For the green curry paste
  4 fresh green chillies, seeded
  1 lemon grass stalk, sliced
  1 small onion, sliced
  3 garlic cloves
  1cm/½in piece galangal or
    fresh root ginger, peeled
  grated rind of ½ lime
  5ml/1 tsp coriander seeds
  5ml/1 tsp cumin seeds
  2.5ml/½ tsp fish sauce
To garnish
  1 fresh red chilli, seeded and cut
    into fine strips
  finely pared rind of ½ lime, finely
    shredded
  fresh Thai purple basil or coriander
    (cilantro), chopped
To serve
  175g/6oz/scant 1 cup Thai
    jasmine rice, (optional)

1 First make the green curry paste: put the chillies, lemon grass, onion, garlic, galangal or ginger, lime rind, coriander seeds, cumin seeds and fish sauce in a food processor or blender and process until they are reduced to a thick paste. Set aside.

2 Bring half the coconut milk to the boil in a large frying pan, then reduce the heat and simmer for about 5 minutes, or until reduced by half. Stir in the green curry paste and simmer for a further 5 minutes.

3 Add the finely sliced chicken breasts to the pan with the remaining coconut milk, bamboo shoots, fish sauce and sugar. Stir well to combine all the ingredients and bring the curry back to simmering point, then simmer gently for about 10 minutes, or until the chicken slices are cooked through. The mixture will look grainy or curdled during cooking, but do not worry as this is quite normal.

4 Meanwhile, prepare the garnish and set aside. Add the rice and saffron to a pan of boiling salted water. Reduce the heat and simmer for 10 minutes, or until tender. Drain the rice and serve it with the curry, garnished with the chilli, lime rind and basil or coriander.

Energy 236kcal/991kJ; Protein 33.8g; Carbohydrate 7.2g, of which sugars 5.9g; Fat 8.3g, of which saturates 1.6g; Cholesterol 165mg; Calcium 149mg; Fibre 3.1g; Sodium 253mg.

RED CHICKEN CURRY WITH BAMBOO SHOOTS ★

BAMBOO SHOOTS HAVE A LOVELY CRUNCHY TEXTURE. IT IS QUITE ACCEPTABLE TO USE CANNED ONES, AS FRESH BAMBOO IS NOT READILY AVAILABLE IN THE WEST. BUY CANNED WHOLE BAMBOO SHOOTS, WHICH ARE CRISPER AND OF BETTER QUALITY THAN SLICED SHOOTS. RINSE BEFORE USING.

SERVES 6

INGREDIENTS
    475ml/16fl oz/2 cups reduced-fat
        coconut milk
    450g/1lb skinless chicken fillets, cut
        into bitesize pieces
    30ml/2 tbsp Thai fish sauce
    15ml/1 tbsp sugar
    475ml/16fl oz/2 cups
        chicken stock
    225g/8oz drained canned bamboo
        shoots, rinsed and sliced
    5 kaffir lime leaves, torn
    chopped fresh red chillies and
        kaffir lime leaves, to garnish
For the red curry paste
    5ml/1 tsp coriander seeds
    2.5ml/1/2 tsp cumin seeds
    12–15 fresh red chillies, seeded
        and roughly chopped
    4 shallots, thinly sliced
    2 garlic cloves, chopped
    15ml/1 tbsp chopped galangal
    2 lemon grass stalks, chopped
    3 kaffir lime leaves, chopped
    4 fresh coriander (cilantro) roots
    10 black peppercorns
    good pinch of ground cinnamon
    5ml/1 tsp ground turmeric
    2.5ml/1/2 tsp shrimp paste
    5ml/1 tsp salt
    15ml/1 tbsp sunflower oil

2 Add the oil, a little at a time, mixing or processing well after each addition. Transfer to a jar and keep in the refrigerator until ready to use.

3 Pour the coconut milk into a large heavy pan. Bring the milk to the boil, stirring constantly until it has separated.

5 Add the chicken fillets, Thai fish sauce and sugar to the pan. Stir well, then cook for 5–6 minutes until the chicken changes colour and is lightly golden and cooked through. Stir the chicken constantly to prevent the mixture from sticking to the bottom of the pan.

6 Pour the chicken stock into the pan, then add the sliced bamboo shoots and the torn kaffir lime leaves. Bring back to the boil over a medium heat, stirring constantly to prevent the chicken from sticking. Then remove the curry from the heat and season with salt and pepper to taste if necessary.

7 To serve, spoon the curry immediately into a warmed serving dish and garnish with chopped red chillies and kaffir lime leaves.

VARIATION
Instead of, or as well as, bamboo shoots, use straw mushrooms. These are available as dried mushrooms or in cans from Asian stores and supermarkets. Whether you are using dried or canned mushrooms, stir into the dish a few minutes before serving the curry.

COOK'S TIP
It is essential to use chicken breast fillets, rather than any other cut, for this curry, as it is cooked very quickly. Look out for diced chicken or strips of chicken (which are often labelled "stir-fry chicken") in the supermarket.

1 Make the red curry paste. Dry-fry the coriander and cumin seeds for 1–2 minutes, then put in a mortar with the remaining ingredients except the oil and pound to a paste.

4 Stir in 30ml/2 tbsp of the red curry paste and cook the mixture for 2–3 minutes, stirring constantly. Remaining red curry paste can be kept in the refrigerator for up to 3 months.

Energy 131kcal/552kJ; Protein 18.8g; Carbohydrate 7.5g, of which sugars 7.2g; Fat 3g, of which saturates 0.6g; Cholesterol 55mg; Calcium 51mg; Fibre 0.5g; Sodium 153mg.

GREEN CHICKEN CURRY ★★

USE ONE OR TWO FRESH GREEN CHILLIES IN THIS DISH, DEPENDING ON HOW HOT YOU LIKE YOUR CURRY. THE MILD AROMATIC FLAVOUR OF THE RICE IS A GOOD FOIL FOR THE SPICY CHICKEN.

2 Heat half the oil in a large frying pan. Cook the diced chicken until evenly browned. Transfer to a plate.

3 Heat the remaining oil in the frying pan. Add the thinly sliced green pepper and stir-fry for 3–4 minutes, then add the chilli and ginger paste. Stir-fry for 3–4 minutes, until the mixture becomes fairly thick.

4 Return the chicken to the pan and add the reduced-fat coconut milk. Season with salt and pepper to taste and bring to the boil, then reduce the heat, half cover the pan and simmer for 8–10 minutes.

SERVES 4

INGREDIENTS
    4 spring onions (scallions), trimmed
        and coarsely chopped
    1–2 fresh green chillies, seeded and
        coarsely chopped
    2cm/¾in piece fresh root
        ginger, peeled
    2 garlic cloves
    5ml/1 tsp Thai fish sauce
    large bunch fresh coriander (cilantro)
    small handful of fresh parsley or
        1 lemon grass stalk, chopped into
        4 sticks and lightly crushed
    30–45ml/2–3 tbsp water
    15ml/1 tbsp sunflower oil
    4 skinless, chicken breast
        fillets, diced
    1 green (bell) pepper, seeded and
        thinly sliced
    600ml/1 pint/2½ cups reduced-fat
        coconut milk
    salt and ground black pepper
    hot coconut rice, to serve

1 Put the spring onions, chillies, ginger, garlic, fish sauce, coriander and parsley or lemon grass in a food processor or blender. Pour in 30ml/2 tbsp of the water and process to a smooth paste, adding a further 15ml/1 tbsp water if required.

COOK'S TIP
Virtually every Thai cook has their own recipe for curry pastes, which are traditionally made by pounding the ingredients in a mortar with a pestle. Using a food processor or blender simply makes the task less laborious.

5 When the chicken is cooked, transfer it, with the green pepper, to a plate. Boil the cooking liquid remaining in the pan for 10–12 minutes, until it is well reduced and fairly thick.

6 Return the chicken and green pepper to the green curry sauce, stir well and cook gently for 2–3 minutes to heat through thoroughly. Spoon the curry over the coconut rice, and serve immediately.

Energy 208kcal/877kJ; Protein 28g; Carbohydrate 8g, of which sugars 7.9g; Fat 7.4g, of which saturates 1.3g; Cholesterol 79mg; Calcium 76mg; Fibre 0.7g; Sodium 237mg.

CHICKEN AND LEMON GRASS CURRY ★

THIS FRAGRANT AND TRULY DELICIOUS CURRY IS EXCEPTIONALLY EASY AND TAKES LESS THAN
TWENTY MINUTES TO PREPARE AND COOK, MAKING IT A PERFECT MID-WEEK MEAL.

SERVES 4

INGREDIENTS

10ml/2 tsp sunflower oil
2 garlic cloves, crushed
500g/1¼lb skinless, boneless
  chicken thighs, chopped into
  small pieces
45ml/3 tbsp Thai fish sauce
120ml/4fl oz/½ cup
  chicken stock
5ml/1 tsp granulated sugar
1 lemon grass stalk, chopped into
  4 sticks and lightly crushed
5 kaffir lime leaves, rolled into
  cylinders and thinly sliced across,
  plus extra to garnish
chopped roasted peanuts
  and chopped fresh coriander
  (cilantro), to garnish
For the curry paste
1 lemon grass stalk,
  coarsely chopped
2.5cm/1in piece fresh galangal,
  peeled and coarsely chopped
2 kaffir lime leaves, chopped
3 shallots, coarsely chopped
6 coriander (cilantro) roots,
  coarsely chopped
2 garlic cloves
2 fresh green chillies, seeded and
  coarsely chopped
5ml/1 tsp shrimp paste
5ml/1 tsp ground turmeric

1 Make the curry paste. Place all the ingredients in a large mortar, or food processor and pound with a pestle or process to a smooth paste.

2 Heat the sunflower oil in a wok or large, heavy frying pan, add the garlic and cook over a low heat, stirring frequently, until golden brown. Be careful not to let the garlic burn or it will taste bitter. Add the curry paste and stir-fry with the garlic for about 30 seconds more.

3 Add the chicken pieces to the pan and stir until thoroughly coated with the curry paste. Stir in the Thai fish sauce and chicken stock, with the sugar, and cook, stirring constantly, for 2 minutes more.

4 Add the lemon grass and lime leaves, reduce the heat and simmer for 10 minutes. If the mixture begins to dry out, add a little more stock or water.

5 Remove the lemon grass, if you like. Spoon the curry into four dishes, garnish with the lime leaves, peanuts and coriander and serve immediately.

Energy 122kcal/512kJ; Protein 17.4g; Carbohydrate 3.7g, of which sugars 3g; Fat 4.3g, of which saturates 0.8g; Cholesterol 85mg; Calcium 77mg; Fibre 1.6g; Sodium 131mg.

YELLOW CHICKEN CURRY ★

THE PAIRING OF SLIGHTLY SWEET LOW-FAT COCONUT MILK AND FRUIT WITH THE SAVOURY CHICKEN AND SPICES IS AT ONCE A COMFORTING, REFRESHING AND EXOTIC COMBINATION.

SERVES 4

INGREDIENTS
300ml/½ pint/1¼ cups
  chicken stock
30ml/2 tbsp thick tamarind juice,
  made by mixing tamarind paste with
  warm water
15ml/1 tbsp granulated sugar
200ml/7fl oz/scant 1 cup reduced-fat
  coconut milk
1 green papaya, peeled, seeded and
  thinly sliced
250g/9oz skinless chicken breast
  fillets, diced
juice of 1 lime
lime slices, to garnish

For the curry paste
1 fresh red chilli, seeded and
  coarsely chopped
4 garlic cloves, coarsely chopped
3 shallots, coarsely chopped
2 lemon grass stalks, sliced
5cm/2in piece fresh turmeric,
  coarsely chopped, or 5ml/1 tsp
  ground turmeric
5ml/1 tsp shrimp paste
5ml/1 tsp salt

COOK'S TIP
Fresh turmeric resembles root ginger in appearance and is a member of the same family. When preparing it, wear gloves to protect your hands from staining.

1 Make the yellow curry paste. Put the red chilli, garlic, shallots, lemon grass and turmeric in a mortar or food processor. Add the shrimp paste and salt. Pound or process to a paste, adding a little water if necessary.

2 Pour the stock into a wok or medium pan and bring it to the boil. Stir in the curry paste. Bring back to the boil and add the tamarind juice, sugar and coconut milk. Add the papaya and chicken and cook over a medium to high heat for about 15 minutes, stirring frequently, until the chicken is cooked.

3 Stir in the lime juice, transfer to a warm dish and serve immediately, garnished with lime slices.

Energy 146kcal/619kJ; Protein 16.4g; Carbohydrate 18.6g, of which sugars 18g; Fat 1.2g, of which saturates 0.3g; Cholesterol 44mg; Calcium 77mg; Fibre 3.5g; Sodium 103mg.

SOUTHERN CHICKEN CURRY ★★

A MILD COCONUT CURRY FLAVOURED WITH TURMERIC, CORIANDER AND CUMIN SEEDS THAT DEMONSTRATES THE INFLUENCE OF MALAYSIAN COOKING ON THAI CUISINE.

SERVES 6

INGREDIENTS
 30ml/2 tbsp sunflower oil
 1 large garlic clove, crushed
 1 chicken, weighing about
  1.5kg/3–3½lb, chopped into
  12 large pieces
 400ml/14fl oz/1⅔ cups reduced-fat
  coconut milk
 250ml/8fl oz/1 cup chicken stock
 30ml/2 tbsp Thai fish sauce
 30ml/2 tbsp sugar
 juice of 2 limes
To garnish
 2 small fresh red chillies, seeded and
  finely chopped
 1 bunch spring onions (scallions),
  thinly sliced
For the curry paste
 5ml/1 tsp dried chilli flakes
 2.5ml/½ tsp salt
 5cm/2in piece fresh turmeric or
  5ml/1 tsp ground turmeric
 2.5ml/½ tsp coriander seeds
 2.5ml/½ tsp cumin seeds
 5ml/1 tsp dried shrimp paste

1 First make the curry paste. Put all the ingredients in a mortar, food processor or spice grinder and pound, process or grind to a smooth paste.

2 Heat the oil in a wok or frying pan and cook the garlic until golden. Add the chicken and cook until golden. Remove the chicken and set aside.

3 Reheat the oil and add the curry paste and then half the coconut milk. Cook for a few minutes until fragrant.

4 Return the chicken to the wok or pan, add the stock, mixing well, then add the remaining coconut milk, the fish sauce, sugar and lime juice. Stir well and bring to the boil, then lower the heat and simmer for 15 minutes.

5 Turn the curry into six warm serving bowls and sprinkle with the chopped fresh chillies and spring onions to garnish. Serve immediately.

VARIATION
For a delicious curry that is even lower in fat, remove the skin before cooking the chicken in step 2.

COOK'S TIP
Use a large sharp knife or a Chinese cleaver to chop the chicken into pieces. Wash the board, knife and your hands thoroughly afterwards in hot, soapy water as chicken is notorious for harbouring harmful micro-organisms and bacteria.

Energy 222kcal/935kJ; Protein 29g; Carbohydrate 9.8g, of which sugars 9.5g; Fat 7.7g, of which saturates 1.7g; Cholesterol 144mg; Calcium 50mg; Fibre 0.4g; Sodium 231mg.

MARMALADE AND SOY ROAST DUCK ★★

Sweet-and-sour flavours complement the rich, fatty taste of duck beautifully. Serve this robustly flavoured dish with simple accompaniments such as steamed rice and pak choi.

SERVES 6

INGREDIENTS

   6 duck breast fillets
   45ml/3 tbsp fine-cut marmalade
   45ml/3 tbsp light soy sauce
   salt and ground black pepper

VARIATIONS

• Marmalade gives the duck a lovely citrus flavour but this recipe also works well if you substitute black cherry jam. Use a little plum sauce instead of the light soy sauce if you like, but not too much as the flavour of the cherries will be swamped.

• If the occasion calls for a little ceremony, roast a whole duck. You will need to prick the skin of the bird all over before roasting, so that the fat, which is trapped in a layer beneath the skin, will be released during cooking. This excess oily matter can then be drained off during cooking.

1 Preheat the oven to 190°C/375°F/ Gas 5. Place the duck breasts skin side up on a grill (broiler) rack and place in the sink.

2 Pour boiling water all over the duck. This shrinks the skin and helps it crisp during cooking. Pat the duck dry with kitchen paper and transfer to a roasting pan.

3 Combine the marmalade and soy sauce, and brush over the duck. Season with a little salt and some black pepper and roast for 20–25 minutes, basting occasionally with the marmalade mixture in the pan.

4 Remove the duck breast fillets from the oven and leave to rest for 5 minutes. Slice the duck breast fillets and serve drizzled with any juices left in the pan.

Energy 160kcal/672kJ; Protein 19.9g; Carbohydrate 5.8g, of which sugars 5.8g; Fat 6.5g, of which saturates 2g; Cholesterol 110mg; Calcium 16mg; Fibre 0.1g; Sodium 645mg.

DUCK AND SESAME STIR-FRY ★★★

THIS RECIPE IS INTENDED FOR GAME BIRDS, AS FARMED DUCK WOULD USUALLY HAVE TOO MUCH FAT.
IF YOU DO USE FARMED DUCK, YOU SHOULD REMOVE THE SKIN AND FAT LAYER.

SERVES 4

INGREDIENTS

250g/9oz skinless wild duck
  breast fillets
15ml/1 tbsp sesame oil
15ml/1 tbsp vegetable oil
4 garlic cloves, finely sliced
2.5ml/½ tsp dried chilli flakes
15ml/1 tbsp Thai fish sauce
15ml/1 tbsp light soy sauce
120ml/4fl oz/½ cup water
1 head broccoli, cut into small florets
coriander (cilantro) and 15ml/1 tbsp
  toasted sesame seeds, to garnish

VARIATIONS

This also works well with pheasant or
partridge in place of the duck.

1 Cut the duck into bitesize pieces. Heat
the oils in a wok or large frying pan and
stir-fry the garlic over medium heat until
it is golden brown – do not let it burn.

2 Add the duck pieces to the pan and
stir-fry for a further 2 minutes, until the
meat begins to brown.

3 Stir in the chilli flakes, fish sauce, soy
sauce and water.

4 Add the broccoli florets and continue
to stir-fry the mixture for about 2
minutes, until the duck pieces are
just cooked through.

5 Serve immediately on warmed plates,
garnished with sprigs of coriander and
sesame seeds.

COOK'S TIP

Large wok lids are cumbersome and can
be difficult to store in a small kitchen.
If you need to cover a wok it may be
easier to just place a circle of baking
parchment against the food surface to
keep cooking juices in.

Energy 156kcal/651kJ; Protein 16.3g; Carbohydrate 1.9g, of which sugars 1.6g; Fat 10.4g, of which saturates 1.7g; Cholesterol 69mg; Calcium 58mg; Fibre 2.3g; Sodium 343mg.

FRUITY DUCK CHOP SUEY ★★★

SKINNING THE DUCK REDUCES THE FAT, BUT THIS IS STILL AN INDULGENT RECIPE. IF THIS WORRIES YOU, USE LESS DUCK AND MORE NOODLES. PINEAPPLE GIVES THE DISH A LOVELY FLAVOUR.

2 Meanwhile, heat a wok. Add the strips of duck and stir-fry for 2–3 minutes, Drain off all but 30ml/2 tbsp of the fat.

3 Add the spring onions and celery to the wok and stir-fry for 2 minutes more.

4 Use a slotted spoon to remove the ingredients from the wok and set them aside. Add the pineapple strips and mixed vegetables, and stir-fry for 2 minutes more.

5 Add the cooked noodles and plum sauce to the wok, then replace the duck, spring onion and celery mixture.

6 Stir-fry the duck mixture for about 2 minutes more, or until the noodles and vegetables are hot and the duck is cooked through. Serve immediately.

COOK'S TIP
Fresh sesame noodles can be bought from large supermarkets – you will usually find them in the chiller cabinets alongside fresh pasta. If they aren't available, then use fresh egg noodles instead and cook according to the instructions on the packet.

SERVES 4

INGREDIENTS
   250g/9oz fresh sesame noodles
   2 skinless duck breast fillets
   3 spring onions (scallions), cut
      into strips
   2 celery sticks, cut into strips
   1 fresh pineapple, peeled, cored
      and cut into strips
   300g/11oz mixed vegetables, such as
      carrots, peppers, beansprouts and
      cabbage, shredded or cut into strips
   90ml/6 tbsp plum sauce

1 Cook the noodles in a large pan of boiling water for 3 minutes. Drain. Slice the duck breast fillets into strips.

Energy 603kcal/2553kJ; Protein 36.3g; Carbohydrate 93g, of which sugars 28.1g; Fat 14.2g, of which saturates 1.7g; Cholesterol 138mg; Calcium 96mg; Fibre 6.9g; Sodium 167mg.

DUCK WITH PINEAPPLE AND GINGER ★★

DUCK IS OFTEN THOUGHT OF AS A MEAT THAT IS HIGH IN FAT, BUT IN THIS RECIPE BONELESS DUCK BREAST FILLETS ARE SKINNED FOR A DISH THAT IS BURSTING WITH FLAVOUR AND LOW IN FAT.

SERVES 3

INGREDIENTS

   2 duck breast fillets
   4 spring onions (scallions), chopped
   15ml/1 tbsp light soy sauce
   225g/8oz can pineapple rings
   75ml/5 tbsp water
   4 pieces drained stem ginger in
     syrup, plus 45ml/3 tbsp syrup
     from the jar
   30ml/2 tbsp cornflour (cornstarch)
     mixed to a paste with a little water
   1/4 each red and green (bell)
     pepper, seeded and cut into
     thin strips
   salt and ground black pepper
   cooked thin egg noodles, baby
     spinach and green beans,
     blanched, to serve

3 Drain the canned pineapple rings, reserving 75ml/5 tbsp of the juice. Add this to the reserved cooking juices in the pan, together with the measured water. Stir in the ginger syrup, then stir in the cornflour paste and cook, stirring until thickened. Season to taste.

4 Cut the pineapple and ginger into attractive shapes. Put the cooked noodles, baby spinach and green beans on a plate, add slices of duck and top with the pineapple, ginger and pepper strips. Pour over the sauce and serve.

1 Strip the skin from the duck. Select a shallow bowl that will fit into your steamer and that will accommodate the duck fillets side by side. Spread out the chopped spring onions in the bowl, arrange the duck on top and cover with baking parchment. Set the steamer over boiling water and cook the duck for about 1 hour or until tender. Remove the duck from the steamer and leave to cool slightly.

2 Cut the duck fillets into thin slices. Place on a plate and moisten them with a little of the cooking juices from the steaming bowl. Strain the remaining juices into a small pan and set aside. Cover the duck slices with the baking parchment or foil and keep warm.

Energy 253kcal/1071kJ; Protein 20.8g; Carbohydrate 33.1g, of which sugars 23.8g; Fat 6.8g, of which saturates 1.4g; Cholesterol 110mg; Calcium 31mg; Fibre 1.1g; Sodium 515mg.

DUCK WITH PLUM SAUCE ★★★

RIPE, JUICY PLUMS ARE THE PERFECT ACCOMPANIMENT FOR DUCK, PROVIDING A FRUITY COUNTERPOINT TO THE RICHNESS OF THE MEAT. THE COLOUR OF THE SAUCE LOOKS BEAUTIFUL, TOO.

SERVES 4

INGREDIENTS
  4 duck quarters
  1 large red onion, finely chopped
  500g/1¼lb ripe plums, stoned
    (pitted) and quartered
  30ml/2 tbsp redcurrant jelly
  salt and ground black pepper

1 Using a metal skewer or a fork, prick the duck skin all over to release the fat during cooking. Place the portions skin side down in a dry frying pan.

COOK'S TIP
The plums must be very ripe or the mixture will be dry and the sauce tart.

VARIATIONS
You can use a white onion instead of a red onion. Fine-cut orange marmalade is a great alternative to the redcurrant jelly.

2 Cook the duck pieces over a medium heat for 10 minutes on each side, or until they are golden brown and cooked right through.

3 Remove the duck from the frying pan using a slotted spoon, place on a plate and keep warm.

4 Pour away all but 30ml/2 tbsp of the duck fat, then stir-fry the onion for about 5 minutes, or until softened.

5 Add the plums to the wok or frying pan and cook for 5 minutes more, stirring frequently. Stir in the redcurrant jelly until dissolved.

6 Replace the duck portions and simmer gently for a further 5 minutes, or until the duck is thoroughly reheated.

7 Season to taste with salt and ground black pepper, before serving with plain egg noodles or boiled rice.

Energy 296kcal/1250kJ; Protein 35.9g; Carbohydrate 20.1g, of which sugars 19g; Fat 11.6g, of which saturates 2.3g; Cholesterol 193mg; Calcium 51mg; Fibre 2.7g; Sodium 199mg.

DUCK WITH PINEAPPLE AND PEPPER ★★

*PINEAPPLE AND DUCK IS A FAVOURITE COMBINATION, BUT THE FRUIT MUST NOT BE ALLOWED TO
DOMINATE. THESE PROPORTIONS ARE PERFECT AND THE DISH HAS A SUBTLE SWEET-SOUR FLAVOUR.*

SERVES 4

INGREDIENTS

    15ml/1 tbsp dry sherry
    15ml/1 tbsp dark soy sauce
    2 small skinless duck breast fillets
    15ml/1 tbsp vegetable oil
    2 garlic cloves, finely chopped
    1 small onion, sliced
    1 red (bell) pepper, seeded and cut
      into 2.5cm/1in squares
    75g/3oz/½ cup drained, canned
      pineapple chunks
    90ml/6 tbsp pineapple juice
    15ml/1 tbsp rice vinegar
    5ml/1 tsp cornflour (cornstarch)
    15ml/1 tbsp cold water
    5ml/1 tsp sesame oil
    salt and ground white pepper
    1 spring onion (scallion), shredded

3 Heat the vegetable oil in a non-stick frying pan or wok and stir-fry the garlic and onion for 1 minute. Add the red pepper, pineapple chunks, duck, pineapple juice and vinegar and toss over the heat for 2 minutes.

4 Mix the cornflour to a paste with the water. Add the mixture to the pan with 1.5ml/¼ tsp salt. Cook, stirring, until the sauce thickens. Stir in the sesame oil and serve immediately, garnished with spring onion shreds.

1 Mix together the sherry and soy sauce. Stir in 2.5ml/½ tsp salt and 1.5ml/¼ tsp white pepper. Put the duck fillets in a bowl and add the marinade. Cover and leave in a cool place for 1 hour.

2 Drain the duck fillets and place them on a rack in a grill (broiler) pan. Cook under a medium to high heat for 10 minutes on each side. Leave to cool for 10 minutes, then cut the duck into bite-size pieces.

VARIATION
Another type of fruit that goes well with duck is physalis or Cape gooseberry. Release each berry from its papery jacket and add to the wok instead of the pineapple.

Energy 171kcal/715kJ; Protein 15.7g; Carbohydrate 10.1g, of which sugars 8.4g; Fat 8.6g, of which saturates 1.5g; Cholesterol 83mg; Calcium 21mg; Fibre 1g; Sodium 355mg.

MARINATED DUCK CURRY ★★

THE DUCK IS BEST MARINATED FOR AS LONG AS POSSIBLE, ALTHOUGH THE FLAVOUR WILL BE
IMPROVED EVEN IF YOU ONLY HAVE TIME TO MARINATE IT FOR A SHORT PERIOD.

2 Meanwhile, bring a pan of water to the boil. Add the squash and cook for 10–15 minutes, until just tender. Drain well and set aside.

3 Pour the marinade from the duck into a wok and heat until boiling. Stir in the curry paste and cook for 2–3 minutes, until well blended and fragrant. Add the duck and cook for 3–4 minutes, stirring constantly, until browned on all sides.

4 Add the fish sauce and palm sugar and cook for 2 minutes more. Stir in the coconut milk until the mixture is smooth, then add the cooked squash, with the chillies and lime leaves.

5 Simmer gently, stirring frequently, for 5 minutes, then spoon into a dish, sprinkle with the coriander and serve with cooked noodles.

VARIATION
This dish works just as well with skinless chicken breast fillets.

SERVES 4

INGREDIENTS
   4 duck breast portions, skin and
     bones removed
   30ml/2 tbsp five-spice powder
   15ml/1 tbsp sesame oil
   grated rind and juice of 1 orange
   1 medium butternut squash, peeled
     and cubed
   10ml/2 tsp Thai red curry paste
   30ml/2 tbsp Thai fish sauce
   15ml/1 tbsp palm sugar
   300ml/½ pint/1¼ cups reduced-fat
     coconut milk
   2 fresh red chillies, seeded
   4 kaffir lime leaves, torn
   small bunch coriander (cilantro),
     chopped, to garnish

1 Cut the duck meat into bitesize pieces and place in a bowl with the five-spice powder, sesame oil and orange rind and juice. Stir well to mix all the ingredients and coat the duck in the marinade. Cover the bowl with clear film (plastic wrap) and set aside in a cool place to marinate for at least 15 minutes.

Energy 182kcal/767kJ; Protein 20.3g; Carbohydrate 7.9g, of which sugars 7.9g; Fat 9.6g, of which saturates 1.9g; Cholesterol 110mg; Calcium 61mg; Fibre 0.6g; Sodium 197mg.

DUCK <u>AND</u> GINGER CHOP SUEY ★★★

CHICKEN CAN ALSO BE USED IN THIS RECIPE, AND WOULD BE LOWER IN FAT, BUT DUCK GIVES A RICHER RESULT AND IS GREAT FOR A SPECIAL TREAT. START MAKING THIS A DAY AHEAD, IF YOU CAN.

SERVES 4

INGREDIENTS
    2 duck breast fillets, about
        175g/6oz each
    30ml/2 tbsp vegetable oil
    1 egg, lightly beaten
    1 garlic clove
    175g/6oz beansprouts
    2 slices fresh root ginger, cut
        into matchsticks
    10ml/2 tsp oyster sauce
    2 spring onions (scallions), cut
        into matchsticks
    salt and ground black pepper
For the marinade
    15ml/1 tbsp clear honey
    10ml/2 tsp Chinese rice wine
    10ml/2 tsp light soy sauce
    10ml/2 tsp dark soy sauce

3 Bruise the garlic with the flat blade of a knife. Heat the wok, then add 10ml/2 tsp oil. When the oil is hot, add the garlic and fry for 30 seconds, pressing it to release the flavour. Discard. Add the beansprouts with seasoning and stir-fry for 30 seconds. Transfer to a heated dish, draining off any liquid.

4 Heat the wok and add the remaining oil. When the oil is hot, stir-fry the duck for 3 minutes until cooked. Add the ginger and oyster sauce and stir-fry for a further 2 minutes.

5 Add the beansprouts, egg strips and spring onions, stir-fry briefly and serve.

1 Remove the skin and fat from the duck, cut the breasts into thin strips and place in a bowl. Mix the marinade ingredients together, pour over the duck, cover with clear film (plastic wrap), and marinate in the refrigerator for 6–8 hours or overnight.

2 Next day, make an egg omelette. Heat a small frying pan and add 15ml/1 tbsp of the oil. When the oil is hot, pour in the egg and swirl around to make an omelette. Once cooked, leave it to cool and cut into strips. Drain the duck and discard the marinade.

COOK'S TIP
If you like the flavour of garlic, add 1–2 crushed cloves with the beansprouts instead of just using it to flavour the oil.

Energy 202kcal/844kJ; Protein 20.3g; Carbohydrate 5.1g, of which sugars 4.3g; Fat 12.8g, of which saturates 2.2g; Cholesterol 144mg; Calcium 29mg; Fibre 0.7g; Sodium 384mg.

DUCK WITH PANCAKES ★★

THIS HAS CONSIDERABLY LESS FAT THAN TRADITIONAL PEKING DUCK, BUT IS JUST AS DELICIOUS.
GUESTS SPREAD THEIR PANCAKES WITH SAUCE, ADD DUCK AND VEGETABLES, THEN ROLL THEM UP.

SERVES 4

INGREDIENTS
   15ml/1 tbsp clear honey
   1.5ml/¼ tsp five-spice powder
   1 garlic clove, finely chopped
   15ml/1 tbsp hoisin sauce
   2.5ml/½ tsp salt
   a large pinch of ground white pepper
   2 small skinless duck breast fillets
   ½ cucumber
   10 spring onions (scallions)
   3 leaves from a head of Chinese
      leaves (Chinese cabbage)
   12 Chinese pancakes (see Cook's Tip)
For the sauce
   5ml/1 tsp vegetable oil
   2 garlic cloves, chopped
   2 spring onions (scallions), chopped
   1cm/½in fresh root ginger, bruised
   60ml/4 tbsp hoisin sauce
   15ml/1 tbsp dry sherry
   15ml/1 tbsp cold water
   2.5ml/½ tsp sesame oil

1 Mix the honey, five-spice powder, garlic, hoisin sauce, salt and pepper in a shallow dish which is large enough to hold the duck fillets side by side. Add the duck fillets, and turn to coat them in the marinade.

2 Cover the dish with clear film (plastic wrap) and leave in a cool place to marinate for 2 hours, or overnight if you have the time.

3 Cut the cucumber in half lengthways. Using a teaspoon scrape out and discard the seeds. Cut the flesh into thin batons 5cm/2in long.

4 Cut off and discard the green tops from the spring onions. Finely shred the white parts and place on a serving plate with the cucumber batons.

5 Make the sauce. Heat the oil in a small pan and fry the garlic gently for a few seconds without browning. Add the spring onions, ginger, hoisin sauce, sherry and water. Cook gently for 5 minutes, stirring often, then strain and mix with the sesame oil.

6 Remove the duck fillets from the marinade and drain. Grill (broil) under a medium heat for 8–10 minutes on each side. Leave to cool for 5 minutes before cutting into thin slices. Arrange on a serving platter, cover and keep warm.

7 Line a bamboo steamer with the Chinese leaves and place the pancakes on top.

8 Pour boiling water into a large pan, to a depth of 5cm/2in. Cover the steamer and place it on a trivet in the pan of boiling water.

9 Steam for 2 minutes or until the pancakes are hot. Serve at once with the duck, cucumber, spring onions and the sauce.

COOK'S TIP
Chinese pancakes can be bought frozen from Chinese supermarkets. Leave to thaw before steaming.

Energy 241kcal/1018kJ; Protein 19.1g; Carbohydrate 29.6g, of which sugars 7.5g; Fat 6.3g, of which saturates 1.1g; Cholesterol 83mg; Calcium 92mg; Fibre 2.6g; Sodium 462mg.

CRISPY ROAST DUCK ★★

THIS DISH IS VIETNAM'S ANSWER TO PEKING DUCK, ALTHOUGH HERE THE SUCCULENT, CRISPY BIRD IS ENJOYED IN ONE COURSE. IN A VIETNAMESE HOME, THE DUCK IS SERVED WITH PICKLED VEGETABLES OR A SALAD, SEVERAL DIPPING SAUCES, AND A FRAGRANT STEAMED RICE.

2 Preheat the oven to 220°C/425°F/Gas 7. Stuff the ginger, garlic, lemon grass and spring onions into the duck's cavity and tie the legs with string. Using a bamboo or metal skewer, poke holes in the skin, including the legs.

3 Place the duck, breast side down, on a rack over a roasting pan and cook it in the oven for 45 minutes, basting from time to time with the juices that have dripped into the pan. After 45 minutes, turn the duck over so that it is breast side up. Baste it generously and return it to the oven for a further 45 minutes, basting it every 15 minutes. The duck is ready once the juices run clear when the bird is pierced with a skewer.

4 Serve immediately, pulling at the skin and meat with your fingers, rather than neatly carving it. Serve with ginger dipping sauce, *nuoc mam gung*, pickled vegetables and salad leaves for wrapping up the morsels.

COOK'S TIP
Leaving the duck uncovered in the refrigerator for 24 hours will allow the skin to dry out thoroughly, ensuring that it becomes crispy when it is roasted.

SERVES 6

INGREDIENTS
1 duck, about 2.25kg/5lb
90g/3½oz fresh root ginger, peeled, roughly chopped and lightly crushed
4 garlic cloves, peeled and crushed
1 lemon grass stalk, halved and bruised
4 spring onions (scallions), halved and crushed
ginger dipping sauce, *nuoc mam gung*, pickled vegetables and salad leaves, to serve
For the marinade
80ml/3fl oz fish sauce
30ml/2 tbsp soy sauce
30ml/2 tbsp honey
15ml/1 tbsp five-spice powder
5ml/1 tsp ground ginger

1 In a bowl, beat the ingredients for the marinade together until well blended. Rub the skin of the duck lightly to loosen it, until you can get your fingers between the skin and the meat. Rub the marinade all over the duck, inside its skin and out, then place the duck on a rack over a tray and put it in the refrigerator for 24 hours.

Energy 210kcal/883kJ; Protein 27.4g; Carbohydrate 5.8g, of which sugars 4.5g; Fat 8.8g, of which saturates 2.7g; Cholesterol 147mg; Calcium 35mg; Fibre 0.8g; Sodium 506mg.

DUCK <u>IN A</u> SPICY ORANGE SAUCE ★★

ALTHOUGH DUCK HAS A DELICIOUSLY RICH FLAVOUR, THE SKIN CAN BE QUITE FATTY AND MAKE THIS MEAT DIFFICULT FOR THOSE FOLLOWING A LOW-FAT DIET. TO REDUCE THE FAT CONTENT OF THIS DISH SIMPLY REMOVE THE SKIN BEFORE SERVING. SERVE WITH STEAMED RICE AND BRIGHT VEGETABLES.

SERVES 4

INGREDIENTS

   4 duck legs
   4 garlic cloves, crushed
   50g/2oz fresh root ginger, peeled and
     finely sliced
   2 lemon grass stalks, trimmed,
     cut into 3 pieces and crushed
   2 dried whole red Thai chillies
   15ml/1 tbsp palm sugar
   5ml/1 tsp five-spice powder
   30ml/2 tbsp *nuoc cham* or *tuk trey*
   900ml/1½ pints/3¾ cups fresh
     orange juice
   sea salt and ground black pepper
   1 lime, cut into quarters

3 Stir in the orange juice and place the duck legs back in the pan. Cover the pan and gently cook the duck for 1–2 hours, until the meat is tender and the sauce has reduced. Season and serve with lime wedges to squeeze over it.

1 Place the duck legs, skin side down, in a large heavy pan or flameproof clay pot. Cook them on both sides over a medium heat for about 10 minutes, until browned and crispy. Transfer them to a plate and set aside.

2 Stir the garlic, ginger, lemon grass and chillies into the fat left in the pan, and cook until golden. Add the sugar, five-spice powder and *nuoc cham* or *tuk trey*.

Energy 234kcal/986kJ; Protein 22.1g; Carbohydrate 26g, of which sugars 24.2g; Fat 6.9g, of which saturates 1.3g; Cholesterol 110mg; Calcium 59mg; Fibre 1.2g; Sodium 137mg.

LAMB, PORK AND BEEF

Balancing relatively small amounts of meat with plenty of vegetables and noodles or rice is standard practice in Thailand and China, so recipes from these regions are good for reducing the amount of red meat you eat. Sizzling Beef with Celeriac Straw, and Beef with Fried Rice illustrate this point perfectly. Sticky Pork Ribs sound wickedly indulgent but are also acceptable, largely because what looks like a generous plateful contains a small proportion of meat to bone.

GLAZED LAMB ★★★

LEMON AND HONEY MAKE A CLASSICALLY GOOD COMBINATION IN SWEET DISHES, AND THIS LAMB
RECIPE SHOWS HOW WELL THEY WORK TOGETHER IN SAVOURY DISHES, TOO.

2 Heat the wok, then add the oil. When the oil is hot, stir-fry the lamb until browned all over. Remove from the wok and keep warm.

3 Add the mangetouts and spring onions to the hot wok and stir-fry for 30 seconds.

4 Return the lamb to the wok and add the honey, lemon juice, coriander and sesame seeds, and season well. Bring the sauce to the boil and bubble for 2–3 minutes until the lamb is cooked through and is well coated in the honey mixture.

SERVES 4

INGREDIENTS
  350g/12oz lean boneless lamb
  15ml/1 tbsp vegetable oil
  175g/6oz mangetouts
    (snow peas), trimmed
  3 spring onions (scallions), sliced
  30ml/2 tbsp clear honey
  juice of ½ lemon
  30ml/2 tbsp fresh coriander
    (cilantro), chopped
  10ml/2 tsp sesame seeds
  salt and ground black pepper

1 Trim any visible fat from the lamb. Using a cleaver or sharp knife, cut the lamb into thin strips.

Energy 223kcal/931kJ; Protein 19g; Carbohydrate 7.8g, of which sugars 7.4g; Fat 13.0g, of which saturates 4.9g; Cholesterol 67mg; Calcium 34mg; Fibre 1.2g; Sodium 78mg.

LAMB SATÉ ★

THESE TASTY LAMB SKEWERS ARE TRADITIONALLY SERVED WITH DAINTY DIAMOND-SHAPED PIECES OF COMPRESSED RICE, WHICH ARE SURPRISINGLY SIMPLE TO MAKE. RESERVE SOME SAUCE FOR DIPPING.

MAKES 30 SKEWERS

INGREDIENTS

1kg/2¼lb leg of lamb, boned
3 garlic cloves, crushed
15–30ml/1–2 tbsp chilli sambal or
5–10ml/1–2 tsp chilli powder
90ml/6 tbsp dark soy sauce
juice of 1 lemon
salt and ground black pepper
spray sunflower oil, for spraying
For the chilli sauce
6 garlic cloves, crushed
15ml/1 tbsp chilli sambal or
2–3 fresh chillies, seeded and
ground to a paste
90ml/6 tbsp dark soy sauce
25ml/1½ tbsp lemon juice
30ml/2 tbsp boiling water
To serve
thinly sliced onion
cucumber wedges (optional)
compressed-rice shapes (see
Cook's Tip)

1 Cut the lamb into neat 1cm/½in cubes. Remove any pieces of gristle, and trim off any excess fat. Spread out the lamb cubes in a single layer in a shallow bowl.

2 Put the garlic, chilli sambal or chilli powder, soy sauce and lemon juice in a mortar. Add salt and pepper and grind to a paste. Alternatively, process the mixture using a food processor. Pour over the lamb and mix to coat. Cover and leave in a cool place for at least 1 hour. Soak wooden or bamboo skewers in water to prevent them from scorching during cooking.

3 Prepare the chilli sauce. Put the crushed garlic into a bowl. Add the chilli sambal or fresh chillies, soy sauce, lemon juice and boiling water. Stir well. Preheat the grill.

4 Thread the meat on to the skewers. Spray the skewered meat with oil and grill, turning often. Brush the saté with a little of the sauce and serve hot, with onion, cucumber wedges, if using, rice shapes and the sauce.

COOK'S TIP

Compressed rice shapes are easy to make. Cook two 115g/4oz packets of boil-in-the-bag rice in a large pan of salted, boiling water and simmer for 1¼ hours until the cooked rice fills each bag like a plump cushion. The bags must be covered with water throughout. When cool, cut each rice slab horizontally in half, then into diamond shapes using a sharp, wetted knife.

Energy 33kcal/139kJ; Protein 3.5g; Carbohydrate 0.6g, of which sugars 0.3g; Fat 1.9g, of which saturates 0.9g; Cholesterol 13mg; Calcium 2mg; Fibre 0.1g; Sodium 86mg.

MONGOLIAN FIREPOT ★★

IT IS WORTH INVESTING IN AN AUTHENTIC HOTPOT OR FIREPOT, JUST TO SEE THE DELIGHT ON YOUR GUESTS' FACES WHEN THEY SPY WHAT YOU HAVE IN STORE FOR THEM. THIS TASTES GREAT TOO.

SERVES 6–8

INGREDIENTS
750g/1²/₃lb boned leg of lamb,
  preferably bought thinly sliced
225g/8oz lamb's liver and/or kidneys
900ml/1½ pints/3¾ cups lamb stock
  (see Cook's Tip)
900ml/1½ pints/3¾ cups
  chicken stock
1cm/½in piece fresh root ginger,
  peeled and thinly sliced
45ml/3 tbsp rice wine or
  medium-dry sherry
½ head Chinese leaves
  (Chinese cabbage), rinsed
  and shredded
100g/3½oz young spinach leaves
250g/9oz fresh firm tofu, diced
115g/4oz cellophane noodles
salt and ground black pepper
For the dipping sauce
50ml/2fl oz/¼ cup red
  wine vinegar
7.5ml/½ tbsp dark soy sauce
1cm/½in piece fresh root ginger,
  peeled and finely shredded
1 spring onion (scallion),
  finely shredded
To serve
Steamed Flower Rolls
bowls of tomato sauce, sweet chilli
  sauce, mustard oil and sesame oil
dry-fried coriander seeds, crushed

COOK'S TIP
When buying the lamb, ask the butcher for the bones and make your own lamb stock. Rinse the bones and place them in a large pan with water to cover. Bring to the boil and skim the surface well. Add 1 peeled onion, 2 peeled carrots, 1cm/½in piece of peeled and bruised ginger, 5ml/1 tsp salt and ground black pepper to taste. Bring back to the boil, then simmer for about an hour until the stock is full of flavour. Strain, leave to cool, then skim and use.

1 Ask the butcher from whom you buy the lamb to slice it thinly on a slicing machine. If you have had to buy the lamb in one piece, however, trim off any fat, then put the leg in the freezer for about an hour, so that it is easier to slice thinly.

2 Trim the liver and remove the skin and core from the kidneys, if using. Place them in the freezer too. If you managed to buy sliced lamb, keep it in the refrigerator until needed.

3 Mix both types of stock in a large pan. Add the sliced ginger and rice wine or sherry, with salt and pepper to taste. Heat to simmering point; simmer for 15 minutes.

4 Slice all the meats thinly and arrange them on a large platter.

5 Place the shredded Chinese leaves, spinach leaves and the diced tofu on a separate platter.

6 Soak the noodles in a bowl of warm or hot water, following the instructions on the packet.

7 Make the dipping sauce by mixing all the ingredients together in a small bowl. The other sauces and the crushed coriander seeds should be spooned into separate small dishes and placed on a serving tray.

8 Have ready a basket of warm Steamed Flower Rolls.

9 Fill the moat of the hotpot with the simmering stock. Alternatively, fill a fondue pot and place it over a burner.

10 Each guest selects a portion of meat from the platter and cooks it in the hot stock, using chopsticks or a fondue fork. The meat is then dipped in one of the sauces and coated with the coriander seeds (if you like) before being eaten with a steamed flower roll.

11 When most of the meat has been eaten, top up the stock if necessary, then add the vegetables, tofu and drained noodles. Cook for a minute or two, until the noodles are tender and the vegetables retain a little crispness. Serve the soup in warmed bowls, with any remaining steamed flower rolls.

Energy 144kcal/606kJ; Protein 12.3g; Carbohydrate 12g, of which sugars 1.2g; Fat 5.1g, of which saturates 1.1g; Cholesterol 128mg; Calcium 193mg; Fibre 0.9g; Sodium 49mg.

MINTED LAMB ★★★

*NO MATTER WHAT CUT YOU USE, LAMB IS A FATTY MEAT, SO CAN'T BE EATEN IN HUGE QUANTITIES.
RELISH THE FLAVOUR OF THIS STIR-FRY AND FILL ANY GAPS WITH COUSCOUS AND A GREEN SALAD.*

SERVES 4

INGREDIENTS
    300g/11oz boneless leg of lamb
    30ml/2 tbsp chopped fresh mint
    ½ lemon
    300ml/½ pint/1¼ cups natural
      (plain) low-fat yogurt
    15ml/1 tbsp sunflower oil
    salt and ground black pepper
    lemon wedges and fresh mint sprigs,
      to garnish

1 Place the lamb on a board. Using a
sharp knife or cleaver, cut the lamb into
6mm/¼in thick slices. Spread out the
slices in a bowl or shallow dish.

2 Sprinkle half the chopped mint over
the lamb, season well with salt and
pepper and use your fingers to work the
flavourings into the meat. Cover the bowl
with clear film (plastic wrap) and leave
the lamb to marinate for 20 minutes.

3 Remove any visible seeds from the
lemon and cut it into wedges, including
the skin. Place the lemon wedges in a
food processor. Process until finely
chopped.

4 Scrape the lemon into a bowl, then
stir in the yogurt and the remaining
chopped mint. Add salt and pepper
to taste, if you like.

5 Heat a wok, then add the oil, trickling
it around the inner rim so that it runs
down to coat the surface. When the oil
is hot, add the lamb and stir-fry for
4–5 minutes until cooked. Garnish with
lemon wedges and fresh mint sprigs,
and serve with the yogurt sauce.

Energy 268kcal/1120kJ; Protein 25.9g; Carbohydrate 5.6g, of which sugars 5.6g; Fat 15.0g, of which saturates 6.6g; Cholesterol 86mg; Calcium 152mg; Fibre 0g; Sodium 159mg.

PORK <u>ON</u> LEMON GRASS STICKS ★

THIS SIMPLE RECIPE MAKES AN INTERESTING DISH. THE LEMON GRASS STICKS NOT ONLY ADD A SUBTLE FLAVOUR BUT ALSO MAKE A GOOD TALKING POINT AT A DINNER WITH FAMILY AND FRIENDS.

SERVES 4

INGREDIENTS
  300g/11oz minced (ground)
    lean pork
  4 garlic cloves, crushed
  4 fresh coriander (cilantro) roots,
    finely chopped
  2.5ml/½ tsp granulated sugar
  15ml/1 tbsp soy sauce
  salt and ground black pepper
  8 x 10cm/4in lengths of lemon
    grass stalk
  sweet chilli sauce, to serve

VARIATION
Slimmer versions of these pork sticks are perfect for parties. The mixture will be enough for 12 lemon grass sticks if you use it sparingly.

1 Place the minced pork, crushed garlic, chopped coriander root, sugar and soy sauce in a large bowl. Season with salt and pepper to taste and mix well.

2 Divide into eight portions and mould each one into a ball. It may help to dampen your hands before shaping the mixture to prevent it from sticking.

3 Stick a length of lemon grass halfway into each ball, then press the meat mixture around the lemon grass to make a shape like a chicken leg.

4 Cook the pork sticks under a hot grill (broiler) for 3–4 minutes on each side, until golden and cooked through. Serve with the chilli sauce for dipping.

Energy 111kcal/467kJ; Protein 17.5g; Carbohydrate 3.3g, of which sugars 1.4g; Fat 3.2g, of which saturates 1.1g; Cholesterol 47mg; Calcium 29mg; Fibre 1g; Sodium 323mg.

STICKY PORK RIBS ★★

MANY PEOPLE ASSUME PORK RIBS TO BE HIGH IN FAT, BUT THESE FALL WELL WITHIN ACCEPTABLE LIMITS. TAKE THE TIME TO MARINATE THE MEAT AS THIS ALLOWS ALL THE FLAVOURS TO PERMEATE.

2 Place the pork ribs in an ovenproof dish and pour the marinade over. Mix thoroughly, cover and leave in a cool place for 1 hour.

3 Preheat the oven to 180°C/350°F/ Gas 4. Cover the dish tightly with foil and bake the pork ribs for 40 minutes. Baste the ribs from time to time with the cooking juices.

4 Remove the foil, baste the ribs and continue to cook for 20 minutes until glossy and brown.

5 Garnish the ribs with chives and sliced spring onion and serve with a salad or rice.

COOK'S TIP

- The ribs barbecue very well. Par-cook them in the oven for 40 minutes as described in the main recipe, then transfer them to the barbecue for 15 minutes to finish cooking. The sauce coating makes the ribs liable to burn, so watch them closely.
- Don't forget finger bowls when serving these. They are not called sticky ribs for nothing.

SERVES 4

INGREDIENTS

   30ml/2 tbsp caster (superfine) sugar
   2.5ml/½ tsp five-spice powder
   45ml/3 tbsp hoisin sauce
   30ml/2 tbsp yellow bean sauce
   3 garlic cloves, finely chopped
   15ml/1 tbsp cornflour (cornstarch)
   2.5ml/½ tsp salt
   16 meaty pork ribs
   chives and sliced spring onion
     (scallion), to garnish
   salad or rice, to serve

1 Combine the caster sugar, five-spice powder, hoisin sauce, yellow bean sauce, garlic, cornflour and salt in a bowl, then mix together well.

Energy 239kcal/1006kJ; Protein 32.4g; Carbohydrate 14.5g, of which sugars 10.9g; Fat 6.1g, of which saturates 2.1g; Cholesterol 95mg; Calcium 17mg; Fibre 0.1g; Sodium 291mg.

DRY-COOKED PORK STRIPS ★★

THIS TASTY DISH IS QUICK AND LIGHT ON A HOT DAY. WITH THE LETTUCE AND HERBS, IT'S A VERY FLAVOURSOME MEAL, BUT YOU CAN SERVE IT WITH JASMINE RICE AND A DIPPING SAUCE, IF YOU LIKE.

SERVES 2

INGREDIENTS

  15ml/1 tbsp sunflower oil
  30ml/2 tbsp fish sauce
  30ml/2 tbsp soy sauce
  5ml/1 tsp sugar
  225g/8oz lean pork fillet, cut into
    thin, bitesize strips
  8 lettuce leaves
  chilli sauce, for drizzling
  fresh coriander (cilantro) leaves
  a handful of fresh mint leaves

VARIATION
Try basil, flat leaf parsley, spring onions
or sliced red onion in these parcels.

1 In a wok or heavy pan, heat the oil, fish sauce and soy sauce with the sugar. Add the pork and stir-fry over a medium heat, until all the liquid has evaporated. Cook the pork until it turns brown, almost caramelized, but not burnt.

2 Use a slotted spoon to lift the pork strips out of the wok. Place the cooked pork on to lettuce leaves, drizzle a little chilli sauce over the top, add a few coriander and mint leaves, wrap them up and serve immediately.

Energy 104kcal/435kJ; Protein 12.5g; Carbohydrate 2.1g, of which sugars 2g; Fat 5.1g, of which saturates 1.2g; Cholesterol 35mg; Calcium 13mg; Fibre 0.2g; Sodium 574mg.

ROASTED AND MARINATED PORK ★★

JAPANESE COOKS OFTEN USE A SOY SAUCE AND CITRUS MARINADE TO FLAVOUR MEAT, ADDING IT
BEFORE OR AFTER COOKING. IF POSSIBLE, LEAVE THE MEAT TO MARINATE OVERNIGHT.

SERVES 4

INGREDIENTS
 600g/1⅓lb pork fillet (tenderloin)
 1 garlic clove, crushed
 generous pinch of salt
 4 spring onions (scallions), trimmed,
  white part only
 10g/¼oz dried wakame seaweed,
  soaked in water for 20 minutes
  and drained
 10cm/4in celery stick, trimmed
  and cut in half crossways
 1 carton mustard and cress
  (fine curled cress)
For the sauce
 105ml/7 tbsp shoyu or other
  soy sauce
 45ml/3 tbsp sake
 60ml/4 tbsp mirin
 1 lime, sliced into thin rings

1 Preheat the oven to 200°C/400°F/
Gas 6. Rub the pork with crushed garlic
and salt, and leave for 15 minutes.

2 Roast the pork for 20 minutes, then
turn the meat over and reduce the
oven temperature to 180°C/350°F/
Gas 4. Cook for a further 20 minutes,
or until the pork is cooked and there
are no pink juices when it is pierced.

3 Meanwhile, mix the sauce ingredients
in a container that is big enough to hold
the pork.

4 When the meat is completely cooked,
immediately put it in the sauce, and
leave it to marinate for at least 2 hours,
or overnight.

5 Cut the white part of the spring
onions in half crossways, then in half
lengthways. Remove the round cores,
then lay the spring onion quarters flat
on a chopping board. Slice them very
thinly lengthways to make fine shreds.

6 Soak the shreds of spring onion in a
bowl of ice-cold water. Repeat with the
remaining parts of the spring onions.
When the shreds curl up, drain and
gather them into a loose ball.

7 Cut the drained wakame seaweed into
2.5cm/1in squares or narrow strips.

8 Slice the trimmed celery very thinly
lengthways. Soak in cold water. When
the shreds curl up, drain and gather
them into a loose ball.

9 Remove the pork from the marinade
and wipe it with kitchen paper to soak
up any excess. Slice the pork into slices
of medium thickness.

10 Strain the marinade into a gravy
boat or jug (pitcher).

11 Arrange the sliced pork on a large
serving plate and place the vegetables
around it. Serve cold with the sauce.

Energy 198kcal/830kJ; Protein 32.6g; Carbohydrate 0.9g, of which sugars 0.9g; Fat 6.2g, of which saturates 2.1g; Cholesterol 95mg; Calcium 24mg; Fibre 0.4g; Sodium 114mg.

CHAR-SIU PORK ★

LEAN PORK FILLET OR TENDERLOIN IS A DENSE MEAT, SO A LITTLE GOES A LONG WAY. IT TASTES WONDERFUL WHEN MARINATED, ROASTED AND GLAZED WITH HONEY, AND CAN BE SERVED HOT OR COLD.

SERVES 6

INGREDIENTS

15ml/1 tbsp vegetable oil
15ml/1 tbsp hoisin sauce
15ml/1 tbsp yellow bean sauce
1.5ml/¼ tsp five-spice powder
2.5ml/½ tsp cornflour (cornstarch)
15ml/1 tbsp caster
  (superfine) sugar
1.5ml/¼ tsp salt
1.5ml/¼ tsp ground white pepper
450g/1lb pork fillet (tenderloin),
  trimmed of fat
10ml/2 tsp clear honey
shredded spring onion (scallion),
  to garnish
rice, to serve

1 Mix the oil, sauces, five-spice powder, cornflour, sugar and seasoning in a shallow dish. Add the pork and coat it with the mixture. Cover and chill for 4 hours or overnight.

2 Preheat the oven to 190°C/375°F/ Gas 5. Drain the pork and place it on a wire rack over a deep roasting pan. Roast for 40 minutes, turning the pork over from time to time.

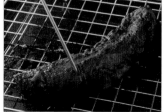

3 Check that the pork is cooked by inserting a skewer or fork into the meat; the juices should run clear. If they are still tinged with pink, roast the pork for 5–10 minutes more.

4 Remove the pork from the oven and brush it with the honey. Leave to cool for 10 minutes before cutting into thin slices. Garnish with spring onion and serve hot or cold with rice.

Energy 117kcal/491kJ; Protein 16.1g; Carbohydrate 2.4g, of which sugars 2g; Fat 4.8g, of which saturates 1.3g; Cholesterol 47mg; Calcium 6mg; Fibre 0g; Sodium 94mg.

CARAMELIZED PORK ⁱ ᴺ BAMBOO ★★★

THIS DISH IS INSPIRED BY THE REFINED IMPERIAL DISHES OF VIETNAM. IN THE PREPARATION OF DISHES FOR THE DEMANDING NINETEENTH-CENTURY EMPEROR TU DOC, CREATIVITY WAS OF THE ESSENCE. EEL IS ALSO GIVEN THIS TREATMENT — IT CAN BE SLIPPED WHOLE INTO THE BAMBOO CAVITY.

SERVES 4–6

INGREDIENTS
- 1 kg/2¼ lb lean pork shoulder, cut into thin strips
- 2 large banana leaves, torn into wide strips
- chopped fresh coriander (cilantro), to garnish
- noodles or rice and *nuoc cham*, to serve

For the marinade
- 45ml/3 tbsp unrefined or muscovado (molasses) sugar
- 60ml/4 tbsp fish sauce
- 3 shallots, finely chopped
- 6 spring onions (scallions), trimmed and finely chopped
- 1cm/½ in fresh root ginger, peeled and finely chopped
- 1 green or red Thai chilli, seeded and finely chopped

1 To make the marinade, gently heat the sugar in a heavy pan with 15ml/1 tbsp water, stirring constantly until it begins to caramelize. Remove from the heat and stir in the remaining ingredients.

2 Place the pork strips in a bowl and add the marinade. Using your fingers, toss the meat in the marinade, then cover and chill for 1–2 hours.

COOK'S TIPS
Bamboo is traditionally used as a cooking vessel in central and northern Vietnam. For this recipe, you will need two bamboo tubes, about 25cm/10in long, split in half lengthways and cleaned. You can find them in some Asian stores, or try a do-it-yourself store.

3 Line the inside of two of the bamboo halves with strips of banana leaf. Spoon in the pork, folding the edges over the top. Place the remaining bamboo halves on top to form tubes again, and then tightly wrap a wide strip of banana leaf around the outside of each tube.

4 Prepare a barbecue. Tie the bamboo parcels with string and cook over the hot barbecue for about 20 minutes. Open up the parcels, check that the pork is cooked, garnish with coriander and serve with noodles or rice and *nuoc cham.*

VARIATIONS
- This method of using a bamboo tube can also be used to cook whole fish on a barbecue.
- If you can't find banana leaves, use thin, flexible cabbage leaves or vine leaves. Alternatively, wrap the tubes in aluminium foil instead.

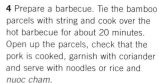

Energy 349kcal/1469kJ; Protein 44g; Carbohydrate 17g, of which sugars 14g; Fat 12g, of which saturates 4g; Cholesterol 142mg; Calcium 71mg; Fibre 1.2g; Sodium 700mg.

AROMATIC PORK WITH BASIL ★★

THE COMBINATION OF MOIST, JUICY PORK AND MUSHROOMS, CRISP GREEN MANGETOUTS AND
FRAGRANT BASIL IN THIS GINGER- AND GARLIC-INFUSED STIR-FRY IS ABSOLUTELY DELICIOUS.

SERVES 4

INGREDIENTS

40g/1½oz cornflour (cornstarch)
500g/1¼lb pork fillet (tenderloin),
  thinly sliced
15ml/1 tbsp sunflower oil
10ml/2 tsp sesame oil
15ml/1 tbsp very finely shredded
  fresh root ginger
3 garlic cloves, thinly sliced
200g/7oz/scant 2 cups mangetouts
  (snow peas), halved
300g/11oz/generous 4 cups mixed
  mushrooms, sliced if large
120ml/4fl oz/½ cup Chinese
  cooking wine
45ml/3 tbsp soy sauce
a small handful of sweet basil leaves
salt and ground black pepper
steamed jasmine rice, to serve

1 Place the cornflour in a strong plastic bag. Season well and add the sliced pork. Shake the bag to coat the pork in flour and then remove the pork and shake off any excess flour. Set aside.

2 Preheat the wok over a high heat and add the oils. When very hot, stir in the ginger and garlic and cook for 30 seconds. Add the pork and cook over a high heat for about 5 minutes, stirring often, until sealed.

3 Add the mangetouts and mushrooms to the wok and stir-fry for 2–3 minutes. Add the Chinese cooking wine and soy sauce, stir-fry for 2–3 minutes and remove from the heat. Just before serving, stir the sweet basil leaves into the pork. Serve with steamed jasmine rice.

COOK'S TIP
For the mushroom medley, try to include fresh shiitake and oyster mushrooms as well as cultivated button (white) ones.

Energy 298kcal/1248kJ; Protein 30.4g; Carbohydrate 14.6g, of which sugars 4.8g; Fat 9.8g, of which saturates 2.4g; Cholesterol 79mg; Calcium 41mg; Fibre 2g; Sodium 903mg.

SWEET-AND-SOUR PORK STIR-FRY ★

THIS IS A GREAT IDEA FOR A QUICK FAMILY SUPPER. REMEMBER TO CUT THE CARROTS INTO THIN MATCHSTICK-SIZE STRIPS SO THAT THEY COOK IN TIME WITH THE REST OF THE INGREDIENTS.

SERVES 4

INGREDIENTS

   450g/1lb lean pork fillet (tenderloin)
   30ml/2 tbsp plain (all-purpose) flour
   5ml/1 tsp sunflower oil
   1 onion, roughly chopped
   1 garlic clove, crushed
   1 green (bell) pepper, seeded
    and sliced
   350g/12oz carrots, cut into
    thin strips
   225g/8oz can bamboo shoots, drained
   15ml/1 tbsp white wine vinegar
   15ml/1 tbsp soft brown sugar
   10ml/2 tsp tomato purée (paste)
   30ml/2 tbsp light soy sauce
   salt and ground black pepper

1 Thinly slice the pork. Season the flour and toss the pork in it to coat.

2 Heat the oil and cook the pork for 5 minutes, until golden. Remove the pork and drain on kitchen paper. You may need to do this in several batches.

3 Add the onion and garlic to the pan and cook for 3 minutes. Stir in the pepper and carrots and stir-fry over a high heat for 6–8 minutes, or until beginning to soften slightly.

4 Return the meat to the pan with the bamboo shoots. Add the remaining ingredients with 120ml/4fl oz/½ cup water and bring to the boil. Simmer gently for 2–3 minutes, or until piping hot. Adjust the seasoning, if necessary, and serve immediately.

VARIATION
Finely sliced strips of skinless chicken breast fillet can be used in this recipe instead of the pork.

Energy 235kcal/988kJ; Protein 25.3g; Carbohydrate 23.9g, of which sugars 16.2g; Fat 4.9g, of which saturates 1.6g; Cholesterol 63mg; Calcium 62mg; Fibre 4.2g; Sodium 637mg.

SWEET AND SOUR PORK ★

THIS IS ONE OF THE MOST POPULAR CHINESE DISHES IN THE WEST, BUT THE TRADITIONAL RECIPE IS WOEFULLY HIGH IN FAT. THIS LOW-FAT VERSION IS JUST AS TASTY.

SERVES 4

INGREDIENTS

15ml/1 tbsp Chinese rice wine or
  dry sherry
350g/12oz lean pork steaks
15ml/1 tbsp vegetable oil
1 garlic clove, finely chopped
½ onion, diced
1 small green (bell) pepper, seeded
  and cut into 2.5cm/1in squares
1 small carrot, sliced
75g/3oz/½ cup drained, canned
  pineapple chunks
30ml/2 tbsp malt vinegar
45ml/3 tbsp tomato ketchup
150ml/¼ pint/⅔ cup pineapple juice
10ml/2 tsp caster (superfine) sugar
10ml/2 tsp cornflour (cornstarch)
15ml/1 tbsp cold water
salt and ground black pepper
rice, to serve

1 Put the sherry in a bowl large enough to hold the pork steaks. Add 2.5ml/½ tsp salt and a large pinch of pepper. Add the pork, turn to coat, then cover and leave to marinate in a cool place for 15 minutes.

COOK'S TIP

This is a great way of giving leftover pork from the Sunday roast a new lease of life. Slice it into bitesize pieces and add it to the wok instead of the freshly cooked pork steaks. It is important that the pork is heated through completely before being served. This will probably take a few minutes longer than the time suggested in the recipe. When it is hot, thicken the sauce and serve.

2 Drain the pork steaks and place them on a rack over a grill (broiler) pan. Grill (broil) under high heat for 5 minutes on each side or until cooked, then remove and leave to cool. Cut the cooked pork into bitesize pieces.

3 Heat a non-stick frying pan or wok, then add the oil. When the oil is very hot, add the garlic and onion and stir-fry for a few seconds, then add the green pepper and carrot and stir-fry for 1 minute.

4 Stir in the pineapple chunks, vinegar, tomato ketchup, pineapple juice and caster sugar. Bring to the boil, lower the heat and simmer for 3 minutes, stirring the mixture once or twice.

5 Meanwhile, put the cornflour in a small bowl. Stir in the water to make a smooth paste.

6 Add the cooked pork to the vegetable mixture and toss over the heat for about 2 minutes.

7 Tip in the cornflour paste. Cook, stirring constantly with the chopsticks or a wooden spoon, until the sauce has thickened slightly. Serve with rice in heated bowls.

VARIATION

Skinless chicken, turkey or duck breast fillets could be used in place of the pork, and you could substitute canned apricots for the canned pineapple, if you like.

Energy 168kcal/709kJ; Protein 19.7g; Carbohydrate 13.6g, of which sugars 13g; Fat 3.8g, of which saturates 1.3g; Cholesterol 55mg; Calcium 20mg; Fibre 1.1g; Sodium 251mg.

STIR-FRIED PORK WITH DRIED SHRIMP ★★

PORK AND SHRIMP ARE A POPULAR FOOD COMBINATION. YOU MIGHT EXPECT THE DRIED SHRIMP TO GIVE A STRONG, FISHY FLAVOUR, BUT INSTEAD IT SIMPLY IMPARTS A DELICIOUS SAVOURY TASTE.

SERVES 4

INGREDIENTS

250g/9oz lean pork fillet
  (tenderloin), sliced
15ml/1 tbsp sunflower oil
2 garlic cloves, finely chopped
45ml/3 tbsp dried shrimp
10ml/2 tsp dried shrimp paste or
  5mm/¼in piece from block of
  shrimp paste
30ml/2 tbsp soy sauce
juice of 1 lime
15ml/1 tbsp palm sugar or light
  muscovado (brown) sugar
1 small fresh red or green chilli,
  seeded and finely chopped
4 pak choi (bok choy) or 450g/1lb
  spring greens (collards), shredded

1 Place the pork in the freezer for about 30 minutes, until firm. Using a sharp knife, cut it into thin slices.

2 Heat the oil in a wok or frying pan and cook the garlic until golden brown. Add the pork and stir-fry for about 4 minutes, until just cooked through.

3 Add the dried shrimp, then stir in the shrimp paste, with the soy sauce, lime juice and sugar. Add the chilli and pak choi or spring greens and toss over the heat until the vegetables are just wilted.

4 Transfer the stir-fry to warm individual bowls and serve immediately.

Energy 175kcal/731kJ; Protein 23.1g; Carbohydrate 6.3g, of which sugars 6.2g; Fat 6.4g, of which saturates 1.4g; Cholesterol 96mg; Calcium 334mg; Fibre 2.4g; Sodium 1223mg.

LEMON GRASS PORK ★★

*CHILLIES AND LEMON GRASS FLAVOUR THIS SIMPLE STIR-FRY, WHILE PEANUTS ADD AN INTERESTING
CONTRAST IN TEXTURE. THE PEANUTS ENRICH THE FLAVOUR WITHOUT SIGNIFICANTLY ADDING FAT.*

SERVES 4

INGREDIENTS

500g/1¼lb boneless pork loin
2 lemon grass stalks,
 finely chopped
4 spring onions (scallions),
 thinly sliced
5ml/1 tsp salt
12 black peppercorns,
 coarsely crushed
15ml/1 tbsp sunflower oil
2 garlic cloves, chopped
2 fresh red chillies, seeded
 and chopped
5ml/1 tsp soft light brown
 sugar
30ml/2 tbsp fish sauce
30ml/2 tbsp roasted unsalted
 peanuts, chopped
ground black pepper
cooked rice noodles, to serve
coarsely torn coriander (cilantro)
 leaves, to garnish

1 Trim any excess fat from the pork.
Cut the meat across into 5mm/¼in
thick slices, then cut each slice into
5mm/¼in strips. Put the pork into a
bowl with the finely chopped lemon
grass, thinly sliced spring onions,
salt and crushed peppercorns; mix
well. Cover the bowl with clear film
(plastic wrap) and leave to marinate
in a cool place or the refrigerator
for 30 minutes.

2 Preheat a wok, add the oil and swirl
it around. Add the pork mixture and
stir-fry over a medium heat for about
3 minutes, until browned all over.

3 Add the garlic and red chillies and
stir-fry for a further 5–8 minutes over a
medium heat, until the pork is cooked
through and tender.

4 Add the sugar, fish sauce and
chopped peanuts and toss to mix, then
season to taste with black pepper. Serve
immediately on a bed of rice noodles,
garnished with the coarsely torn
coriander leaves.

COOK'S TIP
The heat in chillies is not in the seeds,
but in the membranes surrounding them,
which are removed along with the seeds.

Energy 205kcal/856kJ; Protein 27.9g; Carbohydrate 1.8g, of which sugars 1.6g; Fat 9.5g, of which saturates 2.4g; Cholesterol 79mg; Calcium 16mg; Fibre 0.4g; Sodium 88mg.

STIR-FRIED PORK WITH MUSHROOMS ★★★

PORK IS NOW LOWER IN FAT THAN EVER BEFORE, AND IS A GOOD CHOICE FOR A HEALTHY MEAL.
CHOOSE FILLET OR TENDERLOIN, WHICH COOK QUICKLY WHEN CUT INTO FINE STRIPS.

SERVES 4

INGREDIENTS
30ml/2 tbsp vegetable oil
450g/1lb pork fillet (tenderloin),
   cut into fine strips
1 onion, halved and sliced
1 fresh green chilli, seeded
   and chopped
2 garlic cloves, sliced
150g/5oz/1¾ cups oyster
   mushrooms, sliced
200g/7oz green beans, sliced
2 oranges, peeled and cut
   into segments
15ml/1 tbsp clear honey
30ml/2 tbsp sherry
350g/12oz egg noodles, cooked
30ml/2 tbsp sesame oil

1 Heat the oil in a wok or large frying pan until very hot. Stir-fry the pork for 5 minutes until it is tender and cooked through. Remove the pork with a slotted spoon and put it on a plate. Add the onion, chilli, garlic, mushrooms and green beans to the wok and stir-fry the vegetables for 3–5 minutes.

2 Return the pork to the wok. Add the orange segments, honey and sherry, and cook for a further 2 minutes, stirring frequently.

COOK'S TIP
When stir-frying, cut the ingredients into similar size strips so that they cook evenly and quickly, and prepare all the ingredients before you begin cooking.

3 Cook the egg noodles in a pan of boiling water, or according to the pack instructions, until tender. Drain thoroughly, then sprinkle with the sesame oil and toss to coat. Divide the noodles among individual warm serving bowls and spoon the pork stir-fry on top. Serve immediately.

RIBS OF PORK WITH EGG-FRIED RICE ★★★

MEATY PORK RIBS WITH A GLORIOUS MARMALADE AND SOY SAUCE GLAZE ARE GREAT FOR INFORMAL
DINNER PARTIES, AND LOOK IMPRESSIVE WHEN PRESENTED ON A MOUND OF EGG-FRIED RICE.

SERVES 4

INGREDIENTS
2 shallots, chopped
1 garlic clove, chopped
30ml/2 tbsp tomato purée (paste)
45ml/3 tbsp orange marmalade
30ml/2 tbsp light soy sauce
grated rind and juice of 1 orange
grated rind and juice of 1 lemon
1kg/2¼lb meaty pork ribs
salt and ground black pepper
For the egg-fried rice
30ml/2 tbsp vegetable oil
6 spring onions (scallions), sliced
1 red (bell) pepper, seeded
   and chopped
175g/6oz/1½ cups peas
2 eggs, lightly beaten
350g/12oz/1⅔ cups long grain
   rice, cooked and cooled

1 Preheat the oven to 200°C/400°F/ Gas 6. Mix the shallots, garlic, tomato purée, marmalade, soy sauce, orange and lemon rind and juice in a pan. Bring to the boil, stirring all the time, then simmer until reduced to a syrupy glaze. Season with salt and pepper.

2 Arrange the ribs in a roasting pan and drizzle with glaze. Bake for 40 minutes, turning and basting occasionally.

3 Meanwhile prepare the egg-fried rice. Heat the oil in a large frying pan and when it is hot, cook the spring onions, pepper and peas until just tender.

4 Add the lightly beaten eggs. Cook until they are just beginning to set, then beat vigorously, so that the egg mixture breaks up. Add the cooked rice and cook, stirring often, until piping hot. Serve with the glazed ribs.

Top: Energy 243kcal/1016kJ; Protein 26.6g; Carbohydrate 10g, of which sugars 9.1g; Fat 10.5g, of which saturates 2.3g; Cholesterol 71mg; Calcium 61mg; Fibre 2.8g; Sodium 85mg.
Bottom: Energy 317kcal/1323kJ; Protein 36.3g; Carbohydrate 11.8g, of which sugars 7.4g; Fat 14.1g, of which saturates 3.4g; Cholesterol 164mg; Calcium 47mg; Fibre 3.4g; Sodium 147mg.

RICE ROLLS STUFFED WITH PORK ★

IN THIS CLASSIC ASIAN DISH STEAMED RICE SHEETS ARE FILLED WITH MINCED PORK, ROLLED UP AND
THEN DIPPED IN NUOC CHAM. SERVE WITH A MEAT-FREE SALAD FOR A HEALTHY LOW-FAT MEAL.

SERVES 6

INGREDIENTS
    25g/1oz dried cloud ear (wood ear)
      mushrooms, soaked in warm water
      for 30 minutes
    350g/12oz minced (ground) lean pork
    30nl/2 tbsp fish sauce
    10ml/2 tsp sugar
    15ml/1 tbsp sunflower oil
    2 garlic cloves, finely chopped
    2 shallots, finely chopped
    2 spring onions (scallions), trimmed
      and finely chopped
    24 fresh rice sheets, 7.5cm/3in square
    ground black pepper
    nuoc cham, for dipping

COOK'S TIP
To make life easy, prepared, fresh rice
sheets are available in Asian markets.

1 Drain the mushrooms and squeeze
out any excess water. Cut off and
discard the hard stems. Finely chop the
rest of the mushrooms and put them in
a bowl. Add the minced pork, fish
sauce, and sugar and mix well.

2 Heat the oil in a wok or heavy pan.
Add the garlic, shallots and onions. Stir-
fry until golden. Add the pork mixture
and stir-fry for 5–6 minutes, until the
pork is cooked. Season with pepper.

3 Place the fresh rice sheets on a flat
surface. Spoon a tablespoon of the
pork mixture on to the middle of each
sheet. Fold one side over the filling,
tuck in the sides, and roll up to
enclose the filling, so that it resembles
a short spring roll.

4 Place the filled rice rolls on a serving
plate and serve with *nuoc cham* or any
other chilli or tangy sauce of your
choice, for dipping.

Energy 160kcal/670kJ; Protein 13.8g; Carbohydrate 16g, of which sugars 2.4g; Fat 4.4g, of which saturates 1.1g; Cholesterol 37mg; Calcium 13mg; Fibre 0.6g; Sodium 43mg.

STIR-FRIED PORK WITH LYCHEES ★★

THE SWEET, ALMOST SCENTED FLAVOUR OF SUCCULENT LYCHEES MAKES THEM AN EXCELLENT ACCOMPANIMENT FOR ANY MEAT, BUT THEY ARE PARTICULARLY GOOD WITH PORK OR DUCK.

SERVES 4

INGREDIENTS

450g/1lb lean pork fillet
(tenderloin)
30ml/2 tbsp hoisin sauce
15ml/1 tbsp vegetable oil
4 spring onions (scallions), sliced
175g/6oz lychees, peeled, stoned
(pitted) and cut into slivers
salt and ground black pepper
fresh lychees and fresh parsley
sprigs, to garnish

1 Press the meat down on a chopping board, using the palm of your hand, and slice it horizontally into strips. Cut the strips crossways into bitesize pieces and place them in a bowl.

2 Pour the hoisin sauce over the pork and marinate for 30 minutes.

3 Heat the wok until it is very hot, then add the pork and stir-fry for 5 minutes until it is cooked through and the outside is crisp and golden.

4 Add the spring onions and stir-fry for a further 2 minutes.

5 Sprinkle the lychee slivers over the pork, and season well with salt and pepper. Garnish with fresh lychees and fresh parsley, and serve.

Energy 198kcal/833kJ; Protein 24.8g; Carbohydrate 8.7g, of which sugars 8.6g; Fat 7.4g, of which saturates 1.9g; Cholesterol 71mg; Calcium 16mg; Fibre 0.5g; Sodium 202mg.

SAENG WA OF GRILLED PORK ★

PORK FILLET IS CUT IN STRIPS BEFORE BEING GRILLED. SHREDDED AND THEN TOSSED WITH A
DELICIOUS SWEET-SOUR DRESSING, IT MAKES A MARVELLOUS WARM AND LOW-FAT SALAD.

3 Transfer the cooked pork strips to a board. Slice the meat across the grain, then shred it with a fork. Place in a large bowl and add the shallot slices, lemon grass, kaffir lime leaves, ginger, chilli and chopped coriander.

4 Make the dressing. Place the sugar, fish sauce, lime juice and tamarind juice in a bowl. Whisk until the sugar has completely dissolved. Pour the dressing over the pork mixture and toss well to mix, then serve.

VARIATION
If you want to extend this dish a little, add cooked rice or noodles. Thin strips of red or yellow (bell) pepper could also be added. For a colour contrast, add lightly cooked green beans, sugar snap peas or mangetouts (snow peas).

SERVES 4

INGREDIENTS
  30ml/2 tbsp dark soy sauce
  15ml/1 tbsp clear honey
  400g/14oz pork fillet (tenderloin)
  6 shallots, very thinly
    sliced lengthways
  1 lemon grass stalk, thinly sliced
  5 kaffir lime leaves, thinly sliced
  5cm/2in piece fresh root ginger,
    peeled and sliced into
    fine shreds
  ½ fresh long red chilli, seeded and
    sliced into fine shreds
  small bunch fresh coriander
    (cilantro), chopped
For the dressing
  30ml/2 tbsp palm sugar or light
    muscovado (brown) sugar
  30ml/2 tbsp fish sauce
  juice of 2 limes
  20ml/4 tsp thick tamarind juice,
    made by mixing tamarind paste
    with warm water

1 Preheat the grill (broiler) to medium. Mix the soy sauce with the honey in a small bowl or jug (pitcher) and stir until the honey has completely dissolved.

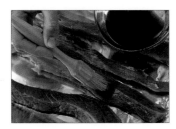

2 Using a sharp knife, cut the pork fillet lengthways into quarters to make four long, thick strips. Place the pork strips in a grill pan. Brush generously with the soy sauce and honey mixture, then grill (broil) for about 10–15 minutes, until cooked through and tender. Turn the strips over frequently and baste with the soy sauce and honey mixture.

Energy 182kcal/767kJ; Protein 22.6g; Carbohydrate 14.3g, of which sugars 13.5g; Fat 4.2g, of which saturates 1.4g; Cholesterol 63mg; Calcium 45mg; Fibre 1g; Sodium 1144mg.

BRAISED BLACK PEPPER PORK ★

THIS DISH IS QUICK TO MAKE, TASTY AND BEAUTIFULLY WARMING THANKS TO THE GINGER AND BLACK PEPPER. IT IS SURE TO BE A POPULAR CHOICE FOR A LOW-FAT FAMILY MEAL.

SERVES 6

INGREDIENTS

 1 litre/1¾ pints/4 cups water
 45ml/3 tbsp *tuk trey* or other fish sauce
 30ml/2 tbsp soy sauce
 15ml/1 tbsp sugar
 4 garlic cloves, crushed
 40g/1½oz fresh root ginger, peeled and
   finely shredded
 15ml/1 tbsp freshly ground
   black pepper
 675g/1½lb lean pork shoulder
   or rump, cut into bitesize cubes
 steamed jasmine rice, crunchy salad
   and pickles or stir-fried greens,
   such as water spinach or long
   beans, to serve

1 In a large heavy pan, bring the water, *tuk trey* and soy sauce to the boil. Reduce the heat and stir in the sugar, garlic, ginger, black pepper and pork. Cover the pan and simmer for about 1½ hours, until the pork is very tender and the liquid has reduced.

2 Serve the pork in individual bowls with steamed jasmine rice. Drizzle the braised juices over it, and accompany it with a fresh crunchy salad, pickles or stir-fried greens, such as the delicious water spinach with *nuoc cham*, or long beans.

Energy 154kcal/647kJ; Protein 24.4g; Carbohydrate 4g, of which sugars 3.7g; Fat 4.5g, of which saturates 1.6g; Cholesterol 71mg; Calcium 13mg; Fibre 0.1g; Sodium 613mg.

PORK AND PINEAPPLE COCONUT CURRY ★

THE HEAT OF THIS COLOURFUL CURRY BALANCES OUT ITS SWEETNESS TO MAKE A SMOOTH AND FRAGRANT DISH. IT TAKES VERY LITTLE TIME TO COOK, SO IT IS IDEAL FOR A QUICK AND TASTY SUPPER BEFORE GOING OUT, OR FOR A MID-WEEK FAMILY MEAL ON A BUSY EVENING.

SERVES 4

INGREDIENTS
- 400ml/14fl oz reduced-fat coconut milk
- 10ml/2 tsp Thai red curry paste
- 400g/14oz lean pork loin steaks, trimmed and thinly sliced
- 15ml/1 tbsp Thai fish sauce
- 5ml/1 tsp palm sugar or light muscovado (brown) sugar
- 15ml/1 tbsp tamarind juice, made by mixing tamarind paste with warm water
- 2 kaffir lime leaves, torn
- ½ medium pineapple, peeled and chopped
- 1 fresh red chilli, seeded and finely chopped

1 Pour the coconut milk into a bowl and let it settle, so that the cream rises to the surface. Scoop the cream into a measuring jug (cup). You should have about 250ml/8fl oz/1 cup. If necessary, add a little of the coconut milk.

2 Pour the coconut cream into a large pan and bring it to the boil.

3 Cook the coconut cream for about 10 minutes, until the cream separates, stirring frequently to prevent it from sticking to the base of the pan and scorching. Add the red curry paste and stir until well mixed. Cook, stirring occasionally, for about 4 minutes, until the paste is fragrant.

4 Add the sliced pork and stir in the fish sauce, sugar and tamarind juice. Cook, stirring constantly, for 1–2 minutes, until the sugar has dissolved and the pork is no longer pink.

5 Add the remaining coconut milk and the lime leaves. Bring to the boil, then stir in the pineapple. Reduce the heat and simmer gently for 3 minutes, or until the pork is fully cooked. Sprinkle over the chilli and serve.

Energy 189kcal/800kJ; Protein 22.1g; Carbohydrate 16.1g, of which sugars 16.1g; Fat 4.5g, of which saturates 1.6g; Cholesterol 63mg; Calcium 55mg; Fibre 1.2g; Sodium 182mg

SWEET AND SOUR PORK, THAI-STYLE ★

IT WAS THE CHINESE WHO ORIGINALLY CREATED SWEET AND SOUR COOKING, BUT THE THAIS ALSO DO IT VERY WELL. THIS VERSION HAS A FRESHER AND CLEANER FLAVOUR THAN THE ORIGINAL. IT MAKES A GOOD ONE-DISH MEAL WHEN SERVED SIMPLY OVER FRESHLY BOILED RICE.

SERVES 4

INGREDIENTS

   350g/12oz lean pork
   15ml/1 tbsp sunflower oil
   4 garlic cloves, thinly sliced
   1 small red onion, sliced
   30ml/2 tbsp Thai fish sauce
   15ml/1 tbsp granulated sugar
   1 red (bell) pepper, seeded and diced
   ½ cucumber, seeded and sliced
   2 plum tomatoes, cut into wedges
   115g/4oz piece of fresh pineapple,
     cut into small chunks
   2 spring onions (scallions), cut into
     short lengths
   ground black pepper
To garnish
   coriander (cilantro) leaves
   spring onions (scallions), shredded

1 Place the pork in the freezer for 30–40 minutes, until firm. Using a sharp knife, cut it into thin strips.

2 Heat the oil in a wok or large frying pan. Add the garlic. Cook over a medium heat until golden, then add the pork and stir-fry for 4–5 minutes. Add the onion slices and toss to mix.

3 Add the fish sauce, sugar and ground black pepper to taste. Toss the mixture over the heat for 3–4 minutes more.

4 Stir in the red pepper, cucumber, tomatoes, pineapple and spring onions. Stir-fry for 3–4 minutes more, then spoon into a bowl. Garnish with the coriander and spring onions and serve.

Energy 168kcal/708kJ; Protein 20.3g; Carbohydrate 13.5g, of which sugars 12.9g; Fat 4g, of which saturates 1.3g; Cholesterol 55mg; Calcium 32mg; Fibre 2g; Sodium 604mg.

CURRIED PORK <u>WITH</u> PICKLED GARLIC ★★

THIS VERY RICH CURRY IS BEST ACCOMPANIED BY LOTS OF PLAIN RICE AND PERHAPS A LIGHT
VEGETABLE DISH. IT COULD SERVE FOUR IF SERVED WITH A VEGETABLE CURRY. IT IS WELL WORTH
INVESTING IN A JAR OF PICKLED GARLIC FROM ASIAN STORES, AS THE TASTE IS SWEET AND DELICIOUS.

SERVES 2

INGREDIENTS
    130g/4½oz lean pork steaks
    15ml/1 tbsp sunflower oil
    1 garlic clove, crushed
    15ml/1 tbsp Thai red curry paste
    130ml/4½fl oz/generous ½ cup
        reduced-fat coconut milk
    2.5cm/1in piece fresh root ginger,
        finely chopped
    30ml/2 tbsp vegetable or
        chicken stock
    30ml/2 tbsp Thai fish sauce
    5ml/1 tsp granulated sugar
    2.5ml/½ tsp ground turmeric
    10ml/2 tsp lemon juice
    4 pickled garlic cloves,
        finely chopped
    strips of lemon and lime rind,
        to garnish

1 Place the pork steaks in the freezer for 30–40 minutes, until firm, then, using a sharp knife, cut the meat into fine slivers, trimming off any excess fat.

2 Heat the oil in a wok or large, heavy frying pan and cook the garlic over a low to medium heat until golden brown. Do not let it burn. Add the curry paste and stir it in well.

3 Add the coconut milk and stir until the liquid begins to reduce and thicken. Stir in the pork. Cook for 2 minutes more, until the pork is cooked through.

4 Add the ginger, stock, fish sauce, sugar and turmeric, stirring constantly, then add the lemon juice and pickled garlic. Spoon into bowls, garnish with strips of rind, and serve.

Energy 160kcal/667kJ; Protein 14.9g; Carbohydrate 6g, of which sugars 5.9g; Fat 8.6g, of which saturates 1.7g; Cholesterol 41mg; Calcium 75mg; Fibre 1.3g; Sodium 126mg.

STIR-FRIED PORK AND BUTTERNUT CURRY ★

THIS CURRY CAN BE MADE WITH BUTTERNUT SQUASH, PUMPKIN OR WINTER MELON. FLAVOURED WITH GALANGAL AND TURMERIC, IT IS DELICIOUS SERVED WITH RICE AND A FRUIT-BASED SALAD, OR EVEN JUST WITH CHUNKS OF FRESH CRUSTY BREAD TO MOP UP THE TASTY SAUCE.

SERVES 6

INGREDIENTS

    10ml/2 tsp sunflower oil
    25g/1oz galangal, finely sliced
    2 red Thai chillies, peeled, seeded
      and finely sliced
    3 shallots, halved and finely sliced
    30ml/2 tbsp *kroeung*
    10ml/2 tsp ground turmeric
    5ml/1 tsp ground fenugreek
    10ml/2 tsp palm sugar
    450g/1lb lean pork loin, cut into
      bitesize chunks
    30ml/2 tbsp *tuk prahoc*
    900ml/1½ pints/3¾ cups
      reduced-fat coconut milk
    1 butternut squash, peeled, seeded
      and cut into bitesize chunks
    4 kaffir lime leaves
    sea salt and ground black pepper
    1 small bunch fresh coriander
      (cilantro), coarsely chopped and
      1 small bunch fresh mint, stalks
      removed, to garnish
    rice or noodles and salad, to serve

2 Stir in the chunks of pork loin and stir-fry until golden brown on all sides. Stir in the *tuk prahoc* and pour in the coconut milk.

COOK'S TIP

Increase the number of chillies if you want a really hot curry.

3 Bring to the boil, add the squash and the lime leaves, and reduce the heat. Cook gently, uncovered, for 15–20 minutes, until the squash and pork are tender and the sauce has reduced. Season to taste. Garnish the curry with the coriander and mint, and serve with rice or noodles and salad.

1 Heat the oil in a large wok or heavy pan. Stir in the galangal, chillies and shallots and stir-fry until fragrant. Add the *kroeung* and stir-fry until it begins to colour. Add the turmeric, fenugreek and sugar.

VARIATION

For a vegetarian option, omit the pork and use baby aubergines (eggplants) instead. The Cambodian flavourings and creamy coconut milk work well with many combinations.

Energy 149kcal/628kJ; Protein 17g; Carbohydrate 10.6g, of which sugars 10.2g; Fat 4.6g, of which saturates 1.5g; Cholesterol 47mg; Calcium 71mg; Fibre 0.7g; Sodium 221mg.

BAKED CINNAMON MEAT LOAF ★

THIS TYPE OF MEAT LOAF IS USUALLY SERVED AS A SUPPER OR LIGHT LUNCH, WITH A FRESH, CRUSTY BAGUETTE. ACCOMPANIED WITH EITHER TART PICKLES OR A CRUNCHY SIDE SALAD, AND SPLASHED WITH PIQUANT SAUCE, IT IS A LIGHT, TASTY DISH FOR ALL THE FAMILY.

SERVES 4–6

INGREDIENTS

30ml/2 tbsp *nuoc mam* or other
   fish sauce
25ml/1½ tbsp ground cinnamon
10ml/2 tsp sugar
5ml/1 tsp ground black pepper
15ml/1 tbsp potato starch
450g/1lb lean minced (ground) pork
30ml/2 tbsp sunflower oil
2–3 shallots, very finely chopped
spray sunflower oil, for greasing
nuoc cham, for drizzling
red chilli strips, to garnish
bread or noodles, to serve

COOK'S TIPS
• Serve the meat loaf as a nibble with drinks by cutting it into bitesize squares or fingers.
• Serve with a piquant sauce for dipping.
• Cut the meat loaf into wedges and take on a picnic to eat with bread and pickles or chutney.
• Fry slices of meat loaf until browned and serve with fried eggs.

VARIATION
For a delicious meat loaf that is even lower in fat, replace the lean minced (ground) pork with chicken breast fillets.

1 In a large bowl, mix together the *nuoc mam*, ground cinnamon, sugar and ground black pepper. Sprinkle over the potato starch and beat until the mixture is smooth.

2 Add the minced pork, the oil, and the very finely chopped shallots to the bowl and mix thoroughly. Cover with clear film (plastic wrap) and put in the refrigerator for 3–4 hours.

3 Preheat the oven to 180°C/350°F/Gas 4. Lightly oil a baking tin (pan) and spread the pork and shallot mixture in the tin in an even layer – when pressed, the potato starch should mean it feels springy.

4 Cover with foil and bake in the oven for 35–40 minutes. If you want the top to turn brown and crunchy, remove the foil for the last 10 minutes.

5 Turn the meat loaf out on to a board and slice it into strips. Drizzle the strips with *nuoc cham*, and serve them hot with bread or noodles.

Energy 158kcal/661kJ; Protein 16.8g; Carbohydrate 7.7g, of which sugars 4.6g; Fat 6.8g, of which saturates 1.5g; Cholesterol 47mg; Calcium 19mg; Fibre 0.8g; Sodium 54mg.

LARP OF CHIANG MAI ★

CHIANG MAI IS A CITY IN THE NORTH-EAST OF THAILAND. THE CITY IS CULTURALLY VERY CLOSE TO LAOS AND FAMOUS FOR ITS CHICKEN SALAD, WHICH WAS ORIGINALLY CALLED "LAAP" OR "LARP". YOU CAN USE PORK AS HERE, BUT DUCK, CHICKEN OR BEEF WOULD WORK JUST AS WELL.

SERVES 4

INGREDIENTS
450g/1lb minced (ground) pork
1 lemon grass stalk, root trimmed
3 kaffir lime leaves, finely chopped
4 fresh red chillies, seeded
    and chopped
60ml/4 tbsp lime juice
30ml/2 tbsp Thai fish sauce
15ml/1 tbsp roasted ground rice
    (see Cook's Tip)
2 spring onions (scallions), chopped
30ml/2 tbsp fresh coriander
    (cilantro) leaves
thinly sliced kaffir lime leaves,
    mixed salad leaves and fresh
    mint sprigs, to garnish

1 Heat a large non-stick frying pan. Add the minced pork and moisten with a little water. Stir constantly over a medium heat for 7–10 minutes until it is cooked. Meanwhile, cut off the lower 5cm/2in of the lemon grass stalk and chop finely.

2 Transfer the cooked pork to a bowl and add the chopped lemon grass, lime leaves, chillies, lime juice, fish sauce, ground rice, spring onions and coriander. Mix thoroughly.

3 Spoon the pork mixture into a salad bowl. Sprinkle sliced kaffir lime leaves over the top and garnish with salad leaves and sprigs of mint.

COOK'S TIP
Use glutinous rice for the roasted ground rice. Put the rice in a frying pan and dry-fry it until golden brown. Remove and grind to a powder, using a pestle and mortar or a food processor. When the rice is cold, store it in a glass jar in a cool and dry place.

THAI BEEF SALAD ★★

A HEARTY AND HEALTHY MAIN MEAL SALAD, PACKED WITH GREEN VEGETABLES, THIS COMBINES TENDER STRIPS OF STEAK WITH A WONDERFUL CHILLI AND LIME DRESSING.

SERVES 4

INGREDIENTS
2 sirloin steaks, each
    about 400g/14oz
1 lemon grass stalk, root trimmed
1 red onion or 4 Thai shallots,
    thinly sliced
1/2 cucumber, cut into strips
30ml/2 tbsp chopped spring
    onion (scallion)
juice of 2 limes
15–30ml/1–2 tbsp Thai fish sauce
Chinese mustard cress, salad cress,
    or fresh coriander (cilantro)
    to garnish

COOK'S TIP
Look out for gui chai leaves in Thai and Asian groceries. These look like very thin spring onions (scallions) and are often used as a substitute for the more familiar vegetable.

1 Pan-fry or grill (broil) the steaks in a large, heavy frying pan over a medium heat, for 6–8 minutes for medium-rare and about 10 minutes for well done. Remove from the pan and allow to rest for 10–15 minutes. Meanwhile, cut off the lower 5cm/2in from the lemon grass stalk and chop it finely.

2 When the meat is cool, slice it thinly and put the slices in a large bowl.

3 Add the sliced onion or shallots, cucumber, lemon grass and chopped spring onion to the meat slices.

4 Toss the salad and season with the lime juice and fish sauce to taste. Transfer the salad to a serving bowl or plate and serve at room temperature or chilled, garnished with the Chinese mustard cress, salad cress or coriander leaves.

Top: Energy 163kcal/682kJ; Protein 25.3g; Carbohydrate 4.4g, of which sugars 1.2g; Fat 4.8g, of which saturates 1.6g; Cholesterol 71mg; Calcium 53mg; Fibre 1.1g; Sodium 620mg.
Bottom: Energy 186kcal/774kJ; Protein 23.3g; Carbohydrate 2g, of which sugars 1.6g; Fat 9.4g, of which saturates 3.8g; Cholesterol 58mg; Calcium 16mg; Fibre 0.4g; Sodium 333mg.

CHILLI AND HONEY-CURED DRIED BEEF ★★

DRYING IS AN ANCIENT METHOD OF PRESERVING FOOD, WHICH ALSO INTENSIFIES THE FLAVOUR OR POTENCY OF MOST INGREDIENTS. IN THIS TRADITIONAL SOUTH-EAST ASIAN DISH THE CHILLIES ADD A WONDERFUL KICK TO THE MEAT WHILE THE HONEY ADDS A SUBTLE SWEETNESS.

2 Using a mortar and pestle, grind the chopped lemon grass, garlic and chillies to a paste. Stir in the honey, *nuoc mam* and soy sauce. Put the beef into a bowl, add the paste and rub it into the meat. Spread out the meat on a wire rack and place it in the refrigerator, uncovered, for 2 days, or until dry and hard.

3 Cook the dried beef on the barbecue or under a conventional grill (broiler) until heated through, and serve it with rice wrappers, fresh herbs and a dipping sauce.

COOK'S TIP
Drying is an ancient method of preserving food, which also intensifies the flavour or potency of most ingredients. In hot countries beef can be dried quickly in the sun, but in cooler areas it dries more slowly, so needs to be put in the refrigerator to prevent it going off.

VARIATION
This recipe also works well with venison. Cut the meat into thin strips and you have a South-east Asian version of the South African *biltong*.

SERVES 6

INGREDIENTS
450g/1lb lean beef sirloin
2 lemon grass stalks, trimmed and chopped
2 garlic cloves, chopped
2 dried Serrano chillies, seeded and chopped
30–45ml/2–3 tbsp honey
15ml/1 tbsp *nuoc mam*
30ml/2 tbsp soy sauce
rice wrappers, fresh herbs and dipping sauce, to serve

1 Trim the beef and cut it across the grain into thin, rectangular slices, then set it aside.

Energy 158kcal/660kJ; Protein 17.3g; Carbohydrate 6.7g, of which sugars 6.6g; Fat 7g, of which saturates 2.9g; Cholesterol 44mg; Calcium 6mg; Fibre 0.1g; Sodium 405mg.

SEARED BEEF SALAD ^{IN A} LIME DRESSING ★★

THIS BEEF DISH IS AN INDO-CHINESE FAVOURITE AND VERSIONS OF IT ARE ENJOYED IN VIETNAM, THAILAND, CAMBODIA AND LAOS. IT IS ALSO ONE OF THE TRADITIONAL DISHES THAT APPEAR IN THE BEEF SEVEN WAYS FEAST IN WHICH SEVEN DIFFERENT BEEF DISHES ARE SERVED.

SERVES 6

INGREDIENTS
  about 7.5ml/1½ tsp sunflower oil
  450g/1lb beef fillet, cut into steaks
    2.5cm/1in thick
  115g/4oz/½ cup beansprouts
  1 bunch each fresh basil and mint,
    stalks removed, leaves shredded
  1 lime, cut into slices, to serve
For the dressing
  grated and juice (about 80ml/3fl oz)
    of 2 limes
  30ml/2 tbsp *nuoc mam*
  30ml/2 tbsp raw cane sugar
  2 garlic cloves, crushed
  2 lemon grass stalks, finely sliced
  2 red Serrano chillies, seeded and
    finely sliced

3 Drain the meat of any excess juice and transfer it to a wide serving bowl. Add the beansprouts and herbs and toss it all together. Serve with lime slices to squeeze over.

1 To make the dressing, beat the lime rind, juice and *nuoc mam* in a bowl with the sugar, until the sugar dissolves. Stir in the garlic, lemon grass and chillies and set aside.

2 Pour a little oil into a heavy pan and rub it over the base with a piece of kitchen paper. Heat the pan and sear the steaks for 1–2 minutes each side. Transfer them to a board and leave to cool a little. Using a sharp knife, cut the meat into thin slices. Toss the slices in the dressing, cover and leave to marinate for 1–2 hours.

COOK'S TIP
It is worth buying an excellent-quality piece of tender beef fillet for this recipe as the meat is only just seared.

Energy 174kcal/727kJ; Protein 18.4g; Carbohydrate 7.3g, of which sugars 6g; Fat 8.1g, of which saturates 3g; Cholesterol 44mg; Calcium 28mg; Fibre 1g; Sodium 52mg.

SUKIYAKI-STYLE BEEF ★★

THIS DISH IS A MEAL IN ITSELF; THE RECIPE INCORPORATES ALL THE TRADITIONAL FOOD ELEMENTS
— MEAT, VEGETABLES, NOODLES AND TOFU — IN A HIGHLY FLAVOURED MUSHROOM BROTH.

SERVES 4

INGREDIENTS
   450g/1lb lean rump (round) steak
   200g/7oz rice noodles
   15ml/1 tbsp vegetable oil
   200g/7oz firm tofu, cubed
   8 fresh shiitake mushrooms, wiped
      and trimmed
   2 medium leeks, sliced into
      2.5cm/1in lengths
   90g/3½oz baby spinach,
      to serve
For the stock
   15ml/1 tbsp caster (superfine) sugar
   90ml/6 tbsp rice wine
   45ml/3 tbsp dark soy sauce
   120ml/4fl oz/½ cup water

1 Trim off the fat from the beef. If you have time, place it in the freezer and leave for 30 minutes. Cut it into very thin slices.

2 Blanch the noodles in boiling water for 2 minutes. Drain well.

3 To make the stock, mix together the sugar, rice wine, soy sauce and water in a small bowl.

4 Heat the wok, then add the oil. When the oil is hot, stir-fry the beef for 2–3 minutes until it is cooked, but still pink in colour.

5 Pour the stock over the beef. Add the tofu, mushrooms and leeks. Toss together over the heat for 4 minutes, until the leeks are tender. Meanwhile, wash and thoroughly drain the baby spinach leaves.

6 Serve immediately with the baby spinach leaves, making sure that each person receives some beef and tofu.

Energy 418kcal/1748kJ; Protein 32.4g; Carbohydrate 42.2g, of which sugars 1.1g; Fat 9.8g, of which saturates 2.5g; Cholesterol 66mg; Calcium 307mg; Fibre 0.7g; Sodium 377mg.

SIZZLING BEEF WITH CELERIAC STRAW ★★★

THE CRISP CELERIAC MATCHSTICKS LOOK LIKE FINE PIECES OF STRAW WHEN COOKED AND HAVE A MILD CELERY-LIKE FLAVOUR THAT IS QUITE DELICIOUS WITH THE STRIPS OF STEAK.

SERVES 4

INGREDIENTS
    450g/1lb celeriac
    30ml/2 tbsp vegetable oil
    1 red (bell) pepper
    6 spring onions (scallions)
    450g/1lb lean rump (round) steak
    60ml/4 tbsp beef stock
    30ml/2 tbsp sherry vinegar
    10ml/2 tsp Worcestershire sauce
    10ml/2 tsp tomato purée (paste)
    salt and ground black pepper

1 Peel the celeriac and then cut it into fine matchsticks, using a sharp knife or a cleaver, if you have one.

2 Heat the wok, then add 15ml/1 tbsp of the oil. When the oil is hot, fry the celeriac matchsticks until golden brown and crisp. Drain well.

3 Cut the red pepper in half lengthways, then remove and discard the core and seeds. Slice each half into 2.5cm/1in wide strips.

4 Trim the spring onions and cut them into similar lengths.

5 Trim any fat from the steak, then chop the lean beef into strips, across the grain of the meat.

6 Heat the wok and add the remaining oil. When the oil is hot, stir-fry the spring onions and pepper for 2–3 minutes.

7 Add the beef strips and stir-fry for a further 3–4 minutes until well browned. Pour in the stock, then add the vinegar, Worcestershire sauce and tomato purée. Stir well and heat through for 1–2 minutes. Season with salt and pepper and serve with the celeriac straw.

Energy 237kcal/994kJ; Protein 26.7g; Carbohydrate 9.3g, of which sugars 8.9g; Fat 10.7g, of which saturates 2.6g; Cholesterol 66mg; Calcium 74mg; Fibre 3.7g; Sodium 123mg.

BEEF AND MUSHROOMS WITH BLACK BEANS ★★

THIS CLASSIC CHINESE DISH IS LOW IN FAT AND OFFERS A GOOD SUPPLY OF MINERALS NEEDED FOR OPTIMUM HEALTH, INCLUDING ZINC AND IRON. SERVE WITH STEAMED VEGETABLES SUCH AS BROCCOLI.

SERVES 4

INGREDIENTS
   30ml/2 tbsp dark soy sauce
   30ml/2 tbsp Chinese rice wine
   10ml/2 tsp cornflour (cornstarch)
   10ml/2 tsp sesame oil
   450g/1lb fillet (beef tenderloin) or
      rump (round) steak, trimmed of fat
   12 dried shiitake mushrooms
   25ml/1½ tbsp salted black beans
   5ml/1 tsp caster (superfine) sugar
   30ml/2 tbsp vegetable oil
   4 garlic cloves
   2.5cm/1in fresh root ginger
   200g/7oz open cap
      mushrooms, sliced
   1 bunch spring onions (scallions),
      sliced diagonally
   1 fresh red chilli, seeded and
      shredded
   salt and ground black pepper

1 In a large bowl, mix together half the dark soy sauce, half the Chinese rice wine, half the cornflour and all of the sesame oil with 15ml/1 tbsp fresh cold water until smooth and thoroughly combined. Add a generous pinch of salt and ground black pepper.

2 If you have time, place the beef in the freezer and leave it for 30 minutes. Cut it into very thin slices, no more than 5mm/¼in thick.

3 Add the slices of meat to the cornflour mixture and rub the mixture into the beef with your fingers. Cover the bowl and set the beef aside for 30 minutes at room temperature.

4 Meanwhile, pour boiling water over the dried mushrooms and leave them to soak for about 25 minutes.

5 Transfer 45ml/3 tbsp of the soaking water to a cup or small bowl. Lift the mushrooms out of the bowl and gently squeeze them to remove any excess soaking water.

6 Using a sharp knife, cut off the mushroom stems. Discard these, then cut the caps in half, and set them aside.

7 Peel the garlic cloves and slice them thinly, using a sharp knife. Peel the ginger and cut the flesh into thin strips.

8 Mash the salted black beans with the caster sugar. In another bowl, combine the remaining cornflour, soy sauce and Chinese rice wine.

9 Heat the oil in a wok, then stir-fry the beef for about 30–45 seconds, until just brown. Transfer it to a plate and set aside.

10 Add the sliced garlic and the strips of ginger to the remaining oil in the wok, stir-fry for 1 minute, then add all the mushrooms and stir-fry for 2 minutes more.

11 Set aside a few tablespoons of the sliced green part of the spring onions, then add the rest to the wok. Add the mashed black bean mixture and stir-fry for 1–2 minutes.

12 Stir in the beef, then add the shiitake soaking water. Add the cornflour mixture and simmer until the sauce thickens.

13 Sprinkle the shredded chilli and the reserved slices from the green part of the spring onions over the beef, and serve immediately.

Energy 208kcal/873kJ; Protein 25.9g; Carbohydrate 4.7g, of which sugars 1.5g; Fat 8.8g, of which saturates 3.5g; Cholesterol 69mg; Calcium 20mg; Fibre 1.1g, Sodium 590mg.

BEEF IN OYSTER SAUCE ★★

THE OYSTER SAUCE GIVES THE BEEF EXTRA RICHNESS AND DEPTH OF FLAVOUR. TO COMPLETE THE DISH, ALL YOU NEED IS PLAIN BOILED RICE OR NOODLES, AND PERHAPS SOME STEAMED GREENS.

SERVES 4

INGREDIENTS
    350g/12oz lean rump (round) steak,
        trimmed of fat
    15ml/1 tbsp vegetable oil
    300ml/½ pint/1¼ cups beef stock
    2 garlic cloves, finely chopped
    1 small carrot, thinly sliced
    3 celery sticks, sliced
    15ml/1 tbsp dry sherry
    5ml/1 tsp caster (superfine) sugar
    45ml/3 tbsp oyster sauce
    5ml/1 tsp cornflour
    15ml/1 tbsp cold water
    4 spring onions (scallions), cut
        into 2.5cm/1in lengths
    ground white pepper
    rice or noodles, to serve

1 Slice the steak thinly. Place the slices in a bowl, add 5ml/1 tsp of the vegetable oil and stir to coat.

2 Bring the stock to the boil in a large pan. Add the beef and cook, stirring, for 2 minutes.

3 Drain the beef, reserving 45ml/3 tbsp of the stock in a small bowl, and set the beef aside on a plate.

4 Heat the remaining oil in a non-stick frying pan or wok. Stir-fry the garlic for a few seconds, then add the carrot and celery and stir-fry for 2 minutes.

5 Stir in the sherry, caster sugar, oyster sauce and a large pinch of pepper. Add the steak to the pan with the reserved stock. Simmer for 2 minutes.

6 Mix the cornflour to a paste with the water. Add the mixture to the pan and cook, stirring, until thickened.

7 Stir in the spring onions, then serve immediately, with rice or noodles.

VARIATION
To increase the number of servings without upping the fat content of the dish, simply add more vegetables, such as (bell) peppers, mangetouts (snow peas), water chestnuts, baby corn cobs and mushrooms.

Energy 162kcal/679kJ; Protein 19.9g; Carbohydrate 5.3g, of which sugars 5g; Fat 6.5g, of which saturates 1.8g; Cholesterol 52mg; Calcium 25mg; Fibre 1g; Sodium 260mg.

STIR-FRIED CHILLI BEEF AND MUSHROOMS ★★

IN THAILAND THIS IS OFTEN MADE WITH JUST STRAW MUSHROOMS, BUT OYSTER MUSHROOMS MAKE A GOOD SUBSTITUTE AND USING A MIXTURE MAKES THE DISH EVEN MORE INTERESTING.

SERVES 6

INGREDIENTS

- 450g/1lb rump (round) steak
- 30ml/2 tbsp soy sauce
- 15ml/1 tbsp cornflour (cornstarch)
- 15ml/1 tbsp sunflower oil
- 15ml/1 tbsp chopped garlic
- 15ml/1 tbsp chopped fresh root ginger
- 225g/8oz/3¼ cups mixed mushrooms such as shiitake, oyster and straw
- 30ml/2 tbsp oyster sauce
- 5ml/1 tsp granulated sugar
- 4 spring onions (scallions), cut into short lengths
- ground black pepper
- 2 fresh red chillies, seeded and cut into strips, to garnish

1 Place the steak in the freezer for 30–40 minutes, until firm, then, using a sharp knife, slice it on the diagonal into long thin strips.

2 Mix together the soy sauce and cornflour in a large bowl. Add the steak, turning to coat well, cover with clear film (plastic wrap) and leave to marinate at room temperature for 1–2 hours.

3 Heat half the oil in a wok or large, heavy frying pan. Add the garlic and ginger and cook for 1–2 minutes, until fragrant. Drain the steak, add it to the wok or pan and stir well to separate the strips. Cook, stirring frequently, for a further 1–2 minutes, until the steak is browned all over and tender. Remove from the wok or pan and set aside.

4 Heat the remaining oil in the wok or pan. Add the shiitake, oyster and straw mushrooms. Stir-fry over a medium heat until golden brown.

5 Return the steak to the wok and mix it with the mushrooms. Spoon in the oyster sauce and sugar, mix well, then add ground black pepper to taste. Toss over the heat until all the ingredients are thoroughly combined.

6 Stir in the spring onions. Tip the mixture on to a serving platter, garnish with the strips of red chilli and serve.

Energy 174kcal/725kJ; Protein 18.1g; Carbohydrate 5.2g, of which sugars 2.7g; Fat 9.1g, of which saturates 3.1g; Cholesterol 44mg; Calcium 11mg; Fibre 0.6g; Sodium 489mg.

ORIENTAL BEEF ★★

THIS SUMPTUOUSLY RICH BEEF MELTS IN THE MOUTH, AND IS PERFECTLY COMPLEMENTED BY THE COOL, CRUNCHY RELISH. USE VERY LEAN MEAT AND CUT OFF ANY OBVIOUS FAT.

SERVES 4

INGREDIENTS
    450g/1lb lean rump (round) steak,
        trimmed of fat
    4 whole radishes, to garnish
For the marinade
    15ml/1 tbsp vegetable oil
    2 garlic cloves, crushed
    60ml/4 tbsp dark soy sauce
    30ml/2 tbsp dry sherry
    10ml/2 tsp soft dark brown sugar
For the relish
    6 radishes
    10cm/4in piece cucumber
    1 piece preserved stem ginger

1 If you have time, place the steak in the freezer for 30 minutes. This firms it so it can be cut very thinly. Remove the steak from the freezer, cut it into thin strips and place it in a bowl.

2 To make the marinade, pour the oil into a bowl and stir in the garlic, soy sauce, sherry and sugar. Pour the mixture over the beef, cover and leave to marinate overnight.

3 To make the relish, use a sharp knife to chop the radishes and cucumber into matchsticks and the ginger into slivers. Mix well together in a bowl.

4 Heat a wok or large non-stick frying pan until it is very hot, then add the meat with the marinade, and stir-fry for 3–4 minutes.

5 Serve the beef immediately with the relish, and garnish each plate with a whole radish.

Energy 169kcal/709kJ; Protein 25g; Carbohydrate 0.6g, of which sugars 0.6g; Fat 7.4g, of which saturates 2.3g; Cholesterol 66mg; Calcium 11mg; Fibre 0.3g; Sodium 70mg.

BEEF WITH TOMATOES ★★

BASED ON A SIMPLE KOREAN DISH, THIS COLOURFUL AND FRESH-TASTING MIXTURE IS THE PERFECT WAY OF SERVING SUN-RIPENED TOMATOES FROM THE GARDEN OR FARMERS' MARKET.

SERVES 4

INGREDIENTS
350g/12oz lean rump (round) steak, trimmed of fat
15ml/1 tbsp vegetable oil
300ml/½ pint/1¼ cups beef stock
1 garlic clove, finely chopped
1 small onion, sliced into rings
5 tomatoes, quartered
15ml/1 tbsp tomato purée (paste)
5ml/1 tsp caster (superfine) sugar
15ml/1 tbsp dry sherry
15ml/1 tbsp cold water
salt and ground white pepper
noodles, to serve

1 Slice the rump steak thinly. Place the steak slices in a bowl, add 5ml/1 tsp of the vegetable oil and stir to coat.

2 Bring the stock to the boil in a large pan. Add the beef and cook for 2 minutes, stirring constantly. Drain the beef and set it aside.

VARIATION
Add 5–10ml/1–2 tsp soy sauce to the tomato purée (paste). You will not need to add any extra salt.

3 Heat the remaining oil in a non-stick frying pan or wok until very hot. Stir-fry the garlic and onion for a few seconds.

COOK'S TIP
Use plum tomatoes or vine tomatoes from the garden, if you can. The store-bought ones are a little more expensive than standard tomatoes but have a far better flavour.

4 Add the beef to the pan or wok, then tip in the tomatoes. Stir-fry for 1 minute more over high heat.

5 Mix the tomato purée, sugar, sherry and water in a cup or small bowl. Stir into the pan or wok, add salt and pepper to taste and mix thoroughly. Cook for 1 minute until the sauce is hot. Serve in heated bowls, with noodles.

Energy 172kcal/723kJ; Protein 20.5g; Carbohydrate 6.7g, of which sugars 6.4g; Fat 6.8g, of which saturates 1.9g; Cholesterol 52mg; Calcium 18mg; Fibre 1.6g; Sodium 74mg.

BEEF STEW WITH STAR ANISE ★★★

THE BEANSPROUTS, CHOPPED SPRING ONION AND CORIANDER ARE ADDED AT THE END OF COOKING FOR A DELIGHTFUL AND FRAGRANT CONTRAST IN TASTE AND TEXTURE.

SERVES 4

INGREDIENTS
    1 litre/1¾ pints/4 cups vegetable or
      chicken stock
    450g/1lb beef steak, cut into slivers
    3 garlic cloves, finely chopped
    3 coriander (cilantro) roots,
      finely chopped
    2 cinnamon sticks
    4 star anise
    30ml/2 tbsp light soy sauce
    30ml/2 tbsp Thai fish sauce
    5ml/1 tsp granulated sugar
    115g/4oz/1⅓ cups beansprouts
    1 spring onion (scallion),
      finely chopped
    small bunch fresh coriander
      (cilantro), coarsely chopped

1 Pour the stock into a large, heavy pan. Add the beef, garlic, chopped coriander roots, cinnamon sticks, star anise, soy sauce, fish sauce and sugar. Bring to the boil, then reduce the heat to low and simmer for 30 minutes. Skim off any foam that rises to the surface of the liquid with a slotted spoon.

2 Meanwhile, divide the beansprouts among four individual serving bowls. Remove and discard the cinnamon sticks and star anise from the stew with a slotted spoon. Ladle the stew over the beansprouts, garnish with the chopped spring onion and chopped fresh coriander and serve immediately.

Energy 221kcal/923kJ; Protein 27.3g; Carbohydrate 4.1g, of which sugars 2.4g; Fat 10.7g, of which saturates 4.3g; Cholesterol 65mg; Calcium 16mg; Fibre 0.8g; Sodium 608mg.

BEET WITH PEPPERS AND BLACK BEAN SAUCE ★★

THE BLACK BEAN SAUCE GIVES THIS LOW-FAT DISH A LOVELY RICH FLAVOUR. THE BEEF IS FIRST SIMMERED IN STOCK AND THEN STIR-FRIED WITH GARLIC, GINGER, CHILLI AND GREEN PEPPER.

SERVES 4

INGREDIENTS

350g/12oz rump (round) steak,
   trimmed and thinly sliced
15ml/1 tbsp vegetable oil
300ml/½ pint/1¼ cups beef stock
2 garlic cloves, finely chopped
5ml/1 tsp grated fresh root ginger
1 fresh red chilli, seeded and
   finely chopped
15ml/1 tbsp black bean sauce
1 green (bell) pepper, seeded
   and cut into 2.5cm/1in squares
15ml/1 tbsp dry sherry
5ml/1 tsp cornflour (cornstarch)
5ml/1 tsp caster (superfine) sugar
45ml/3 tbsp cold water
salt
rice noodles, to serve

1 Place the sliced steak in a bowl. Add 5ml/1 tsp of the oil and stir to coat.

2 Bring the stock to the boil in a large pan. Add the sliced steak and cook for 2 minutes, stirring constantly to prevent the slices from sticking together. Strain the beef through a sieve (strainer) and set aside.

3 Heat the remaining oil in a non-stick frying pan or wok. Stir-fry the garlic, ginger and chilli with the black bean sauce for a few seconds.

4 Add the pepper and a little water. Cook for about 2 minutes more, then stir in the sherry. Add the beef slices to the pan and spoon the sauce over.

5 Mix the cornflour and sugar to a paste with the water. Pour the mixture into the pan. Cook, stirring, until the sauce has thickened. Season with salt. Serve immediately, with rice noodles.

COOK'S TIP
For extra colour, use half each of a green pepper and red pepper.

Energy 146kcal/613kJ; Protein 19.3g; Carbohydrate 2.1g, of which sugars 1.1g; Fat 6.4g, of which saturates 1.8g; Cholesterol 52mg; Calcium 5mg; Fibre 0g; Sodium 115mg.

SIMMERED BEEF SLICES AND VEGETABLES ★★

THIS ONE-POT DISH IS A FAMILY FAVOURITE IN JAPAN. IT IS A GOOD EXAMPLE OF HOW A SMALL AMOUNT OF MEAT CAN BE STRETCHED WITH VEGETABLES TO MAKE A TASTY LOW-FAT MEAL.

SERVES 4

INGREDIENTS

   250g/9oz lean fillet (beef tenderloin)
   or rump (round) steak, trimmed of
   fat and very thinly sliced
   1 large onion
   15ml/1 tbsp vegetable oil
   450g/1lb small potatoes, halved
   then soaked in water
   1 carrot, cut into 5mm/¼in rounds
   45ml/3 tbsp frozen peas, thawed
   and blanched for 1 minute
For the seasonings
   30ml/2 tbsp caster (superfine)
   sugar
   75ml/5 tbsp shoyu
   15ml/1 tbsp mirin
   15ml/1 tbsp sake or dry sherry

1 Cut the thinly sliced beef slices into 2cm/¾in wide strips, and slice the onion lengthways into 5mm/¼in pieces.

2 Heat the vegetable oil in a pan and lightly fry the beef and onion slices. When the colour of the meat changes, drain the potatoes and add to the pan.

3 Once the potatoes are coated with the oil in the pan, add the carrot. Pour in just enough water to cover, then bring to the boil, skimming a few times.

4 Boil vigorously for 2 minutes, then rearrange the ingredients so that the potatoes are underneath the beef and vegetables. Reduce the heat to medium-low and add all the seasonings. Simmer for 20 minutes, partially covered, or until most of the liquid has evaporated.

5 Check if the potatoes are cooked. Add the peas and cook to heat through, then remove the pan from the heat. Serve the beef and vegetables immediately in four small serving bowls.

Energy 263kcal/1110kJ; Protein 17.8g; Carbohydrate 34.7g, of which sugars 15.6g; Fat 6g, of which saturates 1.6g; Cholesterol 37mg; Calcium 37mg; Fibre 2.8g; Sodium 1393mg.

PAPER-THIN SLICED BEEF <u>IN</u> STOCK ★★★

THIS DISH IS GREAT FOR SHARING WITH FRIENDS, AS THE COOKING IS DONE AT THE TABLE. THE
SESAME SAUCE THAT USUALLY ACCOMPANIES IT HAS BEEN OMITTED HERE BECAUSE IT IS HIGH IN FAT.

SERVES 4

INGREDIENTS
600g/1⅓lb lean rump (round) steak
2 thin leeks, trimmed and cut into
thin strips
4 spring onions (scallions), quartered
8 shiitake mushrooms, minus stems
175g/6oz/2 cups oyster mushrooms,
base part removed, torn into
small pieces
½ head Chinese leaves (Chinese
cabbage), cut into 5cm/2in squares
300g/11oz *shungiku*, halved
275g/10oz firm tofu, halved
and cut crossways in 2cm/¾in
thick slices
10 x 6cm/4 x 2½in *dashi-konbu*,
wiped with a damp cloth
For the lime sauce
1 lime
20ml/4 tsp mirin
60ml/4 tbsp rice vinegar
120ml/4fl oz/½ cup shoyu
4 x 6cm/1½ x 2½in *dashi-konbu*
5g/⅛oz dried fish flakes
For the pink daikon
1 piece daikon (mooli), 6cm/2½in
in length, peeled
1 dried chilli, seeded and cut
in strips

1 Make the lime sauce. Squeeze the lime into a liquid measure and make up to 120ml/4fl oz/½ cup with water.

2 Pour the lime juice into a small bowl and add the mirin, rice vinegar, shoyu, *dashi-konbu* and the dried fish flakes. Cover with clear film (plastic wrap) and leave to stand overnight.

3 Make the pink daikon. Using a wooden skewer, pierce the daikon in several places and insert the chilli strips. Leave for 20 minutes, then grate finely into a sieve (strainer). Squeeze out the liquid and divide among four small bowls.

4 Slice the meat very thinly and arrange on a platter. Put the vegetables and tofu on another platter. Fill a flameproof casserole three-quarters full of water and add the dashi-konbu. Bring to the boil, then transfer to a table burner. Strain the citrus sauce and add 45ml/3 tbsp to each bowl of grated daikon.

5 Remove the konbu from the stock. Add some tofu and vegetables to the pot. Each guest picks up a slice of beef, holds it in the stock for a few seconds until cooked, then dips it in the sauce. As the tofu and vegetables are cooked, they are removed and dipped in the same way, and more are added to the pot.

Energy 311kcal/1302kJ; Protein 40.7g; Carbohydrate 7.1g, of which sugars 6g; Fat 12.9g, of which saturates 4.7g; Cholesterol 92mg; Calcium 412mg; Fibre 3.8g; Sodium 887mg.

GREEN BEEF CURRY <u>WITH</u> THAI AUBERGINES ★★

THIS IS A VERY QUICK AND SIMPLE CURRY TO MAKE, SO BE SURE TO USE GOOD QUALITY MEAT.
SIRLOIN IS RECOMMENDED, BUT YOU COULD ALSO USE A TENDER RUMP STEAK INSTEAD.

SERVES 6

INGREDIENTS
450g/1lb lean beef sirloin
15ml/1 tbsp sunflower oil
45ml/3 tbsp Thai green curry paste
600ml/1 pint/2½ cups reduced-fat
  coconut milk
4 kaffir lime leaves, torn
15–30ml/1–2 tbsp Thai fish sauce
5ml/1 tsp palm sugar
150g/5oz small Thai aubergines
  (eggplants), halved
a small handful of fresh Thai basil
2 fresh green chillies, to garnish

1 Trim off any excess fat from the beef.
Using a sharp knife, cut it into long,
thin strips. This is easiest to do if it is
well chilled. Set it aside.

2 Heat the oil in a large, heavy pan or
wok. Add the curry paste and cook for
1–2 minutes, until it is fragrant.

3 Stir in half the coconut milk, a little
at a time. Cook, stirring frequently, for
about 5–6 minutes, until an oily sheen
appears on the surface of the liquid.

4 Add the beef to the pan with the kaffir
lime leaves, Thai fish sauce, sugar and
aubergine halves. Cook for 2–3 minutes,
then stir in the remaining coconut milk.

5 Bring back to a simmer and cook
until the meat and aubergines are
tender. Stir in the Thai basil just before
serving. Finely shred the green chillies
and use to garnish the curry.

COOK'S TIP
To make the green curry paste, put
15 fresh green chillies, 2 chopped lemon
grass stalks, 3 sliced shallots, 2 garlic
cloves, 15ml/1 tbsp chopped galangal,
4 chopped kaffir lime leaves, 2.5ml/
½ tsp grated kaffir lime rind, 5ml/1 tsp
chopped coriander root, 6 black
peppercorns, 5ml/1 tsp each roasted
coriander and cumin seeds, 15ml/1 tbsp
granulated sugar, 5ml/1 tsp salt and
5ml/1 tsp shrimp paste into a food
processor and process until smooth.
Gradually add 30ml/2 tbsp vegetable oil,
processing after each addition.

Energy 174kcal/726kJ; Protein 17.6g; Carbohydrate 5.5g, of which sugars 5.4g; Fat 9.2g, of which saturates 3.3g; Cholesterol 44mg; Calcium 35mg; Fibre 0.5g; Sodium 159mg.

BEEF WITH FRIED RICE ★★

ONE OF THE JOYS OF CHINESE COOKING IS THE EASE AND SPEED WITH WHICH A REALLY GOOD MEAL CAN BE PREPARED. THIS COLOURFUL DISH CAN BE ON THE TABLE WITHIN 15 MINUTES.

SERVES 4

INGREDIENTS
200g/7oz lean beef steak
5ml/1 tsp sunflower oil
2 garlic cloves, finely chopped
1 egg
250g/9oz/2¼ cups cooked
  jasmine rice
½ medium head broccoli,
  coarsely chopped
30ml/2 tbsp dark soy sauce
15ml/1 tbsp light soy sauce
5ml/1 tsp palm sugar or light
  muscovado (brown) sugar
15ml/1 tbsp Thai fish sauce
ground black pepper
chilli sauce, to serve

1 Trim the steak and cut into very thin strips with a sharp knife.

2 Heat the oil in a wok or frying pan and cook the garlic over a low to medium heat until golden. Do not let it burn. Increase the heat to high, add the steak and stir-fry for 2 minutes.

3 Move the pieces of beef to the edges of the wok or pan and break the egg into the centre. When the egg starts to set, stir-fry it with the meat.

4 Add the rice and toss all the contents of the wok together, scraping up any residue on the base, then add the broccoli, soy sauces, sugar and fish sauce and stir-fry for 2 minutes more. Season to taste with pepper and serve immediately with chilli sauce.

COOK'S TIP
Soy sauce is made from fermented soya beans. The first extraction is sold as light soy sauce and has a delicate, "beany" fragrance. Dark soy sauce has been allowed to mature for longer.

Energy 232kcal/975kJ; Protein 16.9g; Carbohydrate 24.5g, of which sugars 5g; Fat 8.1g, of which saturates 2.7g; Cholesterol 77mg; Calcium 52mg; Fibre 1.4g; Sodium 321mg.

RICE

Rice forms the bulk of most meals in South-east Asia.
The dishes are usually combined with a healthy proportion of
vegetables and just small amounts of protein in the shape
of meat, fish or tofu. Many of these recipes contain all the
delicious flavours of classic Asian cooking, such as with Garlic
and Ginger Rice with Coriander, Fried Rice with Mushrooms, and
Sticky Rice Parcels. As rice is low in fat, many of the dishes
contain less than 1 gram of fat per serving.

STEAMED RICE ★

Long grain rice is the most frequently eaten grain in Asia – freshly steamed and served at almost every meal. If the main dish doesn't include noodles, then a bowl of steamed rice – com – or rice wrappers will provide the starch for the meal.

SERVES 4

INGREDIENTS

  225g/8oz/generous 1 cup long grain
    rice, rinsed and drained
  a pinch of salt

1 Put the rice into a heavy pan or clay pot. Add 600ml/1 pint/2½ cups water to cover the rice by 2.5cm/1in. Add the salt, and then bring the water to the boil.

VARIATION
Jasmine rice is delicious and readily available from Asian stores.

2 Reduce the heat, cover the pan and cook gently for about 20 minutes, or until all the water has been absorbed. Remove the pan from the heat and leave to steam, still covered, for a further 5–10 minutes.

3 To serve, simply fluff up with a fork.

Energy 203kcal/864kJ; Protein 4g; Carbohydrate 49g, of which sugars 0g; Fat 1g, of which saturates 0g; Cholesterol 0mg; Calcium 2mg; Fibre 0.3g; Sodium 0mg.

BAMBOO-STEAMED STICKY RICE ★

Sticky rice, or glutinous rice, requires a long soak in water before being cooked in a bamboo steamer. Combine sticky rice with savoury fillings such as mushrooms and Chinese sausage, wrap in lotus leaves and steam to make tasty lunchtime snacks.

SERVES 4

INGREDIENTS
350g/12oz/1¾ cups sticky rice

1 Put the rice into a large bowl and fill the bowl with cold water. Leave the rice to soak for at least 6 hours, then drain, rinse thoroughly, and drain again.

VARIATION
Sticky rice is enjoyed as a sweet, filling snack with sugar and coconut milk and, as it is fairly bulky, it is also served with dipping sauces, light dishes and vegetarian meals.

2 Fill a wok or heavy pan one-third full with water. Place a bamboo steamer, with the lid on, over the wok or pan and bring the water to the boil. Uncover the steamer and place a dampened piece of muslin (cheesecloth) over the rack. Tip the rice into the middle and spread it out. Fold the muslin over the rice, cover and steam for 25 minutes until the rice is tender but firm. The measured quantity of rice grains doubles when cooked.

Energy 314kcal/1314kJ; Protein 7g; Carbohydrate 66g, of which sugars 0g; Fat 1g, of which saturates 0g; Cholesterol 0mg; Calcium 14mg; Fibre 0g; Sodium 0mg.

COCONUT JASMINE RICE ★

THIS RICH DISH IS OFTEN SERVED WITH A TANGY PAPAYA SALAD TO BALANCE THE SWEETNESS OF THE COCONUT MILK AND SUGAR. IT IS ONE OF THOSE COMFORTING TREATS THAT EVERYONE ENJOYS.

SERVES 6

INGREDIENTS
250ml/8fl oz/1 cup water
475ml/16fl oz/2 cups reduced-fat
  coconut milk
2.5ml/½ tsp salt
30ml/2 tbsp granulated sugar
450g/1lb/2⅔ cups jasmine rice

COOK'S TIP
For a special occasion serve in a halved papaya and garnish with thin shreds of fresh coconut. Use a vegetable peeler to pare the coconut finely.

1 Place the measured water, coconut milk, salt and sugar in a heavy pan. Wash the rice in several changes of cold water until it runs clear.

2 Add the jasmine rice, cover tightly with a lid and bring to the boil over a medium heat. Reduce the heat to low and simmer gently, without lifting the lid unnecessarily, for 15–20 minutes, until the rice is tender and cooked through. Test it by biting a grain.

3 Turn off the heat and leave the rice to rest in the pan, still covered with the lid, for a further 5–10 minutes.

4 Gently fluff up the rice grains with chopsticks or a fork before transferring it to a warmed dish and serving.

Energy 306kcal/1286kJ; Protein 5.8g; Carbohydrate 69g, of which sugars 9.1g; Fat 0.6g, of which saturates 0.2g; Cholesterol 0mg; Calcium 40mg; Fibre 0g; Sodium 218mg.

FRAGRANT COCONUT RICE ★

THIS WAY OF COOKING RICE IS VERY POPULAR THROUGHOUT INDONESIA AND THE WHOLE OF SOUTH-EAST ASIA. COCONUT RICE GOES PARTICULARLY WELL WITH FISH, CHICKEN AND PORK.

SERVES 6

INGREDIENTS

   350g/12oz/1¾ cups Thai fragrant rice
   400ml/14fl oz can reduced-fat
     coconut milk
   300ml/½ pint/1¼ cups water
   2.5ml/½ tsp ground coriander
   5cm/2in cinnamon stick
   1 lemon grass stalk, bruised
   1 bay leaf
   salt
   crisp fried onions, to garnish

1 Put the rice in a strainer and rinse thoroughly under cold water. Drain well, then put in a pan. Pour in the coconut milk and water. Add the coriander, cinnamon stick, lemon grass and bay leaf. Season with salt. Bring to the boil, then lower the heat, cover and simmer for 8–10 minutes.

2 Lift the lid and check that all the liquid has been absorbed, then fork the rice through carefully, removing the cinnamon stick, lemon grass and bay leaf.

3 Cover the pan with a tight-fitting lid and continue to cook the rice over the lowest possible heat for 3–5 minutes more. Take care that the pan does not scorch.

4 Pile the rice on to a warm serving dish and serve garnished with the crisp fried onions.

VARIATION
For a quick and easy healthy supper, stir in strips of freshly cooked skinless chicken breast and peas 5–6 minutes before serving and heat through.

COOK'S TIP
When bringing the rice to the boil, stir it frequently to prevent it from settling on the bottom of the pan. Once the rice is nearly tender, continue to cook over a very low heat or just leave to stand for 5 minutes.

Energy 226kcal/945kJ; Protein 4.6g; Carbohydrate 49.9g, of which sugars 3.4g; Fat 0.6g, of which saturates 0.1g; Cholesterol 0mg; Calcium 39mg; Fibre 0.2g; Sodium 75mg.

SAVOURY RICE WITH ROASTED COCONUT ★

ORIGINALLY FROM INDIA AND THAILAND, COCONUT RICE IS POPULAR THROUGHOUT SOUTH-EAST ASIA. RICH AND NOURISHING, IT IS OFTEN SERVED WITH A TANGY FRUIT AND VEGETABLE SALAD, SUCH AS THE ONES MADE WITH GREEN PAPAYA OR GREEN MANGO.

SERVES 4–6

INGREDIENTS

- 400ml/14fl oz/1⅔ cups unsweetened coconut milk
- 400ml/14fl oz/1⅔ cups seasoned chicken stock
- 225g/8oz/generous 1 cup long grain rice, rinsed in several bowls of water and drained
- 115g/4oz fresh coconut, grated

COOK'S TIP

As the coconut shells are often halved and used as bowls, they make a perfect serving vessel for this rice, garnished with fresh or roasted coconut or crispy-fried ginger. In the street, this rice is often served on a banana leaf.

1 Pour the coconut milk and stock into a heavy pan and stir well to combine. Bring the liquid to the boil and stir in the rice. Stir once, reduce the heat and cover the pan. Simmer gently for about 25 minutes, until the rice has absorbed all the liquid. Remove from the heat and leave the rice to sit for 10 minutes.

2 Meanwhile, heat a small, heavy pan. Stir in the fresh coconut and roast it until it turns golden with a nutty aroma. Tip the roasted coconut into a bowl.

3 Fluff up the rice with a fork and spoon it into bowls. Scatter the roasted coconut over the top and serve.

Energy 175kcal/731kJ; Protein 3g; Carbohydrate 33.5g, of which sugars 3.5g; Fat 3g, of which saturates 2g; Cholesterol 0mg; Calcium 28mg; Fibre 0.6g; Sodium 75mg.

RICE CAKES <u>WITH</u> SPICY DIPPING SAUCE ★★

*A CLASSIC THAI APPETIZER, THESE RICE CAKES ARE EASY TO MAKE AND WILL KEEP ALMOST
INDEFINITELY IN AN AIRTIGHT CONTAINER. START MAKING THEM AT LEAST A DAY BEFORE YOU
PLAN TO SERVE THEM, AS THE RICE NEEDS TO DRY OUT OVERNIGHT.*

SERVES 4–6

INGREDIENTS
    175g/6oz/1 cup Thai jasmine rice
    350ml/12fl oz/1½ cups water
    oil, for deep-frying and greasing
For the spicy dipping sauce
    6–8 dried chillies
    2.5ml/½ tsp salt
    2 shallots, chopped
    2 garlic cloves, chopped
    4 coriander (cilantro) roots
    10 white peppercorns
    250ml/8fl oz/1 cup coconut milk
    5ml/1 tsp shrimp paste
    115g/4oz minced (ground) pork
    115g/4oz cherry tomatoes, chopped
    15ml/1 tbsp Thai fish sauce
    15ml/1 tbsp palm sugar or light
        muscovado (brown) sugar
    30ml/2 tbsp tamarind juice (tamarind
        paste mixed with warm water)
    30ml/2 tbsp coarsely chopped
        roasted peanuts
    2 spring onions (scallions), chopped

1 Make the sauce. Snap off the stems
of the chillies, shake out the seeds and
soak the chillies in warm water for
20 minutes. Drain and put in a mortar.
Sprinkle over the salt and crush. Add
the shallots, garlic, coriander and
peppercorns. Pound to a coarse paste.

2 Pour the coconut milk into a pan and
bring to the boil. When it begins to
separate, stir in the pounded chilli
paste. Cook for 2–3 minutes, until the
mixture is fragrant. Stir in the shrimp
paste and cook for 1 minute more.

3 Add the pork, stirring to break up any
lumps. Cook for 5–10 minutes, then stir
in the tomatoes, fish sauce, palm sugar
and tamarind juice. Simmer, stirring
occasionally, until the sauce thickens,
then stir in the chopped peanuts and
spring onions. Remove the sauce from
the heat and leave to cool.

4 Preheat the oven to the lowest setting.
Grease a baking sheet. Wash the rice in
several changes of water. Put it in a
pan, add the water and cover tightly.
Bring to the boil, reduce the heat and
simmer gently for about 15 minutes.

5 Remove the lid and fluff up the rice.
Spoon it on to the baking sheet and
press it down with the back of a spoon.
Leave in the oven to dry out overnight.

6 Break the rice into bitesize pieces.
Heat the oil in a wok or deep-fryer.
Deep-fry the rice cakes, in batches, for
about 1 minute, until they puff up but
are not browned. Remove and drain
well. Serve with the dipping sauce.

Energy 180kcal/750kJ; Protein 2.3g; Carbohydrate 25.7g, of which sugars 2.3g; Fat 7.5g, of which saturates 0.9g; Cholesterol 0mg; Calcium 7mg; Fibre 0.1g; Sodium 136mg.

RED RICE WRAPPED <u>IN</u> OAK LEAVES ★★

THIS IS A SAVOURY VERSION OF A POPULAR SWEETMEAT. OAK TREES DON'T SHED THEIR OLD LEAVES UNTIL NEW ONES APPEAR, SO THEY REPRESENT THE CONTINUITY OF FAMILY LIFE.

SERVES 4

INGREDIENTS
 65g/2½oz/⅓ cup dried aduki beans
 5ml/1 tsp salt
 300g/11oz/1½ cups glutinous rice
 50g/2oz/¼ cup Japanese short
  grain rice
 12 *kashiwa* leaves (optional), to serve
For the *goma-shio*
 45ml/3 tbsp sesame seeds (black
  sesame, if available)
 5ml/1 tsp ground sea salt

1 Put the aduki beans in a heavy pan and pour in 400ml/14fl oz/1⅔ cups plus 20ml/4 tsp water.

2 Bring to the boil, reduce the heat and simmer, covered, for 20–30 minutes, or until the beans look swollen but are still firm. Remove from the heat and drain. Reserve the liquid in a bowl and add the salt. Return the beans to the pan.

3 Wash all of the rice. Drain in a sieve (strainer) and leave for 30 minutes.

4 Bring another 400ml/14fl oz/1⅔ cups plus 20ml/4 tsp water to the boil. Add to the beans and boil, then simmer for 30 minutes. The beans' skins should start to crack. Drain and add the liquid to the bowl with the reserved liquid. Cover the beans and leave to cool.

5 Add the rice to the bean liquid. Leave to soak for 4–5 hours. Drain the rice and reserve the liquid. Mix the rice into the beans.

6 Bring a steamer of water to the boil. Turn off the heat. Place a tall glass in the centre of the steaming compartment. Pour the rice and beans into the steamer and gently pull the glass out. The hole in the middle will allow even distribution of the steam. Steam on high for 10 minutes.

7 Using your fingers, sprinkle the rice mixture with the reserved liquid from the bowl. Cover again and repeat the process twice more at 10 minute intervals, then leave to steam for 15 minutes more. Remove from the heat. Leave to stand for 10 minutes.

8 Make the *goma-shio*. Roast the sesame seeds and salt in a dry frying pan until the seeds start to pop. Leave to cool, then put in a small dish.

9 Wipe each *kashiwa* leaf with a wet dish towel. Scoop 120ml/4fl oz/½ cup of the rice mixture into a wet tea cup and press with wet fingers. Turn the cup upside down and shape the moulded rice with your hands into a flat ball. Insert into a leaf folded in two. Repeat this process until all the leaves are used. Alternatively, transfer the red rice to a large bowl wiped with a wet towel.

10 Serve the red rice with a sprinkle of *goma-shio*. The kashiwa leaves are not to be eaten.

Energy 432kcal/1807kJ; Protein 12.4g; Carbohydrate 78.7g, of which sugars 0.5g; Fat 7.2g, of which saturates 1g; Cholesterol 0mg; Calcium 105mg; Fibre 2.2g; Sodium 5mg.

GARLIC AND GINGER RICE WITH CORIANDER ★

WHEN RICE IS SERVED ON THE SIDE, IT IS USUALLY STEAMED AND PLAIN. THIS MIX OF GARLIC AND GINGER COMPLEMENTS ALMOST ANY VEGETABLE, FISH OR MEAT DISH.

SERVES 6

INGREDIENTS

15ml/1 tbsp sunflower oil
2–3 garlic cloves,
    finely chopped
25g/1oz fresh root ginger,
    finely chopped
225g/8oz/generous 1 cup
    long grain rice, rinsed in
    several bowls of cold water
    and drained
900ml/1½ pints/3¾ cups
    chicken stock
a bunch of fresh coriander (cilantro)
    leaves, finely chopped
a bunch of fresh basil and mint,
    (optional), finely chopped

1 Heat the oil in a clay pot or heavy pan. Stir in the garlic and ginger and fry until golden. Stir in the rice and allow it to absorb the flavours for 1–2 minutes. Pour in the stock and stir to make sure the rice doesn't stick. Bring the stock to the boil, then reduce the heat.

2 Sprinkle the coriander over the surface of the stock, cover the pan, and leave to cook gently for 20–25 minutes, until the rice has absorbed all the liquid. Turn off the heat and gently fluff up the rice to mix in the coriander. Cover and leave to infuse for 10 minutes before serving.

Energy 162kcal/677kJ; Protein 3.7g; Carbohydrate 31.5g, of which sugars 0.3g; Fat 2.2g, of which saturates 0.2g; Cholesterol 0mg; Calcium 25mg; Fibre 0.8g; Sodium 3mg.

SOUTHERN-SPICED CHILLI RICE ★

PLAIN STEAMED RICE IS SERVED AT ALMOST EVERY SOUTH-EAST ASIAN MEAL, BUT SPICY RICE IS POPULAR TOO. A BURST OF CHILLI, TURMERIC AND CORIANDER IS ALL THAT'S NEEDED.

SERVES 4

INGREDIENTS

15ml/1 tbsp sunflower oil
2–3 green or red Thai chillies,
  seeded and finely chopped
2 garlic cloves, finely chopped
2.5cm/1in fresh root ginger, chopped
5ml/1 tsp sugar
10–15ml/2–3 tsp ground turmeric
225g/8oz/generous 1 cup long
  grain rice
30ml/2 tbsp fish sauce
600ml/1 pint/2½ cups water
1 bunch of fresh coriander
  (cilantro), stalks removed, leaves
  finely chopped
salt and ground black pepper

1 Heat the oil in a heavy pan. Stir in the chillies, garlic and ginger with the sugar. As they begin to colour, stir in the turmeric. Add the rice, coating it well, then pour in the fish sauce and the water – the liquid should sit about 2.5cm/1in above the rice.

2 Tip the rice on to a serving dish. Add some of the coriander and lightly toss together using a fork. Garnish with the remaining coriander.

COOK'S TIP
This rice goes well with grilled and stir-fried fish and shellfish dishes, but you can serve it as an alternative to plain rice. Add extra chillies, if you like.

3 Season with salt and ground black pepper and bring the liquid to the boil. Reduce the heat, cover and simmer for about 25 minutes, or until the water has been absorbed. Remove from the heat and leave the rice to steam for a further 10 minutes.

Energy 247kcal/1032kJ; Protein 5.5g; Carbohydrate 48.3g, of which sugars 1.5g; Fat 3.3g, of which saturates 0.4g; Cholesterol 0mg; Calcium 39mg; Fibre 1.1g; Sodium 5mg.

BROWN RICE WITH LIME AND LEMON GRASS ★

IT IS UNUSUAL TO FIND BROWN RICE GIVEN THE THAI TREATMENT, BUT THE NUTTY FLAVOUR OF THE GRAINS IS ENHANCED BY THE FRAGRANCE OF LIMES AND LEMON GRASS IN THIS DELICIOUS DISH.

SERVES 4

INGREDIENTS

2 limes
1 lemon grass stalk
225g/8oz/generous 1 cup brown
 long grain rice
15ml/1 tbsp olive oil
1 onion, chopped
2.5cm/1in piece fresh root ginger,
 peeled and finely chopped
7.5ml/1½ tsp coriander seeds
7.5ml/1½ tsp cumin seeds
750ml/1¼ pints/3 cups
 vegetable stock
60ml/4 tbsp chopped fresh
 coriander (cilantro)
spring onion (scallion) green and
 toasted coconut strips, to garnish
lime wedges, to serve

3 Heat the oil in a large pan. Add the onion, ginger, coriander and cumin seeds, lemon grass and lime rind and cook over a low heat for 2–3 minutes.

4 Add the rice to the pan and cook, stirring constantly, for 1 minute, then pour in the stock and bring to the boil. Reduce the heat to very low and cover the pan. Cook gently for 30 minutes, then check the rice. If it is still crunchy, cover the pan and cook for 3–5 minutes more. Remove from the heat.

5 Stir in the fresh coriander, fluff up the rice grains with a fork, cover the pan and leave to stand for 10 minutes. Transfer to a warmed dish, garnish with spring onion green and toasted coconut strips, and serve with lime wedges.

1 Pare the limes, using a cannelle knife (zester) or fine grater, taking care to avoid cutting the bitter pith. Set the rind aside. Finely chop the lower portion of the lemon grass stalk and set it aside.

2 Rinse the rice in plenty of cold water until the water runs clear. Tip it into a sieve and drain thoroughly.

Energy 235kcal/996kJ; Protein 4.3g; Carbohydrate 47.3g, of which sugars 1.9g; Fat 4.5g, of which saturates 0.8g; Cholesterol 0mg; Calcium 35mg; Fibre 1.9g; Sodium 6mg.

CHINESE LEAVES AND BLACK RICE STIR-FRY ★

THE SLIGHTLY NUTTY, CHEWY BLACK GLUTINOUS RICE CONTRASTS BEAUTIFULLY WITH THE CHINESE LEAVES IN THIS TASTY STIR-FRY, WHICH IS LOW IN SATURATED FAT.

SERVES 4

INGREDIENTS

225g/8oz/1⅓ cups black glutinous rice or brown rice
900ml/1½ pints/3¾ cups vegetable stock
15ml/1 tbsp vegetable oil
225g/8oz Chinese leaves (Chinese cabbage), cut into 1cm/½in strips
4 spring onions (scallions), thinly sliced
salt and ground white pepper
2.5ml/½ tsp sesame oil

1 Rinse the rice until the water runs clear, then drain and tip into a pan. Add the stock and bring to the boil. Lower the heat, cover the pan and cook gently for 30 minutes.

2 Remove the pan from the heat and leave to stand for 15 minutes without lifting the lid.

3 Heat the vegetable oil in a non-stick frying pan or wok. Stir-fry the Chinese leaves over medium heat for 2 minutes, adding a little water to prevent them from burning.

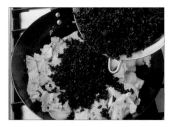

4 Drain the rice, stir it into the pan and cook for 4 minutes, using two spatulas or spoons to toss it with the Chinese leaves over the heat.

5 Add the spring onions, with salt and pepper to taste. Drizzle over the sesame oil. Cook for 1 minute more, stirring constantly. Serve immediately.

Energy 243kcal/1029kJ; Protein 4.8g; Carbohydrate 48.9g, of which sugars 3.8g; Fat 4.5g, of which saturates 0.7g; Cholesterol 0mg; Calcium 37mg; Fibre 2.4g; Sodium 6mg.

NUTTY RICE <u>AND</u> MUSHROOM STIR-FRY ★★

THIS DELICIOUS AND SUBSTANTIAL SUPPER DISH CAN BE EATEN HOT OR COLD WITH SALADS. ONLY A FEW NUTS ARE ADDED, BUT THEY MAKE A SIGNIFICANT CONTRIBUTION TO THE FLAVOUR.

<u>SERVES 4–6</u>

INGREDIENTS

  350g/12oz/1½ cups long grain
    rice, rinsed
  1 small onion, roughly chopped
  250g/9oz/3½ cups field (portabello)
    mushrooms, sliced
  40g/1½oz/⅓ cup mixed nuts (such
    as cashews, peanuts and almonds)
  15ml/1 tbsp vegetable oil
  60ml/4 tbsp fresh coriander
    (cilantro), chopped
  salt and ground black pepper

1 Put the rice in a pan. Add 750ml/
1¼ pints/3 cups of water and bring to
the boil. Cover the pan with a tight-
fitting lid, lower the heat and cook the
rice for 12–14 minutes until just tender.
Drain and refresh under cold water.

2 Heat a wok, then add half the oil.
When the oil is hot, stir-fry the rice for
2–3 minutes. Remove from the heat
and set aside.

3 Add the remaining oil to the pan and
stir-fry the onion for 2 minutes until it
has softened.

4 Mix in the field mushrooms and stir-
fry for 2 minutes. Keep tossing the
mixture, using two spoons or a pair
of chopsticks, until well mixed.

5 Add all the nuts to the wok and stir-fry
for 1 minute. Return the rice to the wok
and stir-fry for 3 minutes. Season and
stir in the parsley. Serve immediately.

Energy 278kcal/1160kJ; Protein 6.8g; Carbohydrate 48.9g, of which sugars 1.2g; Fat 5.8g, of which saturates 0.9g; Cholesterol 0mg; Calcium 32mg; Fibre 1.2g; Sodium 24mg.

FRIED RICE <u>WITH</u> MUSHROOMS ★

A SIMPLE RICE AND MUSHROOM DISH THAT IS VERY LOW IN SATURATED FAT, YET SUFFICIENTLY FILLING TO BE ALMOST A MEAL IN ITSELF. SESAME OIL ADDS A HINT OF NUTTY FLAVOUR.

SERVES 4

INGREDIENTS
  225g/8oz/1¼ cups long grain rice
  15ml/1 tbsp vegetable oil
  1 egg, lightly beaten
  2 garlic cloves, crushed
  175g/6oz/2¼ cups button (white)
    mushrooms or mixed wild and
    cultivated mushrooms, sliced
  15ml/1 tbsp light soy sauce
  1.5ml/¼ tsp salt
  2.5ml/½ tsp sesame oil
  cucumber matchsticks, to garnish

1 Rinse the rice until the water runs clear, then drain thoroughly. Place it in a pan. Measure the depth of the rice against your index finger, then bring the finger up to just above the surface of the rice and add cold water to the same depth as the rice.

2 Bring the water to the boil. Stir the rice, boil for a few minutes, then cover the pan. Lower the heat to a simmer and cook the rice gently for 5–8 minutes until all of the water has been absorbed.

3 Remove the pan from the heat and, without lifting the lid, leave for another 10 minutes before stirring or forking up the rice.

4 Heat 5ml/1 tsp of the vegetable oil in a non-stick frying pan or wok. Add the egg and cook, stirring with a chopstick or wooden spoon until scrambled. Immediately remove the pan from the heat, take out the egg and set aside.

5 Add the remaining vegetable oil in the pan or wok. When it is hot, stir-fry the garlic for a few seconds, then add the mushrooms and stir-fry for 2 minutes, adding a little water, if needed, to prevent burning.

6 Stir in the cooked rice and cook for about 4 minutes, or until the rice is hot, stirring from time to time.

7 Add the cooked egg, soy sauce, salt and sesame oil. Mix together and cook for 1 minute to heat through. Serve the rice immediately, garnished with cucumber matchsticks.

Energy 275kcal/1148kJ; Protein 7.1g; Carbohydrate 50.4g, of which sugars 0.4g; Fat 4.7g, of which saturates 0.8g; Cholesterol 48mg; Calcium 22mg; Fibre 0.5g; Sodium 287mg.

LUNCH-BOX RICE <u>WITH</u> THREE TOPPINGS ★★★

A GREAT DEAL MORE NUTRITIOUS THAN SOME OF THE PACKED LUNCHES TAKEN TO SCHOOL IN THE WEST,
THIS SPECIALITY, ORIGINALLY FROM JAPAN, TOPS RICE WITH THREE DIFFERENT TOPPINGS.

MAKES 4 LUNCH BOXES

INGREDIENTS
  275g/10oz/scant 1²/₃ cups Japanese
    short grain rice cooked using 375ml/
    13fl oz/scant 1²/₃ cups water, cooled
  45ml/3 tbsp sesame seeds, toasted
  salt
  3 mangetouts (snow peas), to garnish
For the yellow topping
  30ml/2 tbsp caster (superfine) sugar
  5ml/1 tsp salt
  3 eggs, beaten
For the pink topping
  115g/4oz cod fillet, skinned
    and boned
  20ml/4 tsp caster (superfine) sugar
  5ml/1 tsp salt
  5ml/1 tsp sake
  2 drops of red vegetable colouring,
    diluted with a few drops of water
For the beige topping
  200g/7oz/scant 1 cup minced
    (ground) chicken
  45ml/3 tbsp sake
  15ml/1 tbsp caster (superfine) sugar
  15ml/1 tbsp shoyu or other soy sauce
  15ml/1 tbsp water

1 To make the *iri-tamago*, mix the sugar and salt with the eggs in a pan. Cook over a medium heat, stirring with a whisk or fork as you would to scramble eggs. When the mixture is almost set, remove from the heat and stir until the egg becomes fine and slightly dry.

2 To make the *denbu*, cook the cod fillet for 2 minutes in a large pan of boiling water. Drain and dry well with kitchen paper. Skin and remove all the fish bones.

3 Put the cod and sugar into a pan, add the salt and sake, and cook over low heat for 1 minute, stirring with a fork to flake the cod. Reduce the heat to low and sprinkle on the colouring. Continue to stir for 15–20 minutes, or until the cod flakes become very fluffy and fibrous. Transfer the *denbu* to a plate.

4 To make the *tori-soboro*, put the minced chicken, sake, sugar, shoyu and water into a small pan. Cook over medium heat for about 3 minutes, then reduce the heat to medium-low and stir with a fork or whisk until the liquid has almost evaporated.

5 Blanch the mangetouts for about 3 minutes in lightly salted boiling water, drain and carefully slice into fine 3mm/⅛in sticks.

6 Mix the rice with the sesame seeds in a bowl. With a wet spoon, divide the rice among four 17 × 12cm/6½ × 4½in lunch boxes. Flatten the surface using the back of a wooden spoon.

7 Spoon a quarter of the egg into each box to cover a third of the rice. Cover the next third with a quarter of the *denbu*, and the last section with a quarter of the chicken topping. Use the lid to divide the boxes, if you like. Garnish with the mangetout sticks.

Energy 516kcal/2162kJ; Protein 29.3g; Carbohydrate 72.2g, of which sugars 17.2g; Fat 11.8g, of which saturates 2.3g; Cholesterol 191mg; Calcium 124mg; Fibre 0.9g; Sodium 370mg.

FESTIVE RICE ★

THIS PRETTY THAI DISH IS TRADITIONALLY SHAPED INTO A CONE AND SURROUNDED BY A VARIETY OF ACCOMPANIMENTS BEFORE BEING SERVED. SERVE AT A HEALTHY SUMMERTIME LUNCH.

2 Heat the oil in a frying pan with a lid. Cook the garlic, onions and turmeric over a low heat for 2–3 minutes, until the onions have softened. Add the rice and stir well to coat in oil.

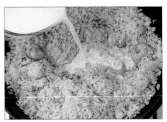

3 Pour in the water and coconut milk and add the lemon grass. Bring to the boil, stirring. Cover the pan and cook gently for 12 minutes, or until all the liquid has been absorbed by the rice.

SERVES 8

INGREDIENTS
    450g/1lb/2⅔ cups jasmine rice
    30ml/2 tbsp sunflower oil
    2 garlic cloves, crushed
    2 onions, thinly sliced
    2.5ml/½ tsp ground turmeric
    750ml/1¼ pints/3 cups water
    400ml/14fl oz can reduced-fat
      coconut milk
    1–2 lemon grass stalks, bruised
For the accompaniments
    omelette strips
    2 fresh red chillies, shredded
    cucumber chunks
    tomato wedges
    fried onions
    prawn (shrimp) crackers

1 Put the jasmine rice in a large strainer and rinse it thoroughly under cold water. Drain well.

COOK'S TIP
Jasmine rice is widely available in most supermarkets and Asian stores. It is also known as Thai fragrant rice.

4 Remove the pan from the heat and lift the lid. Cover with a clean dish towel, replace the lid and leave to stand in a warm place for 15 minutes. Remove the lemon grass, mound the rice mixture in a cone on a serving platter and garnish with the accompaniments, then serve.

Energy 224kcal/939kJ; Protein 4.8g; Carbohydrate 49.5g, of which sugars 4g; Fat 0.6g, of which saturates 0.1g; Cholesterol 0mg; Calcium 44mg; Fibre 0.7g; Sodium 58mg.

STIR-FRIED RICE AND VEGETABLES ★★

THE GINGER GIVES THIS MIXED RICE AND VEGETABLE DISH A WONDERFUL FLAVOUR. SERVE IT AS A VEGETARIAN MAIN COURSE FOR TWO OR AS AN UNUSUAL VEGETABLE ACCOMPANIMENT.

SERVES 2–4

INGREDIENTS

    115g/4oz/generous ½ cup brown
      basmati rice, rinsed and drained
    350ml/12fl oz/1½ cups
      vegetable stock
    2.5cm/1in piece fresh root ginger
    1 garlic clove, halved
    5cm/2in piece pared lemon rind
    115g/4oz/1½ cups
      shiitake mushrooms
    15ml/1 tbsp vegetable oil
    175g/6oz baby carrots, trimmed
    225g/8oz baby courgettes
      (zucchini), halved
    175–225g/6–8oz/about 1½ cups
      broccoli, broken into florets
    6 spring onions (scallions),
      diagonally sliced
    15ml/1 tbsp light soy sauce
    10ml/2 tsp toasted sesame oil

1 Put the rice in a pan and pour in the vegetable stock.

2 Thinly slice the ginger and add it to the pan with the garlic and lemon rind. Slowly bring to the boil, then lower the heat, cover and cook very gently for 20–25 minutes until the rice is tender.

3 Discard the flavourings and keep the pan covered so that the rice stays warm.

4 Slice the mushrooms, discarding the stems. Heat the oil in a wok and stir-fry the carrots for 4–5 minutes until partially tender.

5 Add the mushrooms and courgettes, stir-fry for 2–3 minutes, then add the broccoli and spring onions and cook for 3 minutes more, by which time all the vegetables should be tender but should still retain a bit of "bite".

6 Add the cooked rice to the vegetables, and toss briefly over the heat to mix and heat through. Toss with the soy sauce and sesame oil. Spoon into a bowl and serve immediately.

COOK'S TIP
Keep fresh root ginger in the freezer. It can be sliced or grated and thaws very quickly.

Energy 190kcal/792kJ; Protein 6.3g; Carbohydrate 29.1g, of which sugars 5.6g; Fat 5.4g, of which saturates 0.8g; Cholesterol 0mg; Calcium 63mg; Fibre 3.2g; Sodium 285mg.

CHINESE FRIED RICE ★

ALTHOUGH THE RICE IN THIS RECIPE IS FRIED, WHICH MIGHT RING ALARM BELLS IN TERMS OF FAT, IT CONTAINS ONLY A LITTLE HAM AND COMES IN AT UNDER 4 GRAMS OF FAT.

SERVES 4

INGREDIENTS
  50g/2oz cooked lean ham
  50g/2oz cooked prawns
    (shrimp), peeled
  2 eggs
  pinch of salt
  2 spring onions (scallions),
    finely chopped
  30ml/2 tbsp vegetable oil
  115g/4oz/1 cup green peas, thawed
    if frozen
  15ml/1 tbsp light soy sauce
  15ml/1 tbsp Chinese rice wine or
    dry sherry
  450g/1lb/4 cups cooked white long
    grain rice

1 Dice the cooked ham finely. Pat the cooked prawns dry on kitchen paper.

VARIATIONS
This dish is ideal for using up leftovers. You can use cooked chicken instead of the ham and leave out the prawns, if you like.

2 In a bowl, beat the eggs with a pinch of salt and a few spring onion pieces.

3 Heat a wok. When it is hot, add half the oil, trickling it around the inner rim of the wok so that it runs down to coat the surface. Stir-fry the peas, prawns and ham for 1 minute, then add the soy sauce and rice wine or sherry. Stir to combine, then transfer to a bowl and keep hot.

4 Heat the remaining oil in the wok and add the eggs. Stir over a low heat until lightly scrambled.

5 Add the prawn mixture, rice and the remaining spring onions. Stir to heat thoroughly. Serve hot or cold.

Energy 86kcal/360kJ; Protein 9.8g; Carbohydrate 3.8g, of which sugars 1.2g; Fat 3.7g, of which saturates 1g; Cholesterol 127mg; Calcium 34mg; Fibre 1.4g; Sodium 477mg.

JASMINE RICE WITH PRAWNS AND THAI BASIL ★

THAI BASIL (BAI GRAPAO), ALSO KNOWN AS HOLY BASIL, HAS A UNIQUE, PUNGENT FLAVOUR THAT IS BOTH SPICY AND SHARP. IT CAN BE FOUND IN MOST ASIAN FOOD MARKETS.

SERVES 6

INGREDIENTS

  15ml/1 tbsp sunflower oil
  1 egg, beaten
  1 onion, chopped
  15ml/1 tbsp chopped garlic
  15ml/1 tbsp shrimp paste
  1kg/2¼lb/4 cups cooked jasmine rice
  350g/12oz cooked shelled prawns
    (shrimp)
  50g/2oz thawed frozen peas
  oyster sauce, to taste
  2 spring onions (scallions), chopped
  15–20 Thai basil leaves, roughly
    snipped, plus an extra sprig,
    to garnish

1 Heat 15ml/1 tbsp of the oil in a wok or frying pan. Add the beaten egg and swirl it around to set like a thin omelette.

2 Cook the omelette (on one side only) over a gentle heat until golden. Slide the omelette on to a board, roll up and cut into thin strips. Set aside.

3 Heat the remaining oil in the wok or pan, add the onion and garlic and stir-fry for 2–3 minutes. Stir in the shrimp paste and mix well until thoroughly combined.

4 Add the rice, prawns and peas and toss and stir together, until everything is heated through.

5 Season with oyster sauce to taste, taking great care as the shrimp paste is salty. Mix in the spring onions and basil leaves. Transfer to a serving dish and top with the strips of omelette. Serve, garnished with a sprig of basil.

Energy 311kcal/1316kJ; Protein 16.3g; Carbohydrate 52.6g, of which sugars 0.3g; Fat 5.4g, of which saturates 1.1g; Cholesterol 145mg; Calcium 84mg; Fibre 0.6g; Sodium 125mg.

SPECIAL FRIED RICE ★★★

MORE COLOURFUL THAN OTHER FRIED RICE DISHES AND ALMOST A MEAL IN ITSELF — IDEAL FOR A MIDWEEK SUPPER. IT ALSO COMPLEMENTS SOME OF THE HOT CURRIES FROM THESE REGIONS.

SERVES 4

INGREDIENTS
    50g/2oz/⅓ cup cooked peeled
      prawns (shrimp)
    3 eggs
    5ml/1 tsp salt
    2 spring onions (scallions),
      finely chopped
    60ml/4 tbsp vegetable oil
    115g/4oz lean pork, finely diced
    15ml/1 tbsp light soy sauce
    15ml/1 tbsp Chinese rice wine
    450g/1lb/6 cups cooked rice
    115g/4oz green peas

COOK'S TIP
If you don't have any Chinese
rice wine, substitute dry sherry.

1 Pat the prawns dry with kitchen paper. Put the eggs in a bowl with a pinch of the salt and a few pieces of spring onion. Whisk lightly. Heat half the oil in a wok, add the pork and stir-fry until golden. Add the prawns and cook for 1 minute, then add the soy sauce and rice wine. Remove from the heat and keep warm.

2 Heat the remaining oil in the wok and lightly scramble the eggs. Add the rice and stir well with chopsticks.

3 Add the remaining salt and spring onions, the stir-fried prawns, pork and peas. Toss well over the heat to combine and serve either hot or cold.

Energy 343kcal/1434kJ; Protein 20.2g; Carbohydrate 40.5g, of which sugars 4.2g; Fat 11.2g, of which saturates 1.6g; Cholesterol 124mg; Calcium 91mg; Fibre 2.4g; Sodium 632mg

RICE PORRIDGE ★

A STEAMING BOWL OF THICK RICE PORRIDGE IS A NOURISHING AND SATISFYING BREAKFAST. IT CAN BE MADE PLAIN, OR WITH THE ADDITION OF CHICKEN, PORK, EGG, FISH OR PRAWNS.

SERVES 6

INGREDIENTS

- 15ml/1 tbsp vegetable or groundnut (peanut) oil
- 25g/1oz fresh root ginger, shredded
- 115g/4oz/generous 1 cup long grain rice, rinsed and drained
- 1.2 litres/2 pints/5 cups chicken stock or water
- 30–45ml/2–3 tbsp *tuk trey*
- 10ml/2 tsp sugar
- 450g/1lb fresh fish fillets, boned (any fish will do)
- sea salt and ground black pepper

For the garnish

- 15ml/1 tbsp vegetable or groundnut (peanut) oil
- 2 garlic cloves, finely chopped
- 1 lemon grass stalk, trimmed and finely sliced
- 25g/1oz fresh root ginger, shredded
- a few coriander (cilantro) leaves

1 In a heavy pan heat the oil and stir in the ginger and rice for 1 minute. Pour in the stock and bring it to the boil. Reduce the heat and simmer, partially covered, for 20 minutes, until the rice is tender and the soup is thick. Stir the *tuk trey* and sugar into the soupy porridge. Season and keep the porridge hot.

2 Meanwhile, fill a wok one third full of water. Fit a covered bamboo steamer on top and bring the water to the boil so that the steam rises. Season the fish fillets, place them on a plate and put them inside the steamer. Cover and steam the fish until cooked.

3 For the garnish, heat the oil in small wok or heavy pan. Add the chopped garlic, lemon grass and ginger and stir-fry until golden and fragrant. Add chillies to the mixture, if you like.

4 Ladle the rice porridge into bowls. Tear off pieces of steamed fish fillet to place on top. Sprinkle with the stir-fried garlic, lemon grass and ginger, and garnish with a few coriander leaves.

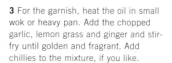

Energy 152kcal/636kJ; Protein 15g; Carbohydrate 17g, of which sugars 1.7g; Fat 2g, of which saturates 0.3g; Cholesterol 35mg; Calcium 11mg; Fibre 0g; Sodium 45mg.

STICKY RICE CAKES <u>WITH</u> PORK ★★★

THESE RICE CAKES ARE SUBSTANTIAL ENOUGH TO SERVE FOR SUPPER, WITH A SALAD AND DIPPING SAUCE. THE LOTUS LEAVES KEEP THE RICE MOIST AND THE MEAT TENDER.

SERVES 2

INGREDIENTS
  15ml/1 tbsp vegetable oil
  2 garlic cloves, chopped
  225g/8oz lean pork, cut into
    bitesize chunks
  30ml/2 tbsp fish sauce
  2.5ml/½ tsp sugar
  10ml/2 tsp ground black pepper
  115g/4oz lotus seeds, soaked
    for 6 hours and drained
  2 lotus or banana leaves,
    trimmed and cut into 25cm/10in
    squares
  500g/1¼lb/5 cups cooked
    sticky rice
  salt

1 Heat the oil in a heavy pan. Stir in the garlic, until it begins to colour, then add the pork, fish sauce, sugar and pepper.

2 Cover and cook over a low heat for about 45 minutes, or until tender. Leave to cool, then shred the pork.

3 Meanwhile, cook the lotus seeds in boiling water for about 10 minutes. When soft, drain, pat dry and leave to cool.

4 Place a quarter of the cooked sticky rice in the middle of each lotus or banana leaf. Place half the shredded pork and half the lotus seeds on the rice.

5 Drizzle some of the cooking juices from the pork over the top. Place another quarter of the rice on top, moulding and patting it with your fingers to make sure the pork and lotus seeds are enclosed like a cake. Fold the leaf edge nearest to you over the rice, tuck in the sides, and fold the whole packet over to form a tight, square bundle. Tie it with string. Repeat with the second leaf and the remaining ingredients.

6 Fill a wok one-third full of water. Place a double-tiered bamboo steamer, with its lid on, on top. Bring the water to the boil, lift the bamboo lid and place a rice cake on the rack in each tier. Cover and steam for about 45 minutes. Carefully open up the parcels and serve.

Energy 555kcal/2343kJ; Protein 32.3g; Carbohydrate 80.9g, of which sugars 2.6g; Fat 13.6g, of which saturates 3g; Cholesterol 71mg; Calcium 65mg; Fibre 1.1g; Sodium 84mg.

CHINESE JEWELLED RICE ★★

KEEP THE BASIC INGREDIENTS FOR THIS DISH IN YOUR KITCHEN AND YOU'LL ALWAYS HAVE THE MEANS TO MAKE A QUICK LOW-FAT MEAL. THE ONLY THING YOU'LL NEED TO BUY IS THE HAM.

SERVES 4

INGREDIENTS
  350g/12oz/1½ cups long grain rice
  30ml/2 tbsp vegetable oil
  1 onion, roughly chopped
  115g/4oz cooked lean ham, visible
    fat removed, diced
  175g/6oz/1¼ cups canned
    white crabmeat
  75g/3oz/½ cup canned water
    chestnuts, drained and cut
    into cubes
  4 dried black Chinese mushrooms,
    soaked, drained and diced
  115g/4oz/1 cup peas, thawed
    if frozen
  30ml/2 tbsp oyster sauce
  5ml/1 tsp sugar

1 Rinse the raw rice under cold water, then cook for 10–12 minutes in 750–900ml/1¼–1½ pints water in a pan with a tight-fitting lid. When the rice is cooked, refresh it in a sieve (strainer) under cold running water. Set aside until required.

2 Heat the wok, then add the oil, trickling it around the inner rim so that it runs down to coat the surface of the wok. When the oil is hot, add the chopped onion and cook until it has softened but not coloured.

3 Add the diced ham, white crab meat, cubed water chestnuts, diced Chinese mushrooms and peas. Mix lightly, then stir-fry for 2 minutes.

4 Stir in the oyster sauce and sugar and mix well to combine thoroughly.

5 Add the rice to the wok. Toss all the ingredients together over high heat, until the rice is heated through.

6 Serve immediately in heated bowls.

Energy 474kcal/1979kJ; Protein 22.5g; Carbohydrate 77.5g, of which sugars 4.3g; Fat 7.8g, of which saturates 1.1g; Cholesterol 48mg; Calcium 86mg; Fibre 1.9g; Sodium 710mg.

FRIED RICE WITH PORK ★★

*THIS IS GREAT FOR USING UP LAST NIGHT'S LEFTOVER RICE, BUT FOR SAFETY, IT MUST BE COOLED
QUICKLY AND KEPT IN THE REFRIGERATOR, THEN FRIED UNTIL HEATED ALL THE WAY THROUGH.*

SERVES 4–6

INGREDIENTS

45ml/3 tbsp vegetable oil
1 onion, chopped
15ml/1 tbsp chopped garlic
115g/4oz tender pork, cut into small
   cubes
2 eggs, beaten
500g/2¼lb/5 cups cooked rice
30ml/2 tbsp fish sauce
15ml/1 tbsp dark soy sauce
2.5ml/½ tsp caster
   (superfine) sugar
To serve
4 spring onions (scallions),
   finely sliced
2 fresh red chillies, sliced
1 lime, cut into wedges

1 Heat the oil in a wok or large frying
pan. Add the onion and garlic and cook
for about 2 minutes until softened.

2 Add the pork to the softened onion
and garlic. Stir-fry until the pork
changes colour and is fully cooked.

3 Tip in the beaten eggs and stir-fry
over the heat until scrambled into small
lumps. Add the rice and continue to stir
and toss, to coat it with the oil and
prevent it from sticking.

4 Add the fish sauce, soy sauce and
sugar and mix well. Continue to fry until
the rice is hot. Spoon into warmed
bowls and serve, with sliced spring
onions, chillies and lime wedges.

COOK'S TIPS
• The rice used in this and similar stir-
fries is usually made the day before and
added cold to the dish.
• If you like, you can drizzle sweet, sour
or hot chilli dipping sauce over the stir-
fries when serving.

CHINESE CLAY POT RICE WITH CHICKEN ★

THIS CANTONESE DISH IS A GREAT FAMILY ONE-POT MEAL. THE TRADITIONAL CLAY POT ENSURES THAT THE INGREDIENTS REMAIN MOIST, WHILE ALLOWING THE FLAVOURS TO MINGLE.

SERVES 4

INGREDIENTS
500g/1¼lb chicken breast fillets, cut into thin strips
5 dried shiitake mushrooms, soaked in hot water for 30 minutes, until soft
1 Chinese sausage, sliced
750ml/1¼pints/3 cups chicken stock
225g/8oz/generous 1 cup long grain rice, washed and drained
fresh coriander (cilantro) leaves, finely chopped, to garnish

For the marinade
30ml/2 tbsp sesame oil
45ml/3 tbsp oyster sauce
30ml/2 tbsp soy sauce
25g/1oz fresh root ginger, finely grated (shredded)
2 spring onions (scallions), trimmed and finely sliced
1 fresh red chilli, seeded and finely sliced
5ml/1 tsp sugar

1 In a bowl, mix together the ingredients for the marinade. Toss the chicken in the marinade, making sure it is well coated. Set aside.

2 Drain the shiitake mushrooms and squeeze out excess water. Remove any hard stems and halve the caps. Add the mushroom caps and the Chinese sausage to the chicken.

3 Bring the stock to the boil in the clay pot. Stir in the rice and bring it back to the boil. Reduce the heat, cover the pot, and simmer on a low heat for 15–20 minutes, until almost all the liquid has been absorbed.

4 Spread the marinated mixture over the top of the rice and cover the pot. Leave to steam for about 10–15 minutes, until all the liquid is absorbed and the chicken is cooked. Garnish with coriander and serve.

Energy 371kcal/1560kJ; Protein 36.2g; Carbohydrate 46.8g, of which sugars 1g; Fat 4g, of which saturates 1.2g; Cholesterol 93mg; Calcium 54mg; Fibre 0.7g; Sodium 721mg.

CHICKEN AND BASIL RICE ★

FOR THIS DISH, THE RICE IS PARTIALLY BOILED BEFORE BEING SIMMERED WITH COCONUT SO THAT IT FULLY ABSORBS THE FLAVOUR OF THE CHILLIES, BASIL AND SPICES.

SERVES 4

INGREDIENTS

350g/12oz/1¾ cups Thai fragrant
   rice, rinsed
15ml/1 tbsp sunflower oil
1 large onion, finely sliced into rings
1 garlic clove, crushed
1 fresh red chilli, seeded and
   finely sliced
1 fresh green chilli, seeded and
   finely sliced
generous handful of basil leaves
3 skinless chicken breast fillets,
   about 350g/12oz, finely sliced
5mm/¼in piece of lemon grass,
   pounded or finely chopped
600ml/1 pint/2½ cups reduced-fat
   coconut milk
salt and ground black pepper

1 Bring a pan of lightly salted water to the boil. Add the rice to the pan and boil for about 6 minutes, until partially cooked. Drain and set aside.

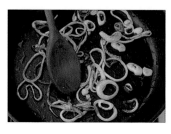

2 Heat the oil in a frying pan and fry the onion rings for 5–10 minutes until golden and crisp. Lift out, drain on kitchen paper and set aside.

3 Fry the garlic and chillies in the oil remaining in the pan for 2–3 minutes, then add the basil leaves and fry briefly until they begin to wilt.

4 Remove a few basil leaves and set them aside for the garnish, then add the chicken slices with the lemon grass and fry for 2–3 minutes until golden.

5 Add the rice. Stir-fry for a few minutes to coat the grains, then pour in the coconut cream. Cook for 4–5 minutes or until the rice is tender, adding a little more water if necessary. Adjust the seasoning.

6 Pile the rice into a warmed serving dish, sprinkle with the fried onion rings and basil leaves, and serve immediately.

Energy 492kcal/2064kJ; Protein 28.8g; Carbohydrate 83.1g, of which sugars 11.6g; Fat 4.8g, of which saturates 0.9g; Cholesterol 61mg; Calcium 83mg; Fibre 1.1g; Sodium 220mg.

FIVE INGREDIENTS RICE ★

THE CHINESE LOVE RICE SO MUCH THEY INVENTED MANY WAYS TO ENJOY IT. HERE, CHICKEN AND
VEGETABLES ARE COOKED WITH SHORT GRAIN RICE MAKING A HEALTHY LIGHT LUNCH DISH.

SERVES 4

INGREDIENTS

    275g/10oz/1¼ cups short
      grain rice
    90g/3½oz carrot, peeled
    2.5ml/½ tsp lemon juice
    90g/3½oz gobo (burdock)
      or canned bamboo shoots
    225g/8oz/3 cups oyster mushrooms
    8 fresh parsley sprigs
    350ml/12fl oz/1½ cups water
      and 7.5ml/1½ tsp instant
      dashi powder
    150g/5oz skinless chicken breast
      fillet, cut into 2cm/¾in chunks
    30ml/2 tbsp soy sauce
    30ml/2 tbsp sake
    25ml/1½ tbsp mirin
    pinch of salt

1 Put the rice in a large bowl and wash well with cold water. Keep changing the water until it remains clear, then tip the rice into a sieve (strainer) and drain for 30 minutes.

2 Using a sharp knife, cut the carrot into 5mm/¼in rounds, then cut the discs into flowers.

COOK'S TIP
Although gobo or burdock is recognized as a poisonous plant in the West, it has been eaten in Japan for centuries. To make it safe to eat, gobo must always be cooked, because it contains iron and other acidic elements that are harmful if they are eaten raw. By soaking it in alkaline water and then cooking it for a short time, gobo becomes edible.

3 Fill a small bowl with cold water and add the lemon juice. Peel the gobo and then slice it with a knife as if you were sharpening a pencil into the bowl.

4 Leave for 15 minutes, then drain. If using canned bamboo shoots, slice them into thin matchsticks.

5 Tear the oyster mushrooms into thin strips. Chop the parsley. Put it in a sieve and pour over hot water from the kettle to wilt the leaves. Allow to drain and then set aside.

6 Heat the dashi stock in a large pan and add the carrots and gobo or bamboo shoots. Bring to the boil and add the chicken. Remove any scum from the surface, and add the soy sauce sake, mirin and salt.

7 Add the rice and mushrooms and cover with a tight-fitting lid. Bring back to the boil, wait 5 minutes, then reduce the heat and simmer for 10 minutes. Remove from the heat without lifting the lid and leave to stand for 15 minutes. Add the wilted herbs and serve.

Energy 312kcal/1308kJ; Protein 16.1g; Carbohydrate 58.4g, of which sugars 2.8g; Fat 1.2g, of which saturates 0.2g; Cholesterol 26mg; Calcium 30mg; Fibre 1.5g; Sodium 566mg.

CHICKEN AND EGG ON RICE ★★

THE AGE-OLD QUESTION OF WHICH CAME FIRST, THE CHICKEN OR THE EGG, IS ADDRESSED IN THIS
ELEGANT DISH. IT IS TRADITIONALLY COOKED IN A LIDDED CERAMIC BOWL.

SERVES 4

INGREDIENTS
    250g/9oz skinless, boneless
      chicken thighs
    4 fresh mitsuba or parsley
      sprigs, trimmed
    300ml/½ pint/1¼ cups water
      and 25ml/1½ tbsp instant
      dashi powder
    30ml/2 tbsp caster (superfine) sugar
    60ml/4 tbsp mirin
    60ml/4 tbsp shoyu or other soy sauce
    2 small onions, sliced thinly
      lengthways
    4 large (US extra large) eggs, beaten
    275g/10oz/scant 1½ cups Japanese
      short grain rice cooked with 375ml/
      13fl oz/scant 1⅔ cups water
    shichimi togarashi (Japanese
      seven-spice powder), to serve
      (optional)

1 Cut the chicken thighs into 2cm/¾in
square bitesize chunks. Chop the roots
of the fresh mitsuba or parsley into
2.5cm/1in lengths. Set aside.

2 Pour the dashi stock, sugar, mirin and
shoyu into a clean frying pan with a lid
and bring to the boil. Add the onion
slices to the pan and lay the chicken
pieces on top. Cook over a high heat for
5 minutes, shaking the pan frequently.

3 When the chicken is cooked, sprinkle
with the mitsuba or parsley, and pour
the beaten eggs over to cover the
chicken. Cover and wait for 30 seconds.
Do not stir.

4 Remove from the heat and leave to
stand for 1 minute. The egg should be
just cooked but still soft, rather than
set. Do not leave it so that the egg
becomes a firm omelette.

5 Scoop the warm rice on to individual
plates, then pour the soft eggs and
chicken on to the rice. Serve
immediately with a little *shichimi-
togarashi*, if you want spicy taste.

COOK'S TIP
Mitsuba, also known as Japanese wild
parsley, tastes like angelica. Cut off the
root before use.

Energy 417kcal/1743kJ; Protein 25.2g; Carbohydrate 56.9g, of which sugars 1.9g; Fat 7.8g, of which saturates 2.1g; Cholesterol 256mg; Calcium 70mg; Fibre 0.2g; Sodium 935mg.

THAI FRIED RICE ★★

THIS SUBSTANTIAL AND TASTY DISH IS BASED ON JASMINE RICE. DICED CHICKEN, RED PEPPER AND CORN KERNELS ARE ADDED, TO GIVE THE DISH AN APPETIZING COLOUR AND EXTRA FLAVOUR.

SERVES 4

INGREDIENTS

   475ml/16fl oz/2 cups water
   50g/2oz/½ cup coconut
     milk powder
   350g/12oz/1¾ cups jasmine
     rice, rinsed
   15ml/1 tbsp sunflower oil
   2 garlic cloves, chopped
   1 small onion, finely chopped
   2.5cm/1in piece of fresh root ginger,
     peeled and grated
   225g/8oz skinless, chicken breast
     fillets, cut into 1cm/½in dice
   1 red (bell) pepper, seeded
     and sliced
   115g/4oz/1 cup drained canned
     whole kernel corn
   5ml/1 tsp chilli oil
   5ml/1 tsp hot curry powder
   2 eggs, beaten
   salt
   spring onion (scallion) shreds,
     to garnish

3 Push the onion mixture to the sides of the wok, add the chicken to the centre and stir-fry for 2 minutes. Add the rice and toss well. Stir-fry over a high heat for about 3 minutes more, until the chicken is cooked through.

4 Stir in the sliced red pepper, corn, chilli oil and curry powder, with salt to taste. Toss over the heat for 1 minute. Stir in the beaten eggs and cook for 1 minute more. Garnish with the spring onion shreds and serve.

1 Pour the water into a pan and whisk in the coconut milk powder. Add the rice and bring to the boil. Reduce the heat, cover and cook for 12 minutes, or until the rice is tender and the liquid has been absorbed. Spread the rice on a baking sheet and leave until cold.

2 Heat the oil in a wok, add the garlic, onion and ginger and stir-fry over a medium heat for 2 minutes.

COOK'S TIP

It is important that the rice is completely cold before being fried.

Energy 508kcal/2127kJ; Protein 24.7g; Carbohydrate 83.9g, of which sugars 8.7g; Fat 8g, of which saturates 1.6g; Cholesterol 135mg; Calcium 57mg; Fibre 1.3g; Sodium 204mg.

STICKY RICE PARCELS ★★

THIS IS A SUPERB DISH, PACKED WITH FLAVOUR. THE PARCELS LOOK PRETTY AND IT IS A PLEASURE TO CUT THEM OPEN AND DISCOVER THE DELICIOUS CHICKEN AND MUSHROOM FILLING INSIDE.

SERVES 4

INGREDIENTS
  450g/1lb/2⅔ cups glutinous rice
  20ml/4 tsp vegetable oil
  15ml/1 tbsp dark soy sauce
  1.5ml/¼ tsp five-spice powder
  15ml/1 tbsp dry sherry
  4 skinless, boneless chicken thighs,
    each cut into 4 pieces
  8 dried Chinese mushrooms, soaked
    in hot water until soft
  25g/1oz dried shrimps, soaked in
    hot water until soft
  50g/2oz/½ cup canned bamboo
    shoots, drained and sliced
  300ml/½ pint/1¼ cups
    chicken stock
  10ml/2 tsp cornflour (cornstarch)
  15ml/1 tbsp cold water
  4 lotus leaves, soaked in warm
    water until soft
  salt and ground white pepper

1 Rinse the glutinous rice in a sieve (strainer) until the water runs clear, then leave to soak in a bowl of water for 2 hours.

2 Drain the rice in a sieve and tip it into a bowl. Stir in 5ml/1 tsp of the oil and 2.5ml/½ tsp salt.

3 Line a large steamer with a piece of clean muslin or cheesecloth.

4 Scrape the soaked rice into the steamer, cover and steam over a large pan of boiling water for 45 minutes, stirring the rice from time to time and topping up the water if needed.

5 Mix the soy sauce, five-spice powder and sherry. Put the chicken pieces in a bowl, add the marinade, stir to coat, then cover and leave to marinate for 20 minutes.

6 Drain the Chinese mushrooms, remove and discard the stems, then chop the caps roughly. Drain the dried shrimps in a sieve.

7 Heat the remaining oil in a non-stick frying pan or wok. When the oil is hot, stir-fry the chicken for 2 minutes, then add the mushrooms, shrimps, bamboo shoots and stock. Mix well and simmer for 10 minutes.

8 Mix the cornflour to a paste with the cold water in a small bowl. Add to the pan and cook, stirring, until the sauce has thickened. Season to taste. Lift the cooked rice out of the steamer and let it cool slightly.

COOK'S TIP
The sticky rice parcels can be made several days in advance and simply re-steamed before serving. If you do this, allow an extra 20 minutes' cooking time to ensure that the filling is hot.

9 With lightly dampened hands, divide the rice into four equal portions. Put half of one portion in the centre of a lotus leaf. Spread it into a round and place a quarter of the chicken on top.

10 Cover with the remaining half portion of rice. Fold the leaf around the filling to make a neat rectangular parcel. Make three more parcels in the same way.

11 Put the rice parcels, seam side down, into the steamer, using two tiers if the parcels are too big to fit in one. Cover and steam over a high heat for about 30 minutes. Serve the parcels on individual heated plates, inviting each diner to unwrap their own.

Energy 565kcal/2369kJ; Protein 37.3g; Carbohydrate 87.1g, of which sugars 0.3g; Fat 6.1g, of which saturates 0.7g; Cholesterol 102mg; Calcium 101mg; Fibre 0.2g; Sodium 336mg.

NOODLES

This chapter introduces a range of recipes that should be in the
repertoire of every cook. Most of the noodles are made from rice
or egg, although you will also find mung bean noodles. Their
almost glassy appearance makes them a popular choice for
stir-fries. Notable low-fat noodle dishes include Steamboat, and
Curried Rice Vermicelli. Recipes such as Pork Chow Mein are
designed to stand alone, but there are also some enticing
accompaniments, including Noodles with Ginger and Coriander.

PLAIN NOODLES <u>WITH</u> FOUR FLAVOURS ★

*A WONDERFULLY SIMPLE WAY OF SERVING NOODLES, THIS DISH ALLOWS EACH INDIVIDUAL DINER
TO SEASON THEIR OWN, SPRINKLING OVER THE FOUR FLAVOURS AS OFTEN AS THEY LIKE. FLAVOURINGS
ARE TRADITIONALLY PUT OUT IN LITTLE BOWLS WHENEVER PLAIN NOODLES ARE SERVED.*

<u>SERVES 4</u>

INGREDIENTS
    4 small fresh red or green chillies
    60ml/4 tbsp Thai fish sauce
    60ml/4 tbsp rice vinegar
    granulated sugar
    mild or hot chilli powder
    350g/12oz rice noodles

1 Prepare the four flavours. For the
first, finely chop 2 small red or green
chillies, discarding the seeds or leaving
them in, depending on how hot you like
your flavouring. Place them in a small
bowl and add the Thai fish sauce.

2 For the second flavour, chop the
remaining chillies finely and mix them
with the rice vinegar in a small bowl.
Put the sugar and chilli powder in
separate small bowls.

3 Cook the noodles until tender,
following the instructions on the packet.
Drain well, tip into a large bowl and
serve immediately with the four flavours
handed separately.

Energy 321kcal/1341kJ; Protein 4.5g; Carbohydrate 72.4g, of which sugars 1g; Fat 0.2g, of which saturates 0g; Cholesterol 0mg; Calcium 12mg; Fibre 0.2g; Sodium 278mg.

FRESH RICE NOODLES ★★

A VARIETY OF DRIED NOODLES IS AVAILABLE IN ASIAN SUPERMARKETS, BUT FRESH ONES ARE QUITE DIFFERENT AND NOT THAT DIFFICULT TO MAKE. THE FRESHLY-MADE NOODLE SHEETS CAN BE SERVED AS A SNACK, DRENCHED IN SUGAR OR HONEY, OR DIPPED INTO A SAVOURY SAUCE OF YOUR CHOICE.

SERVES 4

INGREDIENTS
    225g/8oz/2 cups rice flour
    600ml/1 pint/2½ cups water
    a pinch of salt
    15ml/1 tbsp vegetable oil, plus extra
      for brushing
    slivers of red chilli and fresh root
      ginger, and coriander (cilantro)
      leaves, to garnish (optional)

1 Place the flour in a bowl and stir in some of the water to form a paste. Pour in the rest of the water, beating it to make a lump-free batter. Add the salt and oil and leave to stand for 15 minutes.

COOK'S TIP
You may need to top up the water through one of the slits and tighten the cloth.

2 Meanwhile, fill a wide pan with water. Cut a piece of smooth cotton cloth a little larger than the diameter of the pan. Stretch it over the top of the pan, pulling the edges tautly down over the sides, then wind a piece of string around the edge, to secure. Using a sharp knife, make three small slits, about 2.5cm/1in from the edge of the cloth, at regular intervals.

3 Bring the water to the boil. Stir the batter and ladle 30–45ml/2–3 tbsp on to the cloth, swirling it to form a 13–15cm/5–6in wide circle. Cover with a domed lid, such as a wok lid, and steam for 1 minute, or until the noodle sheet is translucent.

4 Carefully insert a spatula or knife under the noodle sheet and prise it off the cloth. (If it doesn't peel off easily, you may need to steam it a little longer.) Transfer the noodle sheet to a lightly oiled baking tray, brush lightly with oil, and cook the remaining batter in the same way.

VARIATION
Fresh noodles are also delicious cut into strips and stir-fried with garlic, ginger, chillies and *nuoc cham* or soy sauce.

Energy 251kcal/1046kJ; Protein 4g; Carbohydrate 45g, of which sugars 0g; Fat 5g, of which saturates 1g; Cholesterol 0mg; Calcium 24mg; Fibre 1.1g; Sodium 200mg.

RICE NOODLES <u>WITH</u> FRESH HERBS ★

BUN IS THE VIETNAMESE WORD USED TO DESCRIBE THE THIN, WIRY NOODLES KNOWN AS RICE STICKS OR RICE VERMICELLI. HOWEVER, WHEN THE VIETNAMESE TALK ABOUT A DISH CALLED BUN, THEY ARE USUALLY REFERRING TO THIS RECIPE, WHICH COULD BE DESCRIBED AS A NOODLE SALAD.

SERVES 4

INGREDIENTS
   half a small cucumber
   225g/8oz dried rice sticks (vermicelli)
   4–6 lettuce leaves, shredded
   115g/4oz/½ cup beansprouts
   1 bunch mixed basil, coriander
     (cilantro), mint and oregano, stalks
     removed, leaves shredded
   juice of half a lime
   nuoc mam or *nuoc cham*, to drizzle

COOK'S TIP
In the street stalls and cafés of Hanoi, different types of mint, ginger leaves, oregano and thyme provide the herb bedding for this dish, giving it a really distinctive, fragrant flavour.

1 Peel the cucumber, cut it in half lengthways, remove the seeds, and cut into matchsticks.

2 Add the rice sticks to a pan of boiling water, loosening them gently, and cook for 3–4 minutes, or until *al dente*. Drain, rinse under cold water, and drain again.

3 In a bowl, toss the shredded lettuce, beansprouts, cucumber and herbs together. Add the noodles and lime juice and toss together. Drizzle with a little *nuoc mam* or *nuoc cham* for seasoning, and serve immediately on its own, or with stir-fried seafood or chicken as a complete meal.

Energy 225kcal/940kJ; Protein 6.9g; Carbohydrate 47.1g, of which sugars 2.5g; Fat 0.8g, of which saturates 0.1g; Cholesterol 0mg; Calcium 66mg; Fibre 1.8g; Sodium 13mg.

THAI NOODLES <u>WITH</u> CHINESE CHIVES ★★

THIS RECIPE REQUIRES A LITTLE TIME FOR PREPARATION, BUT THE COOKING TIME IS VERY FAST.
EVERYTHING IS COOKED IN ONE HOT WOK AND SHOULD BE EATEN IMMEDIATELY. THIS IS A TASTY
AND SUBSTANTIAL VEGETARIAN DISH, PERFECT FOR A WEEKEND FAMILY GATHERING.

SERVES 4

INGREDIENTS

  350g/12oz dried rice noodles
  1cm/½in piece fresh root ginger,
    peeled and grated
  30ml/2 tbsp light soy sauce
  225g/8oz Quorn (mycoprotein),
    cut into small cubes
  15ml/1 tbsp sunflower oil
  2 garlic cloves, crushed
  1 large onion, cut into
    thin wedges
  115g/4oz fried tofu, thinly sliced
  1 fresh green chilli, seeded and
    thinly sliced
  175g/6oz/2 cups beansprouts
  2 large bunches garlic chives, total
    weight about 115g/4oz, cut into
    5cm/2in lengths
  30ml/2 tbsp roasted peanuts, ground
  30ml/2 tbsp dark soy sauce
  30ml/2 tbsp chopped fresh coriander
    (cilantro), and 1 lemon, cut into
    wedges, to garnish

1 Place the noodles in a bowl, cover
with warm water and leave to soak for
30 minutes. Drain and set aside.

2 Mix the ginger and light soy sauce
in a bowl. Add the Quorn, then set
aside for 10 minutes. Drain, reserving
the marinade.

3 Heat half the oil in a frying pan and
cook the garlic for a few seconds. Add
the Quorn and stir-fry for 3–4 minutes.
Using a slotted spoon, transfer to a
plate and set aside.

4 Heat the remaining oil in the pan and
stir-fry the onion for 3–4 minutes, until
softened and tinged with brown. Add
the tofu and chilli, stir-fry briefly and
then add the noodles. Stir-fry over a
medium heat for 4–5 minutes.

5 Stir in the beansprouts, garlic chives
and most of the ground peanuts,
reserving a little for the garnish. Stir
well, then add the Quorn, the dark soy
sauce and the reserved marinade.

6 When hot, spoon on to serving plates
and garnish with the remaining ground
peanuts, the coriander and lemon.

Energy 444kcal/1857kJ; Protein 16g; Carbohydrate 77.6g, of which sugars 4.3g; Fat 6.5g, of which saturates 0.9g; Cholesterol 0mg; Calcium 230mg; Fibre 5g; Sodium 1227mg.

SESAME NOODLE SALAD ★★★

TOASTED SESAME OIL ADDS A NUTTY FLAVOUR TO THIS ASIAN-STYLE SALAD. IT TASTES BEST WHEN IT IS SERVED WARM, AND IT IS SUBSTANTIAL ENOUGH TO SERVE AS A MAIN MEAL.

3 Meanwhile, make the dressing. Whisk together the soy sauce, sesame and sunflower oils, grated ginger and crushed garlic in a small bowl.

4 Cut the tomatoes in half and scoop out the seeds with a teaspoon, then chop roughly. Cut the spring onions into fine shreds.

SERVES 4

INGREDIENTS
  250g/9oz medium egg noodles
  200g/7oz/1¾ cup sugar snap peas
    or mangetouts (snow peas)
  2 tomatoes
  3 spring onions (scallions)
  2 carrots, cut into julienne
  30ml/2 tbsp chopped fresh coriander
    (cilantro)
  15ml/1 tbsp sesame seeds
  fresh coriander (cilantro), to garnish
For the dressing
  10ml/2 tsp light soy sauce
  15ml/1 tbsp toasted sesame seed oil
  15ml/1 tbsp vegetable oil
  4cm/1½in piece fresh root ginger,
    finely grated
  1 garlic clove, crushed

1 Bring a large pan of lightly salted water to the boil. Add the egg noodles, and bring back to the boil. Cook for 2 minutes.

2 Slice the sugar snap peas or mangetouts diagonally, add to the pan and cook for a further 2 minutes. Drain and rinse under cold running water.

5 Tip the noodles and the peas or mangetouts into a large bowl and add the carrots, tomatoes and coriander.

6 Pour the dressing over the top of the noodle mixture, and toss with your hands to combine. Sprinkle with the sesame seeds and top with the spring onions and coriander.

Energy 323kcal/1364kJ; Protein 10.6g; Carbohydrate 50.1g, of which sugars 5.9g; Fat 10.3g, of which saturates 2.2g; Cholesterol 19mg; Calcium 76mg; Fibre 4.2g; Sodium 301mg.

CHILLED SOMEN NOODLES ★★

AT THE HEIGHT OF SUMMER, COLD SOMEN NOODLES SERVED IN ICE COLD WATER AND ACCOMPANIED BY A DIPPING SAUCE AND A SELECTION OF RELISHES MAKE A REFRESHING MEAL.

SERVES 4

INGREDIENTS
  300g/11oz dried somen noodles
For the dipping sauce
  105ml/7 tbsp mirin
  2.5ml/½ tsp sea salt
  105ml/7 tbsp shoyu
  400ml/14fl oz/1⅔ cups konbu and
    bonito stock or instant dashi
For the relishes
  2 spring onions (scallions), trimmed
    and finely chopped
  2.5cm/1in fresh root ginger, peeled
    and finely grated
  2 fresh shiso or basil leaves, finely
    chopped (optional)
  30ml/2 tbsp toasted sesame seeds
For the garnishes
  10cm/4in cucumber
  5ml/1 tsp sea salt
  ice cubes or a block of ice
  ice-cold water
  115g/4oz cooked, peeled small
    prawns (shrimp)
  orchid flowers or nasturtium flowers
    and leaves (optional)

1 To make the dipping sauce, put the mirin in a pan and bring to the boil to evaporate the alcohol. Add the salt and shoyu and shake the pan gently to mix. Add the konbu and bonito stock or instant dashi. Add the water and bring to the boil. Cook over a vigorous heat for 3 minutes without stirring. Remove from the heat and strain through muslin or cheesecloth. Cool, then chill for at least 1 hour.

2 Prepare the cucumber garnish. If the cucumber is bigger than 4cm/1½in in diameter, cut in half and scoop out the seeds, then slice thinly. For a smaller cucumber, cut into 5cm/2in lengths, then use a vegetable peeler to remove the seeds and make a hole in the centre. Slice thinly.

3 Sprinkle with the salt and leave in a sieve (strainer) for 20 minutes, then rinse in cold water and drain.

4 Bring at least 1.5 litres/2½ pints/ 6 cups water to the boil in a large pan. Have 75ml/2½fl oz/⅓ cup cold water to hand. Put the somen in the rapidly boiling water. When the water foams, pour the glass of cold water in. When the water boils again, the somen are ready. Drain into a colander.

5 Rinse under cold running water, and rub the somen with your hands to remove the starch. Drain well.

6 Put some ice cubes or a block of ice in the centre of a chilled, large glass bowl, and add the somen. Pour on enough ice-cold water to cover the somen, then arrange cucumber slices, prawns and flowers, if using, on top.

7 Prepare all the relishes separately and place them in small dishes or small sake cups.

8 Divide approximately one-third of the dipping sauce among four small cups. Put the remaining sauce in a jug (pitcher) or gravy boat.

9 Serve the noodles cold with the relishes. The guests are invited to put any combination of relishes into their dipping-sauce cup. The cup is then held over the somen bowl, and a mouthful of somen is picked up, dipped into the sauce and eaten. More dipping sauce is added from the jug and more relishes are spooned into the dipping-sauce cups as required.

Energy 368kcal/1554kJ; Protein 15.9g; Carbohydrate 59g, of which sugars 3.5g; Fat 9.2g, of which saturates 0.7g; Cholesterol 56mg; Calcium 97mg; Fibre 2.9g; Sodium 1393mg.

FUSION NOODLES ★

WHAT HAPPENS WHEN ITALIANS SETTLE IN SHANGHAI? THEY EMBRACE THE COOKING STYLE OF THEIR ADOPTED COUNTRY BUT INTRODUCE THEIR FAVOURITE PASTA AND BALSAMIC VINEGAR.

SERVES 6

INGREDIENTS
    500g/1¼lb thin tagliarini
    1 red onion
    115g/4oz shiitake mushrooms
    15ml/1 tbsp vegetable oil
    45ml/3 tbsp dark soy sauce
    15ml/1 tbsp balsamic vinegar
    10ml/2 tsp caster (superfine) sugar
    5ml/1 tsp salt
    5ml/1 tsp sesame oil
    celery leaves, to garnish

1 Cook the tagliarini in a large pan of salted boiling water, following the instructions on the pack.

2 Thinly slice the red onion and the mushrooms, using a sharp knife.

3 Heat a wok, then add the vegetable oil. When the oil is hot, stir-fry the onion and mushrooms for 2 minutes.

4 Drain the tagliarini, then add to the wok with the soy sauce, balsamic vinegar, sugar and salt.

5 Stir-fry for 1 minute, then add the sesame oil, mix well to combine thoroughly and serve garnished with celery leaves.

VARIATION
Use thin egg noodles instead of tagliarini, if you like.

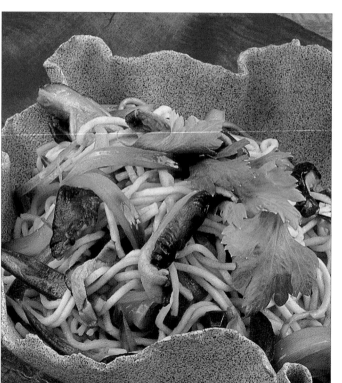

Energy 72kcal/306kJ; Protein 2.7g; Carbohydrate 14.1g, of which sugars 3.1g; Fat 1g, of which saturates 0.1g; Cholesterol 0mg; Calcium 10mg; Fibre 0.9g; Sodium 536mg.

NOODLE, TOFU AND SPROUTED BEAN SALAD ★

THIS CRISP, REFRESHING SALAD IS QUICK AND EASY TO MAKE AND IS BURSTING WITH THE GOODNESS OF FRESH VEGETABLES AND THE FRAGRANT FLAVOUR OF HERBS, RICE VINEGAR AND CHILLI OIL.

SERVES 4

INGREDIENTS

    25g/1oz cellophane noodles
    500g/1¼lb mixed sprouted beans
      and legumes (aduki, chickpea,
      mung, red lentil)
    4 spring onions (scallions),
      finely shredded
    115g/4oz firm tofu, diced
    1 ripe plum tomato, seeded
      and diced
    ½ cucumber, peeled, seeded
      and diced
    60ml/4 tbsp chopped fresh
      coriander (cilantro)
    45ml/3 tbsp chopped fresh mint
    60ml/4 tbsp rice vinegar
    10ml/2 tsp caster (superfine) sugar
    10ml/2 tsp sesame oil
    5ml/1 tsp chilli oil
    salt and ground black pepper

1 Place the cellophane noodles in a bowl and pour over enough boiling water to cover. Leave to soak for 12–15 minutes and then drain and refresh under cold, running water and drain again.

2 Using a pair of scissors, cut the noodles roughly into 7.5cm/3in lengths and put them in a bowl.

3 Fill a wok one-third full of boiling water and place over a high heat. Add the sprouted beans and legumes and blanch for 1 minute.

COOK'S TIP
Fresh sprouted beans are available from most supermarkets.

4 Drain well, then add to the noodles with the spring onions, tofu, tomato, cucumber and herbs.

5 Thoroughly combine the rice vinegar and sugar in a small bowl. Whisk in the sesame oil and chilli oil and add to the noodle mixture.

6 Toss lightly to combine, then transfer the mixure to a salad bowl and chill for 30 minutes before serving.

Energy 114kcal/476kJ; Protein 7.3g; Carbohydrate 11.6g, of which sugars 4.3g; Fat 4.4g, of which saturates 0.6g; Cholesterol 0mg; Calcium 206mg; Fibre 3g; Sodium 15mg.

SICHUAN NOODLES WITH SESAME SAUCE ★★★

NOODLES DRESSED WITH A RICH SESAME PASTE AND CHILLI SAUCE ARE MORE THAN A MATCH FOR THE
CRISP AND COLOURFUL RADISH AND DAIKON SALAD THAT TRADITIONALLY ACCOMPANIES THEM.

SERVES 3–4

INGREDIENTS
  450g/1lb fresh or 225g/8oz dried
    egg noodles
  ½ cucumber, sliced lengthways,
    seeded and diced
  225g/8oz daikon (mooli), peeled
  4–6 spring onions (scallions)
  a bunch of radishes, about 115g/4oz
  115g/4oz/2 cups beansprouts, rinsed
    then left in iced water and drained
  10ml/2 tsp vegetable oil
  2 garlic cloves, halved
  45ml/3 tbsp toasted sesame paste
  5ml/1 tsp sesame oil
  15ml/1 tbsp light soy sauce
  5–10ml/1–2 tsp chilli sauce, to taste
  15ml/1 tbsp rice vinegar
  120ml/4fl oz/½ cup vegetable stock
    or water
  5ml/1 tsp sugar, or to taste
  salt and ground black pepper
  25g/1oz/3 tbsp roasted peanuts or
    cashew nuts, to garnish (optional)

1 If using fresh noodles, cook them in boiling water for 1 minute, then drain well. Rinse the noodles in fresh water and drain again. Cook dried noodles according to the instructions on the packet, draining and rinsing them as for fresh noodles.

2 Sprinkle the diced cucumber with salt and leave for 15 minutes for the salt to draw out the water. Put the cucumber in a colander or sieve (strainer), rinse well, then drain and pat dry on kitchen paper. Place in a large salad bowl.

3 Coarsely grate the daikon using a mandolin or a food processor. Cut the spring onions into fine shreds.

4 Cut the radishes in half and slice finely. Add all the vegetables to the cucumber and toss gently. Set aside.

5 Heat the wok, then add the vegetable oil. When the oil is hot, fry the garlic for about 2 minutes to flavour the oil. Lift out the garlic, using a slotted spoon, and throw it away.

6 Remove the wok from the heat and stir in the sesame paste, with the sesame oil, soy and chilli sauces, vinegar and stock or water. Add a little sugar and season to taste.

7 Warm the mixture through over a gentle heat. Do not overheat the sauce or it will thicken too much.

8 Add the noodles to the sauce and toss together to thoroughly combine.

9 Tip the mixture into a serving dish, garnish with peanuts or cashew nuts, if you like, and serve with the vegetables.

Energy 480kcal/2029kJ; Protein 15.6g; Carbohydrate 84.6g, of which sugars 5.4g; Fat 11.1g, of which saturates 2.9g; Cholesterol 34mg; Calcium 65mg; Fibre 4.8g; Sodium 482mg.

NOODLES WITH GINGER AND CORIANDER ★★

HERE IS A SIMPLE NOODLE DISH THAT IS LOW IN SATURATED FAT AND WOULD GO WELL WITH MOST
ORIENTAL DISHES. IT CAN ALSO BE SERVED AS A LIGHT MEAL FOR 2 OR 3 PEOPLE.

SERVES 4

INGREDIENTS

    handful of fresh coriander (cilantro)
    225g/8oz dried egg noodles
    10ml/2 tsp sesame oil
    15ml/1 tbsp vegetable oil
    5cm/2in piece fresh root ginger,
      cut into fine shreds
    6–8 spring onions (scallions), cut
      into shreds
    30ml/2 tbsp light soy sauce
    salt and ground black pepper

1 Strip the leaves from the coriander stalks. Pile them on to a chopping board and coarsely chop them using a cleaver or large, sharp knife.

2 Bring a large pan of lightly salted water to the boil and cook the noodles according to the packet instructions.

3 Rinse under cold water, drain well and tip into a bowl. Add the sesame oil and toss to coat.

VARIATION

If you don't like the flavour of coriander, use flat leaf parsley.

4 Heat a wok until hot, add the vegetable oil and swirl it around. Add the ginger and stir-fry for a few seconds, then add the noodles and spring onions. Stir-fry for 3–4 minutes, until the noodles are hot.

5 Drizzle over the soy sauce, then sprinkle the chopped coriander on top of the noodles.

6 Add salt and ground black pepper to taste. Toss and serve in heated bowls.

Energy 253kcal/1067kJ; Protein 7.4g; Carbohydrate 41.6g, of which sugars 2.2g; Fat 7.5g, of which saturates 1.6g; Cholesterol 17mg; Calcium 25mg; Fibre 1.9g; Sodium 637mg.

TOASTED NOODLES WITH VEGETABLES ★

SLIGHTLY CRISP NOODLE CAKES TOPPED WITH VEGETABLES MAKE A SUPERB DISH, AND THE VERY GOOD NEWS FOR THE HEALTH-CONSCIOUS IS THAT THE AMOUNT OF SATURATED FAT IS NEGLIGIBLE.

2 Heat 2.5ml/½ tsp oil in a non-stick frying pan or wok. When it starts to smoke, spread half the noodles over the base. Fry for 2–3 minutes until lightly toasted. Carefully turn the noodles over (they stick together like a cake), fry the other side, then slide on to a heated serving plate. Repeat with the remaining noodles to make two cakes. Keep hot.

3 Heat the remaining oil in the clean pan, then fry the garlic for a few seconds. Halve the corn cobs lengthways, add to the pan with the mushrooms, then stir-fry for 3 minutes, adding a little water, if needed, to prevent the mixture from burning. Add the celery, carrot, mangetouts and bamboo shoots. Stir-fry for 2 minutes or until the vegetables are crisp-tender.

SERVES 4

INGREDIENTS

175g/6oz dried egg vermicelli
15ml/1 tbsp vegetable oil
2 garlic cloves, finely chopped
115g/4oz/1 cup baby corn cobs
115g/4oz/1½ cups fresh shiitake
  mushrooms, halved
3 celery sticks, sliced
1 carrot, diagonally sliced
115g/4oz/1 cup mangetouts
  (snow peas)
75g/3oz/¾ cup sliced, drained,
  canned bamboo shoots
15ml/1 tbsp cornflour (cornstarch)
15ml/1 tbsp cold water
15ml/1 tbsp dark soy sauce
5ml/1 tsp caster sugar
300ml/½ pint/1¼ cups
  vegetable stock
salt and ground white pepper
spring onion curls, to garnish

1 Bring a pan of lightly salted water to the boil. Add the egg noodles and cook according to instructions on the packet until just tender. Drain the noodles in a sieve (strainer), refresh under cold water, drain again, then dry thoroughly on kitchen paper.

VARIATION
Sliced fennel tastes good in this stir-fry, either as an addition or instead of the sliced bamboo shoots.

4 Mix the cornflour to a paste with 15ml/1 tbsp cold water. Add to the pan with the soy sauce, sugar and stock. Cook, stirring, until the sauce thickens. Season to taste. Divide the vegetable mixture between the noodle cakes, garnish with the spring onion curls and serve immediately. Each noodle cake serves two people.

Energy 214kcal/893kJ; Protein 7g; Carbohydrate 38.6g, of which sugars 3.5g; Fat 3.4g, of which saturates 0.4g; Cholesterol 0mg; Calcium 44mg; Fibre 2.4g; Sodium 353mg.

STIR-FRIED NOODLES <u>WITH</u> BEANSPROUTS ★★

BEANSPROUTS ARE HIGHLY NUTRITIOUS AND MAKE A VALUABLE CONTRIBUTION TO THIS LOW-FAT DISH, WHICH COMBINES EGG NOODLES WITH RED AND GREEN PEPPERS AND SOY SAUCE.

SERVES 4

INGREDIENTS

- 175g/6oz dried egg noodles
- 15ml/1 tbsp vegetable oil
- 1 garlic clove, finely chopped
- 1 small onion, halved and sliced
- 225g/8oz/4 cups beansprouts
- 1 small red (bell) pepper, seeded and cut into strips
- 1 small green (bell) pepper, seeded and cut into strips
- 2.5ml/½ tsp salt
- 1.5ml/¼ tsp ground white pepper
- 30ml/2 tbsp light soy sauce

3 Stir in the cooked noodles and toss over the heat, using two spatulas or wooden spoons, for 2–3 minutes or until the ingredients are well mixed and have heated through.

4 Season to taste with salt and ground white pepper. Add the soy sauce and stir thoroughly before serving the noodle mixture in heated bowls.

1 Bring a pan of water to the boil. Cook the noodles for 4 minutes until just tender, or according to the instructions on the packet. Drain in a colander, refresh under cold water and drain again.

2 Heat the oil in a non-stick frying pan or wok. When the oil is very hot, add the garlic, stir briefly, then add the onion slices. Cook, stirring, for 1 minute, then add the beansprouts and peppers. Stir-fry for 2–3 minutes more.

Energy 244kcal/1030kJ; Protein 8g; Carbohydrate 39.9g, of which sugars 7.8g; Fat 7g, of which saturates 1.5g; Cholesterol 13mg; Calcium 34mg; Fibre 3.5g; Sodium 352mg.

NOODLES AND VEGETABLES IN COCONUT SAUCE ★

WHEN EVERYDAY VEGETABLES ARE GIVEN THE THAI TREATMENT, THE RESULT IS A DELECTABLE DISH WHICH EVERYONE WILL ENJOY. NOODLES ADD BULK AND A WELCOME CONTRAST IN TEXTURE.

3 Increase the heat to medium, stir in the coconut milk and vegetable stock and bring to the boil. Add the broccoli florets and the noodles, lower the heat and simmer gently for 20 minutes.

4 Meanwhile, make the garnish. Split the lemon grass stalks lengthways through the root. Gather the coriander into a small bouquet and lay it on a platter, following the curve of the rim.

5 Tuck the lemon grass halves into the coriander bouquet and add the chillies to resemble flowers.

6 Stir the fish sauce, soy sauce and chopped coriander into the noodle mixture. Spoon on to the platter, taking care not to disturb the herb bouquet, and serve immediately.

SERVES 6

INGREDIENTS
  10ml/2 tsp sunflower oil
  1 lemon grass stalk, finely chopped
  15ml/1 tbsp Thai red curry paste
  1 onion, thickly sliced
  3 courgettes (zucchini), thickly sliced
  115g/4oz Savoy cabbage,
    thickly sliced
  2 carrots, thickly sliced
  150g/5oz broccoli, stem sliced and
    head separated into florets
  2 × 400ml/14fl oz cans reduced-fat
    coconut milk
  475ml/16fl oz/2 cups vegetable stock
  150g/5oz dried egg noodles
  15ml/1 tbsp Thai fish sauce
  30ml/2 tbsp soy sauce
  60ml/4 tbsp chopped fresh
    coriander (cilantro)
For the garnish
  2 lemon grass stalks
  1 bunch fresh coriander (cilantro)
  8–10 small fresh red chillies

1 Heat the oil in a large pan or wok. Add the lemon grass and red curry paste and stir-fry for 2–3 seconds. Add the onion and cook over a medium heat, stirring occasionally, for about 5–10 minutes, until the onion has softened but not browned.

2 Add the courgettes, cabbage, carrots and slices of broccoli stem. Using two spoons, toss the vegetables with the onion mixture. Reduce the heat to low and cook gently, stirring occasionally, for a further 5 minutes.

Energy 181kcal/766kJ; Protein 7.2g; Carbohydrate 30.4g, of which sugars 12.3g; Fat 4.3g, of which saturates 1.1g; Cholesterol 8mg; Calcium 115mg; Fibre 3.6g; Sodium 559mg.

SWEET AND HOT VEGETABLE NOODLES ★

THIS NOODLE DISH HAS THE COLOUR OF FIRE, BUT ONLY THE MILDEST SUGGESTION OF HEAT. GINGER AND PLUM SAUCE GIVE IT ITS FRUITY FLAVOUR, WHILE LIME ADDS A DELICIOUS TANG.

SERVES 4

INGREDIENTS

130g/4½oz dried rice noodles
15ml/1 tbsp sunflower oil
2.5cm/1in piece fresh root ginger,
  sliced into thin batons
1 garlic clove, crushed
130g/4½oz drained canned bamboo
  shoots, sliced into thin batons
2 medium carrots, sliced into batons
130g/4½oz/1½ cups beansprouts
1 small white cabbage, shredded
30ml/2 tbsp Thai fish sauce
30ml/2 tbsp soy sauce
30ml/2 tbsp plum sauce
5ml/1 tsp sesame oil
15ml/1 tbsp palm sugar or light
  muscovado (brown) sugar
juice of ½ lime
90g/3½oz mooli (daikon), sliced into
  thin batons
small bunch fresh coriander
  (cilantro), chopped
30ml/2 tbsp sesame seeds, toasted

1 Cook the noodles in a large pan of boiling water, following the instructions on the packet. Meanwhile, heat the oil in a wok or large frying pan and stir-fry the ginger and garlic for 2–3 minutes over a medium heat, until golden.

2 Drain the noodles and set them aside. Add the bamboo shoots to the wok, increase the heat to high and stir-fry for 5 minutes. Add the carrots, beansprouts and cabbage and stir-fry for a further 5 minutes, until they are beginning to char on the edges.

3 Stir in the sauces, sesame oil, sugar and lime juice. Add the mooli and coriander, toss to mix, then spoon into a warmed bowl, sprinkle with toasted sesame seeds and serve immediately.

COOK'S TIP
Use a large, sharp knife for shredding cabbage. Remove any tough outer leaves, if necessary, then cut the cabbage into quarters. Cut off and discard the hard core from each quarter, place flat side down, then slice the cabbage very thinly to make fine shreds.

Energy 207kcal/866kJ; Protein 5.6g; Carbohydrate 42.3g, of which sugars 14.2g; Fat 1.6g, of which saturates 0.2g; Cholesterol 0mg; Calcium 94mg; Fibre 4.1g; Sodium 682mg.

NOODLES WITH ASPARAGUS ★★★

THIS DISH IS SIMPLICITY ITSELF, WITH A WONDERFUL CONTRAST OF TEXTURES AND FLAVOURS. TRY TO USE YOUNG ASPARAGUS AS IT IS BEAUTIFULLY TENDER AND COOKS IN MINUTES.

SERVES 2

INGREDIENTS

115g/4oz dried thin or medium
  egg noodles
15ml/1 tbsp oil
1 small onion, chopped
2.5cm/1in fresh root ginger, grated
2 garlic cloves, crushed
175g/6oz young asparagus, trimmed
115g/4oz/2 cups beansprouts
4 spring onions (scallions), sliced
45ml/3 tbsp light soy sauce
salt and ground black pepper

1 Bring a large pan of salted water to the boil. Add the noodles and cook until just tender. Drain, rinse under cold running water and set aside.

2 Heat a wok or frying pan, then add the oil. When the oil is very hot add the onion, ginger and garlic and stir-fry for 2–3 minutes.

3 Add the asparagus and stir-fry for a further 2–3 minutes.

4 Add the noodles and beansprouts and toss over fairly high heat for 2 minutes, to reheat the noodles.

5 Stir in the spring onions and soy sauce and mix well to combine. Season to taste, adding salt sparingly as the soy sauce will add quite a salty flavour.

6 Stir-fry the mixture for 1 minute, then serve immediately.

Energy 339kcal/1427kJ; Protein 12.6g; Carbohydrate 50.1g, of which sugars 7.9g; Fat 11.2g, of which saturates 2.2g; Cholesterol 17mg; Calcium 71mg; Fibre 4.8g; Sodium 1712mg.

FIVE-SPICE VEGETABLE NOODLES ★★

VARY THIS VEGETABLE STIR-FRY BY SUBSTITUTING MUSHROOMS, BAMBOO SHOOTS, BEANSPROUTS, MANGETOUTS OR WATER CHESTNUTS FOR SOME OR ALL OF THE VEGETABLES SUGGESTED BELOW.

SERVES 3–4

INGREDIENTS
225g/8oz dried egg noodles
10ml/2 tsp sesame oil
2 carrots
1 celery stick
1 small fennel bulb
15ml/1 tbsp vegetable oil
2 courgettes (zucchini), halved
 and sliced
1 fresh red chilli, seeded and chopped
2.5cm/1in fresh root ginger, grated
1 garlic clove, crushed
7.5ml/1½ tsp five-spice powder
2.5ml/½ tsp ground cinnamon
4 spring onions (scallions), sliced
thinly sliced fresh red chilli, to
 garnish (optional)

1 Bring a large pan of salted water to the boil. Add the noodles and cook for 2–3 minutes until just tender. Drain the noodles, return them to the pan and toss in the sesame oil. Set aside.

2 Cut the carrot and celery into julienne strips. Cut the fennel bulb in half and cut away the hard core. Cut into slices, then cut the slices into thin strips.

3 Heat the vegetable oil in a wok until very hot. Add all the vegetables, including the chopped chilli, and stir-fry for 7–8 minutes. Add the ginger and garlic and stir-fry for 2 minutes, then add the spices. Cook for 1 minute.

4 Add the spring onions, stir-fry for 1 minute and then stir in 60ml/4 tbsp warm water and cook for 1 minute. Stir in the noodles and toss well together. Serve in heated bowls, sprinkled with sliced red chilli, if you like.

Energy 286kcal/1205kJ; Protein 8.8g; Carbohydrate 44.5g, of which sugars 5g; Fat 9.4g, of which saturates 2g; Cholesterol 17mg; Calcium 54mg; Fibre 3.8g; Sodium 116mg.

VEGETABLE CHOW MEIN ★★★

THE OVERALL FAT CONTENT OF THIS RECIPE IS FAIRLY HIGH, BUT THERE'S ONLY A RELATIVELY SMALL AMOUNT OF SATURATED FAT SO IT IS A PERFECTLY ACCEPTABLE CHOICE FOR AN OCCASIONAL TREAT.

SERVES 4

INGREDIENTS
30ml/2 tbsp vegetable oil
50g/2oz/½ cup cashew nuts
2 carrots, cut into thin strips
3 celery sticks, cut into thin strips
1 green (bell) pepper, seeded
   and cut into thin strips
225g/8oz/1 cup beansprouts
225g/8oz/4 cups dried medium or
   thin egg noodles
15ml/1 tbsp toasted sesame seeds,
   to garnish
For the lemon sauce
30ml/2 tbsp light soy sauce
15ml/1 tbsp Chinese rice wine
   or dry sherry
150ml/¼ pint/⅔ cup vegetable stock
finely grated rind and juice of 2 lemons
15ml/1 tbsp sugar
10ml/2 tsp cornflour (cornstarch)

1 Mix together the soy sauce, Chinese rice wine or dry sherry, stock, lemon rind and juice, sugar and cornflour in a jug (pitcher). Bring a large pan of lightly salted water to the boil.

2 Heat the oil in a wok or large heavy frying pan. Add the cashew nuts, toss quickly over high heat until golden, then remove with a slotted spoon, and set aside.

3 Add the carrots and celery to the pan and stir-fry for 4–5 minutes. Add the pepper and beansprouts and stir-fry for 2–3 minutes more.

4 Meanwhile, cook the noodles in the boiling water for 3 minutes, or according to the instructions on the packet. Drain well and set aside in a warmed serving dish while you make the sauce.

5 Remove the vegetables from the pan with a slotted spoon. Pour in the sauce mixture and cook for 2 minutes, stirring until thick.

6 Return the vegetables to the pan, add the cashew nuts and stir quickly to coat everything in the sauce.

7 Spoon the vegetables and sauce over the noodles. Sprinkle the chow mein with sesame seeds and serve.

VARIATION
You can ring the changes in this recipe by using unsalted peanuts and alternative vegetables such as red or yellow (bell) peppers, courgettes (zucchini), mangetouts (snow peas) or baby corn.

Energy 212kcal/882kJ; Protein 4.2g; Carbohydrate 16.5g, of which sugars 9.9g; Fat 14.4g, of which saturates 2.3g; Cholesterol 0mg; Calcium 50mg; Fibre 2.2g; Sodium 591mg.

MUSHROOMS WITH CELLOPHANE NOODLES ★★

RED FERMENTED TOFU, WHICH IS BRICK RED IN COLOUR, ADDS EXTRA INTEREST TO THIS HEARTY
VEGETARIAN DISH. ITS DISTINCTIVE CHEESE-LIKE FLAVOUR GOES WELL WITH THE MUSHROOMS.

SERVES 3–4

INGREDIENTS
115g/4oz dried Chinese mushrooms
25g/1oz dried cloud ear (wood
   ear) mushrooms
115g/4oz dried tofu
30ml/2 tbsp vegetable oil
2 garlic cloves, finely chopped
2 slices fresh root ginger,
   finely chopped
10 Sichuan peppercorns, crushed
15ml/1 tbsp red fermented tofu
½ star anise
pinch of sugar
15–30ml/1–2 tbsp dark soy sauce
50g/2oz cellophane noodles, soaked
   in hot water until soft
salt

1 Soak the Chinese mushrooms and
cloud ears separately in bowls of hot
water for 30 minutes. Break the dried
tofu into pieces and soak in water
according to the packet instructions.

2 Strain the mushrooms, squeezing as
much liquid from them as possible.
Reserve the liquid. Discard the stems
and cut the caps in half if they are
large. Drain the cloud ears, rinse and
drain again. Cut off any gritty parts,
then cut each cloud ear into two or
three pieces.

COOK'S TIP
Red fermented tofu, sometimes called
red fermented beancurd or just beancurd
cheese, is fermented with rice wine and
salt. It is sold in small cans or jars
and tastes like salty cheese.

3 Heat the oil in a heavy pan and
quickly fry the chopped garlic, ginger
and Sichuan peppercorns for a few
seconds. Add the mushrooms and red
fermented tofu, toss to mix and stir-fry
for 5 minutes.

4 Add the reserved mushroom liquid
to the pan, with sufficient water to
cover the mushrooms completely. Add
the star anise, sugar and soy sauce,
then cover the pan and simmer for
30 seconds. Add the chopped cloud
ears and reconstituted tofu pieces to
the pan. Cover and cook for about
10 minutes.

5 Drain the cellophane noodles, add
them to the mixture and cook for a
further 10 minutes until tender, adding
more liquid if necessary. Add salt to
taste and serve.

Energy 128kcal/533kJ; Protein 4.9g; Carbohydrate 10.3g, of which sugars 0.9g; Fat 7.7g, of which saturates 0.8g; Cholesterol 0mg; Calcium 153mg; Fibre 0.9g; Sodium 360mg.

NOODLES <u>WITH</u> YELLOW BEAN SAUCE ★★★

SERVED SOLO, STEAMED LEEKS, COURGETTES AND PEAS MIGHT BE BLAND, BUT ADD A PUNCHY BEAN SAUCE AND THEY ACQUIRE ATTITUDE THAT EVEN THE ADDITION OF NOODLES CAN'T ASSUAGE.

3 Cover and stand over a wok of simmering water. Steam the vegetables for about 5 minutes, then remove and set aside. Drain and dry the wok.

4 Heat the vegetable oil in the wok and stir-fry the sliced garlic for 1–2 minutes.

5 In a separate bowl, mix together the yellow bean, sweet chilli and soy sauces, then pour into the wok. Stir to mix with the garlic, then add the steamed vegetables and the noodles and toss together to combine.

6 Cook the vegetables and noodles for 2–3 minutes, stirring frequently, until heated through.

7 Divide the vegetable noodles among four warmed serving bowls and sprinkle over the cashew nuts to garnish.

SERVES 4

INGREDIENTS
- 150g/5oz thin egg noodles
- 200g/7oz baby leeks, sliced lengthways
- 200g/7oz baby courgettes (zucchini), halved lengthways
- 200g/7oz sugarsnap peas, trimmed
- 200g/7oz/1¾ cups fresh or frozen peas
- 15ml/1 tbsp vegetable oil
- 5 garlic cloves, sliced
- 45ml/3 tbsp yellow bean sauce
- 45ml/3 tbsp sweet chilli sauce
- 30ml/2 tbsp sweet soy sauce
- 50g/2oz/½ cup cashew nuts, to garnish

1 Cook the noodles according to the packet instructions, drain and set aside.

2 Line a large bamboo steamer with perforated baking parchment and add the leeks, courgettes, sugarsnaps and peas.

Energy 354kcal/1487kJ; Protein 14.6g; Carbohydrate 46.4g, of which sugars 13g; Fat 13.5g, of which saturates 2.7g; Cholesterol 11mg; Calcium 76mg; Fibre 6.8g; Sodium 1008mg.

STIR-FRIED TOFU WITH NOODLES ★★★

TOFU DOES NOT HAVE MUCH FLAVOUR OF ITS OWN, BUT COMBINES WONDERFULLY WELL WITH MIXED VEGETABLES AND A SPICY SAUCE. THIS IS A VERY GOOD WAY OF SERVING IT.

SERVES 4

INGREDIENTS

225g/8oz firm tofu
15ml/1 tbsp vegetable oil
175g/6oz medium egg noodles
5ml/1 tsp cornflour (cornstarch)
10ml/2 tsp dark soy sauce
30ml/2 tbsp Chinese rice wine
5ml/1 tsp sugar
5ml/1 tsp sesame oil
6–8 spring onions (scallions),
    cut diagonally into short lengths
3 garlic cloves, sliced
1 fresh green chilli, seeded
    and sliced
115g/4oz Chinese leaves
    (Chinese cabbage),
    coarsely shredded
50g/2oz/1 cup beansprouts
25g/1oz/¼ cup cashew nuts

1 If the tofu is in water, drain it and pat it dry with kitchen paper. Cut it into 2.5cm/1in cubes.

2 Heat the oil in a wok until it is very hot, then stir-fry the tofu for 1–2 minutes until it is crisp and golden.

3 Remove the tofu with a slotted spoon and drain on kitchen paper. Set aside and keep warm.

4 Cook the egg noodles, following the instructions on the packet. Rinse them thoroughly under cold water in a sieve (strainer), drain well and set aside.

5 In a bowl, blend together the cornflour, soy sauce, rice wine, sugar and sesame oil.

6 Reheat the oil remaining in the wok and, when hot, add the spring onions, garlic, chilli, Chinese leaves and beansprouts. Stir-fry for 1–2 minutes.

7 Meanwhile, toast the cashew nuts in a dry frying pan over medium heat.

8 Add the tofu, noodles and soy sauce mixture to the wok. Cook, stirring, for about 1 minute, until all the ingredients are well mixed. Sprinkle over the toasted cashew nuts. Serve immediately.

Energy 335kcal/1408kJ; Protein 12.3g; Carbohydrate 40.6g, of which sugars 7.5g; Fat 14.9g, of which saturates 2.6g; Cholesterol 13mg; Calcium 328mg; Fibre 2.6g; Sodium 104mg.

TERIYAKI SOBA NOODLES WITH TOFU ★★★

YOU CAN, OF COURSE, BUY READY-MADE TERIYAKI SAUCE, BUT IT IS EASY TO PREPARE AT HOME USING INGREDIENTS THAT ARE NOW READILY AVAILABLE IN SUPERMARKETS AND ASIAN SHOPS.

SERVES 4

INGREDIENTS
350g/12oz soba noodles
250g/9oz asparagus
15ml/1 tbsp toasted sesame oil
30ml/2 tbsp vegetable oil
225g/8oz block firm tofu
2 spring onions (scallions),
  cut diagonally
1 carrot, cut into matchsticks
2.5ml/½ tsp chilli flakes
15ml/1 tbsp sesame seeds
salt and ground black pepper
For the teriyaki sauce
60ml/4 tbsp dark soy sauce
60ml/4 tbsp sake or dry sherry
60ml/4 tbsp mirin
5ml/1 tsp caster (superfine) sugar

VARIATION
Use dried egg or rice noodles instead
of soba noodles, if you prefer.

1 Cook the soba noodles according to the instructions on the packet, then drain and rinse under cold running water. Drain again and set aside.

2 Trim the asparagus, discarding the woody ends.

3 Lay the asparagus in a grill (broiler) pan, brush lightly with sesame oil, then grill (broil) under medium heat for 8–10 minutes, turning frequently, until they are tender and browned. Set aside.

4 Meanwhile, heat the vegetable oil in a wok or large frying pan until it is very hot. Add the tofu to the pan and fry for 8–10 minutes until it is golden, turning it occasionally, using tongs or two wooden spoons, to crisp all sides.

5 Carefully remove the tofu from the wok or pan and leave to drain and cool slightly on kitchen paper. When is has cooled sufficiently, cut the tofu into 1cm/½in slices.

6 To make the teriyaki sauce, mix the soy sauce, sake or dry sherry, mirin and sugar together, then heat the mixture in the wok or frying pan.

7 Toss in the noodles and stir to coat in the sauce. Heat for 1–2 minutes, then spoon into warmed individual serving bowls with the tofu and asparagus. Sprinkle with the spring onions and carrot and sprinkle with the chilli flakes and sesame seeds. Serve immediately.

COOK'S TIP
The asparagus could be steamed for just a couple of minutes instead of being grilled (broiled).

Energy 476kcal/2007kJ; Protein 17g; Carbohydrate 71.6g, of which sugars 6.5g; Fat 13.7g, of which saturates 1g; Cholesterol 0mg; Calcium 332mg; Fibre 4.1g; Sodium 1081mg.

CURRIED RICE VERMICELLI *

SIMPLE AND VERY QUICK TO PREPARE, THIS LIGHTLY FLAVOURED RICE NOODLE DISH WITH
VEGETABLES, PORK AND PRAWNS IS ALMOST A COMPLETE MEAL IN A BOWL.

SERVES 4

INGREDIENTS
  225g/8oz/2 cups dried rice
    vermicelli
  10ml/2 tsp sunflower oil
  1 egg, lightly beaten
  2 garlic cloves, finely chopped
  1 large fresh red or green chilli,
    seeded and finely chopped
  15ml/1 tbsp medium curry powder
  1 red (bell) pepper, thinly sliced
  1 green (bell) pepper, thinly sliced
  1 carrot, cut into matchsticks
  1.5ml/¼ tsp salt
  60ml/4 tbsp vegetable stock
  115g/4oz cooked peeled prawns
    (shrimp), thawed if frozen
  75g/3oz lean ham, cut into cubes
  15ml/1 tbsp light soy sauce

1 Soak the rice vermicelli in a bowl of boiling water for 4 minutes, or according to the instructions on the packet, then drain thoroughly through a sieve or colander, return to the bowl and set aside.

2 Cover the bowl with a damp cloth or with clear film (plastic wrap) so that the vermicelli does not dry out.

3 Heat 5ml/1 tsp of the oil in a non-stick frying pan or wok. Add the egg and scramble until set, stirring with a pair of wooden chopsticks. Remove the egg with a slotted spoon and set aside.

4 Heat the remaining oil in the clean pan. Stir-fry the garlic and chilli for a few seconds, then stir in the curry powder. Cook for 1 minute, stirring, then stir in the peppers, carrot sticks, salt and stock.

5 Bring the mixture to the boil. Add the prawns, ham, scrambled egg, rice vermicelli and soy sauce. Mix well. Cook, stirring, until all the liquid has been absorbed and the mixture is hot. Serve immediately.

Energy 306kcal/1281kJ; Protein 16g; Carbohydrate 50.9g, of which sugars 6.5g; Fat 4.3g, of which saturates 0.9g; Cholesterol 115mg; Calcium 56mg; Fibre 1.8g; Sodium 309mg.

VEGETABLE NOODLES WITH PRAWNS ★★★

DRIED MUSHROOMS ADD AN INTENSE FLAVOUR TO THIS LIGHTLY CURRIED DISH, WHICH MATCHES A COLOURFUL MEDLEY OF VEGETABLES WITH FINE EGG NOODLES AND PRAWNS.

SERVES 4

INGREDIENTS
20g/¾oz/⅓ cup dried
  Chinese mushrooms
225g/8oz fine egg noodles
10ml/2 tsp sesame oil
30ml/2 tbsp vegetable oil
2 garlic cloves, crushed
1 small onion, chopped
1 fresh green chilli, seeded and
  thinly sliced
10ml/2 tsp curry powder
115g/4oz green beans, trimmed
  and halved
115g/4oz Chinese leaves (Chinese
  cabbage), thinly shredded
4 spring onions (scallions), sliced
30ml/2 tbsp soy sauce
115g/4oz cooked prawns (shrimp),
  peeled and deveined
salt

1 Place the mushrooms in a bowl. Cover with warm water and soak them for 30 minutes. Drain, reserving 30ml/ 2 tbsp of the soaking water, then slice.

2 Bring a pan of lightly salted water to the boil and cook the noodles according to the directions on the packet. Drain the noodles in a sieve (strainer), tip into a bowl and toss with the sesame oil.

3 Heat a wok and add the vegetable oil. When it is hot, stir-fry the garlic, onion and chilli for 3 minutes. Stir in the curry powder and cook for 1 minute. Add the mushrooms, green beans, Chinese leaves and spring onions. Stir-fry for 3–4 minutes until the vegetables are crisp-tender.

4 Add the noodles, soy sauce, reserved mushroom soaking water and prawns.

5 Using a pair of chopsticks or two spatulas, toss the mixture over the heat for 2–3 minutes until the noodles and prawns are heated through and thoroughly combined.

Energy 329kcal/1386kJ; Protein 13.4g; Carbohydrate 44.6g, of which sugars 4.5g; Fat 12.1g, of which saturates 2.2g; Cholesterol 73mg; Calcium 71mg; Fibre 3.3g; Sodium 337mg.

NOODLES WITH CRAB AND MUSHROOMS ★★★

THIS IS A DISH OF CONTRASTING FLAVOURS, TEXTURES AND COLOURS, AND IT IS COOKED WITH SKILL AND DEXTERITY. HERE THE CRAB MEAT IS COOKED SEPARATELY TO MAKE IT EASIER.

SERVES 4

INGREDIENTS

- 25g/1oz dried cloud ear (wood ear) mushrooms, soaked in warm water for 20 minutes
- 115g/4oz dried bean thread (cellophane) noodles, soaked in warm water for 20 minutes
- 30ml/2 tbsp vegetable or sesame oil
- 3 shallots, halved and thinly sliced
- 2 garlic cloves, crushed
- 2 green or red Thai chillies, seeded and sliced
- 1 carrot, peeled and cut into thin diagonal rounds
- 5ml/1 tsp sugar
- 45ml/3 tbsp oyster sauce
- 15ml/1 tbsp soy sauce
- 400ml/14fl oz/1⅔ cups water or chicken stock
- 225g/8oz fresh, raw crab meat, cut into bitesize chunks
- ground black pepper
- fresh coriander (cilantro) leaves, to garnish

COOK'S TIP
If you can't find raw crab meat, cooked crab meat would work just as well. Heat up the cooked meat at the end and add to the noodles.

1 Remove the centres from the soaked cloud ear mushrooms and cut the mushrooms in half. Drain the soaked noodles and cut them into 30cm/12in pieces and put aside.

2 Heat a wok or pan and add 15ml/1 tbsp of the oil. Stir in the shallots, garlic and chillies, and cook until fragrant. Add the carrot rounds and cook for 1 minute, then add the mushrooms. Stir in the sugar with the oyster and soy sauces, followed by the bean thread noodles. Pour in the water or stock, cover the wok or pan and cook for about 5 minutes, or until the noodles are soft and have absorbed most of the sauce.

3 Meanwhile, heat the remaining oil in a heavy pan. Add the crab meat and cook until it is nicely pink and tender. Season well with black pepper. Arrange the noodles and crab meat on a serving dish and garnish with coriander.

Energy 292kcal/1224kJ; Protein 16g; Carbohydrate 30g, of which sugars 5g; Fat 13g, of which saturates 2g; Cholesterol 36mg; Calcium 29mg; Fibre 2.5g; Sodium 1000mg.

STIR-FRIED NOODLES <u>IN</u> SEAFOOD SAUCE ★

THE ADDITION OF EXTRA SPECIAL INGREDIENTS SUCH AS CRAB AND ASPARAGUS IN THIS DISH CAN MAKE A SIMPLE STIR-FRY A REAL TREAT THAT IS STILL VIRTUALLY FAT FREE.

SERVES 8

INGREDIENTS

225g/8oz fresh or dried Chinese
   egg noodles
8 spring onions (scallions), cleaned
   and trimmed
8 asparagus spears, plus extra
   steamed asparagus spears, to
   serve (optional)
15ml/1 tbsp sunflower oil
5cm/2in piece fresh root ginger,
   peeled and cut into very fine
   matchsticks
3 garlic cloves, chopped
60ml/4 tbsp oyster sauce
450g/1lb cooked crab meat (all
   white, or two-thirds white and
   one-third brown)
30ml/2 tbsp rice wine
   vinegar
15–30ml/1–2 tbsp light
   soy sauce

1 Put the noodles in a large pan or wok, cover with lightly salted boiling water, place a lid on top and simmer for 3–4 minutes, or for the time suggested on the packet. Drain and set aside.

2 Cut off the green spring onion tops and slice them thinly. Set aside. Cut the white parts into 2cm/¾in lengths and quarter them lengthways. Cut the asparagus spears on the diagonal into 2cm/¾in pieces.

3 Heat the oil in a pan or wok until very hot, then add the ginger, garlic and white spring onion. Stir-fry over a high heat for 1 minute. Add the oyster sauce, crab meat, rice wine vinegar and soy sauce to taste. Stir-fry for about 2 minutes, until the crab and sauce are hot. Add the noodles and toss until heated through. At the last moment, toss in the spring onion tops and serve with a few extra asparagus spears, if you like.

Energy 179kcal/756kJ; Protein 14.1g; Carbohydrate 22.9g, of which sugars 3.1g; Fat 4.1g, of which saturates 0.9g; Cholesterol 49mg; Calcium 82mg; Fibre 1.1g; Sodium 617mg.

STEAMBOAT ★★

MORE COMMONLY KNOWN AS CHINESE FONDUE, THIS DISH CONSISTS OF A SIMMERING POT OF HOT STOCK AT THE CENTRE OF THE DINING TABLE, INTO WHICH INGREDIENTS ARE PLACED TO COOK.

SERVES 8

INGREDIENTS

8 Chinese dried mushrooms, soaked
  for 30 minutes in warm water
1.5 litres/2½ pints/6¼ cups well-
  flavoured chicken stock
10ml/2 tsp rice wine or
  medium-dry sherry
5ml/1 tsp sesame oil
115g/4oz each lean pork and rump
  (round) steak, thinly sliced
1 chicken breast fillet, thickly sliced
225g/8oz raw prawns
  (shrimp), peeled
450g/1lb white fish fillets, skinned
  and cubed
200g/7oz fish balls (from Asian
  food stores)
115g/4oz fried tofu, each
  piece halved
leafy green vegetables, such as
  lettuce, Chinese leaves (Chinese
  cabbage), spinach and watercress,
  cut into 15cm/6in lengths
225g/8oz rice vermicelli
8 eggs
selection of sauces, including soy
  sauce with sesame seeds;
  soy sauce with crushed ginger;
  chilli sauce; plum sauce and
  hot mustard
½ bunch spring onions
  (scallions), chopped
salt and ground white pepper

1 Drain the mushrooms, reserving the soaking liquid. Cut off and discard the stems; slice the caps finely.

2 Pour the stock into a large pan, with the rice wine or sherry, sesame oil and reserved mushroom liquid. Bring the mixture to the boil, then season with salt and white pepper. Reduce the heat and simmer gently while you prepare the remaining ingredients.

VARIATION
Replace the egg in step 5 with long strips of finely cut omelette for an equally delicious result.

3 Put the meat, fish, tofu, green vegetables and mushrooms in bowls on the table. Soak the vermicelli in hot water for about 5 minutes, drain and place in eight soup bowls on a small table. Crack an egg for each diner in a small bowl; place on a side table. Put the sauces in bowls beside each diner.

4 Add the chopped spring onions to the pan of stock, bring it to a full boil and fuel the steamboat. Pour the stock into the moat and seat your guests at once. Each guest lowers a few chosen morsels into the boiling stock, using chopsticks or fondue forks, leaves them for a minute or two, then removes them with a small wire mesh ladle, a fondue fork or pair of chopsticks.

5 When all the meat, fish, tofu and vegetables have been cooked, the stock will be concentrated and wonderfully enriched. Add a little boiling water if necessary. Bring the soup bowls containing the soaked noodles to the table, pour in the hot soup and slide a whole egg into each, stirring until it cooks and forms threads.

Energy 243kcal/1020kJ; Protein 35g; Carbohydrate 4.1g, of which sugars 0.8g; Fat 9.7g, of which saturates 2.6g; Cholesterol 299mg; Calcium 168mg; Fibre 0.4g; Sodium 304mg.

NOODLE CASSEROLES ★★★

NOT QUITE A SOUP NOR YET A STEW, THIS IS SERVED IN INDIVIDUAL CASSEROLES OR POTS. WHEN THE LIDS ARE LIFTED, A POACHED EGG IS REVEALED, NESTLING IN EACH PORTION.

SERVES 4

INGREDIENTS

- 115g/4oz skinless, boneless chicken thighs
- 2.5ml/½ tsp salt
- 2.5ml/½ tsp sake or dry white wine
- 2.5ml/½ tsp light soy sauce
- 1 leek
- 115g/4oz fresh spinach, trimmed
- 300g/11oz dried udon noodles or 500g/1¼lb fresh udon noodles
- 4 shiitake mushrooms
- 4 eggs
- *shichimi-togarishi* or seven-spice powder, to serve (optional)

For the soup

- 1.5 litres/2½ pints/6 cups konbu and bonito stock or instant dashi
- 25ml/1½ tbsp light soy sauce
- 5ml/1 tsp salt
- 15ml/1 tbsp mirin

1 Cut the chicken into small chunks and place in a shallow dish. Sprinkle with the salt, sake or wine and soy sauce.

2 Cut the leek diagonally into 4cm/1½in slices, and place in a bowl. Set aside until needed.

3 Cook the spinach in boiling water for 1–2 minutes, then drain and soak in cold water for 1 minute. Drain again, squeeze lightly, then cut it into 4cm/1½in lengths.

4 If you are using dried udon noodles, boil them according to the packet instructions, allowing 3 minutes less than the stated cooking time. If you are using fresh udon noodles, place them in boiling water, disentangle, then drain.

5 For the soup, bring the konbu and bonito stock or dashi stock, soy sauce, salt and mirin to the boil in a pan, then add the chunks of chicken and the sliced leek. Skim the broth, then simmer for 5 minutes.

6 Use a sharp knife to trim off the hard parts of the shiitake mushroom stems.

7 Divide the udon noodles among four individual flameproof casseroles. Pour the soup, chicken and leeks into the casseroles. Place over medium heat and add the shiitake mushrooms.

8 Gently break an egg into each casserole. Cover and simmer gently for 2 minutes.

9 Divide the spinach among the casseroles and simmer, covered, for a further 1 minute.

10 Serve immediately, standing the hot casseroles on plates or table mats.

11 Sprinkle with *shichimi-togarishi* or seven-spice powder if you like.

VARIATION
Assorted tempura, made from vegetables such as sweet potato, carrot and shiitake mushrooms, or fish such as squid and prawns, could be served in these noodle casseroles, instead of the chicken and the poached egg.

Energy 418kcal/1765kJ; Protein 24.1g; Carbohydrate 59.4g, of which sugars 3.7g; Fat 11.1g, of which saturates 1.7g; Cholesterol 210mg; Calcium 109mg; Fibre 4g; Sodium 576mg.

NOODLES WITH CHICKEN, PRAWNS AND HAM ★★

A MIXTURE OF MEAT AND SEAFOOD WORKS WELL IN A STIR-FRY LIKE THIS ONE. RAID THE REFRIGERATOR FOR YESTERDAY'S LEFTOVERS OR ALTER THE INGREDIENTS TO SUIT WHAT YOU HAVE.

SERVES 4–6

INGREDIENTS
275g/10oz dried egg noodles
15ml/1 tbsp vegetable oil
1 medium onion
1 garlic clove
2.5cm/1in fresh root ginger
50g/2oz/¹⁄₃ cup canned water
  chestnuts, drained and sliced
15ml/1 tbsp light soy sauce
30ml/2 tbsp Thai fish sauce
175g/6oz cooked chicken breast
  fillet, skinned and sliced
150g/5oz cooked lean ham, thickly
  sliced and cut into short fingers
225g/8oz cooked prawn (shrimp)
  tails, peeled
175g/6oz/3 cups beansprouts
200g/7oz baby corn cobs
2 limes, cut into wedges, and
  1 small bunch coriander (cilantro),
  shredded, to garnish

1 Cook the noodles according to the instructions on the packet. Drain well and set aside.

2 Chop the onion, crush the garlic and cut the ginger into fine slivers.

3 Heat a wok or large frying pan, add the oil and fry the onion, garlic and ginger for 3 minutes, until soft but not coloured. Add the chestnuts, soy sauce, fish sauce, chicken, ham and prawns.

4 Add the noodles, beansprouts and baby corn cobs and stir-fry for 6–8 minutes, until heated through. Transfer to a warmed serving dish, garnish with the lime and coriander and serve.

Energy 302kcal/1277kJ; Protein 25.9g; Carbohydrate 35.5g, of which sugars 2.6g; Fat 7.3g, of which saturates 1.7g; Cholesterol 122mg; Calcium 56mg; Fibre 2.4g; Sodium 1031mg.

FIVE-FLAVOUR NOODLES ★★

CABBAGE IS ONE OF THE BEST VEGETABLES FOR STIR-FRYING, AND TASTES GOOD WITH GINGER AND GARLIC IN THIS SIMPLE DISH. TRY TO USE THE SEAWEED; IT ADDS THE FINISHING TOUCH.

SERVES 4

INGREDIENTS
300g/11oz dried thin egg noodles
200g/7oz pork fillet (tenderloin),
   trimmed and thinly sliced
25ml/1½ tbsp oil
10g/¼oz fresh root ginger, grated
1 garlic clove, crushed
200g/7oz/1¾ cups green cabbage,
   roughly chopped
115g/4oz/2 cups beansprouts
1 green (bell) pepper, seeded and cut
   into fine strips
1 red (bell) pepper, seeded and cut
   into fine strips
salt and ground black pepper
20ml/4 tsp *ao-nori* seaweed, to
   garnish (optional)
For the seasoning
   60ml/4 tbsp Worcestershire sauce
   15ml/1 tbsp light soy sauce
   15ml/1 tbsp oyster sauce
   15ml/1 tbsp sugar
   white pepper

1 Cook the egg noodles according to the packet instructions and drain.

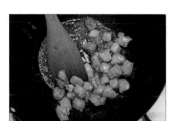

2 Using a sharp chopping knife, carefully cut the pork fillet into 3–4cm/ 1¼–1½in strips and season with plenty of salt and pepper. Next, heat 7.5ml/ 1½ tsp of the oil in a large frying pan or wok and stir-fry the pork until just cooked, then transfer to a dish.

3 Wipe the pan with kitchen paper, and heat the remaining oil. When the oil is hot, add the ginger, garlic and cabbage and stir-fry for 1 minute.

4 Add the beansprouts and stir until softened, then add the green and red peppers and stir-fry for 1 minute, over medium heat. Return the strips of cooked pork fillet to the pan or wok and toss lightly to mix.

5 Add the drained cooked egg noodles. Stir in all the seasoning ingredients together with a little white pepper. Stir-fry for 2–3 minutes. Serve in heated bowls and sprinkle each portion with *ao-nori* seaweed, if you like.

Energy 425kcal/1799kJ; Protein 28.2g; Carbohydrate 62.6g, of which sugars 9.4g; Fat 8.6g, of which saturates 2.6g; Cholesterol 67mg; Calcium 82mg; Fibre 4.4g; Sodium 844mg.

MIXED MEAT NOODLES ∗

A CLASSIC SOUTH-EAST ASIAN DISH THAT ORIGINATED IN SINGAPORE AND HAS BEEN ADOPTED AND ADAPTED BY ITS NEIGHBOURING COUNTRIES. NOODLES ARE STANDARD STREET AND CAFÉ FOOD, AN IDEAL SNACK FOR ANYONE FEELING A LITTLE PECKISH.

SERVES 4

INGREDIENTS
15ml/1 tbsp sesame oil
1 onion, finely chopped
3 garlic cloves, finely chopped
3–4 green or red Thai chillies,
    seeded and finely chopped
4cm/1½in fresh root ginger,
    peeled and finely chopped
6 spring onions (scallions), chopped
1 skinless chicken breast fillet,
    cut into bitesize strips
90g/3½oz lean pork, cut into
    bitesize strips
90g/3½oz prawns (shrimp), shelled
2 tomatoes, skinned, seeded
    and chopped
30ml/2 tbsp tamarind paste
15ml/1 tbsp *nuoc mam*
grated rind and juice of 1 lime
10ml/2 tsp sugar
150ml/¼ pint/⅔ cup water or fish stock
225g/8oz fresh rice sticks (vermicelli)
salt and ground black pepper
1 bunch each fresh basil and mint,
    and *nuoc cham*, to serve

1 Heat a wok or heavy pan and add the sesame oil. Stir in the finely chopped onion, garlic, chillies and ginger, and cook until they begin to colour. Add the spring onions and cook for 1 minute, add the chicken and pork, and cook for 1–2 minutes, then stir in the prawns.

3 Meanwhile, toss the noodles in a large pan of boiling water and cook for a few minutes until tender.

4 Drain the noodles and add to the chicken and prawn mixture. Season with salt and ground black pepper.

5 Serve immediately, with basil and mint leaves sprinkled over the top, and drizzled with spoonfuls of *nuoc cham*.

COOK'S TIP
It's important to serve this dish immediately once the noodles have been added, otherwise they will go soft.

2 Add the tomatoes, followed by the tamarind paste, *nuoc mam*, lime rind and juice, and sugar to the pan and stir well. Pour in the water or fish stock, and stir again before cooking gently for 2–3 minutes. Bubble up the liquid to reduce it.

VARIATIONS
• At noodle stalls in street markets in Thailand and South-east Asia, batches of cold, cooked noodles are kept ready to add to whatever delicious concoction is cooking in the wok.
• At home, you can make this dish with any kind of noodles – egg or rice, fresh or dried.
• Cured Chinese sausage and snails, or strips of squid, are sometimes added to the mixture to ring the changes.

CELLOPHANE NOODLES WITH PORK ★

ADDING CHICKEN STOCK TO A STIR-FRY IN THE FINAL STAGES MIGHT SEEM A BIT STRANGE, BUT THE LIQUID IS ABSORBED BY THE NOODLES, WHICH BECOME BEAUTIFULLY TENDER AND FLAVOURSOME.

SERVES 3–4

INGREDIENTS
115g/4oz cellophane noodles
4 dried Chinese black mushrooms
225g/8oz lean pork fillet (tenderloin)
30ml/2 tbsp dark soy sauce
30ml/2 tbsp Chinese rice wine
2 garlic cloves, crushed
15ml/1 tbsp grated fresh root ginger
5ml/1 tsp chilli oil
30ml/2 tbsp vegetable oil
6 spring onions (scallions), chopped
5ml/1 tsp cornflour (cornstarch)
  blended with 175ml/6fl oz/¾ cup
  chicken stock
30ml/2 tbsp chopped fresh
  coriander (cilantro)
salt and ground black pepper
coriander sprigs, to garnish

1 Put the noodles and mushrooms in separate bowls and cover them with warm water. Leave them to soak for 20 minutes, until soft; drain well.

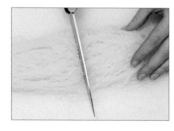

2 Cut the noodles into 13cm/5in lengths. Squeeze any water from the mushrooms, discard the stems and finely chop the caps.

3 Cut the pork into very small cubes. Put into a bowl with the soy sauce, rice wine, garlic, ginger and chilli oil, then leave for about 15 minutes. Drain, reserving the marinade.

4 Heat the oil in a wok and add the pork and mushrooms. Stir-fry for 3 minutes, then add the spring onions and stir-fry for 1 minute.

5 Add the cornflour and stock mixture with the marinade and seasoning.

6 Add the noodles and stir-fry for about 2 minutes, until the noodles absorb most of the liquid and the pork is cooked through. Stir in the coriander. Serve garnished with coriander sprigs.

Energy 198kcal/834kJ; Protein 15.9g; Carbohydrate 24g, of which sugars 1.6g; Fat 4.9g, of which saturates 0.9g; Cholesterol 35mg; Calcium 18mg; Fibre 1.1g; Sodium 487mg.

RICE NOODLES WITH PORK ★★

ALTHOUGH RICE NOODLES HAVE LITTLE FLAVOUR THEMSELVES THEY HAVE THE MOST WONDERFUL ABILITY TO TAKE ON THE FLAVOUR OF THE OTHER INGREDIENTS THEY ARE COOKED WITH.

SERVES 6

INGREDIENTS

450g/1lb lean pork fillet
225g/8oz dried rice noodles
115g/4oz/1 cup broccoli florets
1 red (bell) pepper, quartered
 and seeded
30ml/2 tbsp sunflower oil
2 garlic cloves, crushed
10 spring onions (scallions), trimmed
 and cut into 5cm/2in slices
1 lemon grass stalk, finely chopped
1–2 fresh red chillies, seeded and
 finely chopped
300ml/½ pint/1¼ cups reduced-fat
 coconut milk
15ml/1 tbsp tomato purée (paste)
3 kaffir lime leaves (optional)
For the marinade
45ml/3 tbsp light soy sauce
15ml/1 tbsp rice wine
15ml/1 tbsp oil
2.5cm/1in piece of fresh root ginger

1 Cut the pork into strips about 2.5cm/
1in long and 1cm/½in wide. Mix all
ingredients for the marinade in a bowl,
add the pork, stir to coat and marinate
together for 1 hour.

2 Spread out the rice noodles in a
shallow dish, pour over hot water to
cover and soak for 20 minutes until
soft. Drain.

3 Blanch the broccoli in a small pan of
boiling water for 2 minutes, then drain
and refresh under cold water. Set aside.

4 Place the pepper pieces under a hot
grill (broiler) for a few minutes until the
skin blackens and blisters. Put in a
plastic bag for about 10 minutes and
then, when cool enough to handle, peel
away the skin and slice the flesh thinly.

5 Drain the pork, reserving the marinade.
Heat half the oil in a large frying pan.
Stir-fry the pork, in batches if
necessary, for 3–4 minutes until the
meat is tender. Transfer to a plate and
keep warm.

6 Add a little more oil to the pan if
necessary and fry the garlic, spring
onions, lemon grass and chillies over
a low to medium heat for 2–3 minutes.
Add the broccoli and pepper and stir-fry
for a few minutes more.

7 Stir in the reserved marinade,
coconut milk and tomato purée,
with the kaffir lime leaves, if using.
Simmer gently until the broccoli is
nearly tender, then add the pork and
noodles. Toss over the heat, for 3–4
minutes until the noodles are
completely heated through.

Energy 307kcal/1281kJ; Protein 19.5g; Carbohydrate 35.7g, of which sugars 5g; Fat 9.1g, of which saturates 2.1g; Cholesterol 47mg; Calcium 44mg; Fibre 1.2g; Sodium 116mg.

WHEAT NOODLES WITH STIR-FRIED PORK ★★

THIS DELICIOUS RECIPE IS SIMPLICITY ITSELF WITH A WONDERFUL CONTRAST OF TEXTURES AND TASTE. THE PORK IS MARINATED IN PEANUT OIL WHICH ADDS A MARVELLOUSLY NUTTY FLAVOUR.

SERVES 4

INGREDIENTS
225g/8oz pork loin, cut into thin strips
225g/8oz dried wheat noodles, soaked
    in lukewarm water for 20 minutes
15ml/1 tbsp sunflower oil
2 garlic cloves, finely chopped
2–3 spring onions (scallions),
    trimmed and cut into
    bitesize pieces
45ml/3 tbsp *kroeung*
15ml/1 tbsp fish sauce
30ml/2 tbsp unsalted roasted
    peanuts, finely chopped
chilli oil, for drizzling (optional)
For the marinade
30ml/2 tbsp fish sauce
30ml/2 tbsp soy sauce
15ml/1 tbsp peanut oil
10ml/2 tsp sugar

1 In a bowl, combine the fish sauce, soy sauce, peanut oil and sugar for the marinade, stirring constantly until all the sugar dissolves. Toss in the strips of pork, making sure they are well coated in the marinade. Put aside for 30 minutes.

2 Drain the wheat noodles. Bring a large pan of water to the boil. Drop in the noodles, untangling them with chopsticks, if necessary. Cook for 4–5 minutes, until tender. Allow the noodles to drain thoroughly, then divide them among individual serving bowls. Keep the noodles warm until the dish is ready to serve.

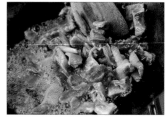

3 Meanwhile, heat a wok. Add the oil and stir-fry the garlic and spring onions, until fragrant. Add the pork, tossing it around the wok for 2 minutes. Stir in the *kroeung* and fish sauce for 2 minutes, adding a splash of water if the wok gets too dry, and tip the pork on top of the noodles. Sprinkle the peanuts over the top to serve.

VARIATION
Wheat noodles are especially popular in Cambodia. Sold dried, in straight bundles like sticks, they are versatile and robust. Noodles drying in the open air, hanging from bamboo poles, are common in the markets. This simple recipe comes from a noodle stall in Phnom Penh. It also tastes excellent when made with fresh egg noodles.

Energy 340kcal/1435kJ; Protein 19.6g; Carbohydrate 46g, of which sugars 4.4g; Fat 9.9g, of which saturates 1.4g; Cholesterol 35mg; Calcium 23mg; Fibre 1.9g; Sodium 41mg.

PORK CHOW MEIN ★★★

PROVING THAT YOU DON'T NEED MASSIVE AMOUNTS OF MEAT TO MAKE A TASTY MEAL, THIS CLASSIC RECIPE TEAMS NOODLES WITH PORK, VEGETABLES AND FRESH HERBS IN A SAVOURY SAUCE.

SERVES 2–3

INGREDIENTS
    175g/6oz medium egg noodles
    275g/10oz pork fillet (tenderloin)
    15ml/1 tbsp vegetable oil
    2 garlic cloves, crushed
    8 spring onions (scallions), sliced
    1 red (bell) pepper, seeded and
        roughly chopped
    1 green (bell) pepper, seeded and
        roughly chopped
    30ml/2 tbsp dark soy sauce
    45ml/3 tbsp dry sherry
    5ml/1 tsp sesame oil
    175g/6oz/3 cups beansprouts
    45ml/3 tbsp chopped fresh flatleaf
        parsley or coriander (cilantro)
    15ml/1 tbsp toasted sesame seeds

1 Soak the egg noodles in warm water according to the packet instructions. Drain well.

2 Thinly slice the pork fillet. Heat the sunflower oil in a wok or large frying pan. Add the pork to the wok or pan, and cook over high heat, stirring constantly, until the meat is golden brown and cooked through.

3 Add the garlic, spring onions and peppers to the wok or pan. Cook the mixture over a high heat, stirring frequently, for 3–4 minutes, or until the vegetables just begin to soften. Reduce the heat slightly.

4 Add the noodles, with the soy sauce, sherry and sesame oil. Stir-fry for 2 minutes. Add the beansprouts and cook for a further 1–2 minutes. Stir in the parsley or coriander and serve in heated bowls. Sprinkle with the sesame seeds.

Energy 453kcal/1906kJ; Protein 30.8g; Carbohydrate 53.7g, of which sugars 11.3g; Fat 14.2g, of which saturates 3.4g; Cholesterol 75mg; Calcium 86mg; Fibre 5.6g; Sodium 896mg.

BEEF NOODLES WITH ORANGE AND GINGER ★★

STIR-FRYING IS ONE OF THE BEST WAYS TO COOK WITH THE MINIMUM OF FAT. IT'S ALSO ONE OF THE QUICKEST WAYS TO COOK, BUT YOU DO NEED TO CHOOSE GOOD QUALITY TENDER MEAT.

SERVES 4

INGREDIENTS
  450g/1lb lean beef, e.g. rump
    (round), fillet (beef tenderloin)
    or sirloin steak
  finely grated rind and juice of
    1 orange
  15ml/1 tbsp light soy sauce
  5ml/1 tsp cornflour (cornstarch)
  2.5cm/1in fresh root ginger,
    finely chopped
  175g/6oz rice noodles
  10ml/2 tsp sesame oil
  15ml/1 tbsp vegetable oil
  1 large carrot, cut into thin strips
  2 spring onions (scallions),
    thinly sliced

1 If you have time, place the beef in the freezer and leave for 30 minutes, then cut it into very thin slices.

2 Place the beef in a bowl and sprinkle over the orange rind and juice. If possible, cover the bowl and leave the beef to marinate for at least 30 minutes.

3 Drain the liquid from the meat into a bowl and set aside, then mix the beef strips with the soy sauce, cornflour and ginger.

4 Cook the noodles according to the instructions on the packet. Drain well, toss with the sesame oil and keep warm.

5 Heat the vegetable oil in a wok or large frying pan. When the oil is very hot, add the beef strips and stir-fry for 1 minute until lightly coloured, then add the carrot and stir-fry for a further 2–3 minutes.

6 Stir in the spring onions and the reserved liquid from the meat, then cook, stirring, until the sauce boils and thickens. Serve immediately with the rice noodles.

COOK'S TIP
The citrus flavours that are such a success in this beef recipe work equally well with chicken or duck. Use thin strips from breast portions and toss in some orange segments just before serving.

Energy 353kcal/1478kJ; Protein 27.2g; Carbohydrate 39.6g, of which sugars 2.6g; Fat 9g, of which saturates 2.5g; Cholesterol 66mg; Calcium 18mg; Fibre 0.6g; Sodium 80mg.

NOODLES WITH BEEF AND BLACK BEAN SAUCE ★★

THIS IS AN EXCELLENT MIXTURE OF FLAVOURS AND TEXTURES — THE COMBINATION OF TENDER BEEF WITH A CHILLI BLACK BEAN SAUCE, TOSSED WITH SILKY-SMOOTH RICE NOODLES IS VERY SATISFYING.

SERVES 4

INGREDIENTS

- 450g/1lb fresh rice noodles
- 30ml/2 tbsp vegetable oil
- 1 onion, thinly sliced
- 2 garlic cloves, finely chopped
- 2 slices fresh root ginger,
  finely chopped
- 225g/8oz mixed (bell) peppers,
  seeded and sliced
- 350g/12oz rump (round) steak, thinly
  sliced against the grain
- 45ml/3 tbsp fermented black beans,
  rinsed in warm water, drained
  and chopped
- 30ml/2 tbsp dark soy sauce
- 30ml/2 tbsp oyster sauce
- 15ml/1 tbsp chilli black bean sauce
- 15ml/1 tbsp cornflour (cornstarch)
- 120ml/4fl oz/½ cup beef stock
  or water
- 2 spring onions (scallions), finely
  chopped, and 2 red chillies, seeded
  and thinly sliced, to garnish

1 Rinse the noodles under hot water until soft, then drain well. Set aside.

2 Heat half the oil in a wok or frying pan, swirling it around. Add the onion, garlic, ginger and pepper slices. Stir-fry for 3–5 minutes, then remove all the ingredients from the wok or pan and keep warm.

3 Add the remaining oil to the wok or pan and swirl to coat. When hot, add the sliced beef and fermented black beans and stir-fry over a high heat for 5 minutes or until they are cooked.

4 In a small bowl, blend the soy sauce, oyster sauce and chilli black bean sauce with the cornflour and stock or water and stir until smooth. Add the mixture to the wok, together with the onion and pepper mixture and cook, stirring, for 1 minute.

5 Add the noodles and mix together lightly. Stir over a medium heat until the noodles are heated through. Taste and adjust the seasoning if necessary. Serve immediately, garnished with the chopped spring onions and thinly sliced chillies.

Energy 567kcal/2376kJ; Protein 25.8g; Carbohydrate 100.4g, of which sugars 4.7g; Fat 5.5g, of which saturates 1.7g; Cholesterol 52mg; Calcium 29mg; Fibre 1.2g; Sodium 338mg.

VEGETABLES AND SIDE DISHES

All of the recipes in this chapter are low in fat, especially

saturated fat, but they are also filling and full of flavour, so

you won't feel any sense of sacrifice. You could combine a

couple of dishes, such as Vegetables with Chiang Mai Spicy

Dip, and Pak Choi with Lime Dressing, and still stay well

within sensible fat limits. If you are looking for a more

substantial vegetable dish, try Braised Aubergines and

Courgettes or Southern-Style Yam.

STIR-FRIED BEANSPROUTS ★

SPROUTED BEANS ARE HIGHLY NUTRITIOUS, ESPECIALLY IF YOU GROW THEM YOURSELF AND USE THEM WHEN THEY ARE REALLY FRESH. THEY MAKE FOR A CRISP AND CRUNCHY STIR-FRY.

SERVES 4

INGREDIENTS

15ml/1 tbsp vegetable oil
1 garlic clove, finely chopped
5ml/1 tsp grated fresh root ginger
1 small carrot, cut into
   fine matchsticks
50g/2oz/½ cup drained,
   canned bamboo shoots, cut
   into fine matchsticks
450g/1lb/8 cups beansprouts
2.5ml/½ tsp salt
large pinch of ground white pepper
15ml/1 tbsp dry sherry
15ml/1 tbsp light soy sauce
2.5ml/½ tsp sesame oil

1 Heat a non-stick frying pan or wok. Add the vegetable oil, just below the rim so that it trickles down to coat the surface. When the oil is hot, add the chopped garlic and grated ginger and stir-fry for 2 minutes.

2 Toss the carrot and bamboo shoot matchsticks into the pan or wok and stir-fry for 2–3 minutes.

3 Add the beansprouts to the pan or wok with the salt and pepper. Drizzle over the dry sherry and toss the beansprouts over the heat for 3 minutes until they have heated through.

4 Sprinkle over the light soy sauce and sesame oil, toss to mix thoroughly, then serve immediately.

COOK'S TIP
Beansprouts keep best when stored in the refrigerator or other cool place in a bowl of cold water, but you must remember to change the water daily.

Energy 76kcal/318kJ; Protein 3.9g; Carbohydrate 6.9g, of which sugars 4.5g; Fat 3.4g, of which saturates 0.5g; Cholesterol 0mg; Calcium 31mg; Fibre 2.3g; Sodium 278mg.

STIR-FRIED CHINESE LEAVES ★

THIS SIMPLE WAY OF COOKING CHINESE LEAVES PRESERVES THEIR DELICATE FLAVOUR. THE RIBS REMAIN BEAUTIFULLY CRUNCHY AND PROVIDE A CONTRAST TO THE SOFTER PARTS OF THE LEAVES.

SERVES 4

INGREDIENTS

675g/1½lb Chinese leaves
(Chinese cabbage)
15ml/1 tbsp vegetable oil
2 garlic cloves, finely chopped
2.5cm/1in piece fresh root ginger,
finely chopped
2.5ml/½ tsp salt
15ml/1 tbsp oyster sauce
4 spring onions (scallions), cut
into 2.5cm/1in lengths

1 Stack the Chinese leaves together and cut them into 2.5cm/1in slices using a sharp knife.

2 Heat a wok or large sauté pan. When the wok or pan is hot, add the oil just below the rim so that it trickles down to coat the surface. When the oil is hot, add the garlic and ginger and stir-fry for 1 minute.

VARIATION
If you are catering for vegetarians, substitute 15ml/1 tbsp light soy sauce and 5ml/1 tsp caster sugar for the oyster sauce.

3 Add the Chinese leaves to the wok or pan and stir-fry for 2 minutes. Sprinkle the salt over and drizzle with the oyster sauce. Toss the leaves over the heat for 2 minutes more.

4 Tip the spring onions into the wok or pan and stir-fry for 1 minute more. Toss the mixture well, transfer it to a heated serving plate or bowl and serve.

Energy 77kcal/321kJ; Protein 2.6g; Carbohydrate 9.8g, of which sugars 9.6g; Fat 3.2g, of which saturates 0.3g; Cholesterol 0mg; Calcium 87mg; Fibre 3.7g; Sodium 74mg.

PAK CHOI WITH LIME DRESSING ★

THE COCONUT DRESSING FOR THIS THAI SPECIALITY IS TRADITIONALLY MADE USING FISH SAUCE, BUT VEGETARIANS COULD USE MUSHROOM SAUCE INSTEAD. BEWARE, THIS IS A FIERY DISH!

SERVES 4

INGREDIENTS
15ml/1 tbsp sunflower oil
3 fresh red chillies, thinly sliced
4 garlic cloves, thinly sliced
6 spring onions (scallions),
  sliced diagonally
2 pak choi (bok choy), shredded
15ml/1 tbsp crushed peanuts
For the dressing
30ml/2 tbsp fresh lime juice
15–30ml/1–2 tbsp Thai fish sauce
250ml/8fl oz/1 cup reduced-fat
  coconut milk

1 Make the dressing. Put the lime juice and fish sauce in a bowl and mix well together, then gradually whisk in the coconut milk until combined.

2 Heat the oil in a wok and stir-fry the chillies for 2–3 minutes, until crisp. Transfer to a plate using a slotted spoon. Add the garlic to the wok and stir-fry for 30–60 seconds, until golden brown. Transfer to the plate.

3 Stir-fry the white parts of the spring onions for about 2–3 minutes, then add the green parts and stir-fry for 1 minute more. Transfer to the plate.

4 Bring a large pan of lightly salted water to the boil and add the pak choi. Stir twice, then drain immediately.

5 Place the pak choi in a large bowl, add the dressing and toss to mix. Spoon into a large serving bowl and sprinkle with the crushed peanuts and the stir-fried chilli mixture. Serve warm or cold.

VARIATION
If you don't like particularly spicy food, substitute red (bell) pepper strips for some or all of the chillies.

Energy 58kcal/244kJ; Protein 2.2g; Carbohydrate 5g, of which sugars 4.8g; Fat 3.5g, of which saturates 0.5g; Cholesterol 0mg; Calcium 113mg; Fibre 1.4g; Sodium 408mg.

SPRING VEGETABLE STIR-FRY ★

*FAST, FRESH AND PACKED WITH HEALTHY VEGETABLES, THIS STIR-FRY IS DELICIOUS SERVED WITH
MARINATED TOFU AND RICE OR NOODLES. TOP THE DISH WITH SESAME SEEDS FOR AN EXOTIC TOUCH.*

SERVES 4

INGREDIENTS

   2 spring onions (scallions)
   175g/6oz spring greens or
     collard greens
   15ml/1 tbsp vegetable oil
   5ml/1 tsp toasted sesame oil
   1 garlic clove, chopped
   2.5cm/1in piece fresh root ginger,
     finely chopped
   225g/8oz baby carrots
   350g/12oz broccoli florets
   175g/6oz asparagus tips
   30ml/2 tbsp light soy sauce
   15ml/1 tbsp apple juice
   15ml/1 tbsp sesame seeds, toasted

1 Trim the spring onions and cut them diagonally into thin slices.

2 Wash the spring greens or collard greens and drain in a colander, then shred finely.

3 Heat a frying pan or wok over high heat. Add the vegetable oil and the sesame oil, and reduce the heat. Add the garlic and sauté for 2 minutes.

4 Add the chopped ginger, carrots, broccoli and asparagus tips to the pan and stir-fry for 4 minutes.

5 Add the spring onions and spring greens or collard greens and stir-fry for a further 2 minutes.

6 Add the soy sauce and apple juice and cook for 1–2 minutes until the vegetables are tender; add a little water if they appear dry.

7 Sprinkle the sesame seeds on top and serve hot.

Energy 105kcal/434kJ; Protein 7.1g; Carbohydrate 9.4g, of which sugars 8.6g; Fat 4.4g, of which saturates 0.7g; Cholesterol 0mg; Calcium 170mg; Fibre 5.9g; Sodium 565mg

SAUTÉED GREEN BEANS ★

THE SMOKY FLAVOUR OF THE DRIED SHRIMPS ADDS AN EXTRA DIMENSION TO THESE GREEN BEANS,
AND BECAUSE THIS DISH IS SO LOW IN SATURATED FAT, YOU CAN EAT IT TO YOUR HEART'S CONTENT.

3 Bring a large pan of lightly salted water to the boil and cook the beans for 3–4 minutes until crisp-tender. Drain, refresh under cold water and drain again. Pat the beans dry with kitchen paper.

4 Drain the dried shrimps, reserving the soaking water for adding to fish soup, if you like.

SERVES 4

INGREDIENTS
    450g/1lb green beans
    25g/1oz dried shrimps
    15ml/1 tbsp vegetable oil
    3 garlic cloves, finely chopped
    5 spring onions (scallions), cut
      into 2.5cm/1in lengths
    15ml/1 tbsp light soy sauce
    salt

COOK'S TIP
Don't be tempted to use too many dried shrimps. As well as being high in salt, dried shrimps have a very strong flavour that could overwhelm the more delicate taste of the beans.

1 Put the dried shrimps in a bowl and pour over the warm water to cover. Stir, cover the bowl with clear film (plastic wrap) and leave to soak for 1 hour.

2 Using a sharp knife, trim the green beans neatly, then bunch them together on a board and slice them in half.

5 Heat the oil in a non-stick frying pan or wok until very hot. Stir-fry the garlic and spring onions for 30 seconds, then add the shrimps. Mix lightly.

6 Add the green beans and soy sauce. Toss the mixture over the heat until the beans are hot. Serve immediately.

Energy 64kcal/264kJ; Protein 4.5g; Carbohydrate 4g, of which sugars 2.9g; Fat 3.5g, of which saturates 0.5g; Cholesterol 19mg; Calcium 90mg; Fibre 2.7g; Sodium 163mg.

SPINACH ᵂⁱᵀᴴ TOASTED SESAME SEEDS ★

SEASONAL GREEN VEGETABLES ARE SIMPLY BLANCHED AND COOLED AND FORMED INTO LITTLE TOWERS.
WITH A LITTLE HELP FROM SOY SAUCE AND SESAME SEEDS, THEY REVEAL THEIR TRUE FLAVOUR.

SERVES 4

INGREDIENTS
  450g/1lb fresh spinach
  30ml/2 tbsp shoyu or other soy sauce
  30ml/2 tbsp water
  15ml/1 tbsp sesame seeds
  salt

1 Blanch young spinach leaves in lightly salted boiling water for 15 seconds. For Japanese-type spinach, hold the leafy part and slip the stems into the pan. After 15 seconds, drop in the leaves and cook for 20 seconds.

2 Drain immediately and place the spinach under running water. Squeeze out all the excess water by hand. Now what looked like a large amount of spinach has become a ball, roughly the size of an orange. Mix the shoyu and water, then pour on to the spinach. Mix well and leave to cool.

3 Meanwhile, put the sesame seeds in a dry frying pan and stir or toss until they start to pop. Remove from the heat and leave to cool.

4 Drain the spinach and squeeze out the excess sauce with your hands. Line up the spinach in the same direction on a chopping board, then form it into a log shape of about 4cm/1½in in diameter. Squeeze again to make it firm. With a sharp knife, cut it across into four cylinders.

5 Place the spinach cylinders on a large plate or individual dishes. Sprinkle with the toasted sesame seeds and a little salt, to taste, and serve.

Energy 54kcal/222kJ; Protein 4.1g; Carbohydrate 2.5g, of which sugars 2.3g; Fat 3.1g, of which saturates 0.4g; Cholesterol 0mg; Calcium 218mg; Fibre 2.7g; Sodium 692mg.

ASPARAGUS WITH GALANGAL ★

ONE OF THE CULINARY LEGACIES OF FRENCH COLONIZATION IN VIETNAM AND CAMBODIA IS ASPARAGUS. CAMBODIAN IN STYLE, THIS IS A LOVELY WAY TO EAT ASPARAGUS.

SERVES 4

INGREDIENTS
    15ml/1 tbsp sunfllower oil
    2 garlic cloves, finely chopped
    2 Thai chillies, seeded and finely
      chopped
    25g/1oz galangal, finely shredded
    1 lemon grass stalk, trimmed and
      finely sliced
    350g/12oz fresh asparagus stalks,
      trimmed
    30ml/2 tbsp *tuk trey*
    30ml/2 tbsp soy sauce
    5ml/1 tsp sugar
    15ml/1 tbsp unsalted roasted
      peanuts, finely chopped
    1 small bunch fresh coriander
      (cilantro), finely chopped

1 Heat a large wok and add the oil. Stir in the garlic, chillies, galangal and lemon grass and stir-fry until they become fragrant and begin to turn golden.

2 Add the asparagus and stir-fry for a further 1–2 minutes, until it is just tender but not too soft.

3 Stir in the *tuk trey*, soy sauce and sugar. Stir in the peanuts and coriander and serve immediately.

VARIATION
This recipe also works well with broccoli, green beans and courgettes (zucchini), cut into strips.

Energy 79kcal/327kJ; Protein 4g; Carbohydrate 4.9g, of which sugars 4.5g; Fat 4.9g, of which saturates 0.7g; Cholesterol 0mg; Calcium 53mg; Fibre 2.5g; Sodium 540mg.

THAI ASPARAGUS ★

THIS IS AN EXCITINGLY DIFFERENT WAY OF COOKING ASPARAGUS. THE CRUNCHY TEXTURE IS RETAINED AND THE FLAVOUR IS COMPLEMENTED BY THE ADDITION OF GALANGAL AND CHILLI.

SERVES 4

INGREDIENTS

    350g/12oz asparagus stalks
    15ml/1 tbsp sunflower oil
    1 garlic clove, crushed
    15ml/1 tbsp sesame seeds, toasted
    2.5cm/1in piece fresh galangal,
      finely shredded
    1 fresh red chilli, seeded and
      finely chopped
    15ml/1 tbsp Thai fish sauce
    15ml/1 tbsp light soy sauce
    45ml/3 tbsp water
    5ml/1 tsp palm sugar or light
      muscovado (brown) sugar

VARIATIONS
Try this with broccoli or pak choi (bok choy). The sauce also works very well with green beans.

1 Snap the asparagus stalks. They will break naturally at the junction between the woody base and the more tender portion of the stalk. Discard the woody parts of the stems.

2 Heat the oil in a wok and stir-fry the garlic, sesame seeds and galangal for 3–4 seconds, until the garlic is just beginning to turn golden.

3 Add the asparagus stalks and chilli, toss to mix, then add the fish sauce, soy sauce, water and sugar. Using two spoons, toss over the heat for a further 2 minutes, or until the asparagus just begins to soften and the liquid is reduced by half.

4 Carefully transfer to a warmed platter and serve immediately.

Energy 50kcal/207kJ; Protein 3.4g; Carbohydrate 3.1g, of which sugars 3g; Fat 2.7g, of which saturates 0.4g; Cholesterol 0mg; Calcium 50mg; Fibre 1.8g; Sodium 269mg.

BROCCOLI <u>WITH</u> GARLIC ★

A WONDERFULLY SIMPLE DISH THAT YOU WILL WANT TO MAKE AGAIN AND AGAIN. THE BROCCOLI COOKS IN NEXT TO NO TIME, SO DON'T START COOKING UNTIL YOU ARE ALMOST READY TO EAT.

SERVES 4

INGREDIENTS
 450g/1lb broccoli
 15ml/1 tbsp vegetable oil
 2 garlic cloves, sliced
 30 ml/2 tbsp light soy sauce
 salt

COOK'S TIP
Broccoli is a rich source of vitamin C and folic acid and is also believed to have antioxidant properties.

1 Trim the thick stems of the broccoli and cut the head into large florets.

2 Bring a pan of lightly salted water to the boil. Add the broccoli and cook for 3–4 minutes until crisp-tender.

3 Drain the broccoli thoroughly and transfer it to a heated serving dish.

4 Heat the oil in a small pan. Fry the sliced garlic for 2 minutes to release the flavour, then remove it with a slotted spoon. Pour the oil carefully over the broccoli, taking care as it will splatter.

5 Drizzle the soy sauce over the broccoli, sprinkle over the fried garlic and serve.

VARIATIONS
Cos lettuce or Chinese leaves (Chinese cabbage) taste delicious prepared this way.

Energy 65kcal/271kJ; Protein 5.2g; Carbohydrate 2.7g, of which sugars 2.2g; Fat 3.8g, of which saturates 0.6g; Cholesterol 0mg; Calcium 64mg; Fibre 2.9g; Sodium 543mg.

BROCCOLI WITH SESAME SEEDS ★★★

THIS SIMPLE TREATMENT IS IDEAL FOR BROCCOLI AND OTHER BRASSICAS, INCLUDING BRUSSELS
SPROUTS. ADDING A SPRINKLING OF TOASTED SESAME SEEDS IS AN INSPIRED TOUCH.

SERVES 2

INGREDIENTS
    225g/8oz purple sprouting broccoli
    15ml/1 tbsp vegetable oil
    15ml/1 tbsp soy sauce
    15ml/1 tbsp toasted sesame seeds
    salt and ground black pepper

VARIATIONS
• Sprouting broccoli has been used for
  this recipe, but when it is not available
  an ordinary variety of broccoli, such as
  calabrese, will also work very well.
• An even better choice would be
  Chinese broccoli, which is often
  available in Asian markets under the
  name *gailan*.

1 Using a sharp knife, cut off and
discard any thick stems from the
broccoli and cut the broccoli into long,
thin florets. Stems that are young and
tender can be sliced into rounds.

2 Remove any bruised or discoloured
portions of the stem along with any
florets that are no longer firm and
tightly curled.

3 Heat the vegetable oil in a wok or
large frying pan and add the broccoli.
Stir-fry for 3–4 minutes, or until tender,
adding a splash of water if the pan
becomes too dry.

4 Mix the soy sauce with the sesame
seeds, then season with salt and ground
black pepper. Add to the broccoli, toss
to combine and serve immediately.

Energy 135kcal/558kJ; Protein 6.6g; Carbohydrate 2.7g, of which sugars 2.3g; Fat 10.9g, of which saturates 1.5g; Cholesterol 0mg; Calcium 115mg; Fibre 3.5g; Sodium 545mg.

MORNING GLORY ᵂᴵᵀᴴ GARLIC ᴬᴺᴰ SHALLOTS ★

WATER MORNING GLORY GOES BY VARIOUS NAMES, INCLUDING WATER SPINACH, WATER CONVOLVULUS AND SWAMP CABBAGE. IT IS A GREEN LEAFY VEGETABLE WITH LONG JOINTED STEMS AND ARROW-SHAPED LEAVES. THE STEMS REMAIN CRUNCHY WHILE THE LEAVES WILT LIKE SPINACH WHEN COOKED.

SERVES 4

INGREDIENTS
    2 bunches water morning glory, total
      weight about 250g/9oz, trimmed
      and coarsely chopped into 2.5cm/
      1in lengths
    15ml/1 tbsp sunflower oil
    4 shallots, thinly sliced
    6 large garlic cloves, thinly sliced
    sea salt
    1.5ml/¼ tsp dried chilli flakes

VARIATIONS
Use spinach instead of morning glory, or
substitute young spring greens (collards),
sprouting broccoli or Swiss chard.

1 Place the morning glory in a steamer
and steam over a pan of boiling water
for 30 seconds, until just wilted. If
necessary, cook it in batches. Place the
leaves in a bowl or spread them out on
a large serving plate.

2 Heat the oil in a wok and stir-fry the
shallots and garlic over a medium to
high heat until golden. Spoon the
mixture over the morning glory, sprinkle
with a little sea salt and the chilli flakes
and serve immediately.

Energy 58kcal/240kJ; Protein 2.9g; Carbohydrate 4.2g, of which sugars 2g; Fat 3.4g, of which saturates 0.4g; Cholesterol 0mg; Calcium 113mg; Fibre 2g; Sodium 89mg

VEGETABLES <u>WITH</u> CHIANG MAI SPICY DIP ★

IN THAILAND, STEAMED VEGETABLES ARE OFTEN PARTNERED WITH RAW ONES TO CREATE THE CONTRASTING TEXTURES THAT ARE SUCH A FEATURE OF THE NATIONAL CUISINE. BY HAPPY COINCIDENCE, IT IS AN EXTREMELY HEALTHY WAY TO SERVE THEM.

SERVES 4

INGREDIENTS
  1 head broccoli, divided
  into florets
  130g/4½oz 1 cup green
  beans, trimmed
  130g/4½oz asparagus, trimmed
  ½ head cauliflower, divided
  into florets
  8 baby corn cobs
  130g/4½oz mangetouts (snow peas)
  or sugar snap peas
  salt
For the dip
  1 fresh green chilli, seeded
  4 garlic cloves, peeled
  4 shallots, peeled
  2 tomatoes, halved
  5 pea aubergines (eggplants)
  30ml/2 tbsp lemon juice
  30ml/2 tbsp soy sauce
  2.5ml/½ tsp salt
  5ml/1 tsp granulated sugar

2 Make the dip. Preheat the grill (broiler). Wrap the chilli, garlic cloves, shallots, tomatoes and aubergines in a foil package. Grill (broil) for 10 minutes, until the vegetables have softened, turning the package over once or twice.

3 Unwrap the foil and tip its contents into a mortar or food processor. Add the lemon juice, soy sauce, salt and sugar. Pound with a pestle or process to a fairly liquid paste.

4 Scrape the dip into a serving bowl or four individual bowls. Serve, surrounded by the steamed and raw vegetables.

VARIATIONS
You can use a combination of other vegetables if you like. Use pak choi (bok choy) instead of the cauliflower or substitute raw baby carrots for the corn cobs and mushrooms in place of the mangetouts (snow peas).

1 Place the broccoli, green beans, asparagus and cauliflower in a steamer and steam over boiling water for about 4 minutes, until just tender but still with a "bite". Transfer them to a bowl and add the corn cobs and mangetouts or sugar snap peas. Season to taste with a little salt. Toss to mix, then set aside.

COOK'S TIP
Cauliflower varieties with pale green florets have a more delicate flavour than those with white florets.

Energy 101kcal/422kJ; Protein 9.5g; Carbohydrate 11.9g, of which sugars 10.2g; Fat 2g, of which saturates 0.4g; Cholesterol 0mg; Calcium 98mg; Fibre 6.7g; Sodium 1082mg.

STIR-FRIED GREENS ★

WHEN YOU'VE GOT A SINGLE CHICKEN BREAST FILLET OR SMALL PIECE OF PORK FILLET IN THE REFRIGERATOR, THIS IS THE IDEAL RECIPE TO USE. IT TASTES GREAT AND IS LOW IN FAT.

3 When the meat is cooked, add the sliced stems first and cook them quickly; then add the torn leaves, quail's eggs and chilli. Spoon in the oyster sauce and a little boiling water, if necessary. Cover and cook for 1–2 minutes only.

4 Remove the cover, stir the mixture and add sugar and salt to taste. Stir in the cornflour and water mixture and toss thoroughly. Cook until the mixture is well coated in a glossy sauce.

5 Serve immediately, while still very hot and the colours are bright and positively jewel-like.

COOK'S TIP

As with all stir-fries, don't start cooking until you have prepared all of the ingredients. Cut everything into small, even-size pieces so that the food can be cooked very quickly and all the colours and flavours are preserved.

SERVES 4

INGREDIENTS
    2 bunches spinach or 1 head Chinese
       leaves (Chinese cabbage) or
       450g/1lb curly kale
    3 garlic cloves, crushed
    5cm/2in piece fresh root ginger,
       peeled and cut in matchsticks
    15ml/1 tbsp vegetable oil
    115g/4oz skinless chicken breast
       fillet or pork fillet (tenderloin),
       very finely sliced
    8 quail's eggs, hard-boiled
       and shelled (optional)
    1 fresh red chilli, seeded
       and shredded
    30–45ml/2–3 tbsp oyster sauce
    15ml/1 tbsp brown sugar
    10ml/2 tsp cornflour (cornstarch),
       mixed with 60ml/4 tbsp cold water
    salt

1 Wash the chosen leaves well and shake them dry. Strip the tender leaves from the stems and tear them into pieces. Discard the lower, tougher part of the stems and slice the remainder evenly, with a sharp knife.

2 Fry the garlic and ginger in the hot oil, without browning, for 1 minute. Add the chicken or pork and keep stirring it in the wok until the meat changes colour.

VARIATION

The quail's eggs look very attractive, but if you don't have any, you can substitute some baby corn, halved at an angle.

Energy 111kcal/465kJ; Protein 10.3g; Carbohydrate 8.9g, of which sugars 8.7g; Fat 4g, of which saturates 0.5g; Cholesterol 20mg; Calcium 196mg; Fibre 2.5g; Sodium 358mg.

COURGETTES ^{WITH} NOODLES ★

ANY COURGETTE OR MEMBER OF THE SQUASH FAMILY CAN BE USED IN THIS SIMPLE DISH, WHICH IS LOW IN FAT, YET FILLING ENOUGH TO MAKE A GOOD LIGHT LUNCH FOR FOUR.

SERVES 4

INGREDIENTS

450g/1lb courgettes (zucchini)
1 onion, finely sliced
1 garlic clove, finely chopped
15ml/1 tbsp vegetable oil
2.5ml/½ tsp ground turmeric
2 tomatoes, chopped
45ml/3 tbsp water
115g/4oz cooked, peeled
   prawns (shrimp) (optional)
25g/1oz cellophane noodles
salt

1 Use a potato peeler to cut thin strips from the outside of each courgette so that they have a stripy appearance. Use a sharp knife to cut the courgettes into neat slices.

2 Heat the oil in a wok. Add the onions and garlic and stir-fry for 2 minutes. Add the turmeric, courgette slices, chopped tomatoes and water. If using the prawns, add them to the wok.

3 Put the noodles in a pan and pour over boiling water to cover. Leave for 1 minute and then drain. Cut the noodles in 5cm/2in lengths and add to the vegetables.

4 Cover with a lid and cook in their own steam for 2–3 minutes. Toss everything well together. Season with salt to taste and serve while still hot.

Energy 54kcal/225kJ; Protein 2.1g; Carbohydrate 6.1g, of which sugars 2.7g; Fat 2.5g, of which saturates 0.3g; Cholesterol 0mg; Calcium 24mg; Fibre 1.2g; Sodium 3mg.

ORIENTAL GREEN BEANS ★

THIS IS A SIMPLE AND DELICIOUS WAY OF ENLIVENING GREEN BEANS. THE DISH CAN BE SERVED HOT OR COLD AND, ACCOMPANIED BY AN OMELETTE, MAKES A PERFECT LIGHT LUNCH OR SUPPER.

SERVES 4

INGREDIENTS
    450g/1lb/3 cups green beans
    15ml/1 tbsp vegetable oil
    5ml/1 tsp sesame oil
    2 garlic cloves, crushed
    2.5cm/1in piece fresh root ginger
    30ml/2 tbsp dark soy sauce

1 Steam the beans over a pan of boiling lightly salted water for 4 minutes or until just tender.

2 Meanwhile, peel the ginger, using a sharp knife, slice it into matchstick strips, then chop the strips finely. Heat the vegetable and sesame oils in a heavy pan, add the garlic and sauté for 2 minutes.

3 Stir in the ginger and soy sauce and cook, stirring constantly, for a further 2–3 minutes until the liquid has reduced, then pour this mixture over the warm beans. Leave to infuse for a few minutes before serving.

VARIATIONS
• Substitute other green beans, if you wish. Runner beans and other flat varieties should be cut diagonally into thick slices before steaming. This recipe also works well with mangetouts (snow peas) or sugar snap peas.
• Broccoli goes well with ginger and garlic, but don't steam calabrese broccoli or its vibrant colour will become dull. Blanch the broccoli in boiling water instead.

Energy 62kcal/254kJ; Protein 2.4g; Carbohydrate 4.2g, of which sugars 3.1g; Fat 4.1g, of which saturates 0.6g; Cholesterol 0mg; Calcium 42mg; Fibre 2.5g; Sodium 534mg.

STEAMED AUBERGINE <u>WITH</u> SESAME SAUCE ★

SERVE THIS TASTY VEGETABLE MEDLEY ON ITS OWN, OR AS AN ACCOMPANIMENT TO GRILLED STEAK. IT CONTAINS VERY LITTLE FAT, SO CAN EASILY BE ACCOMMODATED IN A HEALTHY DIET.

SERVES 4

INGREDIENTS

  2 large aubergines (eggplants)
  400ml/14fl oz/1²/₃ cups water
    with 5ml/1 tsp instant
    dashi powder
  25ml/1¹/₂ tbsp caster
    (superfine) sugar
  15ml/1 tbsp shoyu
  15ml/1 tbsp sesame seeds, finely
    ground in a mortar and pestle
  15ml/1 tbsp sake or dry sherry
  15ml/1 tbsp cornflour (cornstarch)
  salt
For the accompanying vegetables
  130g/4¹/₂oz shimeji mushrooms
  115g/4oz/³/₄ cup fine green beans
  100ml/3fl oz/scant ¹/₂ cup water
    with 5ml/1 tsp instant
    dashi powder
  25ml/1¹/₂ tbsp caster
    (superfine) sugar
  15ml/1 tbsp sake or dry sherry
  1.5ml/¹/₄ tsp salt
  dash of shoyu

1 Peel the aubergines and cut them in quarters lengthways. Prick them all over with a skewer, then plunge them into a bowl of salted water. Leave them to stand for 30 minutes.

2 Drain the aubergines and lay them side by side in a steamer, or in a wok half filled with simmering water and with a bamboo basket supported on a tripod inside, for 20 minutes, or until the aubergines are soft. If the quarters are too long to fit in the steamer, cut them in half.

3 Mix the dashi stock, sugar, shoyu and 1.5ml/¹/₄ tsp salt together in a large pan. Gently transfer the aubergines to this pan, then cover and cook over a low heat for a further 15 minutes. Take a few tablespoonfuls of stock from the pan and mix with the ground sesame seeds. Add this mixture to the pan.

4 Thoroughly mix the sake with the cornflour in small bowl, then add to the pan with the aubergines and stock and shake the pan gently, but quickly. When the sauce becomes quite thick, remove the pan from the heat.

5 While the aubergines are cooking, prepare and cook the accompanying vegetables. Wash the mushrooms and cut off the hard base part. Separate the large block into smaller chunks with your fingers. Trim the green beans and cut in half.

6 Mix the stock with the sugar, sake, salt and shoyu in a shallow pan. Add the green beans and mushrooms and cook for 7 minutes until just tender. Serve the aubergines and their sauce in individual bowls with the accompanying vegetables over the top.

BRAISED AUBERGINE AND COURGETTES ★

AUBERGINE, COURGETTES AND SOME FRESH RED CHILLIES ARE COMBINED WITH BLACK BEAN SAUCE IN THIS DISH TO CREATE A SIMPLE, SPICY AND QUITE SENSATIONAL ACCOMPANIMENT TO ANY MEAL.

SERVES 4

INGREDIENTS

  1 aubergine (eggplant), about
    350g/12oz
  2 small courgettes (zucchini)
  2 fresh red chillies
  2 garlic cloves
  15ml/1 tbsp vegetable oil
  1 small onion, diced
  15ml/1 tbsp black bean sauce
  15ml/1 tbsp dark soy sauce
  45ml/3 tbsp cold water
  salt
  chilli flowers (optional), to garnish
    (see Cook's Tip)

COOK'S TIP
Chilli flowers make a pretty garnish.

1 Using a sharp knife, slit a fresh red chilli from the tip to within 1cm/½in of the stem end. Repeat this at regular intervals around the chilli so that you have slender "petals" attached at the stem.

2 Rinse the chilli to remove the seeds, then place it in a bowl of iced water for at least 4 hours until the "petals" curl. Rinse well.

1 Trim the aubergine and slice it in half lengthways, then across into 1cm/½in thick slices.

2 Layer all the slices of aubergine in a colander, sprinkling each layer with salt. Leave the aubergine in the sink to stand for about 20 minutes.

3 Roll cut each courgette in turn by slicing off one end diagonally, then rolling the courgette through 180 degrees and cutting off another diagonal slice, so that you create a triangular wedge.

4 Make more wedges of courgette in the same way.

5 Remove the stalks from the chillies, cut them in half lengthways and scrape out and discard the pith and seeds. Chop the chillies finely.

VARIATION
You can vary the intensity of the chilli in this dish. For a fiery result, retain the chilli seeds and add to the mixture; for a milder result, reduce the amount of chilli or even omit it altogether.

6 Cut the garlic cloves in half. Place them cut side down and chop them finely by slicing first in one direction and then in the other.

7 Rinse the aubergine slices well, drain and dry thoroughly on kitchen paper.

8 Heat the oil in a wok or non-stick frying pan. Stir-fry the garlic, chillies and onion with the black bean sauce for a few seconds.

9 Add the aubergine and stir-fry for 2 minutes, sprinkling over a little water to prevent them from burning. Stir in the courgettes, soy sauce and water. Cook, stirring often, for 5 minutes. Serve hot. Add a garnish of chilli flowers if you like.

Energy 66kcal/276kJ; Protein 3g; Carbohydrate 6.1g, of which sugars 4.2g; Fat 3.5g, of which saturates 0.5g; Cholesterol 0mg; Calcium 34mg; Fibre 2.9g; Sodium 270mg.

FRAGRANT MUSHROOMS IN LETTUCE LEAVES ★

THIS QUICK AND EASY VEGETABLE DISH IS SERVED ON LETTUCE LEAF "SAUCERS" SO IT CAN EASILY BE EATEN WITH THE FINGERS — MAKING THIS A POPULAR TREAT WITH CHILDREN.

SERVES 4

INGREDIENTS
15ml/1 tbsp sunflower oil
2 garlic cloves, finely chopped
2 baby cos or romaine lettuces,
   or 2 Little Gem (Bibb) lettuces
1 lemon grass stalk, finely chopped
2 kaffir lime leaves, rolled in
   cylinders and thinly sliced
200g/7oz/3 cups oyster or chestnut
   mushrooms, sliced
1 small fresh red chilli, seeded
   and finely chopped
juice of ½ lemon
30ml/2 tbsp light soy sauce
5ml/1 tsp palm sugar or light
   muscovado (brown) sugar
small bunch fresh mint, leaves
   removed from the stalks

1 Heat a wok or large, heavy frying pan and add the sunflower oil. Add the finely chopped garlic and cook over a medium heat, stirring occasionally, until golden. Do not let it burn or it will taste bitter.

2 Meanwhile, separate the individual lettuce leaves and set aside.

3 Increase the heat under the wok or pan and add the lemon grass, lime leaves and sliced mushrooms. Stir-fry for about 2 minutes.

4 Add the chilli, lemon juice, soy sauce and sugar to the wok or pan. Toss the mixture over the heat to combine the ingredients together, then stir-fry for a further 2 minutes.

5 Arrange the lettuce leaves on a large plate. Spoon a small amount of the mushroom mixture on to each leaf, top with a mint leaf and serve.

Energy 52kcal/217kJ; Protein 2g; Carbohydrate 3.5g, of which sugars 3.3g; Fat 3.5g, of which saturates 0.5g; Cholesterol 0mg; Calcium 45mg; Fibre 1.8g; Sodium 543mg.

SLOW-COOKED SHIITAKE WITH SHOYU ★★

SHIITAKE MUSHROOMS COOKED SLOWLY ARE SO RICH AND FILLING, THAT SOME PEOPLE CALL THEM "VEGETARIAN STEAK". THIS IS A USEFUL AND FLAVOURSOME ADDITION TO OTHER DISHES.

SERVES 4

INGREDIENTS

20 dried shiitake mushrooms
30ml/2 tbsp vegetable oil
30ml/2 tbsp shoyu
5ml/1 tsp toasted sesame oil

1 Start soaking the dried shiitake the day before. Put them in a large bowl almost full of water. Cover the shiitake with a plate or lid to stop them floating to the surface of the water. Leave to soak overnight.

VARIATION

Cut the slow-cooked shiitake into thin strips. Mix with 600g/1⅓lb/5¼ cups cooked brown rice and 15ml/1 tbsp finely chopped chives. Sprinkle with toasted sesame seeds.

2 Remove the shiitake from the soaking water and gently squeeze out the water with your fingers.

3 Measure 120ml/4fl oz/½ cup of the liquid in the bowl, and set aside.

4 Heat the oil in a wok or a large frying pan. Stir-fry the shiitake over a high heat for 5 minutes, stirring continuously.

5 Reduce the heat to the lowest setting, then add the liquid and the shoyu.

6 Cook the mushrooms until there is almost no moisture left, stirring frequently. Sprinkle with the toasted sesame oil and remove from the heat.

7 Leave to cool, then slice and arrange the shiitake on a large plate.

Energy 66kcal/272kJ; Protein 1.1g; Carbohydrate 0.8g, of which sugars 0.7g; Fat 6.5g, of which saturates 0.8g; Cholesterol 0mg; Calcium 4mg; Fibre 0.6g; Sodium 537mg.

NEW POTATOES COOKED <u>IN</u> DASHI STOCK ★

AS THE STOCK EVAPORATES IN THIS DELICIOUS DISH, THE ONION BECOMES MELTINGLY SOFT AND CARAMELIZED, MAKING A WONDERFUL SAUCE THAT COATS THE NEW POTATOES.

SERVES 4

INGREDIENTS
    15ml/1 tbsp toasted sesame oil
    1 small onion, thinly sliced
    1kg/2¼lb baby new potatoes,
        unpeeled
    200ml/7fl oz/scant 1 cup water with
        5ml/1 tsp instant dashi powder
    45ml/3 tbsp shoyu or other
        soy sauce

COOK'S TIP
Japanese chefs use toasted sesame oil for its distinctive strong aroma. If the smell is too strong, use a mixture of half sesame and half vegetable oil.

1 Heat the sesame oil in a wok or large pan. Add the onion slices and stir-fry for 30 seconds, then add the potatoes. Stir constantly, until all the potatoes are well coated in sesame oil, and have begun to sizzle.

2 Pour on the dashi stock and shoyu and reduce the heat to the lowest setting. Cover and cook for 15 minutes, turning the potatoes every 5 minutes so that they cook evenly.

3 Uncover the wok or pan for a further 5 minutes to reduce the liquid. If there is already very little liquid remaining, remove the wok or pan from the heat, cover and leave to stand for 5 minutes. Check that the potatoes are cooked, then remove from the heat.

4 Transfer the potatoes and onions to a deep serving bowl. Pour the sauce over the top and serve immediately.

Energy 210kcal/890kJ; Protein 4.8g; Carbohydrate 42.4g, of which sugars 4.9g; Fat 3.5g, of which saturates 0.7g; Cholesterol 0mg; Calcium 21mg; Fibre 2.7g; Sodium 829mg

PINEAPPLE <u>WITH</u> GINGER <u>AND</u> CHILLI ★

IN SOUTH-EAST ASIA FRUIT IS OFTEN TREATED AS A VEGETABLE AND TOSSED IN A SALAD. HERE
PINEAPPLE IS COMBINED WITH GINGER AND CHILLI AND SERVED AS A SIDE DISH.

SERVES 4

INGREDIENTS

15ml/1 tbsp sunflower oil
2 garlic cloves, finely shredded
40g/1½oz fresh root ginger, peeled
  and finely shredded
2 red Thai chillies, seeded and
  finely shredded
1 pineapple, trimmed, peeled,
  cored and cut into bitesize chunks
15ml/1 tbsp *tuk trey* or other
  fish sauce
30ml/2 tbsp soy sauce
15ml–30ml/1–2 tbsp sugar
15ml/1 tbsp roasted unsalted
  peanuts, finely chopped
1 lime, cut into quarters, to serve

1 Heat a large wok or heavy pan and add the sunflower oil. Stir in the finely shredded garlic, ginger and chilli. Stir-fry until they begin to colour, then add the pineapple chunks and stir-fry for a further 1–2 minutes, until the edges turn golden.

2 Add the *tuk trey*, soy sauce and sugar to taste and continue to stir-fry until the pineapple begins to caramelize.

3 Transfer to a serving dish, sprinkle with the roasted peanuts and serve with lime wedges.

Energy 136kcal/577kJ; Protein 2.1g; Carbohydrate 22.8g, of which sugars 22.5g; Fat 4.8g, of which saturates 0.6g; Cholesterol 0mg; Calcium 41mg; Fibre 3g; Sodium 539mg.

THAI-STYLE PINEAPPLE ★

THIS DISH MAKES AN INTERESTING ACCOMPANIMENT TO GRILLED MEAT OR STRONGLY FLAVOURED FISH SUCH AS TUNA OR SWORDFISH. IF THE IDEA SEEMS STRANGE, THINK OF IT AS RESEMBLING A FRESH MANGO CHUTNEY, BUT WITH PINEAPPLE AS THE PRINCIPAL INGREDIENT.

SERVES 4

INGREDIENTS

1 pineapple
15ml/1 tbsp sunflower oil
2 garlic cloves, finely chopped
2 shallots, finely chopped
5cm/2in piece fresh root ginger,
  peeled and finely shredded
30ml/2 tbsp light soy sauce
juice of ½ lime
1 large fresh red chilli, seeded and
  finely shredded

VARIATION
This also tastes excellent if peaches or nectarines are substituted for the diced pineapple. Use three or four, depending on their size.

1 Trim and peel the pineapple. Cut out the core and dice the flesh.

2 Heat the oil in a wok or frying pan. Stir-fry the garlic and shallots over a medium heat for 2–3 minutes, until golden. Do not let the garlic burn or the dish will taste bitter.

3 Add the pineapple. Stir-fry for about 2 minutes, or until the pineapple cubes start to turn golden on the edges.

4 Add the ginger, soy sauce, lime juice and chopped chilli. Toss together until well mixed. Cook over a low heat for a further 2 minutes, then serve.

Energy 119kcal/507kJ; Protein 1.3g; Carbohydrate 22.8g, of which sugars 22.4g; Fat 3.2g, of which saturates 0.4g; Cholesterol 0mg; Calcium 42mg; Fibre 2.8g; Sodium 539mg.

SOUTHERN-STYLE YAM ★

THE FOOD OF SOUTHERN THAILAND IS NOTORIOUSLY HOT AND BECAUSE OF THE PROXIMITY TO THE BORDERS WITH MALAYSIA, RICHER CURRY FLAVOURS REMINISCENT OF INDIAN FOOD ARE ALSO FOUND IN HERE TOO. MANY DISHES ARE IN FACT OF CHINESE ORIGIN AND ARE ADAPTED TO LOCAL TASTES.

SERVES 4

INGREDIENTS

90g/3½oz Chinese leaves (Chinese
   cabbage), shredded
90g/3½oz/generous 1 cup
   beansprouts
90g/3½oz/scant 1 cup green
   beans, trimmed
90g/3½oz broccoli, preferably the
   purple sprouting variety, divided
   into florets
15ml/1 tbsp sesame seeds, toasted
For the yam
120ml/4fl oz/½ cup reduced-fat
   coconut milk
5ml/1 tsp Thai red curry paste
90g/3½oz/1¼ cups oyster
   mushrooms or field
   (portabello) mushrooms, sliced
5ml/1 tsp ground turmeric
5ml/1 tsp thick tamarind juice, made
   by mixing tamarind paste with
   warm water
juice of ½ lemon
60ml/4 tbsp light soy sauce
5ml/1 tsp palm sugar or light
   muscovado (brown) sugar

1 Steam the shredded Chinese leaves, beansprouts, green beans and broccoli separately or blanch them in boiling water for 1 minute per batch. Drain, place in a serving bowl and leave to cool.

2 Make the yam. Pour half the coconut milk into a wok and heat gently for 2–3 minutes, until it separates. Stir in the red curry paste. Cook over a low heat for 30 seconds, until the mixture is fragrant.

3 Increase the heat to high and add the mushrooms to the wok or pan. Cook for a further 2–3 minutes.

4 Pour in the remaining coconut milk and add the ground turmeric, tamarind juice, lemon juice, soy sauce and sugar to the wok or pan. Mix thoroughly.

5 Pour the mixture over the prepared vegetables and toss well to combine. Sprinkle with the toasted sesame seeds and serve immediately.

COOK'S TIP

Oyster mushrooms need gentle handling. Tear large specimens apart and don't overcook them or they will be rubbery.

Energy 68kcal/286kJ; Protein 4g; Carbohydrate 7g, of which sugars 6.1g; Fat 2.9g, of which saturates 0.5g; Cholesterol 0mg; Calcium 75mg; Fibre 2.4g; Sodium 1108mg.

TURNIPS WITH PRAWNS AND MANGETOUTS ★

THIS IS SOMETHING OF A CINDERELLA DISH, TRANSFORMING TURNIPS, THOSE SOMEWHAT NEGLECTED VEGETABLES, INTO SOMETHING THAT IS AS SOPHISTICATED AS IT IS SURPRISING.

2 Insert a cocktail stick (toothpick) into the back of each prawn, and gently scoop up the thin black vein running down its length. Very carefully pull the vein out, then discard.

3 Blanch the prawns in boiling water with the vinegar until the colour just changes. Drain. Cook the mangetouts in lightly salted water for 3 minutes. Drain well, then set aside.

4 Remove the saucer from the turnips and add the cooked prawns to the stock for about 4 minutes to warm through. Scoop out the turnips, drain and place in individual bowls. Transfer the prawns to a small plate.

5 Mix the cornflour with 15ml/1 tbsp water and add to the pan that held the turnips. Increase the heat a little bit and shake the pan gently until the liquid thickens slightly.

6 Place the mangetouts on the turnips and arrange the prawns on top, then pour about 30ml/2 tbsp of the hot liquid from the pan into each bowl. Serve immediately.

SERVES 4

INGREDIENTS
  8 small turnips, peeled
  600ml/1 pint/2½ cups water and
  7.5ml/1½ tsp instant dashi powder
  10ml/2 tsp shoyu or light soy sauce
  (use the Japanese pale *awakuchi* soy
  sauce if available)
  60ml/4 tbsp mirin
  30ml/2 tbsp sake
  16 medium raw tiger prawns (jumbo
  shrimp), heads and shells removed
  but with tails left intact
  dash of rice vinegar
  90g/3½oz mangetouts (snow peas)
  5ml/1 tsp cornflour (cornstarch)
  salt

1 Par-boil the turnips in boiling water for 3 minutes. Drain, then place them side by side in a deep pan. Add the dashi stock and cover with a saucer to submerge the turnips. Bring to the boil, then add the shoyu, 5ml/1 tsp salt, the mirin and sake. Reduce the heat to very low, cover and simmer for 30 minutes.

Energy 80kcal/339kJ; Protein 10.4g; Carbohydrate 6.1g, of which sugars 4.6g; Fat 0.6g, of which saturates 0.1g; Cholesterol 98mg; Calcium 87mg; Fibre 2.3g; Sodium 375mg.

FRIED VEGETABLES <u>WITH</u> NAM PRIK ★★

THIS DISH PROVIDES A VERY SIMPLE WAY TO ACHIEVING FIVE FRUIT AND VEGETABLE PORTIONS A DAY IN YOUR DIET, AND IT IS SERVED WITH A PIQUANT DIP FOR MAXIMUM FLAVOUR.

<u>SERVES 6</u>

INGREDIENTS

3 large (US extra large) eggs
1 aubergine (eggplant), halved
   lengthways and cut into long,
   thin slices
½ small butternut squash,
   peeled, seeded and cut into
   long, thin slices
2 courgettes (zucchini),
   trimmed and cut into long,
   thin slices
75ml/5 tbsp sunflower oil
salt and ground black pepper
nam prik or sweet chilli
   sauce, to serve (see
   Cook's Tip)

1 Beat the eggs in a large bowl. Add the aubergine, butternut squash and courgette slices. Toss the vegetables until coated all over in the egg, then season with salt and pepper.

2 Heat the oil in a wok. When it is hot, add the vegetables, one strip at a time, making sure that each strip has plenty of egg clinging to it. Do not cook more than eight strips at a time or the oil will cool down too much.

COOK'S TIP
Nam prik is quite a complex sauce, numbering dried shrimp, tiny aubergines (eggplant), shrimp paste and lime or lemon juice among its ingredients.

3 As each strip turns golden and is cooked, lift it out, using a wire basket or slotted spoon, and drain on kitchen paper. Keep hot while cooking the remaining vegetables. Transfer to a warmed dish and serve with the *nam prik* or sweet chilli sauce as a dip.

Energy 113kcal/468kJ; Protein 5.2g; Carbohydrate 3.6g, of which sugars 3.1g; Fat 8.8g, of which saturates 1.6g; Cholesterol 95mg; Calcium 56mg; Fibre 2g; Sodium 36mg.

PICKLES
AND SALADS

These superb salads are uniformly low in fat but
raise any meal into another dimension with their
fantastic colour, flavour and presentation. The dishes
in this chapter go particularly well with meat,
poultry and seafood dishes. Discover the classic
combinations of crisp, sweet, sharp, spicy and
aromatic flavours in Green Papaya Salad, and
Sweet-and-Sour Cucumber with Mint.

PICKLED VEGETABLES ★

EVERYDAY SOUTH-EAST ASIAN PICKLES GENERALLY CONSIST OF CUCUMBER, MOOLI AND CARROT —
GREEN, WHITE AND ORANGE IN COLOUR — AND ARE SERVED FOR NIBBLING ON, AS PART OF THE
TABLE SALAD, OR AS AN ACCOMPANIMENT TO GRILLED MEATS AND SHELLFISH.

SERVES 6

INGREDIENTS
    300ml/½ pint/1¼ cups white
      rice vinegar
    90g/3½oz/½ cup sugar
    450g/1lb carrots, cut into 5cm/2in
      matchsticks
    450g/1lb mooli (daikon), halved,
      and cut into thin crescents
    600g/1lb 6oz cucumber, partially
      peeled in strips and cut into
      5cm/2in matchsticks
    15ml/1 tbsp salt

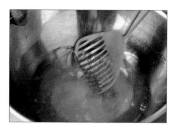

1 In a large bowl, whisk the vinegar with
the sugar, until it dissolves.

2 Add the carrots and mooli to the
vinegar mixture and toss well to coat.
Cover them and place in the refrigerator
for 24 hours, turning them occasionally.

3 Put the cucumber on a plate and
sprinkle with the salt. Leave for 30
minutes, then rinse under cold water
and drain well. Add to the carrot and
mooli and toss well in the pickling
liquid. Cover and refrigerate as before.

4 Lift the vegetables out of the pickling
liquid to serve, or spoon them into a jar
and store in the refrigerator.

Energy 104kcal/438kJ; Protein 1.8g; Carbohydrate 24.5g, of which sugars 24.1g; Fat 0.5g, of which saturates 0.2g; Cholesterol 0mg; Calcium 59mg; Fibre 3.1g; Sodium 31mg

HOT THAI PICKLED SHALLOTS ★

PICKLING THAI SHALLOTS IN THIS WAY DEMANDS SOME PATIENCE, WHILE THE VINEGAR AND SPICES WORK THEIR MAGIC, BUT THE RESULTS ARE DEFINITELY WORTH THE WAIT. THINLY SLICED, THE SHALLOTS ARE OFTEN USED AS A CONDIMENT WITH SOUTH-EAST ASIAN MEALS.

MAKES 2–3 JARS

INGREDIENTS

5–6 small red or green bird's
  eye chillies
500g/1¼lb Thai pink shallots,
  peeled
2 large garlic cloves, peeled, halved
  and green shoots removed
For the vinegar
40g/1½oz/3 tbsp granulated sugar
10ml/2 tsp salt
5cm/2in piece fresh root ginger,
  peeled and sliced
15ml/1 tbsp coriander seeds
2 lemon grass stalks, cut in
  half lengthways
4 kaffir lime leaves or pared strips of
  lime rind
600ml/1 pint/2½ cups cider vinegar
15ml/1 tbsp chopped fresh
  coriander (cilantro)

1 The chillies can be left whole or halved and seeded. The pickle will be hotter if you leave the seeds in. If leaving the chillies whole, prick them several times with a cocktail stick (toothpick). Bring a large pan of water to the boil. Add the chillies, shallots and garlic. Blanch for 1–2 minutes, then drain. Rinse all the vegetables under cold water, then drain again.

2 Prepare the vinegar. Put the sugar, salt, ginger, coriander seeds, lemon grass and lime leaves or lime rind in a pan, pour in the vinegar and bring to the boil. Reduce the heat to low and simmer for 3–4 minutes. Leave to cool.

3 Remove and discard the ginger, then bring the vinegar back to the boil. Add the fresh coriander, garlic and chillies and cook for 1 minute.

4 Pack the shallots into sterilized jars, distributing the lemon grass, lime leaves, chillies and garlic among them. Pour over the hot vinegar. Cool, then seal and store in a cool, dark place for 2 months before eating.

COOK'S TIPS
• Always be careful when making pickles to be sure that bowls and pans used for vinegar are non-reactive, that is, they are not chemically affected by the acid of the vinegar. China and glass bowls and stainless steel pans are suitable. Kilner and Mason jars are ideal containers.
• When packing pickles, make sure that metal lids will not come in contact with the pickle. The acid in the vinegar will corrode the metal. Use plastic-coated or glass lids with rubber rings. Alternatively, cover the top of the jar with a circle of cellophane or waxed paper to prevent direct contact when using metal lids.
• Take care when handling hot jars. Let them cool slightly after sterilizing and before filling to avoid burning yourself. However, do not let them cool down completely, or they may crack when the hot vinegar is poured in.

Energy 135kcal/566kJ; Protein 3.9g; Carbohydrate 30.3g, of which sugars 23.9g; Fat 0.7g, of which saturates 0g, Cholesterol 0mg; Calcium 85mg; Fibre 3.9g; Sodium 12mg.

SOYA BEANSPROUT HERB SALAD ★

*SOYA BEANSPROUTS ARE PARTICULARLY FAVOURED IN ASIA. UNLIKE MUNG BEANSPROUTS, THEY ARE
SLIGHTLY POISONOUS WHEN RAW, BUT ARE FINE TO CONSUME IF PARBOILED BEFORE USING.*

2 Bring a pan of salted water to the boil. Drop in the beansprouts and blanch for a minute only. Drain and refresh under cold water until cool. Drain again and put them into a clean dish towel. Shake out the excess water.

3 Put the beansprouts into a bowl with the spring onions. Pour over the dressing and toss well. Garnish with coriander leaves and serve.

SERVES 4

INGREDIENTS
    450g/1lb fresh soya beansprouts
    2 spring onions (scallions), finely
    sliced
    1 small bunch fresh coriander
    (cilantro), stalks removed
For the dressing
    5ml/1 tsp sesame oil
    30ml/2 tbsp *tuk trey* or other
    fish sauce
    15ml/1 tbsp white rice vinegar
    10ml/2 tsp palm sugar
    1 red chilli, seeded and finely sliced
    15g/½oz fresh young root ginger,
    finely shredded

1 First make the dressing. In a bowl, beat the oil, *tuk trey* and rice vinegar with the sugar, until it dissolves. Stir in the chilli and ginger and leave to stand for 30 minutes to allow the flavours to develop.

Energy 58kcal/245kJ; Protein 3.8g; Carbohydrate 7.9g, of which sugars 5.8g; Fat 1.5g, of which saturates 0.2g; Cholesterol 0mg; Calcium 52mg; Fibre 2.5g; Sodium 11mg

BAMBOO SHOOT SALAD ★

THIS HOT, SHARP-FLAVOURED SALAD IS POPULAR THROUGHOUT SOUTH-EAST ASIA. USE CANNED WHOLE BAMBOO SHOOTS, IF YOU CAN FIND THEM — THEY HAVE MORE FLAVOUR THAN SLICED ONES.

SERVES 4

INGREDIENTS

400g/14oz canned bamboo shoots,
  in large pieces
25g/1oz/about 3 tbsp glutinous rice
30ml/2 tbsp chopped shallots
15ml/1 tbsp chopped garlic
45ml/3 tbsp chopped spring
  onions (scallions)
30ml/2 tbsp Thai fish sauce
30ml/2 tbsp fresh lime juice
5ml/1 tsp sugar
2.5ml/½ tsp dried chilli flakes
20–25 small fresh mint leaves
15ml/1 tbsp toasted sesame seeds

COOK'S TIP
Glutinous rice does not, in fact, contain any gluten — it's just sticky.

1 Rinse the bamboo shoots under cold running water, then drain them and pat them thoroughly dry with kitchen paper and set them aside.

2 Dry-roast the rice in a frying pan until it is golden brown. Leave to cool slightly, then tip into a mortar and grind to fine crumbs with a pestle.

3 Transfer the rice to a bowl and add the shallots, garlic, spring onions, fish sauce, lime juice, sugar, chillies and half the mint leaves. Mix well.

4 Add the bamboo shoots to the bowl and toss to mix. Serve sprinkled with the toasted sesame seeds and the remaining mint leaves.

Energy 88kcal/368kJ; Protein 4.4g; Carbohydrate 11.5g, of which sugars 4.6g; Fat 2.8g, of which saturates 0.4g; Cholesterol 0mg; Calcium 51mg; Fibre 2g; Sodium 274mg.

GREEN PAPAYA SALAD ★

THIS SALAD APPEARS IN MANY GUISES IN SOUTH-EAST ASIA. AS GREEN PAPAYA IS NOT AS EASY TO GET HOLD OF AS MANY OTHER EXOTIC FRUITS, FINELY GRATED CARROTS, CUCUMBER OR EVEN CRISP GREEN APPLE CAN BE USED INSTEAD. ALTERNATIVELY, USE VERY THINLY SLICED WHITE CABBAGE.

SERVES 4

INGREDIENTS

1 green papaya
4 garlic cloves, coarsely chopped
15ml/1 tbsp chopped shallots
3–4 fresh red chillies, seeded
  and sliced
2.5ml/½ tsp salt
2–3 snake beans or 6 green beans,
  cut into 2cm/¾ in lengths
2 tomatoes, cut into thin wedges
45ml/3 tbsp Thai fish sauce
15ml/1 tbsp caster (superfine) sugar
juice of 1 lime
15ml/1 tbsp crushed roasted peanuts
sliced fresh red chillies, to garnish

1 Cut the papaya in half lengthways. Scrape out the seeds with a spoon and discard, then peel, using a swivel vegetable peeler or a small sharp knife. Shred the flesh finely in a food processor or using a grater.

2 Put the garlic, shallots, red chillies and salt in a large mortar and grind to a paste with a pestle. Add the shredded papaya, a small amount at a time, pounding with the pestle until it becomes slightly limp and soft.

3 Add the sliced snake or green beans and wedges of tomato to the mortar and crush them lightly with the pestle until they are incorporated.

4 Season the mixture with the fish sauce, sugar and lime juice. Transfer the salad to a serving dish and sprinkle with the crushed roasted peanuts. Garnish with the sliced red chillies and serve the salad immediately.

Energy 68kcal/286kJ; Protein 1.3g; Carbohydrate 15.9g, of which sugars 15.6g; Fat 0.3g, of which saturates 0.1g; Cholesterol 0mg; Calcium 37mg; Fibre 3.1g; Sodium 543mg.

VIETNAMESE TABLE SALAD ★

WHEN THIS VIETNAMESE-STYLE TABLE SALAD IS SERVED ON ITS OWN, THE VEGETABLES AND FRUIT ARE USUALLY FOLDED INTO LITTLE PACKETS USING LETTUCE LEAVES OR RICE WRAPPERS, AND THEN DIPPED IN A SAUCE, OR ADDED BIT BY BIT TO BOWLS OF RICE OR NOODLES.

SERVES 6

INGREDIENTS

half a cucumber, peeled and sliced
200g/7oz/scant 1 cup beansprouts
2 carrots, peeled and finely sliced
2 unripe star fruit (carambola),
  finely sliced
2 green bananas, finely sliced
1 firm papaya, cut in half, seeds
  removed, peeled and finely sliced
1 bunch each fresh mint and basil,
  stalks removed
1 crunchy lettuce, leaves separated
juice of 1 lime
dipping sauce, to serve

1 Arrange the cucumber, beansprouts, carrots, star fruit, green bananas, papaya, mint and basil attractively on a large plate. Place the lettuce leaves on one side so that they can be used as wrappers.

2 Squeeze the lime juice over the sliced fruits, particularly the bananas to help them retain their colour, and place the salad in the middle of the table. Serve with a dipping sauce.

Energy 94kcal/397kJ; Protein 2.5g; Carbohydrate 20.6g, of which sugars 11.6g; Fat 0.7g, of which saturates 0.1g; Cholesterol 0mg; Calcium 61mg; Fibre 3.4g; Sodium 14mg.

SWEET AND SOUR SALAD ★

This Indonesian-style salad makes a perfect accompaniment to a variety of spicy dishes and curries, with its clean taste and bright, jewel-like colours, and pomegranate seeds, though not traditional, make a beautiful garnish. A wonderful dish for a buffet party.

SERVES 8

INGREDIENTS

1 small cucumber
1 onion, thinly sliced
1 small, ripe pineapple or 425g/
   15oz can pineapple rings
1 green (bell) pepper, seeded and
   thinly sliced
3 firm tomatoes, chopped
30ml/2 tbsp golden granulated sugar
45–60ml/3–4 tbsp white wine vinegar
120ml/4fl oz/¹⁄₂ cup water
salt
seeds of 1–2 pomegranates,
   to garnish

1 Halve the cucumber lengthways, remove the seeds, slice and spread on a plate with the onion. Sprinkle with salt. After 10 minutes, rinse and dry.

2 If using a fresh pineapple, peel and core it, removing all the eyes, then cut it into bitesize pieces. If using canned pineapple, drain the rings and cut them into small wedges. Place the pineapple in a bowl with the cucumber, onion, green pepper and tomatoes.

3 Heat the sugar, white wine vinegar and measured water in a pan, stirring until the sugar has dissolved. Remove the pan from the heat and leave to cool. When cold, add a little salt to taste and pour over the fruit and vegetables. Cover and chill until required. Serve in small bowls, garnished with pomegranate seeds.

VARIATION
To make an Indonesian-style cucumber salad, salt a salad cucumber as described in the recipe. Make a half quantity of the sugar, vinegar and salt dressing and pour it over the cucumber. Add a few chopped spring onions (scallions). Cover and chill. Serve sprinkled with toasted sesame seeds.

Energy 53kcal/224kJ; Protein 0.9g; Carbohydrate 12.3g, of which sugars 12.1g; Fat 0.3g, of which saturates 0.1g; Cholesterol 0mg; Calcium 20mg; Fibre 1.5g; Sodium 6mg

GREEN MANGO SALAD ★

ALTHOUGH THE ORANGE AND YELLOW MANGOES AND PAPAYAS ARE DEVOURED IN VAST QUANTITIES WHEN RIPE AND JUICY, THEY ARE ALSO JUST AS POPULAR WHEN GREEN. THEIR TART FLAVOUR AND CRUNCHY TEXTURE MAKE THEM AN IDEAL INGREDIENT FOR SALADS AND STEWS.

SERVES 4

INGREDIENTS

450g/1lb green mangoes
grated rind and juice of 2 limes
30ml/2 tbsp sugar
30ml/2 tbsp *nuoc mam*
2 green Thai chillies, seeded and
  finely sliced
1 small bunch fresh coriander
  (cilantro), stalks removed,
  finely chopped
salt

1 Peel, halve and stone (pit) the
green mangoes, and slice them into
thin strips.

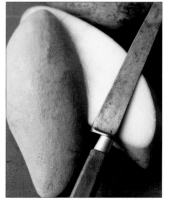

2 In a bowl, mix together the lime rind
and juice, sugar and *nuoc mam*. Add
the mango strips with the chillies and
coriander. Add salt to taste and leave
to stand for 20 minutes to allow the
flavours to mingle before serving.

Energy 69kcal/293kJ; Protein 1.2g; Carbohydrate 16.2g, of which sugars 15.8g; Fat 0.4g, of which saturates 0.1g; Cholesterol 0mg; Calcium 39mg; Fibre 3.6g; Sodium 7mg.

SWEET-AND-SOUR CUCUMBER WITH MINT ★

SHORT, FAT CUCUMBERS ARE A COMMON SIGHT IN THE MARKETS THROUGHOUT SOUTH-EAST ASIA.
THIS SALAD IS A GREAT ADDITION TO A SUMMER BARBECUE OR THE SALAD TABLE, AND IS A
DELIGHTFUL ACCOMPANIMENT TO ANY MEAT, POULTRY, FISH OR SHELLFISH MAIN COURSE.

SERVES 6

INGREDIENTS

2 cucumbers
30ml/2 tbsp sugar
100ml/3½fl oz/½ cup rice vinegar
juice of half a lime
2 green Thai chillies, seeded and
    finely sliced
2 shallots, halved and finely sliced
1 small bunch each fresh coriander
    (cilantro) and mint, stalks removed,
    leaves finely chopped
salt
fresh coriander leaves, to garnish

COOK'S TIP
Decorate the dish with edible flowers,
such as nasturtiums, to add colour.

1 Use a vegetable peeler to remove
strips of the cucumber peel. Halve
the cucumbers lengthways and cut
into slices. Place the slices on a plate
and sprinkle with a little salt. Leave
them to stand for 15 minutes. Rinse
well, drain the slices and pat them dry
with kitchen paper.

2 In a bowl, mix the sugar with the
vinegar until it has dissolved, then stir
in the lime juice and a little salt to taste.

3 Add the chillies, shallots, herbs and
cucumber to the dressing and leave to
stand for 15–20 minutes. Garnish with
coriander leaves and a flower, if you like.

Energy 33kcal/138kJ; Protein 0.9g; Carbohydrate 7.2g, of which sugars 6.9g; Fat 0.2g, of which saturates 0g; Cholesterol 0mg; Calcium 34mg; Fibre 1g; Sodium 5mg.

THAI FRUIT AND VEGETABLE SALAD ★

THIS REFRESHING FRUIT SALAD IS THE PERFECT ACCOMPANIMENT TO ANY SPICY MAIN COURSE DISH.
THE MIXTURE OF FRESH FRUIT SERVES AS A COOLER TO COUNTERACT THE HEAT OF THE CHILLIES
PRESENT IN OTHER DISHES. IT IS A TYPICALLY HARMONIOUS BALANCE OF FLAVOURS.

SERVES 6

INGREDIENTS
1 small pineapple
1 small mango, peeled and sliced
1 green apple, cored and sliced
6 rambutans or lychees, peeled and
  stoned (pitted)
115g/4oz/1 cup green beans,
  trimmed and halved
1 red onion, sliced
1 small cucumber, cut into
  short sticks
115g/4oz/1⅓ cups beansprouts
2 spring onions (scallions), sliced
1 ripe tomato, quartered
225g/8oz cos, romaine or iceberg
  lettuce leaves
For the coconut dipping sauce
30ml/2 tbsp reduced-fat coconut milk
30ml/2 tbsp granulated sugar
75ml/5 tbsp boiling water
1.5ml/¼ tsp chilli sauce
15ml/1 tbsp Thai fish sauce
juice of 1 lime

1 Make the coconut dipping sauce.
Spoon the coconut milk, sugar and
boiling water into a screw-top jar. Add
the chilli and fish sauces and lime
juice, close tightly and shake to mix.

2 Trim both ends of the pineapple with
a serrated knife, then cut away the
outer skin. Remove the central core
with an apple corer. Alternatively,
quarter the pineapple lengthways and
remove the portion of core from each
wedge with a knife. Chop the pineapple
and set aside with the other fruits.

3 Bring a small pan of lightly salted
water to the boil over a medium heat.
Add the green beans and cook for
3–4 minutes, until just tender but still
retaining some "bite". Drain, refresh
under cold running water, drain well
again and set aside.

4 To serve, arrange all the fruits and
vegetables in small heaps on a platter
or in a shallow bowl. Pour the coconut
sauce into a small serving bowl and
serve separately as a dip.

Energy 100kcal/425kJ; Protein 2.3g; Carbohydrate 22.6g, of which sugars 21.7g; Fat 0.7g, of which saturates 0.1g; Cholesterol 0mg; Calcium 50mg; Fibre 3.2g; Sodium 190mg.

AUBERGINE SALAD ★

AN APPETIZING AND UNUSUAL SALAD IS SO TASTY THAT YOU WILL FIND YOURSELF MAKING OVER AND OVER AGAIN. ROASTING THE AUBERGINES REALLY BRINGS OUT THEIR FLAVOUR IN THIS DISH.

SERVES 6

INGREDIENTS
 2 aubergines (eggplant)
 15ml/1 tbsp sunflower oil
 30ml/2 tbsp dried shrimp, soaked in
  warm water for 10 minutes
 15ml/1 tbsp coarsely chopped garlic
 1 hard-boiled egg, chopped
 4 shallots, thinly sliced
  into rings
 fresh coriander (cilantro) leaves and
  2 fresh red chillies, seeded and
  sliced, to garnish
For the dressing
 30ml/2 tbsp fresh lime juice
 5ml/1 tsp palm sugar or light
  muscovado (brown) sugar
 30ml/2 tbsp Thai fish sauce

1 Preheat the grill (broiler) to medium or preheat the oven to 180°C/350°F/ Gas 4. Prick the aubergines several times with a skewer, then arrange on a baking sheet. Cook them under the grill for 30–40 minutes, or until they are charred and tender. Alternatively, roast them by placing them directly on the shelf of the oven for about 1 hour, turning them at least twice. Remove the aubergines and set aside until they are cool enough to handle.

2 Meanwhile, make the dressing. Put the lime juice, palm or muscovado sugar and fish sauce into a small bowl. Whisk well with a fork or balloon whisk. Cover with clear film (plastic wrap) and set aside until required.

3 When the aubergines are cool enough to handle, peel off the skin and cut the flesh into medium slices.

4 Heat the oil in a small frying pan. Drain the dried shrimp thoroughly and add them to the pan with the garlic. Cook over a medium heat for about 3 minutes, until golden. Remove from the pan and set aside.

5 Arrange the aubergine slices on a serving dish. Top with the hard-boiled egg, shallots and dried shrimp mixture. Drizzle over the dressing and garnish with the coriander and red chillies.

VARIATION
For a special occasion, use salted duck's or quail's eggs, cut in half, instead of chopped hen's eggs.

Energy 61kcal/254kJ; Protein 4.8g; Carbohydrate 3.6g, of which sugars 2.8g; Fat 3.2g, of which saturates 0.6g; Cholesterol 57mg; Calcium 75mg; Fibre 1.6g; Sodium 408mg.

LOTUS STEM SALAD ★

IF YOU CANNOT FIND FRESH LOTUS STEMS OR ONES PRESERVED IN BRINE, TRY THIS RECIPE WITH FRESHLY STEAMED, CRUNCHY ASPARAGUS TIPS FOR A LOW-FAT RECIPE THAT TASTES DELICIOUS.

SERVES 4

INGREDIENTS

half a cucumber
225g/8oz jar preserved lotus stems,
  drained and cut into 5cm/2in strips
2 shallots, finely sliced
25g/1oz/½ cup fresh basil
  leaves, shredded
salt
fresh coriander (cilantro) leaves,
  to garnish
For the dressing
  juice of 1 lime
  30ml/2 tbsp *nuoc mam*
  1 red Thai chilli, seeded and chopped
  1 garlic clove, crushed
  15ml/1 tbsp sugar

1 To make the dressing, mix together the dressing ingredients in a bowl and set aside.

2 Peel the cucumber and cut it into 5cm/2in batons. Soak the batons in cold salted water for 20 minutes. Put the lotus stems into a bowl of water. Using a pair of chopsticks, stir the water so that the loose fibres of the stems wrap around the sticks.

3 Drain the stems and put them in a bowl. Drain the cucumber batons and add to the bowl, then add the shallots, shredded basil leaves and the prepared dressing. Leave the salad to marinate for 20 minutes before serving. Garnish with fresh coriander leaves.

COOK'S TIP
If you cannot find the stems, fresh lotus roots make a good substitute and are readily available in Asian markets. They grow in sausage-like links, each one about 18–23cm/7–9in long. Once the mud that coats them has been washed off, a pale beige-pink skin is revealed. When buying fresh lotus roots, choose ones that feel heavy for their size, as this is an indication that they are full of liquid. This means that the roots will absorb the flavours of the dressing while retaining a crunchy texture. They should be peeled and soaked in water with a little lemon juice before being added to the salad, to retain their pale colour.

Energy 40kcal/168kJ; Protein 1.4g; Carbohydrate 8.3g, of which sugars 7.5g; Fat 0.3g, of which saturates 0g; Cholesterol 0mg; Calcium 55mg; Fibre 1.7g; Sodium 573mg.

CABBAGE SALAD ★

THIS IS A SIMPLE AND DELICIOUS WAY OF SERVING A SOMEWHAT MUNDANE VEGETABLE. THE CLASSIC THAI FLAVOURS OF CHILLI AND PEANUTS PERMEATE THIS COLOURFUL WARM SALAD.

SERVES 6

INGREDIENTS
 15ml/1 tbsp sunflower oil
 2 large fresh red chillies, seeded
   and cut into thin strips
 6 garlic cloves, thinly sliced
 6 shallots, thinly sliced
 1 small cabbage, shredded
 15ml/1 tbsp coarsely chopped
   roasted peanuts, to garnish
For the dressing
 30ml/2 tbsp Thai fish sauce
 grated rind of 1 lime
 30ml/2 tbsp fresh lime juice
 120ml/4fl oz/½ cup reduced-fat
   coconut milk

VARIATION
Cauliflower and broccoli can also be
cooked in this way.

1 Make the dressing by mixing the fish
sauce, lime rind and juice and coconut
milk in a bowl. Whisk until thoroughly
combined, then set aside.

2 Heat the oil in a wok. Stir-fry the
chillies, garlic and shallots over a
medium heat for 3–4 minutes, until the
shallots are brown and crisp. Remove
with a slotted spoon and set aside.

3 Bring a large pan of lightly salted
water to the boil. Add the cabbage and
blanch for 2–3 minutes. Tip it into a
colander, drain well and put into a
bowl.

4 Whisk the dressing again, add it to
the warm cabbage and toss to mix.
Transfer the salad to a serving dish.
Sprinkle with the fried shallot mixture
and the peanuts. Serve immediately.

Energy 70kcal/290kJ; Protein 2.2g; Carbohydrate 8.3g, of which sugars 7g; Fat 3.3g, of which saturates 0.5g; Cholesterol 0mg; Calcium 51mg; Fibre 2.2g; Sodium 206mg.

SAMBAL NANAS ★

THESE ARE THE LITTLE SIDE DISHES SERVED AT ALMOST EVERY MALAY MEAL. THIS DISH INCLUDES
CUCUMBER AND PINEAPPLE, BUT IT COULD BE MADE WITH JUST SHRIMP PASTE, CHILLI AND LIME JUICE.

SERVES 10

INGREDIENTS

  1 small or ¹/₂ large fresh
    ripe pineapple
  ¹/₂ cucumber, halved lengthways
  50g/2oz dried shrimps
  1 large fresh red chilli, seeded
  1cm/¹/₂in cube shrimp paste,
    prepared (see Cook's Tip)
  juice of 1 large lemon or lime
  light brown sugar, to taste (optional)

1 Cut off both ends of the pineapple. Stand it upright on a board, then slice off the skin from top to bottom, cutting out the spines. Slice the pineapple, removing the central core. Cut into thin slices and set aside.

2 Trim the ends from the cucumber and slice thinly. Sprinkle with salt and set aside. Place the dried shrimps in a food processor and chop fairly finely. Add the chilli, prepared shrimp paste and lemon or lime juice and process again to a paste.

3 Rinse the cucumber, drain and dry on kitchen paper.

4 Mix the cucumber with the pineapple and chill. Just before serving, spoon in the spice mixture with sugar to taste. Mix well and serve.

COOK'S TIP
The pungent shrimp paste, also called *balachan*, is popular in many South-east Asian countries, and is available in Asian supermarkets. Since it can taste a bit raw in a sambal, dry fry it by wrapping in foil and heating in a frying pan over a low heat for 5 minutes, turning from time to time. If the shrimp paste is to be fried with other spices, this preliminary cooking can be eliminated.

Energy 48kcal/203kJ; Protein 3.2g; Carbohydrate 8.6g, of which sugars 8.5g; Fat 0.3g, of which saturates 0g; Cholesterol 25mg; Calcium 77mg; Fibre 1.1g; Sodium 219mg.

SEAWEED AND RADISH SALAD ★★

HIJIKI IS A MILD-TASTING SEAWEED AND, COMBINED WITH RADISHES, CUCUMBER AND BEANSPROUTS, IT MAKES A REFRESHING SALAD THAT IS THE PERFECT ACCOMPANIMENT TO A RICH MAIN DISH.

SERVES 4

INGREDIENTS
  15g/½oz/½ cup hijiki seaweed
  250g/9oz/1¼ cups radishes, sliced
    into very thin rounds
  1 small cucumber, cut into
    thin sticks
  75g/3oz/1½ cups beansprouts
For the dressing
  15ml/1 tbsp sunflower oil
  15ml/1 tbsp toasted sesame oil
  5ml/1 tsp light soy sauce
  30ml/2 tbsp rice vinegar or 15ml/
    1 tbsp wine vinegar
  15ml/1 tbsp mirin

1 Soak the hijiki in a bowl of cold water for 10–15 minutes until it is rehydrated, then drain, rinse under cold running water and drain again. It should almost triple in volume.

2 Place the hijiki in a pan of water. Bring the water to the boil, then reduce the heat and simmer the hijiki for about 30 minutes or until tender.

COOK'S TIP
Hijiki is a type of seaweed that is popular in Japan. It resembles wakame and is generally sold dried and finely shredded. It is available in many supermarkets and Asian stores.

3 Meanwhile, make the dressing. Whisk the oils with the vinegar and mirin in a bowl until combined, and then whisk in the soy sauce.

4 Drain the cooked hijiki in a sieve (strainer) and arrange it in a shallow bowl or platter with the prepared radishes, cucumber and beansprouts. Pour over the dressing and toss lightly to combine.

Energy 68kcal/280kJ; Protein 1.4g; Carbohydrate 2.8g, of which sugars 2.4g; Fat 5.8g, of which saturates 0.8g; Cholesterol 0mg; Calcium 23mg; Fibre 1.1g; Sodium 276mg.

ASSORTED SEAWEED SALAD ★

SEAWEED IS A NUTRITIOUS, ALKALINE FOOD WHICH IS RICH IN FIBRE. ITS UNUSUAL FLAVOURS ARE A GREAT COMPLEMENT TO FISH AND TOFU DISHES. THIS SALAD IS EXTREMELY LOW IN FAT.

SERVES 4

INGREDIENTS

5g/⅛oz each dried wakame, dried
  arame and dried hijiki seaweeds
about 130g/4½oz fresh
  enokitake mushrooms
15ml/1 tbsp rice vinegar
6.5ml/1¼ tsp salt
2 spring onions (scallions)
a few ice cubes
½ cucumber, cut lengthways
250g/9oz mixed salad leaves

For the dressing

60ml/4 tbsp rice vinegar
7.5ml/1½ tsp toasted sesame oil
15ml/1 tbsp shoyu
15ml/1 tbsp water with a pinch
  of instant dashi powder
2.5cm/1in piece fresh root ginger,
  finely grated

1 Soak the dried wakame seaweed for 10 minutes in one bowl of water and, in a separate bowl of water, soak the dried arame and hijiki seaweeds together for 30 minutes.

2 Trim the hard end of the enokitake mushroom stalks, then cut the bunch in half and separate the stems.

3 Cook the wakame and enokitake in boiling water for 2 minutes, then add the arame and hijiki for a few seconds. Immediately remove from the heat.

4 Drain in a sieve (strainer) and sprinkle over the vinegar and salt while still warm. Chill until needed.

5 Slice the spring onions into thin, 4cm/1½in long strips, then soak the strips in a bowl of cold water with a few ice cubes added to make them curl up. Drain. Slice the cucumber into thin, half-moon shapes.

6 Mix the dressing ingredients in a bowl. Arrange the mixed salad leaves in a large bowl with the cucumber on top, then add the seaweed and enokitake mixture. Decorate the salad with spring onion curls and serve with the dressing.

Energy 26kcal/107kJ; Protein 1.5g; Carbohydrate 2.2g, of which sugars 2g; Fat 1.3g, of which saturates 0.2g; Cholesterol 0mg; Calcium 28mg; Fibre 1.2g; Sodium 272mg.

POMELO AND CRAB SALAD ★

TYPICALLY, A THAI MEAL INCLUDES A SELECTION OF ABOUT FIVE DISHES, ONE OF WHICH IS
TRADITIONALLY A REFRESHING AND PALATE-CLEANSING SALAD THAT FEATURES TROPICAL FRUIT.

SERVES 6

INGREDIENTS

    15ml/1 tbsp sunflower oil
    4 shallots, finely sliced
    2 garlic cloves, finely sliced
    1 large pomelo
    15ml/1 tbsp roasted peanuts
    115g/4oz cooked peeled
        prawns (shrimp)
    115g/4oz cooked crab meat
    10–12 small fresh mint leaves
For the dressing
    30ml/2 tbsp Thai fish sauce
    15ml/1 tbsp palm sugar or light
        muscovado (brown) sugar
    30ml/2 tbsp fresh lime juice
For the garnish
    2 spring onions (scallions),
        thinly sliced
    2 fresh red chillies, seeded and
        thinly sliced
    fresh coriander (cilantro) leaves
    shredded fresh coconut (optional)

1 Make the dressing. Mix the fish sauce, sugar and lime juice in a bowl. Whisk well, then cover with clear film (plastic wrap) and set aside.

2 Heat the oil in a small frying pan, add the shallots and garlic and cook over a medium heat until they are golden. Remove from the pan and set aside.

3 Peel the pomelo and break the flesh into small pieces, taking care to remove any membranes.

4 Grind the peanuts coarsely and put them in a salad bowl. Add the pomelo flesh, prawns, crab meat, mint leaves and the shallot mixture. Pour over the dressing, toss lightly and sprinkle with the spring onions, chillies and coriander leaves. Add the shredded coconut, if using. Serve immediately.

COOK'S TIP
The pomelo is a large citrus fruit that looks rather like a grapefruit, although it is not, as is sometimes thought, a hybrid. It is slightly pear-shaped with thick, yellow, dimpled skin and pinkish-yellow flesh that is both sturdier and drier than that of a grapefruit. It also has a sharper taste. Pomelos are sometimes known as "shaddocks" after the sea captain who brought them from their native Polynesia to the Caribbean.

Energy 71kcal/300kJ; Protein 8g; Carbohydrate 5.8g, of which sugars 5.4g; Fat 2g, of which saturates 0.3g; Cholesterol 51mg; Calcium 53mg; Fibre 0.8g; Sodium 144mg.

CRAB AND CUCUMBER VINEGAR SALAD ★

FOR THE DRESSING, TRY AND USE A JAPANESE OR GREEK CUCUMBER IF POSSIBLE — THEY ARE ABOUT ONE-THIRD OF THE SIZE OF ORDINARY SALAD CUCUMBERS AND CONTAIN LESS WATER.

SERVES 4

INGREDIENTS
  ½ red (bell) pepper, seeded
  pinch of salt
  275g/10oz cooked white crab meat,
    or 2 × 165g/5½oz canned white
    crab meat, drained
  about 300g/11oz Japanese or
    salad cucumber
For the vinegar mixture
  15ml/1 tbsp rice vinegar
  10ml/2 tsp caster (superfine) sugar
  10ml/2 tsp awakuchi shoyu

1 Slice the red pepper into thin strips lengthways. Sprinkle with a little salt and leave for about 15 minutes. Rinse well and drain.

2 For the vinegar mixture, combine the rice vinegar, sugar and awakuchi shoyu in a small bowl.

3 Loosen the crab meat with cooking chopsticks and mix it with the sliced red pepper in a mixing bowl. Divide among four small bowls.

4 If you use salad cucumber, scoop out the seeds. Finely grate the cucumber with a fine-toothed grater or use a food processor. Drain in a fine-meshed sieve.

5 Mix the cucumber with the vinegar mixture, and pour a quarter on to the crab meat mixture in each bowl. Serve cold immediately, before the cucumber loses its colour.

VARIATIONS
• The vinegar mixture is best made using awakuchi shoyu, but ordinary soy sauce can be used instead. It will make a darker dressing, however.
• This dressing can be made into a low-fat substitute for vinaigrette: reduce the sugar by half and add a few drops of oil.

Energy 82kcal/345kJ; Protein 13.3g; Carbohydrate 5.6g, of which sugars 5.4g; Fat 0.8g, of which saturates 0.1g; Cholesterol 50mg; Calcium 100mg; Fibre 0.9g; Sodium 560mg.

THAI PRAWN SALAD ᵂᴵᵀᴴ GARLIC DRESSING ᴬᴺᴰ FRIZZLED SHALLOTS ★

IN THIS INTENSELY FLAVOURED SALAD, FRESH PRAWNS AND A PERFECTLY RIPE MANGO ARE PARTNERED WITH A SWEET-AND-SOUR GARLIC DRESSING HEIGHTENED WITH THE HOT TASTE OF CHILLI. THE CRISP FRIZZLED SHALLOTS ARE A TRADITIONAL ADDITION TO THAI SALADS.

SERVES 6

INGREDIENTS

675g/1½lb medium raw prawns (shrimp), peeled and deveined, with tails intact
finely shredded rind of 1 lime
½ fresh red chilli, seeded and finely chopped
15ml/1 tbsp olive oil, plus extra for spraying
1 ripe but firm mango
2 carrots, cut into long thin shreds
10cm/4in piece cucumber, sliced
1 small red onion, halved and thinly sliced
a few fresh mint sprigs
a few fresh coriander (cilantro) sprigs
15ml/1 tbsp roasted peanuts, coarsely chopped
4 large shallots, thinly sliced and fried until crisp in 5ml/1 tsp sunflower oil
salt and ground black pepper

For the dressing
1 large garlic clove, chopped
10–15ml/2–3 tsp caster (superfine) sugar
juice of 2 limes
15–30ml/1–2 tbsp Thai fish sauce
1 fresh red chilli, seeded and finely chopped
5–10ml/1–2 tsp light rice vinegar

1 Place the prawns in a glass dish with the lime rind, chilli, oil and seasoning. Toss to mix and leave to marinate at room temperature for 30–40 minutes.

2 Make the dressing. Place the garlic in a mortar with 10ml/2 tsp of the caster sugar. Pound with a pestle until smooth, then work in about three-quarters of the lime juice, followed by 15ml/1 tbsp of the Thai fish sauce.

3 Transfer the dressing to a jug (pitcher). Stir in half the chopped red chilli. Taste the dressing and add more sugar, lime juice and/or fish sauce, if you think they are necessary, and stir in light rice vinegar to taste.

4 Peel and stone (pit) the mango. The best way to do this is to cut either side of the large central stone (pit), as close to it as possible, with a sharp knife. Cut the flesh into very fine strips and cut off any flesh still adhering to the stone.

5 Place the strips of mango in a bowl and add the carrots, cucumber slices and red onion. Pour over about half the dressing and toss thoroughly. Arrange the salad on four to six individual serving plates or in bowls.

6 Heat a ridged, cast-iron griddle pan or heavy frying pan until very hot. Spray with a little oil, then sear the marinated prawns for 2–3 minutes on each side, until they turn pink and are patched with brown on the outside. Arrange the prawns on the salads.

7 Sprinkle the remaining dressing over the salads and garnish with the mint and coriander sprigs. Sprinkle over the remaining chilli with the peanuts and crisp-fried shallots. Serve immediately.

COOK'S TIP
To devein the prawns (shrimp), make a shallow cut down the back of each prawn, using a small, sharp knife. Using the tip of the knife, lift out the thin, black vein, then rinse the prawn thoroughly under cold, running water, drain it and pat it dry with kitchen paper.

Energy 156kcal/656kJ; Protein 20.9g; Carbohydrate 8.9g, of which sugars 8.4g; Fat 4.3g, of which saturates 0.7g; Cholesterol 219mg; Calcium 102mg; Fibre 1.4g; Sodium 397mg.

SEAFOOD SALAD <u>WITH</u> FRAGRANT HERBS ★★

THIS IS A SPECTACULAR SALAD. THE LUSCIOUS COMBINATION OF PRAWNS, SCALLOPS AND SQUID, MAKES IT AN IMPRESSIVE CHOICE TO SERVE UP FOR A SPECIAL CELEBRATION.

SERVES 4–6

INGREDIENTS
- 250ml/8fl oz/1 cup fish stock or water
- 350g/12oz squid, cleaned and cut into rings
- 12 raw king prawns (jumbo shrimp), peeled, with tails intact
- 12 scallops
- 50g/2oz cellophane noodles, soaked in warm water for 30 minutes
- ½ cucumber, cut into thin batons
- 1 lemon grass stalk, finely chopped
- 2 kaffir lime leaves, finely shredded
- 2 shallots, thinly sliced
- 30ml/2 tbsp chopped spring onions (scallions)
- 30ml/2 tbsp fresh coriander (cilantro) leaves
- 12–15 fresh mint leaves, torn
- 4 fresh red chillies, seeded and cut into slivers
- juice of 1–2 limes
- 30ml/2 tbsp Thai fish sauce
- fresh coriander sprigs, to garnish

1 Pour the fish stock or water into a medium pan, set over a high heat and bring to the boil. Cook each type of seafood separately in the stock for 3–4 minutes. Remove with a slotted spoon and set aside to cool.

2 Drain the noodles. Using scissors, cut them into short lengths, about 5cm/2in long.

3 Place them in a serving bowl and add the cucumber, lemon grass, kaffir lime leaves, shallots, spring onions, coriander, mint and chillies.

4 Pour over the lime juice and fish sauce. Mix well, then add the seafood. Toss lightly. Garnish with the fresh coriander sprigs and serve.

Energy 339kcal/1420kJ; Protein 27.3g; Carbohydrate 42g, of which sugars 2.3g; Fat 6.8g, of which saturates 0.9g; Cholesterol 219mg; Calcium 148mg; Fibre 1.7g; Sodium 861mg.

CHICKEN AND SHREDDED CABBAGE SALAD ★

IN SOME SOUTH-EAST ASIAN HOUSEHOLDS, A WHOLE CHICKEN IS COOKED IN WATER WITH HERBS TO MAKE A BROTH. THE CHICKEN IS SHREDDED AND SOME IS USED IN A SALAD.

SERVES 6

INGREDIENTS
  450g/1lb chicken, cooked and torn
  into thin strips
  1 white Chinese cabbage, trimmed
  and finely shredded
  2 carrots, finely shredded
  or grated
  a small bunch fresh mint, stalks
  removed, finely shredded
  1 small bunch fresh coriander
  (cilantro) leaves, to garnish
For the dressing
  15ml/1 tbsp sunflower oil
  30ml/2 tbsp white rice vinegar

45ml/3 tbsp fish sauce
juice of 2 limes
30ml/2 tbsp palm sugar
2 red Thai chillies, seeded and
  finely chopped
25g/1oz fresh young root
  ginger, sliced
3 garlic cloves, crushed
2 shallots, finely chopped

1 First make the dressing. In a bowl, beat the oil, vinegar, fish sauce, and lime juice with the sugar, until it has dissolved. Stir in the other ingredients and leave to stand for about 30 minutes to let the flavours mingle.

2 Put the cooked chicken strips, cabbage, carrots and mint in a large bowl. Pour over the dressing and toss well. Garnish with coriander leaves and serve.

Energy 170kcal/715kJ; Protein 20.4g; Carbohydrate 15.8g, of which sugars 13.7g; Fat 3.1g, of which saturates 0.5g; Cholesterol 53mg; Calcium 94mg; Fibre 3.2g; Sodium 60mg.

COLD
DESSERTS

Although desserts have never been central to culinary tradition

in South-east Asia, there are some tasty morsels to be had.

Iced Fruit Mountain, for instance, consists simply of a wide

variety of fresh fruits tumbling over a sculpted sierra of

crushed ice. Flavoured ices are said to have originated in

China, and dishes such as Lychee and Elderflower Sorbet,

Ginger Granita and Orange Sorbet are excellent for

cleansing the palate.

WATERMELON ICE ★

AFTER A HOT AND SPICY THAI MEAL, THE ONLY THING MORE REFRESHING THAN ICE-COLD WATERMELON IS THIS WATERMELON ICE. MAKING IT IS SIMPLICITY ITSELF.

3 Spoon the watermelon into a food processor. Process to a slush, then mix with the sugar syrup. Chill the mixture in the refrigerator for 3–4 hours.

4 Strain the mixture into a freezerproof container. Freeze for 2 hours, then remove from the freezer and beat with a fork to break up the ice crystals. Return the mixture to the freezer and freeze for 3 hours more, beating the mixture at half-hourly intervals. Freeze until firm.

5 Alternatively, use an ice-cream maker. Pour the chilled mixture into the machine and churn until it is firm enough to scoop. Serve immediately, or scrape into a freezerproof container and store in the freezer.

6 About 30 minutes before serving, transfer the ice to the refrigerator so that it softens slightly. This allows the full flavour of the watermelon to be enjoyed and makes it easier to scoop.

SERVES 4–6

INGREDIENTS
90ml/6 tbsp caster
(superfine) sugar
105ml/7 tbsp water
4 kaffir lime leaves, torn into
small pieces
500g/1¼lb watermelon

1 Put the sugar, water and lime leaves in a pan. Heat gently until the sugar has dissolved. Pour into a large bowl and set aside to cool.

2 Cut the watermelon into wedges with a large knife. Cut the flesh from the rind, remove the seeds and chop.

Energy 62kcal/263kJ; Protein 0.1g; Carbohydrate 16.3g, of which sugars 16.3g; Fat 0g, of which saturates 0g; Cholesterol 0mg; Calcium 9mg; Fibre 0g; Sodium 1mg.

LYCHEE AND ELDERFLOWER SORBET ★

THE FLAVOUR OF ELDERFLOWERS IS FAMOUS FOR BRINGING OUT THE ESSENCE OF GOOSEBERRIES, BUT WHAT IS LESS WELL KNOWN IS HOW WONDERFULLY IT COMPLEMENTS LYCHEES.

SERVES 4

INGREDIENTS
175g/6oz/¾ cup caster
    (superfine) sugar
400ml/14fl oz/1⅔ cups water
500g/1¼lb fresh lychees, peeled
    and stoned (pitted)
15ml/1 tbsp elderflower cordial
    or lime syrup
dessert biscuits (cookies),
    to serve (optional)

COOK'S TIP
For the best result, switch the freezer
to the coldest setting before making the
sorbet – the faster the mixture freezes,
the smaller the ice crystals that form,
and the better the final texture of the
sorbet will be.

1 Place the sugar and water in a pan
and heat gently until the sugar has
dissolved, stirring several times.
Increase the heat and boil for 5 minutes.

2 Add the lychees. Lower the heat and
simmer for 7 minutes. Remove from the
heat and pour into a jug (pitcher) or
bowl. Set aside until cool.

3 Purée the fruit and syrup in a
blender or food processor. Place a sieve
(strainer) over a bowl and pour the
purée into it. Press through as much
of the purée as possible with a spoon.

4 Stir the elderflower cordial or lime
syrup into the strained purée, then
pour the mixture into a freezerproof
container. Freeze for 2 hours, until ice
crystals start to form around the edges.

5 Remove the sorbet from the freezer
and process briefly in a food processor
or blender to break up the crystals.
Repeat this twice more, then freeze
until firm. Transfer to the refrigerator
for 10 minutes to soften slightly before
serving in scoops, with dessert biscuits,
if you like.

Energy 249kcal/1064kJ; Protein 1.4g; Carbohydrate 64.7g, of which sugars 64.7g; Fat 0.1g, of which saturates 0g; Cholesterol 0mg; Calcium 31mg; Fibre 0.9g; Sodium 4mg.

COCONUT ICE CREAM ★

ICE CREAM MADE WITH COCONUT MILK AND CONDENSED MILK CAN BE VERY HIGH IN FAT, BUT IN
THIS SPECIALLY ADAPTED LOW-FAT, LOW-CHOLESTEROL RECIPE, REDUCED-FAT VERSIONS ARE USED
TO MAKE THIS DELECTABLE DISH SUITABLE FOR ANYONE FOLLOWING A LOW-CHOLESTEROL DIET.

2 Pour the mixture into the frozen freezer bowl of an ice-cream maker (or follow the appliance instructions) and churn till the mixture has thickened. (This will take 30–40 minutes.)

3 Transfer the mixture to a lidded plastic tub, cover and freeze until the consistency is right for scooping. If you do not have an ice-cream maker, pour the mixture into a shallow container and freeze on the coldest setting.

4 When ice crystals form around the sides of the ice cream, beat the mixture, then return it to the freezer. Do this at least twice. The more you do it, the creamier the mixture will be.

5 Make the sauce. Mix the sugar, measured water and ginger in a pan. Stir over medium heat until the sugar has dissolved, then bring the liquid to the boil. Add the pandan leaf, if using, tying it into a knot so that it can easily be removed with the ginger before serving. Lower the heat and simmer for 3–4 minutes. Set aside till required.

6 Serve the ice cream in coconut shells or in a bowl. Sprinkle with the strips of coconut and serve with the gula melaka sauce, which can be hot, warm or cold.

SERVES 6

INGREDIENTS
    400ml/14fl oz can reduced-fat
      coconut milk
    400ml/14fl oz can reduced-fat
      condensed milk
    2.5ml/¹/₂ tsp salt
For the sauce
    150g/5oz/³/₄ cup palm sugar or
      muscovado (molasses) sugar
    150ml/¹/₄ pint/²/₃ cup water
    1cm/¹/₂in slice fresh root
      ginger, bruised
    1 pandan leaf (if available)
    coconut shells (optional) and thinly
      pared strips of coconut, to serve

1 Chill the cans of coconut and condensed milk very thoroughly. In a bowl, mix the coconut milk with the condensed milk. Gently whisk together with the salt.

COOK'S TIP
Coconut milk takes longer to freeze than double (heavy) cream, so allow plenty of time for the process.

Energy 291kcal/1242kJ; Protein 7g; Carbohydrate 69.4g, of which sugars 69.4g; Fat 0.3g, of which saturates 0.2g; Cholesterol 1mg; Calcium 253mg; Fibre 0g; Sodium 175mg

COCONUT SORBET ★★

DELICIOUSLY REFRESHING AND COOLING, THIS TROPICAL SORBET CAN BE FOUND IN DIFFERENT VERSIONS ALL OVER SOUTH-EAST ASIA. OTHER CLASSIC SORBETS ARE TRADITIONALLY FLAVOURED WITH LYCHEES, PINEAPPLE, MANGOES, WATERMELON, LEMON GRASS AND RED BEANS.

SERVES 6

INGREDIENTS

175g/6oz/scant 1 cup caster
  (superfine) sugar
120ml/4fl oz/½ cup reduced-fat
  coconut milk
50g/2oz/⅔ cup grated or desiccated
  (dry unsweetened shredded) coconut
a squeeze of lime juice

1 Place the sugar in a heavy pan and add 200ml/7fl oz/scant 1 cup water. Bring to the boil, stirring constantly, until the sugar has dissolved completely. Reduce the heat and simmer for 5 minutes to make a light syrup.

2 Stir the coconut milk into the sugar syrup, along with most of the coconut and the lime juice. Pour the mixture into a bowl or freezer container and freeze for 1 hour.

3 Take the sorbet out of the freezer and beat it with a fork, or blend it in a food processor, until it is smooth and creamy, then return it to the freezer and leave for 30 minutes.

4 Remove the sorbet from the freezer again and beat it with a fork, or blend it in a food processor, until it is smooth and creamy. Then return it to the freezer and leave until completely frozen.

5 Before serving, allow the sorbet to stand at room temperature for 10–15 minutes to soften slightly. Serve in small bowls and decorate with the remaining grated coconut.

COOK'S TIP
This refreshing sorbet is very welcome on a hot day, or as a palate refresher during a spicy meal. You could serve it in coconut shells, garnished with sprigs of fresh mint.

Energy 170kcal/717kJ; Protein 0.7g; Carbohydrate 32g, of which sugars 32g; Fat 5.2g, of which saturates 4.5g; Cholesterol 0mg; Calcium 23mg; Fibre 1.1g; Sodium 26mg.

GINGER GRANITA ★

THIS FULL-BODIED GRANITA IS A MUST FOR GINGER LOVERS. SERVED SOLO, IT IS A SIMPLE AND INEXPENSIVE DESSERT, YET IS SMART ENOUGH TO SERVE TO THE MOST SOPHISTICATED GUESTS.

SERVES 6

INGREDIENTS
  150g/5oz/¾ cup caster
    (superfine) sugar
  1 litre/1¾ pints/4 cups water
  75g/3oz fresh root ginger
  a little ground cinnamon, to decorate

1 Bring the sugar and water to the boil in a pan, stirring until all the sugar has dissolved. Take the pan off the heat.

VARIATION
For a stronger ginger flavour, use lemon and ginger tea. Make up 1 litre/1¾ pints/4 cups of the tea and boil it with the sugar before adding the chopped ginger. Cool completely before chilling.

2 Peel the ginger, chop it finely, then stir it into the hot sugar syrup. Leave for at least 1 hour to infuse (steep) and cool, then pour into a bowl and chill.

3 Strain the chilled syrup into a large, shallow plastic container, making sure the depth is no more than 2.5cm/1in.

4 Cover and freeze for 2 hours or until the mixture around the sides of the container has become mushy.

5 Using a fork, break up the ice crystals and mash finely. Return the granita to the freezer for 2 hours more, beating every 30 minutes until the ice becomes soft and very fine with even size ice crystals.

6 After the final beating, return the now slushy granita to the freezer. Serve in tall glasses decorated with ground cinnamon.

COOK'S TIP
Make sure you buy very fresh, young root ginger for this dessert. Look for firm pieces with smooth skin.

RUBY GRAPEFRUIT GRANITA ★

THIS IS SHARPER THAN SOME OTHER GRANITAS, BUT IS VERY REFRESHING. IT LOOKS STUNNING IF YOU SERVE IT IN THE EMPTY GRAPEFRUIT SHELLS, WITH A FEW GRAPEFRUIT SEGMENTS ON THE SIDE.

SERVES 6

INGREDIENTS
  200g/7oz/1 cup caster
    (superfine) sugar
  300ml/½ pint/1¼ cups water
  4 ruby grapefruit
  tiny mint leaves, to decorate

1 Put the sugar and water into a pan. Bring the water to the boil, stirring until the sugar has dissolved. Pour the syrup into a bowl. Leave to cool, then chill.

2 Cut the grapefruit in half. Squeeze the juice, taking care not to damage the grapefruit shells. Set these aside.

3 Strain the juice into a large plastic container. Stir in the chilled syrup, making sure that the depth of the mixture does not exceed 2.5cm/1in.

4 Cover and freeze for 2 hours or until the mixture around the sides of the container is mushy.

5 Using a fork, break up the ice crystals and mash the granita finely.

6 Freeze for 2 hours more, mashing the mixture every 30 minutes until the grapefruit granita consists of fine, even crystals.

7 Select the six best grapefruit shells for use as the serving dishes. Using a sharp knife, remove the grapefruit pulp, leaving the shells as clean as possible on the inside.

8 Scoop the sorbet into the grapefruit shells, decorate with the tiny mint leaves and serve immediately.

COOK'S TIP
Grapefruit shells make very good, eye-catching serving dishes. For a more modern treatment, consider the effect you would like to achieve when halving the grapefruit. They look great when tilted at an angle, or with a zig-zag pattern around the edge. Having squeezed the juice and removed the membrane, trim a little off the base of each shell so that it will remain stable when filled with granita.

Top : Energy 99kcal/420kJ; Protein 0.1g; Carbohydrate 26.1g, of which sugars 26.1g; Fat 0g, of which saturates 0g; Cholesterol 0mg; Calcium 13mg; Fibre 0g; Sodium 2mg.
Bottom: Energy 163kcal/695kJ; Protein 1g; Carbohydrate 42.1g, of which sugars 42.1g; Fat 0.1g, of which saturates 0g; Cholesterol 0mg; Calcium 42mg; Fibre 1.4g; Sodium 5mg.

LEMON SORBET ★

REFRESHINGLY TANGY AND YET DELICIOUSLY SMOOTH, THIS FAT-FREE SORBET QUITE LITERALLY MELTS IN THE MOUTH, AND IS THE PERFECT DESSERT FOR SERVING AFTER A SPICY STIR-FRY.

SERVES 6

INGREDIENTS
    200g/7oz/1 cup caster
      (superfine) sugar
    300ml/½ pint/1¼ cups water
    4 lemons, well scrubbed
    1 egg white
    sugared lemon rind, to decorate

1 Put the sugar and water into a medium pan and bring to the boil, stirring occasionally until the sugar has just dissolved.

2 Using a swivel vegetable peeler pare the rind thinly from two of the lemons so that it falls straight into the pan.

3 Simmer for 2 minutes without stirring, then take the pan off the heat. Leave to cool, then chill.

4 Squeeze the juice from all the lemons and add it to the syrup. Strain the syrup into a shallow freezerproof container, reserving the rind. Freeze the mixture for 4 hours until it is mushy and ice crystals have begun to form around the edges of the mixture.

5 Scoop the sorbet into a food processor and beat until smooth. Lightly whisk the egg white until just frothy. Spoon the sorbet back into the tub, beat in the egg white and return to the freezer for 4 hours. Before serving, transfer the sorbet to the refrigerator for 10 minutes to soften slightly.

6 Scoop into bowls or glasses and decorate with sugared lemon rind.

COOK'S TIP
Cut one third off the top of a lemon and retain as a lid. Squeeze the juice out of the larger portion. Remove any membrane and use the shell as a container. Scoop or pipe sorbet into the shell, top with the lid.

Energy 134kcal/571kJ; Protein 0.7g; Carbohydrate 35g, of which sugars 35g; Fat 0g, of which saturates 0g; Cholesterol 0mg; Calcium 19mg; Fibre 0g; Sodium 12mg.

ORANGE SORBET ★

THE ULTIMATE LOW-FAT TREAT — THESE DELECTABLE ORANGE SORBETS SERVED IN FRUIT SHELLS ARE
FUN TO SERVE AND EASY TO EAT. KEEP SOME IN THE FREEZER FOR IMPROMPTU DESSERTS.

SERVES 8

INGREDIENTS
   150g/5oz/⅔ cup sugar
   juice of 1 lemon
   14 medium oranges
   8 fresh bay leaves, to decorate

1 Put the sugar in a heavy pan. Add half the lemon juice, then add 120ml/ 4fl oz/½ cup water. Heat until the sugar has dissolved, stirring occasionally. Bring to the boil and boil for 2–3 minutes until the syrup is clear.

2 Slice the tops off eight of the oranges to make lids. Scoop out the flesh of the oranges and reserve.

3 Freeze the empty shells and lids until needed. Grate the rind of the remaining oranges and add to the syrup.

4 Squeeze the juice from the oranges, and from the reserved flesh. There should be 750ml/1¼ pints/3 cups.

5 Squeeze another orange or add bought orange juice, if necessary, to make up the volume.

6 Stir the orange juice and remaining lemon juice into the syrup, then add 90ml/6 tbsp cold water.

7 Taste, and add more lemon juice or sugar if you think the mixture needs it, bearing in mind that freezing will dull the taste a little.

8 Pour the mixture into a shallow freezer container and freeze for 3 hours.

9 Turn the orange sorbet mixture into a bowl and whisk thoroughly to break up the ice crystals. Freeze for 4 hours more, until firm, but not solid.

10 Pack the mixture into the hollowed-out orange shells, mounding it up, and set the lids on top. Freeze until ready to serve. Just before serving, push a skewer into the tops of the lids and push in a bay leaf, to decorate.

Energy 152kcal/647kJ; Protein 2.4g; Carbohydrate 37.5g, of which sugars 37.5g; Fat 0.2g, of which saturates 0g; Cholesterol 0mg; Calcium 109mg; Fibre 3.6g; Sodium 12mg.

MANDARINS IN SYRUP ★

MANDARINS, TANGERINES, CLEMENTINES, MINEOLAS; ANY OF THESE LOVELY CITRUS FRUITS ARE
SUITABLE FOR THIS RECIPE, WHICH IS BOTH FAT FREE AND VERY LOW IN ADDED SUGAR.

2 Peel the remaining fruit, removing as much of the white pith as possible. Arrange the peeled fruit whole in a wide dish or bowl.

3 Mix the mandarin juice, sugar and orange flower water and pour it over the fruit. Cover the dish and chill in the refrigerator for at least 1 hour.

4 Bring a small pan of water to the boil. Add the shreds of mandarin rind and blanch them for 30 seconds. Drain and set aside.

5 When the shreds of rind are cold, sprinkle them over the mandarins, with the pistachio nuts. Serve in chilled dessert bowls.

SERVES 4

INGREDIENTS
   10 mandarin oranges
   15ml/1 tbsp icing
    (confectioners') sugar
   10ml/2 tsp orange flower water
   15ml/1 tbsp chopped
    pistachio nuts

1 Thinly pare a little of the rind from one mandarin and use a small, sharp knife to cut it into fine shreds for decoration. Squeeze the juice from two mandarins and set aside.

COOK'S TIP
Mandarin oranges look very attractive if you leave them whole, but you may prefer to separate the segments.

Energy 121kcal/512kJ; Protein 3.2g; Carbohydrate 23.4g, of which sugars 23.3g; Fat 2.3g, of which saturates 0.3g; Cholesterol 0mg; Calcium 112mg; Fibre 4.1g; Sodium 31mg.

RAINBOW DRINK ★

THIS DRINK IS A REAL TREAT. TWO KINDS OF SWEETENED BEANS ARE COLOURFULLY LAYERED WITH CRUSHED ICE, DRENCHED IN COCONUT MILK AND TOPPED WITH JELLIED AGAR AGAR.

SERVES 4

INGREDIENTS
  50g/2oz dried split mung beans,
    soaked for 4 hours and drained
  50g/2oz red azuki beans, soaked
    for 4 hours and drained
  25g/1oz/2 tbsp sugar
For the syrup
  300ml/½ pint/1¼ cups
    coconut milk
  50g/2oz/¼ cup sugar
  25g/1oz tapioca pearls
  crushed ice, to serve
  15g/½oz jellied agar agar, soaked
    in warm water for 30 minutes
    and shredded into long strands,
    to decorate

2 In a heavy pan, bring the coconut milk to the boil. Reduce the heat and stir in the sugar, until it dissolves. Add the tapioca pearls and simmer for about 10 minutes, until they become transparent. Leave to cool and chill in the refrigerator.

3 Divide the beans among four tall glasses, add a layer of crushed ice, then the azuki beans and more ice. Pour the coconut syrup over the top and decorate with strands of agar agar. Serve immediately with straws and long spoons.

1 Put the mung beans and azuki beans into two separate pans with 15g/l/½oz/ 1 tbsp sugar each. Pour in enough water to cover and, stirring all the time, bring it to the boil. Reduce the heat and leave both pans to simmer for about 15 minutes, stirring from time to time, until the beans are tender but not mushy – you may have to add more water. Drain the beans, leave to cool and chill separately in the refrigerator.

COOK'S TIP
Many variations of rainbow drinks are served throughout South-east Asia, some combining ingredients such as lotus seeds, taro, sweet potato, and tapioca pearls with exotic fruits. Served in tall, clear glasses in the markets, restaurants and bars, they are popular in both Vietnam and Cambodia.

Energy 188kcal/800kJ; Protein 6g; Carbohydrate 42g, of which sugars 25g; Fat 0.5g, of which saturates 0.2g; Cholesterol 0mg; Calcium 55mg; Fibre 2.5g; Sodium 87mg.

ICED FRUIT MOUNTAIN ★

WITH ONLY THE MEREST TRACE OF FAT, THIS IS ONE MOUNTAIN YOU CAN CONQUER WITHOUT WORRYING ABOUT THE CONSEQUENCES. IT MAKES A STUNNING CENTREPIECE FOR A SPECIAL MEAL.

SERVES 6–8

INGREDIENTS
1 star fruit (carambola)
4 kumquats
6 physalis
225g/8oz seedless black grapes
1 apple and/or 1 Asian pear
2 large oranges, peeled
8 fresh lychees, peeled (optional)
1 Charentais melon and/or
½ watermelon
225g/8oz large strawberries
caster (superfine) sugar, for dipping
wedges of lime, to decorate

COOK'S TIP
This list of fruits is just a suggestion. Use any colourful seasonal fruits you like.

1 Slice the star fruit and halve the kumquats. Do not remove the hulls from the strawberries. Cut the apple and/or Asian pear into wedges, and the oranges into segments. Use a melon baller for the melon or, alternatively, cut the melon into neat wedges. Chill all the fruit.

2 Prepare the ice cube "mountain". Choose a wide, shallow bowl that, when turned upside down, will fit neatly on a serving platter. Fill the bowl with crushed ice cubes. Put it in the freezer, with the serving platter. Leave in the freezer for at least 1 hour.

3 Remove the serving platter, ice cubes and bowl from the freezer. Invert the serving platter on top of the bowl of ice, then turn platter and bowl over. Lift off the bowl and arrange the pieces of fruit on the mountain.

4 Decorate the mountain with the lime wedges, and serve the fruit immediately, handing round a bowl of caster sugar separately for guests with a sweet tooth.

Energy 56kcal/239kJ; Protein 1.1g; Carbohydrate 13.4g, of which sugars 13.4g; Fat 0.2g, of which saturates 0g; Cholesterol 0mg; Calcium 35mg; Fibre 1.7g; Sodium 17mg.

EXOTIC FRUIT SALAD WITH PASSION FRUIT ★

PASSION FRUIT MAKES A SUPERB DRESSING FOR ANY FRUIT, BUT REALLY BRINGS OUT THE FLAVOUR OF EXOTIC VARIETIES. YOU CAN EASILY DOUBLE THE RECIPE, THEN SERVE THE REST FOR BREAKFAST.

SERVES 6

INGREDIENTS
    1 mango
    1 papaya
    2 kiwi fruit
    reduced-fat coconut or vanilla ice
       cream, to serve
For the dressing
    3 passion fruit
    thinly pared rind and juice of 1 lime
    5ml/1 tsp hazelnut or walnut oil
    15ml/1 tbsp clear honey

COOK'S TIP
Clear honey scented with orange blossom
would be perfect for the dressing.

1 Peel the mango, cut it into three slices, then cut the flesh into chunks and place it in a large bowl. Peel the papaya and cut it in half. Scoop out the seeds, then chop the flesh.

2 Cut both ends off each kiwi fruit, then stand them on a board. Using a small sharp knife, cut off the skin from top to bottom. Cut each kiwi fruit in half lengthways, then cut into thick slices. Combine all the fruit in a large bowl.

3 Make the dressing. Cut each passion fruit in half and scoop the seeds out into a sieve set over a small bowl. Press the seeds well to extract all their juices. Lightly whisk the remaining dressing ingredients into the passion fruit juice, then pour the dressing over the fruit. Mix gently to combine. Leave to chill for 1 hour before serving with scoops of coconut or vanilla ice cream.

Energy 66kcal/278kJ; Protein 1g; Carbohydrate 14.6g, of which sugars 14.5g; Fat 0.8g, of which saturates 0.1g; Cholesterol 0mg; Calcium 26mg; Fibre 2.9g; Sodium 7mg.

MANGO PUDDINGS ★

LIGHT AND SOPHISTICATED, THESE JELLIED MANGO PUDDINGS MAKE DELIGHTFUL DESSERTS. SERVED WITH A SELECTION OF TROPICAL FRUITS, THEY ADD A REFRESHING TOUCH TO THE END OF A MEAL.

SERVES 4

INGREDIENTS
750ml/1¼ pints/3 cups coconut milk
150g/5oz/¾ cup sugar
15ml/1 tbsp powdered gelatine
(gelatin)
1 egg yolk
1 large, ripe mango, stoned (pitted)
and puréed
4 slices ripe jackfruit or pineapple,
quartered
1 banana, cut into diagonal slices
1 kiwi fruit, sliced
4 lychees, peeled
2 passion fruit, split open, to
decorate

1 In a heavy pan, heat the coconut milk with the sugar, stirring all the time, until it has dissolved.

2 Add the gelatine and keep stirring until dissolved. Remove from the heat.

3 Beat the egg yolk with the mango purée. Add the purée to the coconut milk and stir until smooth. Spoon the mixture into individual, lightly oiled moulds and leave to cool. Place them in the refrigerator for 2–3 hours, until set.

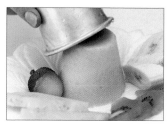

4 To serve, arrange the fruit on individual plates, leaving enough room for the jellies. Dip the base of each mould briefly into hot water, and then invert the puddings on to the plates. Lift off the moulds and decorate with passion fruit seeds.

VARIATION
The tangy fruitiness of mango is particularly delicious in these jellied puddings, but you could substitute papaya, banana, durian or avocado.

Energy 305kcal/1300kJ; Protein 2.9g; Carbohydrate 72.6g, of which sugars 72g; Fat 2.4g, of which saturates 0.8g; Cholesterol 50mg; Calcium 109mg; Fibre 3g; Sodium 216mg.

JUNGLE FRUITS IN LEMON GRASS SYRUP ★

THIS EXOTIC AND REFRESHING FRUIT SALAD CAN BE MADE WITH ANY COMBINATION OF TROPICAL FRUITS — JUST GO FOR A GOOD BALANCE OF COLOUR, FLAVOUR AND TEXTURE.

SERVES 6

INGREDIENTS
    1 firm papaya
    1 small pineapple
    2 small star fruit (carambola), sliced
        into stars
    12 fresh lychees, peeled and stoned
        (pitted) or 14oz/400g can lychees
    2 firm yellow or green bananas, peeled
        and cut diagonally into slices
    mint leaves, to decorate
For the syrup
    115g/4oz/generous ½ cup caster
        (superfine) sugar
    2 lemon grass stalks, bruised and
        halved lengthways

1 To make the syrup, put 225ml/
7½ fl oz/1 cup water into a heavy pan
with the sugar and lemon grass stalks.
Bring to the boil, stirring constantly until
the sugar has dissolved, then reduce
the heat and simmer for 15 minutes.
Leave to cool.

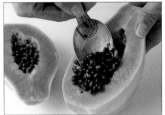

2 Peel and halve the papaya, remove
the seeds and slice the flesh crossways.
Peel the pineapple and slice it into
rounds. Remove the core and cut each
round in half. (Keep the core and slice
it for a stir-fry.)

3 Put all the fruit into a bowl. Pour the
syrup, including the lemon grass stalks,
over the top and toss to combine. Cover
and chill for 6 hours, or overnight.
Before serving, remove the lemon grass
stalks and decorate with mint leaves.

Energy 174kcal/742kJ; Protein 1.3g; Carbohydrate 44.2g, of which sugars 43.4g; Fat 0.3g, of which saturates 0g; Cholesterol 0mg; Calcium 38mg; Fibre 2.7g; Sodium 6mg.

CLEMENTINES IN SPICED SYRUP ★

STAR ANISE IS A VERY USEFUL SPICE. NOT ONLY DOES IT ADD A DELICATE AND AROMATIC FLAVOUR,
BUT IT ALSO MAKES AN ATTRACTIVE DECORATION, ESPECIALLY WITH CITRUS FRUITS.

SERVES 6

INGREDIENTS
350ml/12fl oz/1½ cups sweet
   dessert wine
75g/3oz/6 tbsp caster
   (superfine) sugar
6 star anise
1 cinnamon stick
1 vanilla pod (bean)
30ml/2 tbsp Cointreau or another
   orange liqueur, such as Grand
   Marnier or Van der Hum
1 strip of thinly pared lime rind
12 clementines

1 Put the wine, sugar, star anise and cinnamon in a large pan. Split the vanilla pod and add it to the pan with the lime rind.

2 Bring to the boil, lower the heat and simmer for 10 minutes.

3 Pour the spiced vanilla syrup into a bowl and set aside to cool. When it is completely cold, stir in the Cointreau.

VARIATION
Tangerines or oranges can be used instead of clementines, if you prefer.

4 Peel the clementines. Leave some clementines whole and cut the rest in half. Arrange them in a glass dish. Pour over the spicy syrup and chill overnight.

Energy 143kcal/605kJ; Protein 0.9g; Carbohydrate 23.5g, of which sugars 23.5g; Fat 0.1g, of which saturates 0g; Cholesterol 0mg; Calcium 40mg; Fibre 1g; Sodium 12mg.

PAPAYAS <u>IN</u> JASMINE FLOWER SYRUP ★

THE FRAGRANT SYRUP CAN BE PREPARED IN ADVANCE, USING FRESH JASMINE FLOWERS FROM A HOUSE PLANT OR THE GARDEN. TRY IT WITH ICE CREAM OR SPOONED OVER LYCHEES OR MANGOES.

SERVES 2

INGREDIENTS
105ml/7 tbsp water
45ml/3 tbsp palm sugar or light
  muscovado (brown) sugar
20–30 jasmine flowers, plus a
  few extra flowers, to decorate
  (optional)
2 ripe papayas
juice of 1 lime

COOK'S TIP
Although scented white jasmine flowers are perfectly safe to eat, it is important to make certain that the flowers have not been sprayed with pesticides or any other harmful chemicals. Washing the flowers will not necessarily remove all the residue.

1 Place the water and sugar in a small pan. Heat gently, stirring occasionally, until the sugar has dissolved, then simmer, without stirring, over a low heat for 4 minutes.

2 Pour into a bowl, leave to cool slightly, then add the jasmine flowers. Leave to steep for at least 20 minutes.

3 Peel the papayas and slice in half lengthways. Scoop out and discard the seeds. Place the papayas on serving plates and squeeze over the lime.

4 Strain the syrup into a clean bowl, discarding the flowers. Spoon the syrup over the papayas. If you like, decorate with a few fresh jasmine flowers.

Energy 197kcal/837kJ; Protein 1.6g; Carbohydrate 49.9g, of which sugars 49.9g; Fat 0.3g, of which saturates 0g; Cholesterol 0mg; Calcium 81mg; Fibre 6.6g; Sodium 17mg.

CHINESE FRUIT SALAD ★

FOR AN UNUSUAL FRUIT SALAD WITH AN ORIENTAL FLAVOUR, TRY THIS MIXTURE OF FRUITS IN A TANGY LIME AND LYCHEE SYRUP, TOPPED WITH A LIGHT SPRINKLING OF TOASTED SESAME SEEDS.

SERVES 4

INGREDIENTS

- 115g/4oz/½ cup caster (superfine) sugar
- 300ml/½ pint/1¼ cups water
- thinly pared rind and juice of 1 lime
- 1 eating apple
- 400g/14oz can lychees in syrup
- 1 ripe mango, peeled, stoned (pitted) and sliced
- 1 star fruit (carambola), sliced (optional)
- 2 bananas
- 5ml/1 tsp sesame seeds, toasted

COOK'S TIP

Don't prepare the apples and bananas in advance or they will discolour.

1 Place the sugar in a pan with the water and the lime rind. Heat gently until the sugar dissolves, stirring several times, then increase the heat and bring the mixture to the boil. Boil gently for 7–8 minutes. Remove from the heat and pour the syrup into a jug (pitcher). Set aside to cool.

2 Core the apple, and slice it. Drain the lychees and reserve the juice. Pour the juice into the cooled lime syrup with the lime juice. Place all the prepared fruit in a bowl and pour over the syrup. Chill for about 1 hour. Just before serving, slice the banans into the bowl and sprinkle with toasted sesame seeds.

Energy 259kcal/1102kJ; Protein 2.5g; Carbohydrate 60.4g, of which sugars 59.4g; Fat 2.5g, of which saturates 0.4g; Cholesterol 0mg; Calcium 54mg; Fibre 2.7g; Sodium 5mg.

APPLES AND RASPBERRIES IN ROSE POUCHONG ★

THIS DELIGHTFULLY FRAGRANT AND QUICK-TO-PREPARE ASIAN DESSERT COUPLES THE SUBTLE FLAVOURS OF APPLES AND RASPBERRIES WITH AN INFUSION OF ROSE-SCENTED TEA.

SERVES 4

INGREDIENTS

 5ml/1 tsp rose pouchong tea
 5ml/1 tsp rose water (optional)
 50g/2oz/¼ cup sugar
 5ml/1 tsp lemon juice
 5 dessert apples
 175g/6oz/1½ cups
  fresh raspberries

1 Warm a large teapot. Add the rose pouchong tea and 900ml/1½ pints/3¾ cups of boiling water together with the rose water, if using. Allow to stand and infuse for 4 minutes.

2 Measure the sugar and the lemon juice into a stainless-steel pan. Pour the tea through a small sieve (strainer) into the pan, and stir to dissolve the sugar.

3 Peel the apples, then cut into quarters and core.

4 Add the apples to the pan of syrup. Return the pan to the heat and bring the syrup to simmering point. Cook the apples for about 5 minutes, until just tender.

5 Transfer the apples and syrup to a large metal tray and leave to cool to room temperature.

6 Pour the cooled apples and syrup into a bowl, add the raspberries and mix to combine. Spoon into individual dishes or bowls and serve immediately.

VARIATION

A fruit tea such as rosehip and hibiscus could be used instead of the rose pouchong, or try cranberry and raspberry to highlight the flavour of the berries.

Energy 90kcal/384kJ; Protein 0.9g; Carbohydrate 22.5g, of which sugars 22.5g; Fat 0.2g, of which saturates 0.1g; Cholesterol 0mg; Calcium 21mg; Fibre 2.4g; Sodium 4mg.

PEARS WITH GINGER AND STAR ANISE ★

PEARS POACHED IN SPICED WINE SYRUP BECOME TRANSLUCENT AND BEAUTIFULLY TENDER. THEY LOOK LOVELY SLICED AND PRESENTED ON A DESSERT PLATE AND COATED WITH THE REDUCED SYRUP.

SERVES 4

INGREDIENTS
    1 lemon
    75g/3oz/6 tbsp caster (superfine) sugar
    300ml/½ pint/1¼ cups white
        dessert wine
    5 star anise
    10 cloves
    600ml/1 pint/2½ cups cold water
    7.5cm/3in fresh root ginger
    6 slightly unripe pears
    25g/1oz/3 tbsp drained, preserved
        ginger in syrup, sliced
    whipped cream, to serve

1 Pare the lemon thinly and squeeze the juice. Place in a pan just large enough to hold the pears snugly in an upright position. Add the sugar, wine, star anise, cloves and water. Bruise the ginger and add it. Bring to the boil.

2 Meanwhile, peel the pears, leaving the stems intact. Immerse them in the wine mixture.

3 Return the wine mixture to the boil, lower the heat, cover and simmer for 15–20 minutes or until the pears are tender. Lift out the pears with a slotted spoon and place them in a heatproof dish. Boil the wine syrup rapidly until it is reduced by about half, then pour over the pears. Leave to cool, then chill.

4 Cut the pears into thick slices and arrange these on four serving plates. Remove the ginger and whole spices from the wine sauce, stir in the preserved ginger and spoon the sauce over the pears. Serve with cream.

Energy 235kcal/991kJ; Protein 0.9g; Carbohydrate 46.5g, of which sugars 46.5g; Fat 0.2g, of which saturates 0g; Cholesterol 0mg; Calcium 45mg; Fibre 5g; Sodium 18mg.

COOL GREEN FRUIT SALAD ★

A MONOCHROMATIC FRUIT SALAD CAN LOOK MORE SOPHISTICATED THAN A MEDLEY OF MIXED COLOURS. USE THE FRUITS SUGGESTED OR MAKE UP EXCITING COMBINATIONS OF YOUR OWN.

SERVES 6

INGREDIENTS

   3 Ogen or Galia melons
   115g/4oz green seedless grapes
   2 kiwi fruit
   1 star fruit (carambola)
   1 green-skinned eating apple
   1 lime
   175ml/6fl oz/¾ cup sparkling
     grape juice

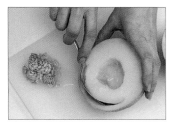

1 Cut the melons in half and scoop out the seeds. Keeping the shells intact, scoop out the fruit with a melon baller, or spoon it out and cut into bitesize cubes. Set the melon shells aside.

2 Remove any stems from the grapes, and, if they are large, cut them in half. Peel and chop the kiwi fruit. Thinly slice the star fruit. Core and thinly slice the apple and place the slices in a bowl, with the melon, grapes, kiwi fruit and star fruit.

COOK'S TIP

If you're serving this dessert on a hot summer day, serve the filled melon shells nestling on a platter of crushed ice to keep them beautifully cool.

3 Thinly pare the lime, cut the rind in fine strips and blanch the strips in boiling water for 30 seconds. Drain, dip in cold water, and drain again. Squeeze the juice from the lime and gently mix it with the fruit.

4 Spoon the prepared fruit into the melon shells and chill in the refrigerator until required. Just before serving, spoon the sparkling grape juice over the fruit and sprinkle it with the blanched lime rind.

Energy 102kcal/436kJ; Protein 1.7g; Carbohydrate 24.4g, of which sugars 24.4g; Fat 0.4g, of which saturates 0g; Cholesterol 0mg; Calcium 46mg; Fibre 1.9g; Sodium 81mg.

SWEET ADUKI BEAN PASTE JELLY ★

BASED ON AGAR-AGAR, A SETTING AGENT MADE FROM SEAWEED, THESE JELLIES LOOK LIKE BLOCKS OF MOUNTAIN ICE IN WHICH SEMI-PRECIOUS STONES HAVE BEEN TRAPPED FOR CENTURIES.

SERVES 12

INGREDIENTS
  200g/7oz can aduki beans
  40g/1½oz/3 tbsp caster
    (superfine) sugar
For the *agar-agar* jelly
  2 × 5g/⅛oz sachets powdered
    agar-agar
  100g/3¾oz/½ cup caster sugar
  rind of ¼ orange in one piece

1 Drain the beans, then tip into a pan over a medium heat. When steam begins to rise, reduce the heat to low.

2 Add the sugar one-third at a time, stirring constantly until the sugar has dissolved and the moisture evaporated. Remove from the heat.

3 Pour 450ml/¾ pint/scant 2 cups water into a pan, and mix with one *agar-agar* sachet. Stir until dissolved, then add 40g/1½oz of the sugar and the orange rind. Bring to the boil and cook for about 2 minutes, stirring constantly until the sugar has all dissolved.

4 Remove from the heat and discard the orange rind.

5 Transfer 250ml/8fl oz/1 cup of the hot liquid into a 15 × 10cm/6 × 4in container so that it fills only 1cm/½in. Leave at room temperature to set.

6 Add the bean paste to the *agar-agar* liquid in the pan, and mix well. Move the pan on to a wet dish towel and keep stirring for 8 minutes.

7 Pour the bean and *agar-agar* liquid into an 18 × 7.5 × 2cm/7 × 3 × ¾in container and leave to set for 1 hour at room temperature, then 1 hour in the refrigerator. Turn upside down on to a chopping board covered with kitchen paper. Leave for 1 minute, then cut into 12 rectangular pieces.

8 Line 12 ramekins with clear film (plastic wrap). With a fork, cut the set kanten block into 12 squares. Put one square in each ramekin, then place a bean and kanten cube on top of each.

9 Pour 450ml/¾ pint/scant 2 cups water into a pan and mix with the remaining kanten sachet. Bring to the boil, add the remaining sugar, then stir constantly until dissolved. Boil for a further 2 minutes, and remove from the heat. Place the pan on a wet dish towel to cool quickly and stir for 5 minutes, or until the liquid starts to thicken.

10 Ladle the liquid into the ramekins to cover the cubes. Twist the clear film at the top. Leave to set in the refrigerator for at least 1 hour. Carefully remove the ramekins and clear film and serve cold on serving plates.

Energy 63kcal/267kJ; Protein 1.2g; Carbohydrate 15.2g, of which sugars 12.8g; Fat 0.1g, of which saturates 0g; Cholesterol 0mg; Calcium 18mg; Fibre 1g; Sodium 66mg.

MANGO ᴬᴺᴰ GINGER CLOUDS ★

THE SWEET, PERFUMED FLAVOUR OF RIPE MANGO COMBINES BEAUTIFULLY WITH PRESERVED GINGER,
AND THIS CHILLED LOW-FAT DESSERT MAKES THE VERY MOST OF BOTH THESE INGREDIENTS.

SERVES 6

INGREDIENTS

   3 ripe mangoes
   3 pieces preserved stem ginger plus
      45ml/3 tbsp syrup from the jar
   75g/3oz/½ cup silken tofu
   3 egg whites
   6 pistachio nuts, chopped

1 Cut the mangoes in half, remove and discard the stones (pits) and peel the fruit, using a sharp knife. Roughly chop the mango flesh.

2 Cut the tofu into rough cubes to make it easier to process.

3 Put the chopped mango in a food processor and add the ginger, the syrup from the jar and the chopped tofu.

4 Process the mixture until it is smooth, then scrape into a mixing bowl.

COOK'S TIP
This dessert can be served lightly frozen. If you prefer not to use ginger, omit the ginger pieces and syrup and use 45ml/ 3 tbsp clear honey instead.

5 Put the egg whites in a bowl and whisk them either by hand or with an electric whisk, until they form soft peaks. Fold them into the mango mixture.

6 Spoon the mixture into wide dishes or tall sundae glasses and cover with clear film (plastic wrap). Chill before serving, sprinkled with the chopped pistachios.

Energy 110kcal/466kJ; Protein 3.9g; Carbohydrate 17g, of which sugars 16.6g; Fat 3.5g, of which saturates 0.5g; Cholesterol 0mg; Calcium 80mg; Fibre 2.3g; Sodium 79mg.

HEAVENLY JELLIES WITH FRUIT ★

DELICATE, VANILLA-FLAVOURED JELLY, SET WITH RIBBONS OF EGG WHITE WITHIN IT, MAKES A MOUTHWATERING AND LIGHT DESSERT THAT TASTES GREAT WHEN SERVED WITH FRESH FRUIT.

SERVES 6

INGREDIENTS

10g/¼oz *agar-agar*
900ml/1½ pints/3¾ cups
  boiling water
115g/4oz/½ cup caster
  (superfine) sugar
5ml/1 tsp vanilla extract
1 egg white, lightly beaten
225g/8oz/1½ cups strawberries
450g/1lb fresh lychees, or 425g/15oz
  can lychees, drained

1 Put the *agar-agar* into a pan. Stir in the boiling water, return to the boil and then lower the heat. Simmer the mixture for 10–15 minutes, stirring occasionally, until the *agar-agar* has dissolved completely.

2 Stir in the sugar. As soon as it has dissolved, strain the syrup through a fine sieve (strainer) placed over a bowl. Return the mixture to the pan.

VARIATION
The jelly can be made with equal amounts of reduced-fat coconut milk and water instead of just water.

3 Immediately stir in the vanilla extract, then gently pour in the egg white in a steady stream; the heat will cook the egg white. Gently stir the mixture just once to distribute the threads of cooked egg white.

4 Pour the mixture into a shallow 28 x 18cm/11 x 7in baking tray and allow to cool. The jelly will set at room temperature, but it will set faster and taste better if it is transferred to the refrigerator to set as soon as it has cooled completely.

5 Hull most of the strawberries, keeping the green part on a few for decoration. If the strawberries are large, cut them into smaller bitesize pieces.

6 If using fresh lychees, peel them and remove the stones (pits). If using canned lychees, drain them in a sieve. Divide them among six small serving dishes or cups, then add some strawberries to each portion.

7 Turn the jelly out of the tray and cut it into diamond shapes to serve with the strawberries and lychees.

Energy 131kcal/559kJ; Protein 1.6g; Carbohydrate 33g, of which sugars 33g; Fat 0.1g, of which saturates 0g; Cholesterol 0mg; Calcium 21mg; Fibre 0.9g; Sodium 14mg.

COCONUT JELLY WITH STAR ANISE FRUITS ★

*THIS JELLY IS PERFECT SERVED WITH PLENTY OF REFRESHING EXOTIC FRUIT. IT MAKES A DELICIOUS
TREAT AFTER ANY ASIAN-STYLE MEAL. THE COMBINATION OF REDUCED-FAT COCONUT MILK WITH
FRESH STAR FRUIT AND LYCHEES MAKES FOR A DELICIOUS AND SURPRISINGLY LOW-FAT DESSERT.*

SERVES 4

INGREDIENTS
  250ml/8fl oz/1 cup cold water
  75g/3oz/⅓ cup caster (superfine)
  sugar
  15ml/1 tbsp powdered gelatine
  400ml/14fl oz/1⅔ cups reduced-fat
  coconut milk
For the syrup and fruit
  250ml/8fl oz/1 cup water
  3 star anise
  50g/2oz/¼ cup caster (superfine) sugar
  1 star fruit (carambola), sliced
  12 lychees, peeled and stoned (pitted)
  115g/4oz/1 cup blackberries

1 Pour the water into a pan and add the
sugar. Heat gently until the sugar has
dissolved. Sprinkle over the gelatine and
heat gently, stirring, until the gelatine
has dissolved. Stir in the coconut milk,
remove from the heat and set aside.

2 Grease an 18cm/7in square tin (pan).
Line with clear film (plastic wrap). Pour
in the milk mixture and chill until set.

3 To make the syrup, combine the
water, star anise and sugar in a pan.
Bring to the boil, stirring, then lower
the heat and simmer for 10–12 minutes
until syrupy. Place the fruit in a
heatproof bowl and pour over the hot
syrup. Cool, then chill.

4 To serve, cut the coconut jelly into
diamonds and remove from the tin.
Arrange the coconut jelly on individual
plates, adding a few of the fruits and
their syrup to each portion.

COOK'S TIP
Coconut milk is available in cans or
cartons. It has a high fat content so look
out for the reduced-fat version which can
be up to 88 per cent fat free.

Energy 246kcal/1051kJ; Protein 4.4g; Carbohydrate 60g, of which sugars 60g; Fat 0.4g, of which saturates 0.2g; Cholesterol 0mg; Calcium 67mg; Fibre 1.5g; Sodium 114mg.

COCONUT CREAM DIAMONDS ★

DESSERTS LIKE THESE ARE SERVED IN COUNTRIES ALL OVER THE ASIA, OFTEN WITH MANGOES, PINEAPPLE OR GUAVAS. ALTHOUGH COMMERCIALLY GROUND RICE CAN BE USED FOR THIS DISH, GRINDING JASMINE RICE YOURSELF — IN A FOOD PROCESSOR — GIVES A MUCH BETTER RESULT.

SERVES 6

INGREDIENTS

75g/3oz/scant ½ cup jasmine rice,
  soaked overnight in 175ml/6fl oz/
  ¾ cup water
350ml/12fl oz/1½ cups reduced-fat
  coconut milk
150ml/¼ pint/⅔ cup reduced-fat
  single (light) cream
50g/2oz/¼ cup caster
  (superfine) sugar
raspberries and fresh mint leaves,
  to decorate
For the coulis
75g/3oz/¾ cup blackcurrants,
  stalks removed
30ml/2 tbsp caster (superfine) sugar
75g/3oz/½ cup fresh or
  frozen raspberries

1 Put the rice and its soaking water into a food processor and process for a few minutes until the mixture is soupy.

2 Heat the coconut milk and cream in a non-stick pan. When the mixture is on the point of boiling, stir in the rice mixture. Cook over a very gentle heat for 10 minutes, stirring constantly.

3 Stir the sugar into the coconut rice mixture and continue cooking for a further 10–15 minutes, or until the mixture is thick and creamy.

VARIATION
You could use other soft fruit in the coulis, such as blackberries or redcurrants.

4 Line a rectangular tin (pan) with baking parchment. Pour the coconut rice mixture into the pan, cool, then chill in the refrigerator until the dessert is set and firm.

5 Meanwhile, make the coulis. Put the blackcurrants in a bowl and sprinkle with the sugar. Set aside for about 30 minutes. Tip the blackcurrants and raspberries into a wire sieve set over a bowl. Using a spoon, press the fruit against the sides of the sieve so that the juices collect in the bowl. Taste the coulis and add more sugar if necessary.

6 Carefully cut the coconut cream into diamonds. Spoon a little of the coulis on to each dessert plate, arrange the coconut cream diamonds on top and decorate with the fresh raspberries and mint leaves. Serve immediately.

Energy 146kcal/616kJ; Protein 2g; Carbohydrate 28.5g, of which sugars 18.5g; Fat 3.1g, of which saturates 2g; Cholesterol 8mg; Calcium 50mg; Fibre 0.8g; Sodium 70mg.

SWEET RICE DUMPLINGS IN GINGER SYRUP ★

THESE RICE DUMPLINGS ARE FILLED WITH MUNG BEAN PASTE AND THEN SIMMERED IN A SYRUP. THE DOUGH IS MADE WITH GLUTINOUS RICE FLOUR TO ATTAIN THE DESIRED SPRINGY, CHEWY TEXTURE.

SERVES 4–6

INGREDIENTS
For the syrup
   25g/1oz fresh root ginger, peeled and
   finely shredded
   115g/4oz/generous ½ cup sugar
   400ml/14fl oz/1⅔ cups water
For the filling
   40g/1½oz dried split mung beans,
   soaked for 6 hours and drained
   25g/1oz/2 tbsp sugar
For the dough
   225g/8oz/2 cups sticky glutinous
   rice flour
   175ml/6fl oz/¾ cup boiling water

COOK'S TIP
These dumplings are popular at Vietnamese weddings. Coloured red with food dye, they represent good fortune.

1 To make the syrup, stir the ginger and sugar in a heavy pan over a low heat, until the sugar begins to brown. Take the pan off the heat and stir in 400ml/14fl oz/1⅔ cups water – it will bubble and spit.

2 Return the pan to the heat and bring to the boil, stirring. Reduce the heat and simmer for 5 minutes.

3 To make the filling, put the soaked mung beans in a pan with the sugar and add the water to cover. Bring to the boil, stirring all the time, until the sugar has dissolved. Simmer for 15–20 minutes until the mung beans are soft. When all the water has been absorbed, pound to a smooth paste and leave until cool. Roll the filling into 16–20 small balls.

4 To make the dough, put the flour in a bowl. Make a well in the centre and gradually pour in the water, drawing in the flour to form a dough. When cool enough to handle, knead the dough for a few minutes, until soft and springy.

5 Divide the dough in half and roll each half into a sausage, about 25cm/10in long. Divide each sausage into 8–10 pieces, and roll each piece into a ball. Take a ball of dough and flatten it in the palm of your hand. Place a ball of the mung bean filling in the centre of the dough and seal it by pinching and rolling the dough. Repeat with the remaining balls.

6 Cook the filled dumplings in a pan of boiling water for 2–3 minutes, until they rise to the surface, then drain. Heat the syrup in a heavy pan, drop in the cooked dumplings, and simmer for a further 2–3 minutes. Serve at room temperature, or chilled.

VARIATION
For a spicy version, the syrup can be flavoured with a mixture of ginger, cloves, aniseed and cinnamon sticks.

Energy 231kcal/975kJ; Protein 2.7g; Carbohydrate 54.7g, of which sugars 24.5g; Fat 0.3g, of which saturates 0g; Cholesterol 0mg; Calcium 23mg; Fibre 0.9g; Sodium 4mg.

STICKY RICE ᴵᴺ BEAN PASTE ★

THIS TEA-TIME SNACK IS AN ABSOLUTE FAMILY FAVOURITE AMONG ALL AGES. IT IS TRADITIONALLY MADE ON BIRTHDAYS AND FESTIVALS, WHEN IT IS DECORATED WITH CAMELLIA LEAVES.

MAKES 12

INGREDIENTS

150g/5oz/scant 1 cup glutinous rice
50g/2oz/⅓ cup Japanese short
   grain rice
410g/14¼oz can aduki beans
   (canned in water, with sugar and salt)
90g/3½oz/6½ tbsp caster
   (superfine) sugar
pinch of salt

1 Mix both kinds of rice in a sieve (strainer), wash well under running water, then drain. Leave for at least 1 hour to dry.

2 Tip the rice into a heavy cast-iron pan or flameproof casserole with a lid, and add 200ml/7fl oz/scant 1 cup water.

3 Cover and bring to the boil, then reduce the heat to low and simmer for 15 minutes, or until a slight crackling noise is heard from the pan.

4 Remove from the heat and leave to stand for 5 minutes. Remove the lid, cover and leave to cool.

5 Pour the contents of the aduki bean can into a pan and cook over a medium heat. Add the sugar a third at a time, mixing well after each addition.

6 Reduce the heat to low and mash the beans using a potato masher. Add the salt and remove from the heat. The consistency should be like that of mashed potatoes. Heat gently to remove any excess liquid. Leave to cool.

7 Wet your hands. Shape the sticky rice into 12 balls, each about the size of a golf ball.

8 Dampen some muslin or cheesecloth and place on the work surface.

9 Scoop up 30ml/2 tbsp of the aduki bean paste and spread it in the centre of the cloth to a thickness of about 5mm/¼in.

COOK'S TIP
Make sure the muslin or cheesecloth is really damp, or the rice mixture will stick to it and prove difficult to remove.

10 Put a rice ball in the middle, then wrap it up in the paste using the muslin. Open the cloth and remove the ball. Repeat until all the rice balls are used up. Serve at room temperature.

Energy 123kcal/518kJ; Protein 3.6g; Carbohydrate 27.1g, of which sugars 9g; Fat 0.3g, of which saturates 0g; Cholesterol 0mg; Calcium 31mg; Fibre 2.1g; Sodium 130mg.

KABOCHA SQUASH CAKE ★

THIS IS A VERY SWEET DESSERT OFTEN MADE WITH ADUKI BEANS, TO BE EATEN AT TEA TIME WITH GREEN TEA. THE BITTERNESS OF THE TEA BALANCES THE SWEETNESS OF THE CAKE.

2 Steam the kabocha squash in a covered steamer for about 15 minutes over a medium heat. It will be ready when a chopstick or skewer can be pushed into the centre easily. Remove and leave, covered, for 5 minutes.

3 Remove the skin from the kabocha. Mash the flesh and push it through a sieve (strainer) using a wooden spoon, or purée it in a blender or food processor. Scrape the purée into a mixing bowl. Add the flour, cornflour, caster sugar, cinnamon, water and beaten egg yolks. Mix well.

4 Roll out a *makisu* sushi mat as you would if making a sushi roll. Wet some muslin or cheesecloth slightly with water and lay it on the mat. Spread the kabocha cake mixture evenly on the wet cloth. Hold the nearest end and tightly roll up the *makisu* to the other end. Close both outer ends by rolling up or folding the cloth over.

5 Put the *makisu* containing the rolled kabocha cake back into the steamer for 5 minutes. Remove from the heat and leave to set for 5 minutes.

6 If serving with fruit, peel, trim and slice the Asian pear and persimmon very thinly lengthways.

7 Open the *makisu* when the roll has cooled down. Cut the cake into 2.5cm/1in thick slices and serve cold on four small plates with the thinly sliced fruit, if using.

SERVES 4

INGREDIENTS
1 × 350g/12oz kabocha squash
30ml/2 tbsp plain
  (all-purpose) flour
15ml/1 tbsp cornflour (cornstarch)
10ml/2 tsp caster (superfine) sugar
1.5ml/¼ tsp salt
1.5ml/¼ tsp ground cinnamon
25ml/1½ tbsp water
2 egg yolks, beaten
To serve (optional)
  ½ Asian pear
  ½ persimmon

1 Cut off the hard part from the top and bottom of the kabocha, then cut it into three to four wedges. Scoop out the seeds with a spoon. Cut into chunks.

Energy 97kcal/409kJ; Protein 4.5g; Carbohydrate 13.8g, of which sugars 4.2g; Fat 3.1g, of which saturates 0.9g; Cholesterol 95mg; Calcium 52mg; Fibre 1.1g; Sodium 37mg.

EXOTIC FRUIT SUSHI ★

*THIS IDEA CAN BE ADAPTED TO INCORPORATE A WIDE VARIETY OF FRUITS, BUT TO KEEP TO THE
EXOTIC THEME TAKE YOUR INSPIRATION FROM THE TROPICS. THE SUSHI NEEDS TO CHILL OVERNIGHT.*

SERVES 4

INGREDIENTS
150g/5oz/²⁄₃ cup short grain
   pudding rice
350ml/12fl oz/1½ cups water
400ml/14fl oz/1²⁄₃ cups reduced-fat
   coconut milk
75g/3oz/⅓ cup caster
   (superfine) sugar
a selection of exotic fruit, such as
   1 mango, 1 kiwi fruit, 2 figs and
   1 star fruit (carambola),
   thinly sliced
30ml/2 tbsp apricot jam, sieved
For the raspberry sauce
   225g/8oz/2 cups raspberries
   25g/1oz/¼ cup icing
      (confectioners') sugar

3 Cut the rice mixture into 16 small
bars, shape into ovals and flatten the
tops. Place on a baking sheet lined with
baking parchment. Arrange the sliced
fruit on top, using one type of fruit only
for each sushi.

4 Place the remaining sugar in a small
pan with the remaining 60ml/4 tbsp
water. Bring to the boil, then lower
the heat and simmer until the liquid
becomes thick and syrupy. Stir in the
jam and cool slightly.

5 To make the raspberry sauce, put
the raspberries in a food processor
or blender, and add the icing sugar.
Process in short bursts, using the pulse
button if your machine has one, until
the raspberries are a purée. Press
through a sieve, then divide among
four small bowls.

6 Arrange a few different fruit sushi on
each plate and spoon over a little of the
cool apricot syrup. Serve with the
raspberry sauce.

1 Rinse the rice well under cold running
water, drain and place in a pan with
300ml/½ pint/1¼ cups of the water.
Pour in 175ml/6fl oz/¾ cup of the
coconut milk. Cook over very low heat
for 25 minutes, stirring often and
gradually adding the remaining coconut
milk, until the rice has absorbed all the
liquid and is tender.

2 Grease a shallow 18cm/7in square tin
(pan) and line it with clear film (plastic
wrap). Stir 30ml/2 tbsp of the caster sugar
into the rice mixture and pour it into the
prepared tin. Cool, then chill overnight.

COOK'S TIP
To cut the rice mixture into bars, turn
out of the tin, cut in half lengthways,
then make 7 crossways cuts for 16 bars.
Shape into ovals with damp hands.

Energy 323kcal/1372kJ; Protein 4.5g; Carbohydrate 77.1g, of which sugars 47g; Fat 0.8g, of which saturates 0.3g; Cholesterol 0mg; Calcium 73mg; Fibre 2.9g; Sodium 118mg.

COCONUT CUSTARD ★★

*THIS TRADITIONAL DESSERT CAN BE BAKED OR STEAMED AND IS OFTEN SERVED WITH SWEET STICKY
RICE AND A SELECTION OF FRESH FRUIT. MANGOES AND TAMARILLOS COMBINE VERY WELL.*

2 Strain the mixture into a jug (pitcher), then pour it into four individual heatproof glasses, ramekins or an ovenproof dish.

3 Stand the glasses, ramekins or dish in a roasting pan. Fill the pan with hot water to reach halfway up the sides of the ramekins or dish.

4 Bake for about 35–40 minutes, or until the custards are set. Test with a fine skewer or cocktail stick (toothpick).

5 Remove the roasting pan from the oven, lift out the ramekins or dish and leave until cool.

6 If you like, turn out the custards on to serving plate(s). Decorate with the mint leaves and a dusting of icing sugar, and serve with sliced fruit.

SERVES 4

INGREDIENTS
    4 eggs
    75g/3oz/6 tbsp soft light
      muscovado (brown) sugar
      or palm sugar
    250ml/8fl oz/1 cup reduced-fat
      coconut milk
    5ml/1 tsp vanilla, rose or
      jasmine extract
    fresh mint leaves and icing
      (confectioners') sugar,
      to decorate
    sliced fruit, to serve

1 Preheat the oven to 150°C/300°F/ Gas 2. Whisk the eggs and sugar in a bowl until smooth. Add the coconut milk and extract and whisk well.

Energy 161kcal/681kJ; Protein 6.5g; Carbohydrate 22.7g, of which sugars 22.7g; Fat 5.7g, of which saturates 1.7g; Cholesterol 190mg; Calcium 57mg; Fibre 0g; Sodium 140mg.

STEAMED CUSTARD <u>IN</u> NECTARINES ★

STEAMING NECTARINES OR PEACHES BRINGS OUT THEIR NATURAL COLOUR AND SWEETNESS, SO THIS IS
A GOOD WAY OF MAKING THE MOST OF UNDERRIPE OR LESS FLAVOURFUL FRUIT.

SERVES 6

INGREDIENTS

6 nectarines
1 large (US extra large) egg
45ml/3 tbsp light
   muscovado (brown) sugar
   or palm sugar
30ml/2 tbsp reduced-fat
   coconut milk

COOK'S TIP
Palm sugar, also known as jaggery, is
made from the sap of certain Asian palm
trees, such as coconut and palmyrah. It
is available from Asian food stores. If you
buy it as a cake or large lump, grate it
before use.

1 Cut the nectarines in half. Using a
teaspoon, scoop out the stones (pits)
and a little of the surrounding flesh.

2 Lightly beat the egg, then add the
sugar and the coconut milk. Beat until
the sugar has dissolved.

3 Transfer the nectarines to a steamer
and carefully fill the cavities three-
quarters full with the custard mixture.
Steam over a pan of simmering water
for 5–10 minutes. Remove from the
heat and leave to cool completely before
transferring to plates and serving.

Energy 119kcal/507kJ; Protein 3.8g; Carbohydrate 25.2g, of which sugars 25.2g; Fat 1.1g, of which saturates 0.3g; Cholesterol 32mg; Calcium 24mg; Fibre 2.3g; Sodium 20mg.

Hot Desserts

Stewed pumpkins, grilled pineapples, fried bananas, and sticky

rice are the most commonly used ingredients in hot desserts,

and they are often cooked with coconut milk. Here you will

find sensational hot delights to end any meal, from a light and

fluffy Golden Steamed Sponge Cake to a warming Sweet Mung

Bean Soup, from sweet Toffee Apples to the ever-popular

Banana Fritters — serve these with a scoop of low-fat vanilla

ice cream for a heavenly treat.

FRIED PINEAPPLE ★★★

THIS IS A VERY SIMPLE AND QUICK DESSERT TO MAKE. THE SLIGHTLY SHARP FLAVOUR OF THE FRUIT
MAKES THIS A VERY REFRESHING TREAT; A SPLASH OF RUM TURNS THIS INTO AN ADULT TREAT.

SERVES 4

INGREDIENTS
  1 pineapple
  40g/1½oz/3 tbsp butter
  15ml/1 tbsp desiccated (dry
    unsweetened shredded) coconut
  60ml/4 tbsp soft light brown
    sugar
  60ml/4 tbsp fresh lime juice
  lime slices, to decorate
  low-fat natural (plain) yogurt,
    to serve

1 Using a sharp knife, cut the top off the pineapple and peel off the skin, taking care to remove the eyes. Cut the pineapple in half and remove and discard the woody core. Cut the flesh lengthways into 1cm/½in wedges.

2 Heat the butter in a large, heavy frying pan or wok. When it has melted, add the pineapple wedges and cook over a medium heat for 1–2 minutes on each side, or until they have turned pale golden in colour.

3 Meanwhile, dry-fry the coconut in a small frying pan until lightly browned. Remove from the heat and set aside.

4 Sprinkle the sugar into the pan with the pineapple, add the lime juice and cook, stirring constantly, until the sugar has dissolved. Divide the pineapple wedges among four bowls, sprinkle with the coconut, decorate with the lime slices and serve with the yogurt.

Energy 238kcal/1004kJ; Protein 1.2g; Carbohydrate 36.2g, of which sugars 36.2g; Fat 11g, of which saturates 7.2g; Cholesterol 21mg; Calcium 47mg; Fibre 2.9g; Sodium 67mg.

BANANA FRITTERS ★★

THESE DELICIOUS DEEP-FRIED BANANAS ARE VERY QUICK TO COOK. AT THE LAST MINUTE, FRY THEM ONCE THE OIL IS HOT SO THAT THE BATTER IS CRISP AND THE BANANA INSIDE IS SOFT AND WARM.

SERVES 8

INGREDIENTS
115g/4oz/1 cup self-raising
   (self-rising) flour
40g/1½ oz/¼ cup rice flour
2.5ml/½ tsp salt
200ml/7fl oz/scant 1 cup water
finely grated lime rind (optional)
8 baby bananas
vegetable oil, for deep frying
strips of lime rind, to garnish
caster (superfine) sugar, for dredging
lime wedges, to serve

1 Sift together the self-raising flour, rice flour and salt into a bowl. Add just enough water to make a smooth, coating batter. Mix well, then add the lime rind, if using.

2 Heat the oil in a deep fryer or wok to 190°C/375°F. Meanwhile, peel the bananas. Dip them into the batter several times until well coated, then deep-fry until crisp and golden.

VARIATION
Instead of lime, add finely grated orange rind to the batter.

3 Drain on kitchen paper. Serve hot, dredged with caster sugar and garnished with strips of lime. Offer the lime wedges for squeezing over the bananas.

COOK'S TIP
Tiny bananas are available from some Asian stores and many larger supermarkets, alternatively use small bananas and cut in half lengthways and then in half again.

Energy 204kcal/855kJ; Protein 3.9g; Carbohydrate 26.6g, of which sugars 14.8g; Fat 9.8g, of which saturates 4.4g; Cholesterol 48mg; Calcium 47mg; Fibre 1.7g; Sodium 75mg.

TROPICAL FRUIT GRATIN ★★

THIS OUT-OF-THE-ORDINARY GRATIN IS STRICTLY FOR GROWN-UPS. A COLOURFUL COMBINATION
OF FRUIT IS TOPPED WITH A SIMPLE SABAYON BEFORE BEING FLASHED UNDER THE GRILL.

SERVES 4

INGREDIENTS
2 tamarillos
½ sweet pineapple
1 ripe mango
175g/6oz/1½ cups blackberries
120ml/4fl oz/½ cup sparkling
  white wine
115g/4oz/½ cup caster
  (superfine) sugar
6 egg yolks

VARIATION
Boiling drives off the alcohol in the wine,
but children do not always appreciate the
flavour. Substitute orange juice if making
the gratin for them. White grape juice or
pineapple juice would also work well.

1 Cut each tamarillo in half lengthways,
then into thick slices. Cut the rind and
core from the pineapple and take spiral
slices off the outside to remove the
eyes. Cut the flesh into chunks. Peel
the mango, cut it in half and cut the
flesh from the stone (pit) in slices.

2 Divide all the fruit, including the
blackberries, among four 14cm/5½in
gratin dishes set on a baking sheet and
set aside. Heat the wine and sugar in a
pan until the sugar has dissolved. Bring
to the boil and cook for 5 minutes.

3 Put the egg yolks in a large heatproof
bowl. Place the bowl over a pan of
simmering water and whisk until pale.
Slowly pour on the hot sugar syrup,
whisking all the time, until the mixture
thickens. Preheat the grill (broiler).

4 Spoon the mixture over the fruit.
Place the baking sheet holding the
dishes on a low shelf under the hot
grill until the topping is golden. Serve
the gratin hot.

GRILLED PINEAPPLE WITH PAPAYA SAUCE ★

PINEAPPLE AND STEM GINGER IS A CLASSIC COMBINATION. WHEN COOKED IN THIS WAY, THE FRUIT
TAKES ON A SUPERB FLAVOUR AND IS SIMPLY SENSATIONAL WHEN SERVED WITH THE PAPAYA SAUCE.

SERVES 6

INGREDIENTS
1 sweet pineapple
melted butter, for greasing
  and brushing
2 pieces drained stem ginger in
  syrup, cut into fine matchsticks,
  plus 30ml/2 tbsp of the syrup
  from the jar
30ml/2 tbsp demerara (raw) sugar
pinch of ground cinnamon
fresh mint sprigs, to decorate
For the sauce
  1 ripe papaya, peeled and seeded
  175ml/6fl oz/¾ cup apple juice

1 Peel the pineapple and take spiral
slices off the outside to remove the
eyes. Cut it crossways into six slices,
each 2.5cm/1in thick. Line a baking
sheet with a sheet of foil, rolling up the
sides to make a rim. Grease the foil with
melted butter. Preheat the grill (broiler).

2 Arrange the pineapple slices on the
lined baking sheet. Brush with butter,
then top with the ginger matchsticks,
sugar and cinnamon. Drizzle over the
stem ginger syrup. Grill (broil) for
5–7 minutes or until the slices are
golden and lightly charred on top.

3 Meanwhile, make the sauce. Cut a
few slices from the papaya and set aside,
then purée the rest with the apple juice
in a blender or food processor.

4 Press the purée through a sieve
placed over a bowl, then stir in any
juices from cooking the pineapple.
Serve the pineapple slices with a little
sauce drizzled around each plate.
Decorate with the reserved papaya
slices and the mint sprigs.

COOK'S TIP
Try the papaya sauce with savoury dishes,
too. It tastes great with grilled chicken
and game birds as well as pork and lamb.

Top: Energy 300kcal/1270kJ; Protein 6.2g; Carbohydrate 52.8g, of which sugars 52.7g; Fat 8.7g, of which saturates 2.4g; Cholesterol 302mg; Calcium 119mg; Fibre 4.6g; Sodium 22mg.
Bottom: Energy 97kcal/415kJ; Protein 0.7g; Carbohydrate 24.7g, of which sugars 24.7g; Fat 0.2g, of which saturates 0g; Cholesterol 0mg; Calcium 33mg; Fibre 2.3g; Sodium 19mg.

TOFFEE APPLES ★★

This is a healthier but just as tasty version of a classic Chinese dessert. This dish retains all the flavour and texture without the fuss and fat of deep-frying.

SERVES 6

INGREDIENTS
25g/1oz/2 tbsp butter
75ml/6 tbsp cold water
40g/1½oz/6 tbsp plain
  (all-purpose) flour
1 egg
1 dessert apple
5ml/1 tsp vegetable oil
175g/6oz/¾ cup caster
  (superfine) sugar
5ml/1 tsp sesame seeds

1 Preheat the oven to 200°C/400°F/ Gas 6. Put the butter and water into a small pan and bring to the boil over a high heat.

2 Remove the pan from the heat and add the flour all at once.

3 Stir vigorously with a wooden spoon until the mixture forms a smooth paste which leaves the sides of the pan clean.

4 Leave the choux paste to cool for 5 minutes, then beat in the egg, mixing thoroughly until the mixture is smooth and glossy.

5 Peel and core the apple, then cut it into 1cm/½in chunks.

6 Stir the chopped apple into the cooled choux paste and place teaspoonfuls of the mixture on a dampened non-stick baking sheet.

7 Bake the choux pastry in the oven for 20–25 minutes until it is brown and crisp on the outside, but still soft on the inside.

8 Remove the baking sheet from the oven and leave the pastry to cool.

9 While the pastries are cooling, gently heat the oil in a clean small pan over a low heat and add the caster sugar.

10 Cook, without stirring, until the sugar has melted and turned golden brown, then sprinkle in the sesame seeds. Remove the pan from the heat.

11 Have ready a bowl of iced water. Add the pastries, a few at a time, to the caramel and toss to coat them all over.

12 Remove with a slotted spoon and quickly dip in the iced water to set the caramel; drain well.

13 Serve immediately. If the caramel becomes too thick before all the choux have been coated, re-heat it gently until it liquefies before continuing.

VARIATIONS
A slightly unripe banana can be used instead of an apple, to ring the changes. Alternatively, use chunks of pear or Asian pear, or even peaches or nectarines.

Energy 192kcal/811kJ; Protein 2.1g; Carbohydrate 36.7g, of which sugars 31.6g; Fat 5.1g, of which saturates 2.6g; Cholesterol 47mg; Calcium 32mg; Fibre 0.4g; Sodium 42mg.

PUMPKIN PUDDING ᴵᴺ BANANA LEAVES ★

TRADITIONALLY NATIVE TO CAMBODIA, THIS IS A DELIGHTFUL PUDDING THAT CAN BE MADE WITH
SMALL, SWEET PUMPKINS, OR BUTTERNUT SQUASH WITH DELICIOUS RESULTS.

1 Bring a pan of salted water to the boil. Add the pumpkin flesh and cook for 15 minutes, or until tender. Drain and mash with a fork or purée in a blender.

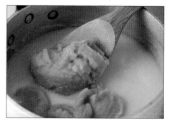

2 In a pan, heat the coconut milk with the sugar and a pinch of salt. Blend the tapioca starch with 15ml/1 tbsp water and 15ml/1 tbsp of the hot coconut milk. Add it to the coconut milk and beat well. Beat the mashed pumpkin into the coconut milk or, if using a blender, add the coconut milk to the pumpkin and purée together.

3 Spoon equal amounts of the pumpkin purée into the centre of each banana leaf square. Fold in the sides and thread a cocktail stick (toothpick) through the open ends to enclose the purée.

4 Fill the bottom third of a wok with water. Place a bamboo steamer on top. Place as many stuffed banana leaves as you can into the steamer, folded side up – cooking them in batches.

5 Cover the steamer and steam parcels for 15 minutes. Unwrap them and serve hot or cold.

SERVES 6

INGREDIENTS
1 small pumpkin, about 1.3kg/3lb, peeled, seeded and cubed
250ml/8fl oz/1 cup reduced-fat coconut milk
45ml/3 tbsp palm sugar
15ml/1 tbsp tapioca starch
12 banana leaves, cut into 15cm/6in squares

VARIATION
You can also try sweet potatoes, cassava or taro root in this recipe.

Energy 76kcal/323kJ; Protein 1.7g; Carbohydrate 17g, of which sugars 13.6g; Fat 0.6g, of which saturates 0.3g; Cholesterol 0mg; Calcium 79mg; Fibre 2.2g; Sodium 46mg.

BAKED RICE PUDDING, THAI-STYLE ★

BLACK GLUTINOUS RICE, ALSO KNOWN AS BLACK STICKY RICE, HAS LONG DARK GRAINS AND A NUTTY TASTE REMINISCENT OF WILD RICE. IT HAS A DISTINCT FLAVOUR AND AN INTRIGUING APPEARANCE.

SERVES 6

INGREDIENTS
    175g/6oz/1 cup white or black
    glutinous rice
    30ml/2 tbsp soft light brown sugar
    475ml/16fl oz/2 cups reduced-fat
    coconut milk
    250ml/8fl oz/1 cup water
    3 eggs
    30ml/2 tbsp granulated sugar

1 Combine the glutinous rice and brown sugar in a pan. Pour in half the coconut milk and the water.

2 Bring to the boil, reduce the heat to low and simmer, stirring occasionally, for 15–20 minutes, or until the rice has absorbed most of the liquid. Preheat the oven to 150°C/300°F/Gas 2.

3 Spoon the mixture into a large ovenproof dish or individual ramekins. Beat the eggs with the remaining coconut milk and sugar in a bowl.

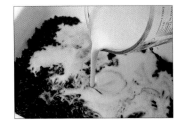

4 Strain the egg mixture into a jug (pitcher), then pour it evenly over the par-cooked rice in the dish or ramekins.

5 Place the dish or ramekins in a roasting pan. Carefully pour in enough hot water to come halfway up the sides of the dish or ramekins.

6 Cover with foil and bake for about 35–60 minutes, or until the custard has set. Serve warm or cold.

COOK'S TIP
Throughout South-east Asia, black glutinous rice is usually used for sweet dishes, while its white counterpart is more often used in savoury recipes.

Energy 198kcal/834kJ; Protein 5.9g; Carbohydrate 36.2g, of which sugars 14.3g; Fat 3.5g, of which saturates 0.9g; Cholesterol 95mg; Calcium 47mg; Fibre 0g; Sodium 124mg.

STEWED PUMPKIN IN COCONUT CREAM ★

FRUIT STEWED IN COCONUT MILK IS A POPULAR DESSERT THROUGHOUT SOUTH-EAST ASIA.
PUMPKINS, BANANAS AND MELONS CAN ALL BE PREPARED IN THIS SIMPLE BUT TASTY WAY.

SERVES 4–6

INGREDIENTS

1kg/2¼lb kabocha pumpkin
750ml/1¼ pints/3 cups reduced-fat
   coconut milk
175g/6oz/¾ cup granulated sugar
pinch of salt
4–6 fresh mint sprigs, to decorate

COOK'S TIP

To make the decoration, wash the
pumpkin seeds to remove any fibres,
then pat them dry on kitchen paper.
Roast them in a dry frying pan, or spread
them out on a baking sheet and grill
(broil) until golden brown, tossing them
frequently to prevent them from burning.

1 Cut the pumpkin in half using a large,
sharp knife, then cut away and discard
the skin. Scoop out the seed cluster.
Reserve a few seeds and throw away
the rest. Using a sharp knife, cut the
pumpkin flesh into pieces that are
about 5cm/2in long and 2cm/¾in thick.

2 Pour the coconut milk into a pan. Add
the sugar and salt and bring to the boil.
Add the pumpkin and simmer for about
10–15 minutes, until it is tender. Serve
warm, in individual dishes. Decorate
each serving with a mint sprig and
toasted pumpkin seeds (see Cook's Tip).

MANGOES WITH STICKY RICE ★

STICKY RICE IS JUST AS GOOD IN DESSERTS AS IN SAVOURY DISHES, AND RIPE MANGOES, WITH
THEIR DELICATE FRAGRANCE AND VELVETY FLESH, COMPLEMENT IT ESPECIALLY WELL.

SERVES 4

INGREDIENTS

115g/4oz/⅔ cup white
   glutinous rice
175ml/6fl oz/¾ cup reduced-fat
   coconut milk
45ml/3 tbsp granulated sugar
pinch of salt
2 ripe mangoes
strips of pared lime rind,
   to decorate

1 Rinse the glutinous rice thoroughly
in several changes of cold water, then
leave to soak overnight in a bowl of
fresh cold water.

COOK'S TIP

Like dairy cream, the thickest and
richest part of coconut milk always
rises to the top. Whenever you open a
can or carton, spoon off this top layer
and use the thinner, lower fat bottom
layer in cooking.

2 Drain the rice well and spread it out
evenly in a steamer lined with muslin or
cheesecloth. Cover and steam over a
pan of simmering water for about
20 minutes, or until the rice is tender.

3 Reserve 45ml/3 tbsp of the cream
from the top of the coconut milk. Pour
the remainder into a pan and add the
sugar and salt. Heat, stirring constantly,
until the sugar has dissolved, then bring
to the boil. Remove the pan from the
heat, pour the coconut milk into a bowl
and leave to cool.

4 Tip the cooked rice into a bowl and
pour over the cooled coconut milk
mixture. Stir well, then leave the rice
mixture to stand for 10–15 minutes.

5 Meanwhile, peel the mangoes, cut the
flesh away from the central stones (pits)
and cut into slices.

6 Spoon the rice on to individual
serving plates. Arrange the mango
slices on one side, then drizzle with the
reserved coconut cream. Decorate with
strips of lime rind and serve.

Top: Energy 164kcal/701kJ; Protein 1.7g; Carbohydrate 40.3g, of which sugars 39.4g; Fat 0.7g, of which saturates 0.4g; Cholesterol 0mg; Calcium 100mg; Fibre 1.7g; Sodium 139mg.
Bottom: Energy 200kcal/846kJ; Protein 3.1g; Carbohydrate 46g, of which sugars 24.3g; Fat 0.8g, of which saturates 0.2g; Cholesterol 0mg; Calcium 32mg; Fibre 2g; Sodium 51mg.

TAPIOCA PUDDING ★

THIS PUDDING, MADE FROM LARGE PEARL TAPIOCA AND COCONUT MILK AND SERVED WARM, IS MUCH LIGHTER THAN THE WESTERN-STYLE VERSION. YOU CAN ADJUST THE SWEETNESS TO YOUR TASTE. SERVE WITH LYCHEES OR THE SMALLER, SIMILAR-TASTING LONGANS — ALSO KNOWN AS "DRAGON'S EYES".

SERVES 4

INGREDIENTS
  115g/4oz/⅔ cup tapioca
  475ml/16fl oz/2 cups water
  175g/6oz/¾ cup granulated sugar
  pinch of salt
  250ml/8fl oz/1 cup reduced-fat
  coconut milk
  250g/9oz prepared tropical fruits,
  such as lychees and papayas
  finely shredded lime rind
  and shavings of fresh coconut
  (optional), to decorate

1 Put the tapioca in a bowl and pour over warm water to cover. Leave to soak for 1 hour so the grains swell. Drain.

2 Pour the measured water in a large pan and bring to the boil over a medium heat. Add the sugar and salt and stir until dissolved.

3 Add the tapioca and coconut milk, reduce the heat to low and simmer gently for 10 minutes, or until the tapioca becomes transparent.

4 Spoon into one large or four individual bowls and serve warm with the tropical fruits. Decorate with the lime rind and coconut shavings, if using.

Energy 324kcal/1384kJ; Protein 1g; Carbohydrate 84.7g, of which sugars 57.2g; Fat 0.4g, of which saturates 0.2g; Cholesterol 0mg; Calcium 51mg; Fibre 1.8g; Sodium 74mg.

TAPIOCA WITH BANANA AND COCONUT ★

POPULAR THROUGHOUT SOUTH-EAST ASIA, THIS IS THE TYPE OF DESSERT THAT EVERYBODY'S MOTHER OR GRANDMOTHER MAKES. SWEET AND NOURISHING, IT IS MADE WITH TAPIOCA PEARLS COOKED IN COCONUT MILK AND SWEETENED WITH BANANAS AND SUGAR.

SERVES 4

INGREDIENTS

550ml/18fl oz/2½ cups water
40g/1½oz tapioca pearls
550ml/18fl oz/2½ cups reduced-fat
  coconut milk
90g/3½oz/½ cup sugar
3 ripe bananas, diced
salt

COOK'S TIP
A pinch of salt added to this recipe enhances the flavour of the coconut milk and counterbalances the sweetness. You can try the recipe with sweet potato, taro root, yellow corn or rice.

1 Pour the water into a pan and bring it to the boil. Stir in the tapioca pearls, reduce the heat and simmer for about 20 minutes, until translucent. Add the coconut milk, sugar and a pinch of salt. Cook gently for 30 minutes.

2 Stir the diced bananas into the tapioca and coconut milk mixture and cook for 5–10 minutes until the bananas are soft but not mushy. Spoon into individual warmed bowls and serve immediately.

Energy 226kcal/964kJ; Protein 1.5g; Carbohydrate 57.2g, of which sugars 45.9g; Fat 0.7g, of which saturates 0.4g; Cholesterol 0mg; Calcium 57mg; Fibre 0.9g; Sodium 154mg.

TAPIOCA AND TARO PUDDING ★

THIS LIGHT AND REFRESHING "SOUP" IS A POPULAR DESSERT CHOICE THROUGHOUT CHINA AND FAR EAST ASIA WITH CHILDREN AND ADULTS ALIKE. IT TASTES VERY CREAMY, BUT IS VERY LOW IN FAT.

3 Peel the *taro* and cut it into diamond-shaped slices, about 1cm/½in thick. Pour the remaining water into a pan and bring it to the boil. Add the *taro* and cook for 10–15 minutes or until it is just tender.

4 Using a slotted spoon, lift out half of the *taro* slices and set them aside. Continue to cook the remaining taro until it is very soft.

SERVES 4–6

INGREDIENTS
    115g/4oz/²/₃ cup tapioca
    1.5 litres/2½ pints/6 cups cold water
    225g/8oz taro
    150g/5oz/²/₃ cup rock sugar
    300ml/½ pint/1¼ cups reduced-fat
       coconut milk

1 Rinse the tapioca, drain well, then put into a bowl with enough water to cover. Leave to soak for 30 minutes.

COOK'S TIP

Taro is a starchy tuber that tastes rather like a floury potato. If it is difficult to locate, use sweet potato instead.

2 Drain the tapioca and put it in a pan with 900ml/1½ pints/3¾ cups water. Bring to the boil, lower the heat and simmer for about 6 minutes or until the tapioca is transparent. Tip into a sieve (strainer), drain well, refresh under cold water, and drain again.

5 Tip the *taro* and cooking liquid into a food processor and process until smooth.

6 Return the *taro* "soup" to the clean pans; stir in the sugar and simmer, stirring occasionally, until the sugar has dissolved, and the mixture is hot.

7 Stir in the tapioca, reserved taro and coconut milk. Cook for a few minutes. Serve immediately in heated bowls or cool and chill before serving.

VARIATION

If children's comments about frogspawn put you off tapioca for life, add fine cooked noodles, such as vermicelli, to the taro soup instead.

Energy 211kcal/901kJ; Protein 0.8g; Carbohydrate 54.8g, of which sugars 30.7g; Fat 0.3g, of which saturates 0.1g; Cholesterol 0mg; Calcium 38mg; Fibre 1g; Sodium 72mg.

GOLDEN STEAMED SPONGE CAKE ★★

CAKES ARE NOT TRADITIONALLY SERVED FOR DESSERT IN CHINA, BUT THIS LIGHT SPONGE IS VERY POPULAR AND IS OFTEN SERVED ON THE DIM SUM TROLLEY AT LUNCHTIME.

SERVES 8

INGREDIENTS
175g/6oz/1½ cups plain
(all-purpose) flour
5ml/1 tsp baking powder
1.5ml/¼ tsp bicarbonate of soda
(baking soda)
3 large (US extra large) eggs
115g/4oz/⅔ cup soft light
brown sugar
45ml/3 tbsp walnut oil
30ml/2 tbsp golden
(light corn) syrup
5ml/1 tsp vanilla extract

3 Add the sifted flour, baking powder and bicarbonate of soda to the egg mixture with the vanilla extract, and beat rapidly by hand or with an electric whisk to form a thick batter that is free from lumps.

4 Pour the batter into the paper-lined steamer or tin. Cover and steam over boiling water for 30 minutes or until the sponge springs back when gently pressed with a finger. Leave to cool for a few minutes before serving.

1 Sift the flour, baking powder and bicarbonate of soda into a bowl. Line an 18cm/7in diameter bamboo steamer or cake tin (pan) with baking parchment.

2 In a mixing bowl, whisk the eggs with the sugar until thick and frothy. Beat in the walnut oil and syrup, then set the mixture aside for about 30 minutes.

VARIATION
Maple syrup can be substituted for golden syrup, but make sure you use the real thing.

Energy 150kcal/632kJ; Protein 4.4g; Carbohydrate 20g, of which sugars 3.3g; Fat 6.5g, of which saturates 1g; Cholesterol 71mg; Calcium 42mg; Fibre 0.7g; Sodium 37mg.

CHURROS ★

*THESE IRRESISTIBLE FRITTERS, SERVED AT EVERY OPPORTUNITY WITH HOT CHOCOLATE OR COFFEE,
CAME TO THE PHILIPPINES WITH THE SPANISH WHO WERE KEEN TO KEEP MEMORIES OF HOME ALIVE.*

MAKES ABOUT 24

INGREDIENTS
450ml/15fl oz/scant 2 cups water
15ml/1 tbsp olive oil
15ml/1 tbsp sugar, plus extra
 for sprinkling
2.5ml/½ tsp salt
150g/5oz/1¼ cups plain
 (all-purpose) flour
1 large (US extra large) egg
sunflower oil, for deep-frying
caster (superfine) sugar,
 for sprinkling

COOK'S TIP
If you don't have a piping (pastry) bag,
you could fry teaspoons of mixture in
the same way. Don't try to fry too many
churros at a time as they swell a little
during cooking.

1 Mix the water, oil, sugar and salt in a
large pan and bring to the boil. Remove
from the heat, and then sift in the
flour. Beat well with a wooden spoon
until smooth.

2 Beat in the egg to make a smooth,
glossy mixture with a piping consistency.
Spoon into a piping (pastry) bag fitted
with a large star nozzle.

3 Heat the oil in a wok or deep fryer to
190°C/375°F. Pipe loops of the mixture,
two at a time, into the hot oil. Cook
the loops for 3–4 minutes until they
are golden.

4 Lift out the churros with a wire
skimmer or slotted spoon and drain
them on kitchen paper. Dredge them
with caster sugar and serve warm.

LECHE FLAN ★

*SERVE THIS TRADITIONAL DESSERT HOT OR COLD WITH CHILLED YOGURT. THE USE OF EVAPORATED
MILK REFLECTS THE 50 YEARS OF AMERICAN PRESENCE IN THE PHILIPPINES.*

SERVES 8

INGREDIENTS
5 large eggs
30ml/2 tbsp caster (superfine) sugar
few drops vanilla extract
410g/14½oz can reduced-fat
 evaporated (unsweetened
 condensed) milk
300ml/½ pint/1¼ cups skimmed milk
5ml/1 tsp finely grated lime rind
strips of lime rind, to decorate
For the caramel
225g/8oz/1 cup sugar
120ml/4fl oz/½ cup water

1 Make the caramel. Put the sugar and
water in a heavy pan. Stir to dissolve
the sugar, then boil without stirring
until golden. Pour into eight ramekins,
rotating to coat the sides.

2 Preheat the oven to 150°C/300°F/
Gas 2. Beat the eggs, sugar and vanilla
extract in a bowl. Mix the evaporated
milk and fresh milk in a pan. Heat to
just below boiling point, then pour on
to the egg mixture, stirring all the time.
Strain the custard mixture into a jug,
add the grated lime rind and cool. Pour
into the caramel-coated ramekins.

3 Place the ramekins in a roasting pan
and pour in enough warm water to come
halfway up the sides of the dishes.

4 Transfer the roasting pan to the oven
and cook the custards for 35–45
minutes or until they just shimmer when
the ramekins are gently shaken.

5 Serve the custards in their ramekin
dishes or by inverting on to serving
plates, in which case break the caramel
and use as decoration. The custards
can be served warm or cold, decorated
with strips of lime rind.

COOK'S TIP
Make extra caramel, if you like, for a
garnish. Pour on to lightly oiled foil and
leave to set, then crush with a rolling pin.

Top: Energy 62kcal/257kJ; Protein 0.9g; Carbohydrate 5.7g, of which sugars 0.9g; Fat 4.1g, of which saturates 0.5g; Cholesterol 8mg; Calcium 10mg; Fibre 0.2g; Sodium 3mg.
Bottom: Energy 320kcal/1361kJ; Protein 10.5g; Carbohydrate 65.7g, of which sugars 65.7g; Fat 3.7g, of which saturates 1.1g; Cholesterol 121mg; Calcium 250mg; Fibre 0g; Sodium 139mg.

Sweet Mung Bean Soup ★

Sweet soups are a popular dessert. In the restaurants and parks along the Perfume River in Vietnam, people often enjoy a delicious sweet bowl of soup made with different sorts of beans, rice, tapioca, bananas or even lotus seeds and root vegetables such as taro.

SERVES 4–6

INGREDIENTS
225g/8oz/1 cup skinned split mung
beans, soaked in water for 3 hours
and drained
500ml/17fl oz/2¼ cups
coconut milk
50g/2oz/¼ cup caster (superfine)
sugar
toasted coconut shavings (optional),
to serve

COOK'S TIP
Be sure to buy the bright yellow, peeled,
split mung beans for this soup rather
than the whole green ones. Split mung
beans are available in Asian stores.

1 Put the mung beans in a pan and
pour in 500ml/17fl oz/2¼ cups water.
Bring the water to the boil, stirring
constantly, then reduce the heat and
simmer gently for 15–20 minutes until
all the water has been absorbed and the
mung beans are soft enough to purée.
Press the beans through a sieve
(strainer), or purée them in a blender.

2 In a large heavy pan, heat the
coconut milk with the caster sugar,
stirring until the sugar has dissolved.
Gently stir in the puréed mung beans,
making sure the soup is thoroughly
mixed and heated through. Serve hot
in individually warmed bowls sprinkled
with toasted coconut shavings, if
you like.

Energy 240kcal/1025kJ; Protein 15g; Carbohydrate 45g, of which sugars 20g; Fat 1g, of which saturates 0g; Cholesterol 0mg; Calcium 57mg; Fibre 0g; Sodium 100mg 00mg.

CASSAVA SWEET ★

THIS TYPE OF SWEET AND STICKY SNACK IS USUALLY SERVED UP WITH A FRESH POT OF LIGHT AND FRAGRANT JASMINE TEA FOR A SNACK. MORE LIKE AN INDIAN HELVA THAN A CAKE, THIS RECIPE CAN ALSO BE MADE USING SWEET POTATOES OR YAMS IN PLACE OF THE CASSAVA.

SERVES 6–8

INGREDIENTS

    butter, for greasing
    350ml/12fl oz/1½ cups coconut milk
    115g/4oz/generous ½ cup palm sugar
    2.5ml/½ tsp ground aniseed
    salt
    675g/1½lb cassava root, peeled
    and coarsely grated

COOK'S TIP

To prepare the cassava for grating, use a sharp knife to split the whole length of the root and then carefully peel off the skin. Simply grate the peeled root using a coarse grater.

1 Preheat the oven to 190°C/375°F/ Gas 5 and grease a baking dish with butter. In a bowl, whisk the coconut milk with the palm sugar, ground aniseed and a pinch of salt, until the sugar has dissolved.

2 Beat the grated cassava root into the coconut mixture and pour into the greased baking dish. Place it in the oven and bake for about 1 hour, or until it is golden on top. Leave the sweet to cool a little in the dish before serving warm or at room temperature.

Energy 254kcal/1086kJ; Protein 1g; Carbohydrate 64g, of which sugars 25g; Fat 1g, of which saturates 1g; Cholesterol 2mg; Calcium 39mg; Fibre 1.8g; Sodium 0.2g.

PANCAKES WITH RED BEAN PASTE ★

IT IS COMMON TO FIND SWEETENED RED BEANS IN DESSERTS AND SWEETMEATS. THEY ARE POPULAR BECAUSE THE RICH, RED COLOUR IS TRADITIONALLY ASSOCIATED WITH GOOD FORTUNE.

SERVES 4

INGREDIENTS
600ml/1 pint/2½ cups cold water
175g/6oz/1 scant cup aduki beans,
  soaked overnight in cold water
115g/4oz/1 cup plain
  (all-purpose) flour
1 large (US extra large) egg,
  lightly beaten
300ml/½ pint/1¼ cups semi-
  skimmed (low-fat) milk
5ml/1 tsp vegetable oil
75g/3oz/6 tbsp caster
  (superfine) sugar
2.5ml/½ tsp vanilla extract
fromage frais or natural (plain)
  yogurt, to serve (optional)

1 Bring the water to the boil in a pan. Drain the beans in a sieve (strainer), add them to the pan and boil rapidly for 10 minutes.

2 Skim off any scum from the surface of the liquid, then lower the heat, cover the pan and simmer, stirring occasionally, for 40 minutes or until the beans are soft.

VARIATION
Instead of serving these sweet pancakes with fromage frais, which would increase the fat content of the dessert, try using whipped tofu instead. Cut 450g/1lb firm tofu into squares and put it in a blender with 60ml/4 tbsp golden (light corn) syrup and 10ml/2 tsp vanilla extract. Add 15ml/1 tbsp water. Blitz until it becomes smooth. If the mixture is too thick, add a little more water and blitz again to combine.

3 Meanwhile, make the pancakes. Sift the flour into a bowl and make a well in the centre. Pour in the egg and half the milk. Beat, gradually drawing in the flour until it has all been incorporated. Beat in the remaining milk to make a smooth batter. Cover; set aside for 30 minutes.

4 Heat a 20cm/8in non-stick omelette pan and brush lightly with the vegetable oil. Pour in a little of the batter, swirling the pan to cover the base thinly.

5 Cook the pancake for 2 minutes until the bottom has browned lightly. Flip the pancake over, either with chopsticks or by flipping in the air, and cook the second side for about 1 minute. Slide the pancake on to a plate.

6 Make seven more pancakes in the same way. Cover the pancakes with foil and keep hot.

7 When the beans are soft and all the water has been absorbed, tip them into a food processor and process until almost smooth. Add the sugar and vanilla extract and process briefly until the sugar has dissolved.

8 Preheat the grill (broiler). Spread a little of the bean paste on the centre of each pancake and fold them into parcels, pressing them down with your fingers to flatten.

9 Place on a baking sheet and cook under the grill for a few minutes until crisp and lightly toasted on each side.

10 Serve the hot pancakes immediately, either on their own or with a little fromage frais or low-fat yogurt.

COOK'S TIP
Both the pancakes and the bean paste can be made well in advance and kept frozen, ready for thawing, reheating and assembling when needed.

Energy 368kcal/1562kJ; Protein 17.2g; Carbohydrate 69.1g, of which sugars 24.8g; Fat 4.5g, of which saturates 1.6g; Cholesterol 52mg; Calcium 183mg; Fibre 4.5g; Sodium 59mg.

GLOSSARY

Aduki beans Small, brownish red beans that are often used in sweet recipes.

Anchovy sauce A Chinese salty sauce.

Ao nori Green seaweed flakes.

Arame A brown variety of seaweed.

Asian pear One of several varieties of pears with green, russet or yellow skin.

Atsu-age Thick, deep-fried tofu. These are usually bought in pieces: 1 atsu-age = 1 piece.

Awakuchi shoyu Pale soy sauce.

Balachan The Malay term for shrimp paste.

Bamboo shoots The edible shoots (new bamboo culms that come out of the ground) of bamboo.

Banana blossom hearts The edible deep, purple flower of the banana tree.

Black bean sauce A popular sauce made from salted black beans.

Beansprouts Mung beans and soy beans are the most often used.

Cellophane noodles Noodles made from mung beans.

Chilli bean paste A Chinese paste made from broad beans.

Chinese broccoli A slightly bitter leaf vegetable featuring thick, flat, glossy blue-green leaves with thick stems.

Chinese chives A popular vegetable widely used in Asian cooking.

Chinese five-spice powder A convenient seasoning in Asian cuisine. It incorporates the five basic flavours of oriental cooking – sweet, sour, bitter, savoury, and salty.

Chinese leaves/Chinese cabbage A vegetable with white stem and green leaves.

Below: Mung beans.

Chinese rice wine Made from glutinous rice, this is generally known as *huang ji* (yellow wine) because of its golden amber colour. The best known and best quality rice wine is *Shao Xing*, named after the district where it is made. Dry sherry may be used as a substitute.

Chinese sausage A wind-dried sausage made from pork and pork fat.

Chinese yam A type of yam that can be eaten raw.

Choi sum A mild-tasting brassica.

Chow chow A Chinese relish made from pickled vegetables.

Coconut cream A thick cream made from coconut milk.

Coconut milk A milk made by soaking grated coconut flesh in hot water and then squeezing it to extract the liquid.

Daikon A long, white vegetable of the radish family.

Dashi-konbu Dried kelp seaweed.

Dashi-no-moto Freeze-dried stock granules for making a quick dashi stock with water.

Dashi Light Japanese stock, available in powder form. Stock granules (dashi-no-moto) are also available. Diluted vegetable stock made from a cube maybe be substituted.

Dried black mushrooms Also known as Chinese black mushrooms.

Egg noodles Noodles made with eggs.

Egg thread noodles Very thin egg noodles.

Enokitake Small delicately flavoured mushrooms with slender stalks.

Fish sauce A condiment derived from fish. Also known as nam pla, nuoc mam and tuk trey.

Fermented rice A popular sweetmeat made from fermented cooked glutinous rice.

Galangal Similar to fresh ginger, galangal is a rhizome. The finger-like protruberances of galangal tend to be thinner and paler in colour but the two look similar and are used in much the same way.

Gobo (burdock root) A long, stick-like root vegetable.

Ginger A commonly used as a spice in cuisines throughout the world.

Glutinous rice Often referred to as sweet or sticky rice, glutinous rice comes in two varieties, black and white. The grains clump together when cooked.

Above: Shimeji mushrooms

Hatcho miso Dark brown soybean paste.

Hijiki Twiggy, black marine algae (seaweed) available dried.

Hoisin sauce A thick, sweet bean sauce.

Holy basil A pungent variety of basil also known as hot basil.

Jasmine rice A long-grain rice, also known as fragrant or scented rice, with a slightly nutty flavour.

Japanese seven-spice powder A popular condiment in Japan, also known as Shichimi togarashi. Containing chilli, sesame, poppy, hemp, shiso, sansho and nori.

Kabocha A squash with dark green skin and yellow flesh, and a nutty flavour.

Kaffir lime leaves The leaves of an inedible fruit that impart a distinctive citrus flavour to soups, curries, fish and chicken dishes. The rind is also used in some recipes.

Kapi The Thai term for shrimp paste.

Kiku nori Dried chrysanthemum petals in a sheet.

Konbu Giant kelp seaweed, usually sold dried as dashi-konbu.

Konnyaku A dense, gelatinous cake made from the konnyaku, a yam-like plant.

Kroeung A Cambodian herb paste made from a blend of lemon grass, galangal, garlic and turmeric.

Lemon basil A variety of basil grown in Thailand used in soups and salads.

Lemon grass A herb widely used in Asian cooking.

Long beans The immature pods of black-eyed beans (peas), also referred to as snake beans.

Lotus root A white-fleshed root from the lotus plant.

Luffa squash A green vegetable popular in Asia.

Mirin A mild, sweet Japanese rice wine used in cooking.

Miso Mixture of fermented soybeans and grains that matures into a paste of different strengths.

Mitsuba Aromatic herb used mostly for soups. Member of the parsley family.

Mooli (Daikon) A long, white vegetable of the radish family.

Mung beans A small bean.

Nam pla The Thai term for fish sauce, an essential flavouring in a vast range of savoury dishes.

Nam prik A general term for pungent and hot sauces or dips.

Ngapi Burmese term for shrimp paste.

Nori Dried, paper-thin seaweed product.

Nuoc cham A popular Vietnamese dipping sauce made from chillies.

Nuoc mam The Vietnamese term for fish sauce, an essential flavouring in a vast range of savoury dishes.

Oyster sauce A thick, brown sauce made from oyster extract.

Pak choi/bok choy Loose-leafed brassica with white stems.

Palm sugar Widely used sugar which is extracted from the sap of palm trees.

Plum sauce A popular condiment made from plum juice.

Ramen Thin egg noodles.

Rice flour A flour made by grinding the raw grain to a very fine powder.

Rice noodles Noodles made from rice.

Rice papers Used for wrapping spring rolls.

Rice sticks These flat, thin dried rice noodles resemble linguine and are available in several widths.

Rice vinegar Used extensively, it is vinegar fermented from rice or distilled rice grains.

Rice-pot crust The crust that forms on the base of the pan.

Sake A strong, powerful, fortified rice wine from Japan.

Sansho Ground Japanese pepper with a minty aroma.

Sencha Green tea made from the young leaves.

Sesame oil A commonly used oil extracted from sesame seeds.

Shichimi togarashi *see* **Japanese seven-spice powder**

Shiitaki A variety of fungus with a brown cap and white stem.

Shimeji Meaty-textured mushroom, similar to oyster mushrooms.

Shiro miso Pale yellow soybean paste, lightly flavoured.

Shoyu Ordinary Japanese soy sauce.

Shrimp paste An essential ingredient in a wide variety of South-east Asian dishes, it is made from tiny shrimps which have been salted, dried and pounded and then left to ferment in hot humid conditions.

Sichuan/Szechuan pepper A spice from the ash tree.

Soba Dried buckwheat noodles.

Sod prik A hot and spicy chilli sauce, originally from China but now popular in Thailand and Vietnam.

Somen Very fine wheat noodles.

Soy sauce A popular condiment made from soya beans.

Spring roll wrappers A type of pancake made from flour and water.

Star anise A star-shaped spice closely resembling anise in flavour.

Star fruit Also known as carambola, this is a bright yellow fruit with a bland, slightly sharp flavour.

Straw mushrooms Delicate, sweet and the most popular variety in Thai cooking.

Sukiyaki Wafer-thin meat and vegetables cooked in a sauce.

Tamarind A tart and sour ingredient from the fruit pods of the tamarind tree which is made into a paste or sold in blocks. Tamarind imparts a fruity and refreshing flavour to savoury dishes.

Below: Taro.

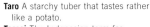

Left: Thai basil.

Taro A starchy tuber that tastes rather like a potato.

Terasi The Indonesian term for shrimp paste.

Tempura A lumpy batter made with ice-cold water for deep-frying fish and sliced vegetables.

Thai basil A herb with an anise flavour.

Tofu A nutritious, coagulated soya bean protein.

Tree ear A dried fungi with a crunchy, chewy texture.

Tuk prahoc The Cambodian term for fish sauce.

Tuk trey A Cambodian fish sauce made by fermenting small fish and salt layered in wooden barrels.

Udon Thick wheat noodles.

Vermicelli rice noodles *see* **rice sticks**

Wakame A curly seaweed, available in a dried form.

Wasabi A Japanese pungent root similar to horseradish, available as a paste or in powder form.

Water chestnuts The Chinese water chestnut is native to China and is widely cultivated in flooded paddy fields in southern China and parts of the Philippines.

Winter melon Also called white gourd or ash gourd or petha, this is a vine grown for its very large fruit, eaten as a vegetable.

Wood ear A dried fungi, also known as cloud ears, with a woody aroma.

Wonton skins Square wrappers made from flour and egg. Round shapes are also available.

Yakitori Skewered grilled chicken.

Yellow bean sauce Made from fermented soya beans. it is also known as brown bean or ground bean sauce.

Yuzu (citron) A citrus fruit the size of a clementine. Lime can be substituted.

INDEX

aduki beans: pancakes with red bean paste 502–3
red rice wrapped in oak leaves 332
sticky rice in bean paste 477
sweet aduki bean paste jelly 470
agar-agar: heavenly jellies with fruit 472–3
rainbow drink 459
sweet aduki bean paste jelly 470
almonds 19
anchovy sauce 22
apples: apples and raspberries in rose pouchong 467
Chinese fruit salad 466
cool green fruit salad 469
iced fruit mountain 460
Thai fruit and vegetable salad 435
toffee apples 488–9
arame seaweed: assorted seaweed salad 441
asian pears 19
asparagus: Asparagus with Crab Meat Sauce 227
asparagus with galangal 404
crab and asparagus soup 60
marinated and grilled swordfish 194
noodles with asparagus 372
spring onions: spring vegetable stir-fry 401
steamed red snapper 193
stir-fried noodles in seafood sauce 382
Thai asparagus 405
udon noodle soup 41
vegetables with Chiang Mai spicy dip 409
teriyaki soba noodles with tofu 378
aubergines 14
aubergine and sweet potato stew with coconut milk 156–7
aubergine curry with coconut milk 150
aubergine salad 436
braised aubergine and courgettes 414–15
fried vegetables with nam prik 423
grilled vegetable sticks 114–15
herb and chilli aubergines 149
steamed aubergine with sesame sauce 413
azuki beans: rainbow drink 459

bamboo shoots 15
bamboo shoot salad 429
beef and vegetables in table-top broth 79
cheat's shark's fin soup 44
chicken and mixed vegetables 236
chicken and vegetable bundles 136
chicken with cashew nuts 245
crispy spring rolls 131
crispy wonton soup 76

cubed chicken and vegetables 240
fish and rice soup 67
hot and sour soup 46
jungle curry 155
popiah 102–103
red chicken curry with bamboo shoots 256–7
sticky rice parcels 354
vegetarian stir-fry with peanut sauce 146–7
five ingredients rice 351
stir-fried beansprouts 398
sweet and hot vegetable noodles 371
sweet-and-sour pork stir-fry 289
banana blossom salad with prawns 209
bananas: banana fritters 485
Chinese fruit salad 466
jungle fruits in lemon grass syrup 463
steamed fish with chilli sauce 177
tapioca with banana and coconut 495
Vietnamese table salad 431
banana leaves: caramelized pork in bamboo 286–7
jungle fish cooked in banana leaves 184
pumpkin pudding in banana leaves 490
red snapper in banana leaves 192
barbecue chicken 249
basil 21
aromatic pork with basil 288
chicken and basil rice 350
Chilli-seared Scallops on Pak Choi 217
griddled squid and tomatoes in a tamarind dressing 201
grilled fish with mung beansprouts 173
sea bass steamed in coconut milk 186
seared beef salad in a lime dressing 309
spicy tofu with basil and peanuts 167
stir-fried chicken with basil and chilli 242
beansprouts 16
beef noodle soup 80–1
duck and ginger chop suey 269
egg foo young – Cantonese style 121
five-flavour noodles 387
noodles with asparagus 372
noodles with chicken, prawns and ham 386
popiah 102–103
prawn and pork soup with rice sticks 55
rice noodles with fresh herbs 360
salmon terikayi 189
seared beef salad in a lime dressing 309
seaweed and radish salad 440
Sichuan noodles with sesame sauce 366
soya beansprout herb salad 428
stir-fried beansprouts 398
stir-fried noodles with beansprouts 369
Thai noodles with Chinese chives 361
tofu and beansprout soup 50
pork chow mein 393
stir-fried tofu with noodles 377
sweet and hot vegetable noodles 371
vegetable chow mein 374
vegetable forest curry 154
Vietnamese table salad 431
beef 31
beef and mushrooms with black beans 312

beef and vegetables in table-top broth 79
beef in oyster sauce 314
beef noodle soup 80–1
beef noodles with orange and ginger 394
beef stew with star anise 318
beef with fried rice 323
beef with peppers and black bean sauce 319
beef with tomatoes 317
beef, vegetable and noodle soup 82
chilli and honey-cured dried beef 308
green beef curry with Thai aubergines 322
noodle and meatball soup 83
noodles with beef and black bean sauce 395
oriental beef 316
paper-thin sliced beef in stock 321
seared beef salad in a lime dressing 309
simmered beef slices and vegetables 320
sizzling beef with celeriac straw 311
steamboat 383
stir-fried chilli beef and mushrooms 315
sukiyaki-style beef 310
Thai beef salad 306–7
tomato and beef soup 78
beer: lobster and crab steamed in beer 226
beetroot: daikon, beetroot and carrot stir-fry 144
black bean sauce 23
beef with peppers and black bean sauce 319
braised aubergine and courgettes 414–15
five-spice squid with black bean sauce 206
mussels in black bean sauce 91
black beans: beef and mushrooms with black beans 312
Chinese-style steamed fish 176
noodles with beef and black bean sauce 395
black glutinous rice 25
Chinese leaves and black rice stir-fry 336
black grapes: iced fruit mountain 460
blackberries: tropical fruit gratin 486–7
blackcurrants: coconut cream diamonds 475
bok choy see pak choi
bread: crispy turkey balls 108
prawn toasts with sesame seeds 127
breadcrumbs: grilled chicken balls on skewers 135
broccoli: broccoli with garlic 406
broccoli with sesame seeds 407
beef with fried rice 323
duck and sesame stir-fry 263
noodles and vegetables in coconut sauce 370
spring onions: spring vegetable stir-fry 401
squid with broccoli 203
tofu and vegetable Thai curry 164–5
rice noodles with pork 391
southern-style yam 421
stir-fried rice and vegetables 341
Thai vegetable curry with lemon grass rice 152–3
vegetables with Chiang Mai spicy dip 409

butternut squash: eel braised in a caramel sauce 197
fried vegetables with nam prik 423
marinated duck curry 268
Northern prawn and squash soup 51
stir-fried pork and butternut curry 303

cabbage: broth with stuffed cabbage leaves 53
cabbage and noodle parcels 111
cabbage salad 438
five-flavour noodles 387
noodles and vegetables in coconut sauce 370
sweet and hot vegetable noodles 371
cake: golden steam sponge cake 497
candlenuts 19
carambola see star fruit
caramelized pork in bamboo 286–7
carp 33
carrots: beef and vegetables in table-top broth 79
beef, vegetable and noodle soup 82
cheat's shark's fin soup 44
chicken and vegetable bundles 136
crunchy summer rolls 122
cubed chicken and vegetables 240
daikon, beetroot and carrot stir-fry 144
escabeche 175
five ingredients rice 351
five-spice vegetable noodles 373
fresh tuna shiitake teriyaki 188
hot and sweet vegetable and tofu soup 49
jungle curry 155
omelette soup 42
picked vegetables 426
simmered tofu with vegetables 160–1
soft-shell crabs with chilli and salt 95
spring onions: spring vegetable stir-fry 401
spiced vegetables with coconut 140
stir-fried beansprouts 398
stir-fried rice and vegetables 341
sweet and hot vegetable noodles 371
sweet-and-sour pork stir-fry 289
vegetable chow mein 374
vegetables and salmon in a parcel 190
Vietnamese table salad 431
cashew nuts 19
chicken with cashew nuts 245
corn and cashew nut curry 151
stir-fried tofu with noodles 377
vegetable chow mein 374
cassava sweet 501
catfish: catfish cooked in a clay pot 196
hot-and-sour fish soup 63
cauliflower: mixed vegetable soup 43
prawn and cauliflower curry 223
spicy cauliflower and ginger samosas 117
tofu and vegetable Thai curry 164–5
vegetables with Chiang Mai spicy dip 409
celeriac: sizzling beef with celeriac straw 311
celery: beef in oyster sauce 314
corn and cashew nut curry 151
five-spice vegetable noodles 373
mixed vegetable soup 43
spiced vegetables with coconut 140
toasted noodles with vegetables 368
vegetable chow mein 374
cellophane noodles 27
cellophane noodle soup 45
cellophane noodles with pork 390

cabbage and noodle parcels 111
cheat's shark's fin soup 44
clay pot of chilli squid 204
courgettes with noodles 411
lettuce parcels 109
noodle, tofu and sprouted bean
 salad 365
noodles with crab and mushrooms
 381
Mongolian firepot 278–9
mushrooms with cellophane noodles
 375
seafood salad with fragrant herbs 446
cherry tomatoes: prawns with yellow
 curry paste 221
chicken 31
 bang bang chicken 233
 barbecue chicken 249
 chicken and basil rice 350
 chicken and egg on rice 352
 chicken and lemon grass curry 259
 chicken and shredded cabbage salad
  447
 chicken and sweet potato curry 237
 chicken and vegetable bundles 136
 chicken rice soup with lemon grass
  70–1
 chicken satay with peanut sauce 232
 chicken teriyaki 235
 chicken with cashew nuts 245
 chicken with hijiki seaweed 243
 chicken with lemon sauce 246
 chicken with mushrooms 244
 chicken with young ginger 250
 Chinese clay pot rice with chicken
  349
 corn and chicken soup 74
 cubed chicken and vegetables
  240
 drunken chicken 108
 five ingredients rice 351
 fragrant grilled chicken 234
 fragrant rice with chicken 252
 ginger, chicken and coconut soup
  68–9
 green chicken curry 258
 grilled chicken balls on skewers
  135
 kabocha squash with chicken sauce
  241
 lettuce parcels 109
 mixed meat noodles 388–9
 noodle casseroles 384–5
 noodles with chicken, prawns and
  ham 386
 red chicken curry with bamboo
  shoots 256–7
 scented chicken wraps 107
 Sichuan chicken with kung po
  sauce 254
 southern chicken curry 261
 soy sauce and star anise chicken
  247
 steamboat 383
 sticky rice parcels 354

stir-fried chicken with basil and
 chilli 242
stir-fried chicken with lemon grass
 251
stir-fried greens 410
stir-fried sweet and sour chicken 253
table-top hotpot 238–9
tiger prawns with ham, chicken and
 egg noodles 218–19
Thai chicken curry 255
Thai fried rice 353
yakitori chicken 134
yellow chicken curry 260
chicken livers: stir-fried giblets with
 ginger 248
chilli bean paste 21
chilli flakes: northern fish curry 182
 snake beans with tofu 163
chilli oil 23
chilli sauce 23
chillies 20
 bamboo shoot, fish and rice soup 67
 beef noodle soup 80–1
 chilli-seared scallops on pak choi 217
 chilli and honey-cured dried beef 308
 clay pot of chilli squid 204
 corn fritters 123
 grilled fish with mung beansprouts
  173
 hot and fragrant trout 170
 hot-and-sour fish soup 63
 hot-and-sour prawn soup 68–9
 jungle curry 155
 jungle fish cooked in banana leaves
  184
 lobster and crab steamed in
  beer 226
 mixed meat noodles 388–9
 pan-steamed mussels with lemon
  grass, chilli and Thai herbs 92
 pak choi with lime dressing 400
 prawn and cauliflower curry 223
 sambal nanas 439
 southern-spiced chilli rice 334
 spiced vegetables with coconut 140
 spicy tofu with basil and peanuts 167
 steamed fish with chilli sauce 177
 steamed mussels with chilli and
  ginger 224
 stuffed chillies 89
 sweet -and-sour cucumber with mint
  434
 Thai fish broth 66
 Thai marinated sea trout 174
 tiger prawns with ham, chicken and
  egg noodles 218–19
 tofu and green bean red curry 162
 tofu soup with mushrooms and
  tomato 47
 tuna with cucumber, garlic and
  ginger 187
 braised aubergine and courgettes
  414–15
 cabbage salad 438
 chilli and honey-cured dried beef 308
 crispy turkey balls 108
 curried rice vermicelli 379
 green papaya salad 430
 herb and chilli aubergines 149
 hot Thai pickled shallots 427
 lamb saté 277
 pineapple with ginger and chilli 419
 plain noodles with four flavours 358
 prawn and pork soup with rice
  sticks 55
 soft-shell crabs with chilli and
  salt 95
 stir-fried chicken with basil and chilli
  242
 stir-fried chilli beef and mushrooms
  315
 stir-fried prawns with tamarind 210

Chinese black mushrooms: cellophane
 noodles with pork 390
Chinese broccoli 14
Chinese cabbage see Chinese leaves
Chinese chestnuts 19
Chinese chives 17
 sea bass with Chinese chives 185
 steamed crab dim sum with Chinese
  chives 129
Chinese fish ball soup 62
Chinese five spice powder 21
Chinese leaves 14
 Chinese leaves and black rice stir-fry
  336
 beef and vegetables in table-top broth
  79
 broth with stuffed cabbage leaves 53
 chicken and shredded cabbage salad
  447
 duck with pancakes 270–1
 mixed vegetable soup 43
 Mongolian firepot 278–9
 noodle and meatball soup 83
 southern-style yam 421
 steamboat 383
 stir-fried Chinese leaves 399
 stir-fried greens 410
 stir-fried tofu with noodles 377
 sweet and sour vegetables with tofu
  166
 table-top hotpot 238–9
 vegetable noodles with prawns 380
Chinese mushrooms: cabbage and
 noodle parcels 111
 cheat's shark's fin soup 44
 Chinese jewelled rice 347
 choi sum and mushroom stir-fry 145
 crispy spring rolls 131
 egg foo young – Cantonese style 121
 grey mullet with pork 183
 lettuce parcels 109
 mini phoenix rolls 104
 mixed vegetables monk-style 142–3
 mushrooms with cellophane noodles
  375
 steamboat 383
 sticky rice parcels 354
 vegetable noodles with prawns 380
 vegetarian stir-fry with peanut sauce
  146–7
Chinese pancakes: duck with pancakes
 270–1
Chinese rice wine: Chinese-style steamed
 fish 176
 sea bass with Chinese chives 185
 squid with broccoli 203
Chinese sausages 31
 Chinese clay pot rice with chicken
  349
 congee with Chinese sausage 77
 popiah 102–103
choi sum 14
 choi sum and mushroom stir-fry 145
chop suey: duck and ginger chop suey
 269
 fruity duck chop suey 264
churros 498–9
cilantro see coriander 21
cinnamon: baked cinnamon meat loaf
 304–5
clams: clams and spring onions 225
 green curried mussels and clams with
  coconut milk 93
clear soup with seafood sticks 56
clementines in spiced syrup 464
cloud ear mushrooms: broth with stuffed
 cabbage leaves 53
 crispy wonton soup 76
 hot and sour soup 46
 mixed vegetables monk-style 142–3
 noodles with crab and mushrooms
  381

rice rolls stuffed with pork 296
mushrooms with cellophane noodles
 375
coconut and seafood soup 57
coconut cream diamonds 475
coconut cream: red snapper in banana
 leaves 192
coconut milk 19
 aubergine and sweet potato stew with
  coconut milk 156–7
 aubergine curry with coconut milk
  150
 baked rice pudding, Thai-style 491
 bamboo shoot, fish and rice soup 67
 cassava sweet 501
 chicken and sweet potato curry 237
 coconut and seafood soup 57
 coconut cream diamonds 475
 coconut custard 480
 coconut ice cream 452
 coconut jasmine rice 328
 coconut jelly with star anise fruits 474
 coconut milk 19
 coconut sorbet 453
 curried pork with pickled garlic 302
 curried seafood with coconut milk 228
 exotic fruit sushi 479
 festive rice 340
 fish in coconut custard 180
 fragrant coconut rice 329
 ginger, chicken and coconut soup
  68–9
 glazed pumpkin in coconut mik 158
 green beef curry with Thai aubergines
  322
 green chicken curry 258
 green curried mussels and clams with
  coconut milk 93
 green prawn curry 220
 jungle curry 155
 mangoes with stick rice 492–3
 marinated duck curry 268
 noodles and vegetables in coconut
  sauce 370
 piquant prawn laksa 52
 potato, shallot and garlic samosas 116
 prawns with yellow curry paste 221
 pumpkin, prawn and coconut soup 54
 pumpkin pudding in banana leaves
  490
 rainbow drink 459
 red chicken curry with bamboo shoots
  256–7
 rice noodles with pork 391
 savoury rice with roasted coconut 330
 sea bass steamed in coconut milk
  186
 sea bass steamed in coconut milk
  186
 snake beans with tofu 163
 southern chicken curry 261
 southern-style yam 421
 spiced vegetables with coconut 140
 spicy green bean soup 40
 steamed custard in nectarines 481
 stewed pumpkin in coconut cream
  492–3
 stir-fried pork and butternut curry 303
 sweet mung bean soup 500
 tapioca and taro pudding 496
 tapioca pudding 494
 tapioca with banana and coconut 495
 tofu and green bean red curry 162
 tofu and vegetable Thai curry 164–5
 Thai fried rice 353
 Thai marinated sea trout 174
 Thai vegetable curry with lemon grass
  rice 152–3
 Thai-style trout 172
cod 32
 Chinese fish ball soup 62
 fish cakes with cucumber relish 128
 seafood wonton soup 58

condensed milk: leche flan 498–9
congee with Chinese sausage 77
coriander 21
  garlic and ginger rice with coriander
    333
  green mango salad 433
  miso broth with tofu 48
  mushrooms with garlic and chilli
    sauce 141
  noodles with ginger and coriander
    367
  piquant prawn laksa 52
  soya beansprout herb salad 428
  sweet -and-sour cucumber with mint
    434
corn: corn and cashew nut curry 151
  corn and chicken soup 74
  green curry puffs 119
  mixed vegetables monk-style 142–3
  sweet and sour vegetables with tofu
    166
  Thai fried rice 353
  Thai vegetable curry with lemon grass
    rice 152–3
  tung tong 118
  vegetables with Chiang Mai spicy dip
    409
  vegetable forest curry 154
courgettes: braised aubergine and
    courgettes 414–15
  chicken and vegetable bundles 136
  courgettes with noodles 411
  five-spice vegetable noodles 373
  fried vegetables with nam prik 423
  noodles with yellow bean sauce 376
  stir-fried rice and vegetables 341
crab 33
  asparagus with crab meat sauce 227
  Chinese jewelled rice 347
  crab and asparagus soup 60
  crab and cucumber vinegar salad 443
  crab cakes with ginger and wasabi 94
  lobster and crab steamed in beer 226
  noodles with crab and mushrooms
    381
  pomelo and crab salad 442
  popiah 102–103
  soft-shell crabs with chilli and salt 95
  steamed crab dim sum with Chinese
    chives 129
  stir-fried noodles in seafood sauce
    382
cucumber: assorted seaweed salad 441
  cellophane noodle soup 45
  crab and cucumber vinegar salad 443
  crunchy summer rolls 122
  fish cakes with cucumber relish 128
  gong boa prawns 216
  lotus stem salad 437
  Oriental scallops with ginger relish 98
  noodle, tofu and sprouted bean
    salad 365
  picked vegetables 426
  popiah 102–103
  sambal nanas 439
  Sichuan noodles with sesame sauce
    366
  sweet -and-sour cucumber with mint
    434
  sweet and sour salad 432
  Thai fruit and vegetable salad 435
  Thai prawn salad with garlic dressing
    and frizzled shallots 444
  tuna with cucumber, garlic and ginger
    187
  Vietnamese table salad 431
  wakame with prawns and cucumber
    86
curried pork with pickled garlic 302
curries: aubergine curry with coconut
    milk 150

chicken and lemon grass curry 259
chicken and sweet potato curry 237
corn and cashew nut curry 151
curried seafood with coconut
    milk 228
green beef curry with Thai aubergines
    322
green chicken curry 258
green prawn curry 220
jungle curry 155
marinated duck curry 268
northern fish curry 182
pork and pineapple coconut curry
    300
prawn and cauliflower curry 223
prawns with yellow curry paste 221
red chicken curry with bamboo shoots
    256–7
southern chicken curry 261
stir-fried pork and butternut curry 303
Thai chicken curry 255
Thai vegetable curry with lemon grass
    rice 152–3
tofu and green bean red curry 162
tofu and vegetable Thai curry
    164–5
vegetable forest curry 154
yellow chicken curry 260
curry pastes 21
curry powders 21

daikon see mooli
daikon, beetroot and carrot stir-fry 144
dashi stock 23
  beef and vegetables in table-top broth
    79
  chicken and egg on rice 352
  chicken with hijiki seaweed 243
  clear soup with seafood sticks 56
  five ingredients rice 351
  new potatoes cooked in dashi stock
    418
  swordfish with citrus dressing 195
dashi-konbu: lemon sole and fresh oyster
    salad 99
dessert wine: clementines in spiced
    syrup 464
dim sum: steamed crab dim sum with
    Chinese chives 129
  steamed flower rolls 130
  steamed pork buns 132
dragon fruit 18
dried golden needles: cellophane noodle
    soup 45
duck 31
  aromatic broth with roast duck, pak
    choi and egg noodles 72–3
  crispy roast duck 272
  duck and ginger chop suey 269
  duck and sesame stir-fry 263
  duck in a spicy orange sauce 273
  duck with pancakes 270–1
  duck with pineapple 267
  duck with pineapple and ginger 265
  duck with plum sauce 266
  fruity duck chop suey 264
  marinated duck curry 268
  marmalade and soy roast duck 262
durian 18

eels 32
  eel braised in a caramel sauce 197
egg foo young – Cantonese style 121
egg noodles 27
  aromatic broth with roast duck, pak
    choi and egg noodles 72–3
  beef, vegetable and noodle soup 82
  firecrackers 126
  five-flavour noodles 364
  five-spice vegetable noodles 373
  gingered prawns with noodles 214
  noodle and meatball soup 83

noodles and vegetables in coconut
    sauce 370
noodles with asparagus 372
noodles with chicken, prawns and
    ham 386
noodles with ginger and coriander
    367
noodles with yellow bean sauce 376
pork chow mein 393
seafood chow mein 205
sesame noodle salad 362
Sichuan noodles with sesame sauce
    366
stir-fried noodles in seafood sauce
    382
stir-fried noodles with beansprouts
    369
stir-fried sweet and sour chicken 253
stir-fried tofu with noodles 377
tiger prawns with ham, chicken and
    egg noodles 218–19
vegetable chow mein 374
vegetable noodles with prawns 380
egg vermicelli: toasted noodles with
    vegetables 368
eggs: baked rice pudding, Thai-style 491
  chicken and egg on rice 352
  corn fritters 123
  fish cakes and vegetables 181
  fried rice with pork 348
  fried vegetables with nam prik 423
  golden steam sponge cake 497
  grilled chicken balls on skewers 135
  leche flan 498–9
  mango and ginger clouds 471
  mini phoenix rolls 104
  omelette soup 42
  popiah 102–103
  ribs of pork with egg-fried rice 294–5
  rolled omelette 120
eggplants see aubergines 14
elderflower: lychee and elderflower
    sorbet 451
enokitake mushrooms: assorted seaweed
    salad 441
escabeche 175
exotic fruit salad with passion fruit 461

fennel: five-spice vegetable noodles 373
  spiced vegetables with coconut 140
fish balls: Chinese fish ball soup 62
  fish cakes and vegetables 181
  steamboat 383
fish cakes: fish cakes and vegetables
    181
fish cakes with cucumber relish 128
fish: bamboo shoot, fish and rice soup
    67
  catfish cooked in a clay pot 196
  Chinese fish ball soup 62
  Chinese-style steamed fish 176
  cubed and marinated raw tuna 100
  curried seafood with coconut milk 228
  escabeche 175
  fish in coconut custard 180
  fish with citrus dressing 195
  fresh tuna shiitake teriyaki 188
  grey mullet with pork 183
  grilled fish with mung beansprouts
    173
  hot and fragrant trout 170
  hot-and-sour fish soup 63
  jungle fish cooked in banana leaves
    184
  lemon sole and fresh oyster salad 99
  marinated and grilled swordfish 194
  northern fish curry 182
  red snapper in banana leaves 192
  red snapper soup 65
  rice in green tea with salmon 64
  rice porridge 345
  salmon terikayi 189

sea bass steamed in coconut milk
    186
sea bass with Chinese chives 185
seafood soup with noodles 61
steamboat 383
steamed fish with chilli sauce 177
steamed fish with five willow sauce
    178–9
steamed red snapper 193
sweet and sour fish 191
swordfish with citrus dressing 195
table-top hotpot 238–9
Thai fish broth 66
Thai marinated sea trout 174
Thai-style trout 172
three sea flavours stir-fry 207
trout with tamarind and chilli sauce
    171
vegetables and salmon in a parcel
    190
fish sauce 22
five willow sauce: steamed fish with five
    willow sauce 178–9

galangal 20
  asparagus with galangal 404
  ginger, chicken and coconut soup
    68–9
  jungle curry 155
  northern fish curry 182
  stir-fried long beans with prawns 211
  stir-fried pork and butternut curry 303
  Thai fish broth 66
  vegetable forest curry 154
galia melons: cool green fruit salad 469
garlic 20
  broccoli with garlic 406
  garlic and ginger rice with coriander
    333
  morning glory with garlic and shallots
    408
  mushrooms with garlic and chilli
    sauce 141
  stir-fried baby squid with ginger, garlic
    and lemon 200
  Thai prawn salad with garlic dressing
    and frizzled shallots 444
  tuna with cucumber, garlic and ginger
    187
giblets: stir-fried giblets with ginger 248
ginger 20
  chicken with young ginger 250
  crab cakes with ginger and
    wasabi 94
  duck and ginger chop suey 269
  duck with pineapple and ginger 265
  ginger, chicken and coconut soup
    68–9
  ginger granita 454–5
  noodles with ginger and coriander
    367
  Oriental scallops with ginger relish 98
  pears with ginger and star anise 468
  pineapple with ginger and chilli 419
  spicy cauliflower and ginger samosas
    117

steamed mussels with chilli and ginger 224
stir-fried baby squid with ginger, garlic and lemon 200
stir-fried giblets with ginger 248
sweet rice dumplings in ginger syrup 476
tuna with cucumber, garlic and ginger 187
ginkgo nuts 19
glutinous rice 25
  baked rice pudding, Thai-style 491
  bamboo shoot salad 429
  congee with Chinese sausage 77
  mangoes with stick rice 492–3
  red rice wrapped in oak leaves 332
  sticky rice in bean paste 477
  sticky rice parcels 354
  sweet rice dumplings in ginger syrup 476
gobo: miso soup with pork and vegetables 75
golden needles: mixed vegetables monk-style 142–3
golden steam sponge cake 497
granitas: ginger granita 454–5
  ruby grapefruit granita 454–5
grapes: cool green fruit salad 469
green beans: fish cakes with cucumber relish 128
  green papaya salad 430
  oriental green beans 412
  sautéed green beans 402
  simmered tofu with vegetables 160–1
  spicy green bean soup 40
  spicy squid salad 202
  steamed aubergine with sesame sauce 413
  stir-fried pork with mushrooms 294–5
  Thai fruit and vegetable salad 435
  tofu and green bean red curry 162
  tofu and vegetable Thai curry 164–5
  vegetables with Chiang Mai spicy dip 409
  Northern prawn and squash soup 51
  vegetable forest curry 154
  vegetable noodles with prawns 380
green mango salad 433
grey mullet 32
  grey mullet with pork 183
grouper 32

haddock: Chinese fish ball soup 62
ham: Chinese fried rice 342
  Chinese jewelled rice 347
  noodles with chicken, prawns and ham 386
  tiger prawns with ham, chicken and egg noodles 218–19
herb and chilli aubergines 149
hijiki seaweed: assorted seaweed salad 441
  seaweed and radish salad 440
hoisin sauce 23
  duck with pancakes 270–1
  sticky pork ribs 282
  stir-fried pork with lychees 297
  char-siu pork 285
honey: char-siu pork 285
  chilli and honey-cured dried beef 308
  glazed lamb 276
hot and sour soup 46
hot and sweet vegetable and tofu soup 49
hot-and-sour fish soup 63
hot-and-sour prawn soup 68–9

ice cream: coconut ice cream 452
iced fruit mountain 460

Japanese cucumber: lemon sole and fresh oyster salad 99
jasmine flowers: papayas in jasmine flower syrup 465
jasmine rice 24

kabocha squash 15
  kabocha squash cake 478
  kabocha squash with chicken sauce 241
kaffir lime leaves 20
  aubergine and sweet potato stew with coconut milk 156–7
  aubergine curry with coconut milk 150
  coconut and seafood soup 57
  fish cakes with cucumber relish 128
  green prawn curry 220
  hot and fragrant trout 170
  hot and sweet vegetable and tofu soup 49
  hot-and-sour prawn soup 68–9
  pan-steamed mussels with lemon grass, chilli and Thai herbs 92
  red snapper in banana leaves 192
  stir-fried pork and butternut curry 303
  tofu and green bean red curry 162
  vegetable forest curry 154
  watermelon ice 450
kiwi: cool green fruit salad 469
  exotic fruit salad with passion fruit 461
konnyaku: cubed chicken and vegetables 240
  fish cakes and vegetables 181
  grilled vegetable sticks 114–15
kroeung: aubergine curry with coconut milk 150
  fish in coconut custard 180
  glazed pumpkin in coconut mik 158
  wheat noodles with stir-fried pork 392
kumquats 18
  iced fruit mountain 460

lamb 31
  glazed lamb 276
  lamb saté 277
  minted lamb 280
  Mongolian firepot 278–9
leche flan 498–9
leeks: chicken and vegetable bundles 136
  noodles with yellow bean sauce 376
  paper-thin sliced beef in stock 321
  sukiyaki-style beef 310
lemon grass 20
  aubergine and sweet potato stew with coconut milk 156–7
  bamboo shoot, fish and rice soup 67
  brown rice with lime and lemon grass 335
  chicken and lemon grass curry 259
  chicken rice soup with lemon grass 70–1
  coconut and seafood soup 57
  corn and cashew nut curry 151
  duck in a spicy orange sauce 273
  green curry puffs 119
  green prawn curry 220
  grilled prawns with lemon grass 88
  hot-and-sour fish soup 63
  hot-and-sour prawn soup 68–9
  jungle curry 155
  lemon grass pork 293
  lemon grass snails 96–7
  northern fish curry 182
  pan-steamed mussels with lemon grass, chilli and Thai herbs 92
  piquant prawn laksa 52
  pork on lemon grass sticks 281
  red snapper in banana leaves 192
  red snapper soup 65

spicy tofu with basil and peanuts 167
steamed fish with chilli sauce 177
steamed mussels with chilli and ginger 224
stir-fried chicken with lemon grass 251
Thai fish broth 66
Thai vegetable curry with lemon grass rice 152–3
Thai-style trout 172
lemon sauce: chicken with lemon sauce 246
lemon sole and fresh oyster salad 99
lemons: lemon sorbet 456
  stir-fried baby squid with ginger, garlic and lemon 200
lettuce: crunchy summer rolls 122
  dry-cooked pork strips 283
  fragrant mushrooms in lettuce leaves 416
  grilled fish with mung beansprouts 173
  lettuce parcels 109
  rice noodles with fresh herbs 360
  sweet and sour prawns 215
  Vietnamese table salad 431
lily buds see golden needles
lime 19
  brown rice with lime and lemon grass 335
  Chinese fruit salad 466
  fried pineapple 484
  green mango salad 433
  red snapper in banana leaves 192
  pak choi with lime dressing 400
  Thai marinated sea trout 174
lion's head meat balls 106
lobster 33
  lobster and crab steamed in beer 226
long beans: jungle curry 155
  snake beans with tofu 163
  stir-fried long beans with prawns 211
long grain rice 24
lotus leaves: sticky rice cakes with pork 346
lotus seeds 19
  sticky rice cakes with pork 346
lotus: lotus stem salad 437
  mixed vegetables monk-style 142–3
luffa squash 15
lychees 18
  heavenly jellies with fruit 472–3
  iced fruit mountain 460
  jungle fruits in lemon grass syrup 463
  lychee and elderflower sorbet 451
  stir-fried pork with lychees 297
  tapioca pudding 494
  Thai fruit and vegetable salad 435

mandarins in syrup 458
mangetouts: aromatic pork with basil 288
  chicken and mixed vegetables 236
  glazed lamb 276
  kabocha squash with chicken sauce 241
  mixed vegetables monk-style 142–3
  salmon terikayi 189
  seafood chow mein 205
  sesame noodle salad 362
  stir-fried prawns with mangetouts 213
  sweet and sour vegetables with tofu 166
  toasted noodles with vegetables 368
  turnips with prawns and mangetouts 422
  vegetables and salmon in a parcel 190
  vegetables with Chiang Mai spicy dip 409
mangoes 18
  Chinese fruit salad 466

exotic fruit salad with passion fruit 461
exotic fruit sushi 479
green mango salad 433
mango puddings 462
mango and ginger clouds 471
mangoes with stick rice 492–3
Thai fruit and vegetable salad 435
Thai prawn salad with garlic dressing and frizzled shallots 444
tropical fruit gratin 486–7
mangosteen 18
marmalade and soy roast duck 262
meat loaf: baked cinnamon meat loaf 304–5
meatballs: noodle and meatball soup 83
milk: leche flan 498–9
mini phoenix rolls 104
mint: Chilli-seared Scallops on Pak Choi 217
  minted lamb 280
  sweet -and-sour cucumber with mint 434
mirin 23
  kabocha squash with chicken sauce 241
miso: miso broth with tofu 48
  miso soup with pork and vegetables 75
mitsuba 21
  clear soup with seafood sticks 56
Mongolian firepot 278–9
monkfish 32
  seafood soup with noodles 61
  Thai fish broth 66
mooli 14
  beef and vegetables in table-top broth 79
  daikon, beetroot and carrot stir-fry 144
  fish cakes and vegetables 181
  fresh tuna shiitake teriyaki 188
  miso soup with pork and vegetables 75
  mixed vegetable soup 43
  picked vegetables 426
  Sichuan noodles with sesame sauce 366
  simmered tofu with vegetables 160–1
  soft-shell crabs with chilli and salt 95
  swordfish with citrus dressing 195
  table-top hotpot 238–9
morning glory with garlic and shallots 408
mung bean thread noodles: Chinese fish ball soup 62
mung beans: rainbow drink 459
  sweet mung bean soup 500
  sweet rice dumplings in ginger syrup 476
mung beansprouts: crunchy summer rolls 122
  grilled fish with mung beansprouts 173
mushrooms 16
  aromatic pork with basil 288

aubergine and sweet potato stew with
    coconut milk 156–7
beef and mushrooms with black
    beans 312
braised tofu with mushrooms 159
chicken and mixed vegetables 236
five ingredients rice 351
fragrant mushrooms in lettuce leaves
    416
fried rice with mushrooms 338
ginger, chicken and coconut soup
    68–9
hot-and-sour prawn soup 68–9
mushrooms with cellophane noodles
    375
mushrooms with garlic and chilli
    sauce 141
noodles with crab and mushrooms
    381
nutty rice and mushroom stir-fry
    337
paper-thin sliced beef in stock 321
southern-style yam 421
stir-fried chilli beef and mushrooms
    315
stuffed sweet peppers 148
tofu and green bean red curry 162
tofu and vegetable Thai curry
    164–5
udon noodle soup 41
vegetables and salmon in a parcel
    190
mussels 33
mussels in black bean sauce 91
green curried mussels and clams with
    coconut milk 93
pan-steamed mussels with lemon
    grass, chilli and Thai herbs 92
steamed mussels with chilli and
    ginger 224
mustard and cress: swordfish with citrus
    dressing 195

nectarines: steamed custard in
    nectarines 481
noodle and meatball soup 83
noodles with beef and black bean sauce
    395
nori: five-flavour noodles 387
rice in green tea with salmon 64
seafood tempura 124–5
seaweed-wrapped prawns 90
nuoc cham 22
nuoc mam 22
baked cinnamon meat loaf 304–5
broth with stuffed cabbage leaves 53
catfish cooked in a clay pot 196
eel braised in a caramel sauce 197
grilled prawns with lemon grass 88
hot-and-sour fish soup 63
jungle fish cooked in banana leaves
    184
pork pâté in a banana leaf 101
tofu soup with mushrooms and
    tomato 47
nutty rice and mushroom stir-fry 337

omelette soup 42
onions 16
orange juice: duck in a spicy orange
    sauce 273
oranges: iced fruit mountain 460
    orange sorbet 457
    stir-fried pork with mushrooms 294–5
oxtail: beef noodle soup 80–1
oyster mushrooms: braised tofu with
    mushrooms 159
    choi sum and mushroom stir-fry 145
    fragrant mushrooms in lettuce leaves
        416
    stir-fried pork with mushrooms 294–5
oyster sauce 22
    beef in oyster sauce 314
    scented chicken wraps 107
oysters: lemon sole and fresh oyster
    salad 99

pak choi 14
    aromatic broth with roast duck, pak
        choi and egg noodles 72–3
    chilli-seared scallops on pak choi 217
    lion's head meat balls 106
    miso broth with tofu 48
    omelette soup 42
    pak choi with lime dressing 400
    vegetarian stir-fry with peanut sauce
        146–7
palm sugar 20
pancakes 28
    pancakes with red bean paste 502–3
pandanus leaves: scented chicken wraps
    107
papayas 18
    exotic fruit salad with passion fruit
        461
    green papaya salad 430
    grilled pineapple with papaya sauce
        486–7
    jungle fruits in lemon grass syrup 463
    papayas in jasmine flower syrup 465
    tapioca pudding 494
    Vietnamese table salad 431
    yellow chicken curry 260
passion fruit: exotic fruit salad with
    passion fruit 461
peanuts 19
    banana blossom salad with prawns
        209
    chicken satay with peanut sauce 232
    herb and chilli aubergines 149
    grilled fish with mung beansprouts
        173
    pomelo and crab salad 442
    snake beans with tofu 163
    spicy curry with basil and peanuts 167
    Thai prawn salad with garlic dressing
        and frizzled shallots 444
    Thai noodles with Chinese chives 361
    tofu and beansprout soup 50
    vegetarian stir-fry with peanut sauce
        146–7
    wheat noodles with stir-fried pork 392
pears with ginger and star anise 468
peas: Chinese fried rice 342
    Chinese jewelled rice 347
    green curry puffs 119
    potato, shallot and garlic samosas 116
    simmered beef slices and vegetables
        320
    spicy cauliflower and ginger samosas
        117
peppers: crab and cucumber vinegar
    salad 443
    curried rice vermicelli 379
    escabeche 175
    five-spice squid with black bean
        sauce 206
    noodles with beef and black bean
        sauce 395

prawns with yellow curry paste 221
    sambal goreng with prawns 222
    stuffed sweet peppers 148
    vegetable chow mein 374
physalis: iced fruit mountain 460
pineapples 18
    duck with pineapple 267
    duck with pineapple and ginger 265
    fried pineapple 484
    fruity duck chop suey 264
    grilled pineapple with papaya sauce
        486–7
    jungle fruits in lemon grass syrup 463
    pineapple with ginger and chilli 419
    pork and pineapple coconut curry
        300
    sambal nanas 439
    sweet and sour pork 290
    sweet and sour salad 432
    Thai fruit and vegetable salad 435
    Thai-style pineapple 420
    tropical fruit gratin 486–7
pistachio nuts: mandarins in syrup 458
    mango and ginger clouds 471
plaice 32
plum sauce 22
    duck with plum sauce 266
    tung tong 118
pomegranates: sweet and sour salad 432
pomelo and crab salad 442
popiah 102–103
porcini mushrooms: beef, vegetable and
    noodle soup 82
gingered prawns with noodles 214
pork 31
    aromatic pork with basil 288
    baked cinnamon meat loaf 304–5
    braised black pepper pork 299
    broth with stuffed cabbage leaves 53
    cabbage and noodle parcels 111
    caramelized pork in bamboo 286–7
    cellophane noodles with pork 390
    char-siu pork 285
    crispy spring rolls 131
    crispy wonton soup 76
    curried pork with pickled garlic 302
    dry-cooked pork strips 283
    egg foo young – Cantonese style 121
    five-flavour noodles 387
    fried rice with pork 348
    grey mullet with pork 183
    larp of chiang mai 306–7
    lemon grass pork 293
    lemon grass snails 96–7
    lion's head meat balls 106
    mini phoenix rolls 104
    miso soup with pork and vegetables
        75
    mixed meat noodles 388–9
    popiah 102–103
    pork and pineapple coconut curry
        300
    pork chow mein 393
    pork on lemon grass sticks 281
    pork pâté in a banana leaf 101
    prawn and pork soup with rice sticks
        55
    ribs of pork with egg-fried rice 294–5
    rice noodles with pork 391
    rice rolls stuffed with pork 296
    roasted and marinated pork 284
    saeng wa of grilled pork 298
    savoury chiffon custards 105
    special fried rice 344
    steamboat 383
    steamed crab dim sum with Chinese
        chives 129
    steamed pork balls with dipping sauce
        133
    steamed pork buns 132
    sticky pork ribs 282

sticky rice cakes with pork 346
    stir-fried pork and butternut curry 303
    stir-fried pork with dried shrimp 292
    stir-fried pork with lychees 297
    stir-fried pork with mushrooms 294–5
    stuffed chillies 89
    sweet and sour pork 290
    sweet and sour pork, Thai-style 301
    sweet-and-sour pork stir-fry 289
    wheat noodles with stir-fried pork 392
potatoes 15
    corn and cashew nut curry 151
    cubed chicken and vegetables 240
    fish cakes and vegetables 181
    green curry puffs 119
    new potatoes cooked in dashi stock
        418
    potato, shallot and garlic samosas 116
    simmered beef slices and vegetables
        320
    simmered tofu with vegetables 160–1
    spicy cauliflower and ginger samosas
        117
    Thai vegetable curry with lemon grass
        rice 152–3
pouchong tea: apples and raspberries in
    rose pouchong 467
prawns 33
    prawns with yellow curry paste 221
    banana blossom salad with prawns
        209
    broth with stuffed cabbage leaves 53
    Chinese fried rice 342
    coconut and seafood soup 57
    courgettes with noodles 411
    crispy spring rolls 131
    curried rice vermicelli 379
    curried seafood with coconut milk 228
    jasmine rice with prawns and Thai
        basil 343
    mixed meat noodles 388–9
    firecrackers 126
    gingered prawns with noodles 214
    gong boa prawns 216
    green prawn curry 220
    grilled prawns with lemon grass 88
    hot-and-sour prawn soup 68–9
    noodles with chicken, prawns and
        ham 386
    Northern prawn and squash soup 51
    piquant prawn laksa 52
    popiah 102–103
    pumpkin, prawn and coconut soup 54
    prawn and cauliflower curry 223
    prawn and pork soup with rice sticks
        55
    prawn toasts with sesame seeds 127
    salt and pepper prawns 87
    sambal goreng with prawns 222
    savoury chiffon custards 105
    seafood chow mein 205
    seafood salad with fragrant herbs
        446
    seafood soup with noodles 61
    seafood tempura 124–5
    seafood wonton soup 58
    seaweed-wrapped prawns 90
    sinigang 62
    special fried rice 344
    steamboat 383
    stir-fried long beans with prawns 211
    stir-fried prawns with mangetouts
        213
    stir-fried prawns with tamarind 210
    stir-fried scallops and prawns 208
    stuffed chillies 89
    sweet and sour prawns 215
    Thai prawn salad with garlic dressing
        and frizzled shallots 444
    three sea flavours stir-fry 207
    tiger prawns with ham, chicken and
        egg noodles 218–19

turnips with prawns and mangetouts
422
vegetable noodles with prawns 380
wakame with prawns and cucumber
86
preserved stem ginger: mango and
ginger clouds 471
pumpkins: glazed pumpkin in coconut
milk 158
pumpkin pudding in banana leaves
490
pumpkin, prawn and coconut soup 54
stewed pumpkin in coconut cream
492–3

quail's eggs: stir-fried greens 410
quorn: Thai noodles with Chinese chives
361

radishes: oriental beef 316
seaweed and radish salad 440
Sichuan noodles with sesame sauce
366
rainbow drink 459
ramen 27
raspberries: apples and raspberries in
rose pouchong 467
coconut cream diamonds 475
exotic fruit sushi 479
raw cane sugar: sea bass steamed in
coconut milk 186
red onions: duck with plum sauce 266
fusion noodles 364
Thai beef salad 306–7
red snapper: red snapper in banana
leaves 192
red snapper soup 65
steamed red snapper 193
redcurrant jelly: duck with plum sauce
266
rice cakes with spicy dipping sauce 331
rice flour 25
Chinese fish ball soup 62
fresh rice noodles 359
rice in green tea with salmon 64
rice noodles 26
beef noodles with orange and ginger
394
fresh rice noodles 359
plain noodles with four flavours 358
rice noodles with fresh herbs 360
rice noodles with pork 391
sukiyaki-style noodles 310
sweet and hot vegetable noodles 371
Thai noodles with Chinese chives 361
tofu and beansprout soup 50
rice paper 29
crunchy summer rolls 122
rice rolls stuffed with pork 296
rice porridge 345
rice vermicelli: curried rice vermicelli 379
mixed meat noodles 388–9
piquant prawn laksa 52
steamboat 383
rice vinegar 23
plain noodles with four flavours 358
sweet -and-sour cucumber with mint
434
rice wine: steamed fish with chilli sauce
177
rice: aubergine curry with coconut milk
150
baked rice pudding, Thai-style 491
bamboo shoot, fish and rice soup 67
bamboo-steamed sticky rice 327
beef with fried rice 323
brown rice with lime and lemon grass
335
chicken rice soup with lemon grass
70–1
chicken with mushrooms 244
chicken and basil rice 350

chicken and egg on rice 352
Chinese clay pot rice with chicken
349
Chinese fried rice 342
Chinese jewelled rice 347
Chinese leaves and black rice stir-fry
336
coconut cream diamonds 475
coconut jasmine rice 328
congee with Chinese sausage 77
exotic fruit sushi 479
festive rice 340
fish in coconut custard 180
five ingredients rice 351
fragrant rice with chicken 252
fried rice with mushrooms 338
fried rice with pork 348
garlic and ginger rice with coriander
333
jasmine rice with prawns and Thai
basil 343
jungle fish cooked in banana leaves
184
lunch-box rice with three toppings
339
nutty rice and mushroom stir-fry 337
red rice wrapped in oak leaves 332
rice in green tea with salmon 64
savoury rice with roasted coconut 330
simmered tofu with vegetables 160–1
southern-spiced chilli rice 334
special fried rice 344
steamed pork balls with dipping sauce
133
steamed rice 326
sticky rice cakes with pork 346
sticky rice parcels 354
stir-fried rice and vegetables 341
Thai fried rice 353
Thai vegetable curry with lemon grass
rice 152–3
tofu and vegetable Thai curry 164–5
rice-pot crust 25
ruby grapefruit granita 454–5
rump steak: beef in oyster sauce 314
beef with peppers and black bean
sauce 319
beef with tomatoes 317
beef, vegetable and noodle soup 82
noodles with beef and black bean
sauce 395
oriental beef 316
paper-thin sliced beef in stock 321
sizzling beef with celeriac straw 311
stir-fried chilli beef and mushrooms
315
sukiyaki-style beef 310

sake 23
chicken and vegetable bundles 136
clams and spring onions 225
fish cakes and vegetables 181
grilled chicken balls on skewers 135
kabocha squash with chicken sauce
241
marinated and grilled swordfish 194
rolled omelette 120
simmered tofu with vegetables 160–1
steamed red snapper 193
vegetables and salmon in a parcel
190
yakitori chicken 134
salmon 32
northern fish curry 182
rice in green tea with salmon 64
salmon terikayi 189
seafood soup with noodles 61
table-top hotpot 238–9
vegetables and salmon in a parcel
190
salt and pepper prawns 87
sambal goreng with prawns 222

sambal nanas 439
samosas: potato, shallot and garlic
samosas 116
scallions see spring onions
scallops 33
chilli-seared scallops on pak choi 217
Oriental scallops with ginger relish 98
seafood chow mein 205
seafood wonton soup 58
stir-fried scallops and prawns 208
three sea flavours stir-fry 207
sea bass 32
hot-and-sour fish soup 63
sea bass steamed in coconut milk
186
sea bass with Chinese chives 185
sea trout 32
see trout
seafood: curried seafood with coconut
milk 228
seafood chow mein 205
seafood salad with fragrant herbs 446
seafood soup with noodles 61
seafood tempura 124–5
seafood wonton soup 58
seafood sticks: clear soup with seafood
sticks 56
seaweed: assorted seaweed salad 441
chicken with hijiki seaweed 243
five-flavour noodles 387
rice in green tea with salmon 64
seaweed and radish salad 440
seaweed-wrapped prawns 90
sesame noodles: fruity duck chop suey
264
sesame noodle salad 362
sesame oil 23
sesame seeds: Sichuan noodles with
sesame sauce 366
sesame seeds 19
broccoli with sesame seeds 407
prawn toasts with sesame seeds 127
southern-style yam 421
spinach with toasted sesame seeds
403
steamed aubergine with sesame
sauce 413
Thai asparagus 405
vegetable chow mein 374
seven spice powder 21
shallots 17
aubergine and sweet potato stew with
coconut milk 156–7
aubergine salad 436
cabbage salad 438
corn and cashew nut curry 151
hot and fragrant trout 170
hot Thai pickled shallots 427
lotus stem salad 437
morning glory with garlic and shallots
408
northern fish curry 182
pomelo and crab salad 442
potato, shallot and garlic samosas 116
sweet and sour vegetables with tofu
166
Thai prawn salad with garlic dressing
and frizzled shallots 444
tofu soup with mushrooms and
tomato 47
shellfish see clams; crab; mussels;
oysters; prawns; seafood; scallops;
shrimp; squid
shiitake mushrooms: beef and
mushrooms with black beans 312
beef and vegetables in table-top broth
79
braised tofu with mushrooms 159
cellophane noodle soup 45
chicken and vegetable bundles 136
chicken with mushrooms 244

Chinese clay pot rice with chicken
349
choi sum and mushroom stir-fry 145
fish cakes and vegetables 181
five-spice squid with black bean
sauce 206
fresh tuna shiitake teriyaki 188
fusion noodles 364
hot and sour soup 46
miso soup with pork and vegetables 75
noodle casseroles 384–5
seafood tempura 124–5
simmered tofu with vegetables 160–1
slow-cooked shiitake with shoyu 417
steamed pork balls with dipping sauce
133
stir-fried rice and vegetables 341
stir-fried scallops and prawns 208
sukiyaki-style beef 310
table-top hotpot 238–9
toasted noodles with vegetables 368
tofu and vegetable Thai curry 164–5
tofu soup with mushrooms and
tomato 47
shimeji mushrooms: steamed aubergine
with sesame sauce 413
shiro miso: marinated and grilled
swordfish 194
shoyu: slow-cooked shiitake with shoyu
417
shrimp: aubergine salad 436
sambal nanas 439
savoury chiffon custards 105
stir-fried pork with dried shrimp 292
sautéed green beans 402
sticky rice parcels 354
see also prawns
shrimp paste 22
Sichuan pepper 20
Sichuan peppercorns: lettuce parcels 109
mushrooms with cellophane noodles
375
salt and pepper prawns 87
singing 212
sirloin steak: beef and vegetables in
table-top broth 79
beef noodle soup 80–1
chilli and honey-cured dried beef 308
Thai beef salad 306–7
snails: lemon grass snails 96–7
snake beans: green papaya salad 430
snake beans with tofu 163
snapper 32
hot-and-sour fish soup 63
red snapper in banana leaves 192
red snapper soup 65
steamed red snapper 193
soba noodles 27
teriyaki soba noodles with tofu 378
sole 32
somen noodles: chilled somen noodles
363
sorbet: coconut sorbet 453
lemon sorbet 456
lychee and elderflower sorbet 451
orange sorbet 457

soy sauce 22
  marmalade and soy roast duck 262
  soy sauce and star anise chicken 247
soya beansprout herb salad 428
spices: spicy squid salad 202
spinach with toasted sesame seeds 403
spinach: egg foo young – Cantonese style
    121
  grilled vegetable sticks 114–15
  hot and sweet vegetable and tofu
    soup 49
  jungle curry 155
  Mongolian firepot 278–9
  noodle casseroles 384–5
  stir-fried greens 410
  table-top hotpot 238–9
  Thai-style trout 172
  Thai vegetable curry with lemon grass
    rice 152–3
spring onions 16
  beef and vegetables in table-top broth
    79
  beef noodle soup 80–1
  beef, vegetable and noodle soup 82
  broth with stuffed cabbage leaves 53
  catfish cooked in a clay pot 196
  Chinese-style steamed fish 176
  clams and spring onions 225
  corn and chicken soup 74
  corn fritters 123
  crispy roast duck 272
  crispy spring rolls 131
  crispy wonton soup 76
  crunchy summer rolls 122
  cubed and marinated raw tuna 100
  drunken chicken 108
  duck and ginger chop suey 269
  duck with pancakes 270–1
  five-spice squid with black bean
    sauce 206
  grey mullet with pork 183
  herb and chilli aubergines 149
  lobster and crab steamed in beer 226
  miso broth with pork 48
  pak choi with lime dressing 400
  paper-thin sliced beef in stock 321
  prawn toasts with sesame seeds 127
  roasted and marinated pork 284
  sautéed green beans 402
  sizzling beef with celeriac straw 311
  soft-shell crabs with chilli and salt 95
  soya beansprout herb salad 428
  special fried rice 344
  spiced vegetables with coconut 140
  spring vegetable stir-fry 401
  steamed fish with chilli sauce 177
  steamed fish with five willow sauce
    178–9
  steamed pork balls with dipping sauce
    133
  steamed red snapper 193
  stir-fried chilli beef and mushrooms
    315
  stir-fried noodles in seafood sauce
    382
  stir-fried rice and vegetables 341

three sea flavours stir-fry 207
trout with tamarind and chilli sauce
    171
yakitori chicken 134
spring roll wrappers 28
  crispy spring rolls 131
  spicy cauliflower and ginger samosas
    117
  tung tong 118
sprouted beans: noodle, tofu and
    sprouted bean salad 365
squid 33
  clay pot of chilli squid 204
  coconut and seafood soup 57
  curried seafood with coconut milk 228
  five-spice squid with black bean
    sauce 206
  griddled squid and tomatoes in a
    tamarind dressing 201
  hot-and-sour fish soup 63
  seafood chow mein 205
  seafood salad with fragrant herbs 446
  seafood tempura 124–5
  spicy squid salad 202
  squid with broccoli 203
  stir-fried baby squid with ginger, garlic
    and lemon 200
star anise: beef stew with star anise 318
  coconut jelly with star anise fruits 474
  eel braised in a caramel sauce 197
  Oriental scallops with ginger relish 98
  pears with ginger and star anise 468
  prawn and cauliflower curry 223
  sea bass steamed in coconut milk
    186
  soy sauce and star anise chicken 247
  stir-fried scallops and prawns 208
star fruit 18
  Chinese fruit salad 466
  cool green fruit salad 469
  exotic fruit sushi 479
  iced fruit mountain 460
  jungle fruits in lemon grass syrup 463
  Vietnamese table salad 431
steamboat 383
steamed flower rolls 130
steamed pork balls with dipping sauce
    133
steamed pork buns 132
straw mushrooms: braised tofu with
    mushrooms 159
  mixed vegetables monk-style 142–3
strawberries: heavenly jellies with fruit
    472–3
  iced fruit mountain 460
stuffed chillies 89
stuffed sweet peppers 148
sugar snap peas: stir-fried sweet and
    sour chicken 253
  noodles with yellow bean sauce 376
sweet and sour fish 191
sweet and sour vegetables with tofu 166
sweet chilli sauce: steamed crab dim
    sum with Chinese chives 129
  steamed pork balls with dipping sauce
    133
sweet potatoes: aubergine and sweet
    potato stew with coconut milk
    156–7
  chicken and sweet potato curry 237
swordfish: marinated and grilled
    swordfish 194
  swordfish with citrus dressing 195
syrup: golden steam sponge cake 497

tagliarini: fusion noodles 364
tamarillos: tropical fruit gratin 486–7
tamarind: griddled squid and tomatoes in
    a tamarind dressing 201
  sambal goreng with prawns 222
  southern-style yam 421
  stir-fried prawns with tamarind 210

trout with tamarind and chilli sauce
    171
  yellow chicken curry 260
tamarind paste 21
tapioca: tapioca and taro pudding 496
  tapioca pudding 494
  tapioca with banana and coconut 495
taro 15
  tapioca and taro pudding 496
tempura: seafood tempura 124–5
teriyaki sauce: chicken teriyaki 235
  fresh tuna shiitake teriyaki 188
  salmon terikayi 189
Thai aubergines: green beef curry with
    Thai aubergines 322
Thai basil: jasmine rice with prawns and
    Thai basil 343
  Thai marinated sea trout 174
tiger lily buds: vegetarian stir-fry with
    peanut sauce 146–7
toffee apples 488–9
tofu 30
  beef and vegetables in table-top broth
    79
  braised tofu with mushrooms 159
  cellophane noodle soup 45
  chicken with mushrooms 244
  crispy spring rolls 131
  fish cakes and vegetables 181
  grilled vegetable sticks 114–15
  hot and sour soup 46
  hot and sweet vegetable and tofu
    soup 49
  mango and ginger clouds 471
  miso broth with tofu 48
  miso soup with pork and vegetables
    75
  mixed vegetable soup 43
  mixed vegetables monk-style 142–3
  mushrooms with cellophane noodles
    375
  noodle, tofu and sprouted bean salad
    365
  paper-thin sliced beef in stock 321
  simmered tofu with vegetables 160–1
  snake beans with tofu 163
  spicy tofu with basil and peanuts 167
  steamboat 383
  stir-fried tofu with noodles 377
  sukiyaki-style beef 310
  sweet and sour vegetables with tofu
    166
  table-top hotpot 238–9
  teriyaki soba noodles with tofu 378
  Thai noodles with Chinese chives 361
  tofu and beansprout soup 50
  tofu and green bean red curry 162
  tofu and vegetable Thai curry 164–5
  tofu soup with mushrooms and
    tomato 47
  vegetarian stir-fry with peanut sauce
    146–7
tomato ketchup: sweet and sour pork
    290
tomatoes: beef with tomatoes 317
  griddled squid and tomatoes in a
    tamarind dressing 201
  sesame noodle salad 362
  sweet and sour salad 432
  tomato and beef soup 78
trout: hot and fragrant trout 170
  Thai marinated sea trout 174
  Thai-style trout 172
  trout with tamarind and chilli sauce
    171
tuk trey 22
  braised black pepper pork 299
  fish in coconut custard 180
  grilled fish with mung beansprouts 173
  stir-fried long beans with prawns 211
tuna 33
  cubed and marinated raw tuna 100

fresh tuna shiitake teriyaki 188
  tuna with cucumber, garlic and ginger
    187
tung tong 118
turkey: crispy turkey balls 110
turnips with prawns and mangetouts
    422

udon noodles 27
  beef and vegetables in table-top
    broth 79
  noodle casseroles 384–5
  udon noodle soup 41

vegetables with Chiang Mai spicy dip 409
vegetarian stir-fry with peanut sauce
    146–7
vermicelli: prawn and pork soup with
    rice sticks 55
  red snapper soup 65
  rice noodles with fresh herbs 360
  seafood soup with noodles 61

wakame seaweed: assorted seaweed
    salad 441
  wakame with prawns and cucumber
    86
walnuts 19
wasabi 22
  crab cakes with ginger and wasabi 94
  cubed and marinated raw tuna 100
water chestnuts 15
  chicken and mixed vegetables 236
  crispy turkey balls 110
  egg foo young – Cantonese style 121
  herb and chilli aubergines 149
  lettuce parcels 109
  lion's head meat balls 106
  mini phoenix rolls 104
  noodles with chicken, prawns and
    ham 386
  prawn toasts with sesame seeds 127
  tung tong 118
watermelon: iced fruit mountain 460
  watermelon ice 450
wheat noodles with stir-fried pork 392
whiting: seafood tempura 124–5
wind-dried sausages see Chinese
    sausages 31
winter melon 15
wonton 28
  crispy wonton soup 76
  seafood wonton soup 58

wonton wrappers: firecrackers 126
  green curry puffs 119
  steamed crab dim sum with Chinese
    chives 129

yakitori chicken 134
yams 15
yellow bean sauce 23
  char-siu pork 285
  noodles with yellow bean sauce 376
  sticky pork ribs 282
yogurt: minted lamb 280